Wigmore Castle, North Herefordshire: excavations 1996 and 1998

by
Stephanie Rátkai

with contributions by

Carol Davidson Cragoe, Greg Campbell, HEM Cool, Anthony Gouldwell, Stephen J Linnane, Phil Mills, Quita Mould, Ruth Shaffrey, David Symons, Richard Thomas, Stephanie Vann, Mariangela Vitolo

Illustrations by

Nigel Dodds (plans and sections)
Jemma Elliot (artefacts and pottery)
Mike Hawkes (floor tile drawings, Chapter 6)

THE SOCIETY FOR MEDIEVAL ARCHAEOLOGY
MONOGRAPH 34

ISSN 0583-9106
ISBN 978-1-909662-19-3

Series editor: Christopher Gerrard
Published by The Society for Medieval Archaeology, London

This publication has been made possible by a grant from English Heritage

The Society for Medieval Archaeology
www.medievalarchaeology.co.uk

Stephanie Rátkai
2015
Wigmore Castle, North Herefordshire: excavations 1996 and 1998,
The Society for Medieval Archaeology Monograph 34,
The Society for Medieval Archaeology, London

Cover drawing by Jemma Elliot

CONTENTS

LIST OF FIGURES

Colour plates

ACKNOWLEDGEMENTS

Stephanie Rátkai would like to thank John Allan, Duncan Brown, Emma Collins and David Williams for help with the identification of imported pottery, and David Barker for comment on the post-medieval and modern pottery. She would also like to thank Martin Brown, for information on the use of gunpowder in the Civil War, Hilary Cool for general encouragement, Brian Kerr for several fruitful conversations about Wigmore and for making available the draft of Jon Cooke's standing fabric report, and Richard Stone for observations about the excavations and archive. She would also like to thank Ian Mortimer for making available draft reports on the lineage and history of the Mortimer family. She is very grateful to Dr Cragoe for assistance in tabulating the historic sources used in Chapter 10, and to Dr Ian Mortimer for kindly providing information of the early Mortimer lineage in advance of its publication. Thanks are also due to English Heritage for their support and funding throughout the project and to Brian Kerr in particular for his help and encouragement. Most of all she would like to thank the late Sarah Jennings, without whom this volume would probably never have been written and to whom it is dedicated.

Carol Davidson Cragoe (Chapter 2) would particularly like to thank Barbara Walters for making available her unpublished research on the Mortimer family.

Quita Mould (Chapter 5) would like to thank the late Colin Slack and colleagues at the then Ancient Monuments Laboratory, now Central Archaeological Service, English Heritage, for undertaking the X-radiography, Margrethe Felter and Susan Bartindale, at York Archaeological Trust, for undertaking the investigative conservation of selected items, Steve Allen, also York Archaeological Trust, for wood species identification and Karen Wilson, Department of Chemistry, University of York, for conducting X-ray fluorescence analysis. She is also grateful for discussions with the following colleagues: Nicholas Hall, Keeper of Artillery at the Royal Armouries, for his useful comments on the ratchet; David Starley for providing value information on the occurrence of copper on medieval arrowheads; the late Geoff Egan for his insights regarding the book clasp and pan weight; Carol Cragoe for information on winching machines; John Clark, Curator Emeritus, Museum of London, and Lindsay Smith for information on curb bits.

Richard Thomas and Stephanie Vann (Chapter 7) are grateful to Sheila Hamilton-Dyer for drawing their attention to the bear bones from Hereford, to Louisa Gidney for suggesting neatsfoot oil preparation as a possible cause of the cattle foot dump, and to Jo Cooper for permitting them to consult the Natural History Museum bird collection at Tring.

In addition Stephanie Vann would like to thank Graham Clark of the Department of Engineering and Tony Gouldwell of the School of Archaeology and Ancient History, University of Leicester, for allowing access to the microscopes, Jane Sidell of English Heritage for her support and guidance, and Richard Thomas of the School of Archaeology and Ancient History, University of Leicester, for his comments on an earlier drafts of eggshell report.

Mariangela Vitolo (Chapter 8) is very grateful to Gill Campbell and David Earle Robinson for their supervision and help during an EPPIC placement in Archaeobotany at English Heritage and to the former for reading and commenting on several drafts of the report for Chapter 8.

SUMMARY

Excavations at Wigmore Castle were carried out in 1996 and 1998 as a precursor to repair and consolidation of the castle by English Heritage. Two areas within the Inner Bailey were excavated: one running up to the Southern Curtain Wall and the other within and around the East Tower. Archaeological deposits had built up to a considerable depth, in places reaching 8.5m.

The castle had remained the honorial *caput* of the Mortimer family from the late 11th century through to 1425, an unusually long tenure amongst Marcher lordships. The Mortimer family became increasingly important players in the history of England, Wales and Ireland, reflected in the family motto *Not from kings but kings from us*. Thereafter, the Mortimer inheritance passed to the Dukes of York and from there to the Crown.

Evidence of the earliest timber castle was found and a clay rampart that was subsequently reduced in height and the area of the Inner Bailey extended, although essentially still on the footprint of the first castle. The evidence indicated that the present site of the castle was that of fitz Osbern's 11th-century castle. Plant remains from the original rampart indicated the landscape in which the castle was built and the differences in the immediate environment when the rampart was reduced and modified.

Part of a substantial 12th-century timber building was uncovered, the excavated part of which had been used as a kitchen. Here remains of a sequence of hearths, cooking pots and food remains were found. The diet was evidently rich and varied, with domesticates, game, fish, wildfowl and eggs. Finds from the late 11th and 12th centuries indicated the possible advent of local pottery production and the importance of the horse in military operations.

The construction of defences in stone probably began in the 12th century. The present standing curtain wall was constructed around 1300 and evidently heralded further work on the castle, both construction and demolition, which a series of lead-melting hearths confirms. Some of this work may be attributable to Roger Mortimer, 1st Earl of March.

The effect of conflict on the castle was indicated by the presence of ballista balls. A number of arrowheads, a possible crannequin and fragments of plate armour, show the continuing martial aspect of the castle and it is possible that some of this material represents the remnants of a castle armoury. A substantial burnt deposit may have resulted from Simon de Montfort's attack on the castle in 1264 or may represent a domestic conflagration.

A possible period of neglect occurred in the later 14th century but by the 15th century the castle was the scene of renewed activity including the rebuilding of the curtain wall. Dietary evidence and some of the artefacts indicate that there was high-status occupation, in which hunting played an important role that continued throughout the 15th century. By the 16th century the castle fabric was beginning to fall into disrepair and evidence of repairs and modifications were noted. Nevertheless, high-status occupation continued and the castle remained to play an important role as a secondary seat of the Council of the Marches. However, by the early 17th century decline at the castle appears to have been terminal. The castle was now owned by the Harley family and it is they who are credited with the pre-emptive slighting of the castle during the Civil War. The slighting is not evident in the excavated areas, and the area in and around the East Tower appears to have been derelict well before the mid-17th century. Pottery, clay pipe and other artefacts which can definitely be ascribed to the Civil War are few. An oxshoe found in the latest deposits may well be associated with the removal of fallen stone for building elsewhere.

Thereafter the castle appears to have been little visited and almost total ruination had set in by the early 18th century. In 1995 the castle was taken into English Heritage Guardianship and has been consolidated and restored as a romantic ruin.

RÉSUMÉ

En préalable à une réparation et consolidation par l'English Heritage, des fouilles archéologiques ont été menées au château de Wigmore en 1996 et 1998. A l'intérieur de la Haute Cour, une zone courant le long de la courtine sud a été fouillée, et une autre à l'intérieur et autour de la tour Est. Les profondeurs des dépôts archéologiques sont considérables, atteignant parfois jusqu'à 8.5 m.

Le château est resté le caput honorial de la famille Mortimer de la fin du XIe siècle jusqu'en 1425, un bail exceptionnellement long parmi la seigneurie de Marcher. La famille Mortimer a joué un rôle de plus en plus important dans l'histoire de l'Angleterre, du Pays de Galle et de l'Irlande, comme le reflète la devise de la famille: *«Not from kings but kings from us»* («nous ne venons pas des rois, mais des rois viennent de nous»). L'héritage Mortimer est ensuite passé aux Ducs de York et de là, à la Couronne.

Des indices du premier château en bois ont été découverts, ainsi que ceux du rempart en terre crue réduit en hauteur par la suite, et de la Haute Cour dont les pourtours restent à l'intérieur du site du premier château même lors de son agrandissement ultérieur. Il semblerait que le site du château actuel corresponde à celui de fitz Osbern qui remonte au XIe siècle. Des restes de plantes provenant du rempart d'origine fournissent des informations relatives au paysage dans lequel le château a d'abord été construit, puis, lorsque le rempart a été réduit en taille et modifié, aux changements environnementaux qui y sont associés.

Parmi les vestiges d'un important bâtiment en bois du XIIe siècle, les restes d'une succession de foyers, de la céramique culinaire et des déchets de nourriture mis au jour dans une partie de ce bâtiment suggèrent que cette dernière servait de cuisine. Le régime alimentaire était visiblement riche et varié, comprenant des poissons domestiques, de pêche sportive, du gibier à plume et des œufs. L'introduction de la production locale de poterie et l'importance du cheval dans les opérations militaires semblent remonter à la fin du XIe siècle et du XIIe siècle.

La construction d'ouvrages défensifs en pierre a probablement débuté au XIIe siècle. La courtine actuellement en place a été érigée vers 1300 et a initié d'autres travaux de construction et de démolition du château, comme l'atteste une série de foyers de fonte de plomb. Une partie de ces travaux peut être attribuée à Roger Mortimer, 1er duc de March.

La présence de boulets de baliste indique que le château a pris part à des conflits. Plusieurs pointes de flèches, un probable cranequin et des fragments d'armure plate montrent une continuité du caractère martial du château. Il est possible qu'une partie de ce matériel corresponde aux restes de l'armurerie. La cause d'un important dépôt brulé peut être attribuée à l'attaque de Simon de Montfort menée sur le château en 1264, à moins qu'il n'ait s'agit d'un incendie domestique.

A la fin du XIVe siècle le château a probablement été laissé à l'abandon, mais au XVe siècle, le château est la scène d'une activité renouvelée avec notamment la reconstruction du mur de courtine. Des vestiges du régime alimentaire et quelques artefacts indiquent une occupation de statut élevé, dans laquelle la chasse occupait un rôle important, et qui s'est prolongée au cours du XVe siècle. Au XVIe siècle, les maçonneries du château ont commencé à se délabrer ; des indices suggèrent des réparations et des modifications. Néanmoins, l'occupation de statut élevé s'est maintenue et le château a continué à jouer un rôle important comme siège secondaire du Conseil des Marches. Cependant, au début du XVIIe siècle, le château finit de décliner. Il appartient alors à la famille Harley qui semble être responsable de la destruction volontaire préemptive du château au cours de la Guerre. La destruction n'est pas évidente, et la zone à l'intérieur et autour de la tour Est apparaît avoir été en état de délabrement bien avant le milieu du XVIIe siècle. Des poteries, des pipes en terre et autres artefacts qui peuvent être attribués avec certitude à la Guerre Civile sont peu nombreux. Un fer à bœuf découvert dans les dépôts les plus récents pourrait être associé au déplacement de pierres tombées et récupérées.

Par la suite le château semble avoir été peu visité et en quasi-totale ruine au début du XVIIIe siècle. En 1995 il est placé sous tutelle de l'English Heritage et a été consolidé et restauré comme ruine romantique.

RIASSUNTO

Gli scavi presso Wigmore Castle furono eseguiti tra il 1996 e il 1998 prima dei lavori di restauro e consolidamento del castello da parte dell'English Heritage. Due aree all'interno della cinta interna sono state indagate: la prima a ridosso del muro della cortina meridionale, la seconda all'interno e intorno alla torre orientale. Il deposito archeologico si era stratificato per uno spessore considerevole, talvolta raggiungendo 8.50 m.

Il castello era rimasto il centro feudale della famiglia Mortimer dalla fine dell'XI secolo fino al 1425, un possedimento eccezionalmente lungo tra le Signorie dei Marches. La famiglia Mortimer divenne un protagonista sempre più importante nella storia di Inghilterra, Galles e Irlanda, rispecchiato nel motto di famiglia "Non dai re ma i re da noi". Successivamente il patrimonio dei Mortimer passò ai Duchi di York e di qui alla Corona.

Sono stati rinvenuti resti del più antico castello in legno insieme ad una fortificazione in argilla che fu successivamente ridotta in altezza mentre l'area della cinta interna fu estesa, pur rimanendo all'interno del tracciato del castello più antico. I dati archeologici suggerirono l'identificazione del sito del castello con quello del castello di XI secolo di fitz Osbern. Resti vegetali rinvenuti nella più antica fortificazione forniscono indicazioni riguardanti il paesaggio nel quale il castello fu costruito e sono indicatori delle differenze nell'ambiente circostante quando la fortificazione fu ridotta e modificata.

E' stata scoperta una parte di un importante edificio in legno di XII secolo, la cui porzione messa in luce era stata usata come cucina, in cui è stata rinvenuta una sequenza di focolari, vasellame per la cottura e resti di cibo. La dieta alimentare era chiaramente ricca e varia, comprendente cacciagione, pesce, selvaggina e uova. I rinvenimenti riferibili al tardo XI e XII secolo hanno indicato la possibile comparsa di produzione locale di ceramica e l'importanza del cavallo nelle operazioni militari.

La costruzione di difese in pietra ha inizio probabilmente nel XII secolo. La cortina muraria attualmente conservata fu costruita intorno al 1300 ed fu evidemente foriera di ulteriori lavori nel castello, sia di edificazione che di demolizione, attestati da una serie di fornaci per la fusione del piombo. Alcuni di questi lavori possono essere attribuiti a Roger Mortimer, 1° Conte di March.

L'occorrenza di un conflitto era attestata nel castello dalla presenza di palle-proiettili per balista. Un gruppo di punte di freccia, un possibile cranequin e frammenti di lastre di corazza, mostrano il perdurare della funzione bellica del castello ed è possibile che parte di questo materiale rappresenti ciò che resta di un'armeria del castello stesso. Un cospicuo deposito di bruciato può essere la conseguenza dell'attacco al castello da parte di Simon de Monfort nel 1264 o può derivare da un incendio domestico.

Un possibile periodo di abbandono si registra nel tardo XIV secolo ma nel XV secolo il castello è oggetto di nuove ristrutturazioni, compresa la ricostruzione del muro di cortina. I reperti alimentari e alcuni manufatti indicano che il castello era occupato da persone di elevato status sociale, in cui la caccia aveva un importante ruolo che continuò attraverso il XV secolo. Nel XVI secolo le strutture del castello cominciarono ad andare in rovina e sono documentati restauri e modifiche. Ciononostante continuò l'occupazione da parte di persone di rango elevato e il castello mantenne un ruolo importante come sede secondaria del Concilio dei Marches. All'inizio del XVII secolo tuttavia, il lento declino dell'edificio sembra giungere al suo termine. Il castello apparteneva all'epoca alla famiglia Harley e a loro viene attribuito l'abbandono preventivo del castello durante la guerra civile. Questo abbandono non è documentato nelle aree scavate: l'area all'interno e intorno alla torre orientale era in stato di abbandono ben prima della metà del XVII secolo. Ceramica, pipe di terracotta e altri manufatti che possono essere attribuiti al periodo della guerra civile sono scarsi. Un ferro per bue rinvenuto nei depositi più recenti può essere associato al traino di pietrame caduto reimpiegato per costruire altrove. In seguito il castello sembra essre stato scarsamente frequentato e all'inizio del XVIII secolo si era consumata una pressoché totale distruzione. Nel 1995 il castello è stato inserito sotto la tutela dell'English Heritage ed è stato consolidato e restaurato come rovina romantica.

1
INTRODUCTION

H E M Cool and Stephanie Rátkai

1.1 ENGLISH HERITAGE'S INVOLVEMENT WITH WIGMORE CASTLE

Wigmore Castle (Herefordshire, NGR SO 408693, HSMR No. 179) lies in North Herefordshire, some 13km to the south-west of Ludlow Castle, Shropshire (Figure 1.1). It is one of the many early post-Conquest castles which are so abundant in the Welsh Marches (PLATE 1). English Heritage took the castle, which is a Scheduled Ancient Monument (Hereford SAM 5), into Guardianship in November 1995. The castle was extremely ruinous and the unexpected collapse of part of the Southern Curtain Wall (Figure 1.2) necessitated both the consolidation of the castle and an exploration into why the fabric was unstable. In contrast to most Guardianship castle sites, it was decided to consolidate the castle but then restore it to a 'romantic ruin', replete with wild plants and shrubs (see Coppack 2002; 2005; see Chapter 2).

Following this, a major conservation project of the monument was put in place. As part of this, Marches Archaeology was commissioned to carry out excavations within the Inner Bailey (see Figure 3.1). The initial plan was for three areas to be excavated. One was completed in 1996. This was adjacent to the curtain wall in the Inner Bailey between the South and South-West Towers, with an aim of exploring the level to which archaeological deposits survived within the castle walls. The second area was within and adjacent to the East Tower, and the aim of the excavation was to inform the consolidation process with respect to the instability of the tower and the reasons for this instability. Work here was undertaken between February and April 1998 and was referred to as 1998A. Further excavations took place here in September 1998 and were referred to as 1998B. Work on the proposed third area, a partly buried but substantially complete undercroft, never took place because it had become a roost for bats. Natural was reached in 1996; the full sequence was not established in 1998 (see Chapter 3). The archive report for 1996 was completed in 1998 (Stone and Appleton-Fox 1998), and in the same year an interim archive report for the first season of excavation that year was also drafted (Appleton-Fox 1998). It should be noted that some confusion was occasioned by Marches Archaeology's use of Area A as a synonym for the 1996 excavations and Area B for the 1998 excavations, when A and B were also used to denote the two separate seasons of excavation in 1998. In this volume the use of 'Area A' and 'Area B' has been avoided.

In January 2008 the Director's Office, Research and Standards of English Heritage commissioned three separate pieces of work on the archive through Dr Carol Davidson Cragoe. Nic Appleton-Fox of Marches Archaeology was commissioned to complete the stratigraphic narrative for 1998, to incorporate the results of the second season in September of that year. David Kendrick was commissioned to produce a report on, and archive of, the architectural stone and tilestones. Barbican Research Associates were commissioned to produce first a project outline and then an assessment and project design of all the other artefacts and the environmental evidence. The report on the architectural stone was completed in February 2008. The artefactual and ecofactual assessment and project design were submitted to English Heritage on 4 March of the same year, and the up-dating of the 1998 stratigraphic narrative was completed in May 2008. English Heritage then commissioned Barbican Research Associates to produce an updated version of their project design to integrate the results of the work completed by Kendrick and Appleton-Fox. This project design (Cool and Rátkai 2008) formed the basis of a proposal to publish the results of the excavations, which has ultimately led to this volume.

1.2 THE EXCAVATIONS

This volume presents the results of the three seasons of excavation undertaken at Wigmore Castle. It can be seen from the above that the two areas chosen for excavation were not in any way dictated by wider archaeological imperatives and the excavated areas were correspondingly small. This was further compounded by an exceptionally deep series of deposits, some 8m deep in the case of the 1996 excavation, which resulted in a very small area indeed being exposed at the base of the trench, due to safety considerations. The areas were not chosen to answer any specific research questions regarding the layout of the castle, its history, its role as a Marcher castle or as a principal seat of the Mortimer family.

Although the excavated sites were chosen in furtherance of the consolidation of the castle, they nevertheless were situated within one of the premier

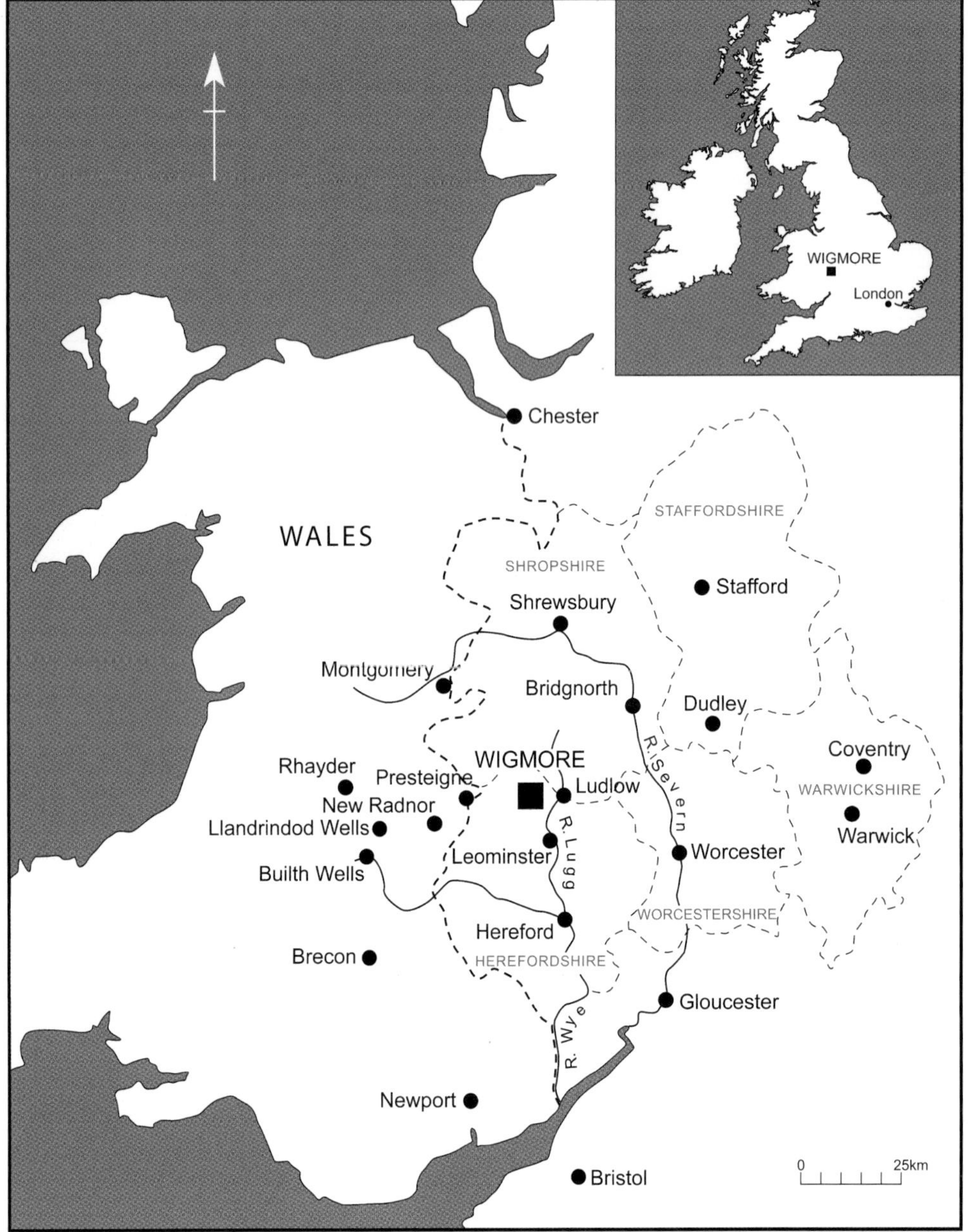

FIGURE 1.1
Location plan of Wigmore

Marcher castles and the honorial caput of the highly influential Mortimer family, later the earls of March, whose story is inextricably entwined with that of the Plantagenet kings. The self-perceived prestige of the family can be seen in its motto *Not from kings but kings from us*. The castle was an important staging post for attacks into Welsh lands, was besieged on several occasions and was the recipient of a number of royal visits. In the history of the Marches, the castle can be seen as nothing less than significant (see Chapter 2). For this reason alone the results of the archaeological investigations are worthy of dissemination and publication.

This volume aims to publish the excavation results and artefactual and ecofactual assemblages from the castle and view them in their own context but also in that of other Marcher castles and that of the powerful family for whom Wigmore Castle was its chief seat. A detailed survey of the standing fabric of the castle has been made by Jon Cooke on behalf of English Heritage and is to be published as a separate volume (Cooke forthcoming). An early draft of this (Cooke 2008) was made available to the project team. Dr Cragoe was commissioned by English Heritage to research the documented history of the Mortimer family and their castle at Wigmore. Both pieces of work formed quite separate projects from the one undertaken in this volume. Abstracts from both Cragoe's and Cooke's work, amongst others, do, however, provide the information in Chapter 2, which aims to give a general view of the history and standing fabric of the castle for the reader, a detailed exploration of either having been specifically excluded by the project brief from this volume.

FIGURE 1.2
Collapse of part of the Southern Curtain Wall (copyright: English Heritage, 1995)

1.3 THE PRIMARY ARCHAEOLOGICAL RECORD

A substantial archive was available for consultation. However, by the time of writing up the stratigraphic narrative (Chapter 3) the original excavators had left the profession and were no longer available for consultation. This is unfortunate since a vital link in the excavation process had been lost. Inevitably, closer inspection of the site record revealed lacunae — the record for the second season of excavation around the East Tower, for example, is incomplete — and some contradictory information, which may have been more easily resolved, had the original excavators been involved. In addition, the low-light, very cramped conditions, particularly evident in the lower reaches of the 1996 excavation were, to say the least, challenging for those trying to record what they saw. The restricted extent of the areas excavated also made the relationship of many of the layers and features difficult to interpret during excavation. Nevertheless, some clear strands of the castle's history could be determined and a good stratigraphic sequence was apparent in the 1996 excavations. The sequence in the area outside the East Tower was less good because of truncation of an already small area by a large cut feature and several subsidiary later cuts.

The photographic record has suffered because of the depth of excavation and attendant poor light quality. The drawn record has been affected by the absence of single-context planning so that the full extent of several contexts is not known for certain. However, few excavations, even those conducted in better circumstances, have an immaculate record, and under the difficult conditions, the Wigmore excavation teams are to be commended for what they did achieve.

1.4 RESEARCH AIMS AND POTENTIAL

One of the purposes of this volume is to bring Wigmore Castle more to the attention of the wider scholarly community. As was noted in several of the assessment reports prepared for the Project Research Design (Cool and Rátkai 2008), knowledge of what was being used, the material culture and daily life during the medieval period in the area in which Wigmore lies is very sparse. Indeed, it could be described as something of a black hole, a situation little changed from the 1990s when Wigmore was one of the towns examined as part of the Central Marches Historic Towns Survey (Dalwood 2005). Wigmore, therefore, offers well stratified sequences that have the potential to form the regional framework for the pottery and faunal remains. The animal bone provides a particularly good dataset since it is closely dated and well preserved, and has the potential to address several key avenues of enquiry such as the impact of the Black Death on diet and animal husbandry techniques, the emergence of technological innovations and the development and ritualisation of the hunt in the later medieval period.

Currently there are scant references to Wigmore in the castle literature. This seems to be because of its poor state of preservation and its isolation, which stand in marked contrast to the erstwhile importance of the castle and the Mortimer family for much of the medieval period, revealed through the documentary sources. The epitaph of Roger Mortimer (d. 1282) gives a taste of the sway the family held:

> Here lies buried Roger the pure, Roger Mortimer the second, called Lord of Wigmore by those who held him dear. While he lived all Wales feared his power, and given as a gift to him, all Wales remained his. It knew his campaigns, he subjected it to torment
>
> (Mortimer 2004, 9).

In Thompson (1987, 20) it is noted that the establishment at Ludlow of the Council of the Marches in Wales in the reign of Edward IV transferred authority 'from the largely defunct marcher castles'. The evidence from the excavations at Wigmore clearly raise the question of how defunct these castles actually were, a topic which is more fully explored in Chapters 9 and 10. Analysis of the material culture evidenced at the castle provides comparanda for the castle's local, regional and national context, and provides a basis from which to explore to what extent the material culture reflects the fact that it has come from a castle occupied by a major aristocratic family.

There are several areas where the analysis of the data from the excavations can extend our knowledge of the castle. It has been possible to establish the date and level of occupation from the 11th century onwards and to explore the evidence for the structures and for the diet and eating practices of the inhabitants. This, in turn, can inform or provide a useful counter-balance to data derived from the study of the documentary sources and from survey of the standing fabric. The wealth of historical information distilled from Dr Cragoe's work about the people living in the castle and the trajectory of its occupation can be compared, for example, with archaeological evidence, to see whether it reflects it or is at odds with it.

At a more theoretical level, it has been possible to examine the nature of the site formation processes. It has been noted that the sequences at Wigmore are very deep and questions have been raised as to why this should be so and whether this might explain why the curtain wall was raised. This is a difficult aim to explore as the deposits at so many castle sites in the past were emptied rather than excavated and so detailed evidence that could be used as comparanda is missing from many of them. It has also become apparent that the redeposition of ceramic building material can be useful in exploring taphonomic processes. This has never been explored in a site of Wigmore's status before.

1.5 THE FORMAT OF THE VOLUME

This volume follows, to a certain extent, a pattern typically seen in many excavation reports with separate free-standing chapters on the stratigraphy, the artefacts and environmental and ecofactual remains (Chapters 3–8). These are introduced by a summary of the history of the site and the Mortimer family, and of the standing fabric (Chapter 2). The results of Chapters 3–8 have been integrated to form Chapter 9 which attempts to plot the development of the castle and highlight aspects of life there. The final chapter (Chapter 10) sets the castle and the Mortimer family in the context of other English and Welsh castles, but more specifically those within the Central March.

2
HISTORICAL AND ARCHITECTURAL OVERVIEW

Carol Davidson Cragoe

> It is impossible to contemplate the massive ruins of Wigmore Castle, situate on a hill, in an Amphitheatre of mountains, whence its owner could survey his vast estates from his square palace, with four corner towers on a keep, at the south-east corner of his double trench'd outworks, without reflecting on the instability of the grandeur of a family, whose ambition and intrigue made more than one English Monarch uneasy on his throne, yet not a memorial remains of their sepultures.
>
> (Gough 1789, II, 454–455).

2.1 INTRODUCTION

Richard Gough's comments are, if anything, truer today than when he wrote in 1789. Wigmore Castle was the site of war and intrigue, folly and grandeur, yet of this home of the ancestors of the kings and queens of England little remains to be seen. An extraordinarily evocative site, it remains entirely uncleared with very little visible beyond verdant lumps and bumps (Figure 2.1) that belie its past significance. Wigmore was taken into State Guardianship in 1995, and its ruins continued to decline until the restoration and conservation project by English Heritage in the late 1990s that sparked the excavations discussed in this monograph. This chapter surveys the historical sources and some of the fabric evidence for the castle, its development and its decline. It makes use of unpublished research on the Mortimers by Barbara Wright. It also draws on a range of unpublished English Heritage reports on aspects of the site prepared in the course of the late 1990s restoration project, notably those of Graham Brown (2002) and Jon Cooke (2008).

2.2 SOURCES AND PREVIOUS INVESTIGATIONS

The documentary evidence for Wigmore is less extensive than it is for many castles, notably the royal castles. The site was in private hands for much of its history, and so the sources have not survived as well as they might, if the papers had been kept in the royal archives. The Harley papers in the British Library and the Nottinghamshire Archives's Portland of Wellbeck Collection are useful for the castle's later history, and The National Archives (TNA) has a collection of material relating to the castle during the periods when it was under royal control. Unfortunately what would be key sources, such as account books from the Mortimer period, do not survive. A mention of a room full of 'old writings' at the castle in 1574 suggests that more survived at that date (BL MS Lansdowne 19 fol 38; Mortimer 2003, 277–278, n.12).

Wigmore Castle's fame as the home of Roger (V) Mortimer (1287–1330), the lover of Queen Isabella, wife of King Edward II, ensured it a place in early topographical and antiquarian histories, both published (Camden 1637; Gough 1789) and unpublished (Buchanan-Brown 1999; Blount 1675; Botzum and Reeves 1997), but their architectural descriptions are limited. G T Clark's article on the castle (Clark 1874), reprinted in his book on *Mediaeval military architecture* (Clark 1884) is much more useful, as he appears to have seen many features of the castle, especially in the Shell Keep area, that are no longer visible. There are some 18th- and 19th-century topographical prints and drawings, many collected in the Pilley Collection in the Hereford City Library, and others held by the British Library, as well as a few early photographs, also largely held in the Pilley Collection.

Of these images, the well-known Buck print of 1733 (Figure 2.2) is the most useful as it was made closest in time to the most significant destruction event in the castle's history: its slighting some 90 years previously during the Civil War. Extremely detailed on close inspection, comparison of this image with the surviving fabric suggests that it was made from detailed sketches made on site, although the perspective is slightly problematic in places. It provides evidence for features seen in fragmentary form by Cooke (2008), such as openings in the curtain wall, the form of the South-West Tower, and the postern gate in the curtain wall above it. The print is also the primary evidence for features now no longer visible, notably the hall complex in the middle of the site and large parts of the keep tower, which survived in a much more complete form at that date (Figures 2.3–2.5).

The Deare watercolour of 1766 (Figure 2.6) provides an interesting contrast to the Buck print

FIGURE 2.1
Interior of the Shell Keep, looking east (photograph: Carol Davidson Cragoe)

FIGURE 2.2
Wigmore Castle, engraving by Samuel and Nathaniel Buck, 1733 (copyright: English Heritage)

FIGURE 2.3
The Shell Keep (detail from Figure 2.2)

FIGURE 2.4
The Gatehouse and remains of the hall range (detail from Figure 2.2)

FIGURE 2.5
The south-west part of the Inner Bailey (detail from Figure 2.2)

with regard to the central area, as it shows both the remains of the North-East Tower and a very substantial survival of tall masonry remains in the central area, making it clear that Buck did not misplace his depiction of the North-East Tower. Deare also shows what may have been an additional small tower or turret between the East and North-East Towers, but unfortunately the image is insufficiently detailed to provide more information about the precise nature of the remains.

The Hearne and Byrne engraving of 1806 (Figure 2.7) provides evidence for now lost vaulting and other features in the Donjon Tower. Other early images of the castle include two sketches of 1800 by Edward Blore in the British Library (BL MS Add 42023, fols 25–26), an engraving in the 1808 *Beauties of England* (Brayley and Britton 1805) and several poor quality sketches and watercolours in the Hereford City Library, Pilley Collection. Together, the later 18th- and 19th-century images confirm the gradual decline of the site, notably the erosion of masonry features and the build up of foliage and deposits on and around the walls.

In the 20th century, the castle and the surrounding earthworks were surveyed in summary form by Edward Downham *c*1895–1906 (BL MS Add 37650, fol 44) and his work printed in the Victoria County History volume (VCH 1908, 247). Both the castle and the village buildings, including the church, were surveyed in considerably more detail by the Royal Commission for Historical Monuments in 1932 for its *Herefordshire* 3rd volume (RCHM 1934). The unpublished notes of the survey of the castle (RCHM 1932) held in the National Monuments Record (NMR) are particularly useful as they contain sketches, not included in the published volume, of several now lost or invisible features, including the Gatehouse portcullis arch (Figure 2.8) and some early walling apparently still *in situ* (Figure 2.9).

The NMR also has a collection of early and mid-20th-century photographs of the site, although the very overgrown condition of the site made photography as difficult then as now. There are other early photographs in the Hereford City Library, Pilley Collection, including an early postcard showing the Outer Bailey under the plough (Figure 2.10).

The sale of the site in 1987 to a new private owner, and the subsequent collapse (unrelated to the change in ownership) of part of the curtain wall in 1988, prompted a flurry of private, scholarly investigations. Part of the Outer Bailey was the subject of a resistivity survey in 1988 (Redhead 1990a; 1990b). It was also the subject of visits by castle scholars, notably Shoesmith (1998) and Stirling-Brown (1988), whose notes explore the history, dating, and form of the site. The monument was taken into State Guardianship in 1995, and is now managed by English Heritage as a free site. Once in Guardianship, the castle was the subject of an innovative research and conservation programme

FIGURE 2.6
Wigmore Castle, watercolour by Deare, 1766 (copyright: The British Library Board. British Library K Top 15 111.b)

FIGURE 2.7
The remains of the Donjon Tower and Shell Keep, drawn by Thomas Hearne and engraved by William Byrne, 1806 (copyright: Carol Davidson Cragoe)

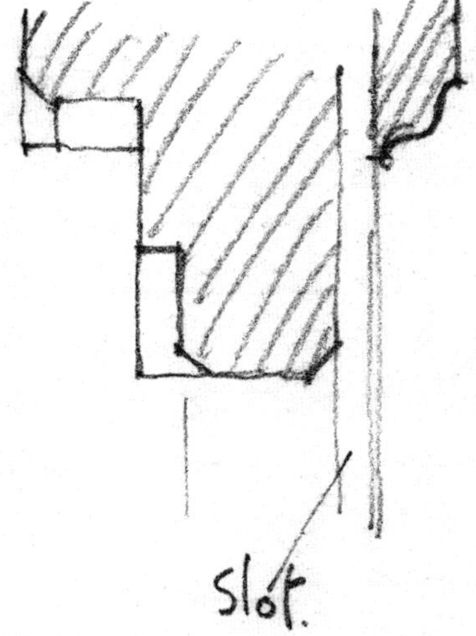

FIGURE 2.8
Sketch of the portcullis arch, 1932, from unpublished notes by the Royal Commission for Historic Monuments (copyright: English Heritage)

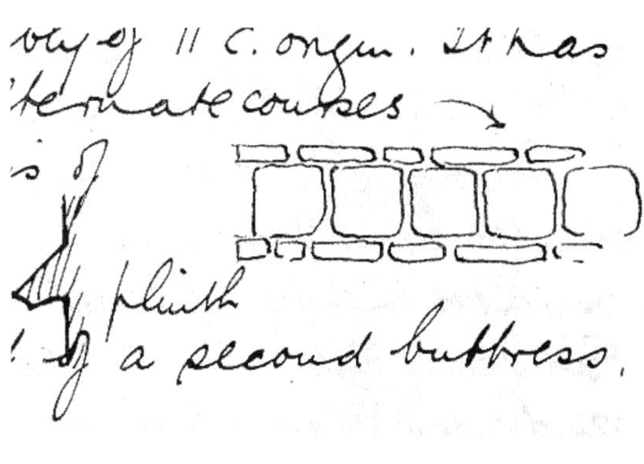

FIGURE 2.9
Sketch of possible Norman masonry in the Shell Keep, 1932, from unpublished notes by the Royal Commission for Historic Monuments (copyright: English Heritage)

FIGURE 2.10
Postcard showing Wigmore Castle, around 1900 (copyright: Hereford City Library, Pilley Collection)

intended to stabilise the masonry, while at the same time preserving the wild and unrestored character of the site that had developed unhindered since the mid-17th century. As well as the two excavations that form the subject of this monograph, there was a detailed survey of the visible masonry of the entire site (Cooke 2008) that revealed much about the castle's history and structural development. A further resistivity survey of the upper part of the Outer Bailey was undertaken (Payne 2007), as was a topographical survey (Barratt 1998). Archaeological investigators from the RCHM undertook their own landscape survey of the castle and its surroundings, including the evidence for the adjacent deer park (Brown 2002). A draft guidebook was also prepared, but never published (Coppack nd).

The initial presentation of the site was minimal, with only a single panel focussing on the conservation project and its rationale, but the desire for new, more detailed site presentation materials in 2008 led to the present author being commissioned to undertake further research. As part of this work, the archaeological artist Dominic Andrews was commissioned to create a new reconstruction

FIGURE 2.11
Reconstruction of Wigmore Castle in the 14th century, by Dominic Andrews (copyright: English Heritage)

drawing taking into account all the evidence gathered from work on the site to that date (Figure 2.11; PLATE 3) to replace a reconstruction by Bryan Byron of 1995. The work on developing Andrews's reconstruction suggested a number of previously unremarked upon features, including a possible outer perimeter wall encompassing the ditch at the back of the site, to the north-west of the Shell Keep, and details of the arrangement of the moat between the Inner and Outer Baileys. Evidence from all of these sources is incorporated into this chapter.

2.3 WIGMORE IN THE LANDSCAPE

Wigmore is located in the north-western corner of Herefordshire, only a few kilometres from the Shropshire and Welsh borders (Figure 1.1). The castle is located roughly equidistant between the Rivers Teme and Lugg, the former having an important crossing point at Leintwardine to the north where the road from mid-Wales (now the A4113) met the Roman road north from Hereford (now largely the A4110) (Figure 2.12). It was one of many castles built along the Welsh Marches in the wake of the Norman Conquest. Other fortified sites in the vicinity of Wigmore included Croft Castle, Richards Castle, Brampton Bryan (Herefordshire), Clun, Hopton Castle, Ludlow and Stokesay (Shropshire). Like other castles of its period (Liddiard 2005, 197–221), the castle at Wigmore would have dominated a wide landscape. The castle was in a prominent position on a steep ridge. Associated features nearby included parks, forests, fishponds, and a monastery, Wigmore Abbey, founded by the Mortimers, that served as the burial place for many generations of the family, as well as a planned town, all of which stamped Mortimer authority over the area.

The placename 'Wigmore' has been variously interpreted. Suggestions include Wicga's moor from a personal name, Welsh *gwig mawr* ('big wood', from Welsh *gwig* for glade or wood), and insect or bug moor from 'wigca' or 'wig' for insect (Ekwall 1990, 518). Gelling suggested that the 'wig' or insect in question was a beetle, and therefore that the name was intended to refer to a blister bog, in which pools and marshes appear to move (Gelling 1984; Coplestone-Crow 1989; Mills 2003), but a buggy or insect-filled moor would be equally likely, especially as the marsh below the castle was not drained until the post-medieval period and still retains some water even today (Figure 2.13).

A further, and also plausible, alternative would read the first element simply as 'wīg', an Old English word for war (Bosworth and Toller 1898; 1921), and therefore Wigmore as either a moor where a battle took place or a defended moor, so-named after the castle itself. Some weight to this last interpretation may come from an annotation in the 1160–70 Herefordshire Domesday, which describes the castle as 'Wigemore in Merstona' (Galbraith and Tait 1950), suggesting that the castle was named separately to the settlement.

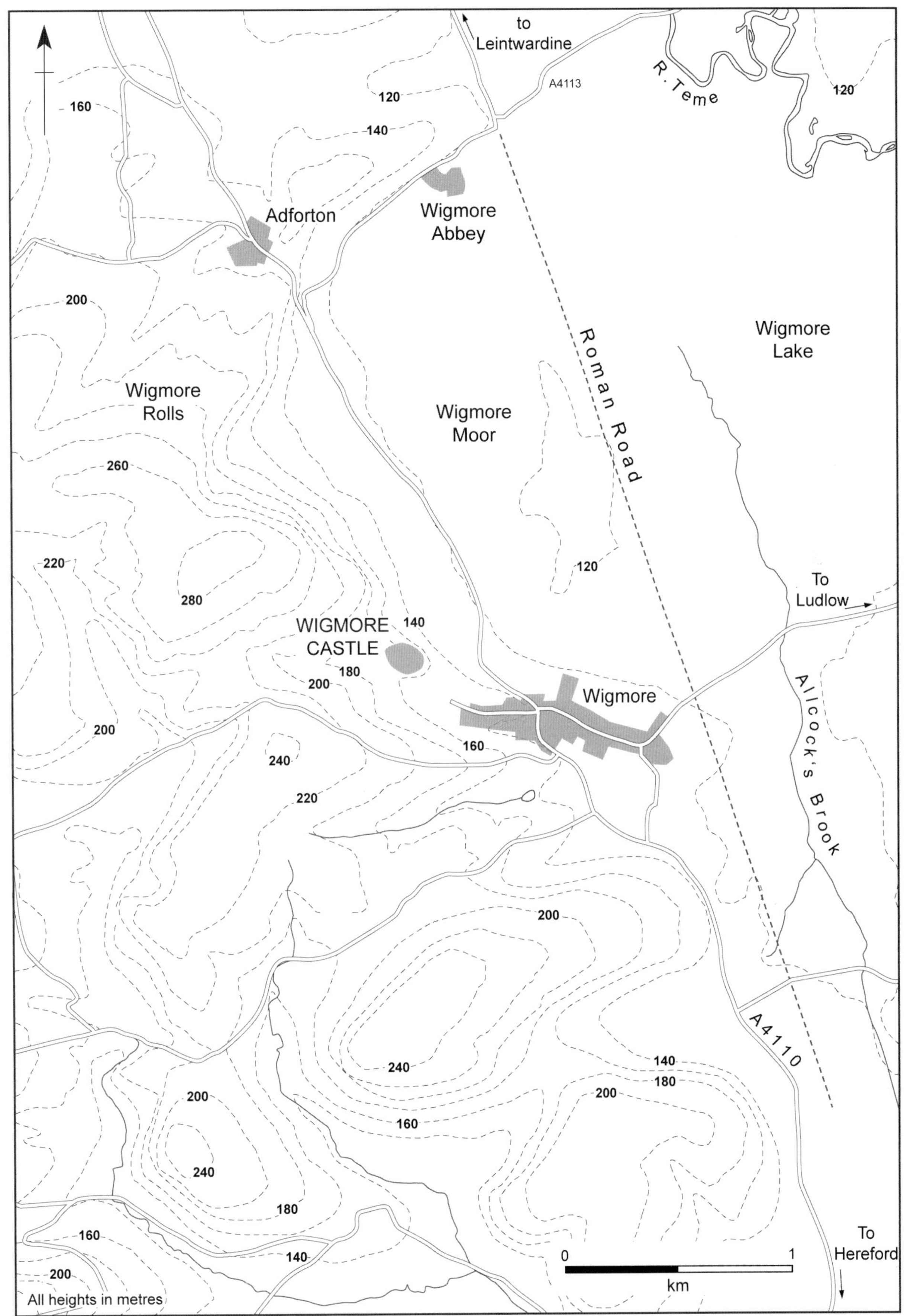

FIGURE 2.12
Wigmore Castle and its immediate landscape

FIGURE 2.13
Wigmore Moor (mere) following floods in June 2008, looking north-west (photograph: Carol Davidson Cragoe)

2.4 FORM OF THE CASTLE

At its greatest extent, the castle (Figure 2.14) comprised an Outer Bailey, an Inner Bailey, and a Shell Keep with a Donjon Tower at the very top of the site. This plan, probably the work of the castle's founder William fitz Osbern, who used a similar plan at his castle at Chepstow (Monmouthshire), cleverly exploits the site's natural topography to enhance its defences. The castle, the parish church, and part of the associated town are built on a steep, narrow ridge that rises towards the north-west from the low-lying ground of Wigmore Moor. At the lowest point on the moor, the ground is only 110m above OD, but it rises sharply along the ridge with the church at 150m, the castle's Outer Bailey at about 160m, the Inner Bailey around 170m, and the Shell Keep at 185m. The land continues to rise behind the castle to the north-west, and the highest ground is in Wigmore Rolls, formerly the deer park, where the land rises to 188m, but it slopes off sharply on both sides of the ridge (Figure 2.15). In addition to the steep sides of the ridge, and the rising ground leading up to the Shell Keep, a natural depression behind the keep to the north appears to have been deepened to create a ditch that is now approximately 30m deep. To the east, the marshy ground of the moor would also have formed a defence.

The large, trapezoidal Outer Bailey (Figure 2.14) is now visible only as earthworks, but the two resistivity surveys of the area (Redhead 1990a; 1990b; Payne 2007) showed that it was seemingly once enclosed by stone walls, perhaps replacing a timber palisade. The Outer Bailey was divided into two parts on different levels by a roadway; evidence for stone buildings was found within the upper, northern, part, and there may have been other buildings in the lower, southern, part which has not been surveyed. The Outer Bailey was separated from the Inner Bailey by a double ditch, possibly once a wet moat, with an intermediate bank with outworks, although this arrangement appears to be a 14th-century alteration to a large, late 11th- or 12th-century single ditch (Brown 2002). The intermediate bank had a wall with four open-backed mantlet towers (Shoesmith 1998, 4), and work by Andrews and the present author for Andrews' reconstruction drawing suggested that this wall continued, probably as a timber palisade for much of its length, around the entire site, taking in the ditch at the rear of the site (Figure 2.11).

The Inner Bailey, enclosed by a stone curtain wall, still partly standing, had at least four mural towers, a main Gatehouse, and a postern gate high on the west side (Figure 2.16). The curtain walls may be 12th-century in origin and probably replaced a timber palisade, evidence for which was found in the 1996 excavation (see Chapter 3). The core of the Gatehouse is late 12th- or early 13th-century and is bonded to the adjacent section of curtain wall, but the early 13th-century East Tower appears to be an addition to a pre-existing section of wall (Cooke 2008). The rest of the mural towers were built or rebuilt in the 14th century (Cooke 2008), and, where they survive, have ogee-headed windows. There may have been another small tower or turret between the East and North-East Towers, now entirely lost. A tall fragment of masonry shown in this position in the

FIGURE 2.14
Plan of Wigmore Castle, showing location of the Outer Bailey (copyright: English Heritage)

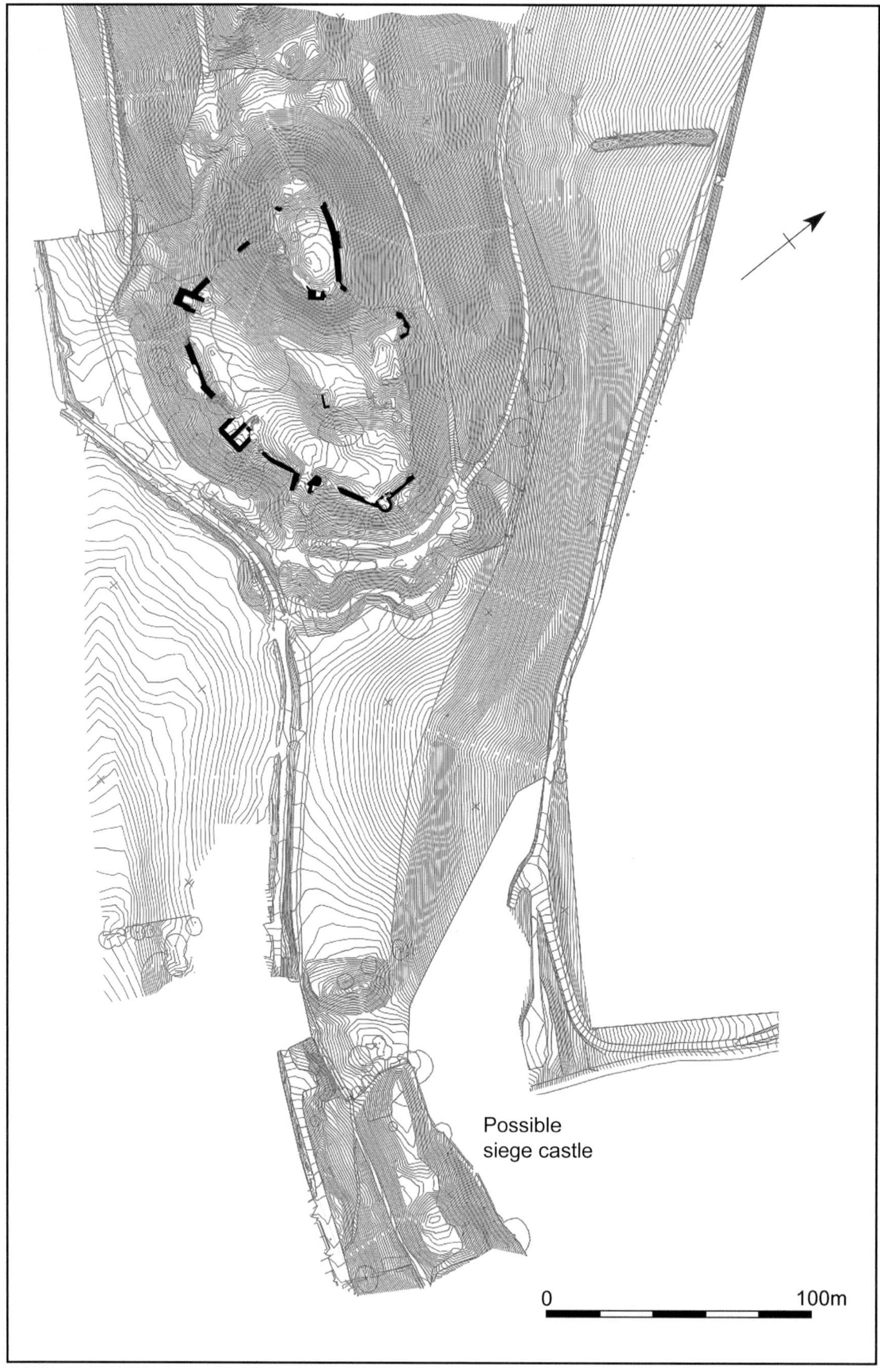

FIGURE 2.15
Detailed topographical survey of Wigmore Castle

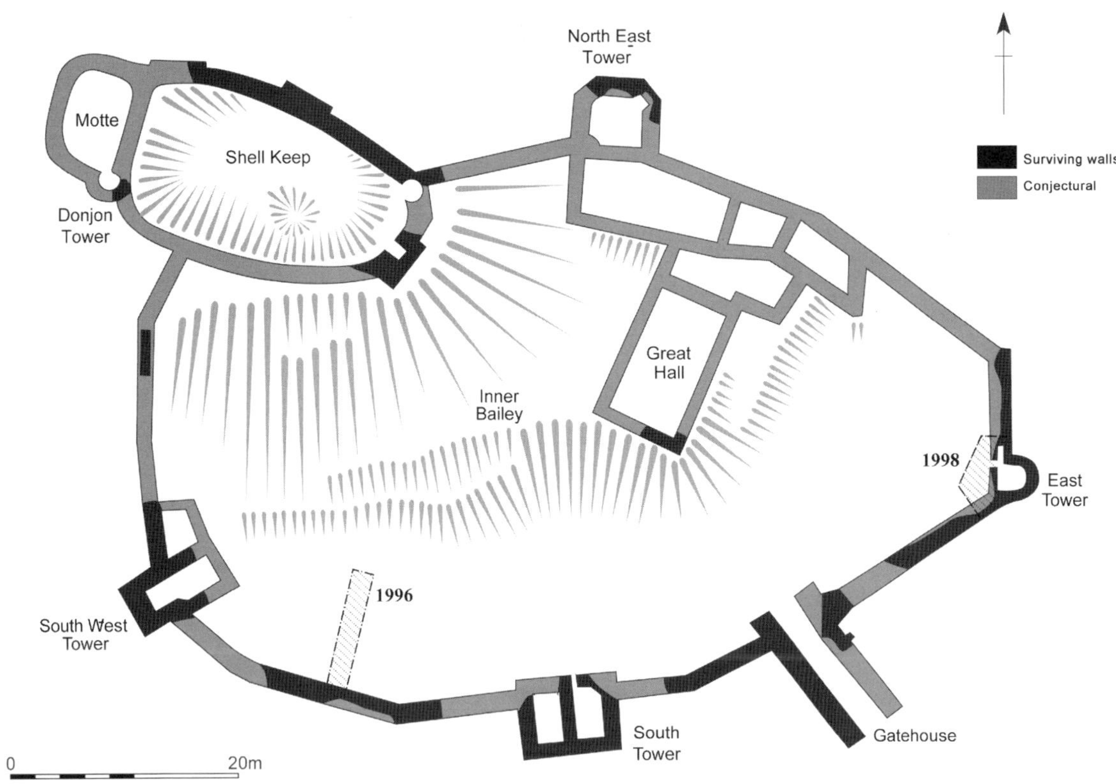

FIGURE 2.16
Plan of the Inner Bailey and Keep, showing surviving (in black) and conjectured (in grey) masonry

FIGURE 2.17
Wigmore Castle, engraving by V Green and F Jukes after a painting by W Hodges, 1778 (copyright: The British Library Board. British Library K Top 15 111.c)

1778 Green and Jukes engraving (Figure 2.17) may represent the remains of this turret, and Shoesmith (1998, 5) noted the presence of what he interpreted as the remains of a semi-circular turret or tower on this stretch of curtain wall.

In the centre of the Inner Bailey was the hall and chamber block complex, now visible only as earthworks and a few masonry fragments. Substantial masonry remains are visible in this area in both the 1773 (Figure 2.4) and 1778 engravings (Figure 2.17). The latter, taken from a different angle from the earlier one, makes it clear that these were indeed the remains of the hall, and not of the North-East Tower, which is also visible in that view. The Buck shows the principal structure as two storied (the floor possibly inserted) and with what appears to be a four-centred arch. There is documentary evidence for a richly furnished chapel (TNA E163/4/48 (2a) and E163/4/48 (5b) + (5c); BL MS Add 60584), but no fabric can be associated with it today.

Both the 1996 and 1998 excavations and the fabric survey (Cooke 2008) revealed considerable evidence for timber buildings built against the back of the Inner Bailey curtain wall for almost its entire circumference, and there were probably additional buildings in the centre of the Inner Bailey. The excavations and Cooke's survey also found evidence that parts of the curtain wall were rebuilt in the 15th century, and there is some evidence for work on the South Tower. At the top of the site was a Shell Keep with at least one mural tower, and possibly more, and physical evidence for additional buildings against its inner face (Cooke 2008). The Shell Keep was accessed by a gateway at its south-east corner, and there was also access on the south-west side. At the summit of the site was a motte and donjon tower that now survives only as a tall, narrow fragment of the former staircase. The 1806 Hearne and Byrne print (Figure 2.7) provides some evidence for this tower, and in particular, shows apparently round arches and vaulting, suggesting it was 12th-century in origin.

Other earthworks probably associated with the castle include a group of mounds immediately to the east of the Outer Bailey, possibly siege works associated with the siege of 1155 (Figure 2.15), and a mound immediately to the north-west of the castle beyond the outer ditch, which may also have been a siege castle (Brown 2002). There may have been additional fortified outworks beyond the park to the north-west (SMR 32589).

2.5 THE CASTLE DEER PARKS AND OTHER RELATED FEATURES

The ridge behind the castle to the north-west, now known as Wigmore Rolls, was enclosed as a deer park in the Middle Ages and early modern periods (Figure 2.18). As well as providing a hunting ground, the parks also formed a natural larder for game meat. Part of the park pale can be seen in Wigmore Rolls (SMR 32603), a post-medieval holloway may follow its course further north (SMR 32610), and another bank and ditch seen as earthworks in Wigmore Rolls may also have been associated with the park or with woodland management in the area (SMR 32581). Other parks and forests on nearby Mortimer lands included the free chase or forest at Deerfold about 6.5km south-west of the castle, and the park at Gatley about 3km south-east of the castle on the other side of the moor. A little further away were the parks at Pembridge and Thornbury in Herefordshire, and Earnwood and Cleobury Mortimer in Shropshire, and the free chases or forests at Bringewood and Mocktree in Shropshire and Wyre in Worcestershire (*CPR* Edward I, 1292–1301, 628). The park at Gatley was sold and disparked in the 1550s, probably in 1557 (*CPR* Philip and Mary, 1557–58, 266), and Deerfold was separated from the Wigmore lands in 1591, when it was leased by the Crown for the support of the iron works at Bringewood. In the early 17th century, part of Deerfold was enclosed, with the rest enclosed in 1810–28 (Tonkin 1984, 292–293). Wigmore park, directly behind the castle to the north, was cleared in the 1660s and early 1670s as part of a wider reorganisation of the landscape around Wigmore by Edward Harley (NRO DD/P6/9/1/9).

Brown (2002) suggested that the park boundary on the east encompassed the area below the castle to the north-east that is enclosed by a pair of parallel banks and ditches, now partly ploughed out (Figure 2.18). Where they survive, the banks have hedges probably dating to the mid-17th century (David Lovelace pers comm), which suggests that the hedges date to the clearance and partial enclosure of the castle site in the 1660s, but does not necessarily date the banks on which they stand. There are a number of problems and questions relating to this area. Firstly, the ditches have banks on their outer sides, suggesting that the enclosure was to keep animals out, rather than keep them in. Secondly, although Brown suggested that the park's eastern boundary ran along the road, both banks appear to continue across the road and to be part of a larger field system that might perhaps pre-date the road and therefore be pre-11th century. The northern of the two banks may indeed be continued in field boundaries as far as the line of the old Roman road. English Heritage's National Mapping Programme (NMP) noted evidence for ploughing in the southern part of the ditched area and also in all of the corresponding area on the other side of the road (Figure 2.18).

As well as the parks, there was demesne, arable and meadow. Other agricultural features associated with the castle included a garden with a courtyard and barns (TNA C133/114(8)), a dovecot (TNA C133/114(8), E142/27 and E372/177(46)), fish-ponds (TNA C133/114(8), E142/27, E372/177(46) and E163/4/48; *CPR* Henry IV, 1405–1408, 219; *CIPM* XXII, Henry IV, 453), and what are described as 'ditches' or 'two ditches' below the castle (TNA C133/114(8), E142/27, E372/177(46)). It has been suggested that these were the two ditches which ran eastwards from the castle down to the moor (Brown 2002), but it may also refer to the moat and associated water system, including a ditch or stream running along the west side of the Outer Bailey. Further afield there was a pond 'below the vill at Wigmore', and another very large fishpond at Burrington (Bayliss 1958–60, 44–45).

Wigmore Moor

The low-lying area to the north of the castle is known as Wigmore Moor or Mere, and may give the place its name. It would have been wet and boggy at all times in the Middle Ages, and would have been actively flooded in wet weather. The inventories of 1322 and 1324 include an item of 10 drums for hunting wildfowl: 1322 *taboribus pro riparia* (TNA E154/1/11B), 1324: *x. tabours pur la Rivere* (TNA E163/4/48 (2a)), almost certainly for use on the moor. The Enclosure Act of 1772 included 103 acres 1 rood 27 perches on Wigmore Moor, and also provided for the cutting of drains on the moor (Tonkin 1975). It is not clear when the rest of the moor was enclosed, but the enclosure process, with its regular field boundaries, was complete by the time of the tithe map of 1845. Some of the moor drainage may actually have taken place before the 1770s, as the Great Drain was also referred as the New Drain in this period, suggesting the presence of earlier drains (Tonkin 1975, 294). To the south-west of the castle, Barnet wood and Woodhampton wood (or Wood wood) were enclosed in 1772 (Tonkin 1975), and an area around Deerfold wood was enclosed in 1810–28, the rest of Deerfold having been enclosed in the mid-17th century (Tonkin 1984).

2.6 THE TOWN OF WIGMORE

Wigmore today is only a small village, but it preserves the fossilised boundaries of many medieval burgage plots. The remains of the former market place, in the centre of the village where the lane leading up to the castle meets the main road (A4110), are also visible (Dalwood 2005) (Figure 2.19). The town had an irregular cross-shaped plan formed by the main road, the road to the castle and that leading eastwards across the moor. There were three gates, which were certainly in use at the time of the town fairs, and presumably at other times as well. These were called the Hereford, Ludlow and Welsh gates (Smith 2002, 362), and must have stood on the roads to the south, east and north respectively, with that leading west into the castle guarded by the castle itself. On the 1845 tithe map (HRO L319) there was a tollgate on the road leading north where a lane branched off onto the moor, but it is unclear if this represents the position of a medieval gate. Also on the tithe map,

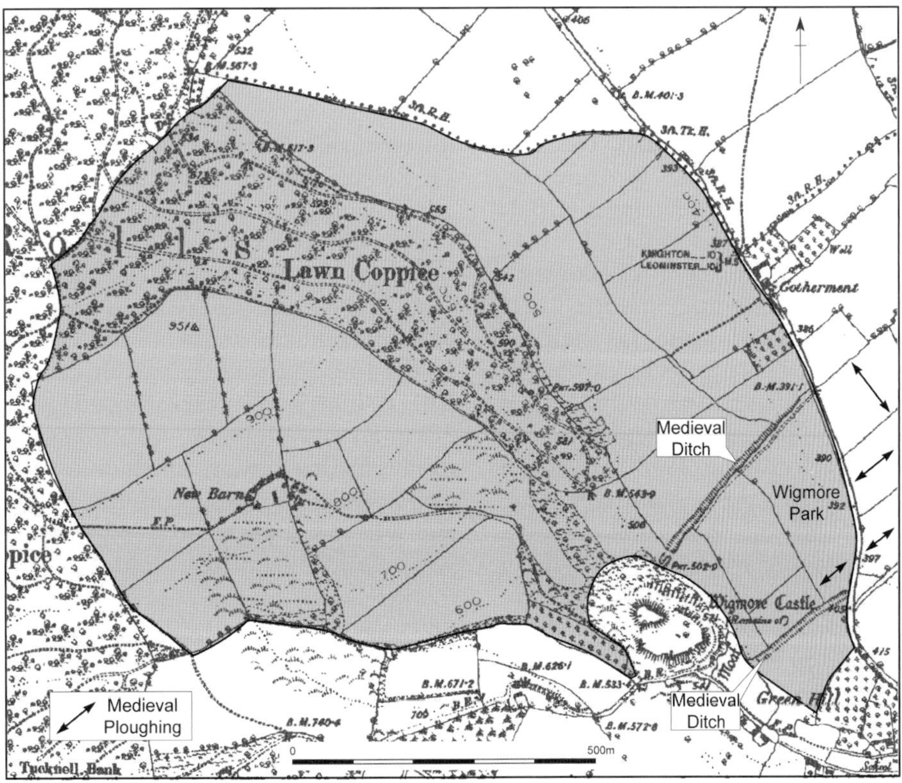

FIGURE 2.18

Wigmore park, showing medieval ditches running down to the moor and evidence of medieval ploughing

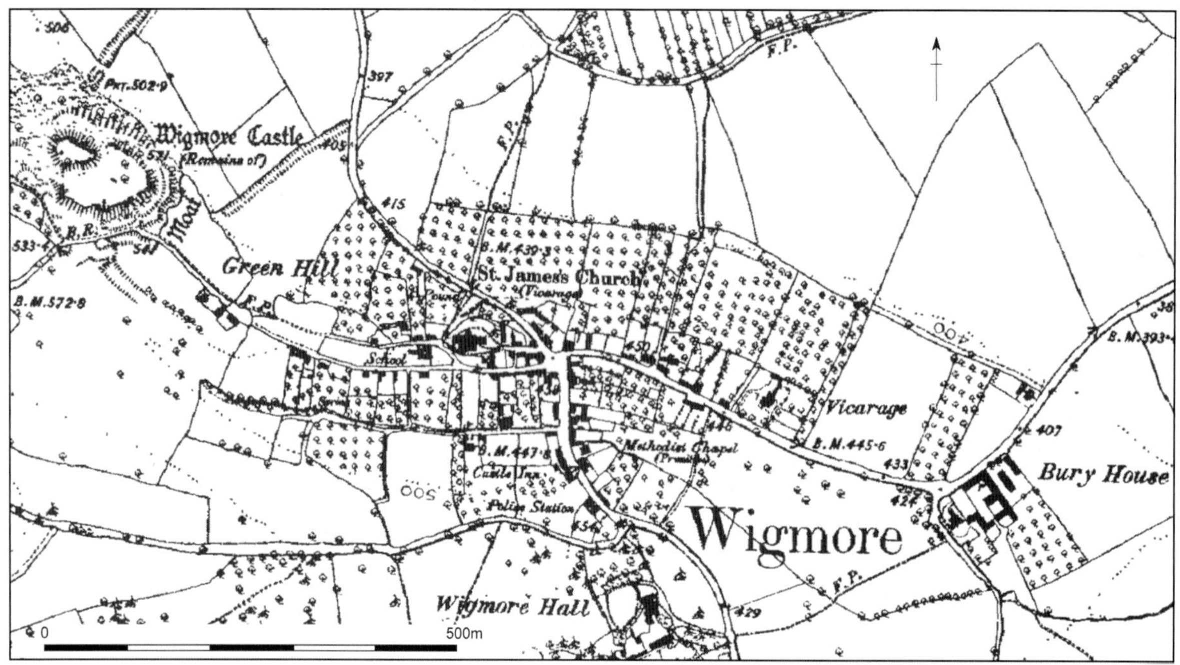

FIGURE 2.19
Wigmore town, showing burgage plots and the former market place (first edition Ordnance Survey, 1886)

the northern, upper section of the Outer Bailey is called 'Courthouse Close', presumably referring to the use of a building there as the manorial court, but it is not known if this was a medieval or post-medieval designation.

No documentary or archaeological evidence has been found to suggest a substantial pre-Conquest settlement at Wigmore, although there may have been a small hamlet there (see below). The present town of Wigmore, with its planned layout, was founded at the same time as the castle or very shortly thereafter. It grew quickly, and, by the time of Domesday, it rendered £7 (DB 179v, 183v). By the early 14th century it had 140½ burgages (*CIPM* IV, Edward I (29–35), 157–166; TNA C133/114), which compares favourably to the 102¾ burgages in Cleobury Mortimer (Shropshire) and the 262½ burgages in New Radnor (Radnorshire) at the same date (Beresford 1967, 257). The Enclosure Act of 1772 listed 37 burgess holders having between them a total of 140 and 1/6th burgage plots, plus 1/15th allocated to the manor (Tonkin 1975, table I), a virtually identical figure to the 140½ burgages of the early 14th century. Despite the presence of burgesses and burgage plots, Wigmore apparently never had a royal charter as such, nor was it ever a parliamentary borough. In the early 1640s, the Harleys made attempts to have their son Edward elected as an MP for the putative borough of Wigmore, but this came to nothing (Eales 1990).

A market and a fair at Wigmore were first mentioned in Edmund (I) Mortimer's *inquisition post mortem* of 1304, but both were almost certainly already in existence by 1272 (O'Donnell 1970, 190), and it is likely that both had ancient origins, probably dating to the later 11th- or early 12th-century foundation of the town. A measure of the importance of the market at Wigmore can be seen in the fact that by 1500, it was one of only nine markets surviving in Herefordshire (the others being at Bromyard, Hereford, Kington, Ledbury, Leominster, Pembridge, Ross and Weobley). It was in decline by the late 17th century, but the market hall still appears on the tithe map of 1845 (HRO L319; O'Donnell 1970, 191).

The fair at Wigmore, however, persisted much longer than the market. The medieval fair was held on 25 July, and in 1610, Sir Thomas Harley was granted a licence for another fair on 25 April. Both fairs would have been principally livestock markets, with animals coming from Wales into England, with cattle and oxen being the main commodity in April, and lambs and horses sold in July (Smith 2002, 358). In the late 17th and early 18th centuries, the fairs had catchment areas that extended for approximately 32km around Wigmore, with some buyers coming from further away, including Worcestershire, Oxfordshire, Northamptonshire, Buckinghamshire and Wiltshire (Smith 2002, 362–368). The fair dates were changed in 1751 to 6 May and 5 August. The market house, in existence in 1845, had gone by 1885, and the August fair ceased in the late 19th or very early 20th century. The May fair continued as a pleasure fair until 1965. It is likely that the Shrewsbury–Hereford railway, opened in 1852, helped to end the fairs' utility as droving became a thing of the past (Smith 2002, 376).

Wool was another major commodity sold in Wigmore. A wool merchant, Philip de Wigmore of Ludlow, is mentioned in 1272, when he was given licence to export 20 sacks of wool, a not inconsiderable amount (*CPR* 1266–72, 692), and in 1338, the merchants of the society of Peruzzi bought at Wigmore 35 of the 200 sacks of wool they were licensed to buy in England (*CCR* 1337–40, 499). Wool was still being sold in Wigmore at the July fair in the early 18th century (Smith 2002, 362). There was apparently also some cloth-making in the area, as a woman from near Wigmore was selling cloth in Ludlow in the late 13th century (Miller 1965, 71), and some leather-working trades. For instance, a glover from Leintwardine was mentioned in a court case of 1399 (*CCR* 1396–99, 275).

The parish church

The parish church of St James, Wigmore was built in the later 11th century (Figure 2.20). Tonkin (2002, 1) suggested that the roughly circular shape of the churchyard is indicative of an earlier origin, but there is no other evidence for this, and the shape of the churchyard may have been determined as much by the topography of the ridge as anything else. Although not mentioned in Domesday, by around 1100 it was a small collegiate church with three canons. The history of Wigmore Abbey assigns its foundation to Ralph (I) Mortimer (Dickinson and Ricketts 1969, 415), but this may refer to the establishment of the canons rather than to the church itself, as the church must be contemporary with the town. Alternatively this may provide a foundation date for both town and church by Ralph Mortimer in the later 1070s, somewhat after the establishment of the castle.

The canonries associated with St James, Wigmore, were subsequently assigned to the Victorine abbey founded at Shobdon by Oliver de Merlimond, steward to the Mortimers, *c*1130. At some point in the mid-12th century, perhaps in the late 1150s or 1160s, the abbey was moved from Shobdon to Eye and then to the parish church in Wigmore. The site proved too steep and cramped, however, and a new abbey church was built some time in 1172–79 at Adforton, just to the north-east of Wigmore (Dickinson and Ricketts 1969, 417; Breen 2001). The abbey church became the principle mortuary chapel of the Mortimers, leaving the parish church for the use of the townsfolk.

The nave of Wigmore parish church is late 11th century and preserves much herringbone masonry of this period; its large size reflects the church's original use as a collegiate church. The original chancel was demolished and rebuilt longer and narrower in the early 14th century; the chancel arch and south aisle are also early 14th century and the West Tower is dated by the RCHM (1934, 205) to the mid-14th century. The 14th-century rebuilding almost certainly dates to the time of Roger (V) Mortimer, and is probably contemporary with his rebuilding of the castle.

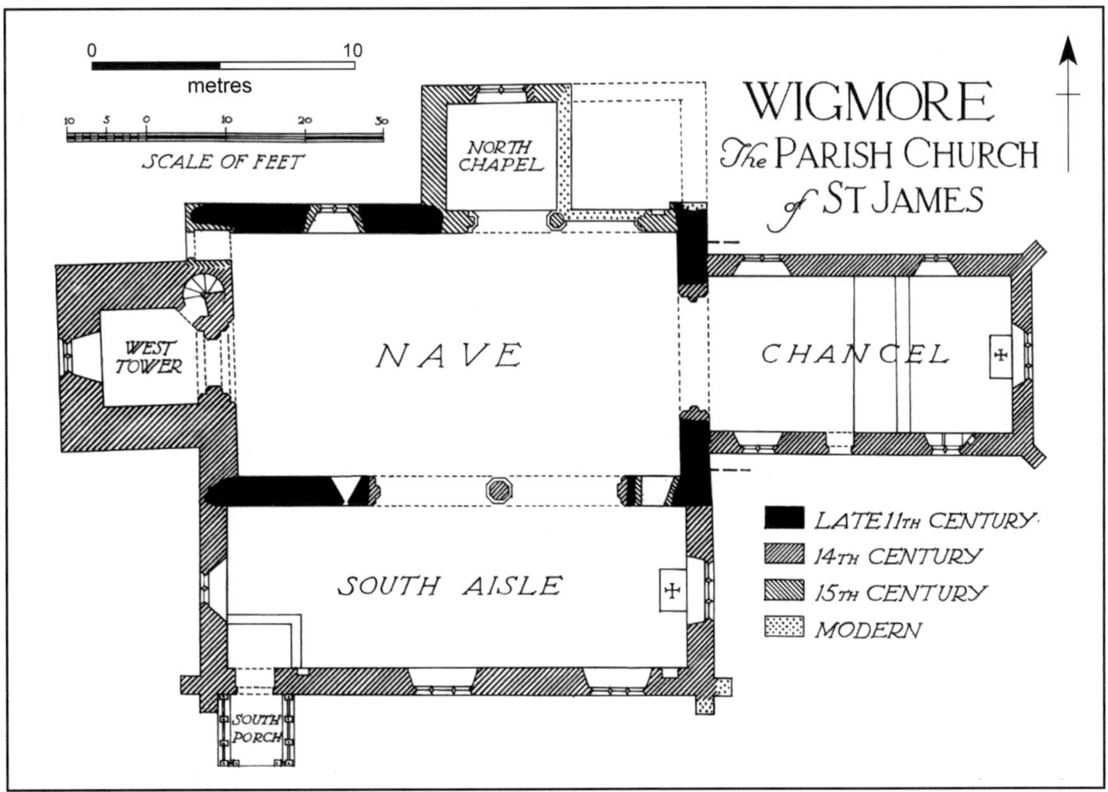

FIGURE 2.20

Plan of the medieval church of St James, Wigmore (after RCHM 1934, MD93_00236) (copyright: English Heritage)

Writing in 1645, Symonds noted that the church had glass with the arms of Mortimer in the east window of the south aisle. He also noted the presence of a tomb slab ('a flat stone') in the south aisle with 'the portrait of a man in armour' (Symonds 1859, 262). This effigy was said by Blount, writing in 1675, to be John Wigmore of the House of Euston. Tonkin (2002, 4) suggested that this aisle was built as the chantry of St Mary, or Lady Chapel, mentioned in the will of John Lenthall and in documents from the time of the Dissolution (*CPR* Edward VI, 1547–48, 352). The combination of the early 14th-century architectural detailing and Mortimer glass lends weight to an attribution of the aisle's construction to Roger (V) Mortimer.

The North Chapel was dated by the RCHM (1934, 204–205) to the 15th century, but by Tonkin (2002) to the mid-14th century. The latter seems more likely. Of the North Chapel, Blount noted that:

> In the windows you may see the remains of excellent stained glass, with the arms of Bohun, Montacute [Montagu], Mortimer and Badlesmere in several places, and in the borders white roses, castles and flowers de Lires [fleurs de lys] painted. There Mortimers armes are thus blazoned by a skilful herald...
>
> (HRO CF50/248 fol 139v, formerly HCL FLC 942.44).

The combination of these four families must indicate that the North Chapel was the work of Roger (VI) Mortimer, 2nd Earl of March (1328–60), whose wife was Philippa Montacute (or Montagu). His mother was Elizabeth Baddlesmere, who married William de Bohun, 1st Earl of Northampton, as her second husband. Therefore, this dates the North Chapel to the mid-14th century, and not to the 15th century as suggested by the RCHM. Both the glass and the monument are now lost.

The North Chapel was used as an elaborate family pew for the Kevill-Davies family of Croft Castle in the 18th century, and was reduced in size and remodelled in 1865. The south porch is also 19th century (RCHME 1934, 203–205). The chancel has good 15th-century stalls, the pulpit is early 16th-century, and the font is medieval, but the church was otherwise refurnished and extensively restored in 1864 by G F Bodley.

2.7 HISTORY AND DEVELOPMENT OF WIGMORE CASTLE

Prehistoric to pre-Conquest development

Although the castle itself was founded in the post-Conquest period, there was some activity in the area nearby from an earlier date. Several early sites have been found in Wigmore Rolls to the north of the castle, including a possible barrow (SMR 32586, SO38726978), and a large rectangular earthwork enclosure, 60m x 50m, probably the remains of an Iron Age or Romano-British farmstead (SMR 32597, SO38937004). A sub-circular enclosure or camp seen in field boundaries has also been identified in Deerfold to the south of the castle (SMR 31641, SO37806840).

There is evidence for Roman-period activity in the general vicinity of Wigmore, most notably in the Roman town at Leintwardine just to the north (Brown 1996). A Roman road ran north–south from Hereford to Leintwardine and passed just to the east of the Wigmore spur across the lower ground (Figure 2.12). It then ran across the moor and near the site of what later became Wigmore Abbey. Sections of it survived in the 12th century, when it was referred in the Wigmore Abbey chronicle as Stanway or Stone Way (Dickinson and Ricketts 1969, 440–441), although it is unclear if this refers to the stretch of road to the north of the abbey still visible today as a lane, or to the now lost section to the south. There is also evidence of a temporary Roman camp about 136m square with its west side adjacent to the Roman road in the area of Bury Court farm at the base of the Wigmore spur (SMR 6350, SO42006900), but the archaeological excavations did not reveal any evidence for Roman occupation on the castle site itself, nor has any been previously posited.

The Roman road was on very low-lying ground, and ran close, probably too close, to the wet mere area of the moor. Today, an approximately 7.5km stretch of the Roman road across Wigmore vale between Yatton, north of Aymestry, and the bridge at Leintwardine is bypassed by what is now the A4110. This road, which follows higher ground above the valley bottom, passes through the centre of Wigmore village and was almost certainly constructed between *c*1070 (when the castle was built) and 1086 (the first reference to Wigmore Borough). The lowest-lying sections of the Roman road probably went out of use at the same time, although the stretch north of Wigmore Abbey may have been retained or rebuilt by the abbey as a link to the bridge at Leintwardine to the north. A further road at right angles linked the abbey to the new main road. The new line of the road would not only have improved its utility in the wetter months, but also made it easier to defend as it now passed just below the castle.

There is no evidence for extensive Anglo-Saxon settlement at Wigmore. Wigmore stands on what was in 1066 waste called Merestun or Merestone, held by Gunnfrothr for King Edward as part of the manor of Kingsland (DB fol 179v and 183v). Gunnfrothr was almost certainly the same man as Gunnvarthr, who held a compact estate in the area including Brampton Bryan and Lingen (C P Lewis pers comm). The ridge on which Wigmore stands is at the centre of this holding. The name Merestun or Merestone suggests that there was some form of settlement (or tun) by the mere (lake or wet ground), but this is unlikely to have been more than a small agricultural hamlet, and it is possible that it was no more than a historical memory of earlier occupation in the area. To date the archaeological record has not revealed evidence of substantial settlement in or around Wigmore village or castle in the pre-Conquest period.

Neither is there any evidence for earlier fortification of the castle site. The fallacious suggestion that the present-day castle at Wigmore stands on the site of Winingamere, a fortification built by Edward the Elder in 971, was first mooted by William Camden in the early 17th century (Camden 1637, 619). It is possible that this represented a local legend which had grown up in the later Middle Ages, perhaps in the late 14th century in connection with the hagiography of the Mortimers as descendent of the kings of England, Wales, Scotland and Ireland that developed when Roger (VII) Mortimer, 4th Earl of March (1374–98), was considered heir presumptive to the English throne (Giffin 1941). Despite the fact that scholars such as Armitage (1904, 439) have discounted this idea as implausible on historical grounds, it was still repeated in the literature on the castle well into the 20th century (e.g. Howse 1950, 19). In a recent article, however, Haslam definitively proved that Edward the Elder's fortification at Wingamere was, in fact, near the present-day Newport in Essex (Haslam 1988).

Late 11th century

Domesday records that Wigmore Castle was built by Earl William [fitz Osbern], often incorrectly called Earl of Hereford (DB 183v; DNB, 'William fitz Osbern'). He probably also founded the town of Wigmore, worth £7 in 1086 (DB 183v) and the parish church. Fitz Osbern, one of the Conqueror's closest associates, and one of the largest post-Conquest land holders, built a string of castles along the Welsh border, including Chepstow, Monmouth (Monmouthshire), and Clifford (Herefordshire), as well as refortifying Shrewsbury (Shropshire) and Hereford (Herefordshire). He was killed in February 1071, and therefore, Wigmore's foundation must date to the period 1067–70. William fitz Osbern was succeeded by his son, Roger de Breteuil, Earl of Hereford, but in 1075 Roger was deprived of his lands and imprisoned for his part in the Revolt of the Earls. He was never released and died in prison at some point in the late 11th century (DNB, 'Roger de Breteuil').

It was probably after Roger de Breteuil's imprisonment in 1075 that Wigmore passed to the Mortimer family, although it is possible that the transfer occurred immediately after fitz Osbern's death. By the time of Domesday, the castle was held by Ralph (I) de Mortimer (deceased in or after 1104), but it is again unclear if it had passed directly to him from Roger de Breteuil, or if it was initially held by his father, Roger (I) de Mortimer (floruit *c*1054–1080). It has been suggested that Roger (I), a distant cousin of the Conqueror with whom the Conqueror had fallen out, never came to England but always remained in Normandy during the late 11th century (DNB, 'Roger (I) de Mortimer'). Therefore, it seems likely that the grant was directly to Ralph and not to his by then elderly father.

The late 14th-century *Wigmore Chronicle* suggests that Ralph (I) de Mortimer won the castle from Eadric or Edric the Wild (Dugdale 1830, vi, 349; Renn 1968, 345), but there is no evidence that Eadric ever held Wigmore, much less had a castle there. If these legends have any basis in truth, it is possible that Ralph (I) was given the castle for service against Eadric, which would suggest that Ralph (I) de Mortimer was active in Herefordshire in the late 1060s and early 1070s, before William fitz Osbern's death, as the principal period of Eadric's rebellion was *c*1069–70, after which date he was apparently reconciled to the king (DNB, 'Eadric the Wild'). Perhaps more likely, the Eadric legend reflects the fact that Eadric's lands in Hampshire, Leicestershire and Warwickshire, forfeited after his rebellion, were subsequently given to Ralph (I) de Mortimer, although his lands in Herefordshire and Shropshire were not given to the Mortimers. In any case, by 1086 Ralph (I) also held extensive estates in a total of 14 counties including Shropshire, Hampshire, Lincolnshire, Wiltshire, Yorkshire and elsewhere (Hopkinson 1989, 179). Once in the hands of the Mortimers, Wigmore remained in the family until the failure of the male line in 1425, when it passed through the female line to the Dukes of York and eventually through them to the Crown.

William fitz Osbern's initial foundation at Wigmore was as substantial as his other major castles and, at a minimum, included the areas of the Shell Keep and Inner Bailey. Suggestions that the first castle was a tiny motte and bailey on the site of earthwork mounds to the east of the Outer Bailey (Shoesmith 1998 241) can be discounted. The discovery of what are apparently the remains of the late 11th century bank and possible palisade in the 1996 excavation (Chapter 3) is particularly significant in this respect as it demonstrates that fitz Osbern's defences ran inside, but on approximately the same line as, the later curtain walls. Given the presence of late 11th-century defences in the lower section of the Inner Bailey, it is inconceivable that the area of the present motte and Shell Keep were not also fortified. It also confirms that the first phase at Wigmore was largely a timber castle (Higham and Barker 2004, 59). As well as the timber palisaded curtain wall of the Inner Bailey, the first phase structures on both the Shell Keep and the Donjon Tower were probably also substantial reinforced timber fortifications, as the earliest masonry seen in this area was 12th-century (RCHM 1934), but it is possible that there is some late 11th-century masonry surviving below ground level in the Shell Keep walls and/or in the remains of the Donjon Tower. It is uncertain if the Outer Bailey was part of fitz Osbern's foundation or a later addition; the evidence for this is discussed below in relation to the 1155 siege of the castle. It is also probably to him that the very substantial earthmoving necessary to create the moat or ditch between the Inner and Outer Bailey areas, and the ditch to the immediate north-west of the Shell Keep, can be attributed.

The 12th century

From an early date Wigmore formed an important base for incursions into Wales by the Mortimers. They probably conquered the cantref of Maelienydd, adjoining their Herefordshire and Shropshire holdings, in the late 11th century, and they certainly held it *c*1135 (Hopkinson 1989, 180), although their control of their Welsh lands was rarely secure, and they would lose Maelienydd for much of the late 12th century. Ralph (I) de Mortimer was succeeded sometime in or after 1104 by his eldest son Hugh (I) de Mortimer (d. *c*1148x50), sometimes confused with his own son Hugh (II) de Mortimer who died *c*1181 (DNB, 'Hugh II de Mortimer'; Hopkinson 1989, 182) although this lineage has recently been challenged (see Section 10.3). Hugh (I) appears to have supported King Stephen over the rival claims of Matilda during the Anarchy period in the second quarter of the 12th century, as his lands were exempted from a grant of all of Herefordshire to Robert, Earl of Leicester, in 1144. Instead, Mortimer was a tenant-in-chief of the king. This exemption for the Mortimers from control by an overlord other than the king would be repeated in later years and formed a cornerstone of their undiluted power in the Marches (Hopkinson 1989, 183).

Hugh (I) Mortimer died *c*1148x50 and was succeeded by his eldest son Roger, but little is known of this Roger, who died *c*1153 and was succeeded by his younger brother, Hugh (II) de Mortimer. Hugh (II) almost immediately fell foul of the new King Henry II's policies to reclaim royal castles and impose order on the country. Henry demanded the return of royal castles held by his barons, among them Bridgnorth ('Brug'), Shropshire, held by Hugh (II) apparently on the basis of a grant by Henry I (Hopkinson 1989, 185). Perhaps because he made the mistake of 'estimating the king to be a mere boy and indignant at his activity' (Searle 1980, 159–161), Hugh refused to return Bridgnorth, and in 1155 Wigmore, Cleobury and Bridgnorth were besieged by Henry II (Howlett 1884–89, iv, 184–185; Stubbs 1870–80, i, 162). Cleobury is said to have been destroyed (although it was rebuilt in time for Hugh (II) to die there in 1180x81), and Hugh was apparently trapped within Bridgnorth Castle. He was forced to publicly surrender Bridgnorth to the king in early July 1155, but was otherwise allowed to retain his lands.

Exactly what happened to Wigmore during the siege of 1155 is not clear, but it has been suggested that the earthworks to the east and west of the castle may have been constructed by the king during the siege (Shoesmith 1998, 241). The eastern set of earthworks, a group of three mounds (Figure 2.15) immediately outside the Outer Bailey enclosure on the higher, east side, are particular interesting in this respect. The 1998 geophysical survey recorded anomalies in the mounds that could represent the remains of masonry structures (Payne 2007, 5–6), although whether these were primary or secondary is not known. If these were indeed related to the 1155 siege, then they indicate the approximate position of the outer defences of the castle in this period, and thus demonstrate that the Outer Bailey was also in existence and had reached its full extent by the mid-12th century. On the other hand, Brown preferred to see them as castle outworks of an unknown date (Brown 2002, 17).

Hugh (II) de Mortimer was also notable for his involvement in the foundation of Wigmore Abbey, which was to become the burial place of the Mortimers. Wigmore Abbey has its origins in a house of Victorine canons founded probably in the 1130s at Shobdon (Herefordshire) by Oliver de Merlimond, steward of Hugh (I) de Mortimer. The house moved several times, including briefly to Wigmore parish church, before Hugh (II) gave them a site at Adforton to the north-east of the castle in 1172. The foundation stone was laid in 1172 and the church was dedicated in 1179. Hugh (II) was buried there, beginning a tradition of Mortimer burials at the abbey (Dickinson and Ricketts 1969). Later chroniclers speak of very fine Mortimer memorials in the abbey church (Given-Wilson 1997, 46–47), but these were all lost at the Reformation when virtually all of the abbey, except for the 14th- and 15th-century abbot's lodging, now a private house, was destroyed (Brakspear 1933; Breen 2001).

Hugh (II) was succeeded by his son Roger (II) de Mortimer (d. 1214), who was heavily involved in struggles with the Welsh. At the time of his father's death, Roger (II) was in prison for his part in the death of Cadwallon ap Madog, the then ruler of Maelienydd, who was killed by Roger's men while under a royal safe-conduct. Roger was apparently released *c*1182 and by 1195 had brought Maelienydd under Mortimer control again (Hopkinson 1989; DNB, 'Hugh (II) de Mortimer'), almost certainly using Wigmore as his principal base from which to do so. Roger (II)'s involvement with the Welsh brought him into conflict with the king again in 1191, when he was said to be plotting with the Welsh, and probably with Prince John, against the king, Richard I, who was then absent from England on crusade (Hopkinson 1989, 188). The royal chancellor and chief justiciar, William Longchamp, apparently attacked Wigmore at that time (Appleby 1963, 30). Roger (II) was exiled for his part in the rebellion, but it is uncertain if he actually left England, perhaps because of Longchamp's fall from power later that year. Certainly in 1192, Roger (II) received 10 marks from the king for his campaign against the Welsh, and in 1194, he was once again serving the king against the Welsh (Crump 1997, 119).

Roger (II) also played his part in one of the defining events in both English and French history, the loss of Normandy in 1204. Although the Mortimers were deprived of their eponymous ancestral lands at Mortemar in the Pays de Caux by Duke William before the Conquest, like many of the Anglo-Norman barons, they retained extensive estates in Normandy throughout the late 11th and 12th centuries. A supporter of King John, Roger (II) was arrested and imprisoned at Dieppe in 1205, but was eventually ransomed for 1,000 marks and had returned to England by 1207 at the latest. As Hopkinson noted, the loss of his Norman lands was a blow to Roger, but it is likely that they had already diminished in value, and his English and Welsh lands, stretching over 13 counties, held great scope for expansion (Hopkinson 1989, 189).

Rebuilding of the castle in stone

At some point in the 12th century, work began to rebuild Wigmore Castle in stone. The first area rebuilt was probably the Shell Keep and Donjon Tower at the top of the site. Hearne and Bryne's engraving of 1806 (Figure 2.7) hints at the presence of round, Norman or Romanesque arches in the vaulting of the Donjon Tower, although it is insufficiently detailed to be certain. Writing in 1874, Clark believed that there was late 11th- or 12th-century Norman work in the Shell Keep and Donjon Tower (Clark 1874), although so much has been lost since Clarke's time that it is difficult to know exactly what he saw. The Royal Commission on Historical Monuments inspectors noted 'a considerable quantity of rough ashlar work with alternate courses of squared and small stone' in the north wall of the Shell Keep (RCHM 1934, 208), dating this masonry to the 12th century; an unpublished sketch of this masonry (Figure 2.9) survives in their notes (RCHM 1932). This stretch of walling was apparently entirely overgrown by the late 1990s, as Cooke could not see it, but he noted the presence of many reused, small, squared blocks in the later medieval work (Cooke 2008). If these blocks were contemporary with the masonry seen by the RCHM, it suggests that there were substantial, early, masonry structures in the Shell Keep that were subsequently rebuilt.

An offset seen at the base of the curtain wall in the 1996 excavations (see Chapter 3) is possibly the first phase of the construction of the stone-built Inner Bailey curtain walls. It is highly likely that the walls to which this offset belonged were built before 1250, probably in the later 12th century, but the archaeological evidence is too inconclusive to be certain of this dating. The dating rests on the structural relationship between the curtain wall, the D-shaped East Tower, and the Gatehouse.

The D-shaped East Tower, with its fireplace and garderobe, was dated by Cooke (2008) to the early 13th century. Investigations suggested that it is an addition to the curtain wall, and therefore, provides a *terminus ante quem* for the construction of the wall itself. The tower, therefore, places the wall in the later 12th or very early 13th century. Unlike the East Tower, however, the first phase of the tower Gatehouse is structurally bonded to the curtain wall, and therefore must also date to the same later 12th- or very early 13th-century building phase as the walls themselves. The Gatehouse was built as a three-storey tower with an attached garderobe on the ditch side (Cooke 2008).

The bailey encompassed by the new stone curtain walls was similar in shape to, but slightly larger than, its predecessor as the evidence for a timber palisade also seen in the 1996 excavation indicates that the rebuilt wall was situated outside the line of the palisade it replaced but on the same alignment; the lower levels were not excavated in 1998, but it is likely that the wall in that area also follows the line of the earlier defences.

Aside from the Gatehouse, the first phase curtain wall may not have had stone-built mural towers, as the East Tower was an addition of the 13th century (Cooke 2008). The South-East, South and North-East Towers appear to be wholly 14th century (Cooke 2008), but it is possible that one or more of the latter stands on unexcavated earlier foundations. There may have been an additional tower or turret between the East and North-East Towers, but its date is unknown (see above).

The 13th century

The loss of Normandy, and with it the Mortimer's Norman lands, in 1204 focussed their attention on Wigmore. Roger (II) de Mortimer died in 1214 and was buried at Wigmore Abbey. He was succeeded by his eldest son Hugh (III), who was closely involved in the ongoing struggles with the Welsh, particularly against Llywelyn ab Iorwerth (*c*1173–1240), also known as Llywelyn the Great, who had recaptured Maelienydd in 1214 (DNB, 'Hugh (II) de Mortimer' and 'Llywelyn ab Iorwerth'). In 1223 King Henry III granted Hugh (III) 20 marks for building works at Wigmore (Pipe Rolls, 7-8 Hen III, 34). This grant was part of a larger parcel of royal grants for castle buildings, including 10 marks for works at Guildford The king visited Wigmore on 13 September 1233 during a trip which also included Leominster (Herefordshire) and Shrewsbury (Shropshire), and was probably part of a campaign against Richard Marshall at Hay, Ewyas and Usk (*CCR* 1231–34, 262; *CPR* Henry III, 1232–47, 25–27; DNB, 'Henry III'). Both the grant and the visit need to be seen in the context of considerable strife with the Welsh in this period.

It is not clear exactly what building works the royal grant related to, or whether additional construction was undertaken in preparation for the royal visit, but it is clear that there was construction ongoing at the castle in the early 13th century. The Inner Bailey defences were completed, and the D-shaped East Tower, which has a fireplace and garderobe, was added to the curtain wall around this time. Cooke (2008) suggested that the tower probably served as a withdrawing chamber from a complex of timber-framed buildings, probably high-status lodgings ranges, built against the curtain wall. It is possible that this tower was built for the king's visit, but as there was also other work in this area at about the same time, including heightening the curtain wall between the tower and the gatehouse, it may have been an unrelated project to improve both the castle's defences and its accommodation.

Hugh (III) de Mortimer died childless in 1227 and was succeeded by his younger brother Ralph (II) de Mortimer (d. 1247) (DNB, 'Hugh (II) de Mortimer'; *CPR* Henry II, 1225–32, 171). In 1230 Ralph (II) made an important political match when he married Gwladus Ddu (d. 1251), the daughter of Llywelyn ab Iorwerth and his wife Joan, the illegitimate daughter of King John (Hopkinson 1991; Crump 1997; DNB 'Llywelyn ab Iorwerth' and 'Joan [Siwan]'). Ralph (II) may have recovered some of the Welsh lands held by Llywelyn at the time of his marriage, but he did not regain Maelienydd until after Llywelyn's death in 1240, and even then found it necessary to see off with force continued Welsh claims. Ralph (II) de Mortimer died in 1246 and, like his brother and forefathers, was buried at Wigmore Abbey (Jones 1973, 241).

His son Roger (III) de Mortimer (1231–82) was underage at the time of his father's death, but in early 1247 paid 2,000 marks to gain his inheritance (DNB, 'Roger (III) de Mortimer'). The same year, he married Maud de Briouze or Braose (d. 1300/1), the wealthy co-heiress of William (V) de Briouze and Eva Marshall, herself the daughter and co-heiress of William (I) Marshall. Maud brought with her, although not until 1259, the lordship of Radnor and parts of Brecon, and from her Marshall forbears, the first of the Mortimer lands in Ireland. Roger (III) continued to be active in service against the Welsh, struggling, and not always succeeding, to keep control of his lands there.

As well as the Welsh wars, Roger (III) and Wigmore Castle were caught up in the Barons' Wars of the early 1260s (Hopkinson 1991). In 1264, Wigmore along with other of Mortimer's lands in Wales and the Marches, including Radnor, fell to a baronial army led by Simon de Montfort (DNB, 'Roger (III) de Mortimer'). In the case of Wigmore, however, the statement that de Montfort had 'levelled all his [Mortimer's] castles, pillaged all his lands, and burnt his manors and vills' (Rothwell 1975, 173) may be an overstatement as there is no substantial physical evidence for large-scale destruction at Wigmore in this period (but see Chapter 9) and the castle was apparently back in Mortimer's hands, and in use, very quickly thereafter. It is possible that either Wigmore or Radnor was commanded by Maud Mortimer at that time (Carpenter 2000, 201). In May 1265, Wigmore played a key part in the escape from prison at Hereford of Prince Edward (later Edward I), when the prince was brought by Mortimer to Wigmore before going on to Ludlow (Jones 1973, 255).

From Ludlow, Prince Edward, Mortimer and his other supporters, including the earl of Gloucester, rode to the battle of Evesham (Worcestershire), where Simon de Montfort was defeated. It has recently been conclusively demonstrated that it was Roger (III) de Mortimer who struck the fatal blow that killed Simon de Montfort (Laborderie *et al* 2000, 405). De Montfort's head was cut off, his testicles removed and draped over his nose, and the whole, horrible package was sent back to Wigmore to Roger's wife Maud (Rothwell 1975, 183; Carpenter 2000, 183 and 201). What she did with it is not recorded, although it has been suggested that the skull may have hung in the hall at Wigmore in the early 14th century (Mortimer 2003, 9). Such ritual humiliation of the despised dead, and of living political prisoners, was commonplace in Wales and the Marches in the 12th and 13th centuries (Insley 2008), but one cannot help wondering whether the dispatch of the grisly remains specifically to Maud Mortimer was a recognition of an unrecorded humiliation she had suffered at the hands of de Montfort the previous year.

Roger (III) de Mortimer remained a close friend and ally of Edward I throughout the rest of his life, and was able to gain exceptional privileges and freedoms for his Marches estates, including those around Wigmore, which should otherwise have been subject to ordinary English law, even as Edward I made attempts to reign in ancient baronial privileges (Hopkinson 1991, 39). Roger (III) officially retired in 1279, hosting a lavish 'round table' tournament at Kenilworth Castle over three days for 100 knights and 100 ladies. During the feast, wine tuns bound with gilt were received from the 'Queen of Navarre' (Blanche de Navarre, wife of Edmund, Duke of Lancaster, Edward I's brother and holder of Kenilworth in the late 13th century). Opened, they proved to contain gold. The casks were subsequently exhibited at Wigmore Abbey (Giffin 1941, 111–112). Despite his so-called retirement, Roger (III) continued to be involved in the struggle against the Welsh, but on 26 October 1282 he died at his manor of Kingsland (Herefordshire) and was buried at Wigmore Abbey (DNB, 'Roger (III) de Mortimer').

Roger (III)'s eldest son Ralph (III) predeceased his father, dying in 1274, and so Roger (III) was succeeded by his second son, Edmund (I) de Mortimer (*c*1255–1304). Roger (III)'s third son, Roger (IV) (*c*1256–1326, 1st Lord Mortimer of Chirk), became an important lord in the Marches in his own right (DNB, 'Roger (IV) Mortimer'). Edmund (I) Mortimer had been destined for the church, and there was some delay in his receiving his father's lands (*CPR* Edward I, 1281–92, 39), which some scholars have suggested indicates that he was not held in high regard by the king (DNB, 'Roger (IV) Mortimer'), but more likely, the delay simply indicated a need to have him released from canonical orders of some form before he could take up military tenure at Wigmore and elsewhere.

Edmund (I) played no less of a role in attempts to subdue the Welsh than his ancestors. In late 1282, for instance, he was part of the force that killed Llywelyn ap Gruffudd, Prince of Wales and grandson of Llywelyn ab Iorweth, a key event in the English struggle for control of Wales (Hopkinson 1995, 303–304; DNB, 'Llywelyn ap Gruffudd'). There can be no doubting that Wigmore Castle was extremely important for the Mortimers in the later 13th century as their main power base. King Edward I stayed at Wigmore in December 1283 and held a chancery there on 22 December 1283 (*CCR* 1279–88, 284). There are also letters dated at Wigmore on 11 and 12 December, suggesting an extended visit (*CPR* Edward I, 1281–92, 107–108), which included other sites in Herefordshire, Shropshire and the Marches. In 1283, the Welsh baron Cadwgan Goch of Arllechwedd complained to the king that 'although he was admitted to the king's grace in this present war... Edmund Mortimer, without observing any rule of right, keeps the said Cadwgan bound in iron chains in his castle at Wigmore' (TNA SC1/18 (163)). Where in the castle Cadwgan was held is not known.

The castle in the later 13th century

Cooke's survey suggested that the majority of the visible fabric of the castle, including the curtain wall mural towers and the extension of the Gatehouse, was built in the early 14th century by Roger (V) Mortimer (Cooke 2008). This confirmed the traditional dating of this masonry. Remfry's suggestion (2000, 22) that much of the visible masonry is datable to the mid-13th-century tenure of Roger (III) Mortimer can be discounted on both architectural and archaeological grounds. On the other hand, it seems improbable that neither Roger (III) nor Edmund (I) Mortimer did anything to the castle, even if it was only to make improvements to timber-framed lodgings buildings in advance of the king's visit in 1283, but conclusive physical evidence for work in this period remains to be found.

Both the manor court at Wigmore (*CIPM* III, Edward I, 189–190), and its parks (*CPR* Edward I, 1292–1301, 628; *CIPM* 4, Edward I, 157–166; TNA C133/114), were mentioned for the first time during the tenure of Edmund (I) Mortimer, but it is almost certain that this was a function of the increasing number of written records in this period and the royal drive to clarify older rights (Clanchy 1993), rather an indication that these were new features at that time.

The early 14th century

Edmund (I) Mortimer died at Wigmore Castle in July 1304 of injuries received in a skirmish at Builth (Mortimer 2003, 16). His teenage son Roger (V) Mortimer (1287–1330) was briefly a ward of Edward II's favourite Piers Gaveston (*CPR* 1301–1307, 308), but he was soon able to buy his succession, probably early in 1305 (Mortimer 2003, 19–20), and in 1306 he was given full control of his lands by the king (*CCR* 1301–1307, 377). Roger (V) had already married Joan de Geneville (or Joinville) *c*1300–1301. The exact date of their marriage is not known, but by the time of his father's death, they already had one or two children (Mortimer 2002, 13–14). Joan's inheritance, which would come from her grandfather and her mother, would eventually include Ludlow Castle as well as substantial lands in Ireland and elsewhere.

Roger (V)'s life has been extensively discussed in recent years (Mortimer 2002; Dryburgh 2002). He spent much of the 1310s in Ireland, having received his de Geneville Irish lands in 1307, and he was also active in quelling revolts in Wales. When in the Marches, he spent a considerable amount of time at Wigmore (BL Harley 1240, fols 40r, 41r, 56v, 58v, 425v; Haines 1978, 218; Mortimer 2002, 304–318), as Ludlow does not seem to have come into his control until after his return from exile in the late 1320s, probably following the death of his mother-in-law during his absence abroad, although the precise date is unknown (Paul Dryburgh pers comm). The marriage in 1316 of Roger (V)'s eldest son Edmund (II) to Elizabeth, the 3-year-old daughter of Bartholomew Baddlesmere, one of the richest men in England, was also the context for many of the guests setting out from Wigmore for the siege of Bristol (Mortimer 2002, 78–80).

Initially a supporter of King Edward II in the tumultuous politics of the early 14th century, in 1321 Roger (V) Mortimer finally joined the side of the rebels. He took part in the siege of Cardiff Castle, and is said to have put its constable into prison at Wigmore (DNB, 'Roger (V) Mortimer'). Outflanked by the king at Shrewsbury, Roger (V) and his uncle Roger (IV) Mortimer of Chirk surrendered to the king in January 1322 and were imprisoned in the Tower of London. Roger (IV) of Chirk died in the Tower in 1326, but on 1 August 1323, Roger (V) managed to escape and fled to France. Once there, he joined forces with Edward II's queen, Isabella, who became (or perhaps already was) his lover. In 1326, they invaded England, and Edward II was captured in November of that year. Edward II was forced to abdicate in favour of his son, Edward III (1312–77) in early January 1327. Isabella was named regent, but as her lover and close companion, Mortimer was *de facto* ruler of England from then until his execution in 1330. Mortimer was created Earl of March in October 1328.

The 14th-century rebuilding

At some point during Roger (V)'s tenure, Wigmore Castle was substantially rebuilt and improved. A two-storey additional structure was added to the front of the Gatehouse, and the late 11th-century ditch or moat between the Inner and Outer Baileys was reshaped and divided into two parallel sections by an outwork with four mantlet towers. The lodgings provision was improved with the addition of the South, South-West and North-East Mural Towers to the Inner Bailey curtain wall. The North-East Tower appears to have served as a solar for a first-floor chamber block, now lost, against the back of the curtain wall. There was additional work on the Shell Keep, where the South-East Tower was also added or remodelled. There may also have been work on the Donjon Tower, but not enough survives to be certain (Cooke 2008).

It is unclear how much of this work was carried out before Roger (V)'s imprisonment in 1321, and how much after his return in 1326, but it seems likely that at least some of the work must date to the period between 1307 and 1321. Inventories taken in 1324–25 when the castle was in royal hands show lavish furnishings with rich textiles and plate (TNA E163/4/48 (2a), E163/4/48 (5b) + (5c); BL MS Add 60584; see also the similar Wigmore inventories of 1331: TNA E101/333/4 and E372/179 (22.d.); Larking 1858; Swynnerton 1914). There was a substantial stock of arms and armour, food stuffs, edible and working animals, and even a collection of games, including a chessboard. The inclusion of swans in the inventory as something possessed by Roger (V) may very well indicate a wet moat, presumably between the Inner and Outer Baileys, where such birds could be kept under some form of control, such as wing clipping and used for display rather than these simply being migratory swans on the mere or some other local water source. There were also peacocks, again birds for display. A hall and a chapel are specifically mentioned, and a kitchen, numerous chambers and farm buildings are implied by lists of relevant contents. Outside the castle there were ditches and fishponds, as well as several parks.

In 1328, following the marriage celebrations of two of his daughters at Hereford, Roger (V) entertained Isabella and Edward III at Ludlow, apparently in a new lodgings range there (Thompson 1889, 57). His biographer has suggested that this demonstrates the lodgings at Wigmore were not completed until 1329 (Mortimer 2002, 207). It is certainly possible that there was work underway at Wigmore in this period, as Roger asked the king for lead from the royal castle at Hanley (*CCR* 1327–30, 293). All the work at Wigmore must certainly have been completed by 1329, when Roger held an Arthurian-themed tournament there attended by Edward III, Isabella and most of the nobles of England (Thompson 1889, 284). Edward III gave Mortimer a goblet with the arms of France and Navarre, his mother's family (TNA E101/384/1 fols 16v and 18v), possibly a reference to the gifts given to Roger (III) in 1279 by Blanche of Navarre at the Kenilworth round table tournament. Nonetheless, Roger (V)'s proud behaviour on the occasion, when he is said to have dressed as King Arthur, with Isabella dressed as Guinevere, and the real king left on the sidelines, provoked scorn even from his own family. His son Sir Geoffrey is said to have called him 'the King of Fools' (Brie 1908, 262).

On 19 October 1330, Roger (V) Mortimer was captured at Nottingham Castle by supporters of Edward III, who at the age of nearly 18 had grown tired of the increasingly overbearing rule of his mother and her lover. Mortimer was executed at Tyburn (Middlesex) on 29 November 1330. His body was taken to the Grey Friar's in Coventry (Thompson 1889, 62), probably at the request of Queen Isabella, who had one of her main manors there (Mortimer 2002, 242). Repeated requests by Roger's widow Joan to have the body brought to Wigmore Abbey appear to have come to nothing (*CCR* 1330–33, 403; *CPR* 1330–34, 196), and it has been suggested that Isabella persuaded her son to block these requests and leave Roger's body near her (Harding 1985; Wright 1998, 25–26). After her husband's death, Joan Mortimer appears to have lived mainly at Ludlow, her family home, but this was not the end for Wigmore.

The later 14th and early 15th centuries

Following Roger (V) Mortimer's death in 1330, the castle was briefly in royal hands, but it was returned to his son Edmund (II) Mortimer in October 1331. Unfortunately, Edmund died in December of the same year, leaving an infant son, Roger (VI) Mortimer (1328–60). After Edmund (II) Mortimer's death, King Edward III stayed at Wigmore again in late July and August 1332, basing his retinue there, although he also visited other places in the area during this time (*CPR* Edward III, 1330–1334, 320–326, 329, 332, 334, 352–353; *CCR* 1330–33, Edward III, 481–482, 488, 580–581, 583–584, 587, 593–594,

596). He must have been attracted as much by the opportunity to drive home his conquest of his rival as he was by Wigmore's well-stocked parks and the rich lodgings built only a few years previously for the royal visit of 1329.

Despite the actions of his grandfather, as he reached manhood the young Roger (VI) Mortimer was greatly esteemed by Edward III and was allowed to regain his lands at an early age, beginning with Wigmore in 1342 (*CCR* 1341–43, 456; *CPR* Edward III, 1340–43, 489). Other lands were gradually also returned to him over the next few years (Figure 2.21).

A close companion of the king, he was a founder member of the Order of the Garter in 1348, and in 1354 the title Earl of March was restored to him. He is known to have raised men from Wales for the king, almost certainly using Wigmore as a base from which to do so. He died in 1360 while campaigning in France, once again leaving a young heir, Edmund (III) Mortimer (1352–81). Edmund (III) Mortimer, 3rd Earl of March, also had a very brief but distinguished career. In 1368 he married Philippa of Clarence, granddaughter of Edward III, who brought with her vast estates in Ireland and elsewhere. He died in Ireland in 1381 of an illness.

Roger (VII) Mortimer (1374–98), 4th Earl of March and 6th Earl of Ulster, was apparently considered a serious claimant to the English throne should Richard II die childless, and he may have been nominated by Richard II as his heir in 1385 (DNB, 'Roger (VII) Mortimer'). The claim came through his mother Philippa of Clarence, granddaughter of Edward III. Summoned to Parliament in Shrewsbury in January 1398, he is said to have been greeted by 20,000 people wearing parti-coloured hoods in red and white in his honour (Given-Wilson 1997, 38–39). In the event, Roger predeceased the king, like his father, dying in Ireland. He was apparently the victim of 'friendly fire', killed by his own men while dressed in Irish clothing (DNB, 'Roger (VII) Mortimer'). He was brought back to Wigmore Abbey for burial.

At the time of his father's death in 1398, Edmund (V) Mortimer (1391–1425), 5th Earl of March and 7th Earl of Ulster, was still only a child. Following the fall of Richard II, Henry IV made Edmund and his younger brother Roger (d. *c*1413), royal wards, and

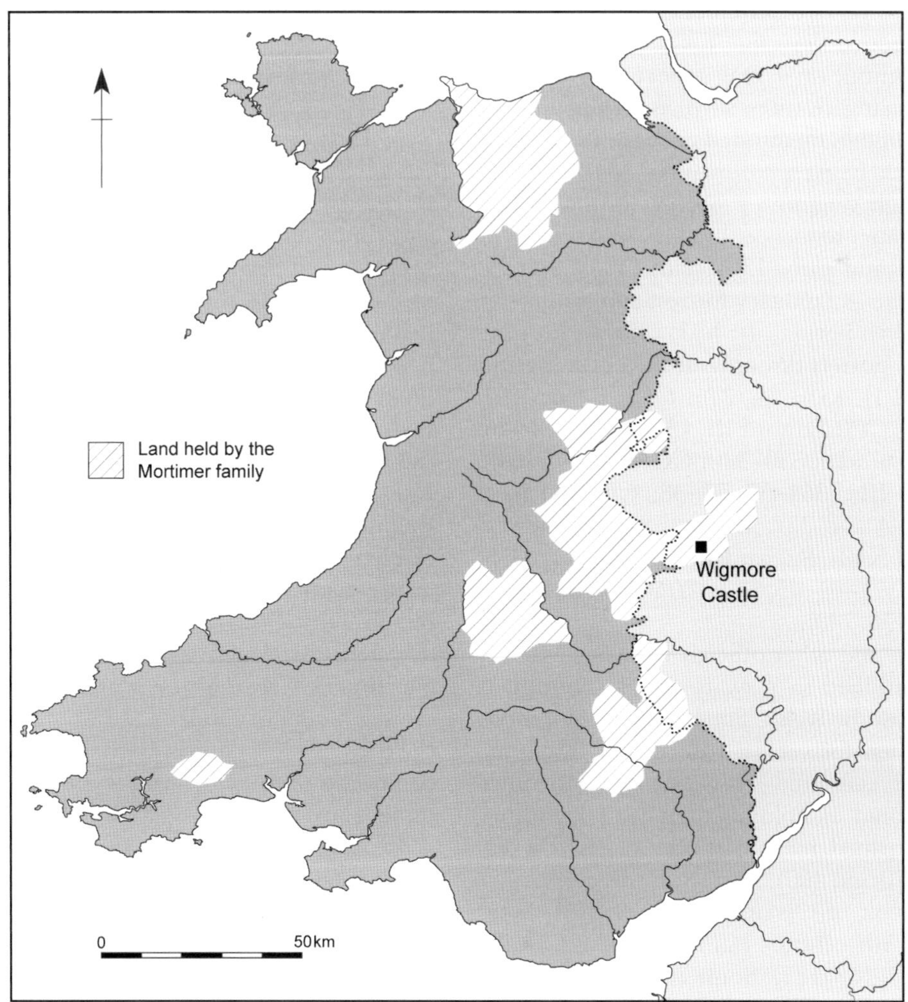

FIGURE 2.21

The Mortimer estates in Wales and the Marches in the mid-14th century (copyright: English Heritage)

for a period they were prisoners at Berkhampstead Castle (Hertfordshire), a clear recognition of their potential claim to the English throne. Until 1413, when he was able to take control of them, Edmund's estates, including Wigmore, were under royal control. In 1423 Edmund was appointed king's lieutenant in Ireland like his father and grandfather before him, and like them, he died there, of plague, at Trim (Co. Meath) in January 1425, leaving no children (DNB, 'Edmund (V) Mortimer'). Edmund Mortimer's heir was his late sister Anne's 12-year-old son, Richard, Duke of York (1411–60), father of the future King Edward IV. Richard was granted livery of his estates, including Wigmore, in 1432 (DNB, 'Richard, Duke of York').

The castle in the later 14th and early 15th centuries

In the 1425 inquest *post-mortem* for Edmund (V) Mortimer, Wigmore Castle was said to be 'derelict and worth nothing' (*CIPM* XXII, 510). This has led some commentators to assume that the castle went out of use after the death of Roger (V) Mortimer in 1330, but other documentary evidence does not bear this out. This statement may have been intended to reduce the value for the inquest (C P Lewis pers comm), or it may reflect the decay of income producing features such as the fishponds, dovecot, and ditches mentioned in the 14th-century sources without being a commentary on the castle per se. Although Wigmore probably was little used as an aristocratic residence by the Mortimers in the later 14th and early 15th centuries, the castle continued in use as a military fortress and as a prison throughout this period. It had official keepers, constables and porters throughout the entire period (*CPR* Edward II, 1330–34, 276; *CPR* Edward III, 1330–34, 264; *CPR* Edward III, 1358–61, 545–546; *CIPM* X, Edward III, 530–540; *CCR* 1360–64, 39; *CPR* Edward III, 1364–67, 37–38; *CPR* Richard II, 1381–85, 94 and 227; *CCR* 1381–85 Richard II, 144; *CIPM* XVII, Richard II, 434 and 437–438; *CPR* Henry IV, 1401–05, 112; *CIPM* XXII, Henry IV, 453, 475–476, 740).

The keepers and other officials were necessary as the castle continued to play its part in continued vigilance against the Welsh. The keeper of Wigmore was to raise men for war in 1367 (*CCR* 1364–68, 371), and several mid-14th-century Mortimer tenants are noted as holding their land by virtue of providing armed men at Wigmore (*CIPM* XI, Edward III, 270 and 400). The castle was garrisoned during the revolt of Owain Glyn Dŵr in the first years of the 15th century (*CPR* Henry IV, 1401–1405, 137–140, 168, 187). Some repairs were made to the castle *c*1333 (TNA C 145/124 (18) A, B and C), and while there is little other definitive archaeological or structural evidence for building works to the castle during the later 14th and early 15th centuries, at the very least, it must have been kept in sufficient repair to allow its continued use.

Wigmore Castle also continued to act as the centre of lordship for the Honour and Liberty of Wigmore. Rents from the borough regularly collected there, and the manor courts were fully functional (*CIPM* XI, Edward III, 530–540, 421; *CCR* 1409–14, 207). The parks were stocked and maintained by parkers and foresters (*CPR* Richard II, 1381–85, 94; *CCR* 1381–85, 144; *CIPM* XVII, Richard II, 434 and 437–438; *CPR* Henry IV, 1401–05, 112; *CPR* Henry IV, 1401–05, 192), and the borough, markets, and fairs continued to function.

Glass, now lost, in the North Chapel, Wigmore parish church, must indicate the work of Roger (VI) Mortimer, 2nd Earl of March (1328–60) (see above). It is possible this also indicates work by Roger (VI) at the castle; certainly it indicates a continued interest in Wigmore on his part. Wigmore Abbey also retained its function as the principal burial place of the Mortimers, and in 1379, a chantry was established at the abbey with two chaplains to pray for the souls of Edmund (III) Mortimer, his wife Philippa of Clarence, and his mother Philippa Montacute (or Montagu), wife of Roger (VI) (*CPR* Richard II, 1377–81, 412). Adam of Usk recorded the elaborate inscriptions of their tombs (Given-Wilson 1997, 46–47).

The 15th century

Richard, Duke of York (1411–60), the son of Anne Mortimer and heir through her to the estates of his uncle, Edmund (V) Mortimer, was knighted in 1426 and in 1432 was given livery of his lands, including Wigmore (DNB, 'Richard of York'). His paternal grandfather, Edmund of Langley, first Duke of York (1341–1402), was the fifth (fourth surviving) son of Edward III, and his mother was the great-granddaughter of Edward III's second son, Lionel. With this ancestry, Richard's claim to the English throne was strong; in 1460 he unsuccessfully challenged Henry VI for the Crown. Richard died at the Battle of Wakefield on 30 December 1460, but in early February 1461, his elder son Edward defeated the Lancastrian forces at the battle of Mortimer's Cross. On 1 March 1461, Edward was crowned king of England as Edward IV, and so from the date of his accession until it was sold at the very beginning of the 17th century, Wigmore Castle was under royal control.

In his biography of Richard, Duke of York, Johnson suggested that Richard's Welsh and Marcher estates were administered largely from Ludlow (Johnson 1991, 14–15). It is true that the castle largely disappears from the documentary sources during the second quarter of the 15th century, but this appears to be at least partially a function of the survival of the sources, rather than an accurate reflection of the state of the castle itself. In general, throughout the entire period from the late 11th to the mid-15th century, the castle only appears in the documents when there was a change of ownership, with an attendant inquest *post-mortem*, or during the minority of an heir, when it was under royal control. At other times, it simply continued to function, but in ways which are now unrecorded as the privately held documents have been lost.

Certainly when the castle reappears in the sources in late 1459, after Richard, Duke of York had fled following his defeat at Ludford Bridge in October of that year, there is nothing to suggest that it had gone out of use in the intervening 34 years. It appears that Wigmore continued to function both as a castle and as a centre of local lordship through the mid-15th century, independent of Ludlow. The castle, honour and lordship had its own receiver in 1459 and 1460, and a constable is mentioned in 1460 (*CPR* Henry VI, 1452–61, 530, 573, 550). In early 1461, Wigmore almost certainly served as a principal staging point for the Yorkist troops in advance of the battle of Mortimer's Cross, a few miles to the south on the road from Wigmore. In 1462, a grant to William Langely, groom of 'le picherhous', recognised his 'good service to the king's father and the king at Northampton, Wakefield and Wigmore' (*CPR* Edward IV, 1461–67, 143).

Like Roger (VIII) Mortimer, a significant part of the dynastic claims of Richard, Duke of York, and his son Edward IV rested on their descent, through Anne Mortimer, Roger (VII) Mortimer's daughter, from Edward III. In consequence, Wigmore retained a very important symbolic significance as the principal seat of the Mortimers. This is indicated by the grant to Edward IV's son, the infant prince of Wales and future Edward V, of a large group of estates beginning with the honour and castle of Wigmore (*CPR* Edward IV, Edward V and Richard III, 1477–85, 59).

Edward IV was seemingly a great builder, apparently undertaking major works at Windsor, Greenwich and Eltham, among other places. At some point in the 15th century, probably during his reign, Wigmore Castle was repaired, although the extent of the work is unclear. Cooke (2008) noted repairs to the South Tower and curtain walls on the south side, and there was some internal refitting in the South Tower, and perhaps elsewhere. In 1870 the basement of the South Tower was discovered, and tiles said by Bound (1876, 31) to be 'of very good workmanship … [with] the fleur-de-lis of France, quartered with the Royal arms of England (Edward IV)' were discovered amidst the rubble. There may also have been work on the Gatehouse and other areas. The castle's continuing military significance is indicated by the grant in May 1483, shortly after Edward IV's death in April, to Henry, Duke of Buckingham, of Wigmore and other Welsh castles with the 'authority to place soldiers in them for their safe custody … receiving the accustomed fees for himself … and for the soldiers and archers in the said castles' (*CPR* Edward IV, Edward V and Richard III, 360). Following this grant, the Duke of Buckingham, too, may have carried out some work at the castle that is not now visible.

The 16th century

Wigmore formed an important part of the early Tudor Crown estates. It was part of the estates held by Arthur, Prince of Wales, in the very late 15th and early 16th centuries, and subsequently by Princess Mary, later Mary I (*CPR* Henry VII, 1485–94; *LPR* Henry VIII, IV, 496). The castle continued in use throughout the 16th century, and it was one of the relatively few royal castles of medieval origin retained by Henry VIII, probably in response to the continued threat of disturbance along the Welsh Marches (Colvin 1968). In 1528, the castle was said to be 'very ruinous' and money for its repair was requested from Cardinal Wolsey (*LPR* Henry VIII, IV, 4096), although it is not clear if this was forthcoming or if any work was carried out at this time. Despite the need for repairs, it is clear that it was still in use. For instance, in the early 1530s, Thomas Croft, son of Sir Edward Croft, receiver general of the earldom of March, dated letters at Wigmore, suggesting that he was in residence there (*LPR* Henry VIII, V, 506; VI, 946; VII, 377). There is no direct evidence for royal visits to the castle in the very late 15th or 16th centuries, although it possible that Prince Arthur went there during his stay at Ludlow, where he died in April 1502. Instead, it seems clear that Wigmore Castle was primarily a working fortress and prison in the Tudor period.

In December 1534, Roland Lee, Bishop of Coventry and Lichfield and Lord President of the Council of the Marches in Wales, wrote that Wigmore was 'utterly decayed in lodgings for want of timely repair', but he noted that 'the walls are good, the lead [possibly from the recently dissolved Wigmore Abbey] will help, and plenty of timber is at hand' (*LPR* Henry VIII, VII, 1571). He spent at least £100 on the works (Auden 1909, 372). Lee seems to have spent some time living at Wigmore, as several of his letters in 1537 are dated there (*LPR* Henry VIII, XII/1, 545, 806, 969), and it was probably at this time that the repairs, said in May of that year to 'go forth well' (*LPR* Henry VIII, XII/1, 1148), were undertaken. There may have been further works in 1538–1539, when Lee was requesting 'a warrant for the stones, iron, lead and glass [from Wigmore Abbey] for the repairs of the King's castle' (*LPR* Henry VIII, XIII/1, 1042) and resisting attempts to sell this material as he did 'not know what will be needed for the repair of the castle of Wigmore' (*LPR* Henry VIII, XIV, 86, 155).

The castle was further repaired by a later president of the Council of the Marches, Sir Henry Sydney (1559–86) (Auden 1909, 372; Skeel 1904,

88). A survey made in 1584 noted that 'the houses buildings walls and other edifices of the said castle being very ruinous and decayed will not without great charges be repaired' (BL Lansdowne 82, fols 199r–v). This survey also provides evidence for there having been two bridges into the park and castle, both of them in very poor condition by that date. As well as being a centre for lordship in the area, with courts apparently held there, there is evidence that Wigmore was used as a prison: Lee wrote to Cromwell about a prisoner kept 'in the porter's lodge [presumably the Gatehouse] and castle of Wigmore' (*LPR* Henry VIII, XIII/1, 1042), and there are also other contemporary references to prisoners held at Wigmore (*LPR* Henry VIII, XIII/1, 519), numbering up to 40 at times (*LPR* Henry VIII, XII/2, 1094). The castle may also have been used in connection with the exploitation of the park at Wigmore, and of the neighbouring parks and chases at Deerfold, Gatley, and Bringewood among others, and the king's lodge in Wigmore park was built or rebuilt *c*1543 (*LPR* Henry VIII, XVIII/1, 445).

The 17th century

In 1595 the borough of Wigmore, with the lands, lordship, honour, manor and castle of Wigmore and many other Marches holdings, was granted to Gelly Meyrick and Henry Lindley, followers of the earl of Essex (*CPR* Elizabeth I, CCCIII, 110–113). Writing in 1645, Symonds (1859, 262) claimed that Meyrick had lived in the castle. Having joined the earl of Essex in rebellion, Gelly Meyrick was executed in 1601 (DNB, 'Gelly Meyrick'). His lands were forfeited to the Crown, and the same year Wigmore Castle, Wigmore Borough and the adjoining estates were sold to Thomas Harley of Brampton Bryan (TNA DD/4P/12/19), who was steward of Wigmore in the late 16th century (LPL S.3199). The castle soon passed to his son Robert Harley (1579–1656), probably on the occasion of the latter's marriage to Ann Barrett in February 1603 (DNB, 'Sir Robert Harley'). The suggestion in the DNB (at the time of writing) that her dowry was used to purchase Wigmore cannot be correct, as the castle had already come into the Harleys' possession by the time of the marriage, unless the dowry was provided early to buy the castle before the marriage.

It is likely that Thomas Harley's family lived at least some of the time in the castle itself, although whether in the hall range or in another part of the site is unclear. Robert Harley was apparently born in Wigmore as he was baptised in the parish church there (HRO AD 60/1 for 1579/1580). He may also have lived there as an adult in the early 17th century, but after Robert's third marriage in 1623, to Brilliana Conway, his father Thomas Harley conveyed the remainder of his estates, including Brampton Bryan, to the couple. Subsequently, Robert and Brilliana Harley probably lived mainly at Brampton Bryan, which, judging by post-Civil War claims for compensation following its destruction, was extremely richly furnished. Nonetheless, Wigmore appears to have remained in use in the early 17th century, and at a minimum retained some military and penal functions up to the early years of the Civil War. An undated 17th-century note in Robert Harley's hand refers to 'the repayre of the old house in the castle and the old gate for a house of correction', at a cost of 2s 2d (TNA DD 4P/56/19/214), a small sum that suggests only minor repairs were needed.

In 1647, however, another note in Robert Harley's hand notes 'that Mr Davyes have 2 or 3 loade of ye stone fallen down at ye castle' (NA DD 4P/63/58/1), provides a clear indication that the castle had been slighted at some point in the Civil War. Exactly how and when the castle was destroyed is unclear. A reference in a contemporary diary for November 1645 claimed that 'Harley ruined it at the beginning of the Parliament' (Symonds 1859, 262). Robert and Brilliana Harley were, unusually for Herefordshire landowners, Parliamentarians. Robert Harley was closely involved with Parliament in the early 1640s, and their son Edward (1624–1700) fought for the Parliamentarian forces. Brilliana stayed mainly in Herefordshire, and notably withstood a Royalist siege at Brampton Bryan in the summer of 1643, before dying of an illness on 29 October 1643. Brampton Bryan was catastrophically sacked and burned in 1644.

Exactly how and when Wigmore was slighted is not entirely clear, but it is likely that it was destroyed by the Harleys because they did not have the resources to defend both Wigmore and Brampton Bryan and, preferring to defend their principal residence, they did not wish to see Wigmore fall into enemy hands and held against them. In a letter to her husband, dated 16 October 1643, only a few weeks before her death, Brilliana wrote that

> … your sarjeant is made a captain and has soldiers billeted in Amstry and Darvell [Aymestry and Deerfold, both near Wigmore]. They say they will send soldiers to Wigmore Castell. I have put some in who I hope will keep it. Colonell Massey could spare not but 8 men and a barrell of powder and a smale quantity of Match …
>
> (BL MS Add 7004, unfoliated).

There are no further references to Wigmore being garrisoned or otherwise occupied, and it is possible that the powder and match to which Brilliana Harley referred were used to slight the castle around this time, either under her direction or by her husband after her death.

Comparison of the Buck print of 1733 (Figure 2.2) with the site as it stands today suggests that the major portion of the destruction seen today had already occurred by the early 18th century, and therefore is probably largely attributable to demolition around the time of the Civil War, although further clearance of the site may have taken place in the 1660s by Edward Harley. By 1733 a large section of the North Curtain Wall was already lost, the Shell Keep and its tower were in ruins, the hall range was largely demolished, the front of the Gatehouse was gone, all of the roofs were lost, and there were no buildings standing along the inside of the curtain wall. Deare's watercolour of 1766 (Figure 2.6) shows the castle in a similar state, but from a different angle. Given the scarcity of men noted by Brilliana Harley, a simple method such as the judicious application of the barrel of gun powder to key parts of the site, such as the curtain wall, Gatehouse and Keep, seems the most likely cause of destruction. Parts of the castle may also have been burned at this time, although it is also possible that salvageable timber and other materials were removed from the site after the end of the war.

In the 1660s and early 1670s, Edward Harley was actively involved in exploiting his Wigmore estates, including felling the timber in the park, apparently to clear it for conversion to agriculture (TNA DD/P6/9/1/9). From this date, Wigmore simply stood as a ruin in the middle of an entirely agricultural landscape. The antiquarian and writer John Aubrey visited Wigmore in the later 17th century in connection with a proposed history of Herefordshire (Buchanan-Brown 1999), and made sketches of an ogee-headed window and a door with a shouldered arch (Figure 2.22), but it is not clear what part of the castle these came from. They may be from the South Tower.

The 18th and 19th centuries

Throughout the 18th and 19th centuries, Wigmore remained a part of the Harley estate. The core of the castle was probably used largely as pasture, but some of the flatter areas of the Outer Bailey and the park behind the castle were ploughed for much of the period (Brydges 1789, 545). In 1778, Green and Jukes placed a yoked horse in the foreground of their image (Figure 2.17), and a late 19th- or early 20th-century postcard (Figure 2.10) shows the upper part of the Outer Bailey ploughed. Looking at the topographical drawings and early photographs, it is also possible to see the development of tree and ivy cover on the site, with relatively little in the 1733 engraving (Figure 2.2), and increasingly more in the watercolour of 1766 (Figure 2.6), the engraving of 1778 (Figure 2.17), and the 19th-century and early 20th-century images (Figures 2.10 and 2.23).

The relative scarcity of 18th- and early 19th-century images suggests that Wigmore was not extensively visited as a tourist site, especially in comparison to well-known sites like Tintern, for which many hundreds of images survive. Nonetheless, the existence of a late 19th or very early 20th-century printed postcard (Figure 2.10) suggests that there was a degree of interest in the site.

The 20th century

There were calls for the castle's restoration in the early 20th century by the Woolhope Club (Anon. 1911, 300), but nothing was done. In 1921, the Harleys' Wigmore estate was broken up and sold. The division between the upper and lower parts of the Outer Bailey, in existence since at least the time of the 1845 tithe map (HRO L319) and probably since the disuse of the site in the mid-17th century, was preserved in this sale. The castle and its surroundings were divided into two plots, with the boundary running down the middle of the Outer Bailey along the line of the former entrance road, and thence close up around the Inner Bailey

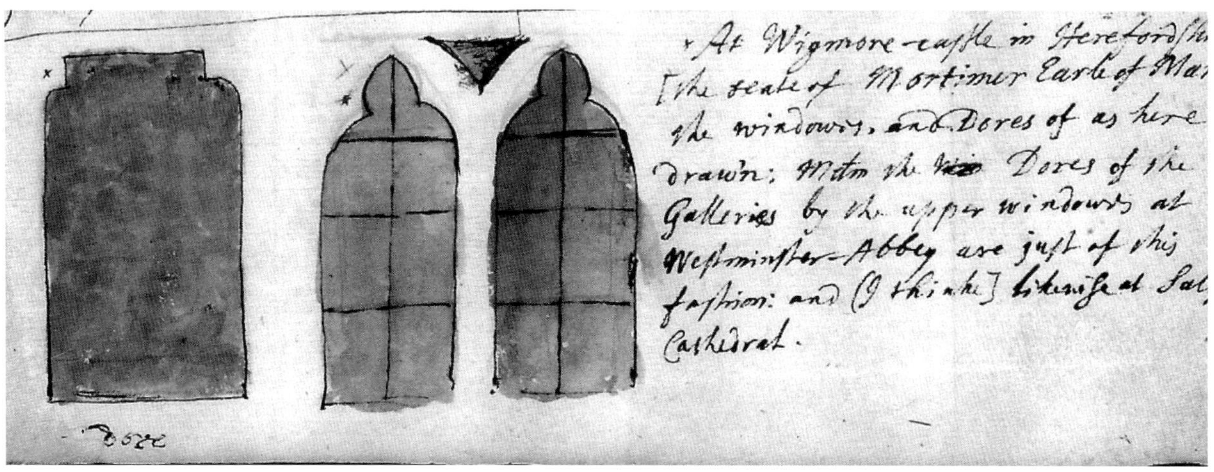

FIGURE 2.22

Late 17th-century sketch of a window and shouldered doorway at Wigmore Castle, John Aubrey's manuscript notes for a proposed history of Herefordshire (copyright: The Bodleian Library, University of Oxford, MS Top. Gen. c. 25, fol 158r)

Figure 2.23
Wigmore Castle, photograph c1900 (copyright: Hereford City Library, Pilley Collection)

Figure 2.24
The inner face of the Gatehouse arch, looking south (photograph: Carol Davidson Cragoe)

FIGURE 2.25
The Gatehouse, looking north-west. Note the depth of fill accumulated below the arch (photograph: Carol Davidson Cragoe)

FIGURE 2.26
The Gatehouse arch in 1932, looking south-east (copyright: English Heritage)

to the south of the castle. The castle, the upper part of the Outer Bailey and the land to the north was one parcel. The southern part, known as Greenhill Farm and including the lower section of the Outer Bailey and the possible site of former fishponds, was a separate plot, and they remain in divided private ownership (EH Registry MP 017/01/03).

Collapse of the portcullis arch

At some point in the mid-20th century, the portcullis arch of the Gatehouse collapsed, a fact not previously recognised. In 1874, J T Clark described the Gatehouse and noted that 'the rib of the central portal remains, with a drop arch and square portcullis groove' (Clark 1874, 107). The RCHM inspectors, who visited in 1932 (RCHM 1932), also noted the portcullis, and in the printed volume described the gateway as having 'a segmental pointed head of three orders, the outer moulded, the two inner chamfered. Between the outer and second order is the slot for the portcullis' (RCHM 1934, 208). Their record sketch (Figure 2.8), not reproduced in the printed volume, shows a moulded outer order, probably dating to the 14th century, with a clear indication of the portcullis slot between it and the chamfered order behind it. Today, the portcullis slot is no longer visible, and it seems likely that it collapsed at some point after the RCHM inspectors visited. Comparison of the sketch with the surviving section of the arch (Figure 2.24) shows that the slot was on the outer, south, face of the arch as the profile of the inner, north, face matches that shown in the RCHM sketch.

The date of the collapse is unknown, but it had certainly occurred by the time the site came into Guardianship in 1995. The scheduling description, written in around 1959, mentions the portcullis slot and the outer order, but an examination of the RCHM volume held by the English Heritage library suggests that the descriptions for Wigmore were simply copied from the entries in the Commission volume and that the inspectors did little more than ensure that the buildings being listed still stood, a common practice during the compilation of the early lists and schedules. The collapse almost certainly took place before scheduling in 1959, as it seems unlikely that such a significant fall of masonry would have gone entirely unnoticed after the site had come under statutory protection. Some confirmation for a late 1930s or 1940s date for the collapse is given by the fact that neither the portcullis slot, nor its collapse, is mentioned by Stirling-Brown, who claimed to have been visiting the site for several decades before writing about it in 1988; Shoesmith also makes no mention of it (Shoesmith 1998). Much of the fill currently choking the Gatehouse arch (Figure 2.25) must be rubble from the fall, as early 20th-century photographs in Hereford City Library and in the NMR show considerably more of the jambs exposed (Figure 2.26). Cooke (2008)

FIGURE 2.27
The Inner Bailey in June 2008, looking east (photograph: Carol Davidson Cragoe)

noted the use of cement mortar repairs to the walling around the surviving part of the arch, which may be an undated repair following the collapse of the outer skin. He also noted that the surviving arch appears to be rebuilt, as the voussoirs do not sit comfortably on the jambs, but this rebuilding may have occurred when the portcullis was remodelled in the 14th century.

The conservation project

Little else was done to the castle in the mid-20th century, but its sale in 1987 to its present owner, John Gaunt, and the dramatic collapse of part of the South Curtain Wall in 1988, returned it to the public gaze. Following protracted negotiations, the site came into State Guardianship in 1995. Once in Guardianship, Wigmore became the subject of an innovative conservation programme by English Heritage. The intention of this project was to retain the 'romantic ruin' nature of the site, while at the same time repairing the recent damage and preventing further catastrophic collapse of the remaining masonry. Destructive vegetation was removed and the masonry beneath conserved, but less invasive species such as ferns and wildflowers were carefully preserved and then replaced to create 'soft-capping' that both protected the wall tops and retained the unique appearance of the site (Tolley *et al* 2000; Channer 2001). As part of this project, the two excavations discussed in this volume were carried out in conjunction with works to stabilise the walls. The initial presentation by English Heritage of the site, which is free and open to the public at all times, was minimal, with only a single graphics panel detailing the conservation project. An additional panel with a reconstruction drawing made in 1995 was placed in the village, at the entrance to the track leading up to the site. In 2008–2009, however, further research was undertaken, and new, more explanatory graphics panels installed. Nonetheless, the site remains extremely evocative and is a haven for wildlife and unusual flora (English Nature 1997) (Figure 2.27).

3

THE EXCAVATIONS

Stephen J Linnane

3.1 INTRODUCTION

There were two seasons of excavation at Wigmore Castle both intended to resolve questions concerning structural stability within the standing masonry after recent or threatened collapse (Figure 3.1). During the course of the excavations context numbers were allocated to individual features and deposits, running from 001 to 407 within the 1996 excavations and 501 to 729 in the 1998 excavations. Context groups have been created by combining context numbers bearing structural and stratigraphic associations and these are designated CG96 or CG98 within the following text. The groups have been used as a basis for interpretation within the relevant finds analyses. The division of the site stratigraphy into 11 identifiable Phases was again based on stratigraphic associations and finds, principally pottery, analysis (Figure 3.2). Detailed descriptions of all contexts and their stratigraphic relationships can be found in the archive. The archive will be stored on the Archaeological Data Service (ADS) website.

3.2 THE 1996 EXCAVATIONS

Introduction and standing fabric

Excavations were undertaken between May and October 1996 within the Inner Bailey of the castle directed by Richard Stone for Marches Archaeology under contract to English Heritage (Figure 3.3). A trench, 3.00m wide, was excavated by hand, running from north to south, starting above the remains of the slighted Southern Curtain Wall to the south of the Inner Bailey and extending northwards into the bailey for a distance of 10.00m. The trench was located 14.00m to the west of the South Tower and 19.00m to the east of the West Tower and was excavated to a maximum depth of 8.00m revealing the inner face and foundations of the possibly three-period Curtain Wall (Figures 3.4 and 3.5). Because of the depth, the trench sides were shuttered and also stepped to such an extent that deposits towards the base of the trench were exposed only over an area of 4.00m by 1.00m and only approximately 1.00 square metre of the natural subsoil was exposed.

During the course of the 1996 excavation some 407 context numbers were allocated, these have been divided into 29 context groups consisting of contemporary features and deposits. The context groups were then placed within one of the 11 phases based on stratigraphic and finds analysis.

The extant masonry

The Southern Curtain Wall

An account of the surviving masonry of Wigmore Castle is provided in Chapter 2 of this volume. Within the 1996 excavations only a portion of the Southern Curtain Wall was exposed. The curtain wall ran from west to east between the South and the West Towers and the excavation was sited approximately midway between the two. Prior to excavation the top and northern, inner face of the Curtain Wall was covered by turf and topsoil. The southern, outer, face of the wall survived to a height of 5.80m with an unknown depth surviving below the current ground surface.

Excavation revealed the slighted wall core and an 8.00m deep elevation of the inner face. No excavation took place against the external face but masonry recording undertaken by Lancaster University Archaeological Unit for English Heritage noted two phases of construction with that part to the west of the excavation being faced from top to bottom in the same manner as the Phase 8 wall exposed by excavation whilst the wall to the east was not so well coursed and may be associated with the earlier, Phase 5 wall found in excavation below the later wall.

The excavations revealed two, possibly three, phases of construction. The inner face of the upper, later portion of the wall was exposed to a depth of 3.60m (Figures. 3.6 and 3.7), and was constructed of alternating thin and thick courses of well-cut rectangular mudstone blocks bedded in hard off-white mortar, 013 of CG96 09, Phase 8. The wall was built on a plinth of large unworked slabs which formed a slightly projecting course overlying the masonry of the earlier wall and was constructed within trench 405 of CG96 09, Phase 8. The later wall overhung the earlier by an offset of some 0.20m. Built into the upper wall was a rectangular recess 1.50m wide, 0.80m deep and with a minimum height of 1.15m. The base of the recess was at a height of 174.58m OD and a square put-log hole (0.15m by 0.15m and of uncertain depth) was built into the Curtain Wall at a similar height and 1.40m to the west of the recess. The put-log hole would

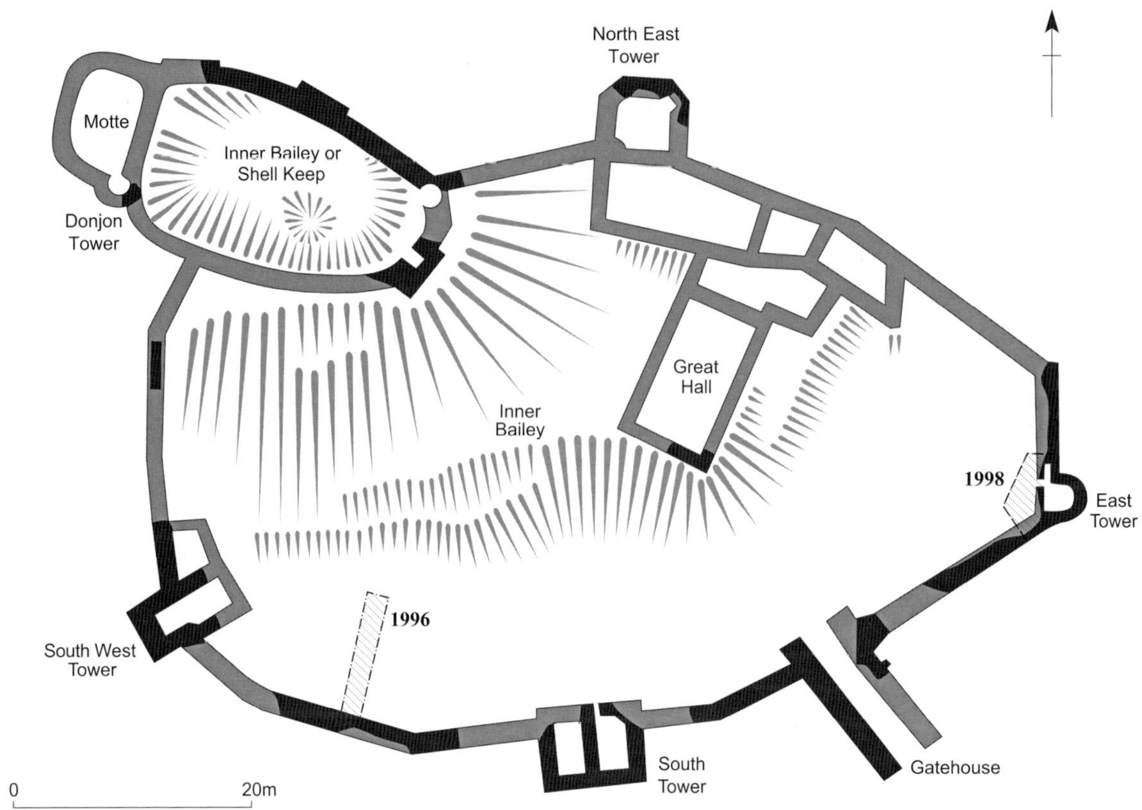

FIGURE 3.1
Location plan of the 1996 and 1998 excavations

Phase	Date/Century	Site	Activity
1	Post-1066 to early 12th	1996 1998	Timber and earthwork defences No deposits excavated
2	Early to late 12th	1996 1998	Construction and use of timber kitchen No deposits excavated
3	Early to mid-13th	1996 1998	Re-surfacing and pits, curtain walls? Construction of curtain walls?
4	Mid- to late 13th	1996 1998	Significant deposits of charcoal and re-surfacing Construction of East Tower
5	Late 13th to early 14th	1996 1998	Rebuild of curtain wall Gravel surface and occupation deposits above
6	Early to mid-14th	1996 1998	Re-surfacing and lead-melting hearths Deposits disrupted
7	Mid- to late 14th	1996 1998	Construction and use of stone building Deposits disrupted
8	Early to mid-15th	1996 1998	Rebuild of curtain wall Large pit and ditches, re-build of East Tower?
9	Mid-15th to late 16th	1996 1998	Re-surfacing, domestic debris and blocking of recess Plaster floor and internal structural post-holes
10	Late16th to mid-17th	1996 1998	Decay and slighting? Limited activity, partial decay
11	Mid-17th to late 20th	1996 1998	Accumulation of deposits after abandonment

FIGURE 3.2
Table showing the phasing given to the excavations

FIGURE 3.3
General view of the site prior to commencement of excavation, looking east (photograph: Marches Archaeology)

appear to have been far too small to have functioned as a joist socket. The purpose of the recess has not been ascertained, although there was evidence of burning on the base and back wall of the cut, the primary function of a fireplace seems unlikely as it did not possess sandstone dressings or a brick/tile lining as might have been expected at this period. Although the presence of the recess might suggest the existence of a building attached to the Curtain Wall no convincing evidence of a structure was found within the excavation trench. Two surfaces post-dating the reconstruction of the Curtain Wall were noted (045 of CG96 06, Phase 9 and 033 of CG96 04, Phase 9) but these were probably laid as external surfaces and both were found at over 0.60m below the level of the recess at heights of 173.75m and 174.00m OD. At a later date, within the 16th century, the recess was partially blocked with a poorly constructed wall, 038 of CG96 05, Phase 9.

The lower section of the Southern Curtain Wall, 389 of CG96 16, Phase 5, was built within construction trench 292 of CG96 17, Phase 5. The wall was built of irregular blocks of grey/green mudstone, was poorly coursed and bonded with a bright red, sandy mortar. The face of the wall was exposed for a depth of 3.60m at which point a slight offset occurred. Below the offset, the wall continued down for a further 2.10m with a slight batter. The lower portion of the wall was very poorly constructed and its face was heavily smeared with the same red mortar as used to bond the wall. At the very base of the wall an offset of 0.20m width was noted and it is possible that this offset was all that remained of an earlier curtain wall whose upper masonry and construction trench were removed during the Phase 5 reconstruction — the 1998 excavation suggested that the earliest curtain walls dated to Phase 3. It seems probable that the Curtain Wall was partially slighted during the Civil War or its immediate aftermath, and that time, vegetation and robbing later contributed to its eventual partial burial.

The excavations

By the time the natural subsoil had been reached at a depth of 168.20m OD the dimensions of the trench had been reduced to 4.00m by 1.00m. Prior to occupation of the site, the natural ground surface would have sloped downwards from north to south and consisted of blue/grey clay with yellow mottling and mudstone inclusions. The earliest feature noted was pit 407, fill 406 (compact pale grey clay), cutting the natural subsoil. This feature may have been of archaeological significance but was only partially excavated, had ill-defined edges and no datable finds and may best be viewed as a probable tree bole.

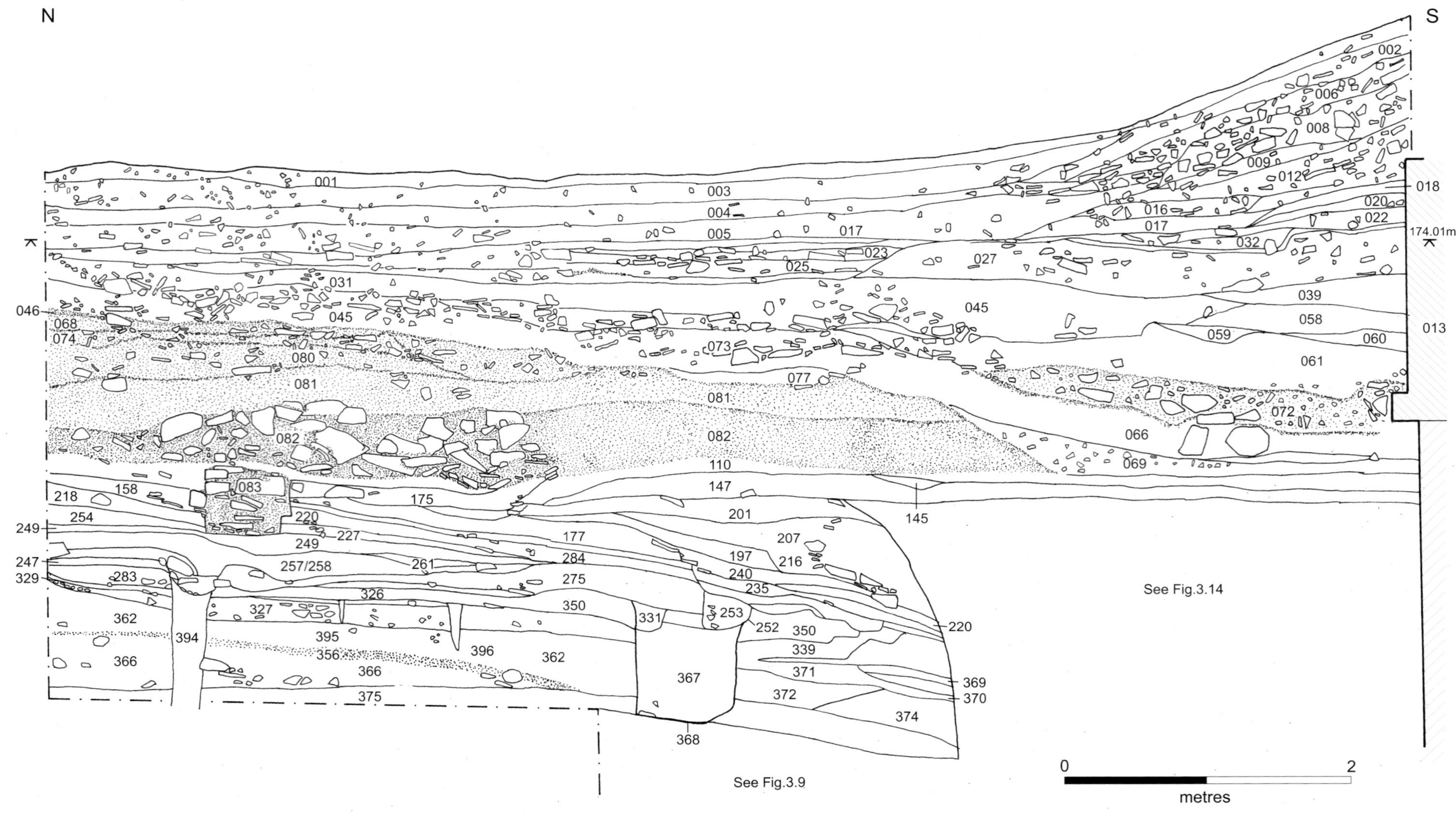

FIGURE 3.4
West-facing trench section, 1996 excavations

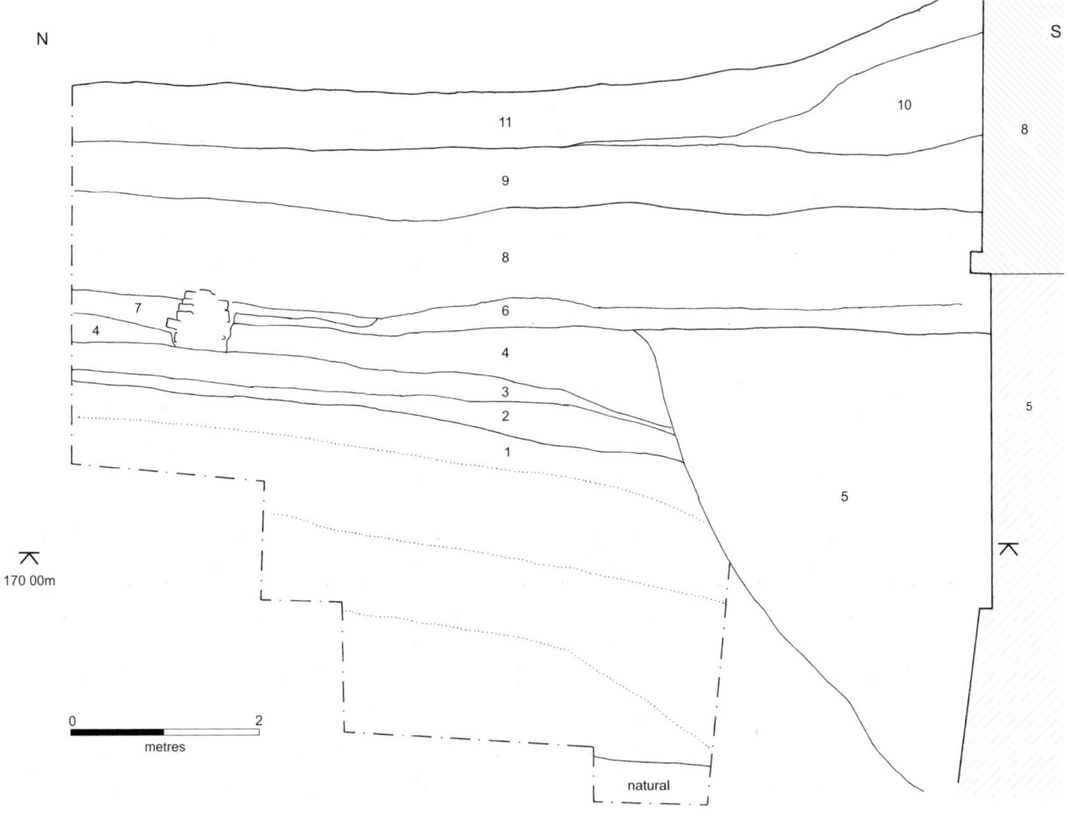

FIGURE 3.5
Simplified west-facing trench section, showing Phases 1 to 11

Phase 1: post-conquest to early 12th century

The earliest deposits encountered appeared to be associated with a clay bank or terrace, probably associated with timber defences at the time of the first fortification of the site (Figures 3.8, 3.9 and 3.10).

Context Group 29: clay bank

Immediately overlying the natural subsoil and partially filling pit 407 was an irregular deposit of blue/grey clay 362/387 containing some mudstone inclusions and with good organic preservation. The deposit possibly represented an initial turf-bank, built as the first phase of the early earthwork defences. The overlying deposits consisted of clay dumps (see Figure 3.10) interspersed with lenses of blue clay containing organic remains. In total the depth of deposits within this group was over 2.00m with the upper surface at 171.30m OD. It is probable that the group represents the position of a defensive bank encircling the Inner Bailey during the early, timber phase of the castle's construction.

A waterlogged timber post 378, of uncertain diameter but 1.18m long (Sample 61), survived adjacent to a possible post-pit of 0.20m diameter, 380 (fill 379). The post-pit was excavated into deposit 382 (Figure 3.8A), a compact blue clay deposit 0.40m deep with brown silt 383 above. Context 383 may have formed an occupation surface contemporary with the post. It is possible that the post formed part of a timber palisade associated with the earliest defences of the site. In section (see Figures 3.4 and 3.9) these lower deposits below 383 tended to slope down to the south suggesting that they were part of a bank whilst those dumped above were more level suggesting that any slope was further to the south or that they were deposited against a revetment.

Phase 2: 12th century

Two large post-holes and a hearth plus a number of lesser features revealed the location of a substantial timber building, possibly built against the outer defences — probably still of timber at this stage (Figures 3.8B and 3.11). The finds assemblage indicated that the building was used as a kitchen.

Context Group 26: timber building

Immediately overlying the Phase 1 deposits considerable activity occurred including pits, post and stake-holes and clay and ash spreads indicating the construction and occupation of a substantial timber building (see Figures 3.8B and 3.11). The

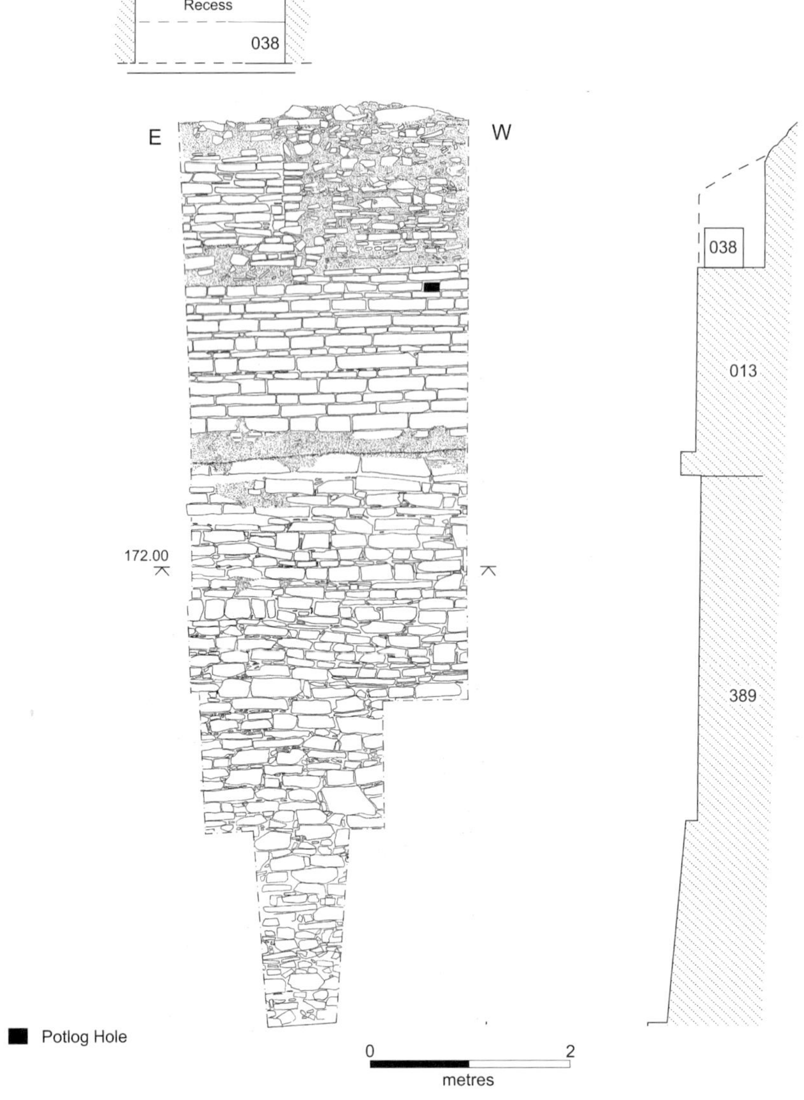

FIGURE 3.6
North-facing elevation, plan and section of the Southern Curtain Wall

FIGURE 3.7
The Southern Curtain Wall 013 of CG96 09, Phase 8, showing recess, put-log hole and later blocking, looking south (photograph: Marches Archaeology)

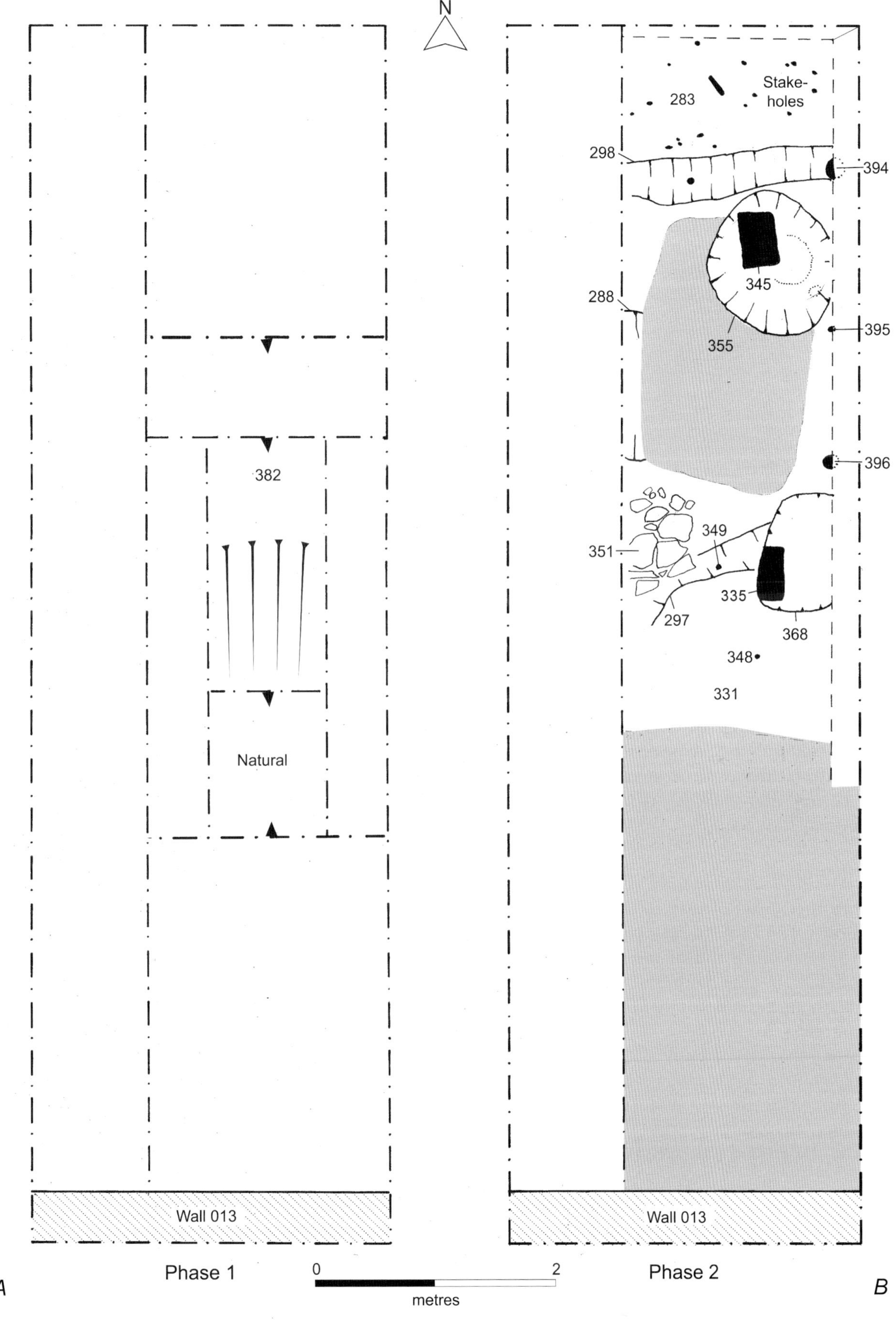

FIGURE 3.8
Plans of the 1996 trench showing Phases 1 and 2

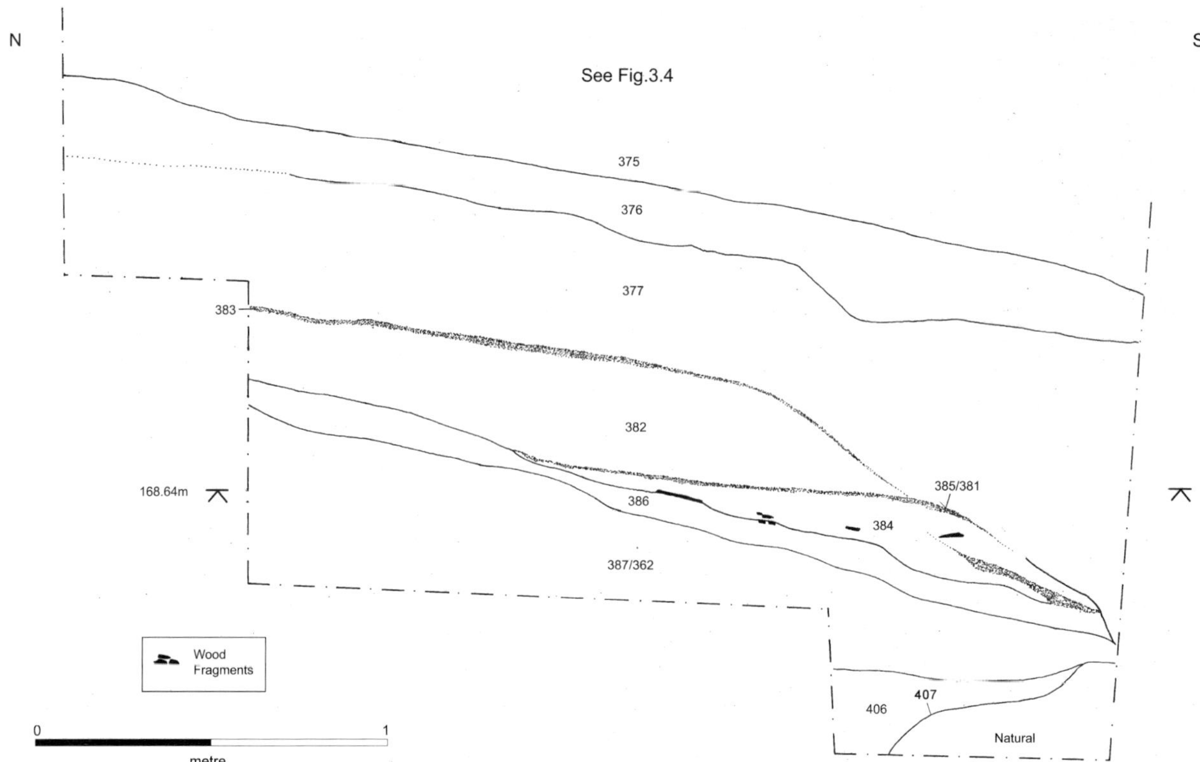

FIGURE 3.9
West-facing trench section showing Phase 1 deposits

stratigraphy was disrupted by large pit cluster, CG96 24, Phase 3, dividing the area into north and south sections and only 8 square metres were available for excavation at this level, at approximately 171.70m OD. Pottery from these layers indicated occupation within the 12th century.

To the north

Within the northern section the principal feature was post-pit 355, fill 353. The pit was located 2.00m from the northern end of the excavation and was sub-circular in plan with an average diameter of *c*1.00m, a maximum depth of 0.50m and steeply sloping sides leading to a flat base. The pit was excavated into clay deposit 327 of CG96 29, Phase 1, and was intended to take a substantial timber post, post-pipe 345, fills 343 and 344. The rectangular post-pipe was located towards the central, northern edge of the pit and measured 0.45m from north to south by 0.30m.

Stake-hole 332 was located to the east of the post-pipe whilst post-hole 394 and two stake-holes 395 and 396 were noted during cleaning of the eastern trench section after excavation had been completed but appeared to be stratigraphically associated. The post-hole 394 was 0.25m in diameter, over 0.90m deep and had been driven from deposit 329. Pit 337, fill 336 and stake-hole 341 (fill 340) were located to the south-east of post-pit 355; pit 337 was 0.50m in diameter by 0.25m deep. Deposit 325/326, a brown silty clay, and 333, a yellow clay, had formed around and above some of these features.

To the south

Overlying 338 and 350 of CG96 27, Phase 2, ash and clay lenses, 295, 303–306, 330 and 331 were associated with features connected to the timber building.

Located some 3.00m to the south of post-pit 355 was 368, fill 367, another sub-rectangular post-pit extending below the eastern trench section. The pit measured 0.92m from north to south by 0.60m and was 0.64m deep with near vertical sides leading to a flat base. The fills contained stone packing around rectangular post-pipe 335, fill 334, which had dimensions of 0.45m from north to south by 0.25m and was 0.60m deep. The pipe was located within the south-western corner of the post-pit and the distance between the two pipes, 345 and 335, centre to centre, was 2.70m.

Apparently later than the backfilling of pit 368 and earlier than stone-built hearth 351 of CG96 27, an irregular gulley 297, fill 296, ran from west to east across the trench and was 0.50m wide by 0.12m deep.

Pit 288, fill 276, was located on the western edge of the site between the two post-pits and appeared to have been associated with this phase but had

FIGURE 3.10
The bank deposits of CG96 29, Phase 1, mid-excavation, looking south (photograph: Marches Archaeology)

been badly truncated by Phase 3 pits and neither its dimensions nor its purpose were established.

Context Group 27: hearth

Located approximately 1.00m to the west of post-pipe 335 and overlying 365 of CG96 29, Phase 1, was hearth 398, which had at least three periods of use. The earlier periods consisted of spreads of charcoal 361 and 390/359 separated by yellow clay lenses 360 and 350. Associated with this early use was a single layer of irregular stone slabs, 373, which formed an alignment running from east to west and which may have been the remnants of a paved area or possibly the footing for a timber wall beam. These features were followed by the construction of 351, a stone slab hearth base extending beyond the western section of the trench with an approximate diameter of 1.00m. The stones were overlain by red-tinged silt 339 (heat affected) and by charcoal deposit 338. A stake-hole 349/347 of 0.025m diameter was located towards the east of the hearth. The stake-hole was 0.05m deep and was angled at 45 degrees to the west.

Context Group 28: stake-holes and gulley

Located some 0.50m to the north of post-pipe 335 was gulley 298 (fill 299), running from east to west and 0.30m wide by 0.15m deep. The gulley had apparently been cut into the backfill of post-pipe 394 and may have functioned as an eaves drip to the timber building of CG96 26. In a cluster within and to the north of the gulley, cutting clay surface 283 and overlain by 280 of CG96 25, Phase 3, a total

FIGURE 3.11
Post-holes and hearth of CG96 26 and 27, Phase 2, looking south (photograph: Marches Archaeology)

of 22 possible stake-holes were identified, 300–302, 307–324, 342. These varied in shape and size and some may not have been archaeological. Typically the stake-holes were round with a diameter of 0.05m and depth of 0.15m. No discernible pattern has been identified. The stake-holes were contemporary with the timber structure and are considered to have been associated with an activity external to it.

Phase 3: early to mid-13th century

Levelling deposits and a sequence of intercutting pits of uncertain purpose lay below a level occupation surface but there was no significant construction activity (Figure 3.12A).

Context Group 25: levelling deposits and two stake-holes

Once the Phase 2 timber building had gone out of use, a sequence of clay, rubble, mortar and silt deposits, 275, 277–280 and 284–287, formed a level surface at 171.85m OD and may have been intended as levelling dumps. These deposits were cut by the pits of CG96 24. Two stake-holes, 285 and 286, of around 0.05m diameter were cut into the surface of 280.

Context Group 24: three intercutting pits

Located towards the north of the trench, cutting surface 280 of CG96 25, Phase 3, and underlying surface 257 of CG96 28, Phase 3, were three intercutting pits. The earliest pit, 282, fill 281, had dimensions of 2.10m from north to south by 1.10m with a maximum depth of 0.50m and was cut by pit 271, fills 274 and 270, which was rectangular with dimensions of 1.89m from north to south by 1.28m with a maximum depth of 0.65m. The latest pit, 273, fill 272, was oval, measuring 0.50m north to south by 0.32m, with a maximum depth of 0.21m and cut the northern edge of pit 271. All of the pit fills contained charcoal flecking but few other finds, either domestic or industrial in nature, and no reason for their excavation was deduced. The pits seriously disrupted the stratigraphy of the underlying features and deposits.

Context Group 23: occupation surface

Sealing the fills of the CG96 24 pits and underlying 248 of CG98 22, Phase 4, an uneven spread of yellow clay, 257/258, had been laid to provide a somewhat irregular working surface at a height of 172.04m OD. This surface was overlain by a series of grey clay lenses containing patches of burnt clay, mortar, ash and charcoal 249, 256, 259, 260, 261 and 262. The deposits suggested an occupation surface and pottery of the early 13th century was recovered along with a coin of William II (SF112, Chapter 5).

Phase 4: mid- to late 13th century

A considerable sequence of activity encompassing five distinctive groups none of which indicated substantial building activity within the area although CG96 20 might have indicated the destruction of a timber building (Figure 3.12B).

Context Group 22: numerous clay lenses with a ditch and a possible post-hole

Overlying 284 of CG96 24, Phase 3, and underlying 200/220 of CG96 20 was a complex sequence of deposits and lenses consisting of compact clays, some exhibiting evidence of burning but not necessarily *in situ,* interspersed with grey silt layers, possibly indicating occupation, 221–223, 225, 228–239, 245–248, 251–254 and 255. Within these deposits were two features that should have been broadly contemporary. Ditch 244/364 (fills 242, 243, 250 and 263) ran from west to east parallel with the Southern Curtain Wall, with its surviving northern edge 3.00m from it. The ditch had been heavily truncated by the Curtain Wall's construction trench, 204 of CG96 17, Phase 5, and its purpose was not ascertained. Possible post-hole 358, fill 357, was observed within the eastern trench section and had surviving dimensions of 0.37m from north to south by 0.30m deep.

Context Group 21: five stake-holes

Cutting red gritty surface 177 of CG96 19, and underlying 168 of CG96 16, Phase 6, a line of five stake-holes, 188–192, ran from west to east, interestingly along the same alignment as that of later wall 083 of CG96 11, Phase 7. The stake-holes were, on average, 0.08m in diameter by 0.10m deep and could have supported a fence or wattle wall.

Context Group 20: charcoal-rich deposits 200/220

Overlying 228, 230 and 223 of CG96 22 and underlying 218 of CG96 19 at a height of 172.23m OD, with a maximum depth of 0.10m, was a near-black, charcoal-rich silty clay deposit, 200/220, covering the whole extent of the trench except where it had been removed by later cuts. The deposit was indicative of a significant fire and contained grey ash lenses and burnt red clay inclusions. The deposit might indicate the destruction of a timber building within the vicinity although a dearth of iron nails and other metalwork might disagree with this interpretation. Pottery provided a date of around 1250 for this episode although the presence of a cuboid horseshoe nail (9701110, Chapter 5) indicates a date some two or three decades later.

Context Group 19: levelling and pit

Overlying the charcoal-rich deposit 200/220 of CG96 20, was a sequence of deposits, consisting

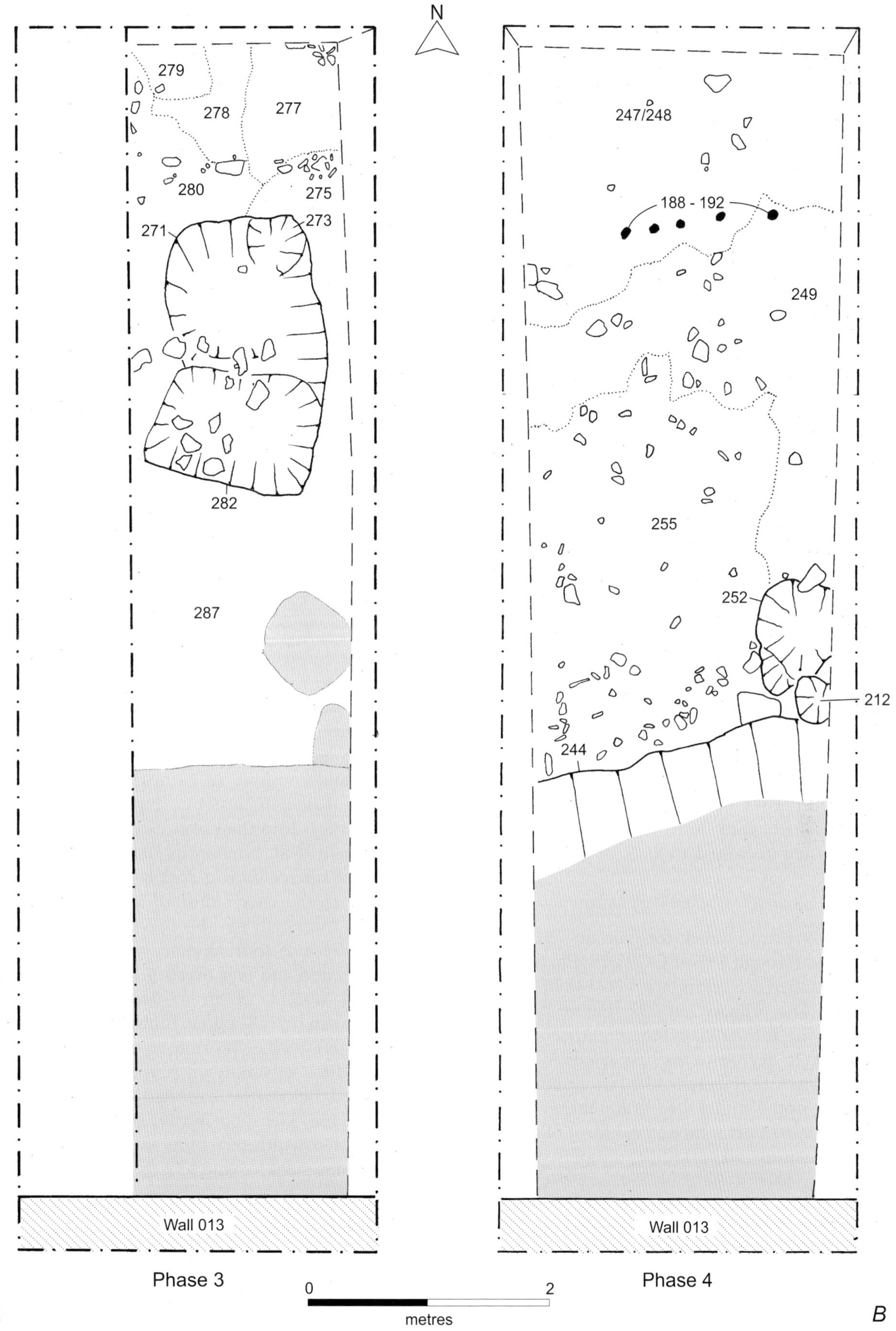

FIGURE 3.12
Plans of the 1996 trench showing Phases 3 and 4

of reddish sand, yellow clay and grey silt, 217–219, cut by pit 252, fills 254 and 240. The pit was bowl-shaped with a diameter of 0.77m and maximum depth of 0.55m; the upper fill contained stone slabs which may possibly have been intended as post packing. Layer 177/193 overlay the fills of pit 252 and consisted of ash and red silt with some small areas of metalling. Overlying these deposits was a further sequence of layers 213–217 which in turn underlay 205/210, a dump of compact green/brown clay, interpreted as a levelling layer of redeposited natural. All underlay 403 of CG96 18.

Context Group 18: occupation activity

Overlying and cut into surface 205/10 was a sequence of deposits and pits indicative of activity in the area immediately preceding construction of the Southern Curtain Wall in Phase 5. Pit 403, fill 402, was seen only when the western trench section was re-cut and its true dimensions and purpose were not established. The deposits overlying the pit contained ash and charcoal and consisted of grey silty clays and more compact clays denoting ground levelling and occupation activity: 401, 404, 201, 202 and 206–208. Pit 212, fill 211, cut 404, extended beyond the western trench section and was circular, bowl-shaped with an estimated diameter of 1.00m and depth of 0.12m. A possible post-hole, 157 (fill 156) and deposits 197–199, within a potential cut, were stratigraphically associated.

Phase 5: late 13th to early 14th century

The Southern Curtain Wall was constructed or reconstructed with finds from its construction trench dated to around 1300.

Context Group 17: Curtain Wall construction

The construction trench for Curtain Wall 389 was excavated through 197 of CG96 25, Phase 4, whilst the fills underlay level surface 144/147 of CG96 16, Phase 6. The primary cut 292 (Figure 3.13A) was 3.90m wide at the top and the slightly concave side sloped at *c*70 degrees to the base at a depth of 4.80m at 168.50m OD (Figure 3.14). Two re-cuts 185 and 204 were noted within the fills and these may be explained as attempts at tidying the form of the trench as construction and backfilling progressed. Deposits containing level stone slabs, 391 and 291, were laid intermittently, presumably intended to provide stable working surfaces or possibly even to support the base of timber scaffolding. The fills within the cut consisted of layers of green and yellow clay, gritty red/brown mortar-rich silts and occasional deposits containing significant quantities of domestic debris; 203 and 178/179 — the uppermost fill (see also Chapter 9, Figure 9.12, for the fill sequence).

The wall itself was constructed of roughly coursed, grey/green mudstone blocks bonded with bright red mortar (Figure 3.15). At a depth of 3.60m within the trench, a slight offset was exposed at 169.40m OD, after which the wall continued down for a further 1.05m with a slight batter at which point there was a further offset and the wall returned to the vertical (see Figure 3.14). At the base of the construction trench and foot of the exposed curtain wall, at a height of 167.70m OD, was a 0.20m wide offset. It is possible that this feature represented the remnants of an earlier period of curtain wall construction, the upper masonry and construction trench of which was removed in the Phase 5 building campaign. The 1998 excavations certainly indicated the possibility of stone-built curtain walls in Phase 3 of the sequence, in the early 13th century.

Phase 6: early to mid-14th century

The Southern Curtain Wall had been constructed and a new clay surface was created at a height of 172.35m OD. The area was now used intensively for the melting of lead, possibly obtained from earlier demolition activity. The ceramic finds indicate that this activity was taking place within the first half of the 14th century.

Context Group 16: occupation surface

After the construction of Curtain Wall 389 of CG 96 17, Phase 5, and the backfilling of its construction trench, a new level surface, 144/147, was laid across the southern part of the site at a height of 172.35m OD. The new surface was intended to consolidate the site and consisted of compact green clay with frequent stone inclusions (Figure 3.13B). The deposit was 0.15m thick and extended 6.00m from the Curtain Wall. Numerous later features cut the new level surface and in part it was scorched red, 162, due to the later industrial activities occurring on it. To the north of 144/147 a yellow/grey clay surface, 176, was contemporary with it, fulfilled the same function and was overlain by 169, a patch of metalling around 1.00m in diameter which was itself overlain by 168, a grey/brown silty clay deposit some 0.10m thick — possibly an occupation surface. A small ditch of unknown purpose, 175 (fill 174), was noted below the eastern trench section and underlay 168. The ditch was visible for 2.30m, had an estimated width of 0.50m and was 0.17m deep with sloping sides leading to a flat base.

Context Group 15: lead-working activity

Overlying surface 144/147 of CG96 15 and associated with lead smelting hearth 114 of CG96 14 were several deposits and pits (Figure 3.16). 171 was a 0.06m square stake-hole located to the west of the hearth and cutting its fill 165. Depression 164 (fill 163) was circular with a diameter of 0.30m and maximum depth of 0.06m located 1.00m to the north-west of the hearth whilst 161 was another

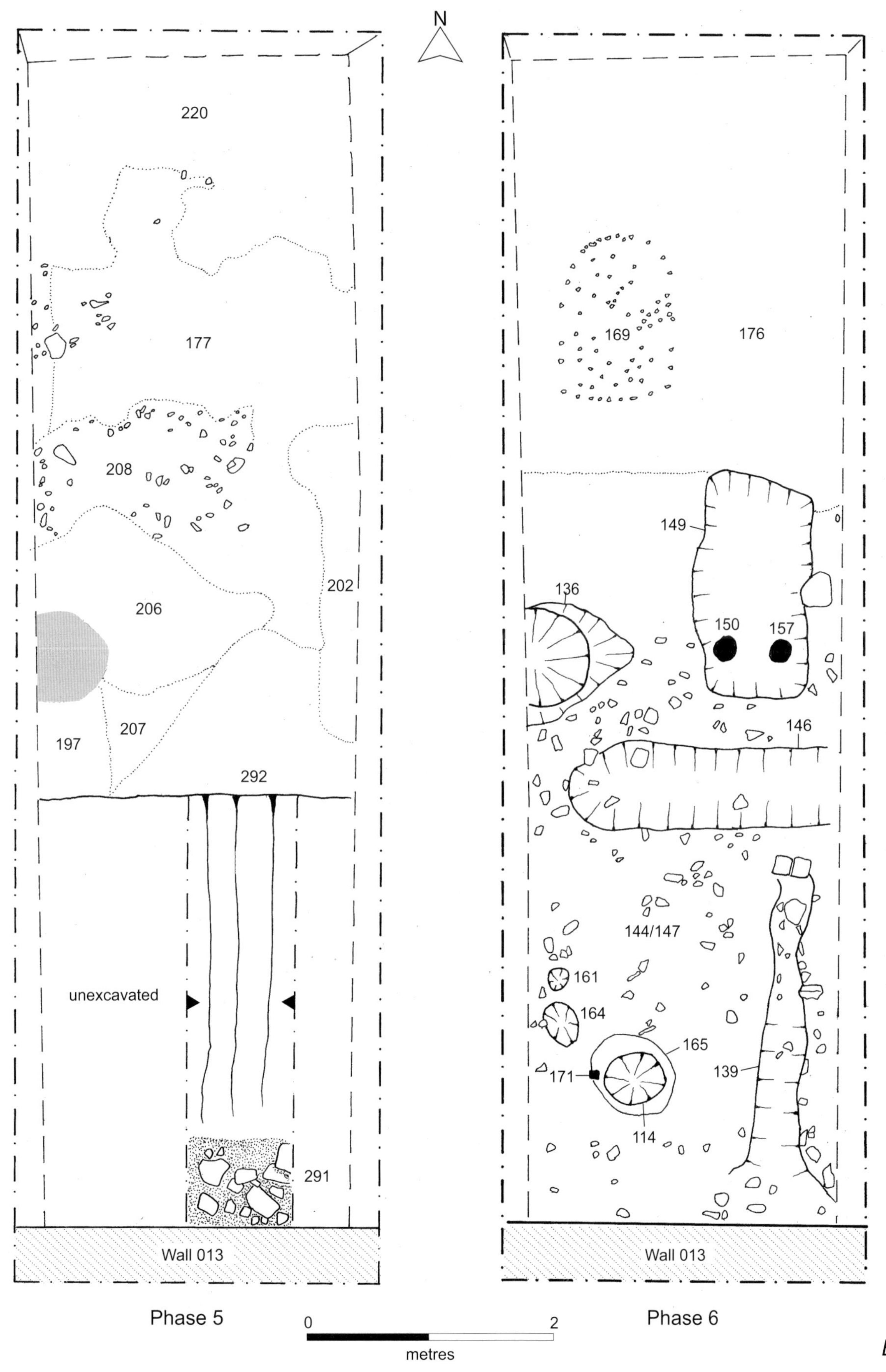

FIGURE 3.13
Plans of the 1996 trench showing Phases 5 and 6

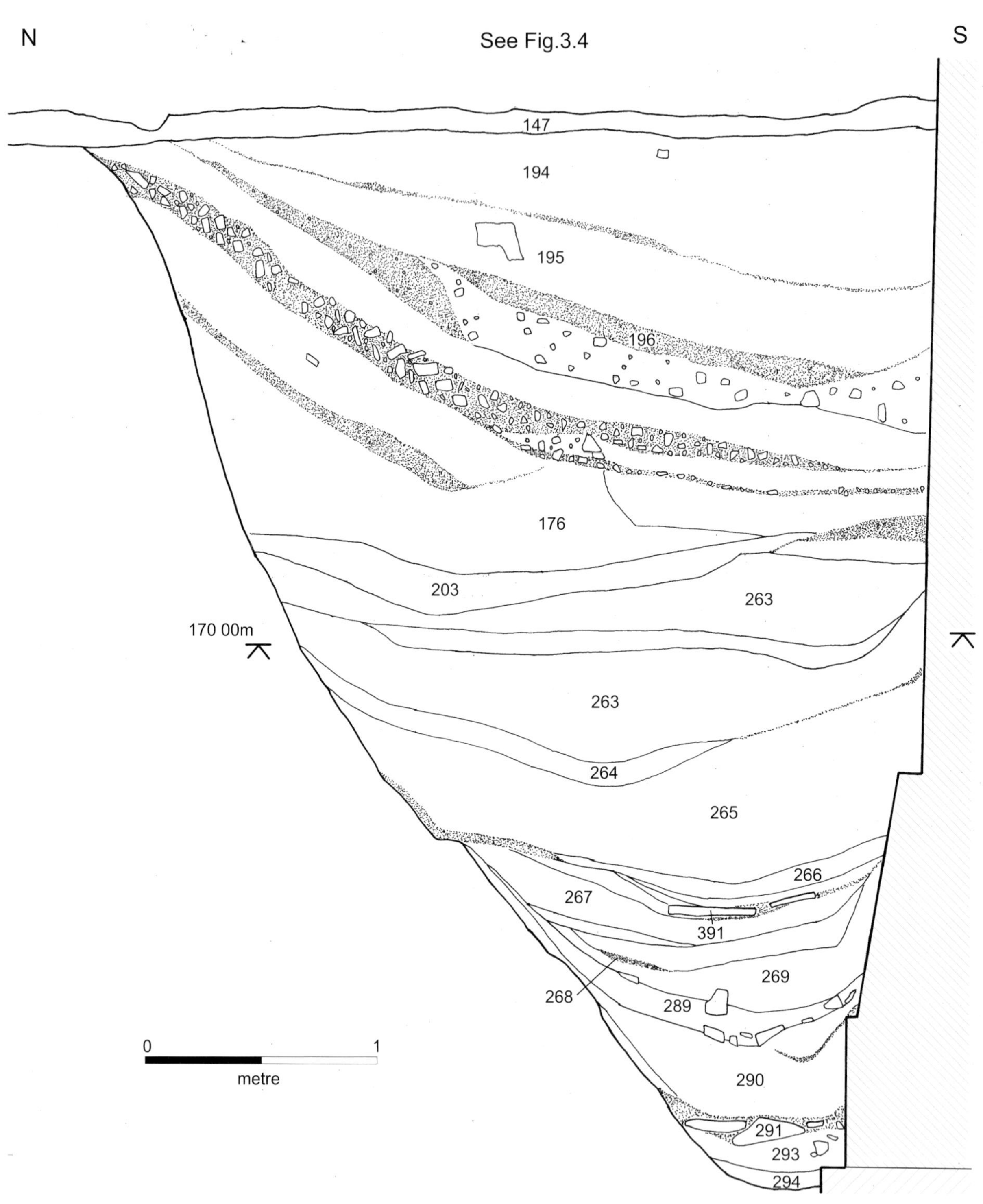

FIGURE 3.14
West-facing section through construction trench 292 of CG96 17, Phase 5

FIGURE 3.15
Construction trench 292 of CG96 17, Phase 5, showing slab surface 391 towards the base, looking south (photograph: Marches Archaeology)

small depression immediately to the north of 164. 154 (fill 153) was a very irregular depression with an ashy fill and may have been caused by animal or root action. Gulley 139 ran from north to south for a distance of 2.70m before petering out close to the curtain wall. The gulley was 0.60m wide, 0.10m deep and contained charcoal-rich fills 137, 140 and 141. Charcoal and ash-rich spreads 137, 138, 140–143, 152 and 153 overlay 144/147 of CG96 16 and were associated with the early lead-melting process.

Context Group 14: lead-melting hearth 114

Located some 1.20m to the north of the Curtain Wall, a bowl-shaped, circular pit of 0.66m diameter by 0.23m deep was excavated into occupation surface 144/147. The pit was used as a bowl hearth for melting scrap lead and had two phases of usage. The earliest retained deposits consisting of brown silt 173, white lead oxide 172, and brown clays 170 and 167 whilst the secondary, smaller pit contained red burnt clay 166, blue/white lead slag 165, molten lead 159 and grey charcoal and ash 113.

Context Group 13: lead-working spreads and ephemeral features

Overlying lead-working pit 114 of CG96 14 and underlying 092 of CG96 10, Phase 7, were a series of thin spreads, 102/112 (notable for its concentration of chicken bones), 109, 110/121, 115, 126, 124, 127, 128, 129, 132, 133, 145, 146, 148, 149, 150 and 151/108, consisting of compact yellow clay, ash, charcoal and burnt clay, mostly containing evidence of lead-working. These deposits were cut by the later lead-working hearth 136 of CG96 12 and resulted from the lead-working and attempts to maintain a level working area around the pit.

A shallow ditch 146 (fill 145) was located in the middle of the trench, running from east to west. The ditch was 0.60m wide by 0.10m deep, ended in a rounded terminal to the west and extended beyond the trench edge to the east.

A rectangular pit 149 (fill 151) with dimensions of 1.80m from north to south by 1.00m and 0.25m deep was excavated about 0.50m to the north of ditch 146. The pit had two circular depressions at its

FIGURE 3.16
Lead-melting hearth 114 of CG96 14, Phase 6, mid-excavation, looking south (photograph: Marches Archaeology)

base, 150 and 157 (fills 151 and 156), with diameters of 0.20m, which may have been truncated post-holes.

Context Group 12: lead-melting hearth 136

A circular, bowl-shaped pit with a diameter of 1.00m and depth of 0.30m was excavated for use as a lead-melting hearth. The hearth was re-cut at least once and contained two lead-rich deposits. The original cut, 136, contained a lead-rich fill 135, overlain by burnt clay 134 and 130. The re-cut, 120, contained lead-rich fill 119 and charcoal-rich fill 118. The upper fills consisted of 111, 116 and 117, associated spreads were charcoal 098/103 and red burnt clay 097. The overlying deposit 085 appeared to have been laid as a level gravel surface immediately after the melting process had ceased.

Phase 7: mid- to late 14th century

During this phase a building was constructed some 7.00m to the north of the Curtain Wall with a doorway to the south (Figure 3.17A). Three floor surfaces would suggest a reasonable period of usage, possibly going out of use at the same time as the Phase 5 Curtain Wall was demolished and reconstructed in Phase 8.

Context Group 11: wall 083, construction, occupation and demolition

To the north of the site, wall 083 was constructed running from east to west. The wall sat in construction trench 400, fill 399, and was 0.60m wide, survived for three courses above a foundation offset and was built of reused, grey sandstone showing tooling marks and a single, X-shaped mason's mark. The northern face retained areas of white plaster suggesting it was internal to the building. The wall extended 0.80m from the western section where it was faced off. This face appeared to have a shallow vertical slot within the masonry, presumably intended to take a timber door jamb. Running eastwards from this slot was an irregular, single course of flat stones, 187. This feature may have been intended either as a threshold or as a support for a timber sill. The wall re-appeared within the eastern section but was not faced and any part that may have contained an eastern door jamb had been demolished. Immediately to the north of the wall and contemporary with its construction was a gulley, 227, which ran from west to east and was 0.66m wide by 0.18m deep with a rounded terminal. The gulley extended beyond the western trench edge. Stratigraphically the gulley was contemporary with wall 083 but it was sealed by the first floor surface 158 and may have been slightly earlier. There were no associated finds. To the south of the wall, mortar spread 125 was also stratigraphically contemporary. To the north of the wall (the building's interior) was a sequence of deposits which apparently denoted the construction of a clay floor 158 and occupation deposits above 160, 101 and 100. Clay 096 may have denoted a new floor surface which extended through the doorway and was cut by narrow gulley 095, fill 094, which had been excavated into the occupation deposits

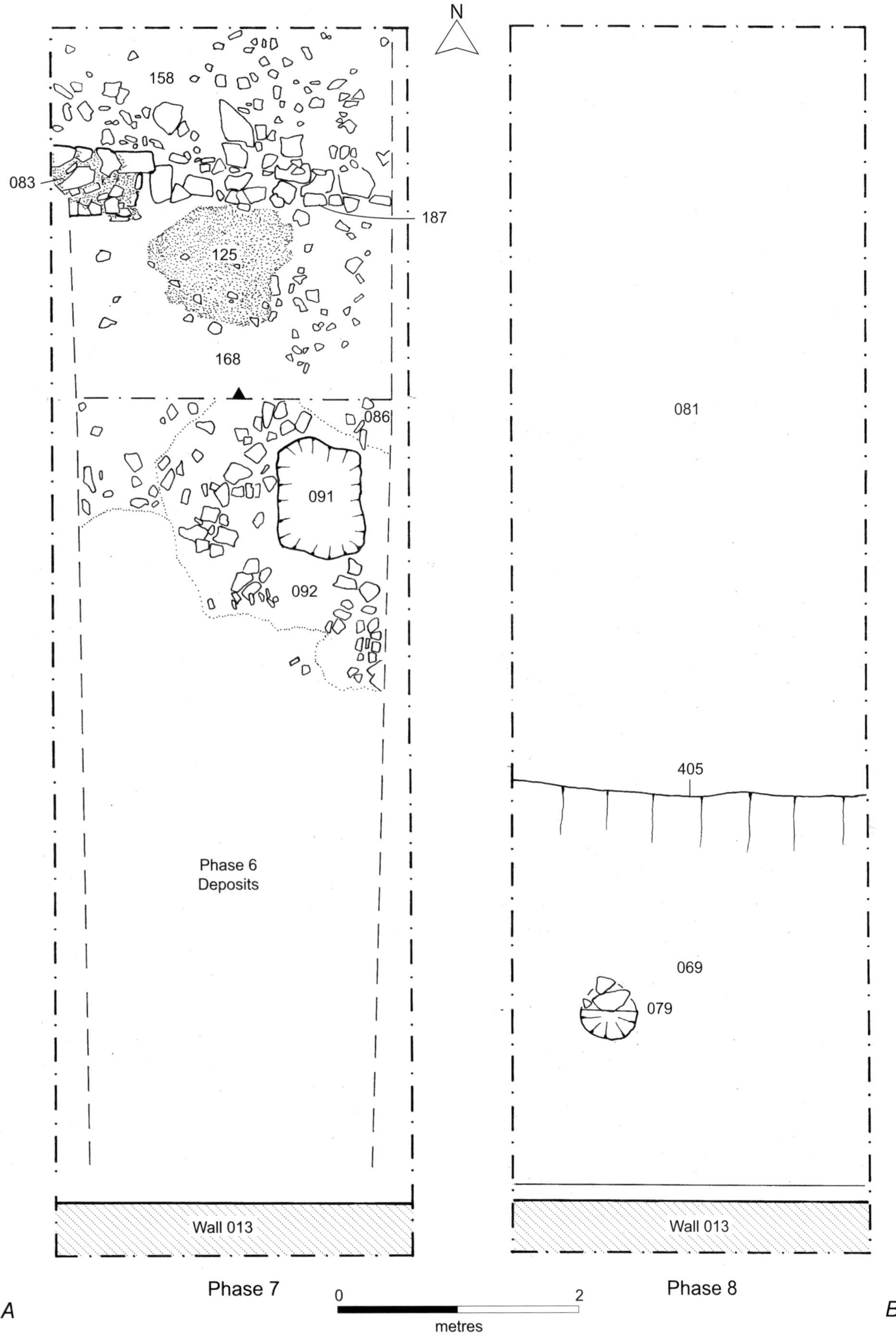

FIGURE 3.17
Plans of the 1996 trench showing Phases 7 and 8

along the same alignment as 187 and was possibly intended to take a timber sill beam across a re-designed doorway. Green-tinged clay 093 may have been the last floor surface with 084, an overlying occupation deposit containing wall plaster, possibly indicating that by this time the building was already falling into disuse. To the south of the wall (the building exterior) was an irregular mortar surface, 125, about 1.00m in diameter which may have been intended as a hard-wearing surface in the area of the proposed entrance. The mortar was overlain by a series of clays and silts denoting occupation 099, 104–107, 122 and 123. After disuse, green clay 088 was deposited over the wall footings and extensive rubble demolition deposits, 081 and 082 of CG96 9, Phase 8, sealed the whole area.

Context Group 10: deposit and rectangular pit

Overlying 102 and the other thin spreads of CG96 13, Phase 6, were 092 and 086, two deposits of compact, grey/brown clay at an average height of 172.50m OD. A rectangular pit, 091, had been excavated into this deposit, located in the centre of the trench and slightly to the east (Figure 3.17A). The pit had dimensions of 0.97m from north to south by 0.71m with an average depth of 0.35m and the fills consisted of charcoal-rich silt 090, overlain by a tumble of flat stones 089 and sealed by orange/brown sandy clay 087. The purpose of the pit was not determined. This group underlay 082 of CG96 09, Phase 8.

Phase 8: early to mid-15th century

During this phase a major reconstruction of the curtain wall was undertaken with significant ground disturbance internally (Figures 3.6, 3.7 and 3.17B). Dating evidence for the date of the reconstruction is scarce but seems to favour a date in the 15th century. Notably, no obvious well made ground surface was identified as having capped the demolition/construction deposits.

Context Group 08: rebuild of Curtain Wall

As part of what must have been a major castle refurbishment, the Phase 5 Curtain Wall was reduced in height to the contemporary ground level at 172.65m OD. Red mortar and rubble deposits 081 and 082 were formed as a result of that demolition to a depth of about 0.80m. In order to reconstruct the new wall a large cut, 405, was excavated through the rubble deposits, measuring 3.40m wide by 0.80m deep with an irregular gently sloping side (Figure 3.17B). The masonry of the reconstructed Curtain Wall 013 is described above. During this phase a sequence of deposits of varying consistency, including clays, silts and gravels (nearly all with some rubble), were deposited into the base of the construction trench (067–070, 074–077 and 080). An unexplained feature was bowl-shaped pit 079, located close to the Curtain Wall with a diameter of 0.65m and maximum depth of 0.40m and a fill consisting of a large central stone surrounded by packing stones within a sandy matrix, 078. All these deposits were overlain by 073/066 of CG96 09, although the two groups might properly be combined as a single activity.

Context Group 09: rubble dumps

A series of dumped deposits (057, 060–066/073, 071 and 072) containing rubble and with varying quantities of clay and gravel, having a generally red/brown colouring, appears to attest to continued levelling of the ground surface possibly with waste demolition and building material from the reconstruction of the Curtain Wall. The pottery assemblage from this group would indicate a date within the 15th century. Dumping continued until cut 405 was full, and deposits then extended further north within the trench.

Phase 9: mid- to late 15th century

This phase (Figures 3.18, 3.19 and 3.20) represents a significant build up of dumps of varying materials, including two possible floor surfaces, a significant dump of domestic debris and the blocking of the alcove within the Southern Curtain Wall.

Context Group 07: levelling dumps for surface 045 of CG96 06

Underlying surface 045 of CG96 and overlying 062 of CG96 08, Phase 8, was a further sequence of deposits (046, 047, 048, 053, 055, 056, 058 and 059). The deposits consisted of yellow clays, brown silts, decayed mortar and included a charcoal-rich layer, 049. The group seems to have been intended as make up for surface 045 but could possibly be associated with the underlying group CG96 08, Phase 8.

Context Group 06: occupation surface 045 and overlying dumps

Overlying 053 and 048 of CG96 07 and underlying 035 of CG96 03 was a confusing sequence of deposits (027, 031, 034, 039, 040, 041, 042, 043, 044, 050, 051, 052 and 054) consisting of loams, clays, gravels, mortar and rubble to an average depth of 0.70m. No coherent activity could be identified within these deposits and they appeared to indicate a period of abandonment. The pottery from within this group dated from the 13th to the 16th centuries, although the underlying surface, 045, was closely datable to the later 15th century on numismatic evidence (SF75, Chapter 5). This level surface consisted of brown gritty clay with some stone admix, covered most of the trench and may have been purposefully laid as a levelling surface at a height of 173.75m OD

(Figure 3.18). It seems probable that the overlying deposits developed in the later 15th and early 16th centuries.

Context Group 04: plaster floor 033

In the early part of the 16th century an irregular, off-white plaster floor, 033, was laid over deposit 027 of CG96 06 at a height of 174.00m OD (Figures 3.19 and 3.20). The floor surface survived in the south-west part of the trench and it is a point of debate as to whether the surface was located within a building. The surface was contemporary with CG96 03 and abutted the Curtain Wall, where it had a thickness of 0.30m, thinning to 0.07m before fragmenting at a distance of 3.70m from the wall. The deposit was initially interpreted as collapsed rendering from the Curtain Wall but this seems to be unlikely and the deposit may have been an attempt to create a level working surface late in the life of the castle, although there were no associated finds and it is possible that the deposit resulted from the dumping of waste plaster.

FIGURE 3.18

Occupation surface 045 of CG96 06, Phase 9, looking south (photograph: Marches Archaeology)

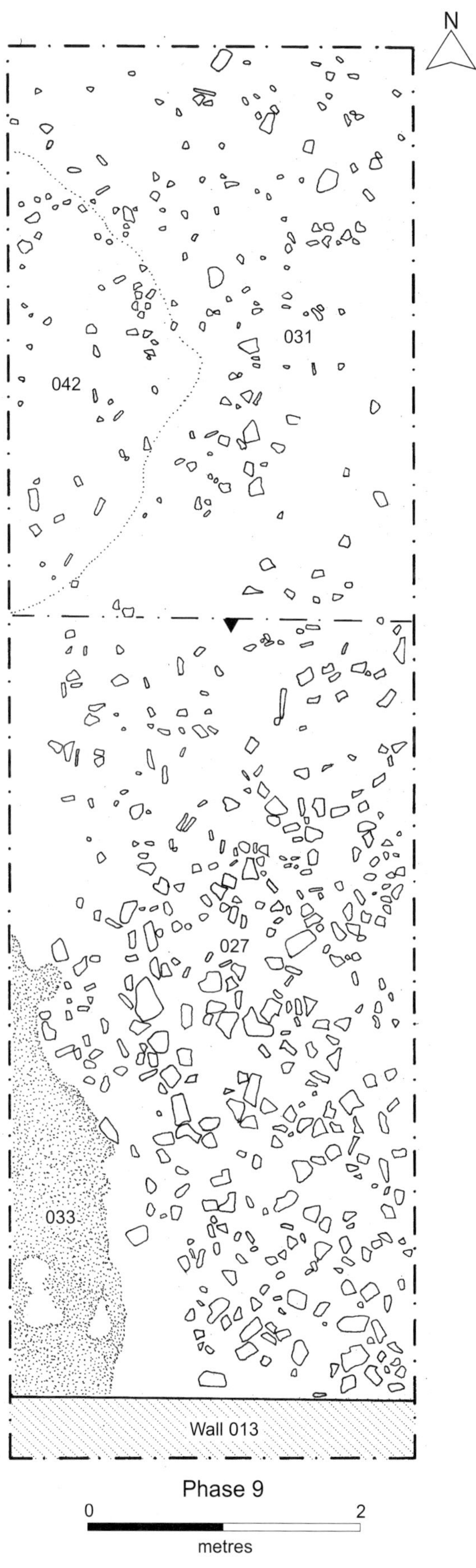

FIGURE 3.19

Plan of the 1996 trench showing Phase 9

FIGURE 3.20
Plaster floor 033 of CG96 04, Phase 9, looking west (photograph: Marches Archaeology)

Context Group 03: domestic debris

Overlying 043 of CG96 06, Phase 9, and underlying possible turf line 024 of CG96 02, Phase 10, was a group of three deposits (025, 030 and 035) which formed a moderately level surface at approximately 174.00m OD in the central and northern part of the trench. The deposits consisted of dark grey/brown charcoal-rich silty clays containing moderate quantities of small- and medium-sized rubble with clean yellow clay and sand lenses. The deposits were rich in finds of all categories, suggesting the dumping of domestic debris. The pottery would indicate a 16th century date for its deposition.

Context Group 05: blocking of recess in Curtain Wall 013

Built into the Phase 8 Curtain Wall 013 and contemporary with it was a rectangular recess, 1.50m long and 0.80m deep but of unknown height due to collapse of the upper masonry courses; the purpose of the recess has not been ascertained (Figures 3.6 and 3.7). The recess was partially blocked by a poorly constructed wall which survived for seven courses and was set back a distance of 0.11m from the face of wall 013 and partially in bond with it. Within the recess, behind the blocking wall, were two deposits: medium brown silty clay 036 overlying rubble, and decayed mortar 037. These deposits produced later 16th-century pottery. Just as the purpose of the recess remains obscure, so does the reason for blocking it.

Phase 10, 16th to mid-17th century: decay and slighting?

Phase 10, Context Group 02: rubble dumps

Overlying 030 of CG96 03, Phase 9, and underlying 006 and 007 of CG96 01, Phase 11, was a sequence of rubble, loam, gravel and mortar dumps. The deposits had built up against Curtain Wall 013 and extended northwards where they rapidly thinned from a maximum depth of 1.20m where they abutted the curtain wall. The rubble dumps appeared to be of 17th-century date and deposit 023 was interpreted as associated with the Civil War slighting whilst 024, a level grey/brown loam deposit, a possible turf line, formed during a period of disuse prior to the slighting. Eight fragments of medieval window glass were found in the layers between these two contexts but most of the glass was found in rubble deposits above 023. Deposit 029 consisted of a dark grey, charcoal-rich deposit containing nails and animal bone and was similar to the deposits of CG96 03, Phase 9, although separated stratigraphically.

Phase 11, mid-17th to late 20th century: abandonment, decay and root disturbance

Context Group 01: turf and topsoil

Prior to excavation the alignment of the trench lay over a significant bank which had formed above the reduced Curtain Wall to a height of 176.30m OD. The bank sloped steeply to the south to meet the outer face of the Curtain Wall and somewhat more gently to the north where the ground surface became more level within the Inner Bailey at a height of 174.70m OD. The surface consisted of course grass and shrubs. Banked up against and over the curtain wall and extending into the bailey was a sequence of deposits primarily consisting of grey/brown loams with turf and topsoil overlying all, 001–007. Only one spread of rubble, 006, fell within this group and this seemed to be of no particular significance. The combined depth of these deposits was some 0.60m. The deposits seem to be the result of vegetation growth and decay during the period of abandonment following the Civil War slighting of 1643 (but see Chapter 4) and overlay rubble dumps of CG96 02, Phase 10.

3.3 THE 1998 EXCAVATIONS

Introduction and standing fabric

The 1998 excavation was located in the south-eastern corner of the Inner Bailey where the East Tower had been constructed in the angle formed by the junction of the Southern and Northern Curtain Walls (see Figure 3.1). Excavations were undertaken between February and April 1998, and a second campaign in September of that year (Figure 3.21). The excavations were directed by Nic Appleton-Fox for Marches Archaeology under contract to English Heritage. The work involved the excavation of the East Tower interior and an irregular trench to the west with an approximate area of 40 square metres. The excavation eventually reached a depth of about 3.00m; at this depth, due to battering of the trench sides and truncation by later features, the area available for excavation had been reduced to approximately 10 square metres. During the course of the 1998 excavation, some 229 context numbers were allocated; these were then divided into 33 context groups consisting of contemporary features and deposits. The context groups were then placed within one of the 11 phases based on stratigraphic and finds analysis (Figure 3.2).

The extant masonry

The following masonry description (Figure 3.22–3.24) is an amalgamation of information obtained from the excavation archive and from a preliminary draft report on the survey of the standing fabric (Cooke 2008) which will be published as an English Heritage Research Report (Cooke forthcoming). Context numbers allocated to the extant masonry during excavation are shown in Figure 3.23.

The Northern Curtain Wall: 536, 599, 679, 680 and 681

This wall extended for 12.50m northwards from the East Tower and survived to a height of 8.00m externally and 3.00m internally. The wall was constructed of coursed mudstone with occasional, possibly re-used, sandstone blocks. External features included square put-log holes in regular rows and columns and a battered sandstone course at 1.00m above the present ground surface, features identical to those found on the East Tower. A row of distinctive round put-log holes located 2.20m below the present wall top may have supported a wooden fighting platform. The northern end of the wall contained sandstone quoins at the point where it changed its alignment to run towards the North-East Tower. The wall was 2.00m thick with the remnants of the parapet being 0.70m wide and surviving to a height of 0.50m above the wall-walk, traces of which survived. At the junction with the East Tower, the curtain wall was designed to accommodate a garderobe chamber, the square outlet of which is visible in the lower exterior of the wall. The external face of this wall was in bond with the East Tower and was probably part of the same reconstruction. For the most part the interior face had been robbed or had collapsed and was only seen within the excavation below a height of 173.00m OD. The excavation revealed a

FIGURE 3.21

General view of the site early in the excavation in 1998, looking north (photograph: Marches Archaeology)

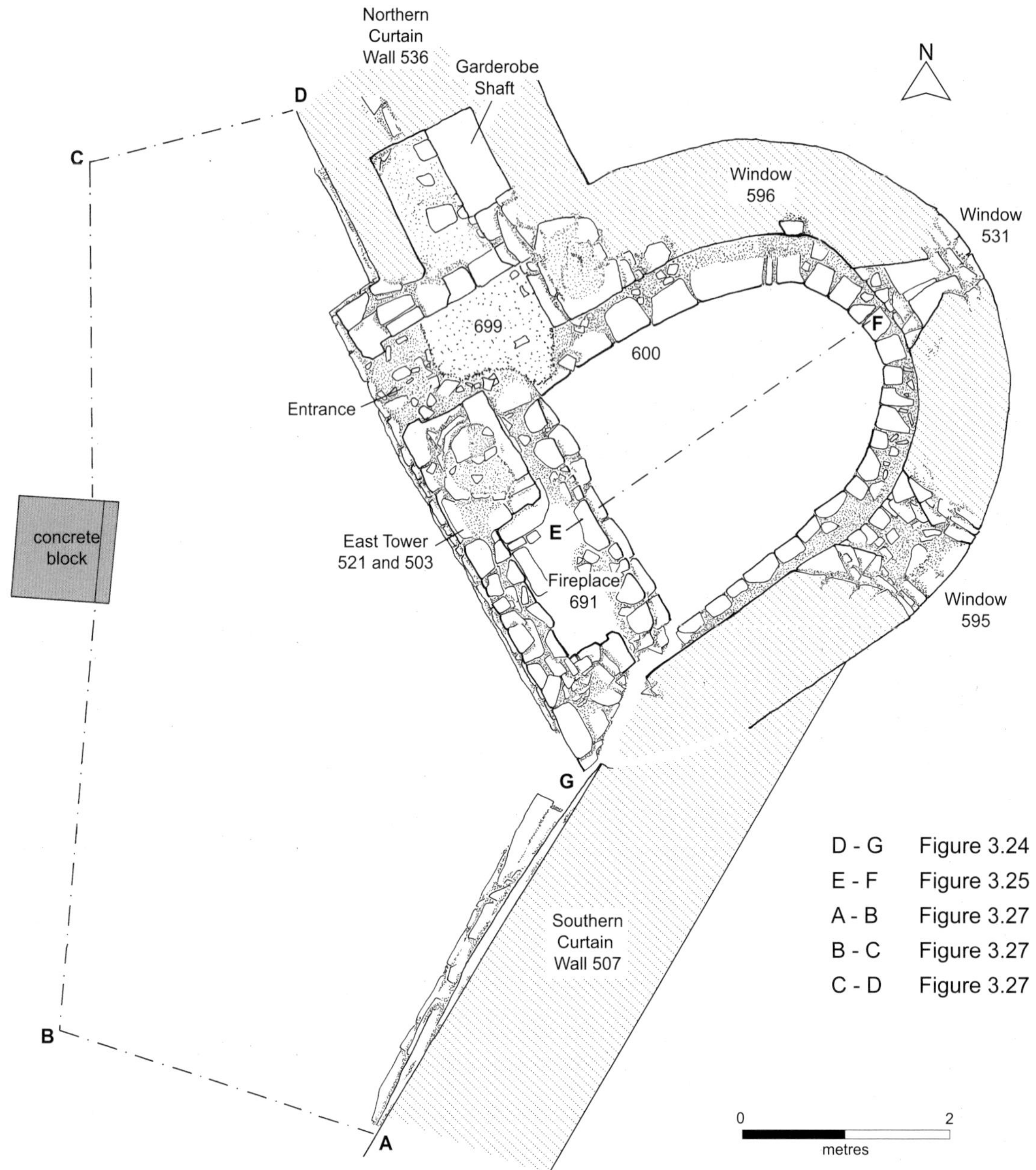

FIGURE 3.22

Plan of the East Tower and 1998 trench showing masonry details and the location of sections (Figures 3.25 and 3.27) and elevation (Figure 3.24)

	Northern Curtain	Eastern Tower	Southern Curtain	Phase
Demolition and decay	599	548, 598, 543,535, 534, 546, 533	597	10 and 11
Features	699 mortar floor	691 fireplace, 595, 596 and 531 windows	-	8
Upper Masonry	536	503, 521	507	8
Lower Masonry	679 680 681	600, 601, 642, 678, 683,684, 676, 701, 704,		4
Earlier Walls?	-	726	682	3

FIGURE 3.23

Table showing context numbers allocated to the extant masonry

poorly faced coursed mudstone wall bonded with tan brown mortar with no off-sets or batters. Excavation records allotted five context numbers to this wall, from the top: 599 decay, 536 bonded to 503, 679 butted by 503, 680 butted to 601 and 681 bonded to 678, all of the East Tower. This irregular sequence might indicate that the Northern Curtain Wall and the East Tower were contemporary builds; this is strongly supported by similarities in their external elevations. Excavation adjacent to this wall ceased at 169.80m OD, within the fills of ditch 658 of CG98 15, Phase 8, and no construction trench was identified. It would appear that the visible aspect of this wall was contemporary with the reconstruction of the East Tower in Phase 8 but it is highly probable that lower courses belonged to an earlier period contemporary with the early courses of the Southern Curtain Wall tentatively dated to Phase 3.

The East Tower

This D-shaped tower was square backed with a semi-circular frontage projecting eastwards with external dimensions of 4.50m from north to south by 5.00m. The tower was located in the south-eastern corner of the Inner Ward and had been inserted into the angle created by the junction of two sections of curtain wall here referred to as the Northern and Southern Curtain Walls. The masonry of the upper part of the tower consisted of poorly coursed, irregular-shaped local mudstone and very occasional sandstone blocks bedded in an off-white mortar (Figure 3.24). The lower masonry was bonded with red mortar and contained a basement room with internal dimensions of 2.60m from west to east by 2.20m enclosed by walls 1.15m thick. This chamber must have been accessed via a trapdoor and ladder from the floor above. The upper masonry was thinner at 0.85m wide, leaving an offset ledge of 0.30m around the tower interior at a height of 171.74m OD, which would have supported a timber floor. The change in mortar from red to white, the difference in wall thickness and the junctions between tower and curtain walls led the excavators to believe that the tower had undergone a major rebuild. In the 1996 excavations red mortar is associated with the Phase 5 Curtain Wall whilst white mortar is used in the Phase 8 rebuild and also in the Phase 7 building of CG96 11. The exterior of the tower, however, shows no change at all and the arrangement of put-log holes in both tower and Northern Curtain Wall is consistent from top to bottom suggesting either that both structures were completely re-faced during the putative rebuild or that there was no rebuild at all. The architectural detail within the surviving masonry is, for example, unlike that within the rest of the castle's towers. There is no definitive archaeological evidence to indicate a rebuild of the tower other than the change in colour of the mortar from red, in the basement, to off-white throughout the upper masonry. The earliest deposits excavated from within the basement dated to the 15th century, possibly late in the century, and appear similar to Phase 8 material from outside the tower (see Chapter 9). However, although the deposition of the lower basement layers could indicate a tower rebuild in Phase 8, immediately preceding their deposition, the evidence is by no means conclusive.

The interior dimensions of the upper chamber were 3.00m from west to east by 2.80m. A number of features within the masonry indicate that the tower was of use not only as a defensive structure but may also have been used as a lodging chamber.

Entrance

The entrance into the tower was located at the northern end of the western wall and consisted of a sandstone threshold at a height of 171.68m OD and chamfered sandstone jambs with internal rebates leading to a passageway 0.86m wide. The northern jamb had been damaged where the lower hinge pin for the door had been removed, indicating that the door opened inwards to the north. The passageway contained a doorway to the north which led to a small chamber containing a garderobe shaft, whilst a second door to the south led into the tower interior. The remains of an off-white plaster floor, 699, were uncovered within the passageway at a height of 171.73m OD.

Garderobe

A doorway, 0.52m wide with chamfered sandstone jambs, was located in the northern face of the entrance passage and led via a sandstone step up to a rectangular chamber located within the Northern Curtain Wall with dimensions of 1.10m from west to east by 0.85m with the floor at a height of 172.08m OD. In the eastern corner a rectangular shaft measuring 0.85m by 0.50m was built into the floor, a garderobe chute with surviving slots built into the masonry above intended to accommodate a timber seat arrangement.

Windows

Within the upper masonry of the tower were the remains of three splayed windows. The window opening to the north-east, 596, was badly damaged by a large tree bole occupying the whole of the opening. Only one sandstone block survived *in situ* at the base of the eastern side of the splay. Both sides of the splayed window opening to the east, 531/2, survived and incorporated sandstone blocks. Internally the splay was estimated at 0.90m wide. The sill for this window partially survived at a height of 172.57m OD and the window reveals survived to a height of 0.60m above the sill. The window

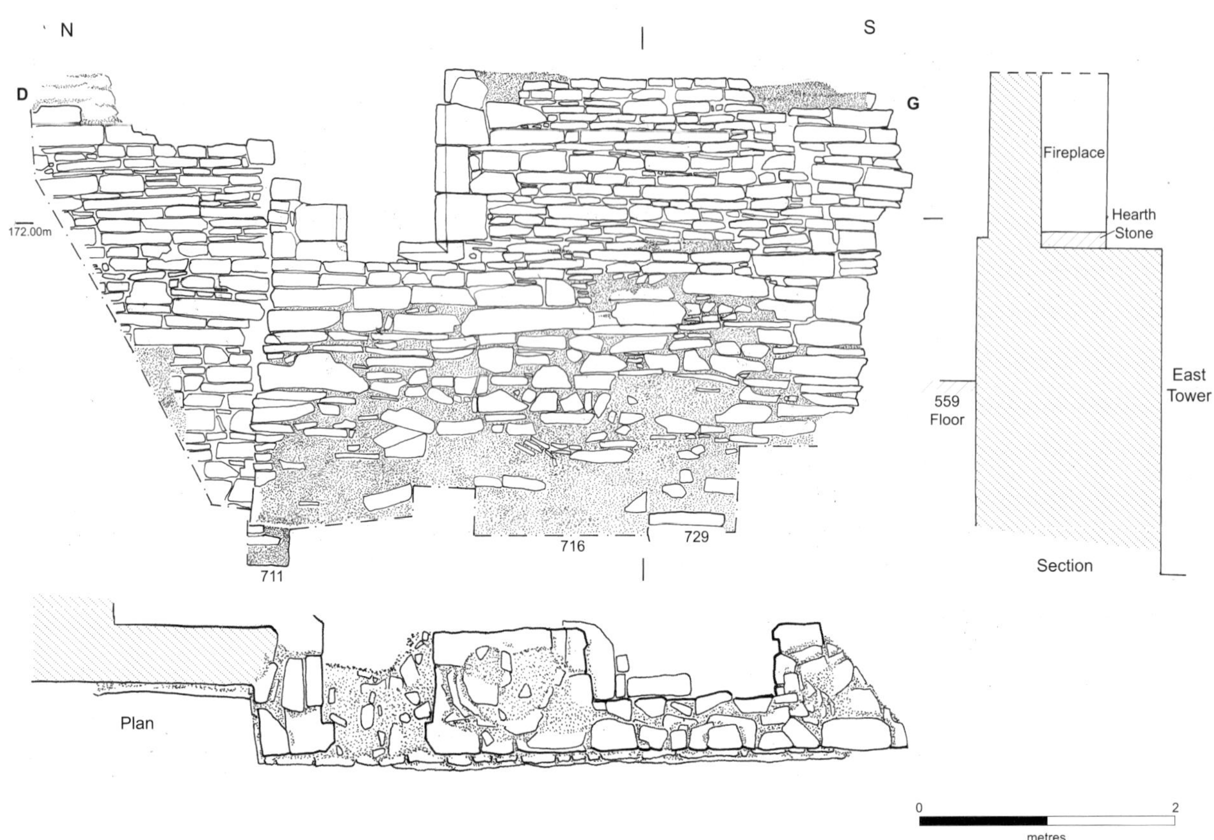

FIGURE 3.24
Elevation and section of the west face of the East Tower

opening to the south-east, 595, had been robbed of masonry detail and was represented by a ragged hole within the masonry with dimensions on the internal face of 3.28m high by 1.58m. The external openings of all windows had been robbed of their sandstone dressings. It seems probable from the surviving masonry that these windows were all identical and were designed as arrow loops providing flanking fire along the faces of both adjoining curtain walls and outwards to the east.

Fireplace

Located at the southern end of the west wall was a fireplace, 691. The opening was 1.43m wide by 0.57m deep with the height estimated at 0.92m at which height a regular gap within the masonry suggested a lintel had once been placed. The base retained fragments of the stone-slabbed hearth at a height of 171.86m OD, whilst the jambs were of dressed sandstone with external and internal chamfers.

The Southern Curtain Wall: 507, 597 and 682

This wall extended for a distance of 17.00m from the East Tower towards the gatehouse to the south-west. It was constructed of coursed mudstone with very few sandstone blocks. The wall stood to a height of 7.00m externally and 1.00m internally but no trace of the wall-walk or parapet has survived. Put-log holes, visible in the external face, were of a very different character to those of the Northern Curtain Wall and East Tower being more irregular and there was no evidence for the battered sandstone course noted in those structures. Within the excavation, a length of 3.40m with a depth of a little more than 2.00m was exposed, and, within this expanse, approximately half of the facing stones had collapsed with one hole penetrating the full width of the masonry. At a height of 171.90m OD the wall developed an irregular offset of some 0.20m width. The base of the wall, 682, below 171.40m OD consisted of poorly faced, coursed mudstone with an intact render facing and was battered at 15 degrees from the vertical. No construction trench for the wall was noted and excavation of deposits in the vicinity ceased on top of deposit 653 of CG 18, Phase 4. The uppermost part of the Southern Curtain, 507, was bonded into the upper masonry of the East Tower, 521, is considered to be contemporary with that build, and has been tentatively assigned to Phase 8 of the 15th century. The lower portion of the wall extended below the rear wall of the East Tower and was not in bond; it is suggested that the lower part of this wall pre-dates both the initial construction of the East Tower in Phase 4 and the visible part of the Northern Curtain Wall, possibly dating to Phase 3 of the early 13th century.

Summary

It seems probable that the Outer Bailey was surrounded with masonry defences within Phase 3 of the castle's development in the early 13th century. These walls were partially rebuilt when the D-shaped East Tower was inserted into the south-eastern corner in the later 13th century in Phase 4. The tower and associated wall stretches were remodelled again in Phase 8, within the 15th century. Excavations have shown that associated structures built against the rear of the tower and curtain walls existed at various periods of use but the excavations were too limited in scale to describe their form or function. This part of the castle appears to have become neglected in the later 16th century and gradually decayed thereafter.

The East Tower: internal deposits

Although, according to written sources, the castle apparently suffered periods of neglect during the 15th and 16th centuries, it was not recorded as having been subjected to demolition until the partial slighting of 1643. The depth of deposits excavated from within the basement of the East Tower might suggest that the floor over the basement had already been removed prior to their deposition, beginning in the later 15th century (Figures 3.25 and 3.26).

Phase 10: 16th to mid-17th century

Having been constructed in Phase 4 and remodelled in Phase 8, the basement room of the East Tower was filled in with deposits dating from the ?late 15th to the 17th centuries. After detailed finds analysis, this group was divided into three sub-groups: 11a, b and c. The ceramic evidence suggested that these would broadly relate to activity within the 15th, 16th and 17th centuries respectively.

Context Group 11, sub-groups a, b and c: early infill (equals CG98 04)

Excavations within the East Tower ceased on the upper surface of 670, a deposit of bright green clay with decayed mudstone inclusions at an average height of 169.10m OD. The surface of this layer sloped down from west to east with a fall of 0.40m over a distance of 2.50m, suggesting that the surface could not have functioned as a purposeful floor. It is possible that 670 was a remnant of an earthen bank associated with the Phase 1 timber castle, however, no construction trench for the surrounding masonry was identified and this would suggest that 670 was deposited within the already built tower, merely another dump within the tower.

The overlying deposits (665, 644, 648, 643, 640 and 630, sub-group a) generally consisted of compact brown silty clays (Figure 3.25). Overlying 648 within this sequence was a spread of pale pink/grey ash, 643, located in the north-western corner of the tower immediately below the tower entrance. The uppermost layer within this sequence was 630, a deposit consisting of dark red/brown silty clay which formed a level surface across the whole tower interior at 169.88m OD. This flat surface may have formed an earthen floor at approximately 1.90m below the timber floor above. Pottery from 665 and the layers above has been dated to the late 15th century.

Overlying 630 was a further sequence of layers: 629, 628, 622, 621, 611, 618, 614 and 610 (sub-group b), generally consisting of brown silty clay loams with some inclusion of mudstone rubble, mortar and charcoal. Located against the northern wall of the tower and overlying 611 was a thin spread of charcoal-rich silty clay, 618, and a yellow/brown burnt deposit, 614. The deposits measured 0.70m by 0.70m and indicated the location of a small fire. Overlying the remains of the fire was 610, a deposit of loose brown silty clay, which formed a level surface at 170.68m OD. The deposition of this last sequence of infill ensured that the space could no longer be used as a room; the height between the upper surface of 610 and the upper floor being now only 1.00m. Pottery from these deposits was dated to the second half of the 16th century.

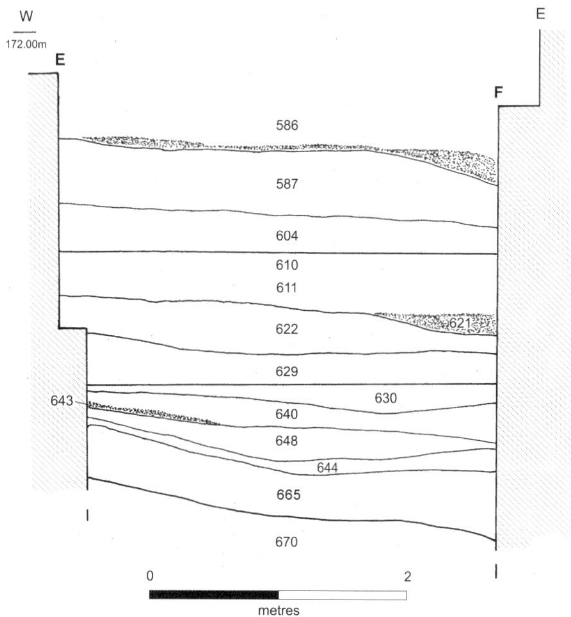

FIGURE 3.25
The East Tower interior: south-facing composite section

FIGURE 3.26
The East Tower interior: mid-excavation, looking east (photograph: Marches Archaeology)

Deposits 604 and 587 (sub-group c), overlying 610, were of a totally different nature, consisting of mudstone rubble within a matrix of brown loam containing mortar fragments. These deposits also produced 16th-century pottery. Overlying 587 was a spread of pale off-white mortar, 586, and a number of stone slabs, 567, immediately in front of the fireplace, apparently displaced from the hearth, indicating that at this stage the tower was already becoming ruinous.

Within the passageway leading from the Inner Bailey to the tower interior, rubble deposit 556 produced 17th-century pottery. This deposit overlay 698, medium brown gritty silt, which in turn overlay plaster floor 699.

Phase 11: mid-17th to late 20th century

After partial slighting in 1643, the castle was allowed to decay through weathering and partial robbing until the current period of restoration.

Context Group 10: demolition and decay

Further rubble deposits, 513, 510 and 509, containing plaster and mortar fragments in a pale grey sandy silt matrix overlay 567 of CG98 11c, Phase 10. Within this sequence, overlying 513 were two charcoal-rich lenses, 512 and 511, located within the fireplace recess, possibly revealing a last use of the fireplace when the tower was already badly decaying. All deposits lay below 501 of CG98 01, Phase 11, the turf and topsoil.

East Tower: external deposits

Phase 3: early to mid-13th century

This phase represents perhaps the remains of the reduced Phase 1 clay bank and slight evidence for masonry construction (Figures 3.22 and 3.27).

Context Group 22: clay deposit 727 and 725

The earliest deposit encountered during the 1998 excavations consisted of a level — except where disrupted by later features — green clay deposit, 727, that extended across the exposed area at a height of 169.30m OD and remained unexcavated. The deposit predated all the surrounding masonry and was overlain by 725, a thin, patchy, gritty red/brown layer which may have been formed through the use of mortar and which may have been a working surface associated with the construction of stone curtain walls within this phase. The deposit produced a single sherd of pottery of uncertain date (see Chapter 4). It is possible that green clay 727 equated to the upper or reduced surface of

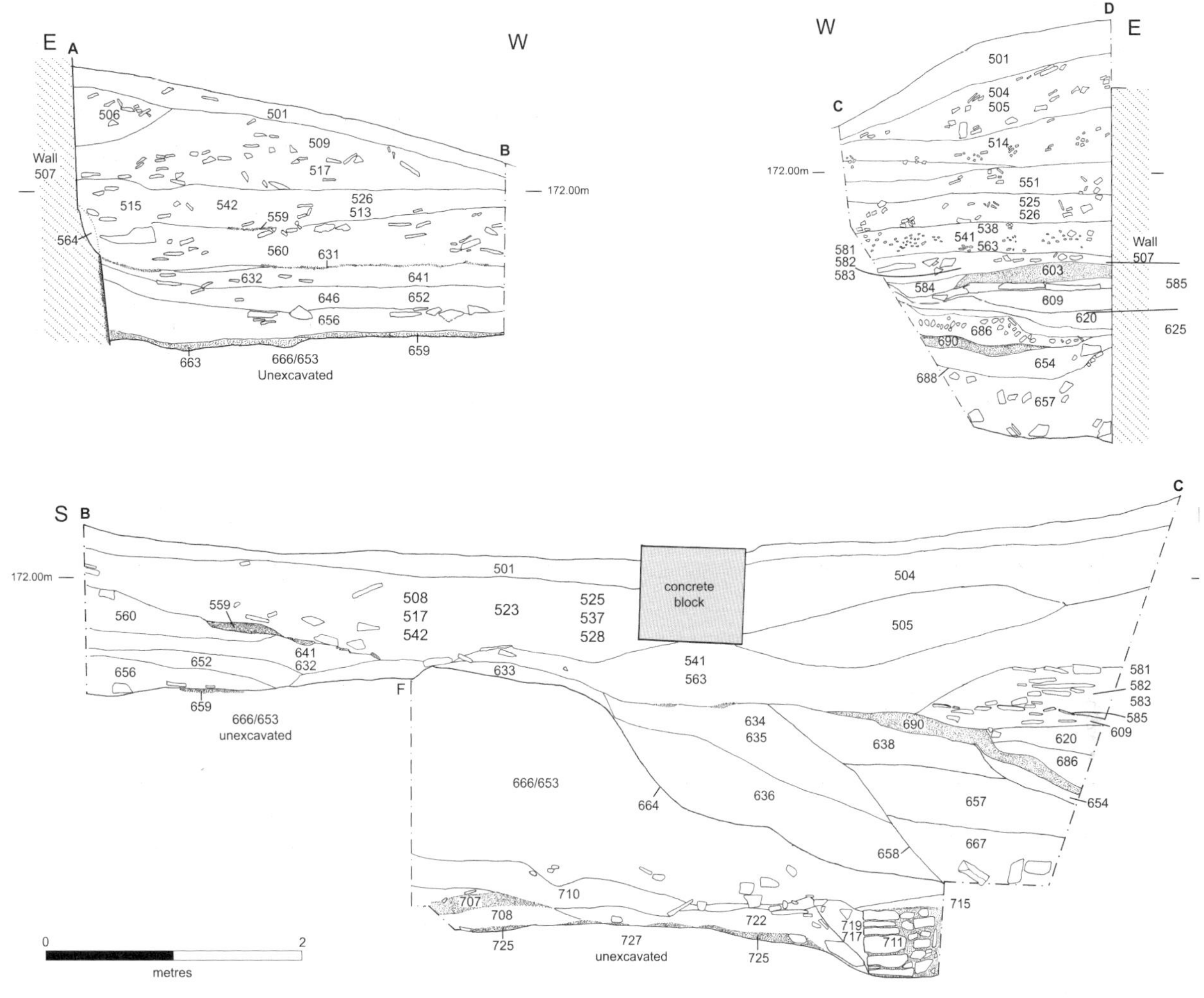

FIGURE 3.27
North, east and south-facing sections in the main trench

the Phase 1 clay bank or terrace noted in the 1996 excavations, uncovered at a height of 171.30m OD, and which may have been associated with early earth and timber defences.

Phase 4: mid- to late 13th century

It is probable that stone curtain walls had already been constructed by this period (Figures 3.27, 3.28, 3.29 and 3.30). In Phase 4 the East Tower was constructed along with a building which ran westwards from the back of the East Tower into the Inner Bailey.

Context Group 09: clay deposits

Above 725 of CG98 22, Phase 3, was a sequence of brown clay deposits with varying quantities of mudstone inclusions and with an average depth of 0.35m (707, 708, 710, 712, 716 and 722). These deposits formed a level surface for Phase 4 construction activity at a height of 169.65m OD. The upper deposit, 710, was cut by 717 and 676, the construction trenches for the East Tower and internal wall 711. Pottery from this group was dated to *c*1250.

Context Group 23: construction trench for East Tower foundation 683

A construction trench, 676, for the first phase of construction of the East Tower was noted where it survived undisturbed by later cuts. The construction trench cut deposit 712 of CG98 09, Phase 4, and was 0.50m wide by 0.50m deep, with its western side sloping at 25 degrees to meet the tower foundation which itself was battered at 20 degrees. The cut was filled with green clay, 703, which extended beyond the confines of the construction trench across the site as an extensive level deposit. Deposit 703 was in turn overlain by green clay deposit 653 of CG98 18.

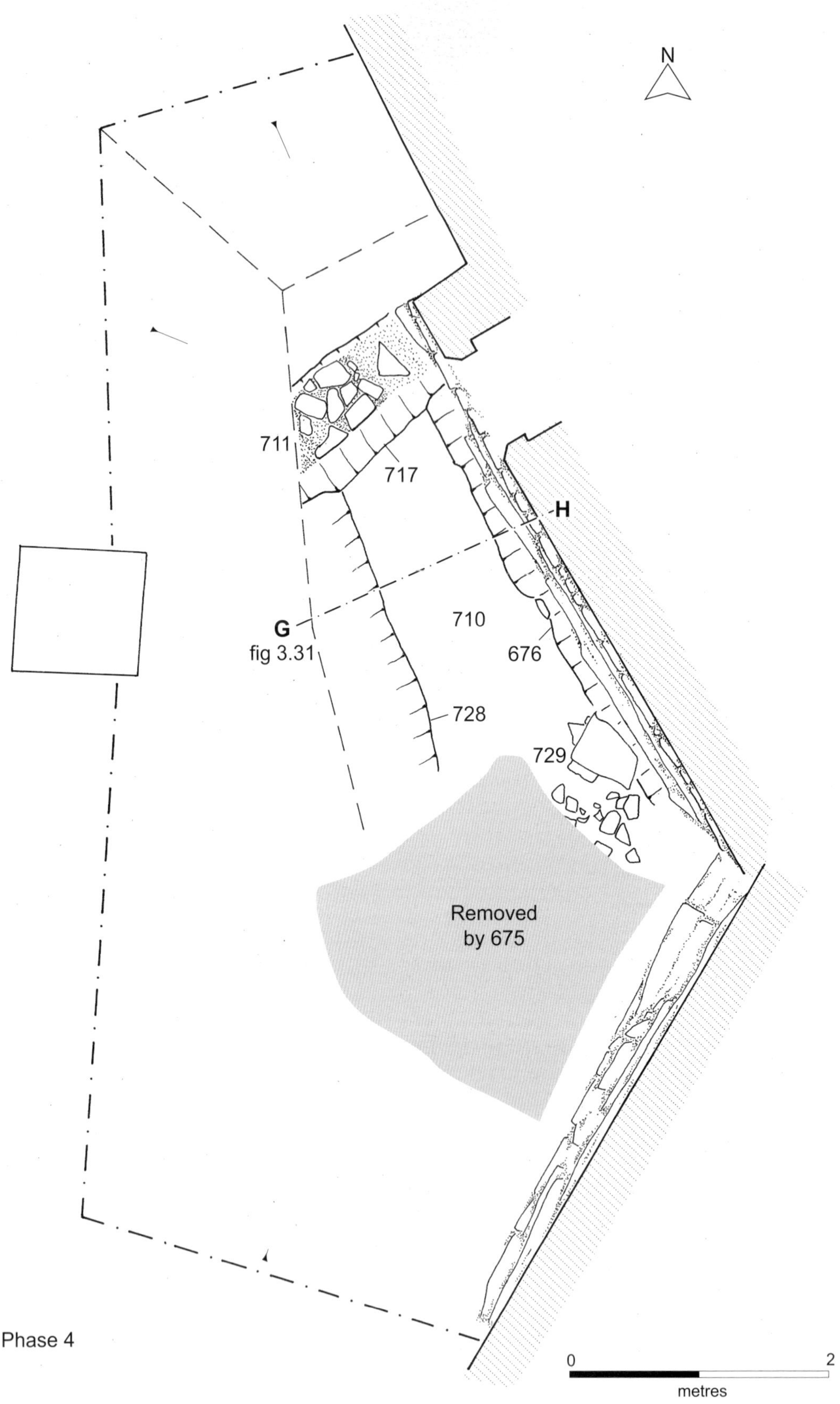

FIGURE 3.28
Plan of the 1998 trench showing Phase 4 features

FIGURE 3.29
Construction trench 676 of CG98 23 and ditch 728 of CG98 24 Phase 4, post-excavation, looking east (photograph: Marches Archaeology)

FIGURE 3.30
Wall foundation 711 of CG98 25, Phase 4, looking south (photograph: Marches Archaeology)

Context Group 24: cut 728, fills 706 and 713

A cut ran from north to south parallel with the East Tower foundation and approximately 1.50m to its west. The cut was 0.60m deep with a flat base and near vertical eastern side. To the west it extended beyond the site boundary whilst to the north it was cut by the construction trench for wall 711 and to the south it was truncated by Phase 8 features. The purpose of the cut was not established but finds from its fill suggested a date within the 13th century.

Context Group 25: wall 711, construction trench 717, fill 719 and stone cluster 729

Following closely on the construction of the Phase 4 East Tower, a wall was constructed running westwards from its north-west corner. The wall foundation, 711, was 0.56m deep by 0.60m wide, constructed of clay-bonded mudstone rubble and with only the southern face coursed, although poorly. The wall was constructed within trench 717 which had a vertical northern face, a flat base of 0.60m width and a southern face sloping at 45 degrees with green clay fill, 719.

The wall foundation abutted the north-western corner of the East Tower and presumably enclosed a structure extending to the west from the tower back. No floor surface was identified to associate with wall 711 but a small spread of mudstone rubble 729 was located 3.00m to its south at a height of 169.80m OD, measuring 0.60m square and apparently sitting within a cut. This feature may have been the remains of an associated wall but was not fully investigated.

Context Group 18: 715 and levelling deposit 653/666

Layer 715 overlay the reduced foundation of wall 711 of CG98 25, extended to the north and consisted of brown clay with a high charcoal content. Overlying 715 was a substantial deposit consisting of pale green clay with decayed mudstone, charcoal and mortar inclusions which extended across the whole excavation area and sealed the redundant features of CG98 23, 24 and 25. The deposit appears to have been intended to create a new, level occupation surface at a height of 170.36m OD.

Phase 5: late 13th to early 14th century

Build up of deposits to create a gravel floor surface and occupation deposits above.

Context Group 33: deposits and a pit

Confined to the eastern part of the site, a sequence of deposits overlay 653 of CG98 18, Phase 4 but was badly disrupted by pit 675 of CG98 17, Phase 8. The deposits consisted of rubble within a grey/brown silt 637, red/brown silty gravel, 673 and green clays 672 and 689. A solitary sub-circular pit 685 (fill 687) was cut into 689 with an average diameter of 0.45m and unknown depth, possibly a post-pit. The nature of the limited excavation made it difficult to interpret this group which produced pottery of the mid-14th century and seems to have been contemporary with gravel floor surface 659/663 of CG98 21.

Context Group 21: gravel floor surface and overlying occupation deposits

Deposits 659 and 663 overlay 653/666 of CG98 18, Phase 4, and were located at the southern end of the site, abutting the rendered face of the Southern Curtain Wall at a height of 170.90m OD. The deposits consisted of orange/brown pea gravel with some small mudstone inclusions with a maximum depth of about 0.12m. They formed a level floor surface, the full extent of which was not established due to truncation by later, Phase 8, features. The overlying layers, 646, 652 and 656, consisted of grey silts with a total depth of 0.35m and a level upper surface at 171.40m OD. Because of the depths of the overlying silt deposits it seems probable that the floor surface was external. A jeton with a probable deposition date of 1325–50 and associated ceramics would suggest a date within the first half of the 14th century.

Phases 6 and 7: 14th century

No contexts were assigned to Phases 6 and 7 within the 1998 excavation due to the massive disruption to the stratigraphy of the site by Phase 8 pits and ditches.

Phase 8: early to mid-15th century

Two little understood, intercutting ditches and a pit were overlain by make-up deposits for a plaster floor (Figures 3.31, 3.32, 3.33 and 3.34).

A large irregular pit with near vertical sides was excavated against the Southern Curtain Wall 507, cutting 637 of CG98 33, Phase 5. The pit was not fully excavated and hence its precise dimensions were not determined but estimated at 3.00m in diameter with a minimum depth of 1.50m. The fill consisted of a grey/brown loam which the excavator suggested indicated vegetation growth on the pit sides whilst the pit was open. The pit was later backfilled with rubble which was in turn cut by ditch 664 of CG98 16. The pottery recovered was of 15th-century date.

Context Group 16: ditch 664, fills 671, 669, 668 and 636

A ditch was excavated through the fill of pit 675 of CG98 17. The ditch ran to the west from Curtain Wall 507 then turned to run northwards, extending beyond the site boundary to the north-west. The ditch was around 2.40m wide by 1.50m deep with a splayed, U-shaped profile, and its fills contained considerable quantities of demolition debris.

Context Group 15: ditch 658, fills 667, 660, and 657/661

Located to the north of the site was a curving ditch running from the northern section southwards then turning to the west and running beyond the western section. The ditch was 1.20m wide by 1.00m deep with sides sloping at *c*45 degrees, leading to an irregular flat base. The fills contained a high quantity

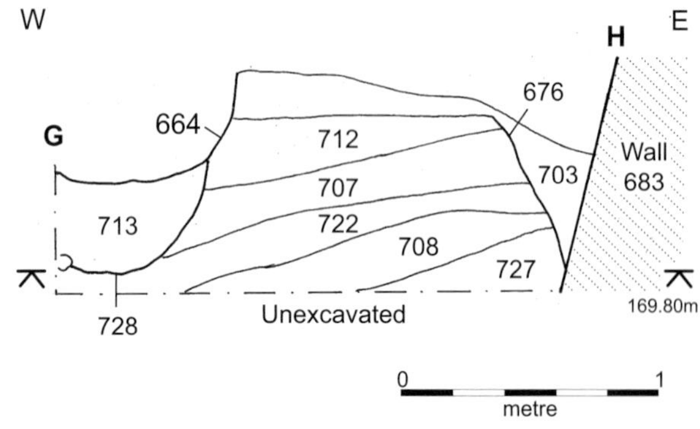

FIGURE 3.31

South-facing section showing Phase 4 features and deposits

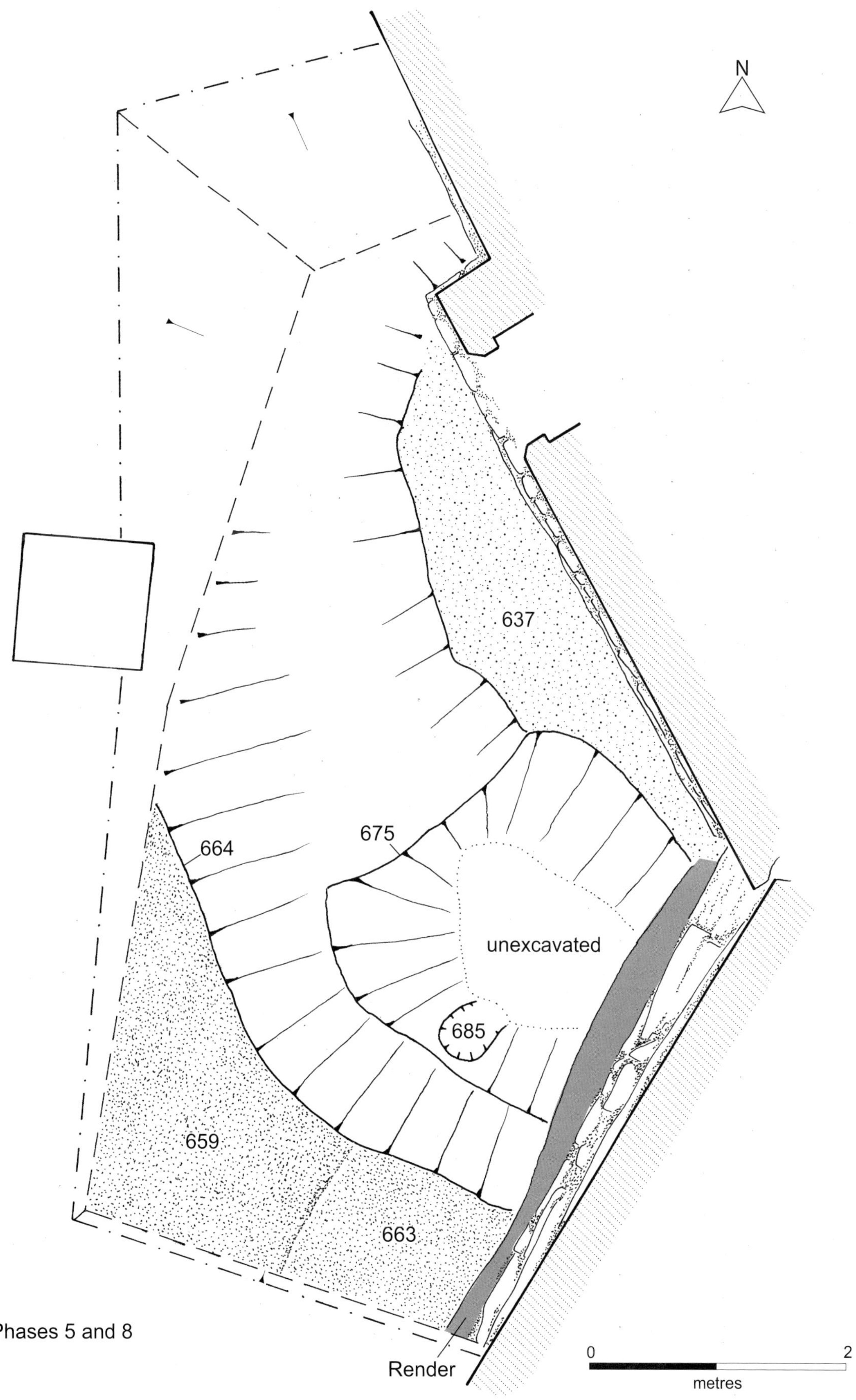

FIGURE 3.32
Plan of the 1998 trench showing Phase 5 and Phase 8 features

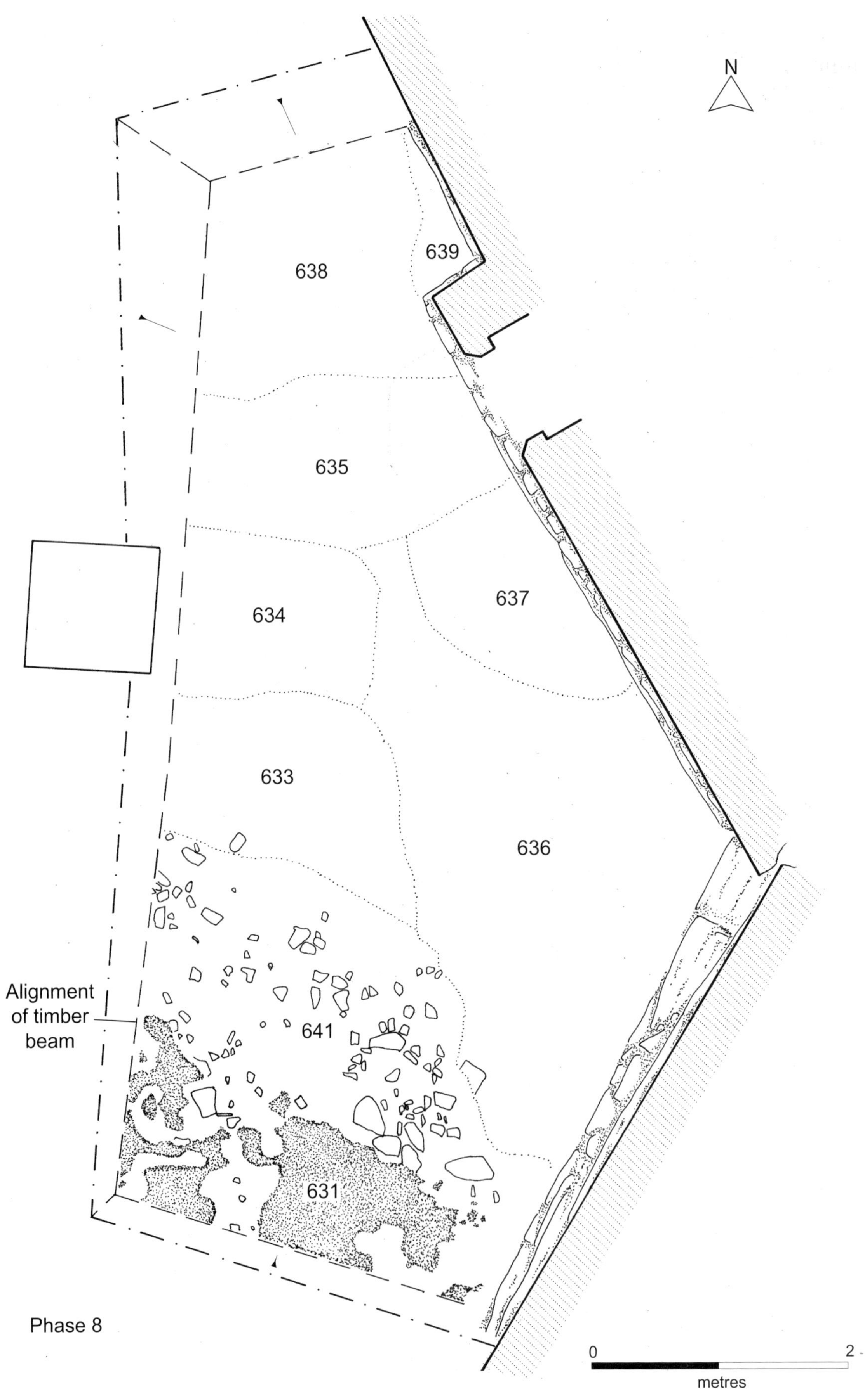

FIGURE 3.33
Plan of the 1998 trench showing Phase 8 features

FIGURE 3.34
Plaster floor 631 of CG98 20, Phase 8, showing distinct north edge, looking east (photograph: Marches Archaeology)

FIGURE 3.35
Ditches and pit of CG98 15–17, Phase 8, looking south (photograph: Marches Archaeology)

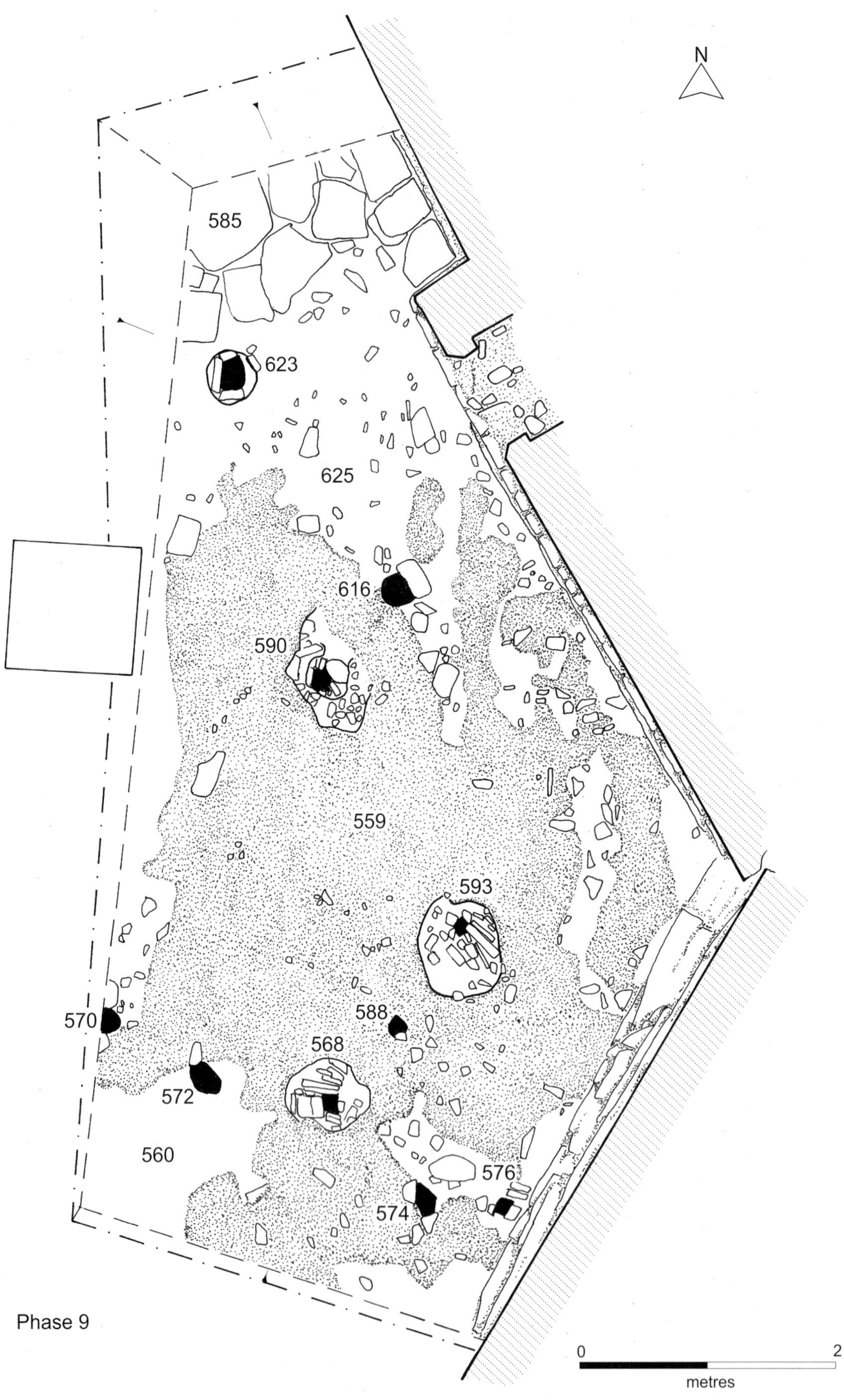

FIGURE 3.36
Plan of the 1998 trench showing Phase 9 features

of pinkish mortar and some decayed mudstone. The ditch cut 636, the upper fill of 664 of CG98 16 and underlay 647 of CG98 14, Phase 9, although this may in fact have been its upper fill.

Context Group 20: plaster floor surface 631 and make-up layers

Located to the south of the area, overlying 646 and 651 of CG98 21, Phase 5, and underlying 560 etc of CG98 12, Phase 9, was a level plaster floor above a series of deposits, mixes of loam, sand and mortar, presumably intended as make up for the plaster floor (Figures 3.33 and 3.34). The plaster floor consisted of a deposit of yellow/white to pink plaster with a minimum depth of 0.02m laid at a height of 171.40m OD. The floor extended beyond the southern and western trench sections and sloped up where it met Curtain Wall 507 to the east. Its northern edge, located some 1.50m from the southern trench boundary, was vertical and very regular, suggesting that it had been laid against a wooden beam running at right angles to the Curtain Wall – iron nails found along this alignment would suggest that a timber partition may have formed the edge and that the floor was laid internal to a wooden structure built against the Curtain Wall and extending to the west and south beyond the trench limits. The pottery produced by these deposits was similar to that from CG98 21 and dating places both groups between *c*1250 and 1400.

Phase 9: mid-15th to late 16th century

A pit, make-up layers and a plaster floor cut by later post alignments and a stone slab floor attest to significant activity taking place in the 16th century (Figures 3.35, 3.36, 3.37 and 3.38).

Context Group 19: pit 688 fills 654, 655 and 690

Cutting 661/657 of CG98 15 and underlying 647 of CG98 14 was a shallow, sub-circular pit which extended beyond the western and northern trench sections. The pit had an estimated diameter of 1.20m with a maximum depth of 0.40m and the fills contained a portion of an articulated horse skeleton. It is possible that the upper fill, mortar deposit 690, was intended as a seal to the backfilled pit.

FIGURE 3.37
Plaster floor 559 of CG98 08, Phase 9, with associated post-holes, looking north (photograph: Marches Archaeology)

Context Group 14: probable Phase 8 ditch fills

In the course of the excavation a series of deposits, mostly mudstone rubble in a gritty brown silt matrix, 634, 635, 638 and 647, were identified as levelling deposits below plaster floor 559 of CG08. Further analysis indicated that the deposits were more likely to have been fills of Phase 8 ditches: 658 of CG15 (658 and 647) and 664 of CG16 (635 and 634). The method of excavation created contamination within the finds assemblage from overlying deposits within CG12 and consequently the CG14 finds assemblage dated from the 14th to the 16th centuries, hence the appearance of this group within Phase 9.

Deposit 647 was notably different to the other contexts in that it contained a higher dark silt content and was rich in animal bone and other finds.

Context Group 12: make up for plaster floor 559

This group was confined to the south-west corner of the site and consisted of deposits of rubble within a clay/loam matrix, 539/560 and 562, overlying 625 which was a more extensive deposit, consisting of decayed mudstone in a yellow sand matrix. Context 579 was allocated to the interface between the upper surfaces of the group and the plaster floor above.

Context Group 08: plaster floor 559/608

A plaster floor was laid over the make-up deposits of CG98 12 and 14 at an average height of 171.10m OD (Figure 3.37). The surface was located in the southern part of the site and extended beyond the site boundaries to south and west whilst butting up against the masonry of the East Tower and the Southern Curtain Wall. The floor consisted of two or three skims of lightly bonded, off-white plaster with a maximum depth of 0.05m. It is possible that the plaster was laid as a base for a stone slab floor which was subsequently robbed. It is probable that the floor was intended to be internal to a building backing onto the Eastern Tower but the form and extent of the associated building has not been established. No obvious occupation deposits were noted overlying the floor whilst the post-holes of CG98 06 and 07 were cut through this floor and must have been later, internal divides. The entrance threshold leading into the East Tower was at a height of 171.68m OD, some 0.50m above the floor surface in that area, suggesting the need for a step to gain access.

Context Group 06: post alignment

Figure 3.38 tabulates the context numbers allocated to post-holes within CG98 06 and 07, Phase 9. Located within the southern part of the site, cutting mortar floor surface 559 of CG98 08 and underlying 542 of CG98 04, Phase 10, were five post-holes that formed an alignment running from north-west to south-east, perpendicular to the Southern Curtain Wall. The alignment probably continued beyond the western site boundary. Two of the post-pits were substantial, having stone packing designed to hold posts 0.20m square and with a maximum depth of 0.45m. The other three were less substantial. It seems probable that the post settings were designed to support an internal wooden partition running westwards from the Southern Curtain Wall and internal to whatever building encompassed the associated plaster floor of CG98 08.

Group 06					
Fill	571	573	569	575	577
Stone packing	619	|	606	|	605
Cut	570	572	568	574	576
Group 07					
Fill	589	594	591/2	615	624
Stone packing	|	607	613	617	627
Cut	588	593	590	616	623

FIGURE 3.38
Table showing context numbers allocated to post-holes within CG98 06 and 07, Phase 9

Context Group 07: post alignments

A further two post-holes, 588 and 593, ran to the north-east from post-hole 568 of CG98 06 whilst another two, 590 and 623, ran northwards from 593 to create an aisle some 2.00m wide along the back of the East Tower. A last post-hole, 616, was located 0.80m to the north-east of 590.

Context Group 05: stone slab floor 585 and associated deposits

A stone-slabbed floor surface at a height of 171.28m OD was located to the north of the site, inserted into the angle between the Northern Curtain Wall and the East Tower and extending beyond the site boundary to west and north (Figure 3.39). The slabs were irregular in size (the largest 0.72m by 0.66m by 0.05m) and formed a surface sloping slightly down to the west. The deposits underlying the floor (609, 620, 626, 639, 662 and 686) may have been deliberately laid as make up and consisted of sandy silt, rubble and gravel layers to a depth of 0.60m. Deposit 686 overlay 590 of CG98 19 but was also recorded as overlying plaster floor 559 of CG98 08 and this would suggest that the slab floor was later than the plaster floor.

Phase 10: 16th to mid-17th century

Despite documented activity on the castle site the deposits and associated finds assemblages appear to indicate limited activity and partial decay (Figure 3.40).

Context Group 13: early decay, probably the same as CG98 04

Located to the north of the site were a series of mortar and rubble deposits, 563, 580–583 and 602, overlying slab floor 585 of CG98 05, Phase 9. The group was generally 0.30m deep with its level upper surface at 171.50m OD. The base deposit 603 lay on top of the slab floor and banked up against the Northern Curtain Wall. It contained significant quantities of mortar and may have been indicative of the building's decay.

Context Group 04: early decay (537, 538, 540, 541, 542, 544, 545, 547, 549, 555, 557, 558, 561, 565 and 566), probably the same as CG98 13

Overlying plaster floor 559 of CG98 08, Phase 9, and the post-hole sequence associated with that floor and lying below surface 523 of CG98 02, Phase 11, was another sequence of deposits which consisted of mortar, loam and rubble mixtures and which generally contained pottery dating from the 16th century. It seems probable that these deposits related to a period of neglect when structures within the immediate vicinity were decaying and/ or were deliberately being demolished. Within these dumps was deposit 544, a mound of rubble in a mortar matrix located adjacent to the entrance into the East Tower. This may represent the remains of a stepped arrangement to gain access into the tower. The finds from this context group bear similarities to those from CG98 11, Phase 10, from within the East Tower.

Phase 11: mid-17th to late 20th century
(Figure 3.40)

After partial slighting in 1643 the castle was allowed to decay through weathering and partial robbing until the current period of restoration.

Context Group 02: demolition and decay (502, 504, 506, 505/508/515, 514, 516, 517, 519, 522, 523, 525, 526, 551, 552 and 564)

Overlying CG98 04 and below 501 of CG98 01 was a group of deposits built up against the masonry to the east. The base layer of this group, 523, was 0.05m deep and consisted of a level surface of medium grey/ brown loam with small mortar fragment inclusions at an average height of 171.70m OD, identified as a turf line. The finds assemblage from this context included a decorative horse-bit datable to the 17th

FIGURE 3.39
Stone slab floor 585 of CG98 05, Phase 9, looking south (photograph: Marches Archaeology)

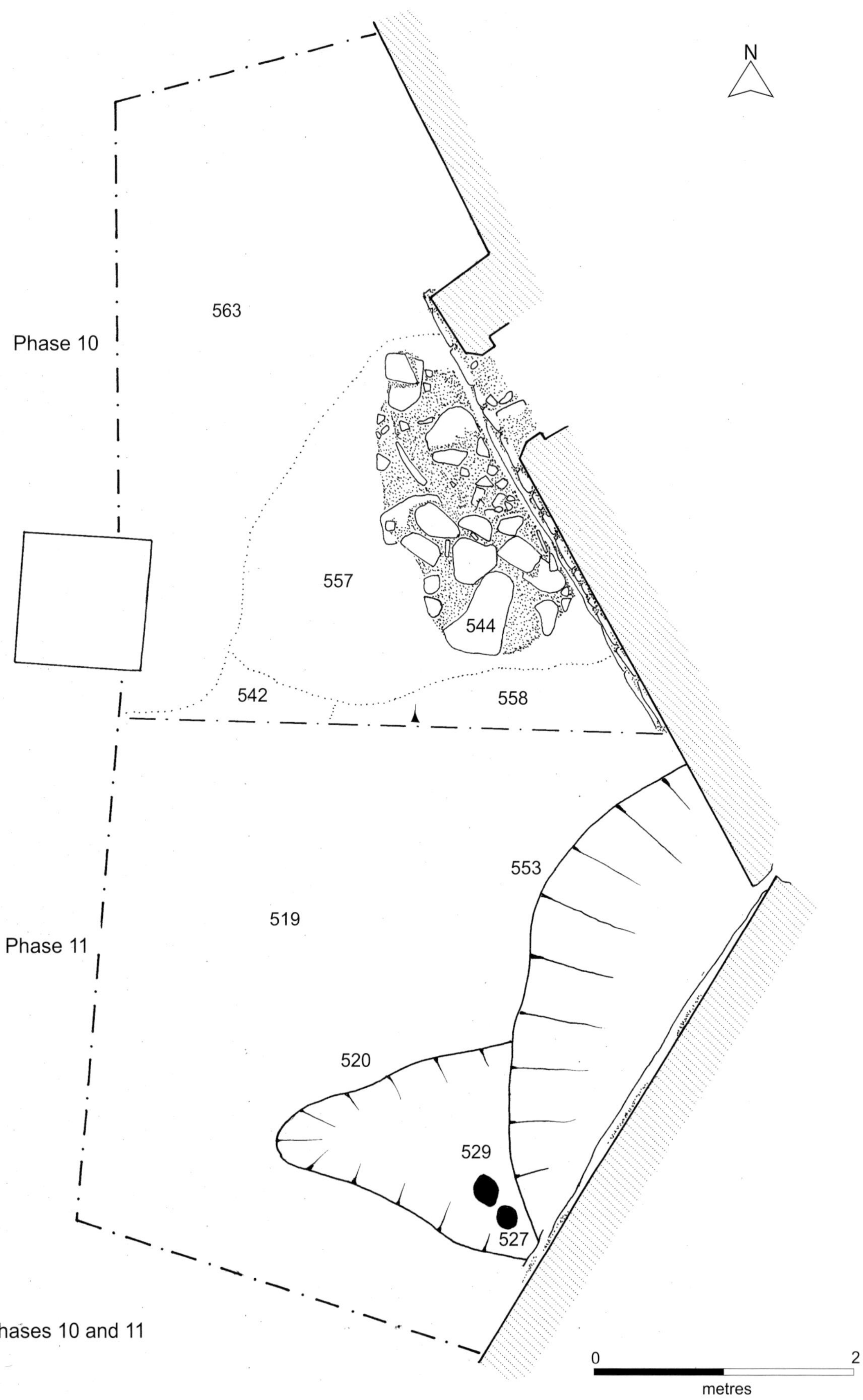

FIGURE 3.40
Plan of the 1998 trench showing Phase 10 and 11 features

century (Chapter 5, no. 14). The overlying layers all contained varying quantities of rubble and mortar with some loam admix. The finds assemblage from within these deposits spanned the period from the 17th century to the present day, although some deposits within the group contained finds of only the 15th/16th century and these deposits may have been transported from elsewhere within the castle site.

Context Group 03: pit 520, fill 518/524, post-holes 527 and 529, fills 528 and 530

Lying within the deposits of CG98 02, Phase 11, below 517, cutting 519 and located to the west of the Southern Curtain Wall, was a shallow pit with dimensions of 1.40m from west to east by 1.10m with a maximum depth of 0.15m. The fill consisted of loose, dark grey, silty clay with pebble inclusions. At the base of the pit were two circular post-holes with diameters of 0.15m and 0.25m and a maximum depth of 0.09m. It is possible that the post-holes predated pit 520 and were originally deeper but had been truncated by the pit. It has been suggested that they may have been intended to take timber props to support the collapsing curtain wall.

Context Group 01: turf and topsoil 501

A deposit of medium brown clay loam covered the whole of the excavation area including the East Tower interior and surrounding masonry to a depth of some 0.15m at an average height of 172.80m OD; it overlay 502 of CG98 22, Phase 10, and 509 of CG98 10, Phase 11. A pit, 553 fill 554, had recently been excavated into the angle between the East Tower, 503, and Southern Curtain Wall, 507, and was still partially open at the commencement of the excavation. A large cubic concrete block with dimensions of 0.85m was embedded into 501 at the western edge of the site but its purpose remains unknown.

Wall 507 then turned to run northwards, extending beyond the site boundary to the north-west. The ditch was around 2.40m wide by 1.50m deep with a splayed, U-shaped profile, and its fills contained considerable quantities of demolition debris.

4

THE POTTERY

Stephanie Rátkai

4.1 INTRODUCTION AND METHODOLOGY

The ceramic datasets

Two areas were excavated in three campaigns: one in 1996 (coded Wig 96A) and two in 1998 (coded Wig 98A and Wig 98B). The former area lay adjacent to the Southern Curtain Wall and the latter within and around the East Tower. The excavated remains and the pottery sequence are very different in the two areas. Wigmore 1996 contained a good stratigraphic sequence from the construction of the castle through to the Civil War destruction and the castle's subsequent abandonment. There is some residuality but in general there is good reason to have confidence in the ceramic sequence. The one drawback with this area is the very deep stratigraphy that necessitated careful shoring and the inevitable gradual reduction in the excavated area at deeper levels. The possibility in lower levels of intrusive features being undetected must be entertained.

In contrast, Wigmore 1998 contained primarily pottery from destruction and demolition dumps, mostly dating from late in the life of the castle. The very nature of this material favours residuality and contamination.

The report is divided into three main sections. The first section gives a general overview of the pottery, the significant fabrics, functional diversity, possible sources for the pottery and chronological trends. The second section details the pottery information in relation to the stratigraphy and taphonomy for the 1996 excavation and the 1998 excavations. The final section compares the results of the two excavations and sets the ceramics within the wider context of pottery assemblages of the Welsh Marches and castles within the West Midlands.

The pottery illustrations are arranged by phase and context group.

Type series methodology

The medieval fabrics have been mainly catalogued using a hierarchical alpha-numeric system. The initial letter/s usually indicate the most noticeable inclusions on initial examination of the sherd (Figure 4.1). These groups are subdivided numerically by inclusion size and/or density. Thus Fabric MS01 indicates that the most obvious inclusions are mica and siltstone. Further subdivision is possible so that Fabric Q01.1, for example, represents a fabric which is a possible variant of Fabric Q01. Some fabrics have been categorised on the basis of the general type of ware, for example, RW redwares, WW whitewares. Well-known medieval and post-medieval types have been referred to by their common name in the text but given an abbreviated name code (HAMGR for Ham Green ware, TG for Tudor Green, SLPW for slipware, MOT for mottled ware) in the catalogues and tables.

No fabric coding system is perfect. The advantages of this system are that broadly similar groups of fabrics are found together, it is easier to judge which fabrics are likely to have come from a similar clay source, the type series is simpler for other researchers to consult for comparanda, and the results of any further pottery research can be integrated comparatively easily within the hierarchy.

Please note: in order to simplify the text the term 'cooking pot' is used to refer to unglazed medieval jars in the early phases, even if there is no hard evidence, such as sooting or limescale, to indicate they were used for cooking. This is because most of the sherds recorded as 'cpj' (cooking pot/jar) in the databases were sooted or had limescale and it seems unnecessarily perverse to assume that the remaining sherds were not cooking pots also. Issues of vessel function are discussed more fully in the phase discussions.

4.2 OVERVIEW OF THE POTTERY

Fabrics, function and chronology

Detailed fabric descriptions of the medieval pottery can be found in Section 4.5 at the end of this chapter. However, a brief introduction to the more common or chronologically significant medieval and post-medieval pottery is necessary here. Information on the earlier fabrics in use at the castle is derived primarily from the 1996 excavation, whereas information on the later fabrics is an amalgamation of data from the 1996 and 1998 excavations. Figures 4.2 and 4.3 present the pottery data by phase.

The earliest fabrics consist of sandy wares Fabrics Q01 and Q03 which are associated with the construction of the castle and its first use (Figure 4.4, 01–02). Fabric Q01 is broadly similar to Worcester-

Prefix	Description
Q	Predominantly or wholly quartz tempered
MS	Markedly micaceous with silstone temper
S	Predominantly or wholly silstone tempered
RW	Fine orange or red wheel-thrown wares, with little temper, often finely micaceous
R	Contains granitic Malvernian rock fabrics (Fabrics R01–03)
R	Contains schist-like rock fragments (Fabric R10)
WW	Whiteware
MWW	Micaceous whiteware

Code	Name/Description	Suggested date	Source
BESSIN	Normandy stoneware	16th–17thC	Normandy
BLW	Blackware	*c*1550–1650	West Midlands
CIST	Cistercian ware	*c*1475–1550	West Midlands
COLOGNE	Rhenish stoneware	16th–17thC	Cologne
Ham Gr	Ham Green ware	12th–13thC	Bristol
MARTINCAMP	Martincamp	16th–17thC	Normandy
MGW	Modern glazed ware	19th–20thC	Staffordshire
MOT	Post-medieval mottled ware	late 17th–mid 18thC	Staffordshire?
MP	Midlands Purple	15th–16thC	Local?
MS01	Micaceous siltsone tempered ware	13th–14th (15th?)C	Local
MS02	Micaceous siltsone tempered ware	mid 13th–14thC	Local
MS03	Micaceous siltsone tempered ware	late 13th–15thC	Local
MS10	Micaceous siltsone tempered ware	13thC?	Local
MS11	Micaceous siltsone tempered ware	13th–14thC?	Local
MS12	Micaceous siltsone tempered ware	13th–15thC?	Local
MWW	Micaceous whiteware	?	Local?
NfrWW	North French whiteware	late 12th–13thC	Northern France
OOL	Oolitic limestone tempered ware	early 13thC	Gloucestershire
PMIP	Post-medieval iron-poor ware	17th–18thc ?	Local?
Q01	Worcester-type sandy cooking pot ware	late 11th–13thC	Worcestershire or more local imitation
Q01.1	Worcester-type sandy cooking pot ware	late 11th–13thC	Worcestershire or more local imitation
Q02	Worcester-type glazed ware	*c*1150–1250	Worcestershire
Q03	Sandy cooking pot	late 11th–12thC	Local?
Q10	Sandy cooking pot	12thC?	Local?
Q11	Fine, reduced glazed ware	mid 13th–15thC	Herefordshire?
Q20	Quartz and sandstone tempered	12thC	Local?
Q30	Fine glazed ware	15th–16thC	
Q31	Fine reduced ware	13th–14thC	Herefordshire
Q32	Fine reduced ware	mid 13th–15thC	Herefordshire
Q40	Sandy glazed ware	15th–16thC	Shropshire/West Midlands
Q60	Sandy glazed ware	13th–14thC	
Q70	Sandy glazed ware	13th–14thC	
QM01	Fine sandy micaceous ware	13thC?	Herefordshire
R01	Malvernian cooking pot	12th–early 14thC	Malvern Chase area
R02	Malvernian pitcher	late 12th–early 13thC	Malvern Chase area
R03	Malvern Chase ware	*c*1350/75–1600	Malvern Chase area
R10	Schist-tempered ware	14thC?	Anglesey, possibly Ireland
RAEREN	Rhenish Stoneware	16thC	Raeren
RW10	Micaceous redware	*c*1250–1500	Herefordshire
RW11	Fine redware	15th–16thC	Local
RW12	Fine redware	later 16th–17thC	Local
RW12.1	Reduced variant of RW12	17thC?	Local
RW12.2	Fine redware, underglaze white slip	17thC?	Local
RW13	Highly micaceous fine redware	15th–16thC	Local
S01	Siltstone-tempered ware	13th–14thC	Local?
S10	Siltstone-tempered ware	13th–14thC	Local?
S11	Siltstone-tempered ware	13thC?	Local?
S20	Coarse siltstone tempered ware	13thC	Local?
SLPW	Slip-decorated ware	mid 17th–early 18thC	Staffordshire or Salop
TG/TGT	Tudor Green/Tudor Green-type	15th–16thC	Surrey/Hampshire
TGE	Tin-glazed earthenware	17thC	Anglo-Dutch
VITR	Vitrified sherd	post-medieval	
WW01	Fine sandy whiteware	14th–15thC	Surrey/Hampshire?
WW02	Glazed buff ware		
WW10	Sandy glazed whiteware	13th–14thC	West Midlands
YW	Yellow ware	late 16th–17thC	West Midlands

FIGURE 4.1

Designations of the main pottery fabric classes and date and sources of the pottery fabrics

Phase	1	2	3	4	5	6	7	8	9	10	11	Total
Fabric												
Q01	88.3%	50.8%	35.9%	7.6%	0.7%				0.6%			8.7%
Q03	11.7%	0.4%		3.2%	0.6%							0.5%
Q10		1.7%	3.0%									0.3%
Q20		45.9%	10.8%	6.0%								5.5%
R01		1.2%	2.1%	5.8%	0.6%			2.1%	0.4%			1.0%
MS01			16.8%	34.3%	7.0%	10.9%	39.7%	9.3%	11.3%	1.4%		9.2%
MS12			1.0%	0.5%	9.9%	12.9%	20.1%	4.6%	12.1%	0.2%		4.2%
OOL			3.2%									0.2%
S01			4.4%		1.0%	5.9%	2.0%	16.3%	3.1%	0.6%		1.6%
S10			7.5%	23.5%	4.7%	2.0%	2.3%	1.9%	1.2%			3.8%
S20			15.4%	6.3%		2.6%						1.6%
MS10				1.2%								0.1%
Q01.1				0.7%	0.1%	0.9%						0.1%
Q02				5.5%	0.1%		0.6%					0.6%
Q31				1.3%	7.4%							1.1%
R03				0.1%								0.0%
RW10				2.0%		16.2%	3.8%	6.2%	2.2%			1.2%
S11				1.9%	41.0%	39.8%	2.8%		0.3%			6.7%
MS02					26.0%	2.2%	5.9%	1.4%	1.2%			3.9%
Q32					0.6%	0.9%		1.1%	0.8%			0.2%
QM01					0.4%							0.0%
MS03						3.3%	22.9%	15.2%	2.3%			1.8%
MS11						2.4%						0.1%
RW13								4.4%	13.0%			1.8%
Q11								1.3%				0.0%
R02								36.2%	30.4%	16.5%	10.2%	9.8%
CISTBLW									0.3%	2.1%	0.5%	0.5%
MWW									0.9%			0.1%
Q30									8.8%		0.6%	1.2%
Q40									7.3%	4.3%	0.0%	1.6%
R01/R02									0.2%			0.0%
RW12									2.4%	59.4%	67.4%	24.9%
WW01									0.1%			0.0%
WW02									0.7%			0.1%
WW10									0.4%			0.0%
BLW										10.9%	13.4%	4.7%
CIST										0.1%		0.0%
FRECHEN										0.7%		0.1%
MOT										0.1%	0.1%	0.0%
BESSIN										0.1%	0.9%	0.2%
RW12.1										2.5%	0.6%	0.5%
RW12.2										0.4%	0.5%	0.2%
SLPW										0.2%	1.1%	0.3%
YW										0.7%	1.6%	0.5%
COLOGNE											1.0%	0.2%
MARTINC											0.6%	0.1%
PMIP											0.1%	0.0%
RAEREN?											0.1%	0.0%
TGE											0.1%	0.0%
MGW											1.5%	0.3%

FIGURE 4.2

Wigmore 1996: quantification (by percentage weight) of pottery by phase

Phase	3	4	5	8	9	10	11	1998B*	Total
Fabric									
MS11	100.0%								0.0%
MS01		25.9%	20.5%	18.2%	12.5%	7.5%	0.4%	39.2%	14.5%
MS01?			9.1%						1.6%
MS02		1.1%		2.7%	1.5%	2.3%			1.4%
MS03			11.6%	9.8%	16.2%	3.5%		13.4%	7.0%
MS12		4.8%	7.9%	6.9%				9.2%	3.5%
MS12?			2.2%			0.4%			0.5%
Q01		15.9%	1.4%		4.2%	3.2%		9.7%	3.0%
Q20		13.2%	0.5%			0.2%		0.7%	0.7%
RW10		6.9%	14.3%	21.6%	46.0%	8.6%		3.8%	12.4%
S11		32.3%						7.1%	1.8%
Q31			0.8%						0.1%
Q60			5.2%	4.5%		0.6%			1.9%
Q70			0.1%			0.1%			0.0%
R01			5.4%		4.9%	1.1%		1.2%	1.7%
R02			5.2%	15.9%	8.3%	37.8%	13.0%	1.9%	19.5%
R10			10.9%	5.6%	2.3%			2.4%	3.2%
S01			0.8%	1.5%	1.5%	1.1%		2.1%	1.1%
S10			3.4%	1.1%		1.5%	0.9%		1.4%
S20			0.7%						0.1%
RW13				4.3%		3.9%			2.2%
Q40				0.3%		0.1%			0.1%
RW11				2.3%		0.5%			0.6%
TG				4.9%				8.5%	1.6%
NfiWW				0.5%		0.9%			0.4%
CIST					2.6%	11.4%	30.6%		7.7%
COLOGNE						3.4%	9.7%		2.3%
MP						0.3%			0.1%
Q11						0.8%			0.3%
Q32						0.2%			0.1%
RW12						10.3%	15.0%		5.4%
WW02?						0.3%			0.1%
BLW							11.5%		1.3%
VITR							2.2%		0.2%
MOT							12.1%		1.3%
MGW							4.7%		0.5%
HAMGR								0.9%	0.1%

FIGURE 4.3

Wigmore 1998: quantification (by percentage weight) of pottery by phase (pottery from 1998B unphased)*

FIGURE 4.4

Medieval pottery, 01–28, Phases 1–5, 1996 excavations

***01**: Fabric Q01, Phase 1, CG96 29, 362. **02**: Fabric Q01, Phase 1, CG96 29, 374. **03**: Fabric Q01, Phase 2, CG96 27, 338. **04**: Fabric Q01, Phase 2, CG96 27 359. **05**: Fabric Q01, Phase 2, CG96 27, 361. **06**: Fabric Q01, Phase 2, CG96 27, 361. **07**: Fabric Q01, Phase 2, CG96 27, 390. **08**: Fabric Q20, Phase 2, CG96 27 338. **09**: Fabric Q20, Phase 2, CG96 27, 390. **10**: Fabric OOL, Phase 3, CG96 25, 287. **11**: Fabric Q01, Phase 3, CG96 25, 275. **12**: Fabric Q20, Phase 3, CG96 25, 275. **13**: Fabric Q01, Phase 3, CG96 24, 270. **14**: Fabric Q01, Phase 3, CG96 23, 257. **15**: Fabric S20, Phase 3, CG96 23, 260. **16**: Fabric MS01 Phase 3, CG96 23, 249. **17**: Fabric MS12, Phase 3, CG96 23, 249. **18**: Fabric S01, Phase 3, CG96 23, 249. **19**: Fabric MS01, Phase 4, CG96 22, 239. **20**: Fabric Q20, Phase 4, CG96 22, 229. **21**: Fabric S10, Phase 4, CG96 22, 243. **22**: Fabric MS01, Phase 4, CG96 20, 220. **23**: Fabric MS01, Phase 4, CG96 19, 177. **24**: Fabric MS01, Phase 4, CG96 19, 177. **25**: Fabric R01, Phase 4, CG96 19, 177. **26**: Fabric MS01, Phase 4, CG96 18 207. **27**: Fabric MS01, Phase 4, CG96 18, 198. **28**: Fabric MS01, Phase 5, CG96 17, 196*

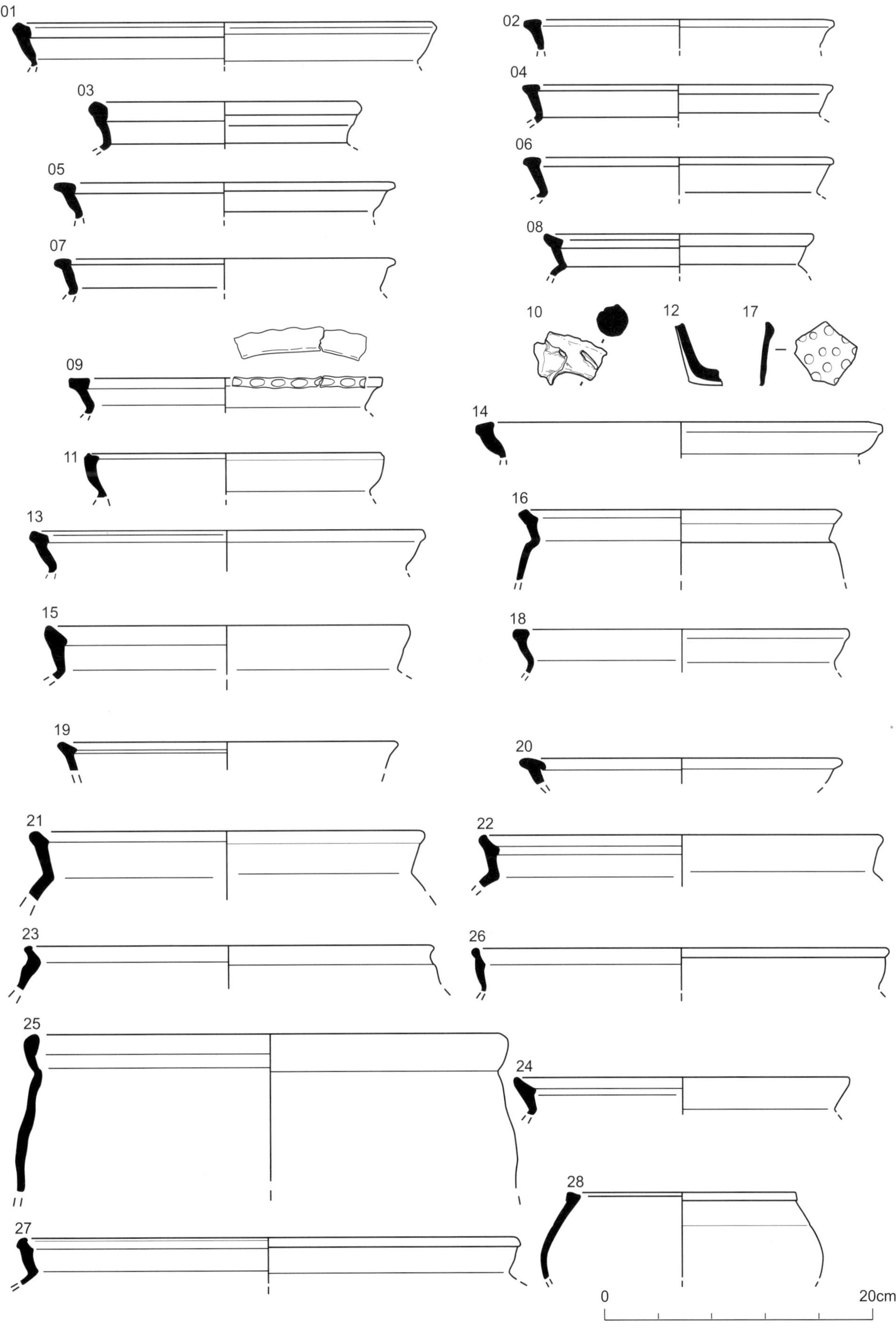
01
02
03
04
05
06
07
08
09
10
12
17
14
11
13
16
15
18
19
20
21
22
23
26
25
24
27
28
0
20cm

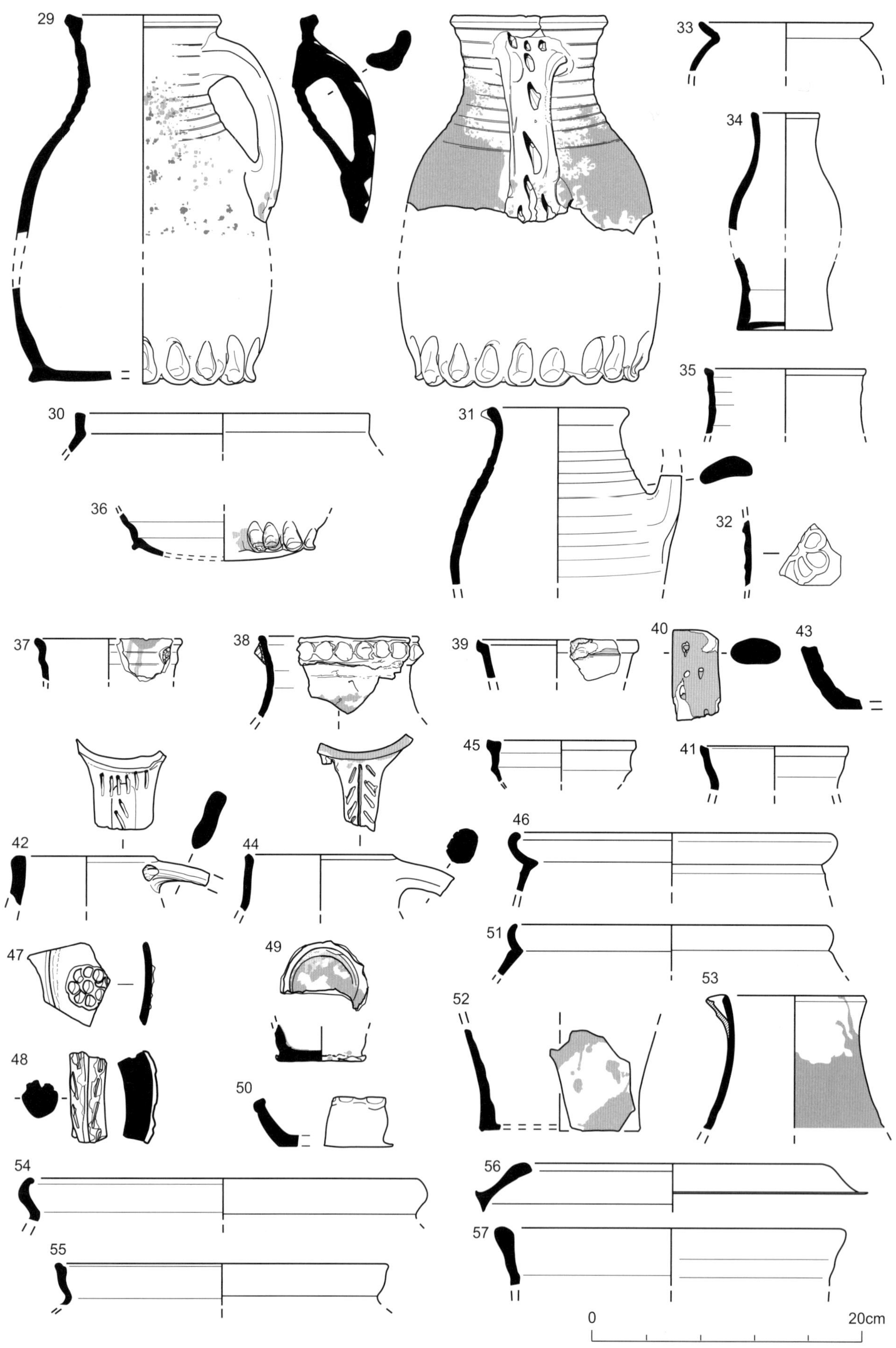
29
30
31
32
33
34
35
36
37
38
39
40
41
42
43
44
45
46
47
48
49
50
51
52
53
54
55
56
57
0
20cm

FIGURE 4.5

Medieval pottery, 29–57, Phases 5–9, 1996 and 1998 excavations

***29**: Fabric MS02, Phase 5, CG96 17, 178. **30**: Fabric S01, Phase 5, CG96 17, 203. **31**: Fabric S11, Phase 5, CG96 17, 178. **32**: Fabric MS12, Phase 5, CG98 33, 673. **33**: Fabric MS12, Phase 5, CG98 33, 673. **34**: Fabric R10, Phase 5, CG98 33, 689, CG98 21, 646; Phase 8, CG98 20, 641 etc. **35**: Fabric MS01, Phase 5, CG98 21, 646. **36**: Fabric MS03, Phase 5, CG98 21, 646. **37**: Fabric RW12, Phase 5, CG98 21, 652. **38**: Fabric MS12, Phase 6, CG96 16, 168. **39**: Fabric S01, Phase 6, CG96 13, 109. **40**: Fabric MS01, Phase 7, CG96 11, 158. **41**: Fabric MS03, Phase 7, CG96 11, 101. **42**: Fabric MS12, Phase 7, CG96 11, 158. **43**: Fabric S10, Phase 7, CG96 11, 187. **44**: Fabric MS03, Phase 8, CG96 09, 076. **45**: Fabric RW13, Phase 8, CG96 08, 061. **46**: Fabric MS01, Phase 8, CG98 15, 667; CG98 20, 632. **47**: Fabric Q60, Phase 8, CG98 17, 674. **48**: Fabric MS12, Phase 8, CG98 16, 669. **49**: Fabric TG, Phase 8, CG98 16, 668. **50**: Fabric MS01, Phase 8, CG98 15, 667. **51**: Fabric S10, Phase 8, CG98 15, 667. **52**: Fabric MS12, Phase 9, CG96 07, 053. **53**: Fabric RW13, Phase 9, CG96 07, 053; CG96 06, 050. **54**: Fabric S10, Phase 9, CG96 06, 051. **55**: Fabric MS01, Phase 9, CG9 06, 050. **56**: Fabric MS01, Phase 9, CG96 06, 050. **57**: Fabric MS12, Phase 9, CG9 06, 44; CG03, 035*

type unglazed ware, as are the vessel forms. These types of cooking pots or jars are known from the late 11th century in Worcester itself and also from the earliest occupation of Hen Domen (Clarke 1982, fabric 3; Vince 1982) in the Welsh Marches, Dudley Castle, West Midlands (personal inspection by the author) and Stafford Castle, Staffordshire (Fabric D12, E05, E21; Rátkai 2007). At present no kiln site has been discovered but the ubiquity of this type of sandy cooking pot in the West Midlands from the late 11th to the 13th centuries — in effect it is a regional type — suggests more than one place of manufacture. A second sandy cooking pot (Fabric Q03) was also found in the early levels of the castle (Phase 1b). This fabric is mainly sandy but also contains very rare inclusions of sandstone, siltstone and what appears to be granitic rock. Despite the presence of granitic rock, the fabric is unlike 'typical' Malvernian unglazed cooking pot ware (Fabric R01) being sandier, lacking mica and without lumps of granitic rock protruding through the surface of the sherds. All the inclusions are rounded, suggesting the clay was derived from a riverine environment.

After the initial construction of the castle, a third type of cooking pot fabric was in existence: Fabric Q20. This is a coarse gritty ware containing quartz/quartzite and lumps of coarse sandstone with poorly cemented grains. Two rim sherds (from one vessel found in 359 and 390; Figure 4.4, 09) were thumbed or finger-pinched, a trait that was not apparent on any of the other early rim sherds. Two examples of glazed vessels in Fabric Q20, probably splash-glazed pitchers, were found in both the 1996 and 1998 excavations. A broad band of square roller-stamping occurred on one Fabric Q20 pitcher sherd (Phase 4, 1998) and incised line decoration on another (Phase 4, 1996). It seems most likely that Fabric Q20 was predominantly a 12th-century fabric — although manufacture at the very end of the 11th century cannot be ruled out.

Unglazed Malvernian cooking pots, Fabric R01, appear slightly after fabric Q20 but are never very common; they reach the apogee of their distribution in the 13th century (Vince 1977; 1985a) and at this time are frequently found in Herefordshire, Worcestershire and even Shropshire, particularly on sites close to or on the River Severn, such as Shrewsbury. At Wigmore there is good reason to believe that some of the Malvernian ware dates to the 12th century partly because of the rim forms and partly because of the entirely black fabric. Malvernian pottery of the 13th and early 14th century is also recorded at the castle with the light brown or pale grey fabrics and in-turned rim characteristic of this period (e.g. Vince 1985a, fig 3, 4–6). Fabric R01 is surprisingly poorly represented, given the comparative frequency of the 14th- to 16th-century oxidised wheel-thrown Malvern Chase ware (Fabric R02) found in the later castle deposits.

How much of the pottery found in Phases 1 and 2 was made locally is open to question. It is quite possible that pottery was brought in from outside the immediate locale during the construction of the castle. This seems to be possible at sites such as Hen Domen and possibly Stafford Castle (Rátkai 2007), but not at Tutbury Castle, Staffordshire, where apparently locally produced cooking pots were found in the earliest layers (Rátkai 2011b). Also of interest is the complete absence of Stamford ware at Wigmore in its early years. In the West Midlands there seems to be no consistency in the presence of this ware. It is found in late 11th-century rampart make-up layers at Tutbury Castle and in early layers at Stafford Castle and Hen Domen but not at Dudley Castle, for example. However, Stafford, Hen Domen and Tutbury all had tenurial/seigneurial links with northern Lincolnshire which may be the primary factor influencing the presence of Stamford ware at these sites.

At Wigmore Castle, Fabric MS01 was the predominant medieval ware. The fabric contained abundant crushed siltstone and golden mica platelets. It first appears in Phase 3, when it may have replaced Fabrics Q01 and Q20, or there may have been some

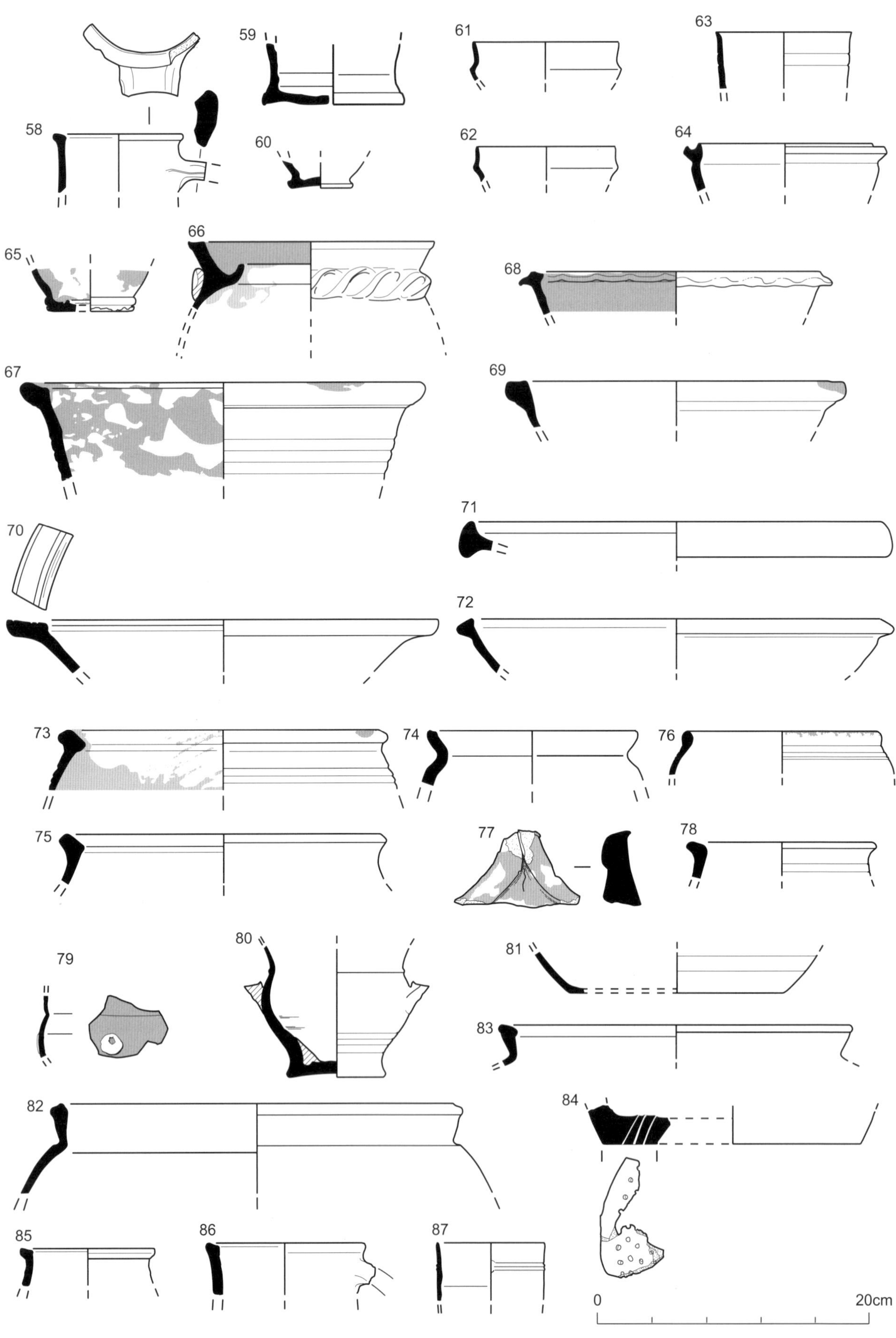
58
59
60
61
62
63
64
65
66
67
68
69
70
71
72
73
74
75
76
77
78
79
80
81
82
83
84
85
86
87
0
20cm

FIGURE 4.6

Medieval pottery, 58–87, Phases 9–11, 1996 and 1998 excavations

***58**: Fabric Q40, Phase 9, CG96 03, 025. **59**: Fabric R02, Phase 9, CG96 03, 025. **60**: Fabric CIST/BLW, Phase 10, CG96 02, 016. **61**: Fabric BLW, Phase 10, CG96 02, 019. **62**: Fabric BLW, Phase 10, CG96 02, 017. **63**: Fabric BLW, Phase 10, CG96 02, 017. **64**: Fabric BLW, Phase 10, CG96 02, 017. **65**: Fabric R02, Phase 10, CG96 02, 021. **66**: Fabric R02, Phase 10, CG96 02, 019. **67**: Fabric RW12, Phase 10, CG96 02, 018. **68**: Fabric RW12, Phase 10, CG96 02, 018; Phase 11, CG01, 007. **69**: Fabric RW12, Phase 10, CG96 02, 018. **70**: Fabric RW12, Phase 10, CG96 02, 017. **71**: Fabric RW12, Phase 10, CG96 02, 017. **72**: Fabric RW12, Phase 10, CG96 02, 012. **73**: Fabric RW12, Phase 10, CG96 02, 017. **74**: Fabric RW12, Phase 10, CG96 02, 017. **75**: Fabric RW12, Phase 10, CG96 02, 017. **76**: Fabric RW12, Phase 10, CG96 02, 011. **77**: Fabric RW12, Phase 10, CG96 02, 009. **78**: Fabric RW12.1, Phase 10, CG96 02, 015. **79**: Fabric CIST, Phase 10, CG98 13, 563. **80**: Fabric CIST, Phase 10, CG98 13, 563. **81**: Fabric MS03, Phase 10, CG98 11, 629. **82**: Fabric Q01, Phase 10, CG98 11, 648. **83**: Fabric Q01, Phase 10, CG98 11, 640. **84**: Fabric RW12, Phase 10, CG98 11, 550. **85**: Fabric RW13, Phase 10, CG98 11, 665. **86**: Fabric RW13, Phase 10, CG98 11, 648. **87**: Fabric BLW, Phase 11, CG96 01, 004*

overlap. In Phase 3 only cooking pot sherds were found but by Phase 4 jug sherds were also present. The jugs, although glazed, appear to have had very little decoration. There is evidence that some jugs were decorated with incised horizontal lines, horizontal combing and possibly stabbing but the vast majority of sherds were undecorated (Figure 4.5, 35). There was one example of a thumbed base, a slashed handle (Figure 4.7, 107) and a stabbed handle (Figure` 4.5, 40). Considering that fabric MS01 was one of the mainstays of the ceramics in use at the castle, it comprises a remarkably dull set of vessels, considering the eminence of the Mortimers and of the castle itself. However, Higham (2000) comments on the prosaic, utilitarian ceramics found at Hen Domen in this phase and it is elsewhere that we must seek indications of wealth and status in castle life.

Fabric MS01 is clearly of fairly local manufacture. It appears to be made from a clay formed from degraded micaceous siltstone and deposits of 'degraded mudstone' were identified at the castle by the excavators. The impetus for production of fabric MS01 may have come from the castle itself. The fabric has been identified at New Radnor, Powys (Water Street Farm WSNR07, Brookside Farm BNR 07A and B, personal inspection by author), Kinnerton near Presteigne, Powys (CHK08, personal inspection by author), Ludlow in Shropshire (Rátkai 2003; 2004; 2006a) and Leominster in Herefordshire (Rátkai 2005; forthcoming a).

A variety of cooking pot forms was found (Figure 4.4, 16, 19, 22–24, 26–28; Figure 4.5, 46, 55) and included imitations of late 13th- or early 14th-century Malvernian cooking pots (Figure 4.5, 46) but the forms of the earlier cooking pots most closely resemble those found in the sandy wares. Cooking pots most commonly had everted, expanded rims with an internal bevel (Figure 4.4, 22, 24). A double dished rim form and a short stubby rimmed form were noted (Figure 4.4, 27 and 23). More specialised cookware was represented by a dripping tray (Figure 4.5, 50) from the 1998 excavations. An unusual globular form, possibly a pipkin (Figure 4.4, 28) and a form with a sharply in-turned rim (Figure 4.5, 56) were both noted in the 1996 excavation.

Fabric MS01 appears to have been first in use in the early 13th century, although a late 12th century date is not an impossibility. It continued in use throughout the 14th century and may have continued into the early 15th century. It is possible that this fabric was replaced by Malvern Chase ware (Fabric R02); either production of fabric MS01 petered out in the later 14th century, opening up the market for the Malvernian potters or the fabric MS01 potters could not compete with the scale of production of the Malvernian industry. The former seems more likely.

In Phase 3, when fabric MS01 first came into use, three other siltstone-tempered wares occurred (Fabrics S01, S10 and S20). These, too, are likely to have been made locally based on the inclusions within the clay body. Fabric S20, the coarsest of the three, was used primarily for cooking pots, although one jug or pitcher sherd with an opaque, cratered yellowish glaze was identified in the 1996 excavations. Fabric S10, possibly a coarser, non-micaceous variant of fabric MS01 was first found as cooking pot sherds in Phase 3; glazed jugs do not appear until Phase 4. In Phase 7 a dripping tray and a bowl were recorded in the 1996 excavations. Fabric S01 cooking pots were found in Phase 3, but thereafter the fabric seems to have been used almost exclusively for jugs. As with fabric MS01 there is little evidence of decoration on the jugs in these siltstone-tempered fabrics. Combed and incised linear decoration is recorded occasionally. There were two slashed strap handles.

A further siltstone-tempered ware, Fabric S11, first appears around the time of the construction of the curtain wall in the 1996 excavations. It is a rather coarse fabric which ought to be relatively early both because of its crudeness and because of sherds from a large jug or pitcher (a form unlikely to occur after

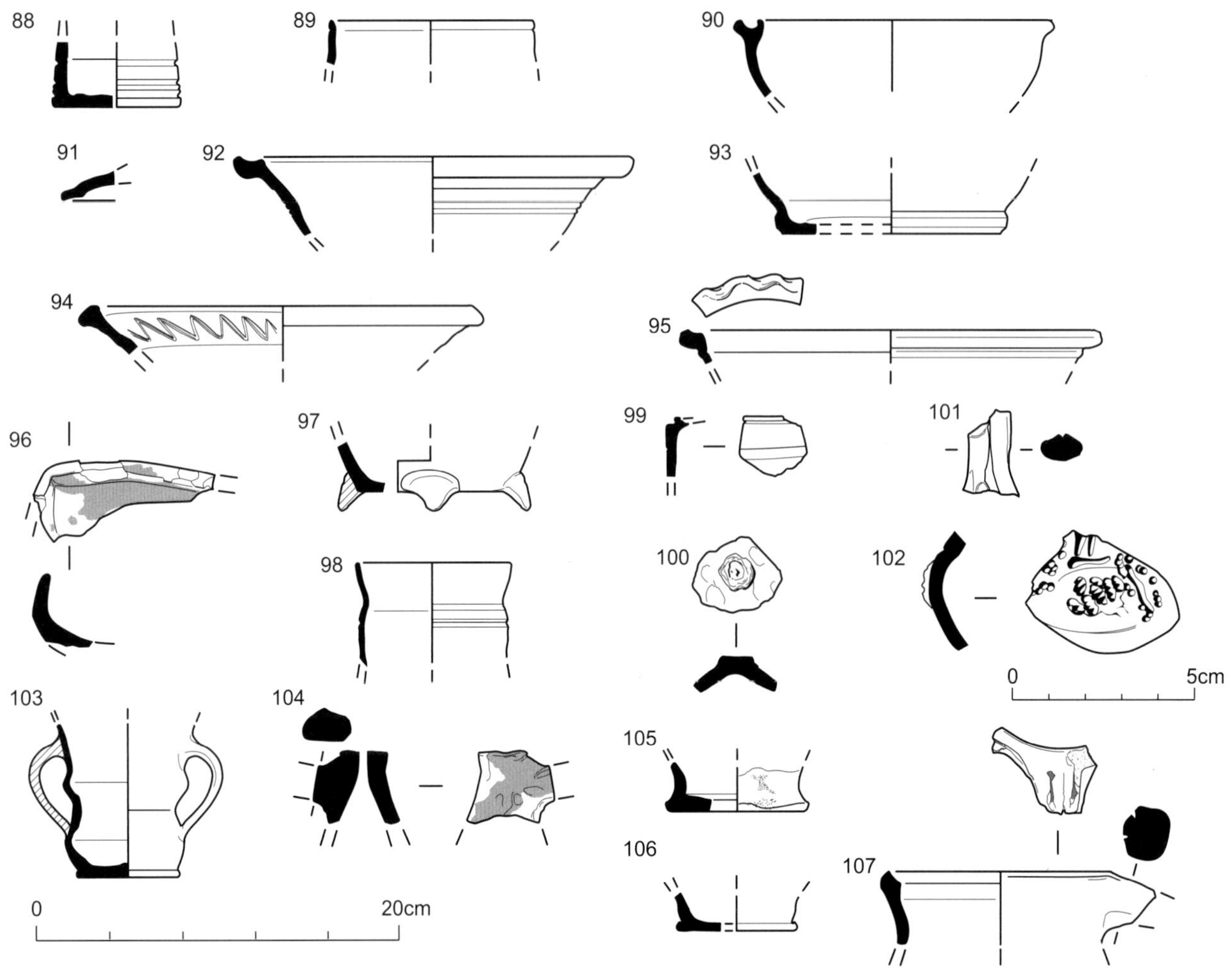

FIGURE 4.7

Medieval pottery, 88–107, Phase 11, 1996 and 1998 excavations and unphased 1998 excavation

***88**: Fabric BLW, Phase 11, CG96 01, 003. **89**: Fabric BLW, Phase 11, CG96 01, 003. **90**: Fabric BLW, Phase 11, CG96 01, 005. **91**: Fabric RW12, Phase 11, CG96 01, 007. **92**: Fabric RW12, Phase 11, CG96 01, 005. **93**: Fabric RW12, Phase 11, CG96 01, 005. **94**: Fabric RW12, Phase 11, CG96 01, 005. **95**: Fabric RW12, Phase 11, CG96 01, 003. **96**: Fabric RW12, Phase 11, CG96 01, 006. **97**: Fabric RW12, Phase 11, CG96 01, 005. **98**: Fabric RW12, Phase 11, CG96 01, 005. **99**: Fabric RW12, Phase 11, CG96 01, 005. **100**: Fabric RW12, Phase 11, CG96 01, 003. **101**: Fabric RW12, Phase 11, CG96 01, 003. **102**: Fabric RAEREN, Phase 11, CG96 01, 002. **103**: Fabric CIST, Phase 11, CG98 02, 519. **104**: Fabric RW12, Phase 11, CG98 02, 525. **105**: Fabric R02, Phase 11, CG98 02, 523. **106**: Fabric CIST, Phase 11, CG98 02, 525. **107**: Fabric MS01, 1998 B, unphased, 695*

*c*1225) which were found in Phase 4 in the 1998 excavations. One of these sherds was decorated with incised horizontal lines and was strongly reminiscent of pitchers from Hen Domen. However, the remainder of the S11 sherds from the 1996 and 1998 excavations were from jugs. The greater part of the jug sherds found in the 1996 excavation were apparently from the same jug (Figure 4.5, 31) (see below). Two plain strap handles were recorded and apart from the pitcher sherd, there were no other decorated sherds apart from three sherds from a finger-impressed base.

Micaceous siltstone-tempered ware MS11 is probably the same fabric as Hereford Fabric A4 (Vince 1985a). It is very infrequent at Wigmore and is found in the earliest recorded context group in 1998 and in levels post-dating the Phase 5 Curtain Wall in the 1996 excavations.

Examination of the 1998 pottery showed that over all there were very few decorated jugs and that jugs in the 'highly decorated' style (*c*1250–1350) were especially poorly represented. Applied 'rosettes' were found on a Fabric MS12 jug, with a glossy dark green glaze and under-glaze white slip. A second jug with an applied rosette and traces of applied curvilinear strip decoration was found in Fabric Q60. Notched applied strips were found on a Fabric MS03 jug and a Fabric RW10 jug. Bands of square roller-stamping were found on two Fabric Q11 jugs. At first sight it is tempting to see the absence of highly decorated wares as reflecting the chronology of the pottery, i.e. most of the pottery post-dates 1325/1350, but the 1996 pottery revealed a similar set of traits, with decoration mostly limited to incised or combed horizontal lines. Rectangular roller-stamping occurred on a Fabric MS03 jug and incised lines and comb teeth impressions were found on three Fabric MS10 sherds (all part of the same vessel). This type of decoration can be paralleled at Haughmond Abbey, to the north-east of Shrewsbury, Shropshire (Rátkai forthcoming b, fig P6, 88) on a jug from an undated clearance deposit. Fabric MS12 jug sherds had examples of roller-stamped decoration and an applied thumbed strip. A pitcher sherd was decorated with circular impressions (Figure 4.4, 17). Other sherds showed that some of the jugs had had finger-impressed bases and there was one sherd from a jug with an applied and thumbed cordon below the rim (Figure 4.5, 38). Further thumbed bases were present in Fabrics S11 and RW10. Slashed strap handles in Fabrics MS02, MS03, MS12 (Figure 4.5, 29, 42 and 44) and a stabbed strap handle in Fabric MS01 (Figure 4.5, 40) were recorded. Plain strap handles were found in Fabrics MS03, MS12, S10 and S11 and a rod handle in fabric S01. Amongst the 1998 pottery, plain strap handles were found in Fabrics MS12 and RW10, and undecorated rod handles in MS01 and MS02, the latter from a small jug. A rod handle with a deep central groove and oblique slashing to either side (Figure 4.5, 48) was found in Fabric MS12. This is a common handle type in central and northern Shropshire (compare Barker 1970, fig. 10 HD113; fig 22 M1; fig. 31 SD16). A slashed strap handle was noted in Fabric MS01. As can be seen from the foregoing there was no correlation between handle type and fabric.

A third important group of fabrics are the fine-bodied, often finely micaceous redwares. Fabric RW10 is similar to Hereford Fabric A7b (Vince 1985a). Knight (1991a, 7) records fine-bodied redwares from Montgomery Castle, there named Herefordshire-type Micaceous ware, but notes that there must have been several production centres utilising the micaceous Devonian Old Red Sandstone clays of Herefordshire, apart from the known production site at Weobley. At Hereford, Fabric A7b first appears around the middle of the 13th century and around 1250–1270 at Montgomery. Knight (1991a, 7) also notes good parallels between micaceous redware from Montgomery and Ludlow. It is likely, then, that the Wigmore Fabric RW10 sherds fall into this sub-group. Fabric RW10 is better represented in the 1998 excavations, particularly in the pre-plaster floor groups (see below).

Fabric RW10 sherds were almost exclusively from jugs, usually with a good quality glossy olive glaze with dark green mottles. A bowl was recorded in the 1996 excavations. The bases from small jugs, possibly used as drinking jugs, were recorded in the 1996 and 1998 excavations. In the former, the base was burnt internally (CG96 03, Phase 9). A small very thin-walled sherd (1998, Phase 9) may have come from a cup. A possible jar and a jug or cistern were also recorded (1998, Phase 10). Unfortunately the fabric RW10 sherds were small and not suitable for illustration. Decorative elements were minimal (see above). One of the Cistercian ware cups from the 1998 excavation appeared to be in Fabric RW10.

Fabric RW13 was similar to Fabric RW10 but very much more micaceous. A similar highly micaceous fabric was recorded at Leominster (Rátkai 2001) which appeared to date from the mid-13th to 15th centuries. However Fabric RW13 seems to date from the later 14th or 15th century at Wigmore. Most of the sherds were from jugs (Figure 4.5, 45 and 53; Figure 4.6, 85–86). A jug found in several contexts in 1996 Phase 9 (Figure 4.5, 53) was characterised by a particularly thick, 'lumpy' olive glaze with dark green mottles. Bowl sherds were found in both the 1996 and 1998 excavations (Phases 8 and 9), a possible bottle (1996, Phase 9) and a jar (1998, Phase 8).

Fabrics Q31, Q32 and QM01 are fine sandy variants of the redwares and were not common. One sherd of Fabric QM01 was found in the 1996 excavation. Fabric Q31 was used primarily for cooking pots and Fabric Q32 for jugs.

Fine sandy, micaceous wares, almost certainly from the Marches, have been found in moat deposits post-dating *c*1300 at Weoley Castle, Birmingham (Rátkai 2011a, Appendix 5, WC Fabrics 10–12). In the 14th century, John de Botetourt, Lord of Weoley Castle, married Joyce de la Zouche Mortimer, a descendant of the Mortimers of Richards Castle, Herefordshire. Joyce herself appears to have been born in Herefordshire. As the fabrics have not been found during excavation in the centre of Birmingham in the Bull Ring (Rátkai 2009), it seems reasonable to assume that the Weoley examples arrived there as items of household baggage.

Fabric RW12 (and its variants Fabric RW12.1 and RW12.2) represents a later development of the redware tradition and spans the late medieval and early post-medieval phases. The fabric is fine but also contains voids from burnt-out organic matter. Fabric RW12.1 is reduced dark grey throughout and the only form represented was a jar (Figure 4.6, 78; 1996, Phase 10). Fabric RW12.2 was characterised by a thick white slip beneath an apple green or clear copper-speckled glaze. Both variants were only found in the 1996 excavations. There are no exact parallels with the later wares from Montgomery Castle but fabric D11, 'brown-glazed redware', is similar (Knight 1991a, 17) although there is a much greater variety of glaze colour at Wigmore, that favours the yellowish tan and olive tones, but the light brown and chestnut colours found at Montgomery are also present. Fabric RW12.2 may find a parallel

Vessel form	Count	Weight (g)	Rim	Base	Illustrations
Unidentified	540	2886	4	12	
Bowl	67	929	19	7	Figure 4.6, 67–72; Figure 4.7, 92–95
Bowl bifid rim	1	15	1		
Bowl flange rim	5	112	4		Figure 4.6, 70
Bowl wall rim	2	91	2		Figure 4.6, 71
Bowl?	4	30			
Jar	29	626	15	5	Figure 4.6, 73–76, Figure 4.7, 99
Jar?	11	75	2		
Jug/jar/cistern	3	45		1	
Jug	1	18			Figure 4.7, 101
Jug/jar	1	35			
Cistern	2	14			
Lid	1	22			Figure 4.7, 91, 100
Lid?	1	3	1		
Drinking vessel	4	13	1		Figure 4.7, 98
Tripod skillet	1	39		1	Figure 4.7, 97
Drip tray/skillet	1	7			
Drip tray	2	103	1	1	Figure 4.7, 96
Chafing dish	5	36	2		Figure 4.6, 77
Watering pot	1	61	1		Figure 4.7, 104
Press/garden furniture	2	90			Figure 4.6, 84
Roof furniture?	1	21			
Total	**684**	**5265**	**53**	**27**	

FIGURE 4.8
Fabric RW12 (later 16th–17th centuries), functional analysis (1996 and 1998)

in the fabric D9 pipkin from Montgomery Castle (Knight 1991a, 16).

Fabric RW12 is not found in the pre-plaster floor deposits in the 1998 excavation and is first found in the 1996 excavation, late in Phase 9 (CG96 05) where it occurs with Cistercian ware/blackware and Malvern Chase ware. The fabric is also found used for Cistercian/blackware and blackware vessels. All the evidence points to fabric RW12 being dated to the beginning of the 16th century and continuing in use into the 17th century. Certainly in 1996 Phases 10 and 11 it is the dominant fabric.

Fabric RW12 forms constitute a broad range of table and kitchen wares (Figure 4.8). Bowls were most common and were found in two sizes: smaller vessels, possibly used at table, with diameters of around 18 and 23cm, and larger bowls, probably used as kitchen wares, around 29–39cm in diameter. This latter group included the wall-rim (e.g. Figure 4.6, 71) and flange-rim bowls. The wall-rim bowl form is recorded in Gwent from kiln sites dating to the late 16th to early 17th centuries (Clarke *et al* 1985). All the Wigmore Castle examples are from Phases 10 and 11 of the 1996 excavations. Decoration found on the bowls included incised horizontal and wavy lines (Figure 4.7, 94 and unillustrated) and finger-pinched rims, giving a frilled effect (Figure 4.6, 68 and Figure 4.7, 95). A small percentage of the bowls had an external brown slip.

Jars were also well represented. Jar diameters ranged mainly from 12cm to 20cm, although there were two larger diameters of 23cm and 28cm. The lid (Figure 4.7, 100) would be a perfect fit for the jars at the smaller end of the diameter range. At least two cisterns (bung hole jars) were identified. One jar may have had a thumbed neck cordon in imitation of the Malvern Chase ware jars (see below). Otherwise decoration was limited to incised horizontal lines on the exterior of the jars. There was one example of an applied thumbed strip.

Further kitchen wares included skillets and dripping trays. The chafing dishes could have been used either to heat food gently or to keep food warm at table. Only one jug could be identified for certain and a small number of drinking vessels were present.

The above vessels represented mainly utilitarian wares; jars for general storage, jugs and cisterns for liquid storage, wide-mouthed bowls for food preparation, and specialised cooking wares such as the skillet and dripping tray, although not one sherd was sooted. Vessels for food consumption were fewer in number and consisted of drinking vessels and some of the smaller diameter bowls. Two unusual vessels were also noted: a watering pot (Figure 4.7, 104) and a pierced base from a press or possibly a watering pot (Figure 4.6, 84).

Fabric RW12.2 was used for bowls. A cup and strainer were also recorded. There was very little of this fabric and it probably dates from the 17th century.

Another important group of pottery consisted of Malvern Chase ware (Fabric R02), which is the same as Hereford Fabric B4 (Vince 1985a). There is some slight evidence (see below) that this ware may have been in use by the third quarter of the 14th century. Fabric R02 was found in most of the 1998 context groups pre-dating the plaster floor and from Phase 8 onwards in the 1996 excavations. The fabric was well represented in the demolition deposits within the East Tower and clearly was an important component of the pottery in use in the castle in the 15th and 16th centuries. In the 1996 group, this fabric group was overwhelmingly biased in favour of jugs like those illustrated by Vince (1985a, fig 40, 3). Bowls were the next best represented form, closely followed by jars, particularly those with a thumbed neck cordon (such as Figure 4.6, 66). There were two sherds from chafing dishes, two from dripping trays and four sherds from drinking vessels (Figure 4.6, 65). Two small jugs and one small jug or bottle were noted. The functional composition in the 1998 group was different. Only two bowl sherds were present. Jar and jug sherds were fairly evenly matched although there was a greater number of sherds from small jugs or bottles (Figure 4.7, 105). The only other form represented was a chafing dish (not illustrated).

Malvernian wares were uncommon at Montgomery Castle (Knight 1991a) but Vince notes that a 'collection of sixteenth and seventeenth century wares [from the City Wall, Ludlow] contained almost totally Malvernian types' and suggests that the pottery was probably transported to Ludlow along the River Teme (Vince 1997, 298 and 292). Evidence from the 1996 excavation at Wigmore suggests that Fabric R02 was superseded by Fabric RW12 probably around the later 16th century.

Cistercian and blackware forms were of the kind normally encountered in the West Midlands. Cistercian ware was more common on the 1998 excavation, where all the sherds were from cups. Indeterminate Cistercian ware/blackware was only found on the 1996 site. Again most of the sherds were from drinking vessels but one small jug with a black 'metallic' glaze was also present. Blackware was also better represented on the 1996 site, with drinking vessels, particularly straight-sided mugs predominating. A small number of jug sherds were also found. Blackware mugs are known from the second half of the 16th century in Coventry (Woodfield 1981) and the same forms continue in use until at least the mid- to late 17th century. There were also imitations of Rhenish stoneware drinking jug forms. Two lid-seated bowls (Figure 4.6, 64 and Figure 4.7, 90) from CG96 01 and CG96 02 were very late in the stratigraphic sequence and the vessels most probably date to the 17th century. A single blackware sherd with quartz grains embedded in the surface is the only example from the castle of 'quartz-decorated ware' a type known to have been made by the Lingen/Deerfold Forest potters in the 17th century (personal inspection by the author). This is surprising in view of the proximity of the forest to Wigmore but may be evidence of how little 17th-century pottery occurs at the castle. The trailed slip decorated wares are one of the few types of pottery which are unequivocally 17th century in date. Slipware sherds were only found in Phase 11 on the 1996 site. Three or four fabrics were recorded: a fine, 'clean' cream ware with few inclusions, a fine sandy cream ware, a light orange fabric, and an orange-red fabric, similar to Fabric RW12. Bowls with internal white slip trailed decoration were found in all four fabrics. The light orange and orange-red fabric bowls had a reddish external slip coat. These vessels are most likely to date to about the time of the Civil War. However, a cup or small bowl, and a cup, both with a yellow-glazed interior and external white slip trails on a dark brown ground, are unlikely to pre-date the late 17th century (see, for example, Barker and Crompton 2007, 22–24) and are probably more or less contemporary with a few sherds from mottled ware mugs also found in Phase 11. Both these slipware vessels had the fine sandy, cream fabric. This type of slipware was made in both Bristol and the Staffordshire Potteries and either source is possible here. The slipware bowls with the pale orange fabric are most likely to come from Staffordshire but the source of the others is less certain. A trailed slipware bowl of Civil War date with a cream fabric similar to the Wigmore examples was found at Stafford Castle (Rátkai 2007, fig 43, 227) but it is unlikely to have been made in Staffordshire (David Barker pers comm).

Imported Continental pottery

Imported Continental pottery was not especially well represented at Wigmore, amounting to just 43 sherds weighing 279g. All but six sherds came from the 1996 excavations; all but one of the 1996 sherds was from Phase 11. A fine cream-bodied green-glazed ware appears to be a North French import. Two sherds were found in the 1998 excavations in 629 (a fill of the East Tower) and in 633 outside the tower in CG98 20 (Phase 8). The sherds (Fabric NfrWW) date to the late 12th to mid-13th century (Duncan Brown pers comm) and were in good condition despite being found residually. The sherds appeared to be from the same vessel, a jug with a flattened squared rim and a deep thumb print at the base of the handle. A third sherd from the 1996 excavations from 042, CG96 06, Phase 9, had a very similar fabric, although the glaze was clear appearing pale yellow against the body of the pot, with sparse copper speckles. It may also be French but could be a southern English whiteware from the Hampshire/Surrey border area.

The Mortimer estates in France were in Normandy but these were lost in the early years of the 13th century (see Chapter 10). Although it is possible that the North French jug was brought directly to Wigmore as part of the travelling household's baggage, it is more likely that the jug was the result of a trip to Bristol or Chester (given that Mortimer landholdings in Britain were centred on the Marches and North Wales) for provisions not easily obtained locally, including those imported from the Continent such as wine and spices. A single Ham Green sherd found in the 1998 excavation, in unphased context 693, indicates some contact with Bristol as does the fish bone (see Chapter 9).

Later North French imports were represented by Martincamp flask sherds and by Normandy stoneware, likely to be from Bessin (Emma Collins pers comm). Martincamp flask sherds were only found on the 1996 site. Martincamp Type I (buff-coloured fabric) and Type II (highly fired purple-grey fabric) were found residually in Phase 11 deposits. Again, Martincamp flasks are fairly commonplace on castle sites in the 16th and 17th centuries. They are often associated with Civil War deposits but here they are possibly more likely to date to the 16th century.

Bessin stoneware was made in Lower Normandy from *c*1450 to the present day. The fabric resembles Midlands Purple ware and the sherds from Wigmore had a thin, patchy, external brown glaze, although the external surfaces appeared somewhat abraded and glaze coverage may have been better originally. According to Hurst *et al* (1986, 100) the distribution of Normandy Stoneware is mainly coastal in England but also note that it is hard to identify examples from the Midlands because of its similarity to Midlands Purple ware. The presence, therefore, of Bessin stoneware so far inland at Wigmore is noteworthy. Bessin stoneware sherds were found in 021, CG96 02, Phase 10 (a single sherd) and in contexts 003, 005 and 006, Phase 11. The sherds were very fragmentary but two vessels at most seem to be represented. The curvature of one of the larger sherds suggests that it comes from either a jug or tall jar (similar to Hurst *et al* 1986, fig 46, 135 and 141). Hurst *et al* (1986) believe that Normandy stoneware occurs in England mainly from the second half of the 16th century, becoming more frequent in the following century. A 17th-century date is perhaps most likely for the first occurrence of this ware at Wigmore.

Other Continental imports were represented by Rhenish stonewares. The earliest of these was a small sherd of Raeren stoneware found residually in Phase 11. This was decorated with a crude stabbed face mask and dates to the early 16th century (Figure 4.7, 102). It can be directly paralleled by published examples (Gaimster 1997, colour plate 15, no. 75; Hurst *et al* 1986, fig 94, 302), dated to *c*1475–1525. Small sherds of Cologne stoneware were found in Phase 11 (1996 and 1998) and within the East Tower (Phase 10). A Frechen stoneware sherd was found in Phase 10 (1996). Rhenish stonewares are not an uncommon find on castle sites. A good group of decorated drinking jugs was found at Stafford Castle (Rátkai 2007) and in the castle ditch in Newcastle (Gaimster 1997), and plain and decorated types were recorded at Montgomery Castle (Knight 1991a). The Wigmore sherds were quite small but all, save one (above), appeared to be undecorated.

4.3 THE POTTERY: STRATIGRAPHY AND TAPHONOMY

The 1996 excavations

A breakdown of the pottery by context group and phase can be seen in Figures 4.9 and 4.10. The 1996 excavations provided a good stratigraphic sequence with comparatively little residuality.

Phase 1

Three Fabric Q01 cooking pot sherds, all sooted, and representing two vessels (Figure 4.4, 01–02) were found in the turf line 362 which lay immediately beneath the probable clay bank of the first castle. There is no doubt that this pottery is that used by the first castle builders and as such must represent pottery brought in by fitz Osbern's men. No pottery was found within the postulated bank itself. Pottery in rampart make-up material and the turf line beneath it is known at Stafford Castle (Rátkai 2007). Pottery was also noted in the first rampart at Tutbury Castle (Ratkai, 2011b). This pottery seems to indicate the sequence of building of early castles, that is, the motte was thrown up whilst the castle builders camped within what was to become a defended bailey. Sufficient time elapsed for pottery and food remains to accumulate there, which lay beneath or were eventually incorporated into the defensive bank.

The remaining pottery came from a series of dumped layers, interpreted as an early modification to the original defences (Chapters 3 and 9). The pottery from these clay dumps was made up of sooted cooking pot sherds mainly in Fabric Q01 with some Fabric Q03. They are generally small sherds, representing surface scatter material incorporated into the clay dumps. If Fabric Q03 is an early variant of Malvernian cooking pot ware (Fabric R01), then this would suggest that the modifications occurred in the 12th century.

Phase 2

After the rampart had become redundant and the site levelled and extended, a timber building CG96 26 and a hearth CG96 27 were constructed. The hearth seems to have been an internal feature of the building since the comparatively large group of pottery recovered from the hearth, some 160 sherds, would be more in keeping with a domestic hearth within a building. The hearth had three phases of use, not identfiable in the pottery assemblage. Apart from the hearth, most of the pottery was from the southern part of the building. Although a reasonably sized group of sherds was found associated here, the sherds were generally small (average sherd weight 6g). Inside the building, most of the pottery came from layers 304, 305 and 325, and fill 367 of post-

Phase	7	7	6	6	6	6	5	4	4	4	4	3	3	3	2	2	1
Group	**10**	**11**	**12**	**13**	**15**	**16**	**17**	**18**	**19**	**20**	**22**	**23**	**24**	**25**	**26**	**27**	**29**
Q01							0.7%	4.6%	1.0%	6.0%	12.5%	12.7%	69.0%	40.3%	68.0%	46.1%	87.8%
Q03											3.4%				0.5%	0.3%	12.2%
Q03?							0.6%		5.5%								
Q20								4.8%			10.1%	2.3%	10.9%	25.8%	18.7%	53.5%	
Q10														11.9%	7.6%		
R01							0.6%		19.7%		0.6%			8.1%	5.2%		
OOL														12.5%			
S01		2.1%		15.5%	6.7%	2.4%	1.0%					8.9%		1.4%			
S20				6.0%	5.9%				1.2%		12.0%	21.0%	20.1%				
MS01		40.9%		36.9%	12.6%	1.6%	7.0%	33.5%	37.3%	94.0%	29.1%	36.6%					
MS12	95.7%	17.9%		1.2%	11.8%	17.5%	9.9%	2.5%				2.3%					
S10		2.3%		4.8%	4.2%		4.7%	31.5%	17.3%		25.5%	16.3%					
Daub											0.1%						
Q02		0.6%					0.1%		10.1%		5.3%						
Q31							7.4%	2.5%	1.2%		1.1%						
R03											0.3%						
RW10		3.9%		9.5%	47.1%	3.2%		10.4%			0.1%						
RW10					1.7%												
MS10									4.4%								
Q01.1				4.8%			0.1%		2.4%								
S11		2.8%		10.7%	6.7%	65.5%	41.0%	10.2%									
MS02		6.1%	100.0%	6.0%	2.5%		26.0%										
Q32				4.8%			0.6%										
QM01							0.4%										
MS03	4.3%	23.4%				6.0%											
MS11					0.8%	4.0%											
Weight (g)	23	773	2	84	119	252	2670	394	585	67	1045	528	329	295	422	1465	205
Sherd count	3	115	1	23	42	30	207	37	49	4	108	42	29	30	69	160	28
ASW	7.5g	6.5g	2g	3.5g	3g	8.5g	13g	10.5g	12g	17g	9.5g	12.5g	11g	10g	6g	9g	7g

FIGURE 4.9

Wigmore 1996 pottery quantification (by weight) by context group, Phases 1–5

hole 368. There was not a single sherd from CG96 28, which was a cluster of stake-holes outside the building, and a gully, possibly the remains of a partition within the building.

Phase 2 witnesses the introduction of Fabric Q20, a coarse, reduced fabric containing lumps of sandstone. The fabric is very distinctive and may be the product of more local pottery manufacture. One sherd from within the building had an olive-yellow splash glaze, the remaining sherds were from cooking pots, mostly undecorated except for two with thumbed rims (Figure 4.4, 09), consistent with an early date for the fabric. Most of the pottery consisted of Fabrics Q01 (Figure 4.4, 03–07) and Q20 (Figure 4.4, 08–09). Three other fabrics were present in small quantities, Fabric Q03 (one sherd), Fabric Q10 (two sherds) and Malvernian cooking pot (Fabric R01, 5 sherds). The latter tended to be black throughout and of 12th-century date. All the Malvernian pottery was from the southern half of the building, but it was absent from the post-hole fills and hearth CG96 27. There is some evidence that Malvernian pottery was introduced after Fabric Q20.

All the sherds, apart from one, were from cooking pots. Most of the pottery was sooted externally. There were also examples of internal sooting, some of which was heavy. The latter sooting pattern may have derived from the broken sherds being burnt in the hearth rather than during use when complete vessels but other sherds from elsewhere within the building were similarly sooted, so there is a stronger possibility that the sooting represents burnt food remains. Limescale, sometimes heavy, was present on the interior of some Fabric Q01 sherds and on one Malvernian sherd. All but one of the sherds with limescale came from the building, rather than the hearth and this is the only period where limescale is a noticeable attribute of the pottery.

All the pottery is consistent with a 12th-century date. It is not possible to tell whether the pottery in the post-holes was deposited there at the time of construction or on removal of the posts when the building was demolished, although the former seems more likely.

The pottery, fish, animal bone, and artefacts suggest that part of this building was used for cooking, although the building as a whole is probably too large to have just had this single function.

Phase 3

Once the Phase 2 timber structure had gone out of use, a series of possible levelling deposits (CG96 25) were laid down. The pottery in these was much the same as in the previous two phases, with Fabric Q01 (Figure 4.4, 11) being dominant. A Malvernian ware rim sherd (not illustrated but see Viince 1985a, fig 38, 1) had a form which suggested a late 12th- or early 13th-century date. It was the only Malvernian sherd from this group. A sherd of similar date was an oolitic limestone-tempered handle from a pitcher (Figure 4.4, 10). The handle had a raised central rib and oblique slashing and had a light brownish-olive glaze. The source of this ware is likely to be Gloucestershire and is probably the equivalent of Fabric D3 in Hereford, where it is dated to the late late 12th- and early 13th-century (Vince 1985a, 56) This is the only occurrence of an oolitic limestone-tempered ware on both this and the 1998 site. This group also marked the first appearance of siltstone-tempered ware, Fabric S01. The levelling deposits of this group had probably been laid down by *c*1200

Phase	**11**	**10**	**9**	**9**	**9**	**9**	**8**	**8**
Group	**1**	**2**	**3**	**5**	**6**	**7**	**8**	**9**
Q01						9.1%		
R01			1.1%				3.8%	
S01		0.6%	6.8%		1.5%			35.4%
MS01		1.4%	2.0%		17.9%	12.1%	12.9%	5.2%
MS12		0.2%	2.9%		15.3%	41.2%	1.2%	8.6%
S10			0.8%		1.7%			4.1%
RW10			4.7%		0.9%	0.6%	3.2%	9.6%
S11					0.6%			
MS02			3.4%				2.1%	0.7%
Q32					1.5%			2.4%
MS03					4.3%		2.3%	30.2%
Q11								2.7%
R02	10.2%	13.3%	53.0%	34.6%	17.0%	19.4%	66.3%	1.0%
R02?		3.2%						
R01/R02					0.4%			
RW13			3.2%		19.9%	15.2%	8.2%	
WW10					0.4%	2.4%		
MWW					1.7%			
Q30	0.6%				16.1%			
Q40	0.0%	4.3%	20.3%		0.5%			
WW01					0.2%			
WW02			1.7%		0.1%			
CISTBLW	0.5%	2.1%		7.7%				
RW12	67.7%	59.8%		57.7%				
RW12?	0.1%							
BLW	13.4%	10.9%						
CIST		0.1%						
FRECHEN		0.7%						
MOT	0.1%	0.1%						
BESSIN	0.9%	0.1%						
RW12.1	0.6%	2.5%						
SLPW	1.1%	0.2%						
YW	1.6%	0.7%						
COLOGNE	1.0%							
MARTINC	0.6%							
MGW	1.5%							
PMIP	0.1%							
RAEREN?	0.1%							
TGE	0.1%							
Sherd Weight	4558g	3139g	870g	104g	1374g	165g	341g	291g
Sherd Count	837	305	93	20	161	21	58	25
ASW	5.5g	10g	9.5g	5g	8.5g	8g	6g	11.5g

FIGURE 4.10
Wigmore 1996 pottery quantification (by weight) by context group, Phases 6–11

and thus provide a *terminus ante quem* for the Phase 2 building.

Cooking pots were sooted and as in the preceding phases, some on the interior. None of the cooking pots had any decoration. A Fabric Q20 base sherd showed in section details of its construction (Figure 4.4, 12). A roll of clay had been luted onto the exterior base angle to strengthen the pot at this point. A single Fabric Q01 sherd had limescale.

Context group CG96 24, consisted of three intercutting pits. The latest pit, 273, contained no pottery. The earliest pit, 282, contained a small amount of pottery consisting of Fabric Q01 cooking pot sherds, two of which had limescale. There is a strong possibility that these sherds were disturbed from underlying Phase 2 layers when the pit was cut.

The middle pit, 271, contained the greatest amount of pottery. The fills contained, yet again, cooking pot sherds in Fabrics Q01 (Figure 4.4, 13) and Q20. As previously, the sherds were small, so it is difficult to be certain whether this is redeposited material but an abraded Q20 jug sherd is probably from the same vessel found in CG96 25, Phase 3, the levelling over the Phase 2 timber building. This at least indicates some redeposition. Again, limescale was present on some of the cooking pot sherds. This provides another link with the pottery from earlier groups since limescale appears to be a feature of Phase 2 and is not seen after CG96 24, Phase 3. One reasonably large cooking pot body sherd was found in the pit in Fabric S20, a coarse siltstone-tempered ware. This is the first time that this fabric appears in the stratigraphic sequence and the sherd may date to the time of the pit backfilling rather than being redeposited.

The pottery gives no indication as to the likely function of the pits. The middle pit in the sequence was the only one to contain a reasonable amount of pottery and was the only one to contain animal bone. The animal bone was indicative of a high-status diet but also contained a small amount of dog bone. Although the middle pit clearly contained domestic waste there is no reason to assume that this pit or the other two were dug specifically for the disposal of rubbish.

Whatever the function of the intercutting pits in CG96 24, they were sealed by a yellow clay layer, 257, and possible occupation deposits, which formed CG96 23, Phase 3. Layer 257 contained a by now familiar group of Fabric Q01 cooking pot sherds (Figure 4.4, 14) only one of which had limescale. The layer above, 260, contained only a Fabric S20 cooking pot (Figure 4.4, 15) and two base sherds from a Fabric S10 cooking pot. This marks the first appearance of Fabric S10 in the stratigraphic sequence. There is a strong possibility that by now Fabrics Q01 and Q20 were in decline.

Most of the pottery in CG96 23 came from an upper occupation deposit 249. The pottery from here was really quite different from everything which had gone before. Micaceous, siltstone-tempered Fabrics MS01 (Figure 4.4, 16) and MS12 (Figure 4.4, 17) first occurred and further sherds of siltstone-tempered Fabric S01 (Figure 4.4, 18), S10 and S20 were found. Single sherds of Fabrics Q01 and Q20 stand a high probability of being residual. Most sherds were from cooking pots. The one exception was the Fabric MS12 sherd (Figure 4.4, 17). This was from a crude, hand-formed pitcher or jug, decorated with shallow circular impressions. The vessel had a dull, patchy olive to tan glaze. The glaze, decoration and method of manufacture suggest a date in the early 13th century at the latest. The ceramic evidence seems to indicate that the capping of the intercutting pits, CG96 24, and the build up of occupation deposits in CG96 23 took place in the early years of the 13th century.

Phase 4

Further deposits were laid down in CG96 22 in Phase 4 and a cut feature 244/364 was identified. The pottery in the various layers and dumps was pretty much the same as that found in CG96 23, Phase 3. Siltstone-tempered and micaceous, siltstone-tempered fabrics were dominant. Some previously unrecorded fabrics were present such as Worcester-type glazed ware (Fabric Q02) and a possible Malvernian tripod pitcher sherd (Fabric R03), the equivalent of Vince's (1985a) Fabric B2. Both of these fabrics are consistent with a date in the first half of the 13th century. A cooking pot base sherd in Fabric Q31 and a Fabric RW10 sherd which equates to Herefordshire-type Micaceous ware (Knight, 1991a) were noted. Both of these are unlikely to pre-date *c*1250. Two of the Worcester-type glazed ware sherds were found in layer 222 beneath the metalled surface 223, where they were the only pottery recorded. Cross-joining sherds (that is, sherds from the same vessel found in more than one context) were found in the CG96 22 deposits and linked 254 with 229, 245 with 231, and 244 with 239. This indicates a certain amount of disturbance or perhaps rapid deposition of the clay and silt layers. However quickly these deposits formed, the activity they represent was brought to an abrupt end by a large conflagration (CG96 20). On the pottery evidence this would seem to have occurred just after the middle of the 13th century.

The pottery from the cut 244/364 was somewhat different from that recovered from the layers and dumps. Four fills were recorded for the feature. Fill 243 which was towards the top of the fill sequence contained pottery like that recovered from the dumps (Figure 4.11). A second group contained only Fabrics Q01, Q03, Q20, which was exactly the same as pottery recovered from Phases 1 and 2, and a single Malvernian sherd. This ware first appears in Phase 2. Unfortunately, it is impossible to know where the pottery actually came from in

	Post-hole Fill 357		Cut unspecified fill		Cut unspecified fill		Layers		Total	Total
	count	weight	count	weight	count	weight	count	weight	count	weight
Daub			1	1					1	1
Q01	3	19	9	72			5	40	17	131
Q20			7	71			3	35	10	106
Q03			5	36					5	36
R01			1	6					1	6
MS01					3	15	31	289	34	304
S10					5	116	18	150	23	266
S20					7	100	3	25	10	125
Q02							4	55	4	55
Q31							1	11	1	11
R03							1	3	1	3
RW10							1	1	1	1
Total	**3**	**19**	**23**	**186**	**15**	**231**	**67**	**609**	**108**	**1045**

FIGURE 4.11
Wigmore 1996 pottery from CG96 22, Phase 4

the fill sequence since it was marked with the cut number, 244, rather than fill number. Sherds from the same Fabric Q01 cooking pot were found in 244 and in 239, which sealed the backfilled cut. This possibly suggests that the pottery came from high up in the fill sequence. The relationship of the cut to the dump layers in this context group was not established stratigraphically although the feature cut CG96 25 (Phase 3) levelling deposits and perhaps the earlier fill material derived from these deposits. It is possible that post-hole 358 might be associated with the cut. Its fill only contained Fabric Q01 cooking pots sherds. What is uncertain is whether cut 244/364 really contained two fills represented by two distinct groups of pottery, in which case this could represent a later re-cut of an earlier feature, unnoticed at the time of excavation, or whether the pottery from the unspecified fill and from fill 243 were one and the same. It was suggested by the excavators that the cut may have marked the location of the earliest outer defences. The pottery from the unspecified fill would be consistent with an early date. Unfortunately, the available stratigraphic evidence is such that the true nature of the cut can never be known for certain.

In terms of vessel function, jug sherds were still in the minority but were better represented than previously. One slightly odd feature about the glazed sherds is that many of the glazes have opacified to a yellowish-white colour and are often 'lumpy'. Perhaps they have been insufficiently fired, burnt or the soil conditions have had a deleterious effect on them. There are three examples of splash glazes on Fabrics S10 and MS01 and on Worcester-type glazed ware. A hand-formed, Fabric MS01 jug had a finger-impressed base. Cooking pots were found in Fabrics MS01 (Figure 4.4, 19), Q20 (Figure 4.4, 20), S10 (Figure 4.4, 21) and S20, although Fabric Q20 must be residual here. Limescale is not present on the cooking pots in this context group, apart from on one Q01 sherd from cut 244.

All the preceding activity represented by CG96 22 in Phase 4 was sealed by a charcoal-rich horizon (CG96 20). The sherds found within this layer, including a Fabric MS01 cooking pot (Figure 4.4, 22), were not heat affected, so presumably were deposited after the fire. An MS01 jug sherd from this context group was decorated with incised horizontal lines.

Further occupation layers (CG96 19) were found above the charcoal layer. In essence these occupation layers contained the same sort of pottery as that found in CG96 22, below the burnt level. There is clearly some residual material, such as Fabric Q01 and Q03, and Worcester-type glazed ware (Fabric Q02, not illustrated) which has a sudden unaccountable percentage spike here. Although Fabric Q01.1 appears here for the first time, this too should be residual. Fabric MS10 is found for the first time in this context group. Both Q01.1 and MS10 were found only in pit 252, together with sherds of Fabric Q03.

The upper dumps (those above the backfilled pit 252) contained most of the pottery from this context group. There were no Fabric RW10 sherds present although a jug sherd in closely related Fabric Q31 was recorded. Dating evidence for the upper dumps was provided by two Malvernian cooking pot sherds, which dated typologically to the late 13th century. The sherds were quite substantial (Figure 4.4, 25, and unillustrated) and it is odd that Figure 4.4, 25, weighing 100g, was associated with an area of metalling, where sherds would be subject to trample. Two Fabric MS01 cooking pots from the same context as the Malvernian sherds have been illustrated (Figure 4.4, 23–24).

For once, jug sherds were in the majority and were found in Fabrics MS01, Q31, S10, Q02 and MS10. The Fabric MS10 jug was highly decorated with incised vertical lines and comb teeth impressions, although insufficient of the jug remained to ascertain what the complete design would have looked like. The highly decorated style is found on jugs in the period *c*1250 to 1350. Decoration on the MS01 jugs was limited to incised horizontal lines.

To sum up Phase 4, CG96 22 seems to represent a build up of material which ended some time early in the third quarter of the 13th century with a substantial fire (CG96 20). Action must have swiftly followed the conflagration, since the charcoal-rich burnt layer was not apparently dissipated or weathered away but was covered over by further dumps of material (CG96 19). The sherds in both CG96 19 and 22 were generally fairly small (Figure 4.9) and there is certainly a case for some of the pottery being redeposited. However, the greater percentage of glazed sherds, the late 13th-century form of two Malvernian cooking pots and the highly decorated MS10 jug sherds argues strongly for the deposition of CG96 19 in the final quarter of the 13th century at the earliest. The dating of these layers is of the utmost importance as their deposition and that of CG96 18 (below) precedes a phase of construction of the Southern Curtain Wall. Whether this represents the very first building of stone defences is discussed in Chapters 9 and 10.

Context group CG96 18 seems to represent occupation activity immediately before the construction of the curtain wall. No great time need have elapsed between this context group and CG96 19 below. There is no appreciable difference between the pottery from the two groups; Fabric S11 appears for the first time but S11 may be a variant of Fabric S10 which was in use from Phase 3. Fabric MS12 is also found for the first time. Residual pottery such as Fabric Q01 and Q20 (a sherd from a splash-glazed jug or pitcher, possibly part of the same vessel found in Phase 2) is present and the pottery group in general has a rather mixed disturbed look. Fabric MS01 was the best represented fabric and had been dominant since the end of Phase 3. In this context group, only Fabric MS01 cooking pot sherds (Figure 4.4, 26–27) were present, possibly because by now there was a greater availability of other glazed wares. A similar proportion of jug sherds (just under 40% by sherd count) was in the group as in CG96 19. A Fabric S11 jug was decorated with grooving or rilling on the shoulder but there were no examples of any more complex decoration. Two Fabric RW10 sherds came from a jug with a pinched base, with fingernail marks visible on the interior. The jug was burnt on the interior. Fabrics RW10 and S12 are unlikely to pre-date the second half of the 13th century but the dating for CG96 18 rests primarily on the dating of CG96 19 (see above).

Phase 5

Deposit 197 of CG96 18 was cut through by the construction trench for the curtain wall. Most of the sherds in this deposit and the one below, 198, were in Fabrics S10 and S11, neither of which were found in the other contexts in this group. A Fabric MS01 cooking pot sherd was found in 197 also and a Fabric MS01 cooking pot sherd (Figure 4.4, 27) and a Fabric MS12 jug sherd were found in 198.

The curtain wall construction trench (CG96 17) contained a long sequence of fills. The pottery came mainly from the upper fills. Other artefacts (see Chapter 5) were likewise absent from the early fills and substantial amounts of bone were present in only two contexts (see Chapters 7 and 9). The earliest fills with pottery were 263, 264, 265 and 266 which occur above the 'working surfaces', identified within the fill sequence (see Chapter 3). These fills contained cooking pot sherds in Fabrics Q01.1, Q03, MS01, MS02, QM01, S01 and S10 and a jug sherd in Fabric MS12. This was the first occurrence of Fabrics MS02 and QM01. The Fabric Q03 sherds appeared to be part of a vessel from pit 252, in CG96 19. Above these fills was a sterile red gritty layer, 209.

The next set of fills (194, 196 and 203) contained a broadly similar group of fabrics to the earliest fills (Fabrics MS01, MS12, Q01, Q02, Q31, R01, S10 and S11). Fabric Q32 first occurred in this group but the sherds appeared to come from a coil-built jug, which might suggest the fabric is residual here. This set of fills differed from the previous ones in that the majority of the sherds were from jugs (44% by sherd count). Cooking pot sherds were found in Fabric Q01, and represent much earlier residual material in the fills, and in Fabrics S01 (Figure 4.5, 30), S10, MS01 and R01 (Malvernian cooking pot). The R01 cooking pot was a late 13th-century form like (Figure 4.4, 25) (see also Vince 1985a, fig 38, 4) from CG96 22. An unglazed pipkin (Figure 4.4, 28), related to the cooking pots in terms of function, in Fabric MS01, was found in this fill group. It is possible that more of this pot occurred in the previous phase, in 201, CG96 18. If so then some of the Phase 4 occupation debris was finding its way into the backfill material.

Some of the jug sherds in this fill group were decorated. Examples of fine roller-stamping were noted on jug sherds in Fabric MS12. Indistinct incised or impressed decoration was noted on another MS12 sherd. A base sherd in the same fabric had wide-spaced thumb impressions along the base angle. Decoration on Fabric S10 jug sherds comprised wavy combing and a raised, self-clay, ridge or rib. A broad band of rectangular roller-stamping was present on a Worcester-type glazed ware sherd, although the sherd is likely to be residual here.

Although this middle fill sequence was apparently cut (see Chapter 3) and a new sequence of fills (183, 182 and 178) deposited within this, beginning with a sterile red gritty layer, there were sherds from the same vessels found in both fill sequences. Likewise sherds from the same vessels were found in all three fills despite 182 and 183 being separated from 178 by a red gritty layer and rubble. This suggests a fairly rapid backfilling of the top section of the construction trench, if nothing else.

The latest fills (178, 182, 183) contained mostly Fabric S11 jug sherds (115 sherds in total), including Figure 4.5, 31, apart from a substantial section of a Fabric MS02 jug (Figure 4.5, 29) and six sherds from a Fabric MS12 jug. Some of the sherds from these upper fills had pale adhesions which reacted with hydrochloric acid. Given that the mortar used in the wall construction was red, the adhesions may have derived from a plaster render. The Fabric S11 jug (Figure 4.5, 31) had roughly a third of its sherds covered with this limey deposit and all of the Fabric MS12 jug sherds were similarly affected. The likely explanation for this phenomenon is that the sherds were lying on the ground surface through which the construction surface was cut and some became covered or splashed with plaster or render which was being prepared close to the wall construction. Most of the Fabric S11 jug sherds were heavily abraded and this might be an indication that they were subjected to trample. Again, this is consistent with them being exposed on the ground surface. The final backfill of the construction trench presumably was made up primarily of material shovelled in from the ground surface to provide an even surface over rubble 180. It is, of course, purely speculative, but it may be possible that the Fabric S11 jug was actually being used by the labourers, was dropped and broke into many pieces, and lay upon the ground surface, before being incorporated into the trench backfill.

There is some obvious residual material in the backfills, such as Fabrics Q01 and Q02. A cross-join between fill 256 of the construction trench and a fill of pit 252, CG96 19, Phase 4, further demonstrates that redeposited material was present.

Phase 6

Once the construction of the curtain wall had been completed, a substantial level surface 147 was laid (CG96 16, Phase 6). Considering the depth and extent of this layer, there is very little pottery within it and it really looks as if the construction of the curtain wall heralded a 'fresh start'. The seal which this layer, together with contemporary layers 168 and 176, provided is demonstrated by the fact that residual material associated with the early castle is not seen again until late in the castle's history, late in Phase 8 and in Phase 9. It is with a certain degree of confidence, therefore, that we can view the pottery from Phase 6 as genuinely representing the pottery in use after the construction of the curtain wall. The available ceramic evidence seems consistent with Phase 6 dating to around 1300–1325/50.

The principal ceramic component in layer 147 was made of more Fabric S11 sherds from the jug (Figure 4.5, 31) found in the top fills of the curtain wall construction trench. These sherds may have been disturbed from either the construction trench or from ground surface 197 when 147 was laid. Other fabrics from 147 comprised Fabric S01 and Fabric MS03. Typologically Fabric MS03 should date to the 14th and 15th centuries but there is possibly some evidence from the 1998 excavations to suggest that it may have been first made in the late 13th century, although CG98 21, Phase 5, from which the MS03 sherd comes may be contaminated (see Chapter 9). Phase 6 marks the first occurrence of Fabric MS03 in the 1996 excavations.

Other pottery in this context group came from layers 168 and 176. This was made up of Fabrics MS01, MS03, MS11, MS12, RW10 and S01. Of the sherds identifiable to form all but one were from jugs. A Fabric MS12 jug from 168 (Figure 4.5, 38) had a thumbed cordon below the rim giving a 'frilled' effect. This type of rim is paralleled in Hereford Fabrics A3 and A4 (Vince 1985a, fig 31, 8, 12). Typologically this dates to *c*1200–1300 and may indicate that the sherd is one of the rare residual elements here. A Fabric S01 sherd was decorated with horizontal combing.

Once a new surface had been established running back from the curtain wall, the area was used for lead-working (CG96 12, 13, 14 and 15). CG96 15 contained the best pottery group, numbering some 42 sherds, which came from a pit-cutting layer 147. Despite the quantity of sherds, they are very small indeed and must represent scraps lying on the ground surface. A small number of sherds was burnt, presumably by having been caught up in the industrial processes. One MS02 sherd had a cratered deposit on its exterior, which, again, is likely to have derived from its proximity to lead-working.

Jug sherds were dominant in this group. Cooking pots were found in Fabrics S10, S20 and MS01. There were no glazed wares in these fabrics. In essence, the pottery was very little different from that found in CG96 16 and in the upper fills of the curtain wall construction trench. The percentage of Fabric RW10 sherds (see Figure 4.2), suggests a date in the first half of the 14th century.

Although there was considerably less Fabric RW10 found in the other context groups associated with lead-working there seems no reason to believe that there was any long interval of time between CG96 15 and CG96 12, which marked the end of this industrial activity. A Fabric MS01 cooking pot imitating the form of late 13th- or early 14th-century Malvernian cooking pots (Fabric R01), was found in CG96 13 and strengthens the case for a date of around 1300–1325 for Phase 6. A Fabric S01 cooking pot from CG96 13 has been illustrated (Figure 4.5, 39). The final backfilling of the curtain wall construction trench through to the end of the lead-working appears to have taken place in a relatively short time.

Phase 7

After the lead-working had finished a building was constructed (CG96 11). No pottery was found within the construction trench for wall 83 of the building. The pottery from the context group contained more or less the same range of fabrics as seen in Phase 6 and it seems likely that material in the floor make up and found within the stone alignment 187 represents redeposited pottery. Given the apparent barrier formed by the laying of layer 147 in CG96 16, it is surprising to find a small cluster of residual Worcester-type glazed ware sherds in 158 and 187. A group of very small sherds, found in layers 93 and 94, may have been contemporary with the floor's final use. The eight sherds from the layers (Fabrics MS01, MS12, S01 and RW10) weighed a mere 15g in total. Layers 104 and 105 outside the building contained Fabrics MS01, MS12, S10 and S11.

Functional analysis reveals that nearly every sherd came from a jug, including Figure 4.5, 40–42. Four cooking pot sherds, less than 4% of the pottery recovered from this context group, were found in Fabrics S10, S11 and MS01. Two Fabric MS01 bowls and possibly one Fabric S10 bowl were recorded, although the latter could have been part of a dripping tray (Figure 4.5, 43) The only recorded dripping tray in the 1998 excavation came from CG98 15, Phase 8, and seems to suggest that this form was not in use at the castle until the 14th century.

Unfortunately this context group is not closely datable, although the absence of Malvern Chase ware (Fabric R02) may be significant and suggest a date before 1350/75. Also, the increasing proportion of Fabric MS03 may be significant chronologically.

During the lifetime of the CG96 11 building a pit was dug (CG96 10). There is so little material in the pit fill that no discussion or interpretation is possible.

Phase 8

Context Groups CG96 10 and 11 were sealed by layers of rubble, 081 and 082 (CG96 9, Phase 8), interpreted as the dismantling of the curtain wall as a prelude to its rebuilding. Not surprisingly, the rubble contained very little pottery. A sherd from an MS12 jug was highly fired to the extent that it resembled Midlands Purple ware, which would suggest a 15th-century date at the earliest. However, Midlands Purple ware is noticeable by its absence in the excavations, only a single sherd being recovered from within the East Tower, and the MS12 sherd may just be an overfired sherd.

More significantly, CG96 09 is the first context group to contain Malvern Chase ware (Fabric R02). Two very small sherds were found in 77, a layer sealing pit 79, which post-dates the reconstruction of the curtain wall. This gives a possible *terminus ante quem* of *c*1375. Fabric Q11 was also found for the first time in this context group. Fabric MS03 was probably largely contemporary with this group, although one of the jug sherds was decorated with bands of narrow, rectangular roller-stamping which is unlikely to post-date *c*1350. Fabric S01, which is slightly better represented than MS03 in this group, must surely be residual at this point. Unfortunately only 25 sherds were recovered from CG96 09 and given the activity that the group represents, contamination is likely and the results of the pottery analysis skewed. However, the paucity of pottery may reflect a period when the castle was less used than previously.

All the sherds which were identifiable to form came from jugs, such as Figure 4.5, 44, with the exception of two cooking pot sherds (Fabrics MS01 and S10) both of which may be residual here. Sherds from a Fabric MS12 jug were found in a later dumped deposit (45, CG96 6, Phase 9).

Mixed deposits, often containing rubble, continued to accumulate in the following context group (CG96 08). Although this context group may be a continuation of the previous one (see Chapter 3), the pottery from it is notably different and there were no cross-joins between the two groups. The group contains a greater number of sherds, by far the greatest proportion of which was made up of Malvern Chase ware (Fabric R02). This is consistent with a date in the 15th century. This context group marks the first appearance of Fabric RW13 (Figure 4.5, 45), a fabric also probably dating to the 15th century. A small amount of residual material was present, such as MS01 cooking pot and jug sherds, a Fabric R01 cooking pot sherd and a Fabric MS11 jug sherd. The sherd size was small, so the material is clearly redeposited. The most common form was the jug. There was a single Fabric R02 bowl sherd.

The pottery data are somewhat confused. The balance of probabilities is that the curtain wall was reconstructed or repaired in the 15th century. It is possible to see a difference between CG96 09 and CG96 08, although the evidence for 15th-century construction in CG96 9 is equivocal. However, if the two context groups represent quite separate events, then there is no real reason to assume that they were separated by any great time. The pottery and other finds (see Chapter 5) suggest that the CG96 08 deposits have come from a domestic area or building possibly demolished in the aftermath of the new building campaign.

Phase 9

Yet more rubble and other deposits continued to accumulate (CG96 07) before surface 045, CG96 06, was laid. The pottery from the underlying deposits of CG96 07, was very little different from that found in CG96 08, Phase 8, and it becomes increasingly difficult to determine the degree of redeposition and the relative chronology of the various dumps, especially bearing in mind that there were only 21 sherds from CG96 07. There was a whiteware jug sherd (Fabric WW10) with a clear to glossy green glaze and combed decoration. A second sherd, possibly from the same vessel was found in CG96 06.

Most of the sherds were from jugs. Some jugs were quite small and may have acted as drinking vessels. A possible bottle was noted in Fabric RW13. A further sherd (from CG96 07) in the same fabric was from a jug (Figure 4.5, 53), sherds from which were also found across contexts 050 and 051 CG96 06, thus linking the two context groups.

The surface 045 in CG96 06 was another substantial and extensive deposit which sealed the CG96 07 dumps. It was overlain by a sequence of deposits consisting of loams, clays, gravels, mortar and rubble. It might have been expected that surface 045 would form a barrier to contamination and residuality but the continuing presence, in the deposits above 045, of Fabrics S10 (Figure 4.5, 54) and MS01 (Figure 4.5, 55–56) seems to indicate some residuality, although it is just possible that Fabric MS01 continued to be made in the 15th century. There were also five sherds from the MS12 jug (not illustrated), which was first encountered in context 082 (CG96 09, Phase 8). A possible cooking pot in Fabric MS12 (Figure 4.5, 57), probably of 15th-century date, was found in a layer above 045. All the Fabric R02 sherds in this context group were from jugs In Hereford, Vince (1985a, 52) notes that in a series of pits of late 14th- to early 15th-century date, the dominant Malvern Chase ware form was the jug. Fabric Q30 was first found in this context group. The fabric resembles some of the later medieval fabrics found in Shrewsbury.

A coin from 045 (see Chapter 5) could be taken to suggest that the surface was deposited *c*1450–1500, which could push the curtain wall reconstruction back into the first half of the 15th century and suggests that surface 045, and the deposits above, contain redeposited material. The coin evidence (Chapter 5) also links CG96 06 with a period of demolition and construction seen in the 1998 excavations CG98 15, Phase 8.

Context Group CG96 06 is difficult to make sense of, not just in terms of the ceramics, but also in terms of the castle's development. There were numerous cross-joins across the group and also cross-joins between this context group and CG96 07 and CG96 09 (Phase 8), for example, the Fabric RW13 jug (Figure 4.5, 53). It is difficult to believe that any great time elapsed between the deposition of CG96 08, 07 and 06, possibly even from the deposition of CG96 09 over the building (CG96 11). The absence of Cistercian ware suggests that all these deposits pre-date the last quarter of the 15th century, which to a certain extent dovetails with the coin evidence, although Cistercian ware was not that well represented in the 1996 excavations and its absence may not be significant.

Several fabrics appear for the first time in this group (MWW, Q30, Q40, WW01 and WW02) but, given the rather confused nature of the deposits in this context group, there is no guarantee that all of them date to the 15th century.

Jugs are again the best represented form. The Malvern Chase pottery (Fabric R02) was very fragmentary but many of the sherds appear to have come from small jugs (similar to Vince 1985a, fig 40, 2). Two main rim forms were identified: a simple slightly everted rim and one slightly flattened (Vince 1985a, fig 40, 2 and 3), sometimes with a depression on the upper surface. The latter form was slightly more common.

In addition to cooking pots in Fabric MS01 seen above, a possible cooking pot, with heavy external sooting, was recorded in Fabric MS12 (Figure 4.5, 57), and in Fabric S10 (Figure 4.5, 54), which must surely be residual here. An unusual form, with an in-turned rim, possibly roof furniture or a distilling base, was found in Fabric MS01 (Figure 4.5, 56). Bowl sherds were found in Fabrics MS12, RW13 and Q32. In terms of form/function the pottery is consistent with a 15th-century date. A Fabric MS12 lid was a unique find but unfortunately too fragmentary for illustration.

Before the demolition of parts of the castle (Phase 10), interpreted as the Civil War slighting, a final rubbish dump (CG96 03) was deposited on top of all the foregoing dumps and accumulations. The pottery in this group was plentiful and the variety of other finds, faunal remains and marine shell mark this out as a dump of domestic waste. Ninety-three sherds were found in this group. The dominant fabric was Malvern Chase ware (Fabric R02) which here is the second greatest concentration after CG96 08. It is not altogether clear what is residual in this group but Fabrics R01, S01, MS01 and RW10 must surely be so, with a strong possibility that MS02 is also. This context group seems to form a distinct entity, although further sherds of the RW13 jug (Figure 4.5, 53) were noted and a sherd from the MS12 cooking pot (Figure 4.5, 57), both fabrics previously found in CG96 06.

The functional composition of this group is different from the previous dumps. Two Fabric R02 dripping trays were present, three bowls (two in Fabric R02 and one in Fabric RW10) and a cistern in Fabric Q40 (Figure 4.6, 58). Thirteen further sherds in Fabric Q40, and two in Fabric R02 represented a possible three further cisterns. The remaining sherds were from jugs (Figure 4.6, 59) (Fabric R02), excepting three residual cooking pot sherds.

The functional composition is more suggestive of a 16th-century deposit. This then leaves quite a gap until the Civil War demolition. Does the demolition (CG96 02) begin before the Civil War? There is certainly documentary evidence (see Chapter 2) for both the poor condition of the standing fabric and for repairs to the castle immediately after the Dissolution but it is not possible to detect in the Phase 10 dumps (see below) any evidence to support more than a single act of demolition.

Other activity before the demolition deposits of Phase 10 are the creation of a plaster surface (CG96 04) from which there were no finds and the blocking of an alcove (CG96 05) within the curtain wall. Unfortunately, no direct relationship could be established between the latter action and the 16th-century rubbish dump (CG96 03). The group of pottery from the alcove was strikingly different from all that had gone before, both in terms of fabric and functional composition. The function of the alcove and the manner in which the sherds came to be deposited within it are unknown. Three fabrics were represented: Fabrics R02, RW12 and Cistercian/blackware all of which were probably contemporary. This is the first occurrence of Fabric RW12. Three vessel forms were found: cups and drinking vessels in Cistercian/blackware, bowls in Fabrics RW12 and R02, and a Fabric R02 jar. Some 40 percent of the Fabric RW12 and R02 sherds were very heavily abraded. The Cistercian/blackware sherds were completely unabraded.

As the term Cistercian/blackware suggests, the sherds occupy the middle ground between true Cistercian and true blackware. The rounded forms of the vessels set them apart from blackware forms, which tend to be more cylindrical and which would be expected to date to *c*1550–1650. Despite the forms there is a certain crudeness in the manufacture, particularly around the base, which has more in common with blackware. The suggested date for this deposit is *c*1550–1600.

Form	Count	Weight	Rim	Base
Bowl	13	165	1	1
Bowl?	1	14		
Cpj	16	225	7	
Cpj?	1	28	1	
Drip tray	1	102	1	
Drip tray?	1	24	1	
Jug	181	1387	15	7
Jug?	4	44		2
Jug small	2	71		2
Bottle?	1	5	1	
Jug/jar/cistern	6	22		1
Jug/cistern	9	49		
Cistern	2	28		
Jar	1	15		
Drinking vessel	2	5	1	
Cup	2	3		
Lid	1	4	1	
Unknown	51	322	1	1
Total	**295**	**2513**	**30**	**14**

FIGURE 4.12

Wigmore 1996, Phase 9: vessel function

The overall function figures for Phase 9 were once more dominated by jugs (Figure 4.12). Most of the vessels represented were associated with either the storage or consumption of liquids. Storage jars for dry goods and bowls were under-represented, given that both the fabrics and vessel forms suggest that the deposits of Phase 9 date to the 15th and 16th centuries.

Phase 10

Context Group CG996 02 contained the second largest group of pottery (305 sherds). The dominant fabric overall was Fabric RW12. This fabric was also well represented in CG96 05, Phase 9, the blocking of the alcove in the curtain wall. Several fabrics appear for the first time in CG96 02, for example, blackware, Rhenish stoneware, Normandy stoneware, slipwares, yellow wares and a variant of Fabric RW12 (Fabric RW12.1).

When the percentage weight of the fabrics in this group is tabulated (Figure 4.13), the picture is somewhat confused, although this would be expected in a series of dumps. Blackware does not appear in the sequence until context 22 but this probably signifies nothing in terms of dating. A discrete group of dumps (017, 019 and 021) were later than the 'blackware horizon' and, with the exception of context 019, contained a higher than average proportion of Fabric RW12, which may indicate that they are late in the series of dumps; the evidence, nevertheless, is equivocal. Context 017 also contained two yellow ware sherds which are likely to date to the 17th century here. Other late material was represented by a trailed slipware bowl sherd from context 009, towards the top of the dump sequence, a type of pottery that is known from Civil War deposits at Dudley Castle (personal inspection by the author) and at Stafford Castle (Rátkai 2007).

In essence, the dumps appear to contain a mixture of 16th- and 17th-century pottery, with a very small amount of earlier material. As sherds from the same vessels are spread throughout the dumps, it seems unlikely that we are looking at distinct phases of demolition; the generally mixed nature of the pottery has not been helped by tree root and animal burrow disturbance throughout this context group and the subsequent Phase 11 deposits. Pottery from dumps 017, 019 and 021 (see above) contained Fabric Q40 sherds from a vessel found in CG96 03, Phase 9. This group had the appearance of a discrete rubbish dump and, indeed, its appearance below turf line, in context 024 (see below), would tend to confirm this. The cross-joins, then, serve to underline the disturbance in the deposits dating from the later periods of the castle's history and highlight a certain degree of unreliabilty in the pottery data. In addition,

Context	24	23	32	28	22	20	18	16	15	
BLW					2.0%	31.3%	12.6%	8.5%		10.9%
CIST					3.0%					0.1%
CISTBLW							1.9%	23.7%	0.7%	2.1%
FRECHEN										0.7%
MOT	3.1%									0.1%
BESSIN										0.1%
MS01		18.3%								1.4%
MS12							1.2%			0.2%
Q40	27.7%	46.2%								4.3%
R02	18.5%	27.4%	100.0%	100.0%	42.6%	7.4%	2.7%	9.4%		13.3%
R02?										3.2%
RW12	33.8%	8.1%			40.6%	58.8%	79.3%	53.1%	70.5%	59.8%
RW12.1					11.9%		2.3%	5.4%	28.9%	2.5%
S01	16.9%					2.6%				0.6%
SLPW										0.2%
YW										0.7%
Total no.	**11**	**25**	**1**	**2**	**15**	**26**	**39**	**20**	**5**	**305**
Total weight	**65**	**197**	**13**	**16**	**101**	**272**	**483**	**224**	**149**	**3139**

Context	14	12	11	10	9	8	21	19	17	
BLW			23.4%		32.4%	17.2%		7.8%	10.5%	10.9%
CIST										0.1%
CISTBLW			1.2%							2.1%
FRECHEN				95.5%						0.7%
MOT										0.1%
BESSIN							1.8%			0.1%
MS01									0.7%	1.4%
MS12										0.2%
Q40							8.9%	11.8%		4.3%
R02			25.7%		19.1%		22.0%	75.5%	5.7%	13.3%
R02?									10.4%	3.2%
RW12	100.0%	100.0%	49.7%	4.5%	38.2%	82.8%	67.3%	4.9%	70.3%	59.8%
RW12.1										2.5%
S01										0.6%
SLPW					10.3%					0.2%
YW									2.3%	0.7%
Total no.	**3**	**7**	**22**	**2**	**13**	**6**	**22**	**14**	**72**	**305**
Total weight	**7**	**97**	**167**	**22**	**68**	**29**	**168**	**102**	**959**	**3139**

FIGURE 4.13

Wigmore 1996, Phase 10 demolition deposits sequence (earliest 024, latest 017): quantification by percentage sherd weight

some sherds were extremely abraded, whilst others were very 'fresh' looking. Abrasion was spread fairly evenly through Fabrics R02 and RW12 and suggests quite different depositional histories for some of the sherds; some had evidently lain exposed and been weathered and trampled, others may have made a fairly rapid transition from breakage to burial.

Pottery in the possible turfline 024 at the beginning of the Phase 10 dump sequence contained a sherd (2g) initially identified as mottled ware, which dates to the second half of the 17th century at the earliest. It is possible that this has been wrongly identified and is really an RW12 sherd. If it is a mottled ware sherd then it must be intrusive.

Despite some caveats about the ceramic sequence, the group can be seen as a good indicator of the type and range of vessels in use in *c*1550–1640 (Figure 4.14). Drinking vessels were well represented and found in blackware (straight-sided mugs with a carination below the rim; Figure 4.6, 61–62), an imitation Rhenish stoneware drinking jug (Figure 4.6, 63) and a possible barrel-shaped mug (unillustrated), Cistercian ware cups (unillustrated), Cistercian/blackware (cups, e.g. Figure 4.6, 60, and a mug), Rhenish stoneware (Frechen drinking jug, unillustrated), Fabric R02 (a cup Figure 4.6, 65) and RW12 (a cup). Bowls were another well-represented class of vessel. They occurred mainly in Fabric RW12 (Figure 4.6, 67–72) and included flange-rim and wall-rim forms. Bowls in Fabric R02 were not common and were limited to two base sherds and two very small, badly abraded

	No.	Weight	Rim	Base
Drinking vessel	61	337	6	4
Bowl/cup	2	22	1	1
Bowl	56	827	8	6
Chafing dish	1	12	1	
Strainer	1	7		
Jar	23	690	13	2
Jug	31	180	2	1
Small jug	2	13		
Small jug/bottle	1	9		1
Jug?	1	2		
Jug/jar/cistern	9	66		
Total	**188**	**2165**	**31**	**15**

FIGURE 4.14
Wigmore 1996 CG96 02, Phase 10: vessel function

sherds, representing two or three vessels in total. Two yellow ware sherds were from cups or bowls and the trailed slipware sherd was from a bowl. Jars formed another important functional category and were mainly found in Fabric RW12 (Figure 4.6, 73–76) and Fabric R02 (Figure 6.4, 66). Two jars were represented in Fabric RW12.1 (Figure 4.6, 78). A blackware flange-rim bowl or possibly a lid (Figure 4.6, 64), with a purplish-brown, cratered, 'metallic' glaze was a rather more unusual find. A second similar vessel (Figure 4.7, 90) was found in Phase 11. Most jug sherds occurred in Fabric R02, apart from four blackware jug body sherds and seven Fabric Q40 sherds. Possible cistern sherds were found principally in Fabric Q40, with single sherds in Fabric R02 and RW12. The Fabric Q40 sherds were presumably residual from Phase 9. Three less common forms were identified: a possible bottle (Fabric R02), a chafing dish (Fabric RW12, Figure 4.6, 77) and a strainer (Fabric RW12).

The range of vessel forms is nothing special for the period and could be paralleled in many urban sites. A small amount of specialised kitchen ware is evident, such as the chafing dish and the strainer, but this simply does not compare, for example, with the very large quantity of specialised cooking ware dating predominantly to the 16th century, found associated with a late kitchen annexe to the medieval keep at Dudley Castle (personal inspection by the author).

Vessels for liquid consumption and storage are still well represented but the importance of bowls, in particular, and storage jars has grown from the previous phase. Of the eight bowl rims present, 75% were from from wide diameter vessels, more likely to be for food preparation rather than consumption.

Phase 11

Above the rubble dumps of CG96 02 lay mainly humic accumulations which formed CG96 01. This group contained the largest pottery group of all, consisting of 837 sherds. As can be seen from the average sherd weight (Figure 4.10), this material was extremely broken. Surprisingly, there was very little material, if any, likely to pre-date the 15th century and the group of pottery is effectively an amalgam of pottery associated with Phases 9 and 10. Some hitherto unrecorded fabrics were present, such as Cologne and Raeren stoneware and Martincamp Fabrics I and II, which are all likely to pre-date the Civil War slighting of the castle. A tin-glazed eathenware sherd from a small jar or albarello, decorated with blue, green and yellow may date to the Civil War or belong in the second half of the 17th century. Five sherds of mottled ware, weighing a paltry 4g, three slipware drinking vessel sherds (see below) and five rather more substantial 20th-century teapot sherds, presumably representing a picnicking mishap, unequivocally post-date the Civil War.

In terms of the taphonomy of the site, it is not altogether clear where the humic layers and their pottery content (and other finds) came from. A possible explanation is that it had eroded from either the motte itself to the north or from a higher level within the bailey but, if so, the absence of any very early material is puzzling. Also, the cross-joins between CG96 01 and CG96 02 seem contrary to such an explanation. Humic layers, of course, can be generated by natural processes, such as the growth and die-back of vegetation but this does not explain the considerable pottery content. In the 1998 excavation, for example, there is very little pottery in the various demolition layers above the plaster floor (CG98 02–04 and 08–09) and only three sherds within the topsoil (CG98 01). The topsoil within the East Tower (CG98 10) likewise only contained 5 sherds.

There clearly is a higher proportion of pottery which is likely to date to the 17th century in the 1996 excavation, such as the yellow ware and trailed slipware, and by this phase the proportion of Fabric R02 continues to decrease as that of Fabric RW12 and blackware increases. This would suggest some sort of chronological difference between the Phase 11 deposits and those of Phase 10.

The functional analysis of the pottery (Figure 4.15) reveals that drinking vessels were the best represented form, followed by bowls and then jars. This is slightly different from the previous phase where drinking vessels were the least well represented of the three. The much larger size of this pottery group means that the range of forms associated with late medieval and early post-medieval fabrics could be expanded. So, two bifid rim jars with thumbed neck cordons similar to Figure 4.6, 66 (a 16th-century form; Vince 1985a) and two chafing dish sherds were recorded in Fabric R02. Cup sherds, probably part of the vessel Figure 4.6, 65, recorded in the previous phase, were also identified. Flange-rim, bifid rim and wall rim bowls were recorded in Fabric RW12 as well as other bowls types (Figure

	No.	Weight	Rim	Base
Bowl	48	154	20	8
Chafing dish	5	28	1	
Chafing dish/skillet	1	7		
Tripod skillet	1	39		1
Drip tray	2	103	1	1
Drinking vessel	190	659	24	7
Flask	18	56		
Jug	31	234	1	
Jar	20	404	11	4
Cistern	2	14		
Jug/jar/cistern	1	35		
Albarello	1	2		
Lid	2	25	1	
Hollow ware	6	42		
Teapot	5	68		
Roof furniture	1	21		
Total	**334**	**1891**	**59**	**21**

FIGURE 4.15
Wigmore 1996 CG96 01, Phase 11: vessel function

4.7, 92–94). A bowl (Figure 4.7, 94) was the only RW12 bowl to be decorated with an incised wavy line. A bowl with a frilled rim was recorded (Figure 4.7, 95). A handle with a central groove may have been from a jug or a two-handled jar (Figure 4.7, 101). More specialised wares were also recorded in this fabric, such as chafing dishes, a tripod skillet (Figure 4.7, 97) and a dripping tray (Figure 4.7, 96). A small tapering sherd may have been either from a skillet handle or part of a support from the rim of a chafing dish. Other less common forms in this fabric were two drinking vessels (Figure 4.7, 98), a lid sherd (Figure 4.7, 100) and a possible lid (not illustrated). The drinking jug form was found in the Rhenish stonewares, one of which (Raeren) had a trace of impressed decoration (Figure 4.7, 102). There were also imitations of Rhenish stoneware forms in blackware (Figure 4.7, 89). More usual blackware mug forms included a 'corrugated' mug (Figure 4.7, 88). One blackware sherd had a quartz grain embedded in the external surface. The small size of the sherd (1g) makes it difficult to be certain if this was deliberate surface treatment, of the sort favoured by the Lingen or Deerfold potters. Lingen is only three or four kilometers from Wigmore. Four Cistercian/blackware sherds were noted; three form a cup and the fourth decorated with a combed applied white clay strip. The latter sherd resembles pottery found at Ticknall (Spavold and Brown 2005) but a more local source should not be ruled out.

Yellow ware forms (not illustrated) consisted of bowls, a mug, a cup and a possible jar. Identification of the yellow ware forms was hampered by the small sherd size. A lid-seated rim blackware bowl (Figure 4.7, 90) was recorded, the same form as another one (Figure 4.6, 64) from Phase 10, and probably three blackware jugs were represented by body sherds. The jugs and the jar are likely to date to the 17th century.

A maximum of four light-on-dark trailed slipware bowls were present. Sherds from one of them were found in CG96 02, Phase 11 (see above). Two other slipware vessels, large mugs or small bowls, were recorded. These were of a type belonging to the late 17th and 18th centuries and consisted of a dark brown or black-glazed exterior, decorated with white slip trails, and a yellow-glazed interior. This type of slipware was made both in Staffordshire (Barker and Crompton 2007, 22–24) and in Bristol (Barton 1963, 164–167) and it is difficult to distinguish between them.

Flasks were only found in Martincamp I and II fabrics. The former dates to *c*1475–1550 and the latter is common in the 16th century, although there is a 'considerable overlap' (Hurst *et al* 1986, 104) in all three of the Martincamp fabrics, and the type II fabric, for example, has been found in Civil War levels at Dudley Castle (personal inspection by the author).

The pottery from the final phase of the castle's history is primarily associated with vessels of consumption, particularly liquid consumption. Vessels for the storage of liquids are also well represented, as in previous phases. Some of the wider-mouthed Fabric RW12 bowls could have been used for food preparation but those with smaller diameters (18–23cm range) were probably used for the serving or consumption of food. The latter type was more frequent, with 11 bowls; wide-mouthed bowls were represented by seven rim sherds, and two rims were too fragmentary to measure. The functional make up of the group can give no definite answer to from where the pottery derived, since it contains elements of the kitchen, the pantry (or other storage areas) and living areas.

A relatively large percentage of drinking vessels would be fairly typical of Civil War deposits from castles. However, some vessel types one might expect to find are absent. There are, for example, no chamber pots or stool pots as were found at Sandal Castle (Brears 1983), and Dudley Castle (personal inspection by the author). At Sandal Castle, the provenance of the chamber pots suggested that small groups of soldiers were issued with one to share between the group, and seem to be a feature of a military garrison. Their absence at Wigmore, therefore, may be another strand of evidence (see Chapters 9 and 10) indicating very little or no occupation at the castle at about the time of the Civil War. Shallow flange rim bowls, what we might term today dishes or deep plates, for the consumption of food were also absent. This could be interpreted in two contradictory ways. Either metal dishes, such as pewter plates, could have been used, which would suggest rather better-off occupants of the castle in the 17th century, or wooden vessels were in use, which would suggest inhabitants of more modest means.

The 1998 excavations

Outside the East Tower

The pottery from the 1998 excavations did not have the same coherence as that from 1996. It formed about a fifth of the total assemblage and was marked often by very low numbers of sherds from individual context groups. Only three groups, CG98 13, CG98 20 and CG98 21 contained 50 or more sherds (Figures 4.16–4.17). Early levels were not reached even in the 1998B excavations and we are reliant on the 1996 pottery to furnish information about ceramic use in the early years of the castle. A number of sherds came from 1998B contexts for which no records survive (Figure 4.18). There is some early material within these contexts (Fabrics Q01, Q20 and a Ham Green ware sherd, the only occurrence of this fabric on the site) but also later material such as RW10 and R02. It is quite impossible to determine how this pottery and the contexts from which it came might relate to the 1998A excavation, although it is possible that the majority of it came from lower levels in the large pit, outside the tower. The presence of these later fabrics in 1998B need not, therefore, have any effect on the proposed chronology of 1998A.

Early construction: Phases 3 and 4

A number of major events were witnessed in this area of excavation: the construction of the East Tower, the laying of a plaster floor (599) which effectively divided and sealed earlier deposits from the later ones, and the destruction of the East Tower. These provide a framework in which to view the remaining context groups. Some idea of the degree of disturbance in the pre-plaster floor groups is witnessed by a unique find, a ceramic bottle (Figure 4.5, 34) in Fabric R10, sherds from which were found in Context Groups CG98 12, CG98 16–17, CG98 20–21, and CG98 33. Likewise, sherds from a micaceous, siltstone-tempered bowl were found in Context Groups CG98 12, CG98 15, CG98 20–21. Sherds from both these vessels were particularly distinctive and could be tracked easily through the assemblage. There is a strong possibility that there were more examples of cross-joining sherds that were not recognised during cataloguing. For example, a number of small RW10 jugs sherds with a good quality glossy olive glaze with darker green mottles (caused by the addition of copper to the glaze), were found in CG98 14, CG98 16, CG98 17, CG98 20–21 and may also represent parts of the same vessel, smashed into many pieces but surprisingly unabraded.

The construction trench for the East Tower (Phase 4) contained no pottery but a possible nailed binding and a key were found in the fill (see Chapter 5), together with iron slag. A substantial layer 653 which overlay the construction trench fill contained no pottery or other finds. The absence of pottery in the construction trench and overlying layer is unusual and cannot be easily explained, although it is, of course, paralleled by the lower fills of the Southern Curtain Wall construction trench in the 1996 excavations (see above).

A construction trench for a possibly earlier wall 711 (CG98 25, Phase 4) contained a siltstone-tempered pitcher sherd (Fabric S11) which had a dull olive glaze and was decorated with incised horizontal lines. The fabric resembles some of the siltstone-tempered wares found at Hen Domen (see Fabric Type 2 and variants; Clarke 1982, 77). The sherd is likely to date to the 12th century and its weight of 17g suggests that it is probably not residual in the fill (but see below). Fabric S11 first appears in Phase 4 in the 1996 excavations but the fabric is closely related to, if not a variant of, Fabric S10 which first appeared towards the end of Phase 3.

Context Group CG98 22, Phase 3, was another potentially early group. A Fabric MS11 sherd was recovered from 725, a possible occupation surface, which overlay green clay 727 (the earliest context identified on the site), although the description of 725 as a 'red gritty layer' is strongly reminiscent of red mortar deposits within the construction trench for the Southern Curtain Wall CG96 17. This layer overlay another layer which appeared to pre-date all masonry construction in the area. Unfortunately, the sherd recovered from 725 weighed only 2g, so there is some margin for error in its identification. Fabric MS11 is the equivalent of Hereford Fabric A4 (Vince 1985a, 39–40) and is a micaceous ware, containing large, rounded pieces of siltstone. It was not a common fabric at Wigmore. The sherd was from a jug with an orange glaze with dark green copper speckles, and was decorated with horizontal combing. The dating of the sherd is 13th- to 14th-century. A Fabric MS11 sherd was associated with levelling immediately after the construction of the curtain wall in in the 1996 excavations (CG96 16).

Clay dumps (CG98 09, Phase 4) above 725 contained 12 sherds in total. The uppermost dump 710 was cut through by the construction trench for wall 711, dated to the 12th century by the pottery. The pottery from the dumps is somewhat confused. Early material is represented by Q01 cooking pots sherds, a Q20 large jug or pitcher sherd with a dull opaque olive glaze and a deep band of square roller-stamping and an S11 pitcher sherd with a yellowish-olive glaze with copper speckling, all of which could be 12th century or early 13th century in date. Sherds of MS01 cooking pot could date to the later 12th century but here may be more likely to date to the early 13th century. However, the uppermost dump 710, through which the wall construction trench was cut, contained single sherds of MS02 and RW10, both of which were covered in mortary deposits. Two further sherds, recovered from sample

Phase	**9**	**9**	**8**	**8**	**8**	**8**	**5**	**5**	**4**	**4**	**4**	**3**
Group	**12**	**14**	**15**	**16**	**17**	**20**	**21**	**33**	**9**	**24**	**25**	**22**
MS11												100.0%
S11									30.8%		100.0%	
MS01	27.5%	3.1%	43.4%	13.4%		22.5%	23.9%		23.8%	51.7%		
MS01?							10.7%					
Q01		6.9%						9.8%	11.2%	48.3%		
MS02		2.5%		2.0%	5.5%	3.0%			1.4%			
MS12				20.5%			3.8%	32.0%	6.3%			
MS12?								15.6%				
Q20								3.3%	17.5%			
RW10	22.5%	62.3%		11.1%	33.7%	34.2%	16.7%		9.1%			
R10	5.9%			2.3%	19.6%	3.4%	10.1%	15.6%				
S10			8.2%					23.8%				
MS03	21.6%	10.7%		1.7%	6.1%	23.8%	13.5%					
Q31							1.0%					
Q60				0.7%	23.3%		6.0%					
Q70							0.1%					
R01		8.2%					6.3%					
R02	18.6%	1.9%	41.8%	17.1%	11.7%	6.4%	6.0%					
S01		2.5%				4.4%	1.0%					
S20							0.8%					
Q40						1.0%						
NfrWW						1.3%						
RW13			6.6%	10.1%								
RW11				6.7%								
TG				14.4%								
CIST	3.9%	1.9%										
Sherd weight	102g	159g	122g	298g	163g	298g	731g	122g	143g	29g	17g	2g
Sherd count	18	19	11	33	20	51	78	11	12	2	1	1
ASW	5.5g	8g	11g	9g	8g	6g	9g	11g	12g	14.5g	17g	2

FIGURE 4.16

Wigmore 1998 outside East Tower: pottery quantification (by % weight) by context group, Phases 3–9 (beneath plaster floor 559) (ASW = average sherd weight)

Phase	**11**	**11**	**11**	**10**	**10**	**9**
Group	**1**	**2**	**3**	**4**	**13**	**8**
MS03						100.0%
MS01		0.5%			3.2%	
R01					1.4%	
R02		17.6%			31.2%	
RW10					1.4%	
RW11					1.1%	
S01					3.4%	
CIST		41.7%		7.8%	58.2%	
MS02				7.8%		
RW12		20.3%		84.3%		
VITR			75.0%			
BLW	88.4%	5.4%	25.0%			
COLOGNE		13.2%				
S10		1.2%				
MOT	11.6%					
Sherd weight	43g	408g	16g	51g	349g	4g
Sherd count	3	29	2	4	50	1
ASW	14g	14g	8g	12.5g	7g	4g

FIGURE 4.17

Wigmore 1998 outside East Tower: pottery quantification (by % weight) by context group, Phases 9–11 (above plaster floor 559) (ASW = average sherd weight)

	677	692	693	694	695	696	702	709	718
Ham Green			x						
MS01			x		x	x		x	
MS03	x				x				
MS12					x				
Q20		x							
Q01				x		x			x
R01							x		
R02			x						
R10			x						
RW10				x	x				
S01				x		x			
S11					x	x			

FIGURE 4.18

Pottery from Wigmore 1998B excavation (unphased)

2223, were from 710 (Fabrics Q01 and MS01). It is extremely unlikely that MS02 and RW10 pre-date *c*1250. A third sherd (Fabric MS12) which should post-date *c*1250 was found in dump 708, which was below 710. The evidence, therefore, would seem to indicate that wall 711 was constructed after *c*1250 but there is always a nagging doubt that the clay dumps have been contaminated by material from CG98 33 and CG98 21, a series of deposits cut by pit 675, and a gravel surface and associated occupation layers respectively (see below).

One final constructional activity was CG98 24. This was a cut of uncertain purpose. The upper fill, 706, contained two cooking pot sherds, in Fabrics Q01 and MS01 respectively. The pottery suggests a backfill date in the first half of the 13th century.

Pre-plaster floor 559 deposits: Phases 5, 8 and 9

A series of dumps of material were interleaved with a gravel floor, 659 (Phase 5) and associated occupation layers above (CG98 21, Phase 5), and a plaster floor, 631 (Phase 8) and possible make-up layers (CG98 14 and 12, Phase 9), before the well preserved plaster floor (559, CG98 8, Phase 9) sealed everything (Figure 4.16). One of the better sized groups of pottery came from CG98 21.

Layers 666 and 663 CG98 21, below the gravel floor 659, contained a sherd of 12th- or early 13th- century Malvernian cooking pot and a siltstone-tempered cooking pot sherd of similar date, respectively. A second Malvernian cooking pot sherd, probably from the same vessel, was found within the gravel surface. All three sherds were residual. A second sherd in Fabric Q31, which is likely to post-date *c*1250, was found in the gravel floor. Sherds from occupation levels above the gravel floor seemed to form a fairly cohesive group with a minimal amount of residual material (two sherds of Fabric S01). Locally produced Fabric MS01 was dominant and accounted for just over a third of the pottery from this group by weight. Fabrics RW10 and MS03 were the next best represented. Both these fabrics indicate a *terminus post quem* of the mid-13th century for the gravel floor and occupation deposits. Fabric MS03 first appears in the 1996 excavation in Phase 6 and RW10 a little earlier. Malvern Chase ware (Fabric R02) first appears towards the top of the group in contexts 646 and 652. Vince (1985a) dates this ware in Hereford to the late 14th to 17th centuries. A Malvernian cooking pot (Fabric R01) in 652 is of a form dating to the late 13th or early 14th century. The cooking pot had a drilled hole, possibly from a riveted repair. Also in 652 was a small sherd of Fabric Q70, possibly a Boarstall-Brill type.

In terms of vessel function, CG98 21 was composed almost exclusively of jug sherds. A small component was made up of MS01 cooking pot and bowl sherds, although these probably represent only two cooking pots (one wheel-thrown) and a maximum of three bowls. The Fabric R10 bottle (Figure 4.5, 34, see above) was found in this group. An R02 sherd may have come from a bottle or small jug. A preponderance of jug sherds was a feature of Phases 6–8 in the 1996 excavations.

The jug sherds were generally small so there was little diagnostic material and only three vessels were suitable for illustration (Figure 4.5, 35–37). None of the jug sherds was decorated. A Fabric MS03 jug had a thumbed base (Figure 4.5, 36) and was one of the few base sherds in the group. Jug rim sherds in Fabric RW10 (Figure 4.5, 37) and MS01 (Figure 4.5, 35) have also been illustrated.

Independent dating of this group was provided by a copper-alloy jeton from context 652 (SF1762, Chapter 5) with a suggested loss date of *c*1325–50, which would seem about right for the pottery from this context, although a little early for the Malvern Chase ware (Fabric R02). Exactly when this ware first started to be made is not certain. Vince (1985a) suggests that it was first in use in Hereford in the late 14th century. At Droitwich, Hurst (1992) cites Vince for the dating of Malvernian ware there. It is possible that the evidence from Wigmore suggests a start date of around the mid-14th century or the Malvernian ware in 652 and 646 may be contamination from CG98 20 above. Internally the pottery from CG98 21 most closely resembles that from Phases 6 and 7 in the 1996 excavations.

Above CG98 21 were dumps of material (CG98 20) possibly used as make-up for the plaster floor 631. The pottery was largely similar to that found in CG98 21, both in terms of fabric and function. A whiteware jug sherd with a clear glaze with copper green speckles (NFrWW) found in this group is a residual French import.

The relationship between CG98 20 and the underlying CG98 21 is not easy to understand. In terms of the context composition, the silty occupation-type layers above the gravel floor 659 are clearly different from the loam, sand and mortary deposits beneath the plaster floor 631. However, not only is the pottery from the two groups virtually identical in terms of fabrics and function, but sherds from the same vessels are scattered across the two groups and do not only occur at the interface of the two groups. There is very little residual material in either group and all that can be said with any certainty is that the two groups were deposited after the mid-13th century and before the end of the 14th century.

Context Group CG98 33, which it is suggested was contemporary with CG98 21, is rather different in composition, although it contained only a small amount of pottery (11 sherds, weighing 122g) and may not be entirely trustworthy. The group is linked to CG98 20 and CG98 21 by the presence of sherds from the R10 bottle (Figure 4.5, 34) but the group has a noticeable residual component of cooking pots in Fabrics Q01, Q20 and S10. Fabric MS12 (e.g. Figure 4.5, 33) which forms the greater part of this group is only poorly represented in CG98 21. One jug sherd was decorated with an applied rosette and had a good quality, dark green glaze and under-glaze white slip (Figure 4.5, 32). This was the only sherd from this vessel identified from the site. A second unique vessel was found in this group, that of a small jar with an internal and external glossy olive glaze, again in Fabric MS12 (Figure 4.5, 33). Typologically, it is difficult to believe that this vessel is earlier than the 14th century. A second sherd from this vessel was found in CG98 16 in a fill of ditch 664.

Before the second plaster floor, 559, was laid, there was a period of marked disturbance characterised by cut features and demolition debris (CG98 15–17). The earliest feature, 675, situated against the curtain wall, cut CG98 33 and was in turn cut by 664, itself cut by 658. Comparatively little pottery was recovered from their fills. The fill of pit 675 (CG98 17) was broadly similar to that from CG98 20. Sherds from vessels found in CG98 20 and CG98 21 had made their way into the pit fill, including more of the Fabric R10 bottle. Three sherds from a jug decorated with an applied rosette and curvilinear strip (Figure 4.5, 47) were found in the fill. A sherd from the same distinctive vessel was found in CG98 21. Typologically this vessel should date to *c*1250–1350 and finds its nearest parallel at Haughmond Abbey, near Shrewsbury (Rátkai forthcoming b, fig P6, 89). There was a single sherd of R02, thick-walled and glazed that may have come from a jar. If so a 15th-century date is most likely for the sherd.

By the time feature 664 (CG98 16) was backfilled Malvern Chase ware was becoming more prominent, which suggests a date in the 15th century. Other factors pointing to this century are the presence of a Fabric RW13 jar, a Tudor Green cup or bowl base (Figure 4.5, 49), which was chipped and abraded, and an RW11 jug sherd with a bib of brown glaze. The fabric of the latter was similar to Cistercian ware. Sherds from vessels found in CG98 17, CG98 20 (Figure 4.5, 46), CG98 21 and 33 were noted. A rod handle in Fabric MS12 (Figure 4.5, 48) was decorated with vertical and oblique slashing, unlikely to occur after *c*1350. This handle was one of the few chronologically diagnostic sherds for this fabric.

The backfill material in cut 658 (CG98 15) came from the lower fill and shares many of the characteristics of the fill of cut 664; the pottery is probably mainly redeposited material from earlier groups such as the rim of an S10 cooking pot (Figure 4.5, 51), possibly the same vessel as that found in CG98 33, and more of the MS01 cooking pot (Figure 4.5, 46) found in CG98 20 and CG98 16. The functional composition of this group is slightly different. A probably residual Fabric MS01 dripping tray with a thumbed rim (Figure 4.5, 50) was noted in the fill, the first time in the stratigraphic sequence that this form had been identified. The form repertoire for Fabric RW13 was increased by the presence of a bowl and a jug. A Malvern Chase jar sherd may have been part of a jar found in CG98 11, Phase 10 (demolition or decay of the East Tower).

A silver half-groat of Edward III was found in the lower fill of 658 (SF1996). Symons (Chapter 5) suggests a loss date towards the middle of the 15th century as most likely, although with some reservations. Such a date would be perfectly in keeping with the pottery from CG98 15 and CG98 16.

The episode of cut features and dumping of demolition material was followed by preparation of the site for the laying of a plaster floor 559 (CG98 12 and CG98 14, Phase 9) by the dumping of rubble. The rubble layers contained very little pottery and the greater part may well have been disturbed and redeposited from earlier groups. The significant pottery from CG98 12 and CG98 14 was Cistercian ware. The two cup sherds indicate that the plaster floor 559 must have been laid after *c*1480. One, probably residual, sherd of Fabric MS03 was found within the plaster floor itself (CG98 08).

The pottery from the pre-plaster floor groups (excluding CG98 09, CG98 22 and CG98 24) is both commonplace and enigmatic. The dominance of glazed wares, in particular jugs, is precisely what would be expected on most medieval sites in the later 13th to 15th centuries. The paucity of specialised cooking vessels such as the pipkin and dripping tray, which one might expect to be fairly well represented on a castle site, can be explained by the small sample size of both the pottery and the area excavated. The pottery is made up of local or fairly local wares. The fairly local wares such as RW10 and Malvern Chase ware (Fabric R02) are widely distributed within the county. The possible Boarstall-Brill sherd and the Tudor Green sherd, although far from their source of manufacture are, nevertheless, widely traded in England and beyond. Even the possible French import is not so noteworthy — a Saintonge sherd, for example, was found at Leominster (Rátkai 2001) — and presumably arrived at Wigmore via the ports of Bristol or Chester. In short, there is little in the pre-plaster floor groups in terms of fabrics or vessel function which would mark the pottery out as having been found on a castle site.

The enigmatic component finds its expression in the amount of disturbance and residuality evidenced in the pottery from after the construction of the gravel floor up to the point of the construction of the second plaster floor. Sherds from the same vessels are clearly distributed throughout the eight context groups and yet each group represents a quite distinct activity, some of which would cause disturbance and redeposition of material, some of which should not. For a phase which seems to span roughly 200 years, 251 sherds were deposited, which probably represented possibly no more than 25 vessels. Although most of the sherds were small (the average sherd weight for most groups was less than 10g and the highest average sherd weight 11g) they were not especially worn or chipped. Considering the rather limited amount of pottery, there were a surprising number of other artefactual finds (see Chapter 5).

Post-plaster floor 559 deposits: Phases 9–11
(Figure 4.17)

Context Groups CG98 05, CG98 06, CG98 07 and CG98 19 post-dated the plaster floor 559 but did not produce a single sherd of pottery and very few other artefacts.

Early decay over the plaster floor, CG98 04, Phase 10, which also sealed the large post-holes cut through the floor (CG98 07), consisted of several layers but contained very little pottery. A total of four sherds were found which comprised one Cistercian ware cup sherd, a Fabric RW12 jar sherd and another possible jar sherd, and a residual Fabric MS02 jug sherd. The RW12 jar sherd may have had a thumbed neck cordon, imitating the Malvern Chase ware jars. What pottery there was seems to date to the 16th century. There is always a chance that the Cistercian ware sherds found beneath the plaster floor were intrusive, caused by the digging of the CG98 07 post-holes through the plaster floor. The Cistercian ware sherd from CG98 04 was almost at the bottom of the deposit sequence.

The near absence of pottery in this group is interesting and could point to several things. Was, for example, the plaster floor the bedding for a tile or stone flagged floor? If so, then the removal of tiles and flags could have led to the removal of any accumulated finds deposits. If the plaster surface was indeed a floor, then it was kept clean during use, which would be expected, but did not suffer a period of abandonment when debris was dumped or allowed to accumulate. This would suggest a fairly rapid sequence of events from disuse to demolition rather than a slow period of decline and decay.

A second series of demolition deposits (CG98 13, Phase 10) overlay the stone-slabbed floor (CG98 05). These may have been contemporary with CG98 04. The pottery formed a largish group of 50 sherds. The dump immediately overlying the slabs contained no pottery, but layers above this contained a mix of Cistercian ware and Malvern Chase ware (Fabric R02), a Fabric RW11 sherd and four residual sherds (Fabrics R01, MS01, RW10 and S01). The layers were almost certainly deposited around *c*1525–50. Five Cistercian cups were present, one of which was decorated with applied white clay pads (Figure 4.6, 79). A complete base and lower section of one cup was made up of 16 joining sherds (Figure 4.6, 80). Jug and jar sherds were found in Fabric R02. Unlike the Cistercian ware, these tended to be abraded, often quite heavily.

Also in this group was pottery from a possible cut 583, marking the edge of the floor. It contained slightly different pottery from the dump layers over the floor and consisted of six Fabric R02 sherds from a small jug, a Fabric RW10 jar rim and a Fabric MS01 cooking pot sherd which was from the same vessel (Figure 4.5, 46) found in CG98 15 and CG98 16.

Further demolition and decay was witnessed in CG98 02, Phase 11. Considering the number of contexts within this group there was very little pottery. To the north, where most of the deposits were found, 523 was a possible turf line and was at the base of the dumps. This contained Fabric R02 and Cistercian ware (and one residual sherd) suggesting 523 formed in the 16th century. A Fabric R02 bottle or small jug (Figure 4.7, 105) from this context had a vertical band of external soot, suggesting it had been put to some quite specific use. Similar sooting patterns have been noted on ceramic bottles from Shrewsbury at the Owen Owen site (personal inspection by the author). A coin of Henry VIII from 523 had a suggested loss date of *c*1530–50, which seems about right for the pottery.

To the south, pottery was only found in 519 and consisted of a two-handled Cistercian ware cup (Figure 4.7, 103) with an internal deposit. All of the rim was present and the sherd was fairly substantial at 132g. It is possible that this vessel belongs more properly in CG98 04.

What both 519 and 523 seem to demonstrate is that the first phase of demolition and abandonment had occurred by *c*1550. Context 519 was cut by a shallow pit and post-holes for possible wall props (CG98 03). A blackware mug handle and a vitrified sherd possibly from a ceramic bottle were found in this group.

The dump layers to the north over 523 contained a small but interesting group of pottery (Figure 4.19). The only example of a chafing dish from the 1998 excavations was found here, although several were recorded in the 1996 excavations. The first and only occurrence of Rhenish stoneware outside the East Tower was also in 525. Rhenish stoneware is often plentiful on castle sites (compare Stafford

	RO2	RW12	Cistercian ware	Blackware	Cologne stoneware	S10 residual	MS01 residual
Cup			6				
Mug				5			
Drinking jug					3		
Jug	1					1	1
Bottle/small jug	1						
Jar		6					
Chafing dish	1						
Watering pot		1					
Unknown	2	1					
Total sherd count	**5**	**8**	**6**	**5**	**3**	**1**	**1**

FIGURE 4.19

Wigmore 1998 CG98 02, Phase 11: vessel function

Castle, Rátkai 2007) but apparently not so in the area of the East Tower.

The one rare find in this group is the top of a watering pot (Figure 4.7, 104). These vessels had a single narrow opening at the top and a multiply pierced base. The pot was submerged in water, filled and the thumb placed over the top opening, which kept the water within the vessel. Once the thumb was removed from the opening, the water could then flow freely through the perforated base. The watering pot not only shows that there was gardening within the castle but that some of the plants must have been grown in containers, suggesting a decorative, recreational garden.

The date of these dumps is not easy to establish. There is a possibility that the RW12 jar was part of the same vessel found in CG98 04. The blackware mug sherds indicate a deposition date after *c*1550 and through into the 17th century. If the entire pottery group is contemporary then a deposition date of *c*1600 is possible but there really is no way to ascertain the likely degree of residuality. What the ceramics cannot tell us is whether the dumps were deposited before the Civil War, at the time of the Civil War slighting or after the Civil War, or whether the dumps are discrete episodes or represent a gradual process over time.

Within the East Tower: Phases 10 and 11

Excavation within the East Tower ceased before the base of the tower was reached. The archaeology consisted of a series of dumps which were divided into two groups (Figure 4.20). The earlier and more substantial group was CG98 11. This contained the single largest pottery group from the 1998 site. The sherds were small with an average sherd weight of 8g. There is a reasonable amount of residual pottery but this seems to increase in the higher or later dumps (Figure 4.21). This could indicate that surface material was used in the lower dumps and then material was dug out to form the upper fills. There was some evidence that sherds in the tower dumps came from the same vessels as those found outside the tower. The evidence was somewhat limited and consisted of a sherd from a French import and sherds in Fabric Q60 and Fabric Q70, all found in pre-plaster floor levels. A further link was between sherds from a Fabric R02 jar found in pre-plaster floor levels also (see above).

The earliest excavated dump, 665, consisted primarily of 15th-century pottery and was made up mainly of jug sherds, including a Fabric RW13 jug (Figure 4.6, 85). Fragments of this jug were found in several contexts. One or possibly two cisterns (bung hole jars) were found in this group. This was the only group from the excavations that contained Midlands Purple ware. There was no Cistercian ware in CG98 11 but the presence of RW12 in the middle of the fill sequence is more consistent with 16th-century deposition. Fills 610, 604 and 587 only contained Malvern Chase ware and seem to form some sort of interlude before the final fills. Fill 556 could have been deposited any time after the mid-16th century. The minute chip of blackware (<1g) in 550 may date to the 17th century.

	CG98 10, Phase 11	CG98 11, Phase 10
COLOGNE		4.4%
RW13		5.0%
MP		0.4%
MS01		8.8%
MS02		2.7%
MS03		4.5%
MS12?		0.6%
Q01		4.1%
Q11		1.0%
Q20		0.2%
Q32		0.2%
Q40		0.1%
Q60		0.8%
Q70		0.1%
R01		1.1%
R02		40.8%
RW10		10.7%
RW11		0.4%
RW12		10.2%
S01		0.6%
S10		1.9%
NfrWW		1.1%
WW02?		0.4%
MGW	29.5%	
MOT	70.5%	
Sherd weight	88	1416
Sherd count	5	170
ASW	17.6g	8.3g

FIGURE 4.20

Wigmore 1998 East Tower: pottery quantification (by % weight) by context group, Phases 10 and 11

	Earliest →											Latest →			
Context	**665**	**644**	**648**	**643**	**640**	**630**	**629**	**622**	**611**	**610**	**604**	**587**	**550**	**556**	**Total**
RW10	50.0%	25.4%	10.2%	1*	24.0%	41.5%	2.7%		11.4%						10.7%
R02	21.8%	62.7%	10.2%		2.4%		6.8%		70.9%	1*	1*	1*			40.8%
RW13	16.4%		18.7%		2.4%		8.6%								5.0%
MP	5.5%														0.4%
MS03	0.9%		5.4%		20.0%		13.1%								4.5%
MS02	0.9%						14.9%		5.1%						2.7%
Q20	2.7%														0.2%
Q40	1.8%														0.1%
MS01		11.9%	19.3%		19.2%	31.7%	18.1%	10.5%	8.9%						8.8%
Q01			22.3%		14.4%		1.4%								4.1%
S10			13.9%		3.2%										1.9%
Q11					8.0%			21.1%							1.0%
S01					6.4%										0.6%
Q60						26.8%									0.8%
Q70							0.5%								0.1%
R01							6.8%								1.1%
RW12							17.2%						63.1%		10.2%
NfrWW							7.2%								1.1%
WW02?							2.7%								0.4%
MS12?								42.1%							0.6%
RW11								26.3%							0.4%
Q32									3.8%						0.2%
BLW														1*	
COLOGNE													36.9%		4.4%

FIGURE 4.21

Wigmore 1998 East Tower pottery: pottery quantification (by % weight) by context, Phases 10 and 11. 1 denotes 100.0%*

Some changes in the functional component of CG98 11 are also visible (Figure 4.22). Contexts 610, 604 and 587 contained mainly jar sherds, probably indicative of a 16th-century deposition date. These were less well represented earlier in the sequence where jugs predominated. Drinking vessels did not appear until the final two fills. A rare find in context 550 was a thick pierced base in Fabric RW12 (Figure 4.6, 84). This may be the base of the watering pot found outside the tower (Figure 4.7, 104) although it may be a little too thick for this. An alternative interpretation is that is part of something like a cheese-press.

Overall, however, the dominant form within the East Tower backfill was the jug. Drinking vessels and bowls were poorly represented. The relatively high proportion of cooking pots/jars, suggests, as does the relative fabric proportions (see above) that there is a fair amount of residuality in this context group. The Phase 10 deposits from outside the Tower (CG98 04 and CG98 13, Figure 4.23) present a very different picture, although containing much less pottery. Here drinking vessels were the dominant form and jars were better represented.

Above CG98 11 was the topsoil (CG98 10). Only five sherds were found, one of which was a mottled ware sherd with a pale brown fabric and under-glaze white slip dating to the second half of the 17th or 18th century. A 19th-century utilitarian whiteware sherd was also found in this group. The turf and topsoil outside the East Tower (CG98 01) was similarly bereft of pottery and contained three sherds only: a 17th-century blackware mug sherd, a blackware jug sherd and a mottled ware sherd.

4.4 DISCUSSION

As can be seen from the above, there is nothing which would mark out the pottery assemblages as coming from a castle or high-status site. The absence of highly decorated wares is striking and all the more so since their *floruit* coincides with the ownership of the castle by Roger (V) Mortimer, the first Earl of March, a period of lavish displays at the castle. Likewise, more unusual cooking vessels such as pipkins, dripping trays and skillets were poorly represented throughout the assemblage and tend to occur in the later periods of the castle's history.

The Mortimer power base was principally in the Welsh Marches and Wales with, for example, the castles of Ludlow, Montgomery, Chirk, Narberth, Richards Castle, Stapleton Castle, Castell Tinboeth, Cymaron, Pembridge, Cefnllys, Caerphilly, Denbigh, Ewyas Lacy, Elmley, New Radnor, counted amongst their holdings (Figure 4.24; see also Figure 10.1). In addition they were in possession of Bridgnorth Castle, manors in Worcestershire, and lordships were held in virtually every county in southern England

Form	No.	Weight	Rim	Base
Bowl	2	17		1
Bowl?	1	18		
Cooking pot	14	154	2	1
Drinking vessel	4	62		
Jar	9	126	1	
Jar?	16	105	1	
Jug/jar	18	188		2
Jug	50	322	7	3
Jug small	1	11		1
Jug?	4	9		
Jug/cistern	1	21		
Jug/jar/cistern	3	38	1	
Press/garden furniture	2	90		
Ridge tile	1	7		
Unknown	44	248		3
Total	**170**	**1416**	**11**	**12**

FIGURE 4.22

Wigmore 1998 East Tower CG98 11, Phase 10: vessel function

Form	No.	Weight	Rim	Base
Cup	24	207	1	2
Jar	1	29	1	
Jar?	10	56	1	
Jug	4	17		
Jug small	6	31		1
Unknown	7	44		1
Total	**54**	**400**	**3**	**4**

FIGURE 4.23

Wigmore 1998 outside the East Tower CG98 04 and 13, Phase 10: vessel function

from Gloucestershire to Berkshire, and there were substantial holdings in Meath, Connaught and Ulster in Ireland. Despite this, the pottery from Wigmore Castle is staunchly local in character with a handful of exceptions indicating either commercial links or the baggage of the travelling household.

Nearby at Dolforwyn Castle (Powys), which came into Mortimer possession in the late 1270s, and seems to have been largely redundant before the end of the 14th century, the pottery comprised 28% Hereford wares, 25% Chesire Plain, 14% Welsh Border 12% Castell-y-Bere and 2% Malvern (Butler 1997, 203), again suggesting a limited area of supply and one which was substantially local. No ceramic or other finds were associated with the brief period in which the castle was in Welsh hands. At Dryslwyn (Carmarthenshire) a predominantly local supply was augmented by pottery from Bristol and from south-west France (Webster 2007). Webster notes that there was less pottery under English occupation and conjectures that the prestige of the castle when in Welsh hands (that is, before 1288) may have drawn the Bristol and French pottery away from its mainly coastal distribution. At Montgomery Castle (Powys), which perhaps is a better parallel for Wigmore Castle, although no absolute quantification of the pottery is given, it is clear that local products dominate with an admixture of Herefordshire, Malvernian and other West Midlands pottery (Knight 1991a). Wares imported from outside Britain came from the Mediterranean area (archaic maiolica and North African Maghrebi ware), France (Rouen and Saintonge) and possibly Germany (?Langerwehe stoneware). However, these imports were very few in number, and considering a much greater area was excavated at Montgomery Castle, the two North French sherds from Wigmore seem rather more acceptable than would at first appear. The striking difference though, between Montgomery and Wigmore is the range and variety of pottery from the post-medieval period found at the former. Here imported pottery from the Iberian Peninsula, the Mediterranean, North France, Germany and North Italy were found, a good number of which date from the late 16th or 17th centuries, exactly the period when Wigmore seems to be in serious decline.

In terms of the ceramics, the first three phases of occupation at Wigmore Castle are characterised by a rather austere and utilitarian range of vessels, although the dietary evidence (see Chapter 7) indicates markedly high status. Cooking pots predominated in the first two phases and only a small amount of glazed sherds were found in Phase 3. The Phase 1 cooking pot sherds must represent vessels used by fitz Osbern's men as they toiled on the first castle and it is entirely possible that they were brought with them from further south in Herefordshire. What arrangements were made in the following phase for the provision of pottery is unclear. The sandy cooking pots (Fabric Q01) in Phases 1 and 2 cannot be differentiated from each other under x20 magnification, although petrological or chemical analysis might reveal subtle differences. Fabric Q20 may well be a local response to the castle's needs but it appears to have been limited to the 12th century and never replaced Fabric Q01, which seems still to have been in use in the 13th century.

Pottery from Phase 2 is of interest since it is the only group with limescale present on the Fabric Q01 cooking pots. This is indicative of repeated boiling of water within the vessels. This phase also contained particularly high amounts of fish bone and eggshell and it is hard to escape from the conclusion that the timber building and hearth, if not in fact a kitchen, were used at times for cooking. Clearly the absence of limescale on later cooking pots points to quite different methods of cooking from Phase 3 onwards. Sooting patterns on the Phase 2 cooking pots indicate that they were used over an open wood fire. Two vessels seem to have been sunk into the embers since sooting was only found from a little way above the base angle upwards. Other pots may have been

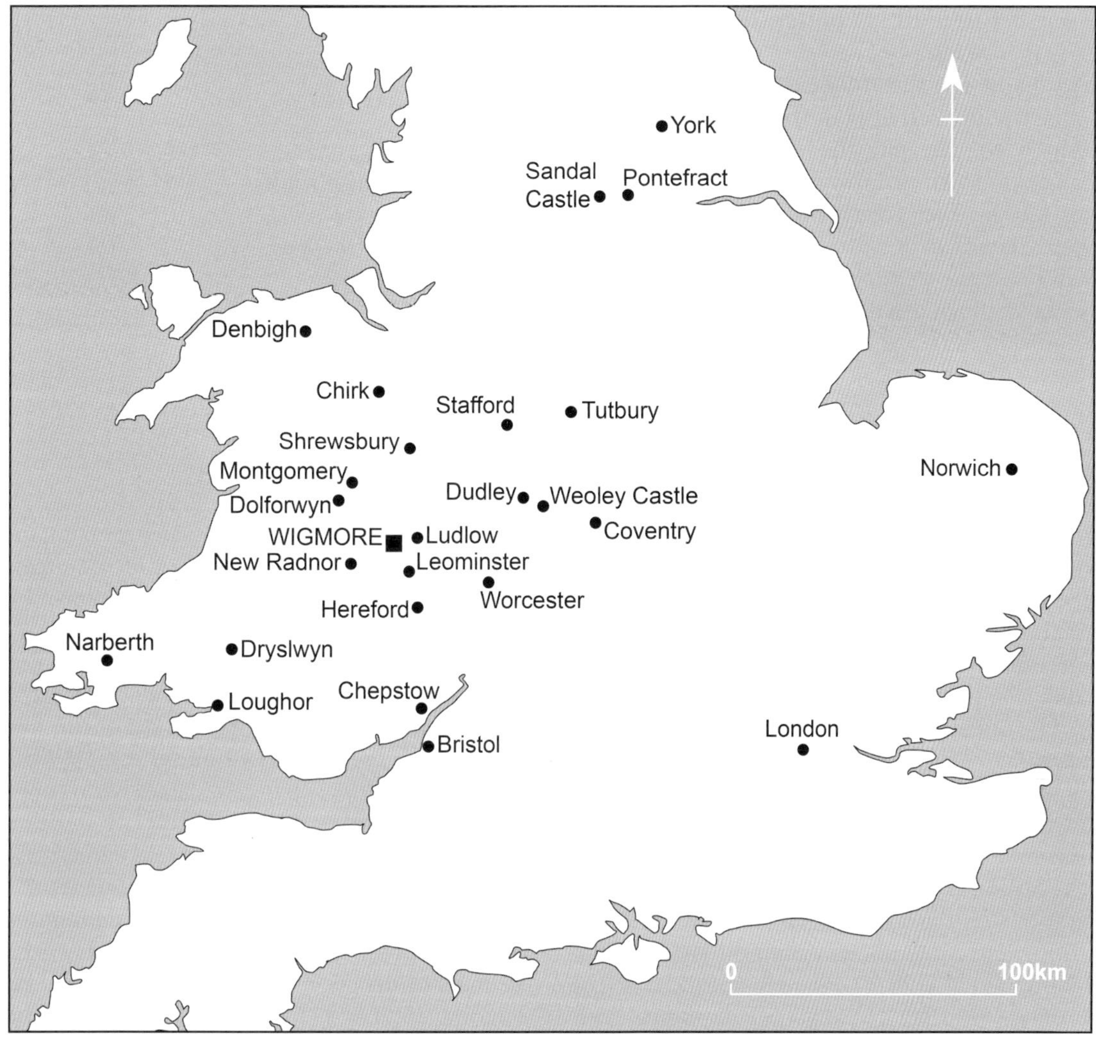

FIGURE 4.24
Principal medieval towns and cities, and castles mentioned in the text

suspended above the fire, resulting in a general all-over soot. A few sherds were unsooted. One unusual sooting pattern was noted on a Malvernian cooking pot found residually in 1996, Phase 5. Here both the interior and exterior were sooted apart from the rim, which might suggest that the pot had been placed in an inverted position in the fire. A striking absence from this and subsequent phase groups was the curfew or fire-cover, a not uncommon find where there are timber buildings. Several, for example, were found at Stafford Castle (Rátkai 2007). It is possible that the Malvernian cooking pot from Phase 5 served as a curfew.

By Phase 3 the major local pottery fabric, Fabric MS01, had come into being and formed a significant proportion of the pottery used at the castle for somewhere between a hundred and two hundred years. The stratigraphic evidence suggests that it was first produced before the middle of the 13th century. In Phase 3 most of the sherds were from cooking pots, with only a few glazed sherds present. The fabric has been found in Ludlow (Shropshire) to the north-east, New Radnor (Radnorshire) to the south-west and Leominster (Herefordshire) to the south. It is possible that pottery production began in the vicinity of Wigmore to serve the castle's needs and certainly there were numerous other castle sites in the area which could also have provided a market. Whether the acquisition by the Mortimers of castles at New Radnor and Ludlow, for example, expanded the market for Fabric MS01 or whether they fell within the normal distribution zone for the ware is impossible to say. On present evidence Fabric MS01 has been found at King Street and Palmers Hall, Ludlow (Rátkai 2004; 2003; 2006a), at Mill Street (Rátkai 2005), Bridge Street (Rátkai forthcoming a), possibly the Buttercross, Leominster (Rátkai 2001), and at Dinmore Manor, midway between Leominster and Hereford (personal inspection by the author). It has not been identified at Acton Burnell, Shrewsbury (Rátkai 2006b) or Montgomery Castle. Strangely, Malvernian cooking pots are a feature of assemblages from New Radnor, Ludlow and Leominster, so their rarity at Wigmore is worthy of note. This may support the contention that MS01 was specifically 'made for' Wigmore consumption, although the Fabric MS01 potters had clearly seen Malvernian cooking pots.

Phases 3 and 4 in the 1998 excavations witnessed some construction activity but the pottery evidence with which to date, say the construction of the East Tower, is lacking. However, the construction trenches for the East Tower and wall 711, and cut 728, were recorded as cutting dumps of material which did contain pottery. The pottery from these dumps was compared with pottery from dumps cut by the curtain wall excavated in 1996 and dated to Phase 5 (Figure 4.25). The two groups were generally similar. The absence of pottery in the East Tower construction trench is paralleled by the lack of pottery in the lower fills of the 1996 Southern Curtain Wall. This would be consistent with an early construction date. However, the 1998 and 1996 pre-construction dumps both contain Fabric RW10 which would seem to indicate construction about the middle of the 13th century at the earliest.

Fabric	Date range	1998	1996
Q01	late11th–12th century	11.20%	4.60%
Q20	12th century	17.50%	4.80%
S10	12th–13th century		31.50%
S11	13th century	30.80%	10.20%
MS01	13th–14th century	23.80%	33.50%
MS02	13th–14th century	1.40%	
MS12	13th–14th century	6.30%	2.50%
RW10	*c*1250–1500	9.10%	10.40%
Q31	*c*1250–1300		2.50%

FIGURE 4.25

Pottery (by % weight) from dumps cut by early construction features

From Phase 5 onwards the pottery from both 1996 and 1998 is dominated by jugs. The two areas cannot be differentiated by function. The 1998 sequence (Phases 5 and 8) beneath the plaster floor is difficult to interpret. Likewise the dating of the phases of construction of the Southern Curtain Wall, CG96 17, Phase 5 and CG96 09, Phase 8, identified in the 1996 excavation is far from certain. It is possible that modifications to the castle fabric seen in the 1996 excavation were contemporary with the laying of the plaster floor 631, CG98 20, Phase 8, outside the East Tower or are possibly broadly contemporary with the cut features, CG98 15 and CG98 16, post-dating floor 631. The ceramics are not particularly helpful here. There is also some evidence to suggest that the lower deposits within the interior of the East Tower were being laid down in the 15th century, possibly before or at the same time as the CG98 15 and CG98 16. There is also a direct ceramic link between CG98 17 and the East Tower backfill. Unfortunately the original interpretation of the stratigraphy below the Phase 9 plaster floor (CG98 12, CG98 14–16) is suspect (see Chapter 9). Nevertheless, a worn and clipped half-groat, with a suggested deposition date well into the first half of the 15th century (Chapter 5), found in CG98 15, suggests that much of the demolition and disturbance occurred in the second or possibly third quarter of the 15th century, after the documentary reference of 1425 (Chapter 2) to the castle being 'worth nothing'.

Although it is always perilous to attempt to link too closely the archaeological record with documentary sources, the construction of the Phase 9 plaster floor outside the East Tower could be associated with the stewardship of the castle by Henry, Duke of Buckingham, in 1483. The documentary evidence certainly seems to suggest that he intended to make ready and garrison Wigmore and other Marcher castles which had come into his possession. The ceramic evidence would not gainsay this interpretation but it nevertheless must remain speculative. Whatever the circumstances of the creation of the plaster floor, it did not appear to have been in use long. A possible second phase of dumping in the East Tower could be contemporary with the construction of the plaster floor and the final dumps contemporary with the final disuse of the floor but again this is speculative. Over on the 1996 site, the first part of Phase 9 is associated with rubble deposits. The absence of Cistercian ware in this rubble may indicate a date before the last quarter of the 15th century but this is by no means certain. In addition, it is unclear whether the preceding series of Phase 8 rubble deposits and the Southern Curtain Wall reconstruction (CG96 09) over the Phase 7 building (CG96 11) represent a series of quite distinct and disparate events, although the presence of a few cross-joining sherds throughout the rubble from Phase 8 through to Phase 9 does tend to suggest otherwise. It is certainly suggestive of a great deal of disturbance. Post-dating the rubble was a quite distinct dump (CG96 03) which had the appearance of a closed group and on initial excavation was described as a 'midden'. Even here, though, there were still cross-joins through to the rubble deposits. Other artefactual and faunal evidence (see Chapters 5 and 7) did however favour the interpretation that this was indeed a dumped deposit. The presence of hearth bottoms in CG96 03 may be further evidence of running repairs to the castle in the 16th century — again works are documented at the castle in the late 1530s. Further refurbishment is evidenced by the blocking of an alcove in the curtain wall which appears to be of a later date and the functional component is quite different from that found in the 'midden' discussed above.

Phase 10 witnesses the slide of the castle into terminal dereliction. The pottery suggests that the East Tower and the exterior area were largely abandoned and probably at least semi-derelict well before the Civil War, since there was no pottery from within or outside the tower, which could be identified as dating to the Civil War with any certainty. In fact, the area outside the tower produced very little pottery at all, which again may be symptomatic of a building or buildings which were little used after the laying of the plaster floor or may have already been derelict. Whatever the precise date of the disuse of the buildings in the area of the 1998 excavations, the ceramic evidence suggests it was earlier than in the 1996 excavations. In the latter area there was a significantly greater amount of pottery from Phase 10, which included pottery datable to the Civil War. However, pottery of this date was not well represented. The presence of large quantities of window glass and other finds in these deposits leave little doubt that they are demolition debris. In contrast, other castles occupied and garrisoned during the Civil War such as Dudley Castle (Rátkai 1987), Montgomery Castle (Knight 1991a), Stafford Castle (Rátkai 2007), Pontefract Castle (Cumberpatch 2002) and Sandal Castle (Brears 1983) have produced very large collections of pottery dating to this period and it is difficult, therefore, to believe that there was any intense occupation in the east and southern part of the Inner Bailey at Wigmore Castle, although that is not to say that the focus of occupation could not have been located elsewhere.

On the 1998 site, in Phase 11, mortar and rubble dumps post-dating the plaster floor and immediately above a turf line containing a coin of Henry VIII with a deposition date of 1530–50 but also a high quality curb bit dating to the 17th century (see Chapter 5) may be further evidence of decay or demolition. Pottery from 525, a layer above the turf line, contained Fabric RW12 and Cologne stoneware, which may suggest a chronological link with one of the late deposits, 550, in the backfill of the East Tower.

The single largest group of pottery came from 1996 Phase 11. Similar humic layers from the 1998 areas contained very little pottery and demonstrate that quite different taphonomic processes were operating in the two areas.

The pottery came mainly from three contexts 003 (397 sherds, 201g), 004 (101 sherds, 487g) and 005 (211 sherds, 1201g), which from the west section can be seen to overlie each other as well as some of the destruction rubble. The earliest layer in this context group (CG96 01) is context 007, although it is possible that this and layer 005 above are one and the same.

All the layers forming CG96 01 (Phase 11) contained Fabric RW12, giving a *terminus post quem* of *c*1550. Of the demolition dumps forming CG96 02 (Phase 10), all those with pottery contained some Fabric RW12 also. Layer 07 (CG96 01), at the base of the sequence, is unusual in that it contains a higher than average amount of Malvern Chase ware (Fabric R02). From the west section drawing, layer 07 overlies rubble 19 of CG96 02, Phase 10, which also contains a higher than average amount of Fabric R02. Both contexts presumably have incorporated pottery from the Phase 9 dumps, where Fabric R02 was dominant. This interpretation is reinforced by cross-joining sherds which show links between the Phase 10 rubble dumps and Phase 9 dumps below. Further cross-joins run throughout the rubble of Phase 10, with and within the Phase 11 humic layers and with pottery from the Phase 9 dumps. Clearly there has been a certain amount of disturbance in the area but the disturbance appears to be localised, that is, the dumps, demolition and humic layers have been disturbed *in situ* rather than comprising material moved from elsewhere.

The average sherd weight of the pottery from Phase 11 is low at just under 5.5g and almost half the average sherd weight of the pottery from Phase 10 (10.3g). The average sherd weight of the pottery from Phase 9 was 8.5g. It is clear therefore that the Phase 11 pottery has suffered a greater amount of wear than the pottery from Phases 9 and 10.

The pottery from Phase 11 was tabulated by stratigraphic sequence to see if any taphonomic factors were evident. With the exception of layer 07, mentioned above, there was no progression in the sequence which might help explain how the humic layers built up over the rubble of Phase 10, since there was little difference between the relative proportions of the wares from the top and bottom of the sequence. A similar tabulation was tried with the Phase 10 demolition rubble. The sequence revealed was similarly unedifying. Fabric RW12 was present in all contexts which contained pottery and the relative proportion of major fabrics or wares (Fabric R02, blackware and Fabric RW12) was very similar. There is, therefore, some difficulty in understanding the taphonomy influencing the deposition of the Phase 11 material. How did so much pottery come to accumulate after the demolition evidenced in Phase 10?

The relative frequency of Cistercian ware and blackware gives some idea of the relative chronology of the 1996 and 1998 sites, which is not necessarily so clear from the overall pottery figures. The demolition of the East Tower or at least the infilling of the basement seems to have occurred earlier than the Civil War slighting of the castle, since there is no pottery which is demonstrably of this date. The tiny chip of blackware from 556 and the Fabric RW12 and Cologne stoneware sherds from 550, both contexts at the very top of the backfill sequence, are as likely to belong to the late 16th century or early 17th century as to the Civil War. A greater amount of disintegration before the Civil War may also be a feature of the area outside the East Tower witnessed by the larger amounts of Cistercian ware compared to blackware.

4.5 FABRIC DESCRIPTIONS

Most of the medieval fabrics are described in this section apart for those that are well-known and have been published elsewhere. References only for the latter fabrics are cited below. Post-medieval fabrics which are presumed local are described here. Further details about the others are given in the main body of the text as appropriate. Figure 4.1 lists all the fabrics mentioned in the text with their common or descriptive name, date range and likely source.

MS01: Figure 4.4, 16, 19, 22–24, 26–28; Figure 4.5, 35, 40, 46, 50, 55, 56; Figure 4.7.107.
Colour: Pale pinkish-brown (very rarely white) surfaces and margins, pale grey core, occasionally dark grey internal surface.
Manufacture: Wheel-thrown or wheel-finished.
Inclusions: quartz: sparse, very fine *c*0.1mm; mica: moderate-abundant, golden flecks to plates up to 2mm, but generally <1mm; siltstone: abundant small fragments generally *c*0.25–0.5mm but occasionally pieces up to 3–4mm.
Glaze: thin yellow with dark green (copper) mottles.

MS02: Figure 4.5, 29
Colour: Orange to pale grey.
Manufacture: Hand formed, wheel finished?
Inclusions: Quartz: Finely sandy matrix with sparse quartz grains up to about 0.5mm; siltstone: sparse rounded 'crushed' odd grains up to *c*0.25mm; mica: moderate golden flecks to platelets visible on surfaces.
Glaze: Glossy olive with darker green (copper) mottles.

MS03: Figure 4.5 , 36, 41 and 44
Colour: Mainly reduced mid grey but merging into pale brown where oxidised towards the external surface.
Manufacture: Probably wheel thrown.
Inclusions: Mica: moderate flecks and small platelets visible on surfaces, some platelets visible in matrix. The matrix appears fine with very small inclusions of quartz *c*0.1mm (but some are *c*0.25mm and there are very rare grains 0.5–1mm). There are very small inclusions of siltstone (but with occasional larger pieces like the quartz).
Glaze: dark green spots and splashes, tan splashes.

MS10: Unillustrated
Colour: White/pale grey, greyish interior surface.
Manufacture: Hand-formed.
Inclusions: Quartz: sparse, very fine <0.1mm, very rare grains up to 0.25mm; siltstone: moderate, ill-sorted, 0.25–3mm, mainly *c*1.00–2.00mm, variable colour, grey, brown or red; organic voids: sparse, blackened; mica: golden flecks and small plates visible on surfaces.
Glaze: Thick, glossy yellowish-olive.

MS11: Unillustrated
This fabric most closely resembles Hereford fabric A4 (Vince 1985a, 39–41). It is different from the other Wigmore micaceous siltstone fabrics in having rare large pieces of siltstone. Vince suggests a source in northern Herefordshire or south Shropshire and its infrequency at Wigmore is therefore puzzling.

MS12: Figure 4.5, 32–33, 38, 42, 48, 52, 57
Colour: Orange to pale yellow grey, some grey reduction in thicker parts of the core.
Manufacture: Wheel-thrown but also possibly hand-formed, wheel-finished. Many of the sherds' surfaces have a 'wiped' look.
Inclusions: Quartz: sparse, rounded and sub-angular, grey or yellow, from <0.1mm 025mm; siltstone: sparse, rounded up to 1mm; voids: sparse, irregular, reaction with HCl; calcite: angular greyish grains, react strongly with HCl; Fe oxide: sparse, rounded, brown, up to 1mm; mica: moderate, flecks visible in matrix and on surfaces; sandstone: rare, white, loosely cemented grains; voids: rare but can be quite large, seem to be from burnt-out organic matter.
Glaze: Olive with copper flecks (the more micaceous sherd), tan with green (copper) mottles.
Comment: A slightly 'granular' textured fabric, inclusions are relatively few, and the fracture is smooth. There may be some sandstone or granitic grains in the fabric.

MWW: Unillustrated
Colour: Putty-coloured to orange.
Manufacture: Coil-built, wheel-finished.
Inclusions: White inclusions: rounded, no reaction with HCl. The matrix is flecked/mottled with this material also, flecks to 0.2mm; Fe oxide: moderate red, rounded, flecks-1.0mm; voids: sparse, elongated and irregular, some from organic, some from calcareous matter; mica: golden, sparse plates visible on surfaces *c*0.25–0.5mm.
Glaze: Overfired, thick, dull, greenish-white.
Comment: There is only a single sherd of this fabric. It may have been badly affected in a conflagration.

NFrWW North French Whiteware: Unillustrated
Colour: Cream.
Manufacture: Wheel-thrown.
Inclusions: Clean very finely sandy matrix with rare larger pink and semi-clear quartz grains up to 0.5mm, sparse silver mica flecks, most visible on the unglazed surfaces.
Glaze: bright green (copper) glaze with darker speckles.

OOL: Figure 4.4, 10
Colour: Brown surfaces and margins, grey core.
Manufacture: ?Probably hand formed.
Inclusions: Abundant fine ooliths and sparse, rounded, red Fe oxide.
Comment: Possibly the same as Vince (1985a) fabric D2. A source in Gloucestershire is likely. The handle of the pitcher (Figure 4.4, 10) has been attached and secured by use of a clay 'dowel'.

Q01: Figure 4.4, 01–07, 11, 13, 14; Figure 4.6, 82–83
Colour: Brown surfaces and margins, grey core, surfaces sometimes black.
Manufacture: Hand formed.
Inclusions: Quartz: ill-sorted, rounded and sub-rounded, white, grey, yellow, rarely clear, 0.5-1mm; organics: sparse voids up to *c*0.5mm; ?mica: sparse 'pinponts' of mica flecks visible on surfaces.
Comment: The fabric and vessel forms are consistent with Worcester-type cooking pots, which first appeared in the late 11th century. Sandy cooking pots of this type are widespread in 12th- and 13th-century levels in the West Midlands.

Q01.1: Unillustrated
Colour: Blackened surfaces, brown margins, black core.
Manufacture: Hand formed?

Inclusions: Quartz: sparse-moderate, rounded, grey, rarely clear, up to 1mm but generally *c*0.5–0.75mm; Fe oxide: sparse-moderate, red-brown, rounded (particularly visible in paler margins; voids: small, irregular) may be burnt out calcareous matter; mica?: rare, small, glistening flecks on surfaces.
Comment: This fabric appears to have been used for cooking pots/jars. There were no form sherds suitable for illustration.

Q02: Worcester-type glazed ware: Unillustrated
See Worcester Fabric 64.1 (Hurst and Rees 1992, 207) and Hereford fabric C2 (Vince 1985a).
Colour: Generally grey with oxidised surfaces although some sherds are reduced throughout.
Inclusions: Quartz: moderate, sub-angular grey quartz 0.25–0.5mm; Fe oxide: sparse, rounded, reddish.

Q03: Unillustrated
Colour: Grey.
Manufacture: Hand formed.
Inclusions: Quartz: off-white to yellowish, abundant, subangular or sub-rounded, 0.25–1mm; sandstone: sub-angular, rare, brownish, loosely cemented grains up to *c*0.5mm; siltstone: very rare, rounded 0.5–0.75mm; ?granitic: rare sub-angular, pale coral pink, 1.0–2.0mm and rare, sub-angular, buff/grey 2.0–3.0mm.

Q10: Unillustrated
Colour: Grey.
Manufacture: Hand formed.
Inclusions: Quartz, abundant, sub-angular, *c*0.25mm; sandstone: rare, light-coloured, loosely cemented grains, subangular, *c*0.5mm; Fe oxide: sparse, reddish, rounded, *c*0.25mm; siltstone: rare, rounded *c*0.25mm.

Q11: Unillustrated
Colour: Grey throughout.
Manufacture: Wheel thrown?
Inclusions: Quartz: moderate, sub-angular, grey (occasionally clear) *c*0.25mm; mica: sparse silver flecks.
Glaze: Glossy, patchy olive with copper mottles.

Q20: Figure 4.4, 8, 9, 12, 20
Colour: Pale brown to pale grey.
Manufacture: Hand formed.
Inclusions: Quartz: moderate, sub-angular, ill-sorted grey and white quartz <*c*0.75mm; sandstone: rare to moderate, loosely cemented grains; mica: sparse-moderate golden flecks and platelets visible on surfaces, rarely in matrix.
Glaze: Very thin clear to yellowish spots/splash glaze.

Q30: Unillustrated
Colour: Light red-brown unglazed surfaces, otherwise mid-grey throughout.
Manufacture: Wheel thrown.
Inclusions: Quartz: sparse, rounded, grey *c*0.1mm with very rare grains *c*0.25mm; siltstone: sparse, rounded, up to 0.5mm but generally *c*0.1–0.25mm; voids: rare, irregular
Glaze: Thick glossy olive to thinner patchier olive.
Comment: Rather dense textured fabric, with very smooth fracture.

Q31: Unillustrated
Colour: Grey-brown, dark brown, black.
Manufacture: Hand formed.
Inclusions: Quartz: abundant, fine generally <0.25mm probably *c*0.10mm; mica: moderate, golden, flecks up to *c*0.25mm visible in matrix, moderate flecks *c*0.5mm visible on surfaces

Q32: Unillustrated
Colour: Mid-grey, one sherd with an internal brown surface
Manufacture: Coil built, wheel-finished.
Inclusions: Quartz: very finely sandy matrix with grains *c*0.1mm or less, very rare larger grains up to 0.5mm; Fe oxide: orange, rounded, from *c*0.25mm to 5mm; Organic voids: sparse *c*0.25–0.5mm.
Mica: Silver flecks visible in matrix, moderate flecks and small platelets visible on unglazed surfaces.
Glaze: Glossy olive with some copper streaking, thin patchy olive almost like a splash glaze.

Q40: Unillustrated
Colour: Surfaces orange to brown, variable grey core depending on wall thickness.
Manufacture: Wheel thrown.
Inclusions: Quartz: sparse, ill-sorted, sub-angular and sub-rounded, grey (rarely clear) mainly 0.5–1mm; Voids: sparse small voids, probably from burnt-out organic material.
Glaze: Spots and splashes of dark greenish brown glaze.
Comment: Surfaces appear to have been 'wiped'.

Q60: Figure 4.5, 47
Colour: Mid-grey, pale grey to orange margins.
Manufacture: Coil made, wheel finished?
Inclusions: Quartz: sparse, sub-angular, generally *c*0.25mm, grey, rarely clear; Fe oxide: sparse, rounded, orange 0.25–0.5mm; mica: sparse, golden flecks and small platelets visible on unglazed surfaces.
Glaze: Thin overfired/burnt or possibly part decayed, dull, opaque, appears to have once been mottled tan-olive.

Q70: Unillustrated
Colour: Buff/pale brown.
Manufacture: Probably wheel-thrown.
Inclusions: Quartz: abundant, fine, well-sorted, generally *c*0.1mm, odd grains *c*0.25mm; mica: rare plates <0.25mm, visible in matrix.
Glaze: Glossy yellow with green mottles.

QM01: Unillustrated
Colour: Light brown surfaces and margins, black core.
Manufacture: Probably hand formed.
Inclusions: Quartz: sparse, rounded and sub-rounded, grey white, ill-sorted 0.25–1mm; Sandstone: sparse, sub-angular, large loosely cemented grains, white-grey; Fe oxide: rare rounded <0.25–1mm.
Voids: generally <0.25, residues within voids react with HCl; mica: abundant, very fine, visible on surfaces and in matrix.

R01: Malvernian Cooking pot Figure 4.4, 25
See Hereford fabric B1 (Vince 1985a), Worcester Fabric 56 (Hurst and Rees 1992, 207).

R02: Wheel-thrown oxidised Malvernian Ware Figure 4.6, 59, 65–66; Figure 4.7, 105
See Hereford fabric B4 (Vince 1985a), Worcester Fabric 69 (Hurst and Rees 1992, 208).

R03: Malvernian Tripod Pitcher ware Unillustrated
See Hereford fabric B2 (Vince 1985a).

R10: Figure 4.5, 34
Colour: Buff to brown surfaces, greyish brown core and margins.
Manufacture: Wheel thrown.
Inclusions: Sparse golden mica platelets up to *c*0.5mm; sparse Fe oxide, rounded 0.25–1mm; sparse quartz, sub-rounded up to 1mm; sparse siltstone, sub-rounded 0.5–1mm; sparse schist sub-angular up to 2mm; sparse igneous rock, light coloured, *c*1.00mm, sub-rounded, sparse organic voids.
Glaze: Pitted olive to yellowish olive with darker green mottles.
Comment: The fabric appears very dense and the inclusions are very poorly-sorted. The single occurrence of this fabric suggests that it is not local. A certain degree of rounding on most inclusions suggests weathering. Schist is widespread in Metamorphic regions and is found in the Scottish Highlands, Anglesey and the Sperrin Mountains, County Tyrone, Ulster (Geological Society of London, (www.geolsoc.org.uk) and elsewhere in Ireland in Wicklow and Galway. Given the Mortimer land holdings, a Welsh source seems most likely but Ireland is not impossible.

RW10: Unillustrated
Colour: Usually orange throughout but some sherds reduced pale grey throughout.
Manufacture: Wheel thrown.
Inclusions: Quartz: sparse, very fine silt-sized grains <0.1mm; voids:sparse elongated organic voids (a chaff or straw impression visible in one sherd); mica: moderate silver mica flecks visible in matrix and on surfaces.
Glaze: glossy olive brown, tan with green (copper) speckles, but also decayed/incorrectly fired in places giving dull opaque green.
Comment: Very fine, dense fabric, with few obvious inclusions.

RW11: Unillustrated
Colour: Orange-brown.
Manufacture: Wheel thrown.
Inclusions: Quartz: abundant, very fine giving a 'granular' texture to the fabric, rare larger grains <0.25mm visible; mica: sparse, mainly visible on surfaces.
Glaze: Brown.

RW12: Figure 4.6, 67-77, 84; Figure 4.7, 91-101, 104
Colour: Orange.
Manufacture: Wheel thrown.
Inclusions: No visible inclusions, the clay body is clean with a slightly granular look. There are rare voids, rarely >0.25mm, which seem to represent burnt out organic matter.
Glaze: Good quality, glossy olive, tan and red-brown.

RW12.1: Figure 4.6, 78
This is essentially a reduced, hard-fired version of RW12. The surfaces are uniformly grey but the core can be purplish-brown or weak red. It is unclear whether the reduction was deliberate, although accidental seems more likely.

RW12.2: Unillustrated
The fabric is indistinguishable from RW12, although a little more brownish in tone. RW12.2 is a sub-group because of the use of a white under-glaze slip. When glazed, the slipped surfaces appear either bright green or pale green with darker green speckles.

RW13: Figure 4.5, 53; Figure 4.6, 85, 86
Colour: Brown.
Manufacture: Wheel thrown.
Inclusions: Mica: abundant, *c*0.01mm; organics: moderate voids from burnt-out organic matter 0.25mm-2.0mm. The clay body has a slightly granular appearance.

S01: Figure 4.4, 18; Figure 4.5, 30, 39
Colour: Generally reduced pale to mid-grey, light brown or pinkish surfaces.
Manufacture: Coil built, wheel finished?
Inclusions: Quartz: very sparse, very fine *c*0.10mm; Siltstone: moderate, red, brown or grey depending on firing, 0.25–2mm but generally <1mm; Voids: sparse, probably organic although one or two very slight reactions to HCl close to the exterior margin, so there may be a little calcareous matter in matrix; sandstone: rare, fine grained, rounded.
Glaze: Olive.

S10: Figure 4.4, 21; Figure 4.5, 43, 51, 54
Colour: Pale grey, brown surfaces, , one sherd with orange interior margin.
Manufacture: Hand formed.
Inclusions: Siltstone: abundant, generally 0.25–1.5mm; Mica: sparse flecks-platelets on surfaces.

S11: Figure 4.5, 31
Colour: Brown.
Manufacture: Coil-built, wheel-finished.
Inclusions: Siltstone: abundant, rounded, 0.25-2.0mm; mica: moderate golden, small platelets *c*0.25mm, smaller flecks visible in clay body; quartz: rare sub-angular grains, 0.25–0.5mm.

S20: Figure 4.4, 15
Colour: Pale to mid grey.
Manufacture: Hand formed.
Inclusions: Siltstone: abundant, rounded, 1-4mm; Mica: moderate, golden, flecks to small platelets; quartz: very rare sub-angular, 1-2mm.
Comment: A very coarse fabric.

Tudor Green: Figure 4.5, 49
For fabric details see Pearce and Vince (1988, 10–11).

WW01: Unillustrated
Colour: White.
Manufacture: Wheel thrown.
Inclusions: Abundant fine quartz <0.01mm: Fe oxide: rare rounded <0.25mm.
Glaze: Clear or pale yellow with green speckles.
Comment: Possibly Tudor Green or Tudor Green-type ware.

WW02: Unillustrated
Colour: Buff to light orange, pale grey core.
Manufacture: Wheel thrown.

Inclusions: Quartz: rare, sub-angular, ill-sorted up to 0.25mm, pinkish or grey depending on firing.
Fe oxide: rare, rounded, up to 0.25mm;Voids: sparse, up to 1mm but generally <0.5mm.
Glaze: Glossy olive.

WW10: Unillustrated
Colour: White to buff fabric, light pinkish-orange interior surface.
Manufacture: Hand formed.
Inclusions: Quartz: moderate to abundant, well-sorted, rounded, pinkish or grey depending on firing conditions, *c*0.25mm; Fe oxide: sparse, red/black depending on firing conditions, rounded, *c*0.25mm.
Glaze: good quality apple green.

Rhenish Stoneware: Figure 4.7, 102
Three types of Rhenish Stoneware were identified: Raeren (Figure 4.7, 102), Frechen and Cologne (see Gaimster, 1997 for detailed descriptions of these wares).

North French Stoneware: Unillustrated
Products from Martincamp and Bessin (Normandy stoneware) were noted (see Hurst *et al* 1986, 100–104).

Cistercian Ware: Figure 4.6, 60, 79–80; Figure 4.7, 103, 106 and Blackware: Figure 4.6, 61–64, 87; Figure 4.7, 88–90
Both these fabrics have in general clean orange, red or occasionally reduced grey bodies similar to RW11, RW12 and RW13.

Yellow ware: Unillustrated
Of the few sherds of yellow ware present, all had a clean white fabric.

Plate 1
Wigmore Castle from the air (copyright: English Heritage)

PLATE 2

Wigmore Castle and village in their setting, viewed from the north. Painting by Dominic Andrews (copyright: English Heritage)

PLATE 3

Reconstruction of Wigmore Castle in the 14th century, by Dominic Andrews (copyright: English Heritage)

Plate 4
Wigmore Castle 1998, excavation within the East Tower, looking north (see Chapter 3) (copyright: English Heritage)

Plate 5
Wigmore Castle 1998, excavation outside the East Tower, looking south-east (see Chapter 3) (copyright: English Heritage)

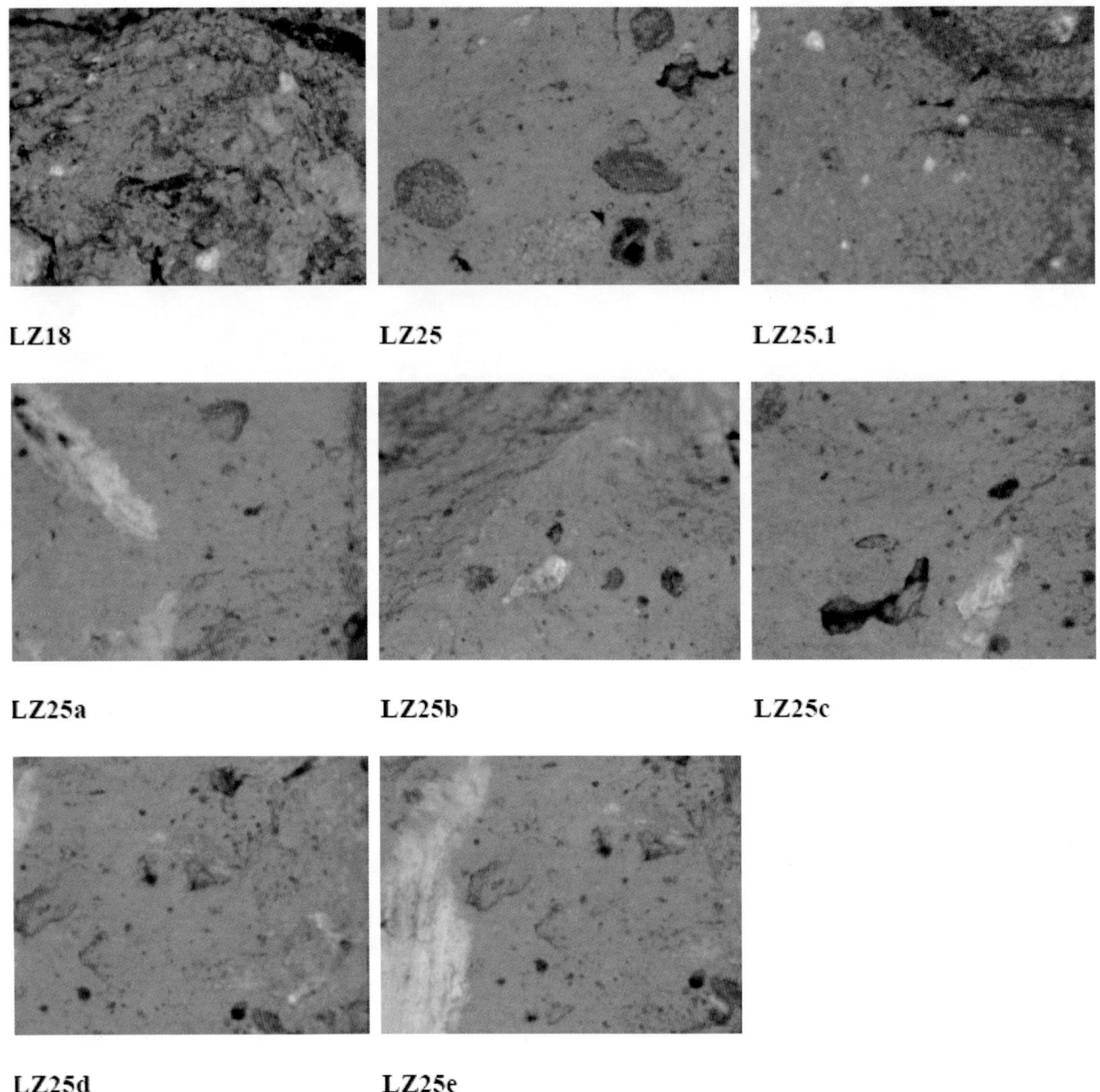

PLATE 6
Photo-micrographs of CBM fabrics LZ18 and LZ25 (see Chapter 6)

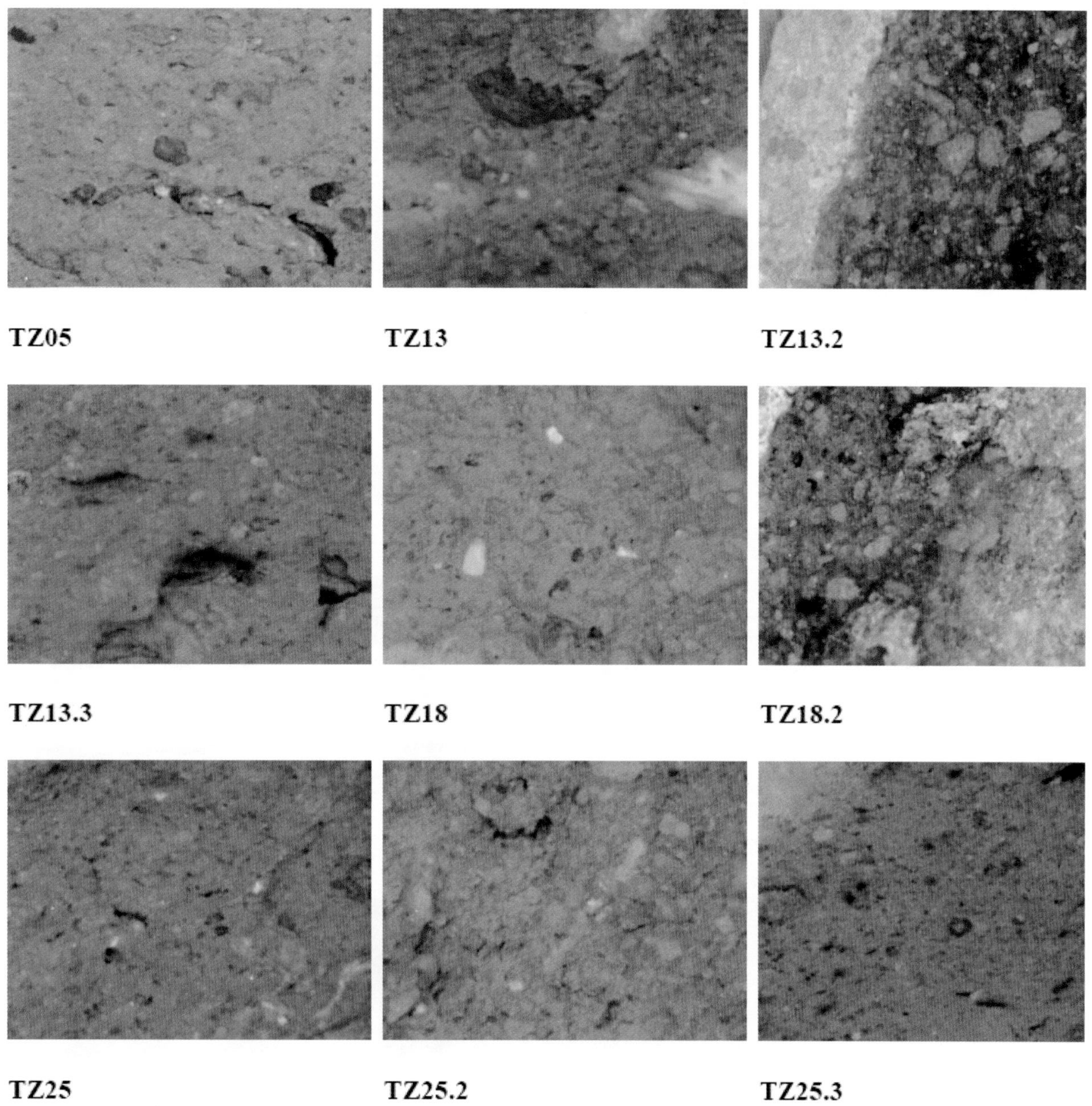

Plate 7
Photo-micrographs of CBM fabrics TZ05, TZ13, TZ13.2–3, TZ18, TZ18.2, TZ25, TZ25.2–3 (see Chapter 6)

Plate 8

Floor tile patterns IP2–4, P1–6 (see Chapter 6)

PLATE 9

Floor tile patterns P7–12, P14, P16 and marbled glaze tile (see Chapter 6)

Plate 10

Floor tiles still in situ in the South Chapel area, Wigmore Abbey, looking east (photograph courtesy of Colin Breen, Queen's University, Belfast)

Plate 11

Floor tiles still in situ in the South Chapel, Wigmore Abbey, looking south (photograph courtesy of Colin Breen, Queen's University, Belfast)

5
THE ARTEFACTS

5.1 THE PORTABLE FINDS

Quita Mould

Nearly 1500 portable finds, chiefly of metalwork, were recovered from excavations at Wigmore Castle, over a thousand from the 1996 excavations (Figure 5.1), a further 462 from the 1998 excavations. The coins (Section 5.3) and objects of worked stone (Section 5.2) have been reported on separately and have not been included in the quantification provided here. The lead-working waste and metal-working debris recovered from the excavations were subject to separate assessment previously (Doonan 1999; Dungworth 2000) and the results of that work, updated to incorporate the refined contextual information, are summarised here with the rest of the metalwork. This material was not seen by the author.

The finds have been considered within broad functional categories and the percentage of each recovered within each phase is given in Figure 5.2. A small number of find types might reasonably be considered within more than one category. For convenience, in the quantification tables all types of buckle have been considered dress accessories, however in the accompanying text they have been discussed as both horse equipment and dress accessories as appropriate. Consequently, the proportion of horse equipment may be slightly under-represented.

The finds comprise principally weapons and armour, horse equipment, small dress accessories, household and domestic items, and structural metalwork, deriving from the buildings. The range of finds recovered is generally consistent with assemblages recovered from excavations at other castles. Tools do appear to be under-represented but this may be due to the limited area investigated at Wigmore Castle and the locations of the interventions undertaken. A small number of individually expensive objects, notably the silver inlaid iron shears, the copper 'brazed' arrowheads and the curb bit, hint at the high status of the owners of the castle.

Few finds relate to the timber castle, though there is good evidence for iron smithing during the 12th century, likely to relate to a phase of castle construction. More than 40% of the portable finds came from contexts attributed to the medieval period and medieval material also occurred residually in later levels. A further 44% of the portable finds came from contexts of 16th- to 17th-century date. From the mid-14th to 15th centuries onward the majority of the finds occurred in dump deposits and levelling layers. Much of the material appears to have been deposited within large dumps dating to the 16th–17th century following decay and disuse of the castle. These dumps contain much redeposited medieval material. Few finds can be directly associated with the Civil War dismantling.

A large group of portable finds were recovered from deposits CG98 11, Phase 10, inside the East Tower, nearly half (43%) coming from a single context (665). While structural finds predominate, military and horse equipment were well represented, much, apparently, occurring residually from previous, medieval, activity. The finds from this group are itemised in Figure 5.3. While the range of material appears to vary little from that seen in earlier contexts representing the castle's occupation, the proportion of weapons and armour and horse equipment in the dumped material, each representing 23% of the group, is higher. The high proportion of dress accessories present in deposits associated with the early years following the castle's disuse in Phase 10, in the 1996 excavations, may suggest that much of the material dumped there came from the more domestic quarters in contrast to the high proportion of weapons, armour and horse equipment in the material dumped at the same date in the area of the 1998 excavations.

Military equipment

A small amount of military equipment came from the 1996 excavations but the majority was recovered from the 1998 excavations, at the south-eastern corner of the Inner Bailey.

Weapons

Arrowheads

Arrowheads are common finds on castle excavations, particularly large and varied groups of 103 arrowheads coming from Carisbrooke Castle (Fairbrother 2000, 141) and 92 from Dryslwyn Castle (Jessop 2007), for example. The typology devised by Jessop (1996) summarising arrowheads

1996 excavations	Phase												
	1	2	3	4	5	6	7	8	9	10	11	u/s	Total
Copper alloy	0	3	1	1	1	0	0	3	2	24	12	1	48
Iron	5	19	9	62	23	144	66	100	265	124	147	6	970
Lead alloy	0	0	0	1	0	3	1	6	1	0	2	0	14
Worked bone	0	1	0	0	0	0	0	0	0	0	4	0	5
Total	**5**	**23**	**10**	**64**	**24**	**147**	**67**	**109**	**268**	**148**	**165**	**7**	**1037**
	(<1%)	**(2%)**	**(1%)**	**(6%)**	**(2%)**	**(14%)**	**(7%)**	**(10%)**	**(26%)**	**(14%)**	**(16%)**	**(<1%)**	

1998 excavations	Phase								
	3	4	5	8	9	10	11	not phased	Total
Copper alloy	0	1	1	0	4	2	2	3	13
Iron	2	21	26	110	38	185	24	19	425
Lead alloy	0	1	3	4	1	8	2	1	20
Worked bone	0	0	0	2	0	0	0	0	2
Amber	0	0	0	1	0	0	0	1	2
Total	**2**	**23**	**30**	**117**	**43**	**195**	**28**	**24**	**462**
	<1%	**5%**	**7%**	**25%**	**9%**	**42%**	**6%**	**5%**	

FIGURE 5.1
Wigmore 1996 and 1998: quantification of portable finds by material type

1996 excavations	Phase										
	1	2	3	4	5	6	7	8	9	10	11
Weapons and armour	0	0	0	3%	0	5%	6%	5%	4%	0	2%
Horse equipment	25%	18%	25%	37%	0	9%	6%	0	12%	8%	22%
Dress accessories	0	18%	0	3%	0	5%	0	5%	8%	39%	26%
Household items	0	28%	12%	3%	40%	**9%**	6%	32%	10%	11%	24%
Tools	0	0	0	0	0	0	6%	5%	1%	2%	4%
Structural fittings	75%	18%	63%	42%	60%	72%	76%	48%	52%	33%	14%
Other	0	18%	0	12%	0	0	0	5%	13%	7%	8%

1998 excavations	Phase					
	4	5	8	9	10	11
Weapons and armour	12%	5%	8%	4%	17%	0
Horse equipment	0	32%	35%	7%	19%	8%
Dress accessories	6%	10%	2%	9%	13%	8%
Household items	38%	5%	13%	4%	8%	8%
Tools	0	0	2%	0	1%	8%
Structural fittings	38%	47%	40%	76%	38%	68%
Other	6%	0	0	0	4%	0

FIGURE 5.2
Wigmore 1996 and 1998: percentage of portable finds by functional category

recovered from many castles, is used here. Seven iron arrowheads were found at Wigmore Castle. A single arrowhead (Figure 5.4, 1) was recovered from the 1996 excavations, a military type (Jessop M1) dating to the late 14th century; it comes from a levelling deposit 044, CG96 06, Phase 9, attributed to the 15th–16th centuries. The majority came from the 1998 excavations where both military and multi-purpose types that could be used for both hunting game and warfare were represented. Only two of the arrowheads (Figure 5.4, 3, and 4; Figure 5.9) were found in contemporary deposits, the remainder occurred residually in later contexts but may be dated by comparison with well-dated arrowheads from elsewhere. One (Figure 5.4, 5) can be dated to the early 13th century (Jessop 1996, MP7), four (Figure 5.4, 3 and 4, 9701858 and 9701692 if complete) to the mid-13th century (Jessop 1996, MP4, MP8, MP8, M5 respectively), and another (Figure 5.4, 2) to the late 14th century (Jessop 1996, M1).

Material	Object	Quantity Context 665	Quantity Other contexts
Copper alloy	pin	1	0
Copper alloy	stud head	0	1
Iron	arrowhead	1	3
Iron	socket	1	0
Iron	chain mail link	1	0
Iron	plate armour fragments	2	8
Iron	buckle	0	2
Iron	spur fragment	6	1
Iron	horseshoe	1	1
Iron	horseshoe nail	2	4
Iron	knife blade	1	0
Iron	key	0	1
Iron	awl	0	1
Iron	hinge	0	1
Iron	hinge staple	0	1
Iron	nailed binding	1	0
Iron	wallhook	0	1
Iron	U-staple	0	1
Iron	stud	1	0
Iron	nail	25	34
Iron	nail shank	13	22
Iron	nail shank fragment	11	8
Iron	strip	0	1
Iron	fragment	0	1
Lead	sheet	1	0
Lead	sheet trimming	3	1

FIGURE 5.3
Finds from CG98 11, Phase 10, the East Tower

Two of the arrowheads were for military use being of Jessop's type M1 (Figure 5.4, 1 and 2) of late 14th-century date, a small socket (9701692) may also be another military arrowhead of Jessop type M5 of mid-13th-century date. One arrowhead recovered was for hunting (Figure 5.4, 4); another broken arrowhead appears to be a second large example (9701858). The other arrowheads present were of types that may have been used for either hunting or warfare (Jessop 1996, MP7, Figure 5.4, 5 and Jessop 1996, MP4 Figure 5.4, 3). The increase in the consumption of venison in the 14th century at Wigmore Castle cannot be correlated with an increase in the proportion of hunting or multi-purpose arrowheads recovered; this may well be because of the limited number found.

It was notable that the barbed arrowheads (Figure 5.4, 5 and 9701858) from Wigmore Castle were rather larger than examples recovered elsewhere (Jessop 1996). One (Figure 5.4, 5) had traces of copper clearly visible when the item was cleaned and copper was detected at two locations at the tip of the blade and also at the socket by X-ray fluorescence analysis (XRF) (Felter and Bartindate 2009). Similarly traces of copper visible when cleaning a late 14th-century military arrowhead (Figure 5.4, 2) were confirmed by XRF. The presence of copper on iron arrowheads is not uncommon but is rarely recorded amongst archaeologically recovered examples. It has been found on an armour-piercing arrowhead of Jessop's type M7 from late 13th- or early 14th-century dumped material in the Lesser Hall at Launceston Castle, Cornwall (Mould 2006, 302, FE9) and was noted on arrowheads from Holm Castle, Tewkesbury, Gloucestershire, and the battle site at Towton (AD 1461) (David Starley pers comm). During a study undertaken at the Royal Armouries, Leeds, on material in their collection, half of the 16 arrowheads investigated were found to have traces of copper on the heads. Only observable when the overlying corrosion products are mechanically removed, it may well be that the use of copper on the heads of iron projectiles is more common than it appears at present, as it remains for the most part undetected unless specifically looked for. Dr David Starley's research suggests that the copper appears to have been used to braze steel cutting edges onto the iron heads. An order for arrowheads intended for warfare made in the year 1359 specified that some had to be 'well brazed, and hardened at the points with steel' (*CPR* 1358–61, 323, quoted in Soden 2007, 120). The occurrence of copper on iron arrowheads of differing types, however, suggests that, on these other styles at least, it was also employed for other uses. Copper 'brazed' arrowheads would appear to be 'top of the range' equipment, requiring a skilled blacksmith with knowledge of the differing properties of iron alloys and increased time to manufacture, and, as such, they reflect the high status of the aristocratic owners of the castle.

Other possible weapons

Two other iron objects might also represent broken weapons but their identifications are far from certain. A fragment of nailed iron strap 20mm wide (SF7533) was found in 13th-century fill 703 of the construction trench 676, CG98 23, Phase 4, for the East Tower. The nailed strap has minerally preserved organic remains on each face, which might suggest it to be a broken scale tang from a weapon, as scale tangs were not commonly used on knives until the 14th century (Cowgill *et al* 1987, 26). The organic remains appear to lie in random directions, however, so that the possibility of the nailed strap coming into contact with wood on both sides during burial cannot be excluded, so that this identification can only be tentatively suggested.

A small iron ratchet (Figure 5.4, 6) was found in a rubble dump deposit (060, CG96 08, Phase 8) associated with the 15th-century rebuilding of the Southern Curtain Wall. The narrow blade is tanged with proportionally large, thick teeth that are not set (angled alternatively to either side) making its use as a saw most unlikely. Comparison with examples used in ratchet suspension mechanisms

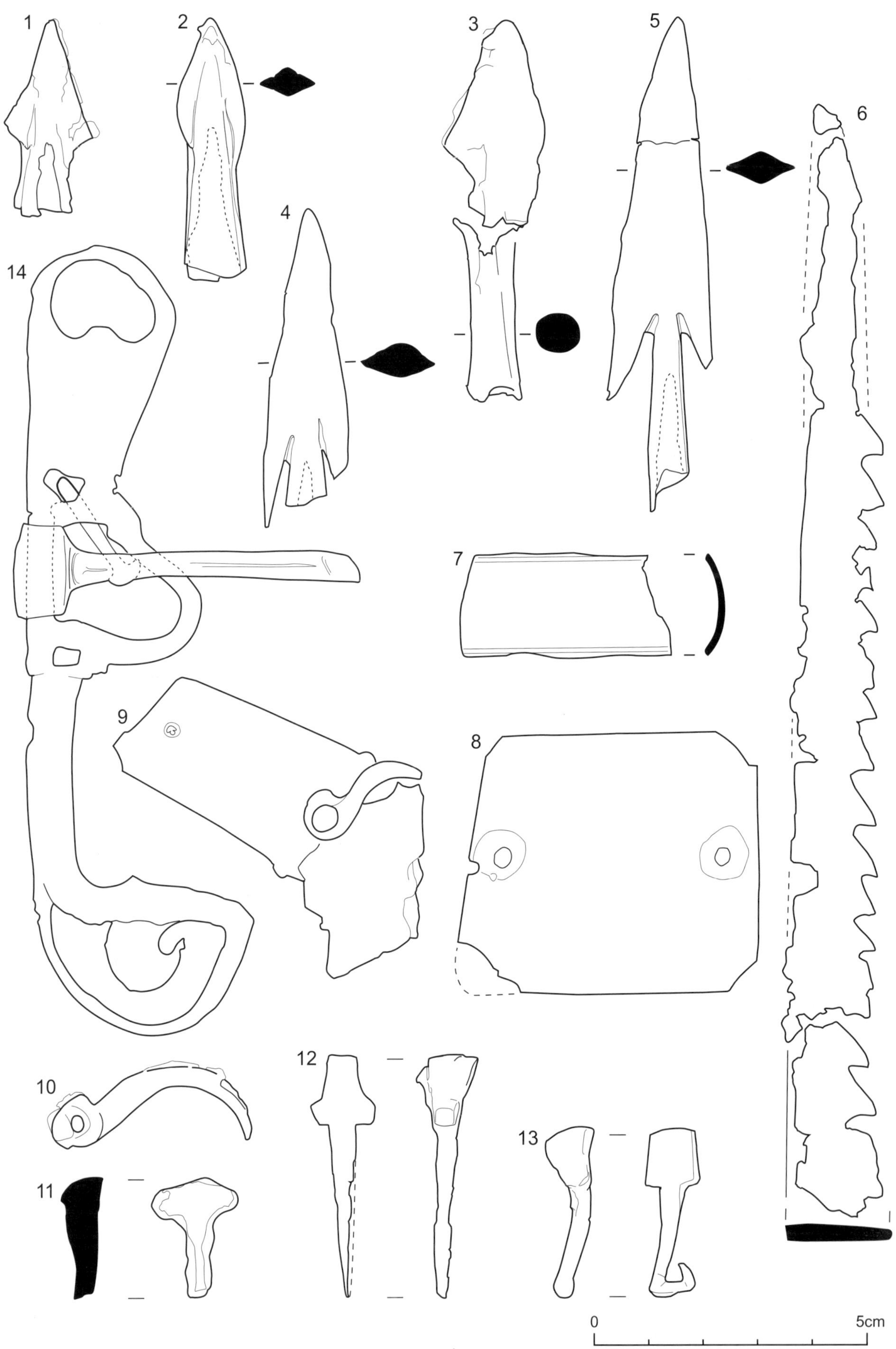

FIGURE 5.4
Illustrated iron artefacts, Nos 1–14

and spit rests associated with the cooking hearth, suggest that the ratchet is rather too small. The possibility exists that it comes from a crossbow rack or cranequin, a device used to span the heavy crossbow. Three machines for bending a crossbow, 7 wooden crossbows with winching machines and 14 of horn with winching machines were listed in an inventory of 1322 (TNA E 154/1/11B) relating to the contents of Wigmore Castle. As attractive as this proposition is, the identification unfortunately remains highly speculative, as the teeth on a crossbow rack are very rounded and the strap itself is thicker (Nicholas Hall pers comm). If the likelihood of the ratchet coming from a crossbow rack is remote, then perhaps the ratchet should best be considered part of the domestic or structural ironwork of the castle considered below.

Armour

Plate armour

Possible plate armour fragments were found in both areas of excavation occurring in two contexts in the 1996 excavations and a further seven in the 1998 excavations. The earliest occurrence (Figures 5.4, 7 and 5.10) came from a clay floor 158, CG96 11, Phase 7, of a building dated to the 14th century. These fragments were narrow with a distinctly curved profile suggesting they come from the fingers of a gauntlet. Plate armour fragments also came from two mid-14th to 15th-century contexts in CG98, Phase 8, a fill 636 of cut 664, CG98 16, Phase 8, and make-up 641, CG98 20, Phase 8, for a gravel floor 651 (Figures 5.4, 8), while a small iron hook (Figure 5.4, 10) likely to come from armour, comparable with another attached to plate armour (Figure 5.4, 9), was recovered from a rubble dump 066, CG96 08, Phase 8, also of this date. Other groups came from two dumps of 16th-century rubbish; one from the 1996 excavations (025, CG96 03, Phase 9), the other (579, CG98 12, Phase 9) from the 1998 excavations. The rest came from 16th- to 17th-century dumped material located both inside and outside the East Tower (CG98 11 and CG98 13 respectively, Phase 10). It is possible that all the plate armour may be of medieval date, as the pieces from 16th-century and later contexts all come from dumps containing earlier material.

The remains of the plate armour recovered are for the most part highly fragmentary and few diagnostic features are preserved, making independent dating difficult. While some do retain original edges, rivets (for example Figure 5.4, 8 and 5.10), rivet holes and, on one occasion, an iron hook (Figure 5.4, 9), others have been recognised only by their thickness, profile and characteristic surface. The degree and nature of the encrustation observed on the plate armour from Wigmore Castle and elsewhere, such as Launceston Castle (Mould 2006, 303–304), is distinctive and while it may well be the result of an initial surface treatment or the subsequent cleaning and polishing that the plate armour underwent when in use, it has not proved possible to confirm this by analysis. Rarely, non-ferrous metal plating is observable in X-radiograph, for example on Figure 5.4, 9 part of group 200990015, but mostly no suggestion of a surface treatment can be discerned. The occurrence of minerally preserved organic remains is also commonly a feature on some plate fragments. A sample of four of the plate armour fragments from Wigmore Castle were investigated (Figure 5.4, 7, 8; 9701933 and 200990015b, Figure 5.10) and two (Figure 5.4, 7 and 8) proved to have a tinned surface, though this was not readily observable in X-radiograph, in contrast to other types of iron objects such as keys and buckles, where this feature can be easily seen. The presence of a tinned surface confirms their identification as plate armour and may go some way to explaining the distinctive corrosion present on other examples, although it could not be detected in all the samples submitted.

Mail links

A riveted iron link from mail (9703007) with a diameter of 11mm was recovered when sieving material from the large demolition dump 665, CG98 11, Phase 10, within the East Tower. In addition, small lengths of used, fine-gauge iron wire (9701308) occurred in a sample of charcoal-rich deposits 220, CG96 20, Phase 4, of late 13th-century date. The wire may possibly have been used in the repair of mail links to make makeshift links or rivets, but see also dress fittings below.

Horse equipment

Horse equipment is usually a common feature of the assemblages from castle excavations and it was well represented at Wigmore Castle. As mentioned previously, the buckles from these excavations have been counted as dress accessories in the tables of functional categories but a number, possibly all, of the iron buckles may well come from horse harnesses and are considered below.

Horseshoes

No complete horseshoes were recovered but the broken branches from ten horseshoes were found. A broken horseshoe (200990029) of Clark's type 2A (Clark 1995, 86), common during the later 11th and 12th centuries, was found on the stone hearth 351, CG96 27, Phase 2, in the timber building dated to the 12th century. Five other broken horseshoes were found in medieval contexts, the remainder coming from later deposits.

At least 67 nails from horseshoes were found. Fiddlekey horseshoe nails, used with Clark's type

1, 2 and 3 horseshoes (Clark 1995, 85–87), were found from the earliest levels onward. Elsewhere fiddlekey nails are found in 10th- to 11th-century contexts (for example, Ottaway 1992, 707) so that the earliest example (Figure 5.4, 11) from Wigmore Castle, recovered from layer 392 above the clay bank of the first timber castle, could represent the earliest Norman activity. The first horseshoe nails of 'eared' type (such as Figure 5.4, 12), associated with horseshoes of Clark's type 3 occurred in 13th-century deposits. A horseshoe nail with a cuboid head (Figure 5.4, 13) used with horseshoes of Clark's type 4, in common use throughout the 14th and 15th century, also occurred in a deposit 245 dated to the 13th century. Type 4 horseshoes are believed to have come into use in London in 1270–1350 (Clark 1995, 96–97), such an early loss of a nail of this type at Wigmore Castle suggests the rider equipped his mount with the most modern horseshoes then available.

Horse bits

A possible broken iron link from a horse bit with a spirally twisted stem and a hooked terminal (9701839) was found in fill 636, CG98 16, Phase 8, dating to the 15th century. A cheek piece and broken bit link from a curb bit (Figures 5.4, 14 and 5.11) came from post-medieval deposits that had accumulated against the curtain wall in the same area of investigation (CG98 02, Phase 11). The iron cheek piece was tin plated (Felter and Bartindale 2009). The curb bit is associated with ridden horses rather than those being driven when used for haulage, and while some illustrations of medieval draught animals fitted with curb bits are known, the curb bit suggests the mount of a member of the gentry (see Clark 1995, 46 for discussion). Though the bit is broken, the short cheeks suggest that the curb bit was 'mild', giving the rider a medium amount of control of his mount but not the very high degree of control necessary for horses used in warfare or tournament. Curb bits recovered by excavation are small in number and appear to vary widely. The Wigmore example can be closely paralleled by another from Battle Abbey, East Sussex (Hare 1985, fig 59, no. 47), recovered along with other horse gear from an area close to the dormitory of the abbey that was later converted into a stable in AD 1810. Spurs from the same location were dated stylistically to the 17th and 18th centuries, so that the Wigmore Castle curb bit, coming from the lowest level of accumulated deposits, is likely to be of similar date, possibly representing one of the few objects associated with the Civil War activity on site. It may be worth noting also that a suggested date of the first half of the 17th century was proposed by H Russell Robinson (Tower Armouries) for a comparable curb bit recovered from the River Thames at Queenhithe in the Museum of London collections (Acc. No. 74.452). The Wigmore Castle, Battle Abbey and Queenhithe curb bits are all notably of small size suggesting they had been used on small horses.

Harness buckles

Eight iron buckles and an iron buckle pin were found. Plain iron buckles with frames sufficiently large to take straps more than 50mm in width are considered to be from horse harness (Egan 1995, 55). No iron buckle from Wigmore Castle attains this size but it is most likely that those with D-shaped and angular frames were from harness and are considered here. No small buckles of a distinctive type used to secure spur leathers were found. Three iron buckle frames could be seen in X-radiograph to be plated with non-ferrous metal, likely to be tin plating, to prevent rusting.

A broken iron buckle frame (200990024) with non-ferrous metal plating came from a late 13th-century occupation surface (168, CG96 16, Phase 6). Two buckles had D-shaped frames. The larger (Figure 5.5, 15) for a strap no more than 40mm (1½ inches) wide, the other (Figure 5.5, 16) took a strap no more than 32mm (1¼ inch) in width. One (Figure 5.5, 15) came from a 16th-century levelling layer (046, CG96 07, Phase 9), the other (Figure 5.5, 16) from demolition dumping 604, CG98 11, Phase 10, in the East Tower, though both may well be of medieval date.

Three iron buckles with angular frames were recovered. The two complete examples (Figure 5.5, 17 and 18), both from 16th-century deposits, were used on straps no wider than 20mm (approximately ¾ inch). A fragment broken from a third example with remains of the pin wrapped around the plated frame (9701944) was found in dumped material (644, CG98 11, Phase 10) within the East Tower. A broken buckle frame of cast copper alloy (200990008) from topsoil, 001, is also of a size (53mm) suitable for harness.

Spurs

Seven pieces broken from iron rowel spurs were part of the large group of material dumped within the East Tower, CG98 11, Phase 10. Their fragmentary condition is such that it is difficult to be certain of the number of spurs present: the six fragments from context 665 represent at least three examples (Figure 5.5, 19, 20 and 21), with another occurring in context 640, CG98 11, Phase 10 (Figure 5.5, 22).

A long, straight neck (shank) with a star rowel with five of the possible eight long points remaining (Figure 5.5, 20) suggests a 15th-century date for one example, while the curved neck and six-pointed rowel of another (Figure 5.5, 22) suggests it may date to the early 15th century. A further fragment (Figure 5.5, 21) appears to be a narrow, curving arm with a small riveted terminal. It is comparable with those on a child's spur probably of early 15th-century date from the Thames at London Bridge (Ellis 1995, 146 and fig 104, no. 353) and also found on a type of spur tentatively assigned to the 16th century (Ward Perkins 1940, C2347, 110 and fig 34); alternatively it is possible that the fragment is a broken rowel box with curved neck rather than a very narrow arm and, therefore, of the same date as the previous example. What independent dating evidence that there is for the spurs suggests a 15th (or possibly at the latest a 16th) century date for the group.

Dress accessories and other personal items

Small dress fittings and personal items were recovered in limited numbers from contexts deriving from the castle's occupation and later abandonment. The general lack of later material is in contrast to the wealth of this category of material found at other castles such as Launceston Castle, Cornwall (Mould 2006), that were popular with 18th- and 19th-century visitors.

Buckles, strap loops and other belt fittings

In all, 12 buckles and a separate buckle pin were present. Four were of copper alloy of which three appear to be dress accessories. The fourth, part of a large cast copper-alloy buckle frame (200990008) found in topsoil, 001, was of a size (53mm in height) suitable for a wide sword belt or harness. A small copper-alloy frame (Figure 5.5, 23) with an ornate outer edge was found in the upper most levelling layer 710 for the construction of wall 711, associated with the East Tower (CG98 09, Phase 4) in the 13th century. It is a well made example comparable with a general type that is long lived, dating from the late 12th through to the late 14th century (Egan and Pritchard 1991, 76). Though an apparently common type, both here and on the continent, they were also worn by those of high status, as an example on the tomb effigy of Berengaria, the queen of Richard I testifies (Egan and Pritchard, 1991, fig 10). This example might best be considered a strap loop, having internal projections, and was designed for use on a narrow strap no more than 15mm (½ inch) wide. It most closely resembles a metal-detected example for which a date *c*1250–1400 is proposed (Whitehead 1996, 22, no. 90). A piece of cast copper-alloy frame (200990024) that may also be a broken buckle was recovered from 14th-century occupation (168, CG96 16, Phase 6). It may be compared with another broken frame fragment from Dryslwyn Castle (Goodall 2007, 257 and fig 9.15, A10) found in the Great Hall in a context dated to 1230–50 (Phase 2a). A cast copper-alloy 'spectacle' buckle (Figure 5.5, 24) with a separate central pin bar of iron was found in a 16th-century rubble dump (647, CG98 14, Phase 9) together with 14th-century pottery. The spectacle buckle is a long-lived style dating to 1350–1720, and buckles with a separate pin (strap) bar were made in small numbers from the 14th century onward (Whitehead 1996, 96), three of lead/tin alloy being found in the city of London (Egan and Pritchard 1991, 102 and fig 65). The small size, separate pin bar and curved profile of the Wigmore Castle buckle, however, strongly suggest it to be a plain shoe or knee buckle dating to *c*1660–1720 (Whitehead 1996, 96–97) and therefore intrusive into this context. This may be one of the few finds associated with the period immediately following the Civil War partial slighting of the castle walls.

While most of the iron buckles have been described with the horse equipment above, one small annular buckle frame of iron (200990017) is a shoe buckle of a type commonly used from the late 14th through to the 16th centuries. The buckle, 16mm in diameter, came from levelling material (043, CG96 06, Phase 9), probably deposited in the 15th or 16th centuries. Another iron ring (200990009) 20mm in diameter, found in topsoil, 002, may be a second example.

Other decorative fittings from belts and girdles were rare. A small (17 x 4mm), rectangular copper-alloy bar mount (9703040) was recovered during sieving of an unphased deposit (721) from the 1998 excavations. It is comparable with others found in the city of London in contexts principally dating to around 1270–1350 (Egan and Pritchard 1991, 211–213 and fig 133).

Pins and lace tags

A small number of copper-alloy (brass) pins were recovered (27 pins and 10 pin stems). Two pieces of broken pin stem (9701313) were retrieved during sieving of a layer 359, within a 12th-century hearth (CG96 27, Phase 2), lacking their heads these broken pins cannot be closely dated but point to the early adoption of new fashions by inhabitants of the castle. A single pin with a wound wire head of Caple type A (Caple 1991) came from a 14th to 15th-century deposit (064, CG96 08, Phase 8). The remainder (90%) came from deposits dating from the 16th century or later.

Only three small copper-alloy lace tags (lace chapes or aiglets) were recovered, occurring singly in deposits of 16th and 16th- to 17th-century rubble and demolition debris. One example (9701804), found in a pit pre-dating the final abandonment of the castle (CG98 03, Phase11), preserved the remains of the lace. A fourth lace tag (SF7526), found in an unphased context during the 1998 excavations, was large, measuring 71mm in length. While it might be suggested that the long lace tag (SF7526) is of 17th century date, similarly large examples have been found in late 13th- to 14th-century contexts in the city of London and this lace tag may well be of

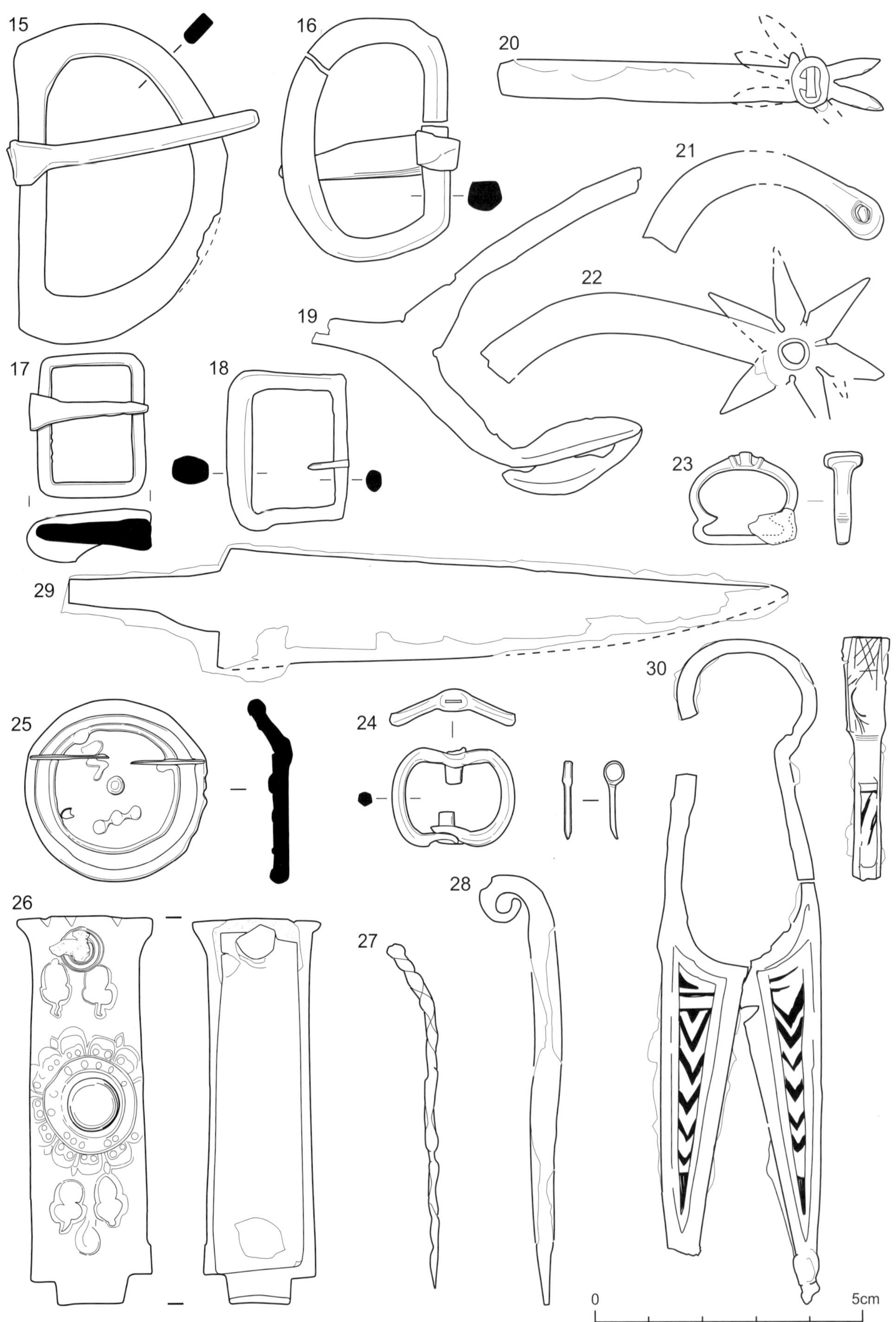

FIGURE 5.5
Illustrated iron, copper-alloy and lead artefacts, Nos 15–30

similar date particularly in the light of the quantity of 13th- to 14th-century material from Wigmore Castle. Alternative uses have been suggested for lace tags of this length that include pens and pin holders (Egan and Pritchard 1991, 286–290).

Later dress fastenings were limited to a 19th-century bone button (9701003) found in the topsoil, 003, and a small disc-shaped iron button (200990031) with non-ferrous metal plating occurring intrusively in a 16th-century deposit (046, CG96 07, Phase 9).

Other decorative items

Small lengths of fine-gauge iron wire (9701308) less than 0.5mm thick were recovered during soil sieving of a 13th-century deposit (220, CG96 20, Phase 4) deriving from a significant fire. Three fragments had a sinuous profile indicating that they had been wound in use. The wire may come from a headdress or hair accessory, perhaps similar to an example, covered with silk thread, found in a late 14th-century context at Baynard House in the city of London (Egan and Pritchard 1991, 296 and fig 194). The context in which the Wigmore wire was found, however, might also suggest the possibility that the wire was used for the repair of mail links and is associated with the military rather than the domestic household.

A rumbler bell of copper-alloy sheet (9701665), 30mm in diameter, was found in a late 15th- or 16th-century rubble dump (560, CG98 12, Phase 9). In the medieval period small bells of this type were worn on dress, on dog collars and on horse harness, any of which might be have occurred in the context of a castle. In London they become common from the late 13th century onward, the plain Wigmore Castle bell being comparable with another example from an early 15th-century context at Trig Lane (Egan and Pritchard 1991, 336–339, no. 1666).

Other personal items

Two small amber beads probably from rosaries were recovered by sieving from the 1998 excavations. The beads are of spherical shape, slightly flattening where the hole has been drilled, and 6–6.5mm in diameter. One (9703042) came from a 15th-century make-up layer (641) for a plaster floor (631, CG98 20, Phase 8), the other (SF7522) from an unphased context (693). They may well be contemporary.

Commerce and literacy

Coins and jetons are considered separately elsewhere (Section 5.3). A pan weight (Figure 5.5, 25 and 5.12) of lead (25.0082g) was recovered from topsoil 003 during the 1996 excavations. The weight has a series of apparently meaningless cast markings on the upper face intended to impress and give a (false) sense of authenticity and reliability to the weight. It is likely to date to the late 16th/17th century (Geoff Egan pers comm).

A book clasp of copper-alloy sheet (Figure 5.5, 26) had remains of a leather strap, 15mm wide and 2mm thick, preserved between the front and back plates. Book clasps of this type occur in contexts dating from the late medieval and early post-medieval periods; of the four from excavations at Winchester one comes from a 14th- to 15th-century context, the others from 16th-century or later deposits (Biddle 1990, 755 and fig 215). The clasp has a raised central boss surrounded by a stamped floral design between acorn motifs, the nature of the decoration suggests the clasp is likely date to the 16th century and is contemporary with the 16th- to 17th-century rubble dump (011, CG96 02, Phase 10) in which it was found. The size of the clasp is such that it may have been used on a bible (Geoff Egan pers comm).

Household items

Like other castle assemblages, household items are well represented, particularly items associated with security, and included a range of domestic utensils and small furniture fittings. Of particular interest are a pair of silver-inlaid iron shears dating to the 13th century. A broken iron candle pricket (9701042) from a later accumulated deposit (007, CG96 01, Phase 11) was the only object associated with lighting to be recovered.

Cooking and eating

A small spirally twisted iron stem (Figure 5.5, 27), likely to be a broken skewer or possibly the handle of a small domestic implement, was found in the lowest fill (367) of a sub-rectangular pit (368, CG96 26, Phase 2) in the 12th-century timber building close to the Southern Curtain Wall. A complete skewer (Figure 5.5, 28) with a scrolled terminal came from a rubble dump (068, CG96 08, Phase 8) associated with the 15th-century rebuilding of the Southern Curtain Wall. Used in the preparation and cooking of roasted meats they hint at quality dining.

A small fragment of copper-alloy sheet (9701055) with a slightly thickened rim that may come from a sheet metal vessel was found in a 16th- to 17th-century rubble dump (022, CG96 02, Phase 10). An iron strap handle mount (9701870) for a more robust, utilitarian vessel such as a bucket was found in the fill cut (658 CG98 15, Phase 8); two broken handle mounts of iron sheet (200990010, 200990012) came from later accumulated deposits (003 and 005, CG96 01, Phase 11).

Two plain iron rings, a figure-of-eight chain link and an S-shaped suspension hook that may have been put to a variety of uses, including pot chain and the suspension of lighting fittings, were present in dumped and later accumulated material (002 and 005, CG96 01, Phase 11; 022, CG96 02, Phase 10; and 035, CG96 03 Phase 9), dating from the 16th century onward (they have been counted as household items in Figure 5.2).

Knives and spoons

The remains of at least nine knives were found, occurring in both areas of excavation, including personal knives, knives used in the preparation of food and possibly for serving. A shield-shaped knife hilt plate of copper-alloy sheet was found in a fill (305) of a pit (368, CG96 26, Phase 2), in the 12th-century timber building. It may be comparable with a mid-13th-century knife from Swan Lane in London (Cowgill *et al* 1987, no. 15), with a composite handle comprising a series of tin plates threaded on the tang, which also has a copper-alloy shoulder plate but other examples directly associated with knives appear to be rare at this date. Two broken knife blades (SF7535, SF7551) and a circular washer crudely cut from lead sheet (SF7550) that may also possibly come from a composite knife handle, were found in 13th-century levelling deposits (CG98 09, Phase 4). A complete knife (Figure 5.5, 29) from a fill (203, CG96 17, Phase 5) of the construction cut, probably dating to around 1300, for the Southern Curtain Wall had remains of the wooden handle present on the tang, however, it was so heavily mineralised that it could only be identified as a ring-porous hardwood. A large broken knife (200990023) from a 14th-century occupation surface (168, CG96 16, Phase 6) is likely to be a kitchen knife used for butchery rather than a knife used at the table. A fragment of another large knife blade (9701093/2) with a downward curving back and a straight edge was amongst a group of domestic metalwork in a mid-14th- to 15th-century dumped deposit (064, CG96 08, Phase 8). A knife (9701073) with a broken scale tang handle and a blade with a blunt, rounded end suggesting it was not used for eating but either for carving or serving at the table (Moore 1999, 71) was found in 16th-century dumped material (25, CG96 03, Phase 9). The point broken from a long knife blade (9701756) and the whittle tang broken from a knife, possibly from the same item, came from a similar deposit (647, CG98 14, Phase 9). A scale tang knife (9701059) with a broken blade was part of a group of domestic metalwork dumped (032, CG96 02, Phase 10) against the Southern Curtain Wall shortly after the abandonment of the castle, while a broken knife blade (9701833) was amongst the material dumped (665, CG98 11, Phase 10) within the East Tower.

A small rectangular piece of bone with a pierced terminal possibly broken from the handle plate of a scale-tanged knife was found in a mid-14th- to 15th-century pit fill (674, CG98 17, Phase 8). Two handle scales from a plain bone handle (9701095, 9701121) were found in two separate later accumulated deposits (002, 003), whereas another scale with a decorative, asymmetrical, downward curving terminal was recovered from another (007), all part of CG96 01, Phase 11.

The fig-shaped bowl of a pewter spoon (9701555) in very poor condition came from dumped material (563, CG98 13, Phase 10) associated with the very early decay of the castle. A similarly shaped spoon bowl of copper alloy (9701802) was found in the topsoil (501, CG98 10, Phase 11). They both have a very small 'rat tail' present on the back of the deeply curved bowl and are likely to date to the beginning of the 16th century.

Other utensils

A pair of iron shears (Figure 5.5, 30) with the handle and blades inlaid with silver were found in the fill (195, CG96 17, Phase 5) of the construction cut for the Curtain Wall. The iron shears, 'blued' to set off the delicate silver inlay, were an expensive and prestigious item clearly with a domestic function, such as cutting sewing threads in needlework, or possibly for hair cutting and beard trimming. They may be compared with two 13th-century examples from Swan Lane in the city of London (Cowgill *et al* 1997, 107 nos 316, 317) each decorated with curvilinear inlaid motifs; another is described as just coming 'from London' (Ward Perkins 1940, 156, fig 48, no. 11). An example from the West Midlands was also recorded at Weoley Castle, Birmingham (Mould 2011). The shears from Wigmore Castle have a more linear design than the other examples.

A broken finger loop from a pair of scissors (9701096) was also found amongst a group of domestic items in a mid-14th- to 15th-century rubble dump (064, CG96 08, Phase 8).

Locks and keys

A piece possibly broken from a lock mechanism (9701093) was found in a rubble dump (064, CG96 08, Phase 8) dating to the mid-14th to 15th century. A padlock (Figure 5.6, 31) with a small, plain, barrel case came from a 16th-century rubbish dump (025, CG96 03, Phase 9). X-radiography suggests it has a bolt with two parallel spines. The size indicates it was used to secure a box or chest or possibly a window shutter. Two copper-plated and decorated iron padlocks of this type were found at Carisbrooke Castle (Fairbrother 2000, fig 56, 101–102), for example, both recovered from the castle interior, one in a medieval post-hole, the other from a later post-medieval (16th–18th century) layer below topsoil. They are comparable with padlocks of Winchester Type C, differing in that the bolt fitted into a broad strap-like extension of the barrel case rather than the more usual L–shaped arm. Padlocks of Winchester Type C in were used for a long period from the 12th through to the 16th century (Goodall 1990,

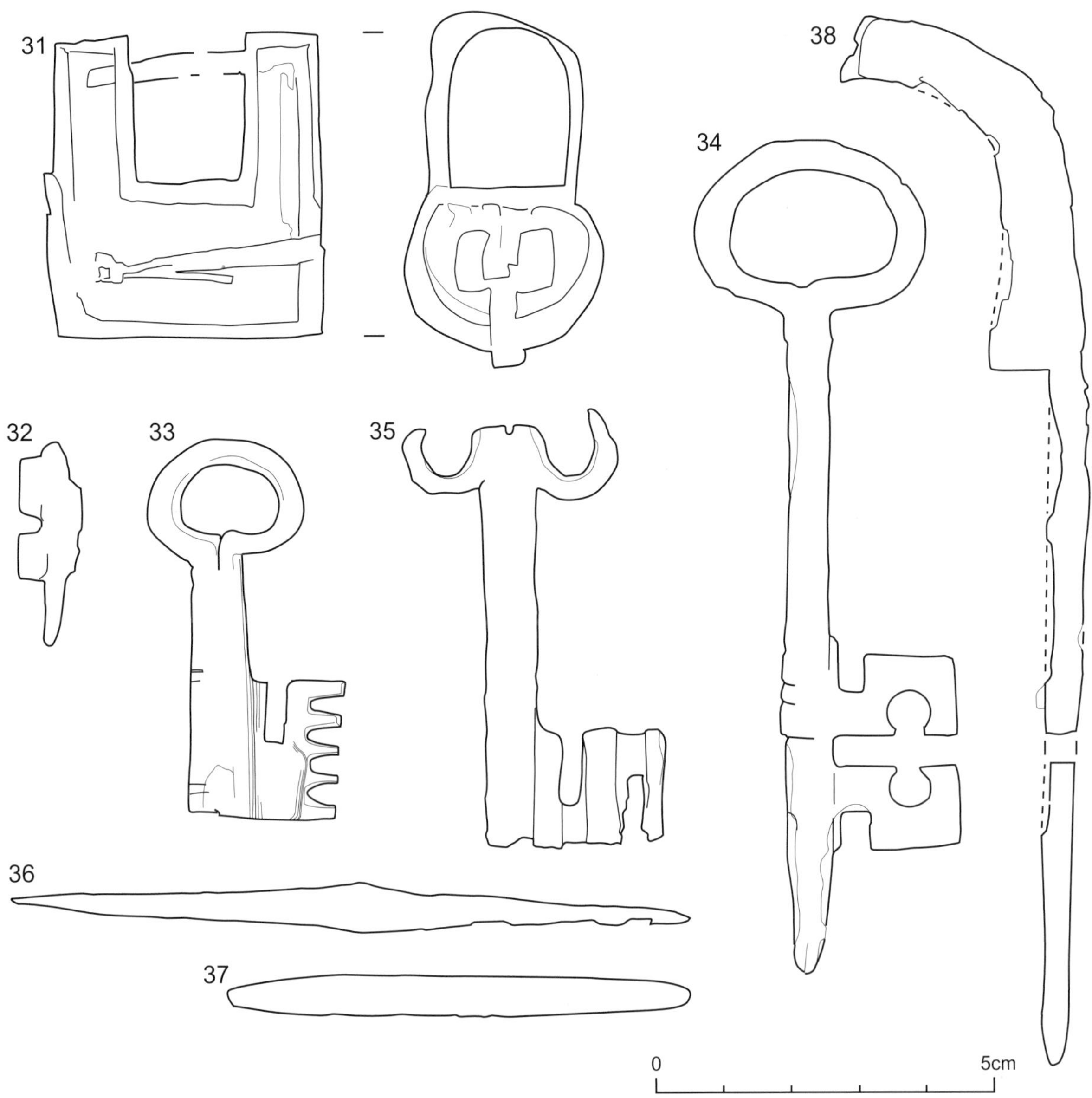

FIGURE 5.6
Illustrated iron artefacts, Nos 31–38

1001), compatible with the late medieval/early post-medieval dating of the examples from Wigmore Castle and Carisbrooke Castle.

Six iron keys were found at Wigmore Castle, all worked mounted locks. The bit broken from a small rotary key (Figure 5.6, 32) of Winchester Type 7 (Goodall 1990, 1007), likely to have been used on a piece of furniture such as a box or cupboard, came from a 13th-century fill (703) of the construction trench (676, CG98 23, Phase 4) for the East Tower. Fragments of a key (20099034) with non-ferrous metal plating were found in a 14th-century occupation surface (168, CG96 16, Phase 6). Other keys came from deposits associated with the disuse of the castle. A small key (Figure 5.6, 33) with a hollow stem, known as a piped shank, to fit on to a pin in the lock came from rubble (028, CG96 02, Phase 10) dumped against the Southern Curtain Wall; being of iron, this particular style of key, Winchester Type 9, can be dated to the post-medieval period (Goodall 1990, 1007). The key had been tin plated. A broken ring key bow with a moulded neck (SF1721) came from material dumped inside the East Tower (640, CG98 11, Phase 10). A large door key (Figure 5.6, 34) of Winchester Type 8 (Goodall 1990, 1007), a type that continued in use into the post-medieval period, and a key with a piped shank and a kidney-shaped bow (Figure 5.6, 35), also likely to be of early post-medieval date, came from a deposit (005, CG96 01, Phase 11) lying just below topsoil, containing finds of 16th- and 17th-century date and thought to represent material from the final occupation of the castle.

Furnishings

Furniture and other fittings were found principally in general levelling and dumping deposits. One exception being a small piece that may be broken from an iron strap mount for a casket, or possibly a broken handle from a small padlock key (9701123), found on the clay floor 158, of the 14th-century stone building. An iron hasp (789710178) from a 16th-century make-up layer (049, CG98 07, Phase 9) was used to close a box or chest. The small number of iron hinges and pieces of nailed iron bindings may come from furniture or doors and shutters. While these are common finds, two pieces of iron binding strap with decorative circular cut-outs (10mm in diameter) are less so. One fragment (9701971) was recovered from a mid-13th- to mid-14th-century occupation deposit (667, CG98 21, Phase 5), the other (9701757) from the fill (646) of cut 658, CG98 15, Phase 8. Varying between 18 and 20mm in width, the two pieces may derive from a single object (there was much disturbance in this area of excavation and redeposition is likely; see Chapters 3 and 9). Each appears in radiograph to have non-ferrous metal plating that would both look attractive and prevent rusting.

Domestic furnishings of copper alloy were limited. A possible furniture fitting in the form a large decorative copper-alloy rivet (9701102) that may be a finial from a handle, was found in the Curtain Wall construction trench backfill (CG96 17, Phase 5). Principally made of copper, the presence of silver in the alloy suggested that the object may have been made of recycled metal (Felter and Bartindale 2009, 9–10). Two plain copper-alloy drape rings (9701084, 9701091) for hanging tapestries and curtains, each 19mm in diameter, were found in mid-15th-century dumps (061, CG96 08, Phase 8 and 076, CG96 08, Phase 9).

Craft tools and agricultural items

Woodworking

A drill bit (9701013) used to drill holes in wood was found in later layer 005, CG96 01, Phase 11, part of a mixed group of principally household items that accumulated following the disuse of the castle. The suggestion of a gouge-like section to the broken tip suggests it to be an auger spoon bit.

Leather-working

Four iron awls, used to make holes in leather, were found and are tools commonly found on castle sites. Leather-workers would be required for the making and repair of harness and other equipment, even if the footwear of the servants was obtained in the locality outside the castle and that of gentry from centres of fashion. The earliest awl to be recovered (Figure 5.6, 36) came from a fill (203, CG96 17, Phase 5) of the construction cut of the Southern Curtain Wall and clearly derived from earlier activity at the castle. The minerally preserved remains of the awl handle made from a ring-porous hardwood were too mineralised to allow species identification. Another, smaller example (Figure 5.6, 37), came from a clay floor (158, CG96 11) within the Phase 7 stone building dating to the 14th century and may also reflect earlier use. A long awl (9701701) comparable with Figure 5.6, 36 occurred in the demolition dump (630, CG98 11, Phase 10) inside the East Tower, while a small awl or tracer (9701553) came from fill of pit 520, CG98 03, Phase 11, dug late in the castle's history.

Horticultural and agricultural activity

The broken iron tooth (200990019) from a rake was found in a dump deposit (080, CG96 09, Phase 8) associated with the rebuilding of the Southern Curtain Wall in the 15th century. An iron collar ferrule (9701518) of a type that might be used on a variety of tool handles to prevent the wooden handles from splitting was found amongst a group of metalwork in the fill of 664, CG98 16, Phase 8.

A small hooked blade (Figure 5.6, 38) with a long tang for insertion into a wooden handle came from a 16th-century make-up layer for surface 045, CG96 07, Phase 9. The slender blade appears to have been extensively sharpened. The implement was probably used for horticulture or gathering fodder for stock. Grafting and pruning knives have curved blades and an unusual knife of this sort may have had a specialised function.

An oxshoe (9701074) from a draught animal used for traction occurred in demolition rubble dump 016, CG96 02, Phase 10 deposited in the 17th century.

Structural metalwork

Structural ironwork

Structural ironwork was, as always, dominated by the number of timber nails found. In the quantification necessary to prepare Figures 5.1 and 5.2 the number of timber nails from each context has been given the value 1 to help offset this bias. In all, 580 complete nails were found, 385 from the 1996 excavations and 195 from those undertaken in 1998. In addition, a further 344 shanks broken from nails were found but lacking heads could not be further categorised with another 207 broken shank fragments. The majority of the nails had flat, angular heads and angular-sectioned shanks but other types, including nails with flat, rectangular heads, smaller nails with flat, 'waisted' (figure-of-eight shaped) heads, nails with L-shaped heads, comparable to joiner's brad nails in use today, and headless nails with rectangular shanks were also present. All these types have been found previously when medieval and post-medieval nail groups have been studied in detail, such as those from the Hospital of St Mary of Ospringe, Kent, for example (Mould 1979) and they are clearly common types used in joinery throughout most of the period. At Wigmore Castle nails with 'waisted' heads, rectangular-headed nails, headless nails and brad nails all occur from the 13th century onwards. It was observed that nails recovered from dumped deposits, particularly those from material dumped inside the East Tower, were often in good condition and not encrusted which may be the result of their immediate burial environment.

A small number of other items of structural ironwork were present including wallhooks and U-shaped staples. The majority of the structural material came from dumped deposits (CG98 13 and CG96 02, Phase 10). They included two broken iron window bars, one (9701610) was still attached to the lead seating that bedded into the stone frame, and an iron window stay (9701040). Much of the lead recovered from the castle derives from fenestration and is described below.

Structural lead

A relatively large amount of lead was recovered from the Wigmore 1996 excavations. Some 35kg of lead was reported on shortly after excavation (Doonan 1999), later a further 1.2kg of lead waste was examined and assessed (Dungworth 2000, 4–5). The results of that work are summarised here. Subsequently a small amount was also retrieved during environmental sampling and bagged with other items of metal. The structural lead that had been allocated small find numbers, including lead sheet, cramps and window cames, has been counted as structural metalwork (Figure 5.2)

Lead waste

There is much lead waste in the form of accumulations shaped like hearth bottoms and spillages, lead solidified from the molten state, in early 14th-century contexts (Figure 5.7). A hearth bottom of lead waste was recovered from the base of a large lead-melting hearth (114, CG96 14, Phase 6) of early 14th-century date, with lead waste, and waste mixed with window cames, coming from the fills (170 and 172) above. A large lead spillage was also present in fill (119) of the re-cut (120) of a second bowl hearth, CG96 12, Phase 6, of the same date.

Two further lead hearth bottoms were found on floor surfaces 093 and 096 in the interior of the stone building, CG96 11, Phase 7, dating to the 14th century. Lead weighing 483g that had solidified in the bowl of a ladle and been subsequently discarded, came from a patch of brown clay (086) close to pit 091, CG96 10, Phase 7. The waste was

Phase	Group	Context	Description	Weight
1996 excavations				
6	12	119	Spillage	5785g
6	12	135	Spillage	242g
6	13	121	Spillage	12g
6	14	167	Spillage	63g
6	14	170	Spillage and cames	1125g
6	14	172	Spillage	3132g
6	15	152	Spillage	52g
6	15	171	Spillage	171g
7	11	88	Spillage	19g
7	11	96	Spillage	67g
10	2	11	Spillage	56g
11	1	5	Spillage	324g
11	1	7	Spillage	87g
6	13	112	Cames/ties	640g
6	14	170	Cames and spillage	1125g
7	11	93	Cames	26g
7	11	101	Cames	67g
10	2	11	Cames	12g
1998 excavations				
4	17	196	Trimming	36g
4	20	200	Sheet trimming	<0.5g
6	12	85	Trimming	40g
6	12	98	Trimming	557g
6	13	102	Trimming	84g
6	13	126	Sheet	14g
6	13	128	Sheet trimming	9g
6	14	113	Trimming	37g
6	15	137	Trimming	1.5g
6	15	140	Offcuts	23g
7	11	100	Sheet trimming	15g
7	11	102	Trimming	5g
7	11	158	Trimming	14g
8	8	61	Sheet offcut	617g
8	8	73	Sheet offcut	323g
8	9	82	Sheet trimming	14g
9	6	43	Sheet	9g

FIGURE 5.7
Lead spillages, window lead, sheet, trimmings and offcuts

composed principally of metallic lead with oxidised surfaces and was consistent with having formed in and around hearths used to melt lead (Dungworth 2000, 5). It would appear that the building was the scene of a major episode of lead melting during the 14th century. The waste lead was found with sheet lead and window cames in the same lead-melting hearths (see below) strongly suggesting it all to be structural leadwork being melted down during demolition.

Window lead

Lead window cames and window ties were recovered principally from a brown clay fill (170) of the 14th-century lead-melting hearth (114) and a layer (112) overlying it, all CG96 14, Phase 6 (Figure 5.7). The close association of window cames and spillage suggests that the cames were in the process of being melted down in the hearth. It is possible that lead was being melted in order that

	Phase 1	Phase 2	Phase 4	Phase 5	Phase 6	Phase 7	Phase 8	Phase 9	Phase 10	Total
Smithing hearth base	3316g		1392g	774g		584g	1344g	4720g	143g	12273g
Vitrified hearth lining	80g									80g
Cinder	310g	6g	3g					39g		358g
Fuel ash slag	1g		86g		41g			39g		167g
Undiagnostic iron slag	550g	49g	518g	67g	4g			929g	68g	2185g
Total	**4257g**	**55g**	**1999g**	**841g**	**45g**	**584g**	**1344g**	**5727g**	**211g**	**15063g**

FIGURE 5.8
Wigmore 1996: iron-smithing slags

it could be recast into cames to re-glaze windows in the immediate vicinity; more likely, perhaps, it was being melted down to be more easily transported for use elsewhere in the castle or further afield.

Roofing lead

Lead sheet, sheet trimmings and offcuts derive from the roofing of buildings or their subsequent repair. A single piece (36g) came from the fill (196, CG96 17, Phase 5) of the construction trench of the Southern Curtain Wall, the remainder from contexts principally associated with lead-melting activity in the early 14th century in CG96 12, 13 and 14, Phase 6, and mid-14th- to 15th-century dump deposits (CG96 08, Phase 8) (Figure 5.7).

Evidence for iron-working

Some 15kg of iron-working slag recovered from the 1996 excavations of a section of the Southern Curtain Wall was examined and assessed (Dungworth 2000). All the types of iron-working slag that could be attributed to a particular activity were found to come from iron smithing, no evidence for smelting was recovered (Figure 5.8).

Evidence for iron smithing came from 12th-century contexts (CG96 29, Phase 1) probably associated with remodelling of the first timber castle. Six complete smithing hearth bottoms, one with hearth lining attached, and four hearth bottom fragments were recovered, all but one fragment coming from a grey/brown clay dump (374); other iron-working waste came from that layer and associated layers above (369, 371, 392). The recovery of smithing hearth bottoms, vitrified hearth lining and cinder suggests that iron smithing was being undertaken within the immediate vicinity at this time (Dungworth 2000, 2).

Iron-smithing slags including hearth bottoms were also recovered from later contexts and were considered likely to be residual or to have derived from another working area some distance from the area of the Southern Curtain Wall investigated (Dungworth 2000, 5). In the light of the contextual information now available, however, one could suggest that there is some evidence for smithing activity on site during the 13th century also. Fragments broken from iron smith hearth bottoms were found in contexts (199, 207, CG96 18, Phase 4) representing 13th-century occupation activity immediately preceding the construction of the Southern Curtain Wall. A complete iron-smithing hearth bottom and fragments from others came from fills 267, 203 and 263 respectively of the construction cut for the Southern Curtain Wall (389, CG96 17, Phase 5), dating to *c*1300. Iron-smithing slags recovered from deposits dating from the mid-14th century onward, though often found in some quantity, occur exclusively in dump deposits. The large amount present in 16th-century dumping might derive from contemporary activity, as six complete iron-smithing hearth bottoms and fragments from others were found in dump 035 and other bottom fragments came from 025 both part of CG96 03 Phase 9, along with other iron-smithing slags. Little cinder and no vitrified hearth lining were present, however.

Illustrated objects

1 Iron arrowhead 200990030, 044, CG96 06, Phase 9
Small central socket with two small fins, now disintegrated, seen in X-radiograph only. Military arrowhead of Jessop Type M1. Length 35mm, width 17mm (measured from X-radiograph). Figure 5.4.

2 Iron arrowhead 9701781, 648, CG9811, Phase 10
Small leaf-shaped blade with large socket with two small curving wings. Military arrowhead of Jessop Type M1. Copper plated. Almost complete. Length 43mm, width 14mm. Figures 5.4 and 5.9, far left.

3 Iron arrowhead SF7530, 707, CG98 09, Phase 4
Small, socketed leaf-shaped blade, fractured. A multi-purpose type of Jessop Type M4. Near complete. Length 65mm, width 17mm (measured from X-radiograph). Figures 5.4 and 5.9, fourth from left.

4 Iron arrowhead 9701766, 652, CG98 21, Phase 5
Triangular blade with central socket reaching to the tip and long barbs to each side, socket and one barb broken. Hunting arrowhead of Jessop Type MP8. Almost complete. Length 48mm, width 16mm. Figures 5.4 and 5.9, second from left.

5 Iron arrowhead 9701784, 644, CG98 11, Phase 10
Long pointed blade with downward facing barbs and long, round-sectioned socket extending well below the barbs. A multi-purpose arrowhead of Jessop Type MP7. Copper plated. Almost complete. Length 89mm, width 19mm. Figures 5.4 and 5.9, third from left.

FIGURE 5.9
Arrowheads: from left 9701781, 9701766, 9701784, SF7530 (photograph: Ian Panter, York Archaeological Trust)

FIGURE 5.10
Plate armour: from top 200099022, 9701933; bottom right 9701722; bottom left 200990015b (photograph: Ian Panter, York Archaeological Trust)

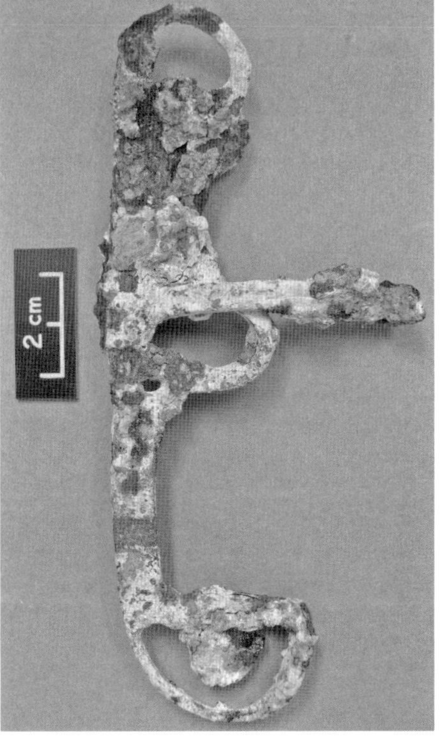

FIGURE 5.11
Curb bit 9701508 (photograph: Ian Panter, York Archaeological Trust)

6 Iron ratchet 9701127, 060, CG96 08, Phase 8
Rectangular-sectioned bar with a series of equally spaced and sized teeth running along one side. The other is straight and plain and extends into a tang at one end, the other end is broken. The teeth have a rectangular section, 2.70mm thick, and are not set indicating this to be a small ratchet and not a saw blade. Almost complete. Surviving length 180mm, max width 18mm. Figure 5.4.

7 Iron plate armour fragments 20099022, 158, CG96 11, Phase 7
Fragments (one illustrated) of narrow plate with curved profile, likely to be broken from the fingers of a gauntlet. Illustrated example tin plated with minerally preserved organic on the interior surface. Incomplete. Surviving length 37mm, width 20mm, thickness 1.7mm. Figures 5.4 and 5.10, top.

8 Iron plate armour fragment 9701722, 641, CG98 20, Phase 8
Rectangular plate with cropped corners and a flat round-headed rivet at each end, slightly curved in profile. Almost complete. Length 54mm, width 45mm, thickness 1.5mm. Figures 5.4 and 5.10, bottom right.

9 Iron plate armour fragments 200990015a, 025, CG96 03, Phase 9
Two pieces of plate, one aligned above the other. At least two original edges, a rivet, and a small curved hook fastening present. Non-ferrous metal plating is visible in X-radiograph. Figure 5.4.

10 Iron armour hook 200990032, 066, CG 08, Phase 8
Small, well-formed, curved hook with pierced ring terminal. Complete. Length 38mm. Figure 5.4.

11 Iron horseshoe nail, 392, CG96 29, Phase 1
Fiddlekey nail with worn head. Complete. Length 22mm, head 16 x 5mm. Figure 5.4.

12 Iron horseshoe nail 9701108, 229, CG96 22, Phase 4
'Earred' nail from horseshoe with rectangular-sectioned straight shank. Complete. Length 43mm, head 14 x 12mm. Figure 5.4.

13 Horseshoe nail 9701110, 245, CG96 22, Phase 4
Nail with cuboid head and clenched shank, not encrusted. Complete. Length 32mm, head 9 x 9mm. Figure 5.4.

14 Iron curb bit 9701508, 523, CG98 02, Phase 11
Cheek and part of a mouthpiece (link) from a curb bit comprising a straight bar with a D-shaped central link articulating with the mouthpiece (bit link) and rein and looped terminals, the upper to take the cheek piece, the lower for the second rein. Tin plated. Incomplete. Length 140mm, bit link surviving length 63mm. Figure 5.4; see also Figure 5.11.

15 Iron buckle 9701077, 046, CG96 07, Phase 9
Large D-shaped frame of rectangular section with a pin with a downward curving terminal wrapped around the integral pin bar. Non-ferrous metal plated. Complete. Length 40mm, height 58mm. Figure 5.5.

16 Iron buckle 9701914, 604, CG98 11, Phase 10
D-shaped frame of round section with pin wrapped around the integral pin bar. Non-ferrous metal plated. Complete. Length 30mm, height 45mm. Figure 5.5.

17 Iron buckle 9701058, 027, CG96 06, Phase 9
Angular, rectangular-sectioned frame with narrowed integral pin bar and pin wrapped around the bar. Complete. Length 23mm, height 28mm. Figure 5.5.

18 Iron buckle 9701662, 560, CG98 12, Phase 9
Rectangular buckle frame with narrowed integral pin bar and thickened rectangular-sectioned outer edge. Complete. Length 25mm, height 28mm. Figure 5.5.

19 Iron spur 9701851, 665, CG98 11, Phase 10
Spur with two broken and distorted sides and a broken, downward pointing neck springing from a crest (heel). Incomplete. Surviving length 74mm, side width 10mm. Figure 5.5.

20 Iron rowel spur neck 9701852, 665, CG98 11, Phase 10
Long straight neck with rowel box and a star rowel with five of the eight long points remaining. Incomplete. Length 74mm, rowel diameter *c*27mm, point length 10mm. Figure 5.5.

21 Iron spur fragment 9701849, 665, CG98 11, Phase 10
Narrow, curving arm of rectangular section with a rounded terminal centrally pieced by a rivet. Incomplete. Surviving length 43mm, width 5 x 3mm. Figure 5.5.

22 Iron rowel spur neck 9701729, 640, CG98 11, Phase 10
Long curving neck with rowel box and six-pointed rowel with lozenge-shaped points. Non-ferrous metal plated. Incomplete. Surviving length 76mm, rowel diameter 36mm, point length 17mm (measured from X-radiograph). Figure 5.5.

23 Copper-alloy strap loop 9707561, 710, CG98 09, Phase 4
Cast D-shaped frame of rectangular section with straight bar, pair of internal ridges and outer frame with three decorative mouldings. Complete. Length 17mm, height (width) 20mm, internal strap width 15mm. Figure 5.5.

24 Copper-alloy two-piece buckle 97071741, 647, CG98 14, Phase 9
Small, cast, spectacle buckle frame of waisted-shape and six-sided section with a curved profile. A scarf joint is centrally placed in one side, originally held together by the insertion of a separate central pin bar of iron, now broken; a fragment of copper-alloy pin also present. Almost complete. Length 23mm, max width (height) 18mm. Figure 5.5.

25 Lead pan weight 9701005, 003, CG96 01, Phase 11
Disc-shaped weight of cast sheet with pair of concentric raised mouldings, a small central raised boss and markings, a small triangular punched mark also present. Complete. Diameter 33mm, thickness 3.05mm, weight 25.0082g. Figures 5.5 and 5.12.

26 Copper-alloy book clasp 9701018, 011, CG96 02, Phase 10
Rectangular clasp comprising a decorated upper sheet and a plain lower sheet held together by a rivet at each end. The upper sheet has a hooked terminal, the other end slightly flared, and is decorated with a central boss surrounded by a stamped floral motif between two pairs of stamped acorn motifs. The clasp is gently curved in profile with remains of a leather strap, 15mm wide and 2mm thick between the sheets. Complete. Length 70mm, max width 25mm. Figure 5.5.

27 Iron skewer 9701114, 367, CG96 26, Phase 2
Slender, spirally twisted stem with pointed tip, curving at the other end. Almost complete. Length 65mm, max width 4mm. Figure 5.5.

28 Iron skewer 9701094, 064, CG96 08, Phase 8
Slender stem with a scrolled head and pointed tip, possibly spirally twisted stem but section now lost through flaking. Complete. Length 78mm, head diameter 12mm. Figure 5.5.

29 Iron knife 9701104, 203, CG96 17, Phase 5
Triangular blade with straight back and edge meeting at a long pointed tip. The centrally placed tang of rectangular

FIGURE 5.12

Lead pan weight 9701005 (photograph: Ian Panter, York Archaeological Trust)

section has much minerally preserved organic remains on one side, identified as a ring-porous hardwood. Complete. Length 135mm, blade length 107mm, width 20mm, back thickness 8mm. Figure 5.5.

30 Iron shears with silver inlay 9701103, 195, CG96 17, Phase 5
Pair of shears with triangular-shaped blades with straight backs and edges tapering to pointed tips, each with a concave curved 'recess' at the junction with the oval-sectioned narrow handles which widen slightly to the strip bow. The blades are decorated with silver inlay comprising a triangular double bordered panel with thick chevrons within and simple linear infilling. The handles and bow are also inlaid, the bow with lozenges with lattice infilling. Almost complete. Total length 121mm, blade length 66mm, width 18mm, bow diameter 26mm, width 9mm. Figure 5.5.

31 Iron barrel padlock 9701060, 025, CG96 03, Phase 9
Small, plain barrel case extending into a wide strap arm into which the bolt fitted. Two parallel spines visible in X-radiograph. Complete. Length 38mm, height 42mm, barrel diameter 24mm. Figure 5.6.

32 Iron key bit SF7538, 703, CG98 23, Phase 4
Broken solid key shank with narrowed pin and broken bit with a central cleft (Winchester Type 7). Incomplete. Length 30+mm, width 9mm. Figure 5.6.

33 Iron key 9701126, 028, CG96 02, Phase 10
Key with oval bow, thick shank with traces of decorative mouldings, now heavily worn, and large bit with upper vertical cleft and four horizontal clefts in the outer edge. The shank is piped for a short pin (Winchester Type 9). Non-ferrous metal plating identified as tin. Complete. Length 57mm bit 20 x 15mm. Figure 5.6.

34 Iron key 9701009, 005, CG96 01, Phase 11
Large key with oval bow, round-sectioned stem with decorative mouldings continuing as a pointed pin beyond the bit. The symmetrical bit has a large central lobed cleft (Winchester Type 8). Non-ferrous metal plating. Complete. Length 120mm, bit 28 x 17mm. Figure 5.6.

35 Iron key 9701011, 005, CG96 01, Phase 11
Key with broken kidney-shaped bow of rectangular-section, thick, hollow stem and thick, solid bit with two vertical clefts. Almost complete. Length 62+mm, bit 18 x 16 x 7mm. Figure 5.6.

36 Iron awl 9701106, 203, CG96 17, Phase 5
Rectangular-sectioned awl with a pointed tip and tang tapering from a distinct shoulder. Minerally preserved organic remains of the wooden handle present. Complete. Length 101mm, max width 8mm. Figure 5.6.

37 Iron awl 200990033, 158, CG 11, Phase 7
Rectangular-sectioned awl tapering to a blunt point at each end, section lost from flaking. Complete. Length 67mm, width 6mm. Figure 5.6.

38 Iron hooked blade 9701079, 049, CG96 07, Phase 9
Narrow blade with curving back and edge, tip now broken, the long rectangular-sectioned tang continues the line of the back. Almost complete. Length 105mm, blade length 50mm, max width 16mm. Figure 5.6.

5.2 THE WORKED STONE OBJECTS
Ruth Shaffrey

The 1996 excavations

The 1996 excavations produced only a gaming board and counters, a large rotary quern and two semi-spherical objects. Smaller-sized finds include a counter associated with the timber building (CG96 26, Phase 2). It is approximately oval and crudely but carefully shaped; it is of a size compatible with the Merels board found in Phase 6. There are also two probable processors. These are also known as hammerstones or pounders and are partly worked stones used for a variety of domestic purposes. They were found in occupation deposits (SF133; 207, CG96 18, Phase 4) and from backfill (SF132; 195, CG96 17, Phase 5) of the Southern Curtain Wall construction trench. The latter is slightly more spherical and may have been intended for use as a projectile, but the wear on both is consistent with use as processors.

The two larger stone finds are a gaming board (Figure 5.13) and a rotary quern. The gaming board is crudely inscribed with the game of Merels (Nine Men's Morris) on one side and was recovered from ground surface 147, CG96 16, Phase 6, along with a single stone pebble, taken to be a counter (SF101). The reverse side of the gaming board is blank and one edge of the game has broken off. The lines of the game have been carelessly incised and irregularly spaced so that the counter recovered with the board would have been too large to have been used on at least two sides of the game.

Despite the apparent popularity of board games in medieval England, stone gaming boards are not particularly common finds and are mainly linked

FIGURE 5.13
Stone gaming board (copyright: English Heritage)

with ecclesiastical institutions, being found carved into window sills, porch seats and steps, particularly at the back of churches (Croft 1987, 2). Boards incised into parts of major structures survive more readily than portable pieces so it is not surprising that a large proportion of surviving gaming boards are on pieces of stone subsequently used in construction, for example at Sparsholt Church (Berkshire) and Scarborough Castle (North Yorkshire) (Coad and Streeten 1982, 260).

There are, however, notable assemblages of portable stone gaming boards, many also associated with churches, for example, Inchmarnock monastery, Bute (where 7 out of 35 boards are for Merels; Ritchie 2008, 119), Whithorn (Dumfries and Galloway) and St Ninian's (Shetland) (Hill 1997, 449) and Tintagel (Cornwall) (Nowakowski and Thomas 1992). Stone gaming boards also have a link with castle sites and several late 12th-century examples have been recovered from Castle Acre Castle, Norfolk (Coad and Streeten 1982, 260) and single examples at the castles of Scarborough, Norwich (Norfolk) and Dover (Kent) (Shirreff 1953, 111). It is possible that this seemingly carelessly scratched gaming board is nothing more than a doodle (Mandl 1999) or mason's mark (Shirreff 1953, 110). The poor quality and the mismatch with the counter suggest it may have been unplayable, like a number of examples from Inchmarnock (Ritchie 2008, 121). However, the board and counters are made from the same stone type and have an appropriate quality of manufacture — perhaps it represents a board intended only for a single use, whose quality was of little importance.

In addition to the gaming board, a fragment of a large rotary quern, measuring approximately 60cm in diameter, was recovered from fill 141 of pit 139, CG96 15, Phase 6. It is much too small to be a millstone, which by the late 13th century were roughly standardised in size at 132–142cm (Langdon 2004, 172); even smaller examples such as that at Castle Donnington (Leicestershire) are in the region of 90cm (Clay and Salisbury 1990, 295–298). Its measurements, however, are large for a medieval rotary quern, which were generally in the range of 25–57cm diameter (Watts 2006, 3) and its size and weight suggest it would have been very difficult to rotate by hand. It is possible that it was rotated with the aid of a mechanical apparatus or additional power, perhaps horse power, but it seems highly doubtful that it was used for the grinding of grain in a standard mill, since it is not likely that one was situated within the castle grounds. One possible interpretation is that it indicates the processing of some other material, for example the grinding of malted grains — these are represented amongst the environmental data and were commonly ground by horse powered mills (Langdon 2004, 151).

The 1998 excavations

The assemblage of worked stone from the 1998 excavations is limited and was mainly recovered from Phase 10 contexts. It includes four discs and one ?processor. The four discs (SF1691, 629, CG98 11, Phase 10; SF1997, 609, CG98 05, Phase 9; SF7501, 630, CG98 11, Phase 10; SF7504, 563, CG98 13, Phase 10) are all of sandstone from the Raglan Mudstone and may be reused roofing material; one of them has a perforation but with wear consistent with suspension rather than being nailed to a surface

(SF1691). One of the discs is blackened on one side (SF7504). The function of these items is unclear. One semi-spherical stone of the same lithology (SF1998, 665, CG98 11, Phase 10) has battering on it suggesting use as a pounder, although it is a soft stone, not particularly suitable for this sort of purpose.

Discussion

The worked stone assemblage from Wigmore Castle is small. It lacks the tools that might be expected in a defensive site, but whose absence might relate to the size of the excavated area. The other recovered finds are typical of occupation sites (the quern) and of castles, even if infrequently found (the gaming board).

5.3 THE COINS AND JETONS

David Symons

A total of seven coins and four jetons were found during excavation. They are discussed by excavated area and by phase.

The 1996 excavations

SF112. Silver cut halfpenny of William II (1087–1100). Cross Voided type, *c*1092–95 (North 1994, no. 853). Moneyer and mint illegible. Weight 0.38g (broken into five pieces and repaired with glue, chipped, some encrustation). From 260, CG96 23, Phase 3, levelling below occupation surface

As Archibald has pointed out, while most hoards of this period contain coins of only one type, suggesting that there was a reasonably systematic replacement of each coin type by its successor, there is a number of hoards that contain multiple types and it is possible that some coins may have remained in circulation for longer than the currency of their particular issue (Archibald 1988, 278). This seems to be still more true of cut fractions (halfpennies and farthings) than of pennies. We also need to take into account the continuing uncertainty about the precise dating of the particular coin types. While the relative order of the successive types is now clear, their absolute dates are not, although we can be confident that Cross Voided most certainly belongs to the 1090s.

In these circumstances it is perhaps best to suggest an approximate date of loss for this coin of *c*1092–*c*1100/1105.

SF75. Copper-alloy jeton, Tournai, 15th century. Weight 1.66g (cracked and with several tiny holes in the flan). From 045, CG96 06, Phase 9, pre-demolition dump, stratigraphically earlier than 034 below.

Obv: fictitious legend. Royal crown with 8 or 9 pellets across the body.

Rev: triple-stranded cross fleur-de-lisée, no quatrefoil at the centre, set in a quatrefoil with 0s at the interior and exterior angles.

A Tournai stock jeton of the 15th century (compare Mitchiner 1988, 223, no. 661 for the obverse and 222, no. 656 for the reverse). The fictitious legend and generally poor striking suggest that this piece belongs later in the sequence of these jetons rather than earlier. Combining this with the fact that it does not exhibit too much wear, a suggested date of loss in the later 15th century seems appropriate.

SF61. Copper-alloy jeton, English, *c*1310–35. Weight 0.97g. From 034, CG96 06, Phase 9, pre-demolition dump.

Obv: Fleur-de-lis between two falcons addorsed, heads turned back; border of large pellets.

Rev: Short cross moline with a single pellet in each quarter; border of large pellets.

This is an example of Berry's Type 8C jeton of Edward II (Berry 1974, 47, pl. 4.11); Mitchiner no. 221 (Mitchiner 1988, 114). It exhibits a degree of wear, suggesting a reasonable time in use. A date of loss around the middle of the 14th century seems likely.

SF22. Probably a contemporary forgery of a copper farthing of Charles I (1625–49), Rose type, Type 1(d)/2 mule (compare Peck 1970, nos 319 ff). Weight 0.94g (poorly struck, worn and corroded). From 005, CG96 01, Phase 11.

Obv: CAROLVS D G MAG BRIT. Two sceptres in saltire through a double-arched crown, no inner circle, i.m. illegible.

Rev: FRAN ET HIB REX. Crowned rose, single-arched crown, i.m. crescent.

The issue of Rose farthings was authorised on 1 March 1636 and it seems that the last type (Type 3) were a Royalist issue from Bristol in 1644. Type 1(d)/2 mules belong somewhere near the beginning of the sequence. This forgery will have circulated at the same time as the genuine coins, suggesting a likely loss in the period *c*1636–50.

SF07. Copper penny of Queen Victoria (1837–1901), dated 1899. Weight 9.33g. From 002, CG66 01, Phase 11.

The design on the coin is still quite sharp, so loss in the first years of the 20th century is probable.

The 1998 excavations

SF1762. Copper-alloy jeton, English, *c*1310–35. Weight 1.30g (corroded). From gravel floor 652, CG98 21, Phase 5.

Obv: Trefoil with uncertain ornaments in the lobes; border of a wavy line and pellets.

Rev: Short cross moline with a single pellet in each quarter; border of large pellets.

This is an example of Berry's Type 11 jeton of Edward II (Berry 1974, 48, pl 4.14); Mitchiner nos 194–195 (Mitchiner 1988, 111). It is quite heavily corroded, but does not appear to be especially worn. A date of deposit in the second quarter of the 14th century, or even slightly later, would be reasonable.

SF1805. Copper-alloy jeton, Tournai, 15th century. Weight 3.72g. From mortar floor 632, CG98 20, Phase 8.

Obv: (Lis) AVE MARIA (annulet) GRACIA. Shield of France modern, single pellet above, three pellets to each side.

Rev: Triple-stranded cross fleur-de-lisée with a quatrefoil centre, in a quatrefoil; V M V M on the internal cusps of the quatrefoil; (pellet/annulet/pellet) in each external angle.

This is another typical example of a Tournai stock jeton; compare those illustrated on Mitchiner (1988, 224–230). Jetons of this type were struck for much of the 15th century. This specimen is relatively unworn so a date of deposit within the same period is likely.

SF1996. Silver half-groat (two pence) of Edward III (1327–77), London mint, Pre-Treaty Series C (issued 1351–52) (North 1991, no. 1148). Weight 1.52g (heavily clipped and worn). From 667, CG98 15, Phase 8, cut feature below Tudor plaster floor.

This coin is quite worn and heavily clipped, having lost 35% of its theoretical issue weight of 2.34g. This suggests that it has been in circulation for a substantial length of time. Indeed, it has lost so much weight that it falls below the theoretical standard weights for the half-groat of 1.94g (introduced in 1412) and 1.56g (introduced in 1464). That said, the wear does not seem sufficient to justify a date of loss as late as the 1460s. Unfortunately this is a subjective judgement, since we can never know the life history of a particular coin. If this specimen had been out of circulation in someone's savings for a considerable period, this would automatically reduce the amount of wear it suffered. Nevertheless, on balance, a date of deposition well into the first half of the 15th century would seem quite reasonable.

SF1657. Silver penny of Edward I (1272–1307). London mint, class 4b (issued *c*1282–89) (North 1991, no. 1024). Weight 1.23g (very slightly chipped). From 560, CG98 12, Phase 9, make up for Tudor plaster floor.

This coin exhibits a fair degree of wear and must have seen a reasonable time in circulation. However, although some pennies of Edward I did remain in use into the 15th century (Archibald 1988, 288–289), albeit in very clipped and worn condition, the weight of this specimen makes it unlikely that it would have remained in circulation too much beyond 1351, when the theoretical weight of the penny was reduced to 18gr/1.17g. In general, circulating coins tended to be at or a little below the theoretical standard, with heavier coins gradually being culled from circulation, although it is clear that occasional coins that were heavier than the current standard might remain in circulation as well (Allen 2005, 58–59). A likely date of deposit for this piece would probably therefore be sometime in the first half of the 14th century.

SF1806. Silver penny of the late 14th century. Uncertain mint, possibly York, although the presence of a quatrefoil at the centre of the reverse is not certain. The obverse legend appears to end with the French title. Weight 0.75g (clipped and very worn). From 629 CG98 11, Phase 10, demolition debris, East Tower.

This coin is very worn and has clearly seen a great deal of use. Its weight has been so reduced by wear and clipping that it could easily have remained in circulation after the weight reduction of 1412, when the theoretical standard for the penny was reduced to 15gr/0.97g, and that of 1464, when the penny standard fell to 12gr/0.78g. Indeed it is clear from hoards such as that from Wyre Piddle (Worcestershire), deposited *c*1467, that pennies of the late 14th century remained in circulation in appreciable numbers well into the later 15th century (Archibald 1970). A date of deposit as late as the 1460s seems reasonable, and this could conceivably be pushed a decade or so later.

SF1803. Silver penny of Henry VIII (1509–47). Durham mint, issued under Bishop Thomas Wolsey (TW by shield and cardinal's hat below), second coinage (issued 1526–29) (North 1991, no. 1811). Weight 0.61g. From turf line, 523, CG98 02 Phase 11.

Although this coin looks fairly worn, the weight is reasonably close to the theoretical standard of 10⅔gr/0.69g which was introduced in 1526 and its appearance probably owes a good deal to poor striking in the mint. It is in any case very unlikely to have remained in circulation much after Henry VIII's drastic debasement of the silver coinage in 1544 and the subsequent base issues of Edward VI in the 1550s. A likely date of deposit is therefore broadly in the period *c*1530–50.

6
BUILDING MATERIALS

6.1 CERAMIC BUILDING MATERIAL
Phil Mills

The ceramic building material (CBM) from Wigmore Castle was examined by context, with material separated into different fabrics (x50 magnification of fresh breaks) and forms, and further grouped by the presence of sooting, glaze, mortar and amount of abrasion on fragments. Photographs of the CBM fabrics are shown in Plates 6 and 7. Basic quantification of the CBM by weight (Wt) and fragment count (No.) is given in Figure 6.1. The data are laid out by 1996 excavation (Wig 1996), the area outside the East Tower (Wig 1998) and the fills within the East Tower (1998 Tower) and also include the small amount of unstratified material. In all other tables 1998 combines data from both within the East Tower and the area outside the tower. Calculations have also been made for: a 'tile equivalent' (TE), a percentage based on the number of corners present (Cnr); 'minimum number of tiles per context' (MT), derived by dividing the number of corners present by the number of corners for a complete piece; and the mean sherd weight (MSW) calculated by dividing the total weight of a group by the number of fragments (Figures 6.2–6.5).

Fabrics and forms

Fired clay Fabric D25

This is a pale, very poorly fired daub. It was found mainly (329g) associated with the Phase 2 hearth, CG96 27, with a small amount coming from an area to the east within the Timber Building, CG96 26.

Floor tile and brick Fabric LZ05: Bredon-type tiles

This is a brick and floor tile fabric. It is yellowish red (5YR5/6) with pale margins. It is hard and has a slightly sandy feel and irregular fracture. Inclusions include abundant quartz at 0.5 mm and grey stone at 0.3mm. This is probably Hereford Fabric A9 (Vince 1985c).

A small quantity of this fabric is intrusive in Phase 4 (surface 722, CG98 09). With the exception of the small quantity of material from Phase 6, there is a steady decline in the quantity of this fabric in subsequent phases, although there is a slightly less linear pattern by weight. This is a pattern expected of material which is first used in Phase 5, with breakages during construction entering the archaeological record, and subsequent appearances in the archaeological record are down to 'decay' and redevelopment.

Several forms have been identified:

—FT1.1 is an oblong plain mosaic tile, with dimensions of 126 x 62 x 28mm, with a thick black or very dark brown glaze on the top surface. Found in decay contexts 537, and 538, CG98 04, Phase 10, and Eastern Tower upper deposit 556, CG98 10, Phase 11.

—FT2.1 is a group of mainly decorated floor tiles with dimensions of 130 x 130 x 28 mm. The bulk of these tiles had impressed decoration. Two types of glazed surface were present. Glaze A was an uneven thick gloss black or very dark brown glaze and Glaze B had a pale green and brown marbled effect. The marbled effect appears to have been achieved by partly combing away a white slip coating and then glazing. Impressed designs associated with the two glaze types are given below. There was an almost complete 'marbled' tile but without any impressed decoration.

Glaze A: Three examples of tiles with an identifiable impressed design were recorded (Figure 6.6); inset lozenges (IP1), floral motifs (IP2) (see Vince 1997, fig 44) and crosess (IP4). A number of tile fragments with this glaze type could have had impressed decoration but insufficient of the tiles survived to be certain.

Glaze B: Two impressed designs were recorded (Figure 6.6): foliate/floral (IP3), linear/curvilinear (IP5). These were only recovered from contexts in Phases 10 and 11.

—FT3.1: a square floor tile with inlaid design, having dimensions 125–130 x 125–130 x 50–75mm. These are present from Phase 8, where they make up 4% of the assemblage by sherd number (Figure 6.8). They include a number of heraldic designs (Figure 6.7; Plates 8 and 9), for which no local parallels could be found in the survey published by Vince and Wilmott (1991), including fleur-de-lys (P1, P14), animals and lions (P2, P4, P5, P9a), leaf fronds (P3) and geometric design (P5, P10) (compare Eames 1980, no. 2103), shields (P7), curved floral border (P8), border with dots (P11), Gothic cross (P12), hunting dog and/or stag design (P16, see Stopford 2005, fig 22.1, design 23.11).

	Wig 1996		Wig 1998		1998 Tower		u/s		Total	
	Wt	No.	Wt	No.	Wt	No.	Wt	No.	Wt	No.
Fired clay	353	30							353	30
Brick	3330	203	799	12					4129	215
Brick/tile	3152	220	671	51	27	7			3850	278
Floor tile	5675	90	22801	245	1744	44	347	4	30567	383
Flat roof tile	1336	50	6376	176	1891	100	367	7	9970	333
Ridge tile	2029	59	4260	74	1065	33	183	3	7537	169
Finial?					15	1			15	1
Total	**15875**	**652**	**34907**	**558**	**4742**	**185**	**897**	**14**	**56421**	**1409**

FIGURE 6.1

Quantification of ceramic building material by weight and count

Wig 96	No. %	Wt %	Cnr %	TE %	MT %	MSW
Phase 1	0.40	3.13				201.50
Phase 2	0.20	1.76	1.79	1.90	4.76	226.00
Phase 3	5.03	2.41				12.40
Phase 4	33.20	13.67				10.65
Phase 5	0.80	0.79				25.25
Phase 6	18.51	1.52	3.57	5.23	4.76	2.12
Phase 7	3.42	3.23	3.57	3.96	4.76	24.41
Phase 8	1.41	6.13	14.29	15.85	9.52	112.57
Phase 9	16.50	18.45	12.50	13.79	19.05	28.93
Phase 10	20.52	48.92	64.29	59.27	57.14	61.66
N / Avg	*497*	*12856*	*56*			*25.9*
Wig 98	**No. %**	**Wt %**	**Cnr %**	**TE %**	**MT %**	**MSW**
Phase 4	1.23	1.00	0.63	0.52	1.47	44.00
Phase 5	2.47	0.66		1.42	1.47	14.50
Phase 8	22.33	20.78	11.39	17.17	17.65	50.26
Phase 9	11.37	4.70	3.16	2.67	4.41	22.34
Phase 10	41.92	46.49	53.80	45.65	44.12	59.90
Phase 11	20.68	26.36	31.01	32.57	30.88	68.82
N / Avg	*730*	*39423*	*158*	*2324*	*68*	*54*

FIGURE 6.2

Ceramic building material by phase

Context	No. %	Wt %	Cnr %	TE %	MT %	MSW
Collapse	9.6	26.1	29.4	27.4	25.8	115.8
Construction layer	9.2	6.7	6.1	5.9	6.7	30.8
Demolition layer	12.9	18.8	22.4	24.8	23.6	62.3
Destruction	4.4	1.7				16.8
Ditch	9.9	12.9	7.0	11.4	10.1	55.6
Feature	0.1	0.1				39.0
Floor layer	1.7	0.5	0.5	0.8	1.1	12.4
Hearth/oven	5.5	0.1				1.1
Layer	0.3	1.0				124.5
Midden	3.5	3.0	2.3	1.7	2.2	36.7
Occupation layer	26.1	11.0	10.7	10.3	10.1	18.0
Pit	4.9	3.6	2.8	3.4	3.4	31.0
Posthole	2.8	1.7	1.9	1.7	3.4	25.5
Rubble dump	8.3	12.0	16.8	12.7	13.5	61.7
Slot	0.2					8.0
Wall	0.6	0.8				56.4
N	*1227*	*52279*	*214*	*2955*	*89*	*42.6*

FIGURE 6.3

Ceramic building material by context class

—FT3.2: a decorated square floor tile with dimensions of 122 x 122 x 100mm (Figure 6.8).
—FT5.1: a reshaped triangular plain mosaic tile, thickness 22mm.
—FT5.2: a triangular, plain mosaic floor tile with dimensions of 160 x 85 x 30mm.

Floor tile Fabric LZ05.1

This fabric is present in small quantities in Phases 8 and 9, but with the highest presence in Phase 10. The only form recognised was a plain mosaic tile, FT1.1. This fabric seems likely to be a sandier variant of TZ05, although its use as a supplement for TZ05, either during the original development, or as subsequent patching, given its presence in Phase 8 seems probable.
—FT1.1: a plain mosaic tile with dimensions of 123 x 26mm and a surface with a matt black glaze. The only example is from 537, CG98 04, Phase 10.

Floor tile and brick Fabric LZ13 (32%)

This is a very low fired, poorly levigated fabric, and was primarily used in the manufacture of sand-moulded bricks, although there are also some fragments of glazed floor tile from Phase 10 and 11. It is possible that some of the early examples of this fabric may be in fact burnt clay. This fabric may equate mainly with Weobley bricks (Vince 1985b) but one thick glazed fragment from 519, CG98 02, Phase 11, contained rare large granitic inclusions and suggests that some of the material was made in the Malvern Chase area, equating to Hereford Fabric B4 (Vince 1985b).

This fabric is found in 374, CG96 29, Phase 1, and in stake-hole fill 367, CG96 26, Phase 2 (see 'Discussion' below). It is most likely to have been initially used from Phase 3. Vince (1985b, 69) notes that brickmaking was an important industry in the Chase in the 16th century.
—Brick 1.1: A hand-made sand-moulded brick with uneven irregular rounded arrises, irregular surfaces, sanded base and smoothed upper surfaces, 110 x 65mm (2½ x 4½ inches). This was present from Phase 4, at 2%, and Phase 5 at 18%, presumably

Fabric	No. %	Wt %	Cnr %	TE %	MT %	MSW
LZ05	26.80	42.10	81.30	76.40	74.20	66.88
LZ05.1	1.20	2.60	3.70	3.40	3.40	89.80
LZ13	31.70	23.80	6.50	5.00	7.90	31.99
TZ05	22.50	14.70	1.40	2.50	3.40	27.87
TZ13	14.50	14.10	6.10	11.00	9.00	41.27
TZ13.2	1.00	0.50				20.17
TZ13.3	2.30	2.30	0.90	1.70	2.20	43.11
N/ Avg	*1227*	*52279*	*214*	*2955*	*89*	*42.61*

FIGURE 6.4

Ceramic building material fabric quantification

Wig 96	No. %	Wt %	Cnr %	TE %	MT %	MSW
TZ13.3	3.02	3.95				33.87
TZ13.2	2.01	1.69				21.70
TZ13	3.02	1.53				13.13
TZ05	11.27	14.01	3.57	7.92	9.52	32.16
LZ13	66.20	39.89	14.29	11.73	14.29	15.59
LZ05.1	0.60	1.63	3.57	3.96	4.76	69.67
LZ05	13.88	37.31	78.57	76.39	71.43	69.51
N/ Avg	*497*	*12856*	*56*			*25.87*
Wig 98	**No. %**	**Wt %**	**Cnr %**	**TE %**	**MT %**	**MSW**
TZ13.3	1.78	1.77	1.27	2.15	2.94	53.77
TZ13.2	0.27	0.06				12.50
TZ13	22.33	18.13	8.23	13.98	11.76	43.86
TZ05	30.14	14.94	0.63	1.08	1.47	26.78
LZ13	8.22	18.56	3.80	3.18	5.88	121.92
LZ05.1	1.64	2.89	3.80	3.23	2.94	94.83
LZ05	35.62	43.64	82.28	76.38	75.00	66.18
N/ Avg	*497*	*12856*	*158*			*54*

FIGURE 6.5

Fabric proportions

Dec	Glaze	Ph	Context		No.	Wt	Cnr
IP1	Black	11	551	Demolition layer	1	80	0
IP2	Black	10	584	Collapse	1	72	0
IP4	Black	11	554	Pit	1	398	2
IP3	Marbled	11	517	Demolition layer	7	651	4
IP3	Marbled	10	563	Collapse	1	341	2
IP5	Marbled	10	23	Rubble Dump	1	45	0

FIGURE 6.6

Wigmore 1998: relief impressed tiles

as a result of remodelling or replacement work, and them most abundantly in Phase 10 at 18%.

Roof tile Fabric TZ05: Hereford Fabric A7

This fabric is present from Phase 5, where it comprises 23% by sherd count of the assemblage. It is absent from Phase 6 and it is residual in subsequent phases, largely as material being reused as hardcore, when the original roof was repaired or replaced with tiles from other sources. The increase in Phases 10 and 11 can be explained by the decay and collapse of other parts of the structure. There are two crested ridge tile forms in this fabric (and a possible finial fragment, see 'Function', below):

—Ridge tile 1.1: brown glazed with small rounded pyramidal crests (Vince 2002a, Hereford, late 13th century).

—Ridge tile 1.2: green glazed with a thin long tapering crest with slashes on one side (Vince 2002a, Hereford mid-13th century).

Roof tile Fabric TZ13: Malvern Chase?

This is a hard red (2.5YR4/6) with light red surfaces (2.5YR7/6) fabric with irregular fracture and granular feel. It has inclusions of abundant sub-rounded quartz with occasional white quartz at 2mm, moderate sub-rounded limestone at 0.4 mm, sparse granitic inclusions at 0.5mm and moderate black sand at 0.2mm. The granitic inclusions suggest a Malvernian source but this fabric is coarser and less well-sorted than Fabric TZ13.3.

—Ridge tile 1.1: a brown-glazed crested ridge tile with rounded pyramidal crests, similar to Vince (2002a) knob ridge tiles, Hereford late 13th century.

Roof tile Fabric TZ13.2: Hereford Fabric A2

This is a hard grey fabric which is sandy with an irregular fracture. It has inclusions of abundant angular limestone at 0.5 mm and some black ironstone and fine transparent quartz. It has a thick green glaze. This equates with Hereford fabric A2 (Vince 1985b).

Roof tile Fabric TZ13.3: Malvern Chase

Malvern Chase tile (Vince 1985b, fabric B4) with a hard fabric. It is red (2.5YR5/6), occasionally with a grey core. It has inclusions of quartz at 0.7mm and granitic lumps. It comprises both ridge and flat tiles from Phase 8 onwards.

—Ridge tile 1.3: This is a ridge tile with rounded knobs along its apex. It is glazed in yellow with green speckle (Vince 2002a, ridge tile with knobbed crests, late 13th century).

Function

The different functional groups of the identified CBM forms are shown in Figure 6.10. Floor tiles are the most common form found in the assemblage, with a small quantity of brick, neither in quantities suggesting *in situ* deposits. The ratios of ridge tile to flat tile fragments are unusual, especially the contrast with the minimum number estimates with weights and number of fragments. This implies that much of the assemblage is residual refuse material. The breakdown of the functional assemblage by phase and area is shown in Figure 6.11. It is interesting to note the appearance of ridge tile and flat tile in

FIGURE 6.7
Decorated floor tiles (see PLATES 8 and 9)

phases and areas together, suggesting their use and disposal together, with the exception of the material deposited in Phase 8 in the 1996 excavations. A small (15g) glazed fabric TZ05 fragment may have been from a decorative piece such as a finial or possibly a louver but the size of the fragment precluded any definite form attribution and the sherd could be part of a pottery jug. It was found within the East Tower, layer 665, where glazed TZ05 ridge tile was found together with numerous glazed jug sherds.

Sooting

Some 2.9% of the stratified assemblage showed signs of sooting and burning (Figure 6.12). Phases 1 and 2 are heavily influenced by the very small sample size. The values for Phases 3, 5 and 7 fall within what has been noted for urban assemblages. The extremely high level of sooting from Phase 8 is of note — this is a level usually associated with industrial sites or hearths. Figure 6.13 shows the figures by phase and area, indicating that both areas show broadly the same pattern, especially the same spike in Phase 8.

Deposition

The proportion of material from each context class for the entire site is shown in Figure 6.3. Given the relatively small size of the assemblage a wide range of context type is represented. This is similar to the pattern observed for the deposition profile at Newark Castle (Mills 2000), for example, and larger

Fabric	Form	Decoration	Phase	Context	Context class	No.	Weight	Cnr	TE %	MT
LZ05	FT3.1	P1	9	560	Construction layer	1	142	2	25	0
LZ05	FT3.1	P10	0	0	Unstratified	1	85	0	0	0
LZ05	FT3.1	P11	*	695	Unstratified	1	140	0	0	0
LZ05	FT3.1	P11	11	3	Topsoil / ploughsoil	1	105	0	0	0
LZ05	FT3.1	P11	11	5	Topsoil / ploughsoil	1	63	0	0	0
LZ05	FT3.1	P12	10	21	Rubble dump	1	77	0	0	0
LZ05	FT3.1	P12	10	24	Rubble dump	3	141	0	0	0
LZ05	FT3.1	P12	11	665	Demolition layer	1	38	0	0	0
LZ05	FT3.1	P12	9	25	Midden	1	13	0	0	0
LZ05	FT3.1	P13	10	537	Collapse	1	168	0	0	0
LZ05	FT3.1	P14	10	537	Collapse	1	47	2	25	1
LZ05	FT3.1	P14	10	558	Collapse	1	151	2	25	0
LZ05	FT3.1	P14	11	519	Demolition layer	1	212	2	25	1
LZ05	FT3.1	P16	10	541	Collapse	1	198	0	0	0
LZ05	FT3.1	P2	8	667	Ditch	1	217	2	25	1
LZ05	FT3.1	P2	9	617	Posthole	3	51	0	0	0
LZ05	FT3.1	P2?	10	14	Rubble dump	1	166	2	25	1
LZ05	FT3.0	P3?	11	599	Demolition layer	1	141	2	25	1
LZ05	FT3.1	P4	10	538	Collapse	1	177	2	25	1
LZ05	FT3.1	P5	10	538	Collapse	1	226	2	25	1
LZ05	FT3.1	P5	11	599	Demolition layer	1	108	2	25	1
LZ05	FT3.1	P5?	11	7	Topsoil / ploughsoil	1	58	0	0	0
LZ05	FT3.1	P6	10	550	Demolition layer	1	83	2	25	1
LZ05	FT3.1	P6	11	523	Demolition layer	1	272	0	25	1
LZ05	FT3.1	P6?	9	25	Midden	1	370	2	25	1
LZ05	FT3.1	P7	8	61	Construction layer	3	618	6	75	1
LZ05	FT3.1	P7?	11	3	Topsoil / ploughsoil	1	47	0	0	0
LZ05	FT3.1	P7?	11	7	Topsoil / ploughsoil	2	39	0	0	0
LZ05	FT3.1	P8	11	517	Demolition layer	1	375	2	50	1
LZ05	FT3.1	P8?	10	563	Collapse	1	73	0	0	0
LZ05	FT3.1	P9	10	537	Collapse	1	514	4	50	1
LZ05	FT3.1	P9	10	538	Collapse	1	284	2	25	1
LZ05	FT3.2	P5	10	20	Rubble dump	2	910	10	125	2

FIGURE 6.8

Catalogue of inlaid tiles, forms FT3.1 and FT3.2 (: unphased)*

medieval urban centres. The largest fragments come from dumps, layers and demolition, as expected. The deposition profiles of the two areas (Wigmore 1996 and Wigmore 1998) show a sharp contrast. There are many more cut features utilised in Wigmore 1996, despite its smaller assemblage size. These differences may be accounted for by more industrial activity in the 1996 excavations, and significantly more refuse dumping in pits, whereas in the 1998 excavations more is related to construction, with some chance refuse disposal in ditch deposits.

Discussion

The earliest ceramic building material in use on the site is fired clay in Phases 1 and 2, probably derived from domestic or industrial hearths or ovens. Brick was recorded in Phase 1 but this occurred with hearth bottoms and is likely to be derived from an industrial process rather than represent intrusive material. Likewise a 'brick' fragment from a post-hole in the Phase 2 Timber Building must represent disturbance of earlier industrial debris or be intrusive from Phase 3. In Phase 3 there seems to be a structure, possibly an oven, incorporating these bricks in close proximity to the area of the 1996 excavations. There is only a small quantity of brick in the assemblage suggesting it was never a major component of construction.

There are plain floor tiles in the archaeological record from Phase 5, and relief decorated and inlaid floor tiles are seen, residually, in Phase 8 in the 1996 excavations, presumably derived from a structure near to that area. However, the deposition profiles in the later phases suggest some mixing of material from different parts of the castle reused as hardcore in construction as was a common occurrence. The floor tiles would have originally been used in a mid- to late-13th-century, high-status or ecclesiastical setting, perhaps a chapel. There are some impressed decorated tiles found residually in Phases 10 and 11 which may have been part of an earlier structure (or part of the same structure) within the castle, but which may have lasted *in situ* for longer than the inlaid tiles. Some further plain coloured tiles were used in structures in the 16th century.

Area	Phase	Colour	No. %	Wt %	Cnr %	TE %	MT %	No.	Wt	Cnr	TE	MT
Wigmore 1998	10	Black	0.69	0.53				144	2991			
Wigmore 1996	10	Brown	8.70	11.40				46	1342			
Wigmore 1998	10	Brown	12.50	24.57				144	2991			
Wigmore 1998	11	Brown	6.06	5.81				33	1875	2	50	2
Wigmore 1998	8	Brown	31.97	40.61	21.43	21.43	22.22	147	7596	14	350	9
Wigmore 1998	9	Brown	13.04	27.65				69	1266			
Wigmore 1998	10	Dark brown	1.39	1.84				144	2991			
Wigmore 1996	10	Green	10.87	8.20				46	1342			
Wigmore 1998	10	Green	10.42	14.68				144	2991			
Wigmore 1998	11	Green	6.06	9.87				33	1875	2	50	2
Wigmore 1996	8	Green	100.00	100.00				1	35			
Wigmore 1998	8	Green	7.48	5.58				147	7596	14	350	9
Wigmore 1996	9	green	14.58	31.24	50.00	50.00	50.00	48	1306	2	50	2
Wigmore 1998	9	Green	5.80	6.40				69	1266			
Wigmore 1996	10	Speckle	13.04	14.83				46	1342			
Wigmore 1998	10	Speckle	4.17	4.01				144	2991			
Wigmore 1998	11	Speckle	3.03	2.67				33	1875	2	50	2
Wigmore 1998	5	Speckle	40.00	77.78				5	36			
Wigmore 1996	9	Speckle	12.50	11.33				48	1306	2	50	2
Wigmore 1998	9	Speckle	7.25	5.37				69	1266			
Wigmore 1998	11	Underlay	3.03	1.17				33	1875	2	50	2
Wigmore 1996	10	Unglazed	65.22	63.93				46	1342			
Wigmore 1998	10	Unglazed	63.19	43.50				144	2991			
Wigmore 1998	11	Unglazed	81.82	80.48	100.00	100.00	100.00	33	1875	2	50	2
Wigmore 1998	5	Unglazed	60.00	22.22				5	36			
Wigmore 1996	7	Unglazed	100.00	100.00				1	40			
Wigmore 1998	8	Unglazed	60.54	53.80	78.57	78.57	77.78	147	7596	14	350	9
Wigmore 1996	9	Unglazed	68.75	55.21	50.00	50.00	50.00	48	1306	2	50	2
Wigmore 1998	9	Unglazed	71.01	54.50				69	1266			
Wigmore 1996	10	Yellow	2.17	1.64				46	1342			
Wigmore 1998	10	Yellow	7.64	10.87				144	2991			
Wigmore 1996	9	Yellow	4.17	2.22				48	1306	2	50	2
Wigmore 1998	9	Yellow	2.90	6.08				69	1266			

FIGURE 6.9

Colour of roof tile by period and area

	No. %	Wt %	Cnr %	MT %	TE %	MSW
Brick/tile	19.20	6.20	3.30	2.20	2.10	13.76
Brick	14.60	6.90	1.40	3.40	1.20	20.26
Finial	0.10					15.00
Floor tile	28.50	56.00	86.90	79.80	81.50	83.72
Ridge tile	12.10	13.10	0.90	2.20	1.70	46.13
Tile	25.50	17.70	7.50	12.40	13.50	29.49
N	*1227*	*52279*	*214*	*89*	*2955*	*42.61*

FIGURE 6.10

Ceramic building material: function

Area	Type	No	Wt	Cnr	TE	MT
Wig 1996	B/T	182	2554	7	62	2
Wig 1996	Brick	171	2851	2	24	2
Wig 1996	Floor tile	65	4940	45	495	15
Wig 1996	Ridge tile	42	1548	1	25	1
Wig 1996	Tile	37	963	1	25	1
Wig 1998	B/T	53	679	0	0	0
Wig 1998	Brick	8	776	1	12	1
Wig 1998	Finial	1	15	0	0	0
Wig 1998	Floor tile	285	24361	141	1912	56
Wig 1998	Ridge tile	107	5325	1	25	1
Wig 1998	Tile	276	8267	15	375	10

FIGURE 6.11

Ceramic building material: function by phase and area

Phase	No. %	Wt %	MT %	Cnr %	TE %	MSW	No.	Wt	Cnr	MT	TE
1	50.0	16.1				65	2	403			
2	100.0	100.0	100.0	100.0	100.0	226	1	226	1	1	12
3	4.0	1.3				4	25	310			
4	0.6	0.3				7	174	2153	1	1	12
5	4.5	3.0				11	22	362		1	33
7	5.9	9.6				40	17	415	2	1	25
8	11.2	16.1	21.4	15.4	12.4	76	170	8980	26	14	499
9	0.6	1.4				61	165	4226	12	7	149
10	2.5	7.4	4.8	3.3	3.5	182	408	24617	121	42	1435

FIGURE 6.12

Ceramic building material: incidence of burning by phase

Phase	Area	No. %	No.
1	Wigmore 1996	50.00	2
2	Wigmore 1996	100.00	1
3	Wigmore 1996	4.00	25
4	Wigmore 1996	0.61	165
5	Wigmore 1996	5.56	18
7	Wigmore 1996	5.88	17
8	Wigmore 1996	14.29	7
8	Wigmore 1998	11.04	163
9	Wigmore 1996	1.22	82
10	Wigmore 1998	3.27	306

FIGURE 6.13

Incidence of burning by phase and area

Roof tiles could date from the mid- to late 13th century. The earliest roof tiles were from the Hereford area and the pattern of supply, with an early component from Malvern Chase also supplying the castle, seems to follow that of Hereford until Phase 8, when Malvernian tile becomes more common. The use of decoration on tiles (Figure 6.9) seems to follow that seen elsewhere, with colour being important in the 14th century, presumably after tiled roofs become more common (Salzman 1952). Colour also seems to have been used to indicate differences in supplier, although there may have been a deliberate attempt for new buildings to have roofs contrasting with the extant roof scape of the castle. The earliest roofs would be unglazed, with green ridge tiles. In the 14th century, green, speckled and brown tiles were most common, and the new build in the mid-14th to 15th century, marked by new suppliers, was also marked by the return of unglazed tiles and brown ridge tiles for new buildings.

The functional make up of the assemblage is consistent with material which comprises both building rubble, the refuse from any construction activity being dumped in middens, pits and ditches, and selected material being reused as hardcore. The appearance of much of the material as hardcore is somewhat underlined by the high level of burning exhibited in the material laid down in Phase 8, compared to the other phases.

6.2 THE ROOF STONES FROM THE 1998 EXCAVATIONS AND THEIR PETROLOGY

Ruth Shaffrey

A total of 90 fragments of stone roofing were individually examined by hand and assigned to groups. Several different stone types were identified within the assemblage, of which the three most prevalent were thin sectioned. Further details of the petrological analysis can be found in the archive report along with descriptions of the stone roofing by phase.

Only two fragments were recovered from the 1996 excavations, both are small fragments which cannot be absolutely identified as roofing and one of these is sufficiently thick to have been used for flooring. The remainder was recovered during the 1998 excavation including 15 complete specimens.

Description

The area around Wigmore Castle is extremely variable geologically, which means that a great variety of stones were available for use (Rosenbaum 2007), although not necessarily in any great quantities. This variety is reflected in the stone roofs of the region, which reveal rocks of Ordovician, Silurian and Devonian age. As might be anticipated in an area with such diverse geology, analysis of the roof stones from Wigmore Castle revealed a broad variation of silty and sandy stones that can be grouped into four broad lithology types (Figure 6.14).

Type	Lithology	Fragments
1	Old Red Sandstone (Raglan Mudstone formation)	54
2	Downton Castle Sandstone	4
3	Old Red Sandstone	7
4	Whitcliffe Beds Sandstone/siltstone	25
	Total	**90**

FIGURE 6.14

Roof stones by lithological type

	Phase 4	Phase 5	Phase 8	Phase 9	Phase 10	Phase 11	Unphased	Total
Complete roof-stone	-	-	2	1	5	7	3	18
Roof-stone fragment	3	-	10	20	19	2	3	57
Unworked, probable roof or floor-stone fragment	-	-	-	2	-	-	-	2
Unworked, probable roof-stone fragment	5	1	1	2	2	-	2	13
Total	**8**	**1**	**13**	**25**	**26**	**9**	**8**	**90**

FIGURE 6.15
Number of roof-stone fragments by phase

The grey-green siltstones and fine-grained sandstones from the Whitcliffe Beds formation were the most locally available stone used at Wigmore Castle on the roof and could have been collected within 1km of the castle to the south. There are other extensive exposures in most directions within only a short distance.

The most numerous stone amongst the assemblage is a fine-grained sandstone from the Raglan Mudstone formation of the Old Red Sandstone. Although sandstones from these beds are known to have been used for roofing in Ludlow itself (Hughes 2003) and the Wigmore Castle roof stones matched reference samples collected from the eastern side of Ludlow, provenancing them is somewhat problematic as there are many small sources. The closest source was approximately 9km to the south near Shirl Heath, and located close to the main north–south road which passed Wigmore Castle. However, it is equally plausible that the stone came from near Ludlow and the links between Ludlow and Wigmore Castle, suggest Ludlow as a more likely source.

Another stone which could have been sourced near Ludlow is the Downton Castle sandstone, which outcrops in and around Ludlow and slightly nearer to Wigmore Castle between Wootton and Downton Castle. It was popular both for roofing and as a freestone (Scard 1990, 57) but occurs only in small quantities in the roof and main fabric of Wigmore Castle. It is not possible to be more precise about the source, but it certainly has a 'local' origin. Other lithologies which provided small quantities of stone may have been imported over slightly greater distances, in particular, seven distinctively purple coloured fragments of Old Red Sandstone. These are an excellent match with stone from Credenhill, some 25km to the south. However, there may have been other small outcrops of the same stone nearer the castle capable of providing the small numbers apparently utilised.

Some prominent local stones are noticeable by their absence, in particular the Ordovician sandstones, such as the Hoar Edge Grit and the Chatwall sandstones (for example Horderley stone). The sources for these are all northwards of Wigmore Castle (Toghill 1990, 81).

Discussion

Although three small fragments were recovered from 13th-century contexts (Phase 4), stone roofing first appears in the archaeological record in significant numbers from Phase 8 in the mid-14th to 15th century (Figure 6.15). There are insufficient Phase 4 fragments to be sure that any of the castle buildings were roofed with stone at that time. The vast majority were discarded in contexts associated with the decay of the castle in Phases 10 and 11. These later phases in particular produced a number of complete examples, and although the documentary evidence indicates that the roof was dismantled for use elsewhere (see Chapter 2), some complete roof stones may have been surplus to requirements.

This assemblage does not indicate any chronological changes to roof-stone supply. Most lithologies occur in all phases and although the Downton Castle sandstone occurs only in 16th- and 17th-century contexts associated with the decay of the castle, its use is likely to have been associated with earlier phases of construction. The small quantity of this lithology, in comparison to other lithologies present, may suggest it was used in very limited amounts and possibly of limited duration.

It is clear from an analysis of the stone roofing that, in keeping with the variation of stone available in the area, Wigmore Castle was not supplied by a single source. It is possible that the different types reflect the long time period over which the castle was constructed and modified, and the changing links of those involved. However, it may equally indicate that the use of a single stone type was not considered essential to the appearance of the castle. Although the stone types are quite different in appearance when fresh, they take on a very similar appearance with weathering and over time, meaning that stone could be obtained from the easiest or cheapest sources, regardless of its appearance.

7

THE FAUNAL REMAINS

7.1 MAMMAL AND BIRD BONES

Richard Thomas and Stephanie Vann

This chapter presents the results of the detailed analysis of the hand-collected and sieved animal bones recovered from excavations at Wigmore Castle (Wigmore 1996 and Wigmore 1998). While two large medieval and post-medieval faunal assemblages from elite sites in the Midlands have recently been published (Sadler and Jones 2007; Thomas 2005a), there have been no detailed zooarchaeological analyses of castles located in the Marches. This site therefore fills an important gap in our knowledge of human-animal interactions in Herefordshire, central England and nationally.

The size of the assemblage and the tight chronological control enables existing ideas regarding the exploitation of animals and dietary preferences throughout the medieval and early modern periods to be tested. In addition to contributing to two of the primary research aims of the Wigmore Castle Project — to explore the status and the material culture of the occupants of the site — a detailed analysis of the faunal remains contributes to a number of key avenues of research within contemporary medieval and early modern archaeology, such as: the impact of the Black Death on diet and animal husbandry techniques (Thomas 2005a; 2006; 2007a); the emergence of technological innovations within agriculture (Langdon 1986; Thomas 2005b); and the elaboration of hunting rituals (Thomas 2007b).

Methods

All mammal and bird bone fragments (hand-collected and sampled) deriving from stratigraphically secure deposits were subjected to macroscopic examination. Species identification was achieved using the comparative reference collection of modern specimens at the School of Archaeology and Ancient History, University of Leicester, and the Natural History Museum's Bird Group, Tring. Morphologically similar species were identified using published criteria: Boessneck (1969), Kratchovil (1969), and Payne (1985) for sheep/goat; and MacDonald (1992) for galliformes. Fragments of mammal bone that could not be attributed to a taxonomic group equal or lower than genus were categorised as small, medium or large mammal or bird. All specimens were zoned using the criteria of Dobney and Reilly (1988).

Two methods of ageing were employed in this analysis: epiphyseal fusion and the eruption sequence and subsequent wear of mandibular teeth. Epiphyses were considered to be fusing once 'spicules of bone… [had]… formed across the epiphyseal plate joining the diaphysis to the epiphysis but open areas were still visible between epiphysis and diaphysis' (Albarella *et al* 1997, 12). Once this line of fusion had closed, an epiphysis was considered to be completely fused. Bird bones were recorded as juvenile if the ends of the bones appeared porous. Mammal bones were divided into three age classes (early fusing, middle fusing, late fusing; after Reitz and Wing 1999, table 3.5).

Tooth wear stages were recorded on the permanent and deciduous fourth premolars and the permanent molars of cattle (Grant 1982), sheep (Payne 1973; 1987) and pigs (Grant 1982), on both isolated and mandibular teeth. Pigs were sexed using the morphology of the mandibular canine and its alveolus (Schmid 1972, 80).

Measurements were taken on all fused bones primarily using the standards of von den Driesch (1976), although supplementary measurements of the humerus and metapodia were taken following Bull and Payne (1988) and Davis (1992) respectively. The minimum and maximum diameters at the base of horncores were also taken. In general, unfused bones were not measured, although exceptions were made for foetal and neonatal specimens to provide an indication of age. No measurements were taken on burnt or calcined specimens due to the problems of shrinkage (Shipman *et al* 1984), or on specimens that were excessively abraded or affected by pathology or butchery.

All bones exhibiting signs of disease or injury were examined macro-morphologically and systematically recorded (after Vann 2008a; Vann and Thomas 2006). In addition, the degenerative changes of the lower limb bones of cattle were recorded using the scoring criteria developed by Bartosiewicz *et al* (1997). Evidence of gnawing, butchery and burning were recorded on all identifiable elements. Both carnivore and rodent gnawing marks were identified. Three types of butchery marks were recorded ('cut', 'chop' and 'saw' marks) and their anatomical location and

		Phase											Total
		1	2	3	4	5	6	7	8	9	10	11	
Hand-collected	Total fragments	247	667	637	1488	1118	573	1067	753	2449	1973	1617	12589
	Identifiable	67	123	133	366	362	133	683	167	541	216	255	3046
	% identifiable	27.1	18.4	20.8	24.6	32.3	23.2	64.0	22.1	22.0	10.9	15.7	24.2
6mm residue	Total fragments	3	1402	147	413	-	48	51	-	132	-	-	2196
	Identifiable	-	25	2	3	-	-	8	-	4	-	-	42
	% identifiable	-	1.7	1.3	0.7	-	-	15.6	-	3.0	-	-	1.9
Flot	Total fragments	-	268	13	56	1	31	21	-	484	55	-	929
	Identifiable	-	19	1	2	1	-	2	-	10	1	-	36
	% identifiable	-	7.0	7.6	3.5	100.0	-	9.5	-	2.0	1.8	-	3.8

FIGURE 7.1
Number and percentage of fragments and identifiable animal bone specimens by phase from Wigmore 1996

		Phase							Total
		3	4	5	8	9	10	11	
Hand-collected	Total fragments	-	1	216	491	682	1565	474	3487
	Identifiable	-	1	49	84	120	423	132	809
	% identifiable	-	100.0	22.6	17.1	17.6	27.0	27.8	23.2
6mm residue	Total fragments	-	-	585	1338	124	685	269	3001
	Identifiable	-	-	36	46	8	39	109	238
	% identifiable	-	-	6.1	3.4	6.4	5.6	40.5	7.9
4mm residue	Total fragments	7	122	26	-	15	3	88	91
	Identifiable	-	-	-	-	-	1	-	1
	% identifiable	-	-	-	-	-	33.3	-	1.1

FIGURE 7.2
Number and percentage of fragments and identifiable animal bone specimens by phase from Wigmore 1998

direction was recorded following Lauwerier (1988) with supplementary codes from Sykes (2007a). Burnt bones were recorded as 'singed', 'burnt' or 'calcined', depending on the degree of exposure to fire. Bone preservation was recorded on a four-point scale (after Harland *et al* 2003).

The mammal and bird bones

Considering the small scale of the archaeological intervention, a substantial assemblage of 22,405 mammal and bird bone fragments was examined from the excavated deposits at Wigmore Castle. The majority of these (15,714 fragments) derived from the 1996 excavations and of these, 3125 were recovered from flots and residues (the remainder were hand-collected). The 1998 excavations produced 6691 fragments of animal bone of which 3262 derived from samples.

Figures 7.1 and 7.2 present the distribution of hand-collected and sieved bone fragments by phase for the two seasons of excavation. While some periods of occupation are better represented than others, the distribution between the 11 phases is fairly even, enabling the exploration of diachronic variation at the site. Although the data for Phase 11 (17th–20th century) are presented for completeness, the significance of the trends within this group should be treated with caution, since an unknown quantity of residual material dated to the 16th century was indicated by the ceramic evidence.

Taphonomy

Before attempting any interpretation of animal bones it is essential to consider the taphonomic processes that led to the transformation of the life assemblage into the sample assemblage (Reitz and Wing 1999, fig 5.1). The processes to be considered here are: recovery efficiency, burning, gnawing and post-depositional degradation (butchery is considered for individual taxa below).

The hand-collected identifiable assemblage was generally well preserved with the majority exhibiting limited abrasion (Figures 7.3 and 7.4). This suggests that disposal occurred relatively promptly following butchery and/or consumption, and that the soil conditions were amenable to

	Phase											Total
	1	2	3	4	5	6	7	8	9	10	11	
1	1.85	0.00	0.00	0.67	0.00	0.00	0.00	2.86	0.00	0.51	0.00	0.34
2	66.67	70.43	65.83	65.32	86.75	66.67	86.10	71.43	62.90	60.10	52.08	71.77
3	31.48	29.57	33.33	33.67	12.85	33.33	13.61	25.71	36.20	38.89	46.88	27.44
4	0.00	0.00	0.83	0.34	0.40	0.00	0.29	0.00	0.90	0.51	1.04	0.45
Total %	**100**	**100**	**100**	**100**	**100**	**100**	**100**	**100**	**100**	**100**	**100**	**100**

FIGURE 7.3

Preservation of hand-collected identifiable post-cranial bones by phase from Wigmore 1996.

Key (after Harland et al 2003): 1: Majority of surface fresh or even slightly glossy, very localised or powdery patches. 2: Bone surface lacks fresh appearance but solid, very localised flaky or powdery patches. 3: Surface solid in places, but flaky or powdery on up to 49% of specimen. 4: Surface flaky or powdery over 50% of specimen

	Phase						Total
	4	5	8	9	10	11	
1	0.0	0.0	0.8	0.0	0.0	0.0	0.1
2	100.0	63.2	68.9	71.3	71.5	67.6	69.7
3	0.0	34.5	30.3	28.8	27.7	31.6	29.5
4	0.0	2.3	0.0	0.0	0.8	0.7	0.7

FIGURE 7.4

Preservation of hand-collected identifiable post-cranial bones by phase from Wigmore 1998 (key: see Figure 7.1)

	1996		1998	
	Fill	Layer	Fill	Layer
1	0.2	0.4	2.2	0.0
2	89.8	64.0	65.2	70.1
3	9.8	35.1	32.6	29.2
4	0.1	0.6	0.0	0.7

FIGURE 7.5

Preservation of hand-collected identifiable post-cranial bones by context type (key: see Figure 7.1)

bone survival. There is evidence for poorer bone preservation in later phases of occupation amongst the 1996 material and better preservation during Phases 5 and 7. The latter is primarily due to the inclusion of well preserved, and presumably rapidly deposited, dumps of cattle and chicken lower limb bones (see below).

Comparison of preservation rates by the two primary context types predictably reveals that bones recovered from fills were generally better preserved than those from layers (Figure 7.5). Overall, the bones from the 1996 excavations were slightly better preserved, a fact supported by the marginally higher proportion of identifiable hand-collected bones (Figures 7.1 and 7.2).

The gnawing data support the view that most bones were rapidly disposed of; 9.1% of identifiable hand-collected post-cranial bones were gnawed from Wigmore 1996 compared with 13.3% from Wigmore 1998. These values are comparable with average values of 12.5% recorded from medieval and post-medieval deposits at Dudley Castle, West Midlands (Thomas 2005a, 13). Only two examples of rodent gnawing were discovered, both from Wigmore 1998 dating to the 16th century (Phase 9). All other recorded gnawing marks from both Wigmore 1996 and Wigmore 1998 had been inflicted by carnivores. The lower proportion of gnawing marks from the 1996 excavations is consistent with the lower abrasion rates exhibited by bones from this area.

Unsurprisingly, gnawing marks were more frequently recorded on identifiable hand-collected bones from layers than fills in both assemblages (Figure 7.6). This indicates that bones which became incorporated into occupation surfaces were more accessible to dogs.

Clear temporal variation in the proportion of gnawed bone at Wigmore Castle is visible, when the data from the two areas of excavation are pooled (Figure 7.7). These data demonstrate high levels of gnawing in Phase 1 (albeit from a small sample), followed by declining proportions until Phase 7. Thereafter, however, the proportion of gnawed bones increases over time until another peak is reached in Phase 10. This variation could be connected to differences in activity at the site. The lowest proportion of gnawing coincides with a major remodelling of the castle when greater opportunities perhaps existed for the rapid disposal of food waste. This is supported by better bone preservation in Phase 5 and Phase 7 contexts (Figure 7.3). In contrast, the increased proportion of gnawing from Phase 8 onwards corresponds to the gradual decay and demolition of the castle when there was perhaps less concern for prompt rubbish disposal. The latter trend is also independently verified by the bone preservation data.

The proportion of identifiable burnt material at Wigmore was very low, making it an insignificant factor affecting assemblage formation: only 16 singed, burnt or calcined bones were identified, 13 of which derived from hand-collected samples.

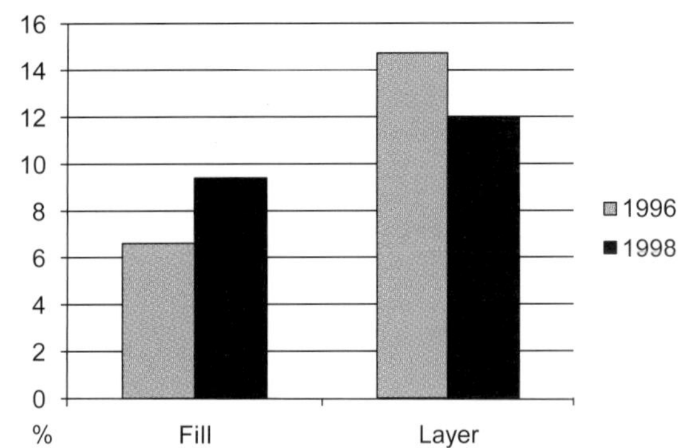

FIGURE 7.6

Proportion of gnawed bones by context type

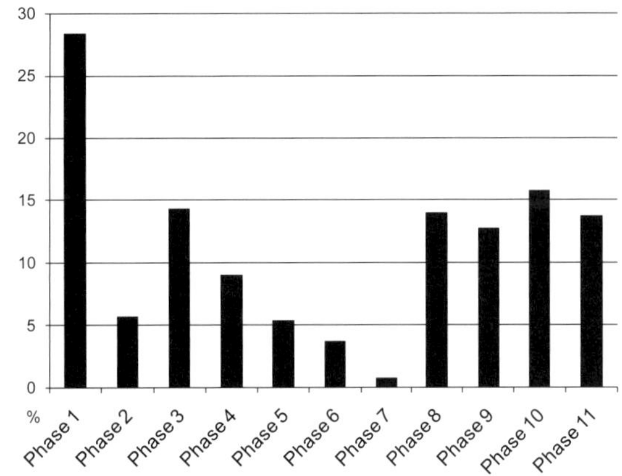

FIGURE 7.7

Percentage of hand-collected gnawed bones by phase

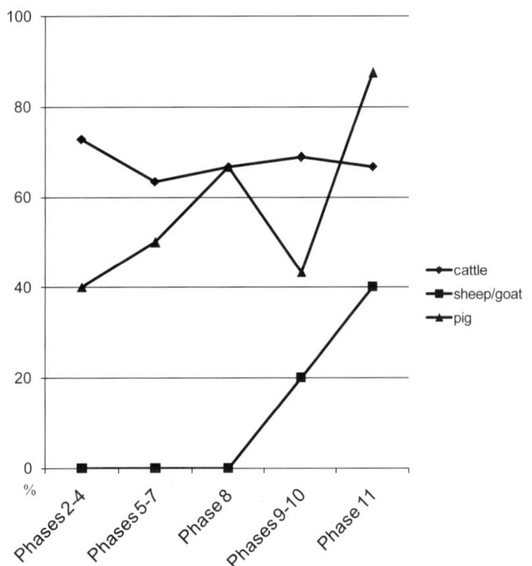

FIGURE 7.8

Percentage of loose teeth out of the total number of loose teeth and mandibles by phase. Closely dated phases have been merged to improve sample sizes

One method that can be employed to assess the degree of fragmentation and the efficiency of recovery is the ratio of loose mandibular teeth to mandibular teeth still held within the jaw. This index relies on the assumptions that fragmented assemblages will contain higher proportions of loose teeth and that loose teeth will be missed in less well-recovered assemblages. The combined data for Wigmore 1996 and Wigmore 1998 reveal that the majority of cattle and pig teeth was recovered loose, indicating a high degree of fragmentation (Figure 7.8). A higher proportion of loose teeth were recovered for cattle and pig, which probably reflects the biases of hand-collection: loose cattle and pig teeth are much larger and therefore more visible than sheep/goat teeth. The only significant temporal variation in these data is the increased proportion of loose teeth from Phase 9. Like the other taphonomic indicators, this suggests that the bones from the final phases of occupation were less well preserved.

Analysis of the percentage of fragments contributed by the different animal groups by recovery method reveals a pattern that conforms to previous experimental work (Payne 1972; 1975). Large mammals were far less common in the 6mm and 4mm residues, while medium mammals, small mammals and birds were better represented (Figure 7.9). Because the zooarchaeological analysis is based primarily upon the analysis of hand-collected bones, consideration must be given to the fact that the hand-collected assemblage is biased in favour of the larger fragments, larger anatomical elements and the larger taxa.

In summary, the taphonomic analysis suggests that bone preservation was slightly better in 1996 contexts. A few temporal differences require consideration in the foregoing analysis. For example, the higher proportion of gnawing and poorer bone preservation in Phase 1 and Phases 8–11 is likely to have led to the preferential destruction of low density skeletal elements (or parts of skeletal elements) and the bones from very young animals. Conversely, the bones from Phases 5–7 may exhibit better preservation of the unfused bones of young animals and lower density skeletal elements.

Species representation

In keeping with contemporary sites, the faunal assemblage from Wigmore Castle is dominated by the bones of domestic taxa (Figures 7.10–7.15). However, as befits a high-status site, a considerable proportion of wild birds and mammals was also recovered, testifying to the diversity of habitats required to provision the aristocratic household. Not all the animals recovered from the site represent the refuse of human consumption however. Several commensal and intrusive species are present, although these are not discussed in detail.

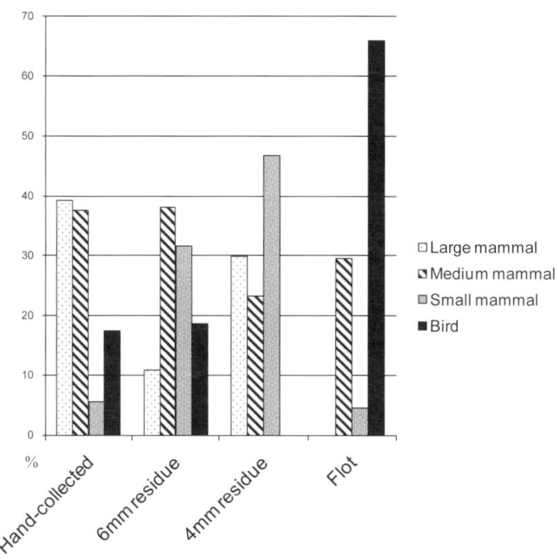

FIGURE 7.9
Relative proportion of different animal groups by recovery method

Domestic mammals

When quantified by the total number of identified specimens (Figure 7.16), cattle (*Bos taurus*) are the most abundant domestic mammal, followed by pig (*Sus scrofa*) and sheep/goat (*Ovis aries/Capra hircus*). Unfortunately, once the data are broken down by phase, species and skeletal element, the samples are too small to provide a meaningful calculation of the minimum number of individuals (MNI) or the minimum number of animal units (MAU).

The majority of the cattle, sheep and pig bones were recovered isolated and disarticulated. However, the fill of the Phase 5 Curtain Wall construction trench from Wigmore 1996 contained an abundance of mostly adult cattle bones (only two unfused metaphyses were recorded from this deposit) deriving from a minimum of 21 animals and dominated by the bones of the head and lower limb (Figures 7.17–7.18). The elemental profile is typical of primary butchery waste and can be connected to the removal, processing and disposal of bones of low meat value and/or to hide preparation, since the bones of the lower limb and head are often left within the skins to maintain the shape of the hide and act as handles. The butchery evidence presented below suggests that the former interpretation is more likely.

The fact that cattle are the most abundant species at Wigmore Castle is typical of English castle sites (Grant 1988, fig 8.2) and while the high proportion may have been over-emphasised by taphonomic biases, beef was by far the most commonly consumed meat (Figures 7.19–7.21). Although the medieval period has been traditionally characterised as one in which sheep were 'of particular importance', the archaeological evidence does not always substantiate this, particularly where castle sites are concerned (Grant 1988, 151). The fact that high proportions of pig are present, particularly in the earlier phases of occupation, is also characteristic of English castle sites (Grant 1988, fig 8.2), a probable consequence of elite dietary preference, the potential of aristocratic estates to keep large numbers of pigs, the use of pigs as food rents (Sykes 2007a, 42) and/or the fact that pigs were not multi-purpose animals and were only exploited for their meat.

Analysis of the relative proportion of cattle, sheep/goat and pig bones by phase reveals three clear trends (Figure 7.16): the relative contribution of cattle remains fairly stable over time apart from the mid-14th to mid-15th century (Phases 5–7), when a peak is reached; a rise in the relative proportion of sheep/goat occurs throughout the occupation of the site; a decline in the relative abundance of pig occurs over time.

These trends are not exclusive to Wigmore Castle and are mirrored at contemporary sites (Figures 7.19–7.21). Unfortunately, the sample from Phase 1 is too small to compare with contemporary Norman sites; however, comparison of 73 mid-12th to mid-14th-century sites reveals that Wigmore Castle is set slightly apart from the main group of elite sites in this period by virtue of its lesser emphasis on sheep (Figure 7.19). By the mid-14th to 16th centuries, following the rise in importance of sheep and a slight decline in the relative abundance of pig, Wigmore resembles contemporary castle sites more closely. In the post-medieval period (16th–18th centuries) many castle sites appear more urban in character (at least in terms of the relative abundance of the primary domesticates). This is probably a consequence of the diminishing popularity of castles as aristocratic residences (Pounds 1990, 296–297) and the deliberate destruction of many of the castles that were used as Royalist strongholds during the Civil War. The fact that Wigmore Castle maintains its elite character in the 16th and 17th centuries (Phase 11 data are not included here) is worthy of attention and testifies to the continuation of high-status dining when the castle was managed by the Council of the Marches and kept in repair as a prison. Although the consumption of mutton had increased at all sites in this period, it is striking that the focus at Wigmore Castle remained on cattle.

The dominance of cattle and the paucity of sheep at Wigmore Castle is replicated at medieval and post-medieval sites in this region (here defined as Herefordshire and Worcestershire; Figure 7.22) and probably reflects the suitability of local grazing and livestock availability rather than consumer preference. This is perhaps surprising given Herefordshire's prominence within the medieval wool trade (Owen 1991, 240), but there is historical evidence to support this view. Based upon the 'number of acres in each county from which each sack of wool came which was contributed, presumably on an equitable basis, to the 30,000 sacks granted to Edward III

	Phase											Total
	1	**2**	**3**	**4**	**5**	**6**	**7**	**8**	**9**	**10**	**11**	
Cattle	22	12	36	110	327	30	28	49	116	68	77	875
Sheep/goat	3	11	8	21	7	11	10	19	68	60	85	303
Sheep	–	–	–	–	–	–	–	–	4	1	2	7
Pig	23	29	23	90	16	17	16	28	106	28	32	408
Equid	1	1	7	3	1	0	0	0	0	0	1	14
Dog	1	6	10	11	–	–	–	1	20	0	2	51
Dog/fox	–	–	–	–	–	–	–	–	1	–	1	2
Cat	1	9	1	48	–	–	–	–	2	–	1	62
Red deer	7	–	–	–	–	–	–	3	21	1	–	32
Fallow deer	–	–	–	6	4	3	4	19	42	16	18	112
Roe deer	5	5	2	–	1	–	1	1	–	–	1	16
Red/fallow deer	–	–	–	–	2	–	–	–	–	–	–	2
Fallow/roe deer	–	–	–	3	1	–	1	1	1	1	–	8
Rabbit	–	–	–	–	–	–	–	–	2	–	10	12
Hare	–	10	12	11	–	–	–	–	1	–	–	34
Brown bear	1	–	–	–	–	–	–	–	–	–	–	1
Mustelid	–	–	–	–	–	–	–	–	–	1	–	1
Rat/water vole	–	–	–	–	–	1	1	–	1	2	–	5
Small rodent	–	–	–	–	–	1	–	–	–	–	–	1
Amphibian	–	1	1	–	–	–	–	1	1	–	–	4
Domestic fowl	1	33	28	36	2	62	604	29	101	30	16	942
Goose	–	1	1	18	–	4	6	6	24	3	5	68
Duck	1	–	–	1	–	–	1	–	1	–	–	4
Teal/garganey	–	–	–	2	–	–	1	–	2	–	–	5
Grey partridge	–	–	1	1	–	–	2	2	4	1	–	11
Pigeon/dove	–	2	–	2	1	1	–	–	–	1	–	7
Woodcock	–	3	3	3	–	1	2	3	14	1	1	31
Corvid	–	–	–	–	–	–	–	–	1	–	–	1
Raven	–	–	–	–	–	–	–	–	–	1	–	1
Jackdaw	–	–	–	–	–	–	–	–	4	–	1	5
Heron	–	–	–	–	–	1	–	–	–	–	–	1
Snipe	–	–	–	–	–	–	–	2	1	–	–	3
Peafowl	–	–	–	–	–	–	–	–	–	1	–	1
Swan	–	–	–	–	–	–	3	–	2	–	–	5
Lapwing	1	–	–	–	–	–	–	–	1	–	–	2
Dunlin	–	–	–	–	–	–	–	1	–	–	–	1
Large turdidae	–	–	–	–	–	–	–	1	–	–	–	1
Small turdidae	–	–	–	–	–	1	2	1	–	–	2	6
Medium wader	–	–	–	–	–	–	1	–	–	–	–	1
Total identified	**67**	**123**	**133**	**366**	**362**	**133**	**683**	**167**	**541**	**216**	**255**	**3046**
Small bird	–	–	–	–	–	1	–	–	–	–	–	1
Medium bird	–	–	3	9	–	4	3	2	7	1	–	29
Large bird	–	–	–	–	–	–	1	–	–	1	–	2
Small mammal	1	20	2	33	–	8	1	2	43	7	1	118
Medium mammal	30	143	40	141	51	34	66	129	282	272	119	1307
Large mammal	49	52	61	144	137	35	69	147	278	211	142	1325
Unidentified	100	329	398	795	568	358	244	306	1298	1265	1100	6761
Total	**247**	**667**	**637**	**1488**	**1118**	**573**	**1067**	**753**	**2449**	**1973**	**1617**	**12589**

FIGURE 7.10

Uncorrected number of hand-collected specimens present (NSP) from Wigmore 1996. Antler fragments not included

by Parliament in 1341' Herefordshire had the fifth lowest density of sheep in medieval England (Trow-Smith 1957, 141).

The increasing abundance of sheep in the medieval and early modern period, coupled with a reduction in the relative numbers of pigs is well attested in both documentary sources and the zooarchaeological record (Albarella 2006; Campbell 1991, 157; Campbell and Overton 1993, 78; Grant 1988; Sykes 2006; Woolgar 1999, 133). The cause of these changes is two-fold: a reduction in the availability of woodland; and the rise of the wool trade.

In the early medieval period woodland provided an important space in which large herds of pigs were kept in a loosely managed, semi-feral state, albeit overseen by swineherds (Salisbury 1994, 56; Wiseman 2000, 34), grazing upon pasture,

	Phase								Total
	2	3	4	5	6	7	9	10	
Sheep/goat	1	-	-	-	-	-	3	1	5
Pig	-	1	1	1	-	-	-	-	3
Rabbit	-	-	-	-	-	-	1	-	1
Hare	1	-	-	-	-	-	-	-	1
Domestic fowl	13	-	1	-	-	2	3	-	19
Grey partridge	3	-	-	-	-	-	-	-	3
Woodcock	-	-	-	-	-	-	1	-	1
Small turdidae	1	-	-	-	-	-	2	-	3
Total identified	**19**	**1**	**2**	**1**	**-**	**2**	**10**	**1**	**36**
Medium bird	-	-	-	-	1	-	2	-	3
Medium mammal	-	-	-	-	-	-	2	3	5
Unidentified	249	12	54	-	30	19	470	51	885
Total	**268**	**13**	**56**	**1**	**31**	**21**	**484**	**55**	**929**

FIGURE 7.11

Uncorrected number of specimens present (NSP) from flot from Wigmore 1996. Antler fragments not included

	Phase							Total
	1	2	3	4	5	7	9	
Pig	-	4	-	1	-	-	-	5
Rabbit	-	-	-	1	-	1	-	2
Hare	-	2	-	-	-	-	1	3
Small rodent	-	-	1	-	-	3	-	4
Amphibian	-	1	-	-	-	-	-	1
Domestic fowl	-	15	-	1	-	4	2	22
Goose	-	2	-	-	-	-	-	2
Woodcock	-	1	1	-	-	-	1	3
Total identified	**-**	**25**	**2**	**3**	**-**	**8**	**4**	**42**
Medium bird	-	-	-	-	-	1	-	1
Small mammal	-	1	-	6	-	-	3	10
Medium mammal	-	8	10	10	-	-	9	37
Large mammal	-	5	-	-	-	-	-	5
Unidentified	3	1363	135	394	48	42	116	2101
Total	**3**	**1402**	**147**	**413**	**48**	**51**	**132**	**2196**

FIGURE 7.12

Uncorrected number of specimens present (NSP) from 6mm residues from Wigmore 1996. Antler fragments not included

roots and rhizomes for most of the year, but also consuming beech mast and acorns on a seasonal basis (Trow-Smith 1957, 81–82). During the 12th and 13th centuries, however, increasing pressure was exerted upon woodland as the population rapidly expanded and there was growing need to increase the land available for arable cultivation. Although it is important to stress that woodland and forest were not synonymous, it has been estimated that woodland coverage in England shrank by 5% between 1086 and 1350, equating to 'an average destruction of 17½ acres per day' (Rackham 1986, 88). The decline in woodland availability meant that pigs would have required feeding in different ways. As Wiseman (2000, 41) notes, 'the alternatives to grazing, acorns, beech mast and all the other products of the forest, were cereals and pulses'. However, the latter foodstuffs were expensive and also required for human consumption. It is perhaps not surprising therefore that large-scale pig-keeping of the kind witnessed in the earlier medieval period became unsustainable. Indeed the zooarchaeological evidence from other sites indicates that during the 14th century there was a shift in pig husbandry towards enclosed management, which enabled greater control to be exerted over breeding and feeding (Hamilton and Thomas 2012).

A contributing factor in the decline in the proportion of pig was the changing nature of the agricultural landscape in the later 14th century. In the early medieval period, the higher proportion of pigs may have reflected the fact that they were the best way of maximising the available resources, when grazing land for cattle and sheep was at a premium due to the intensification of arable farming (Grant 1988, 159). The decline in their proportion in the 14th century may have been a consequence of the conversion of arable to pasture following the collapse of the grain market and population depletion after the Black Death, which made the raising of cattle and sheep for meat more attractive to farmers, since they were less labour intensive and more profitable (Grant 1988, 159; Wiseman 2000, 40). Moreover, a degree of incompatibility existed between pig-

	Phase						Total
	4	5	8	9	10	11	
Cattle	1	11	14	26	147	19	218
Sheep/goat	-	4	19	17	16	15	71
Sheep	-	2	2	-	2	1	7
Goat	-	-	-	-	-	1	1
Pig	-	11	14	16	26	5	72
Equid	-	-	-	1	31	-	32
Dog	-	-	7	8	42	4	61
Dog/fox	-	-	1	-	-	-	1
Cat	-	-	2	-	3	-	5
Fallow deer	-	2	6	9	50	1	68
Red/fallow deer	-	-	-	-	1	-	1
Fallow/roe deer	-	2	-	-	-	-	2
Sheep/goat/roe deer	-	1	-	-	-	-	1
Rabbit	-	-	2	4	46	57	109
Hare	-	1	-	-	1	-	2
Mole	-	-	-	1	-	-	1
Microtinae	-	-	-	3	-	-	3
Rat/water vole	-	-	2	1	-	-	3
Bank vole	-	-	-	-	1	-	1
Amphibian	-	-	-	3	-	-	3
Domestic fowl	-	8	8	17	47	25	105
Goose	-	7	3	7	1	2	20
Duck	-	-	1	1	1	-	3
Grey partridge	-	-	-	2	2	1	5
Pigeon/dove	-	-	1	0	1	-	2
Woodcock	-	-	2	4	1	-	7
Corvid	-	-	-	-	2	-	2
Snipe	-	-	-	-	-	1	1
Medium wader	-	-	-	-	1	-	1
Large turdidae	-	-	-	-	1	-	1
Total identified	**1**	**49**	**84**	**120**	**423**	**132**	**809**
Medium bird	-	-	2	2	1	1	6
Small mammal	-	1	5	10	1	35	52
Medium mammal	-	18	23	42	62	107	252
Large mammal	-	14	52	63	144	117	390
Unidentified	-	134	325	445	934	82	1920
Total	**1**	**216**	**491**	**682**	**1565**	**474**	**3429**

FIGURE 7.13

Uncorrected number of hand-collected specimens present (NSP) from Wigmore 1998. Antler fragments not included

	Phase					Total
	5	8	9	10	11	
Cattle	6	5	2	4	2	19
Sheep/goat	5	11	1	7	4	28
Sheep	2	-	-	-	-	2
Goat	-	-	-	-	1	1
Pig	5	6	4	4	5	24
Fallow deer	3	3	-	4	1	11
Dog	1	-	-	2	-	3
Rabbit	-	1	-	1	73	75
Hare	-	3	-	1	2	6
Mole	-	2	-	-	1	3
Rat	-	2	-	-	-	2
Bank vole	-	-	-	1	2	3
Rat/watear vole	-	1	-	1	1	3
Field mouse	-	1	-	-	-	1
Small rodent	-	-	-	1	3	4
Amphibian	-	-	-	2	1	3
Domestic fowl	9	8	1	8	12	38
Goose	3	1	-	-	-	4
Pigeon/dove	-	1	-	2	-	3
Woodcock	1	1	-	1	-	3
Small turdidae	1	-	-	-		1
Large turdidae	-	-	-	-	1	1
Total identified	**36**	**46**	**8**	**39**	**109**	**238**
Large bird	1	-	-	-	-	1
Medium bird	1	8	-	-	1	10
Unid. bird	-	1	-	2	-	3
Small mammal	-	5	2	-	31	38
Medium mammal	18	26	4	9	18	75
Large mammal	6	11	-	3	9	29
Unidentified	523	1241	110	632	101	2607
Total	**585**	**1338**	**124**	**685**	**269**	**3001**

FIGURE 7.14

Uncorrected number of specimens present (NSP) from 6mm residues from Wigmore 1998. Antler fragments not included

	Phase						Total
	3	4	5	9	10	11	
Sheep/goat	-	-	-	-	1	-	1
Rabbit	-	-	-	-		14	14
Medium mammal	-	-	1	-	-	5	6
Large mammal	-	1	1	1	-	6	9
Unidentified	7	121	24	14	2	63	231
Total	**7**	**122**	**26**	**15**	**3**	**88**	**261**

FIGURE 7.15

Uncorrected number of identified specimens present (NSP) from 4mm residues from Wigmore 1998. Antler fragments not included

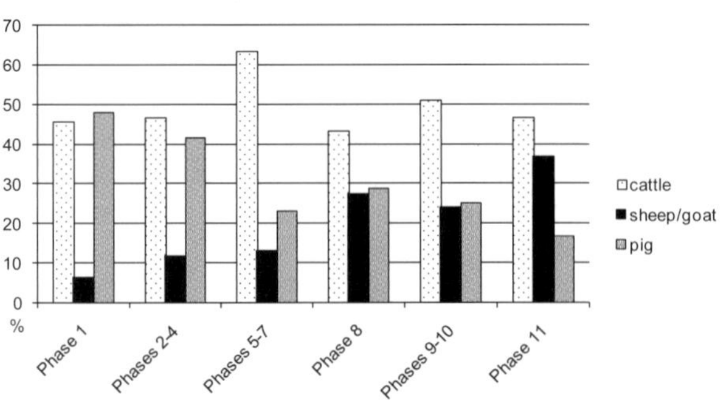

FIGURE 7.16

Relative proportion of hand-collected cattle, sheep/goat and pig by phase. The Phase 5 dump of cattle feet has been excluded. Closely dated phases have been merged to improve sample sizes

	No.
Mandible	19
Maxilla	4
Loose tooth	25
Humerus	2
Radius	1
Carpal	22
Metacarpal	75
Pelvis	2
Femur	1
Patella	1
Tibia	4
Astragalus	3
Calcaneum	1
Tarsal	18
Metatarsal	48
Metapodial	19
Proximal phalanx	6
Medial phalanx	6
Distal phanlanx	7
Total	**264**

FIGURE 7.17

Skeletal distribution of cattle fragments from group 17 (the fill of a mid-13th to mid-14th-century curtain wall construction trench)

FIGURE 7.18

A sample of the cattle bones from group 17. The total length of the scale is 20cm

keeping and pasture, because of the destructive feeding habits of pigs (Wiseman 2000, 31).

The steady increase in the relative abundance of sheep/goat almost certainly attests to the expansion of the wool and cloth industries. Historical sources confirm the rise of the wool trade in the early 12th century; a trend that is also supported by zooarchaeological evidence (Hurst 2005, 51–55; Sykes 2006, fig 5.1). Ryder (1983, 455–457) places the height of wool production between the late 12th and mid-14th centuries. However, it is clear that the shift from arable to pasture in the wake of the Black Death increased the relative importance of sheep. In Norfolk, for example, as a proportion of livestock units, sheep increase from 21.1% in the period 1250–1349 to 32.6% in 1350–1449 (Campbell and Overton 1993, 79). Indeed, woollen manufacture was growing rapidly at the end of the 14th century and throughout the 15th century in England (Davis 1924, 333). The price of wool continued to rise in the 16th century; between 1540 and 1546, for example, the price almost tripled from 6s 8d a 'tod' to 20s 8d after having already risen between 1510 and 1520 (Hibbert 1988, 173). The wool of Herefordshire sheep was held in particularly high esteem; a petition presented by the House of Commons in 1454 regarding recommended export prices, for example, lists the wool from Leominster as more expensive than any other (Curtler 1908, 408).

Regarding the other domestic species, horse (*Equus* sp.), dog (*Canis familiaris*) and cat (*Felis catus*) were present throughout the occupation of the site, albeit in small numbers. With the exception of 27 fragments of a partial dog skeleton from a Phase 11 context (604) and 24 fragments of a Phase 10 partial horse skeleton from a layer of demolition rubble, these animals are represented by isolated and disarticulated fragments. This is typical of medieval sites and one that is representative of their treatment as commodities in death (Thomas 2005c). It is likely that these animals were not eaten, although there are indications that their flesh was occasionally exploited (see below). Goat (*Capra hircus*) was represented by only two bones (a horncore and a deciduous fourth premolar), suggesting that this species was of marginal economic importance. All post-cranial bones upon which the sheep/goat distinction could be attempted were identified as sheep.

Domestic birds

One of the most striking features of the animal bone assemblage from Wigmore Castle is the predominance of domestic fowl; even following the exclusion of a Phase 6 deposit of lower leg bones, they are numerically the most abundant species. No pheasant (*Phasianus colchicus*) or guinea fowl (*Numida meleagris*) bones were identified so it seems likely that they mostly, if not completely, derive from chickens (*Gallus gallus*), and are considered as such henceforth. Goose (*Anser* sp.) and duck (*Anas* sp.) have been classified as domestic birds for analytical purposes, although separating domestic and wild goose and duck is problematic, notwithstanding the additional complication of inter-breeding; however, the *Anser* sp. and *Anas* sp. bones at Wigmore Castle were all within the size range expected of domestic forms.

Analysis of the relative proportion of chicken, goose and duck by phase is presented in Figure 7.23 and reveals a steady decline in the exploitation of domestic birds from Phase 8 onwards. The abundance of chickens in the mid-13th to mid-14th century derives mainly from 593 fragments from an

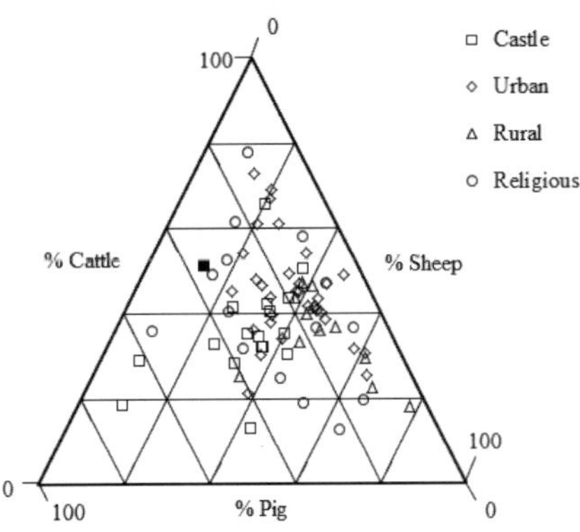

FIGURE 7.19

Relative proportion (%NISP) of cattle, sheep and pig at 73 sites dating to the mid-12th to mid-14th century (the site data primarily derive from Albarella and Pirnie 2008; Sykes 2007a; and Thomas 2005a). The Phase 5 dump of cattle feet has been excluded. Wigmore Castle is represented by a filled symbol

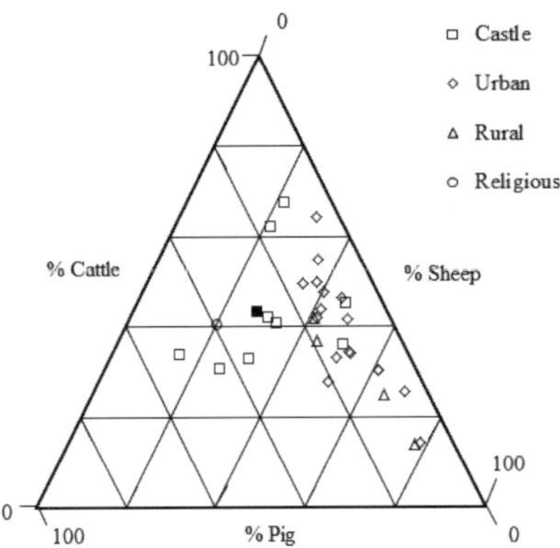

FIGURE 7.20

Relative proportion (%NISP) of cattle, sheep and pig at 32 sites dating to the mid-14th to 16th century (the site data primarily derive from Albarella and Pirnie 2008; and Thomas 2005a). Wigmore Castle is represented by a filled symbol

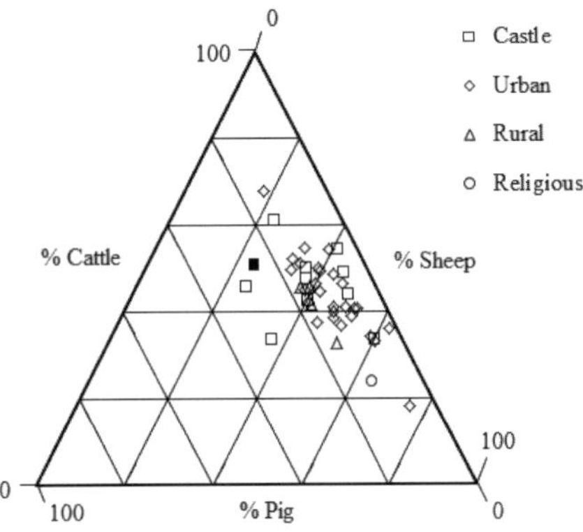

FIGURE 7.21

Relative proportion (%NISP) of cattle, sheep and pig at 35 sites dating to the 16th to 18th centuries (the site data primarily derive from Albarella and Pirnie 2008; and Thomas 2005a). Wigmore Castle is represented by a filled symbol

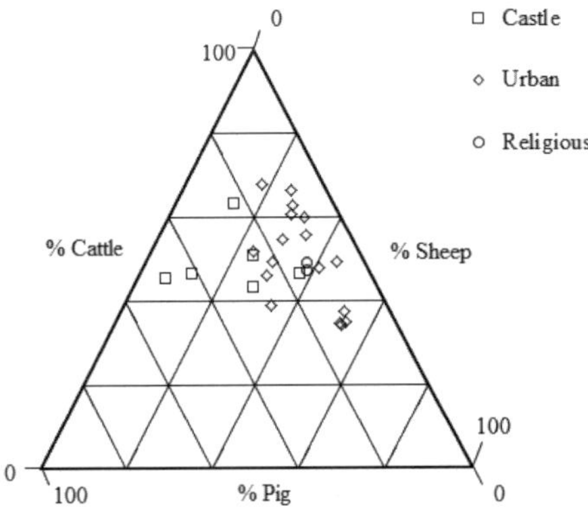

FIGURE 7.22

Relative proportion (%NISP) of cattle, sheep and pig at 12 sites in Herefordshire and Worcestershire dating to the medieval and post-medieval periods (the site data primarily derive from Albarella and Pirnie 2008). The Wigmore Castle data are presented using the same phase groups employed in Figure 7.16

early 14th-century context (102, CG96 13, Phase 6) representing a minimum of 39 birds (Figure 7.24). This assemblage is dominated by elements of the lower hind limb especially the tarsometatarsus and phalanges (Figure 7.25) and is indicative of primary butchery waste; the rest of the carcasses were presumably consumed and disposed of elsewhere. An additional 34 chicken bone fragments derived from CG96 11 contexts dated to the early 14th century; of these, 29 fragments derived from the lower leg. Why such a large number of chickens were butchered and deposited (presumably as a single event) is difficult to establish, but it certainly hints at a major food consumption episode. Intriguingly, this may correspond to one of the major events held at Wigmore Castle during the first half of the 14th century that included: celebrations on the marriage of Roger's young son Edmund to Elizabeth, the infant daughter of Bartholomew de Badlesmere; a tournament held by Roger de Mortimer in 1329 and attended by Queen Isabella, her son Edward III and most of the nobles of England, for which the castle formed the backdrop; and the visit of Edward III to the castle in 1333. Thirty-nine fragments from at least two partial chicken skeletons were also deposited amongst mudstone rubble (587) within the East Tower in Phase 10.

Wild mammals

The abundance of deer at Wigmore Castle is typical of elite sites (Sykes 2007b, fig 11.3). During the medieval period, the hunting of deer was restricted

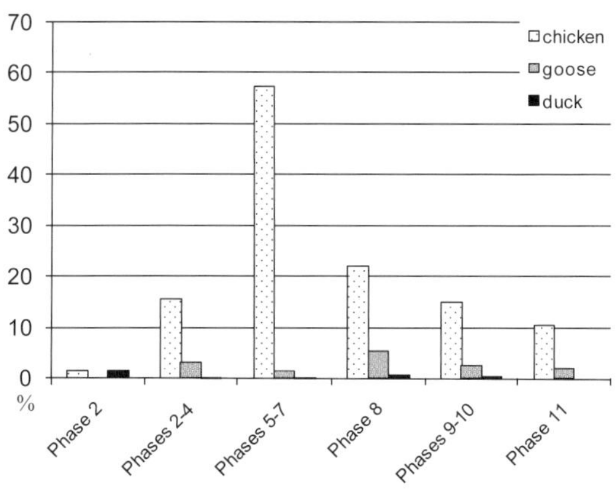

FIGURE 7.23
Relative proportion (%NISP) of hand-collected chicken, goose and duck out of the total number of identifiable bones

FIGURE 7.24
A sample of the chicken lower hind-limb bones from context 102, CG96 13, Phase 6

to the highest members of society and the right to hunt, own a deer park and have the appropriate knowledge and language to correctly adhere to the rituals of the hunt, were important markers of aristocracy (Thomas 2007b). While the hunt provided dietary diversity (in the form of venison), it also served a number of important social functions: it was viewed as a means of ensuring preparedness for war and relieving idleness and sin (Almond 2003, 13–16), and doubtless provided valuable opportunities to make and re-establish social connections.

Calculation of the relative proportion of deer over time (Figure 7.26) reveals a steady increase in abundance from Phase 2 until Phase 8, followed by a subsequent decline. The highest proportion of deer was recovered from Phase 1 contexts; the sample size for this phase is relatively small (NISP=60), but this may indicate the importance of hunting as a demonstration of secular power and resource control by the earliest Norman lords. William fitz Osbern who constructed the first castle at Wigmore, was a relative and close advisor to William the Conqueror, and was therefore one of the leading nobles in England in this period. The late medieval increase in deer exploitation is witnessed at other castle sites in England and Wales (Figure 7.27) and reflects greater emphasis on wild mammals more generally throughout the medieval period (Sykes 2004a, illus. 3). This trend is partly connected to the rise in the number of parks in the medieval period. Between 1086 and the early 14th century the number of parks in England had increased from 32 to approximately 3200, as a countermeasure against the decline in woodland, relaxation of forest law, a rise in status seeking and the growth in importance of local lords (Stamper 1988, 140; Cantor 1965). Wigmore Castle itself is noted as having parks with deer in 1304 and 1361. Changing consumption behaviour following the Black Death may have also contributed to an increased emphasis on wild animals amongst the aristocracy (see below).

The abundance of deer in Phase 8 could also reflect the occupation of the site by Edward, Duke of York, and his family, and the rebuilding of the 15th century. A high proportion of pig (Figure 7.20) was also recovered from this phase and seems to contradict the idea that the castle was 'derelict and worth nothing' as reported in the *inquisition post mortem* of 1425 (see Chapters 2, 9 and 10). In the 16th century (Phase 9), during the reign of Henry VIII, Roland Lee, President of the Council of the Marches, was also active at Wigmore, which may account for the continued emphasis on deer. During the Civil War, however, the walls of the castle were partially destroyed, the site was left in a ruinous state, and the deer parks were ploughed up. The fact that high numbers of deer bones were present in Phase 10 deposits probably reflects the inclusion of residual 16th-century material, since there was nobody really living in the castle in the aftermath of the Civil War and there may have been only little occupation from the early 17th century.

Element	**No.**
Skull	5
Atlas	1
Cervical vertebra	2
Lumbar vertebra	3
Humerus	1
Ulna	1
Carpal	23
Tibiotarsus	2
Tarsometatarsus	130
Phalanx	380
Terminal phalanx	45
Total	**593**

FIGURE 7.25
Body part representation of chicken bones in context 102

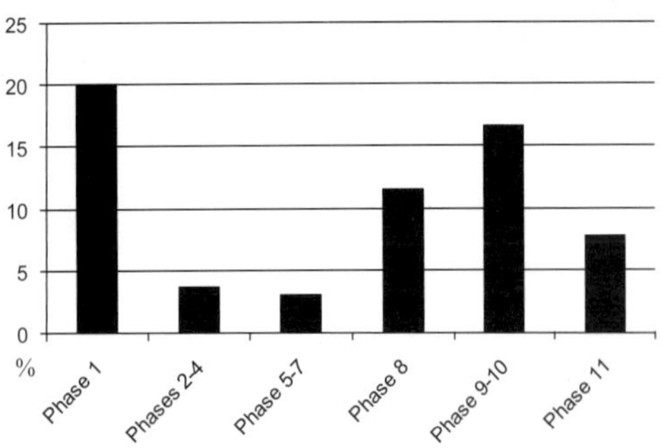

FIGURE 7.26

Relative proportion of deer out of the total proportion of hand-collected cattle, sheep/goat, pig and deer by phase (the Phase 5 dump of cattle feet has been excluded)

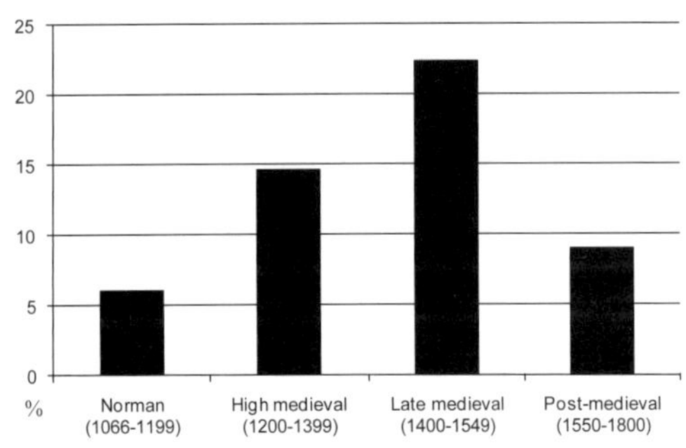

FIGURE 7.27

Relative proportion of deer (out of the total number of hand-collected cattle, sheep/goat, pig and deer) at 26 castle sites in England and Wales (site data primarily derive from Thomas 2005a)

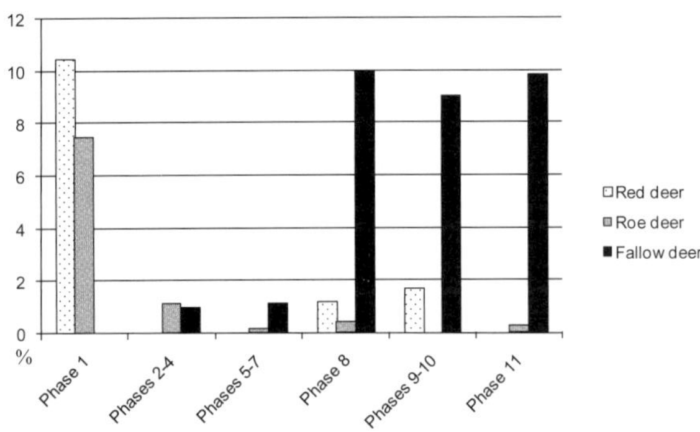

FIGURE 7.28

Relative proportion of red, fallow and roe deer out of the total proportion of identifiable hand-collected bones by phase

Context	Phase	NISP	MNI
510 (sample 2104)	11	25	1
510	11	28	2
523 (sample 2116)	11	33	2
550	10	22	1
622	10	12	1

FIGURE 7.29

Contexts containing partial rabbit skeletons

Analysis of temporal variation in the three species of deer present at Wigmore Castle reveals a growing emphasis on fallow deer (*Dama dama*) and a decline in red deer (*Cervus elaphus*) and roe deer (*Capreolus capreolus*) (Figure 7.28). It now seems certain that the fallow deer was re-introduced into England by the Normans (Sykes 2004b). The increased popularity of this species is seen on elite sites throughout England (Sykes 2007a, 67) and reflects the decimation of woodland and the rise of park hunting; fallow deer are a communal, herd-dwelling and grazing species, making them far more suited to enclosed park environments than red and roe deer (Yalden 1999, 153).

Following deer, the next most abundant wild mammals at Wigmore Castle were rabbit (*Oryctolagus cuniculus*) and hare (*Lepus europaeus*). The dietary contribution of rabbit is difficult to assess because their burrowing habits mean that they can accumulate within archaeological deposits during and after the site was occupied. Seven partial rabbit skeletons came from post-medieval contexts (Figure 7.29) and stratigraphic evidence argues against the idea that they were intrusive: contexts 510, 550 and 622 are all within the East Tower and there is no evidence of burrowing; context 523 is a turf horizon before all the decay destruction proper. Additionally, three rabbit bones displayed evidence of butchery marks, which provides direct evidence for their consumption in the early modern and later post-medieval periods. The fact that rabbits were not recorded at the site before the 13th century is worthy of note. The first documentary reference to rabbits in England occurs in the 12th century, although by the 14th century they became much more numerous (Bailey 1988; Veale 1957).

Like deer, the hare was a highly regarded beast of venery in the medieval period (Cummins 1988, 120–131). The hand-collected data from Wigmore Castle suggests that hare coursing was more popular (or at least relatively more frequent) during the 12th-13th centuries than it was subsequently (Figure 7.30).

Other wild mammals, such as rats, mice, moles and voles, were present but only in small numbers: it is likely that these represent intrusive or commensal species. One mustelid bone may testify to the occasional exploitation of small fur-bearing animals. A couple of very large pig specimens were tentatively identified as wild boar, although these were too fragmentary to confirm metrically.

By far the most intriguing wild mammal present in the animal bone assemblage from Wigmore Castle is a first phalanx of a brown bear (*Ursus arctos*) found in Phase 1 (Figure 7.31). Because brown bears were extirpated from Britain by the early medieval period (Hammon 2010, 100), this specimen must have been imported. It is noteworthy that this bone was recovered from a period characterised by high-status consumption. The fact that the specimen was a foot bone and exhibited multiple cut marks, suggests that it derived from a fur or a paw, rather than from a baited animal: foot bones were usually left within furs. That said, while bears are generally considered to be indigestible, bear paws have been described as a 'celebrated delicacy' (Simon 1952, 399). Only six other medieval sites have yielded the skeletal remains of brown bear to date (Hammon 2010, 98).

Wild birds

Previous studies have noted a greater diversity and proportion of wild bird species at elite sites in the medieval period (Albarella and Thomas 2002; Serjeantson 2006; Sykes 2004a; Thomas 2007a; Yalden and Albarella 2009) and Wigmore Castle is no exception. The most abundant wild birds were woodcock (*Scolopax rusticola*) and grey partridge (*Perdix perdix*), and these species are amongst the most numerous wild bird species on elite sites. Partridges were often raised within the confines of parks and warrens and considerable sums of money were invested in their upkeep (Sykes 2004a, 96); access and exploitation were strictly controlled therefore. Woodcocks are also frequently recorded on elite sites as well as in contemporary documentary sources (Hieatt and Butler 1985, 182), which may again testify to control over their exploitation, since they prefer woodland and scrub habitats and were usually taken using 'specialized netting techniques' (Yalden and Albarella 2009, 138). They may have also been favoured because their omnivorous feeding habit means that they carry a lot of meat for their size (Simon 1952, 612).

Other wild bird species present in small numbers at the site that are worthy of note for their associations with elite diet include swan (*Cygnus* sp.), peafowl (*Pavo cristatus*), grey heron (*Ardea cinerea*), teal/garganey (*Anas crecca/querquedula*) and waders (dunlin, *Calidris alpina*; lapwing, *Vanellus vanellus*; snipe, *Gallinago gallinago*).

The status of the remaining wild birds present at the site (pigeons, corvids and thrushes) is unclear: such species were consumed in the medieval period (Hieatt and Butler 1985, 3), but because they live in close proximity to human settlements they could have been accidentally incorporated into the archaeological record. No butchery marks were observed on these taxa.

To assess changing patterns of wild bird exploitation over time, the relative proportion of high-status wild birds was calculated out of the total number of bird bones for each period (Figure 7.32) following the methods of Albarella and Thomas (2002). These data reveal a greater contribution of high-status wild birds in the later medieval period, followed by a sharp decline in the post-medieval period. The highest values occur in Phase 1 and, although the sample size for this phase was very small (NISP=3), it adds weight to the idea that very high-status consumption occurred in this period, possibly connected to the tenure of William fitz Osbern. The post-medieval decline can probably be attributed to the changed status of Wigmore Castle after the Civil War destruction in 1643 and subsequent abandonment. The fact that high proportions of high-status wild birds were present in Phase 8 contexts provides a further indication of high-status occupation of the site in this period. That said, the increased relative emphasis on wild birds in the later medieval period has been witnessed at other elite residences: on castle sites, for example, the proportion rises from approximately 5% in the 11th–12th centuries to between 10% and 20% (or higher in some instances) in the later medieval period (Sykes 2004a; Thomas 2007a, fig 7-4). This trend is consistent with the idea that aristocratic diet diversified in the face of rising living standards amongst the peasantry in the wake of the Black Death and Peasant's Revolt (Thomas 2007a). In the early medieval period, the consumption of large quantities of meat set the aristocratic diet apart and as living standards rose, peasants began to consume more meat (Dyer 1988). The elite establishment reacted by issuing sumptuary laws, which sought to restrict meat consumption. The sumptuary law of 1363, for example, specified that the lower classes should be limited to eating 'once a day of flesh or of fish' (Pickering 1762, 164). Because these laws could not be enforced, aristocratic diet shifted

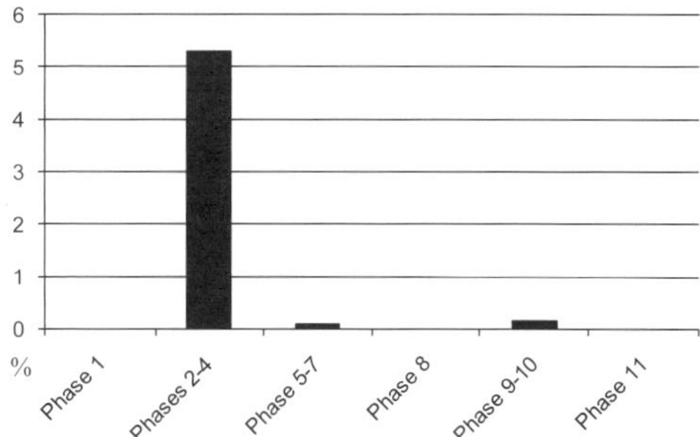

FIGURE 7.30

Percentage of hand-collected hare bones by phase out of the total number of identifiable bones present

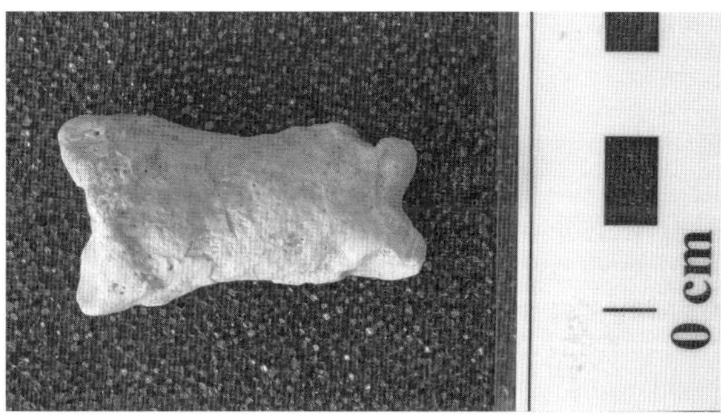

FIGURE 7.31

The first phalanx of a European brown bear

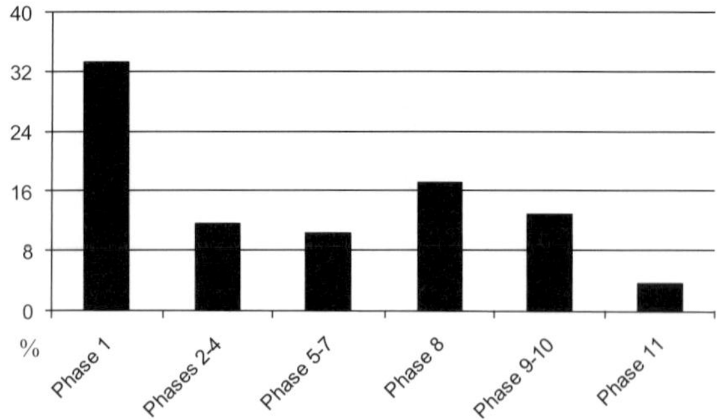

FIGURE 7.32

Percentage of hand-collected high-status wild bird bones by phase out of the total number of bird bones (the Phase 6 dump of chicken feet has been excluded from this analysis)

its emphasis to foodstuffs that were still beyond the financial reach or access of the majority of the population, which in part included greater emphasis on wild birds and mammals. The fact that the rise in wild bird consumption coincides with the expansion of parks and deer hunting, is unsurprising, since parkland would have provided an ideal habitat for some of these species.

Body part representation

To explore the changing nature of animal procurement for the principal domestic mammals, the distribution of body parts by phase has been charted (Figures 7.33–7.35). Due to the small size of the samples, it is only possible to compare medieval and post-medieval phases broadly. For cattle and sheep/goat (Figures 7.33–7.34), all body parts were represented indicating that complete animals were transported to the site 'on the hoof' and processed there. Whilst some elements were less well represented than others, recovery and taphonomic factors are implicated. For example, cattle metapodia, astragali and calcaneii were the most abundant elements; however, these are dense and large elements that have high survival potential. Conversely, some elements present in lower proportions, such as the proximal femur, are less dense than other anatomical zones (Lyman 1994, table 7.6), and therefore more susceptible to post-depositional degradation. The fact that sheep/goat phalanges were less abundant than cattle phalanges further testifies to the biases against smaller elements of hand-collection. There was, however, a slightly greater emphasis on the major meat-bearing elements (e.g. scapula, humerus, radius and tibia) for sheep/goat, which suggests that more dressed mutton carcasses were arriving on site — a typical pattern observed at medieval sites in England (e.g. Albarella and Davis 1996; Albarella *et al* 1997; Jones *et al* 1985; Gidney 1991a; 1991b; Thomas 2005a). With respect to temporal variation, there appears to be greater emphasis on selected sheep/goat body parts (rather than whole carcasses) in the post-medieval period, with lower proportions of low meat value body parts (e.g. mandibles, phalanges, tarsals and metatarsals) and a corresponding rise in some high meat value body parts (e.g. humerus, pelvis and tibia). There is similar (albeit less clear cut) evidence for cattle with lower proportions of metapodials and higher proportions

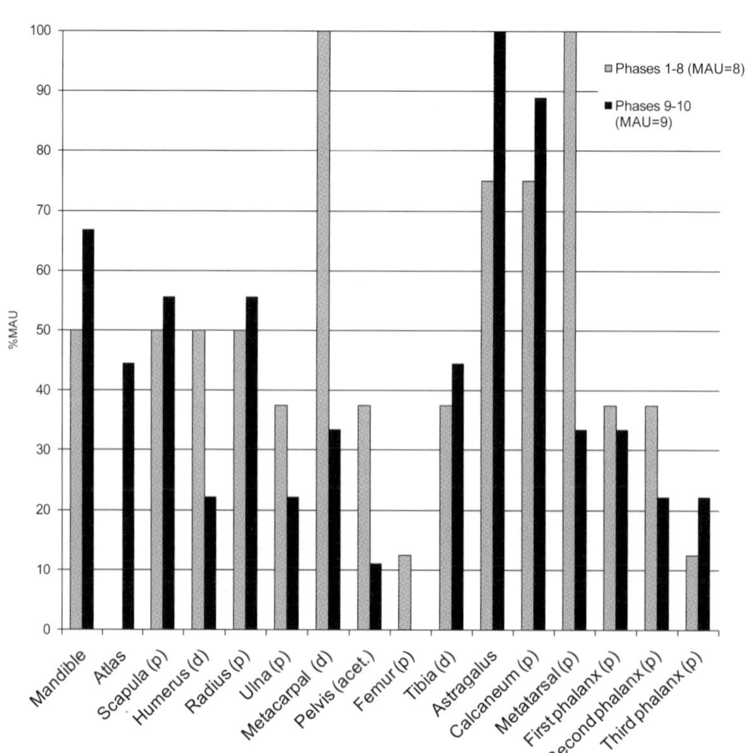

FIGURE 7.33

Body part representation for cattle. The Phase 5 dump of cattle feet has been excluded (p: proximal; d: distal)

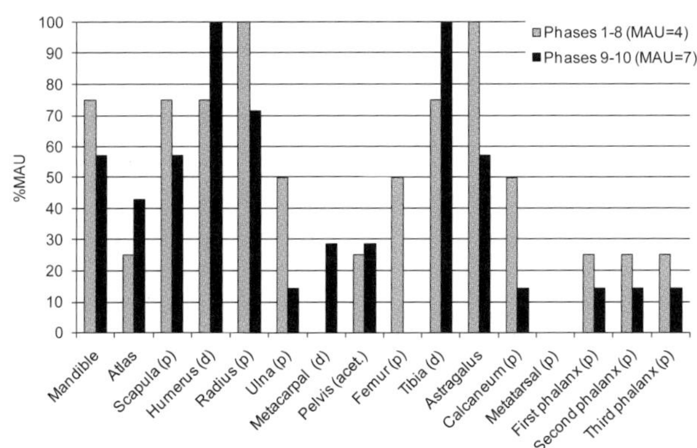

FIGURE 7.34
Body part representation for sheep/goat (p: proximal; d: distal)

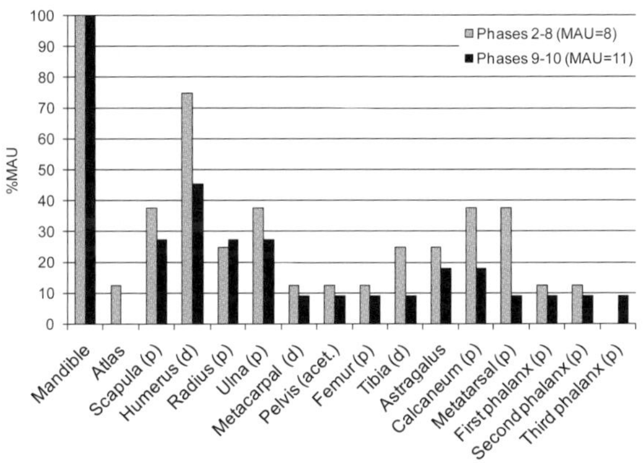

FIGURE 7.35
Body part representation for pig (p: proximal; d: distal)

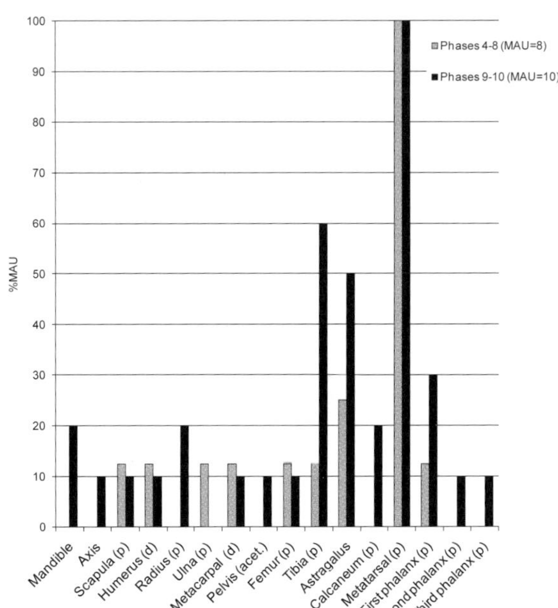

FIGURE 7.36
Body part representation for fallow deer (p: proximal; d: distal)

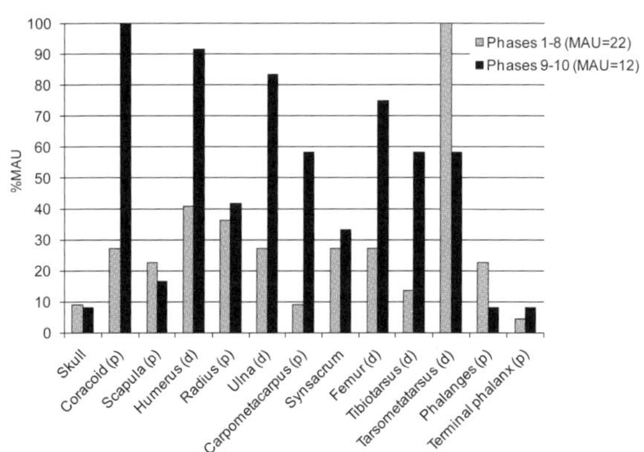

FIGURE 7.37
Body part representation for chicken (p: proximal; d: distal)

of radii and tibiae in the post-medieval period. This probably reflects the growing reliance on food procured from markets and the commercialisation of the meat trade (Rixson 2000).

Consideration of body part representation for pig reveals less even representation of skeletal elements, with a much higher proportion of mandibles and fore-limb elements compared with hind-limb bones (Figure 7.35). The abundance of pig teeth and mandibles is typical of English medieval and post-medieval sites (e.g. Connell and Davis 1997; Grant 1985; Jones *et al* 1985; Maltby 1982; Thomas 2005a). While the young age at slaughter of pigs (see below) would have made the soft, greasy post-cranial bones more susceptible to destruction by carnivores and post-depositional degradation, the manner of pig butchery and procurement may have also contributed to this patterning. Medieval historical sources indicate that domestic pigs were frequently preserved by smoking, salting or air-drying (Woolgar 1999, 116). The lack of post-cranial bones may therefore reflect the fact that more pork was consumed as filleted joints. Documentary sources also reveal that brawn made from the head and foreparts of a boar or pig was regarded as a delicacy in the medieval period (Wilson 1973, 88). Indeed, roast boar's head was a 'favourite entrée for the first course of an English feast' and is frequently mentioned in late 14th-century recipes (Hieatt and Butler 1985, 173). The data in Figure 7.35 demonstrate a lower emphasis on post-cranial bones in the post-medieval period, but this probably reflects the higher proportion of gnawing and poorer bone preservation in this period (see above).

Analysis of body part representation for fallow deer (Figure 7.36) reveals a predominance of hind-limb elements, a pattern widely replicated at contemporary elite sites (Sykes 2007b; Thomas 2007b). This distribution probably reflects the selective butchery and redistribution of deer carcasses described in medieval hunting treatises as the 'unmaking' (Almond 2003, 64; Brewer 1992, 85; Hands 1975, 76; Rooney 1987). Variation exists between the different manuals but in general: one shoulder was given to the forester; the other shoulder was presented to the individual that 'unmade' the deer or the best hunter; the pelvis was left for the raven (*corbyn*); and the hind-limbs (haunches) were kept for the lord. While some of the deer must have derived from the estate of the castle, it is also likely that haunches of deer were gifted as acts of *largesse*. The presence of some fore-limb elements does indicate that the prescribed redistribution of deer carcasses was not always adhered to, possibly more so in the post-medieval period.

Consideration of body part representation for chicken (Figure 7.37) unsurprisingly reveals that most elements are present, indicating the consumption of complete birds on site. The pattern of distribution is uneven, although this is probably a consequence of recovery and taphonomic biases. For example, the skull, scapula and phalanges are poorly represented across all phases. The terminal phalanges is amongst the smallest recorded elements while the skull and scapula are particularly fragile. As with cattle and sheep/goat, there appears to be a greater emphasis on imported joints in the post-medieval period.

Mortality profiles

For cattle, the evidence from tooth eruption and attrition reveals that very few animals were slaughtered in the first couple of years of life. The peak age at slaughter was 3–6 years, when approximately 50% of the animals were slaughtered (Figure 7.38). These animals were presumably killed once they had attained their maximum size. This pattern varies slightly from broadly contemporary elite sites where greater numbers of cattle were slaughtered later in life after they had fulfilled other functions within the agricultural round (such as pulling ploughs and carts). Unfortunately, only four ageable mandibles derived from post-medieval deposits; however three of these were aged to the first year of life, suggesting a younger slaughter age.

The epiphyseal fusion data support the dental evidence by revealing that the majority of cattle were slaughtered beyond the point at which their skeleton was fully matured (Figure 7.39). Differences in slaughter age between phases are evident, although the patterns are rather complex. The greatest slaughter of young animals occurs in the 12th–13th century, a pattern that could be associated with higher status consumption. A slightly greater emphasis on the slaughter of cattle in their third or fourth year of life occurred in the 16th–17th century. This could indicate the presence of faster maturing breeds, the rise of the dairy industry and the decreasing reliance on cattle as traction animals as noted on contemporary sites (Albarella 1997). However, it could also testify to high-status consumption, although given the history of the site, this had probably ceased in the 17th century. It should be observed that the younger age of slaughter observed in the 12th–13th and 16th–17th centuries may have been underestimated, due to the higher levels of carnivore gnawing in these periods (Figure 7.7).

For sheep/goat, the presence of only 12 ageable mandibles precludes any detailed analysis of slaughter age on the basis of tooth eruption and wear, although it is worth noting that all but two of these derived from animals slaughtered less than two years of age. The fusion data for the medieval period is compounded by the paucity of sheep at the site; consequently, all medieval phases have been combined (Figure 7.40). These data reveal that most sheep/goat were kept beyond adulthood in the medieval and early post-medieval period. The

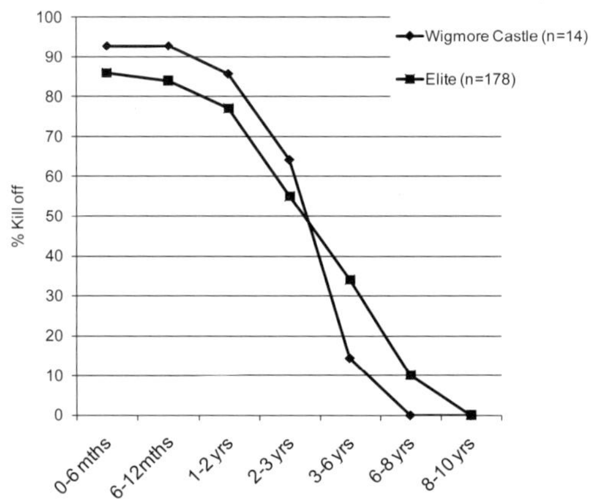

FIGURE 7.38
Tooth eruption and wear data for Phases 5–8 cattle mandibles from Wigmore Castle compared with average values for elite sites dating to the mid-12th to mid-14th centuries (after Sykes 2007a, 35). Age categories follow Halstead (1985)

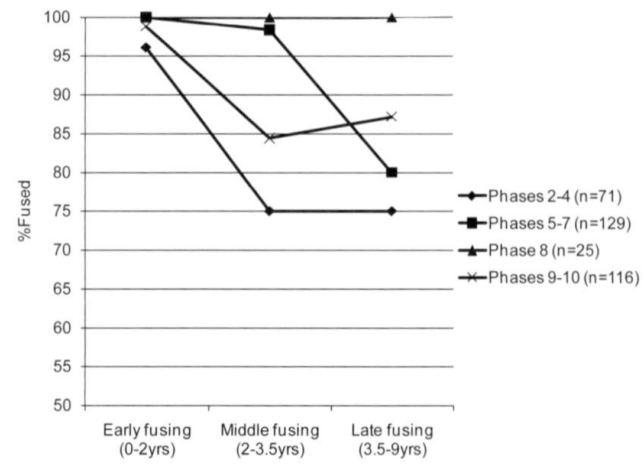

FIGURE 7.39
Epiphyseal fusion data for cattle (age categories follow Reitz and Wing 1999, table 3.5)

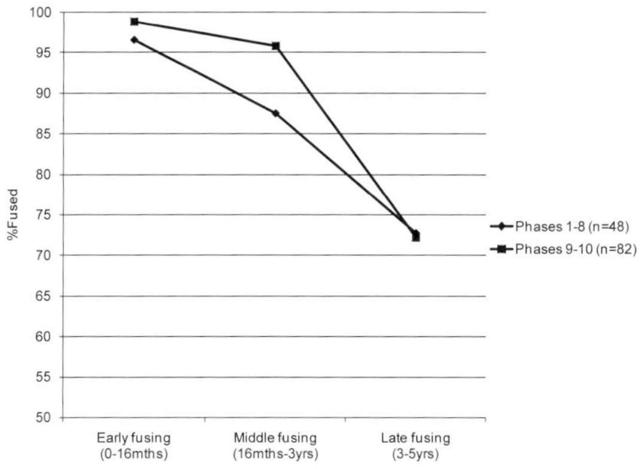

FIGURE 7.40

Epiphyseal fusion data for sheep/goat (age categories follow Reitz and Wing 1999, table 3.5)

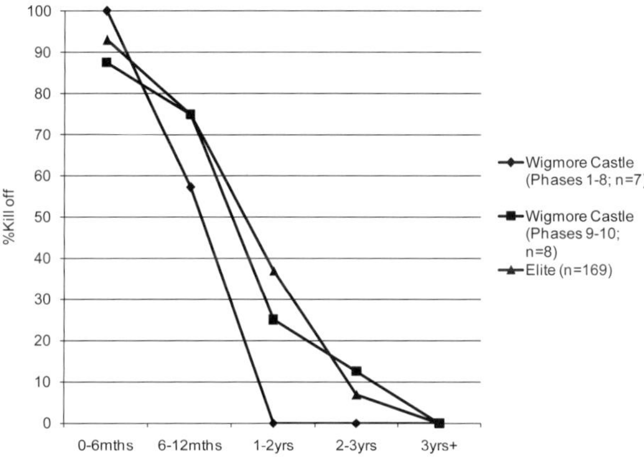

FIGURE 7.41

Tooth eruption and wear data for pig mandibles from Wigmore Castle compared against average values for elite sites dating to the mid-12th to mid-14th centuries (after Sykes 2007a, 35). Age categories follow Payne (1973)

slight increase in slaughter age from the medieval period to the 16th–17th century probably reflects the expansion of the wool and cloth industries, a pattern that has been observed widely in Britain (e.g. Albarella and Davis 1994; 1996; Albarella *et al* 1997; Grant 1985; Maltby 1979; 1982; Thomas 2005a).

Unlike cattle and sheep, pigs were almost exclusively exploited for their meat and lard, and this is reflected in the age distribution diagrams (Figures 7.41–7.42). Based on tooth eruption and wear, the majority of animals were slaughtered within the first two years of life, a pattern that demonstrates a greater emphasis on the tender meat from young animals than broadly contemporary elite sites (Figure 7.41). This pattern is confirmed by the epiphyseal fusion data (Figure 7.42), although it is clear that some animals were kept beyond two years of age. In the 16th–17th centuries the average age of slaughter for pigs increases. This is surprising considering the fact that faster maturing types of pigs were probably present by this period and runs counter to the trend witnessed at contemporary sites (Albarella *et al* 1997; Dobney *et al* 1996; Maltby 1979).

There are insufficient data to convincingly explore the age at slaughter for red and roe deer; however, the fallow deer at Wigmore Castle were almost exclusively represented by adult animals. All of the mandibles recorded belonged to animals in their third or fourth year (Chaplin and White 1969) and only six out of 53 post-cranial bones with recordable fusion status were unfused. The fact that the majority of the deer were slaughtered as adults is unsurprising. Firstly, fallow deer usually only give birth to a single fawn each year (Chapman and Chapman 1975, 146), consequently it would have been impractical to slaughter a high proportion of young animals without compromising the sustainability of the population. Secondly, medieval hunting treatises emphasise the fact that only adult animals should be taken during the hunt (Cummins 1988).

Analysis of the relative proportion of juvenile chicken bones (Figure 7.43) reveals that throughout the medieval and early post-medieval periods the majority of birds were slaughtered as adults, presumably after these birds had attained their maximum size and been exploited for their eggs. Indeed, the average proportion of juvenile chickens at Wigmore Castle is somewhat lower than the values recorded at contemporary sites (Maltby 1982; Serjeantson 2006, fig 9.7; Thomas 2005a). The fact that a relatively higher proportion of juvenile chickens occurred in Phase 8 could further attest to high-status consumption habits in this period.

Sexing

Only 16 pig canines could be sexed from Wigmore Castle: nine boars and seven sows. Although the samples are small, the slaughtering of greater numbers of males is more typical of 'consumer sites', since sows would have been preferred for stock breeding.

A total of 43 chicken tarsometatarsi could be sexed, based on the state of spur formation (Figure 7.44). In the medieval period there is a slight predominance of hens (or at least chickens exhibiting no evidence of a spur) while in the post-medieval period there is a much higher relative proportion of males. A predominance of hens is typical of medieval assemblages and supports the ageing data by reflecting an emphasis on egg production (Serjeantson 2006, 138). The increased proportion of males in the post-medieval period has been witnessed at other archaeological sites (e.g. Thomas 2005a, 69) and further demonstrates a growing emphasis on meat production. Complicating these data is the fact that even mature male tarsometatarsi may not show any sign of a spur, let alone those that were slaughtered before the fusion of the spur to the shaft occurred (Sadler 1990, 41); however, biometrical analysis of

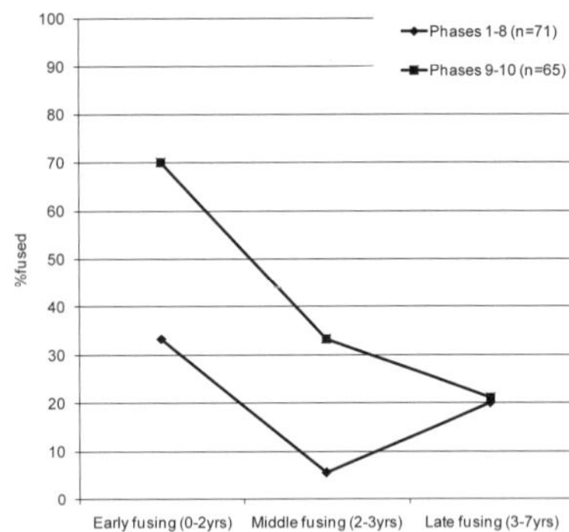

FIGURE 7.42

Epiphyseal fusion data for pig (age categories follow Reitz and Wing 1999, table 3.5)

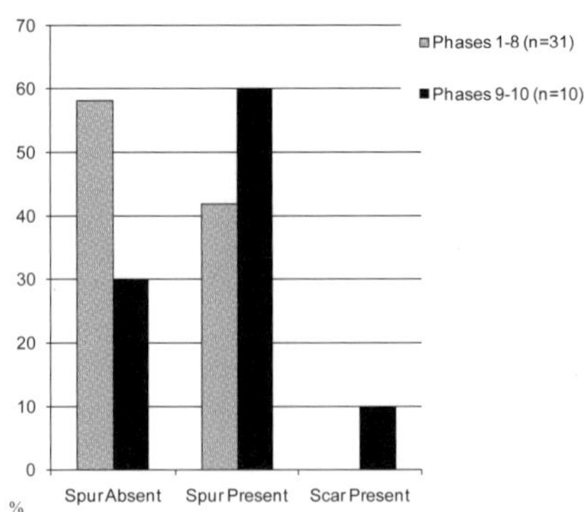

FIGURE 7.44

Spur formation in chicken tarsometatarsi

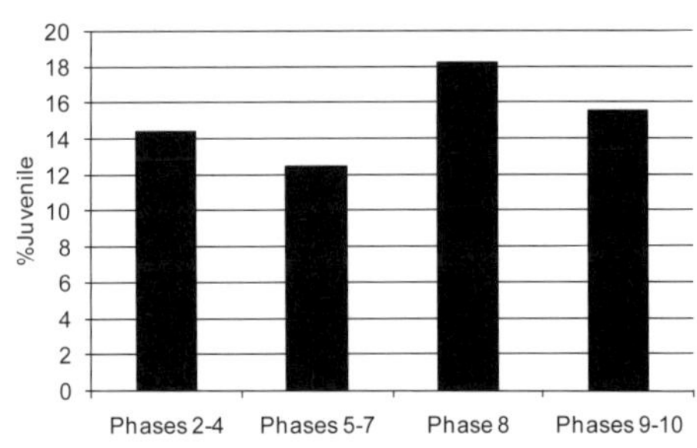

FIGURE 7.43

Relative proportion of juvenile chicken bones by phase. The Phase 6 dump of chicken feet has been excluded from this analysis

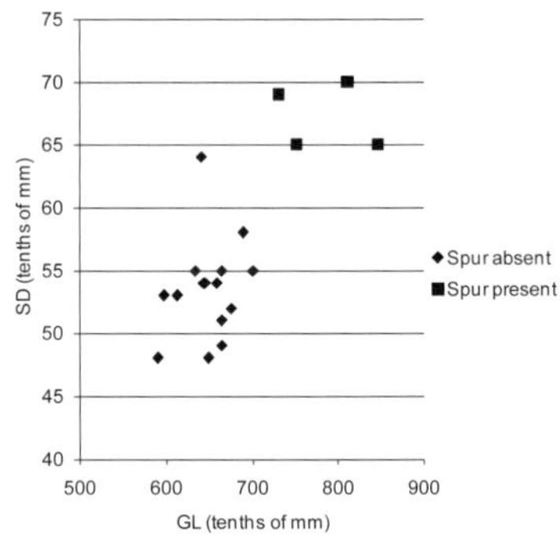

FIGURE 7.45

Biometrical analysis of sexed chicken tarsometarsi (Phases 2–10 combined)

the sexed tarosmetarsi indicates only one possible specimen without a scar that might have been male (Figure 7.45). A further method of assessing the proportion of hens in an archaeological population of domestic fowl is through the identification of medullary bone, which is produced in the marrow cavity of the long bones to offset calcium loss during egg production (Lentacker and Van Neer 1996). Although, complete chicken long bones were not systematically broken to identify this condition, the fact that three cases were recovered from the 13th century (Phase 4) compared with only one from Phase 11, supports the trend observed in the spur formation data.

Biometrical analysis of fallow deer distal tibia for medieval and post-medieval phases combined (Figure 7.46) reveals two distinct clusters, which doubtless reflect the sexual dimorphism of this species (Chapman and Chapman 1975, 33). These data indicate that slightly more bucks were hunted than does, which accords with the preferences articulated in medieval hunting manuals (Cummins 1988, 32, 84).

While there are insufficient metrical data to examine the sexual composition of the sheep from Wigmore Castle, the data for cattle from the mid-13th to mid-14th centuries (Phases 5–7; which primarily derive from the dump of feet) do permit such an assessment. Previous studies have demonstrated that measurements of the distal metacarpal are the most effective discriminators of sex in cattle (e.g. Higham 1969; Thomas 1988; Zalkin 1960). In Figure 7.47 the distal breadth is plotted against the medial condyle depth and reveals the presence of two clusters of data that could indicate the presence of a large group of cows and a smaller group of bulls/oxen. Unfortunately, the paucity of metacarpal measurements in other phases precludes the analysis of temporal variation in the sex profile.

Biometry

In order to provide a statistically viable sample to explore diachronic changes in the size and shape of the livestock at Wigmore Castle a log scaling technique has been employed. This technique involves converting all measurements to logarithms by relativising each against a standard (Simpson *et al* 1960). A positive value indicates that the archaeological specimen is larger than the standard, a negative value that it is smaller, while zero indicates that the standard and archaeological specimen are

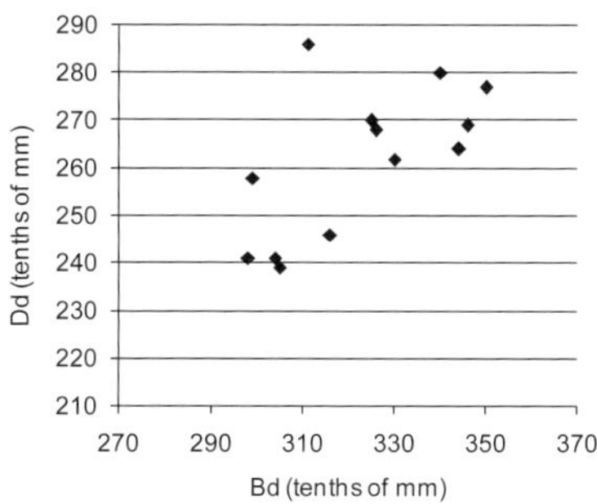

FIGURE 7.46

Scatter diagram of fallow deer tibia distal breadth (Bd) against distal depth (Dd) (Phases 4–10 combined)

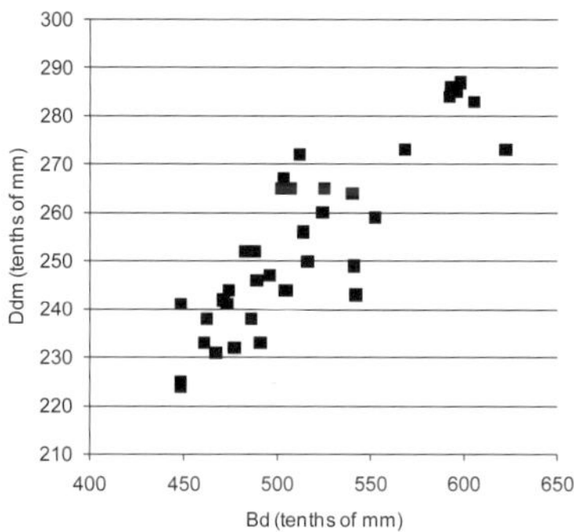

FIGURE 7.47

Scatter diagram of distal epiphysis breadth (Bd) against the medial condyle breadth (Ddm) for Phase 5 cattle metacarpals

identically sized. Wherever possible, measurements taken in different anatomical planes (e.g. lengths, breadths and depths) were combined, because these are highly correlated and thus permit the exploration of both shape and size change. Where samples were small, all post-cranial bones were combined on the same axis, although this inevitably leads to a loss of data resolution, it does permit crude assessment of size change, which would otherwise be impossible.

Unfortunately there were too few measureable cattle teeth to explore diachronic change; however, analysis of cattle post-cranial bone measurements (Figure 7.48) reveals that they were considerably smaller in all phases of occupation than the later 14th-century specimens from Dudley Castle (used as the standard), which witnessed a dramatic increase in size in this period (Thomas 2005a, figs 53–55). Moreover, the cattle from Wigmore Castle appear to have a different shape from the specimens from Dudley Castle: they are longer relative to their breadths and depths. It should be observed, however, that the cattle from Dudley Castle are slightly broader than those from contemporary sites (Thomas 2005a, 36).

While the mean values generally increase over time, particularly in the 16th–17th centuries, coinciding perhaps with the historically attested introduction of larger Dutch stock into the region (Trow-Smith 1957, 208–209), there are no statistically significant variations between consecutive phases, other than an increase in breadth measurements between Phases 5–7 and Phases 9–10 (U=1221; *P*=0.00). Detailed analysis of the metrical data reveals that the narrowness of the specimens in the mid-13th to mid-14th century is due to the presence of a large number of short and slender metapodials in the dump from group 17 (Figure 7.49). The fact that it is primarily the metapodia that exhibit a size difference suggests that it is due to the sexual composition of the specimens: as noted above, cattle metapodia are the most effective discriminators of sex. An abundance of narrow and slender metapodia therefore suggests the presence of large numbers of cows, a fact supported by the sexing data presented in Figure 7.47. The cows of Herefordshire were known for their diminutive conformation. For example, Curtler (1908, 412), albeit writing of the 18th century, notes that 'the Herefordshire cow was small, extremely delicate and very feminine in character, but there was an extraordinary difference between the cow and the ox bred from her, the latter being often three times the weight of the dam'.

Comparison of the greatest length of the astragalus reveals that the late medieval cattle at Wigmore Castle are statistically identical to cattle at contemporary sites in central England such as Dudley Castle, West Midlands (1262–1321), St Peters Lane, Leicester (1200–1400) and West Cotton, Northamptonshire (1100–1400) (Figures 7.50–7.51). However, they are statistically significantly larger than the cattle from sites in the south-west and north-east, like Launceston Castle (Cornwall) and Prudhoe Castle (Northumberland). The only larger contemporary cattle came from mid- to late-14th-century Dudley Castle, which witnessed a dramatic size increase in this period.

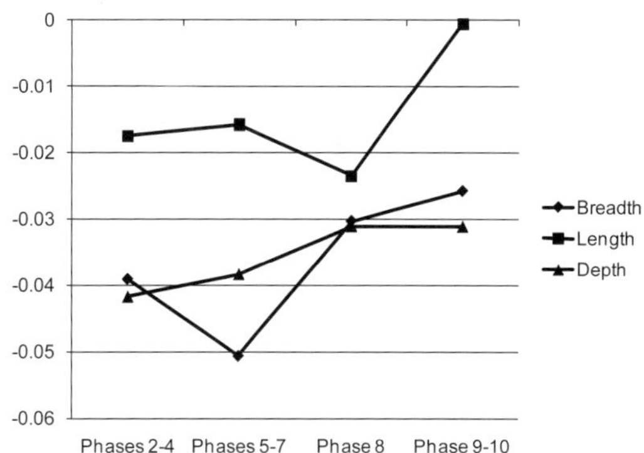

FIGURE 7.48

Mean log values of cattle post-cranial bone measurements by phase. The standard derives from the mean values from Phase 6 (1321–1397) cattle from Dudley Castle (Thomas 2005a)

Measurement	n	Mean
Metapodial (GL)	2	-0.05
Metapodial (Bd)	54	-0.07
Astragalus (GL)	5	-0.02
Astragalus (Bd)	6	-0.03
Phalanx (GL)	17	0.01
Phalanx (Bd)	17	-0.01

FIGURE 7.49

Comparison of mean log values for different measurements from the Phase 5 cattle dump

Site	Date	n	Mean	U	P
Dolforwyn Castle	1274–1390	36	577.42	151	0.45
Dudley Castle	1262–1321	7	581.29	29	0.60
	1321–1397	24	633.71	40	0
Launceston Castle	Late 13thC	34	549.21	47	0
	15thC	62	555.63	119	0
Prudhoe Castle	13thC	26	564.50	81.5	0.09
	13th to mid-14thC	35	563.17	88	0.02
St Peter's Lane	1200–1400	9	589.11	44.5	1.00
West Cotton	1100–1250	31	598.42	116	0.24
	1250–1400	21	609.05	64.5	0.09
Wigmore Castle	12th to mid-14thC	10	589.40	-	-

FIGURE 7.50

Mann-Whitney U-tests of astragalus greatest length measurements from 12th- to mid-14th century contexts at Wigmore Castle and contemporary later medieval sites: Dolforwyn Castle (Stephen Rowland pers comm); Dudley Castle (Thomas 2005a); Launceston Castle (Albarella and Davis 1996); Prudhoe Castle (Davis 1987); St Peter's Lane (Gidney 1991a); West Cotton (Albarella and Davis 1994)

The post-medieval data reveal no statistically significant variation between the cattle astragali from Wigmore Castle and contemporary sites. That said, it is clear that the mean size of the astragalus is considerably greater at Launceston Castle, Castle Mall and early 17th-18th century Prudhoe Castle. This reflects the fact that greater increases in cattle size occurred at these sites in the late medieval and post-medieval periods.

The metrical data for sheep/goat at Wigmore Castle reveals a gradual increase in size over time (Figure 7.52). This pattern is clearly exemplified by plotting the mean log values by phase (Figure 7.53). Statistical analysis of these data using a Mann-Whitney U-test reveals that the size increase between the 12th-13th century (Phases 2–4) and the mid-14th-15th century (Phase 8) is statistically significant (U=38; P=0.03). This represents another early example of stock improvement in medieval England; the earliest previously recorded increase was recorded at mid-late 14th-century Dudley Castle (Thomas 2005a; 2005b). This finding adds to the growing corpus of evidence that stock improvement in the medieval and post-medieval periods occurred

Site	Date	n	Mean	U	P
Castle Mall	Late 16th–18thC	7	642.57	16	0.18
Dudley Castle	1533–1750	21	612.81	81	0.90
Launceston Castle	16thC–1650	38	633.45	107.5	0.20
	1660–1840	34	649.26	84	0.10
Prudhoe Castle	Early to mid-16thC	11	599.00	37	0.59
	mid-16th to early 17thC	26	595.19	78.5	0.31
	early 17th–18thC	11	630.27	33	0.39
Wigmore Castle	12th to mid-14thC	8	613.00	-	-

FIGURE 7.51

Mann-Whitney U-tests of astragalus greatest length measurements from 16th to 17th century contexts at Wigmore Castle and contemporary post-medieval sites: Castle Mall (Albarella et al 1997); Dudley Castle (Thomas 2005a); Launceston Castle (Albarella and Davis 1996); Prudhoe Castle (Davis 1987)

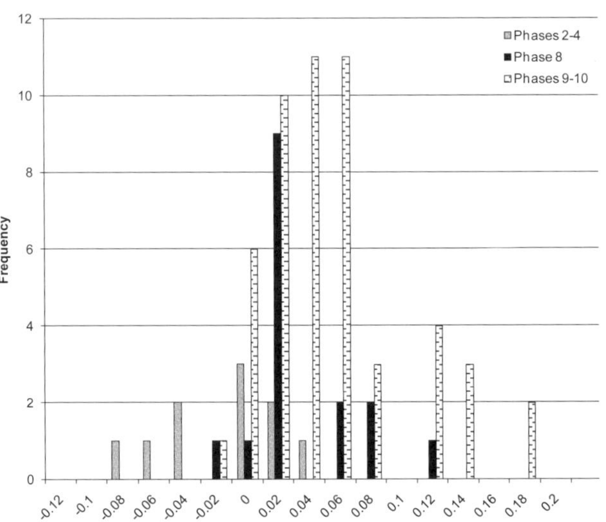

FIGURE 7.52

Histogram of sheep/goat post-cranial bone measurements (all log-scaled values combined). The standard is drawn from Phase 6 (1321–1397) at Dudley Castle

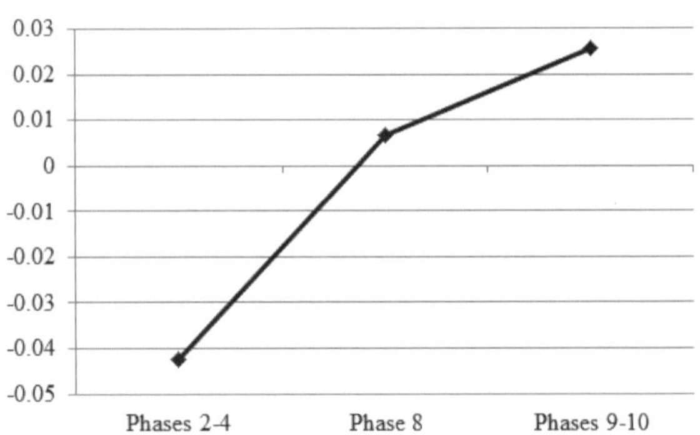

FIGURE 7.53

Mean log-scaled values of sheep/goat post-cranial bones from Wigmore Castle. The standard is drawn from Phase 6 (1321–1397) at Dudley Castle

as part of a long-term, gradual process, varying in its timing across time and space (and by species), that may have been stimulated by changes in society and economy following the Black Death (Thomas 2005b).

Unfortunately, the paucity of the sheep/goat metrical dataset from Wigmore Castle does not permit the analysis of dental measurements or detailed inter-site analysis other than for the post-medieval period (Figure 7.54). The latter reveals that the Phase 9–10 sheep/goat tibiae breadths from Wigmore Castle are on average smaller than those from contemporary sites; the difference is statistically significant at Camber Castle (East Sussex), Little Lane and St Peter's Lane, Leicester and Lincoln. This conclusion is consistent with the historical record; writing of the 17th century, Curtler (1908, 409) notes that the wool of the Herefordshire sheep was still the 'finest in England, but the sheep were small and did not generally beat a fleece of more than 1lb'.

The young age of the pig bones, means that there were too few measurable specimens to undertake a detailed analysis of shape and size change over time; however, by combining all measurements on the same axis it is possible to observe that the pigs from Phases 9–10 were larger than those from medieval phases (Figure 7.55). The dataset for the teeth is much smaller, but the pattern is replicated (Figure 7.56), indicating that the difference in size was brought about by selective breeding or the introduction of new genetic stock.

A comparison of pig post-cranial bone measurements from Phases 9–10 with contemporary sites (Figure 7.57) reveals that the Wigmore specimens are on average smaller than those found elsewhere; however that difference is only statistically highly significant at Lincoln (1600–1750).

The metrical sample for chicken is sufficiently robust to chart both size and shape change by phase (Figure 7.58). This analysis reveals a gradual increase in the average size of chickens over time. Statistically significant variation was recorded in length (U=44; P=0.0240) and breadth (U=840.5; P=0.0002) measurements between Phases 5–7 and Phases 9–10. An

Site	Date	n	Mean	U	P
Camber Castle	Mid-16th to 1637	77	268.57	208.5	0
	1637–18th century	39	270.03	109.5	0
Castle Mall	Late 16th–18th century	31	255.19	158.5	0.27
Dudley Castle	1533–1750	45	257.24	212.5	0.14
Launceston Castle	16th century–1650	53	244.60	305.5	0.53
	1660–1840	50	257.62	234.0	0.12
Lincoln	1600–1750	17	267.47	58.0	0.03
Little Lane	Mid-16th to mid-17th century	51	262.06	191.0	0.02
St Peter's Lane	16th–17th century	11	264.55	37.0	0.05
Yatersbury	16th–17th century	39	248.15	250.0	0.95
Wigmore Castle	16th–17th century	13	247.23	-	-

FIGURE 7.54

Mann-Whitney U-tests of tibia distal breadth measurements from 16th- to 17th-century contexts at Wigmore Castle and contemporary post-medieval sites: Camber Castle (Connell and Davis 1997); Castle Mall (Albarella et al 1997); Dudley Castle (Thomas 2005a); Launceston Castle (Albarella and Davis 1996); Lincoln (Dobney et al 1996); Little Lane (Gidney 1992); St Peters Lane (Gidney 1991c); Yatesbury (Sykes 2001)

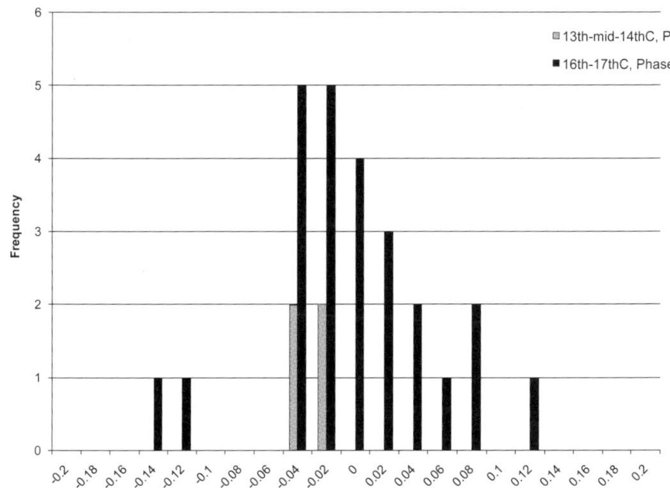

FIGURE 7.55

Pig post-cranial bone log-scaled values combined. The standard is drawn from Phase 5 (1262–1321) at Dudley Castle

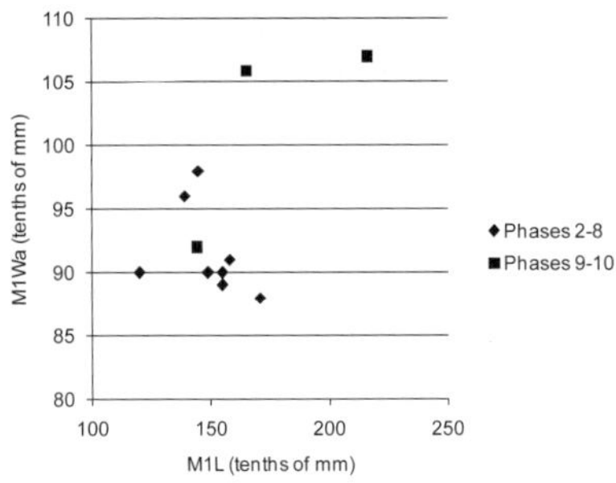

FIGURE 7.56

Metrical analysis of pig mandibular first molars

Site	Date	n	Mean	U	P
Castle Mall	Late 16th–18th century	13	0.02	79.0	0.09
Dudley Castle	1533–1750	12	0	100.0	0.58
Launceston Castle	1600–1650	22	0.01	173.5	0.36
Lincoln	1600–1750	13	0.06	41.0	0
Wigmore Castle	16th–17th century	19	-0.01	-	-

FIGURE 7.57

Mann-Whitney U-tests of post-cranial bone measurements from 16th- to 17th-century contexts at Wigmore Castle against contemporary post-medieval sites: Castle Mall (Albarella et al 1997); Dudley Castle (Thomas 2005a); Launceston Castle (Albarella and Davis 1996); Lincoln (Dobney et al 1996). The standard is drawn from Phase 5 (1262–1321) at Dudley Castle

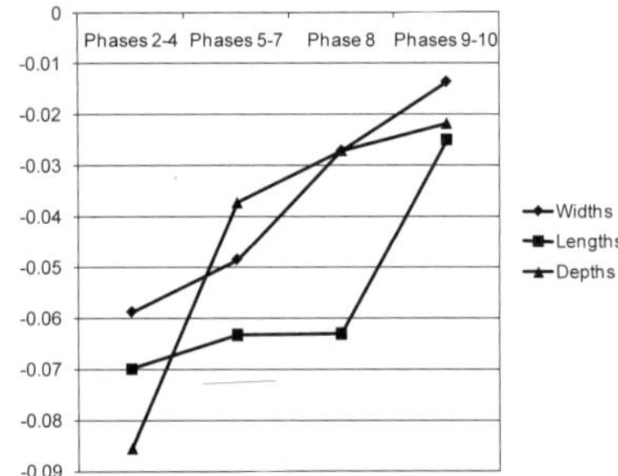

FIGURE 7.58

Mean log-scaled values of chicken post-cranial bone measurements by phase. The standard derives from the mean values from Phase 6 (1321–1397) chickens from Dudley Castle

increase in the size of chicken in the later medieval and early post-medieval periods is well attested at contemporary sites (Albarella *et al* 1997; Dobney *et al* 1996; Maltby 1979; Sadler 2007; Thomas 2005a). It is clear from Figure 7.58 that the chickens from all phases at Wigmore Castle are smaller than those from later 14th-century contexts at Dudley Castle. Comparison of distal tarsometatarsus breadth measurements from Phases 5–7 at Wigmore Castle with contemporary medieval sites (Figure 7.59) reveals that this difference is statistically significant. The chickens from late-13th-century Launceston Castle were also significantly larger than those from Wigmore. The Phase 9–10 chickens from Wigmore Castle were on average smaller than the birds from Camber Castle (East Sussex), Castle Mall, Norwich (Norfolk) and Dudley Castle (West Midlands), although this difference is not statistically significant (Figure 7.60). The Wigmore specimens are larger than those from deposits dated to the 16th-century to 1650 at Launceston Castle and this is statistically significant, although the sample size is very small at the latter site.

The metrical dataset for other species is too poor to provide any meaningful information about size change over time. Only two horse bones were sufficiently complete to yield greatest length measurements from which withers heights could be determined. Both specimens came from Phase 10 deposits and yielded estimates of 12 and 13 hands (based on the withers height calculations of Kiesewalter 1888), indicating the presence of ponies rather than horses. Only three dog bones provided greatest length measurements from which shoulder heights could be estimated. All three derived from Phase 9–10 contexts and produced heights of 41.15cm, 46.52cm and 67.21cm (withers height calculations follow Harcourt 1974). These values are well within the range observed at contemporary sites (e.g. Thomas 2005a, fig 127).

Butchery

In total, 16% of hand-collected and identifiable post-cranial bones at Wigmore Castle exhibited butchery marks. Thirty-one red and fallow deer antler fragments were also recovered, of which five exhibited butchery marks indicating the exploitation of antler as a raw material; both shed and unshed antlers were used. The majority of butchery marks on post-cranial bones was inflicted by knives and cleavers and they are characteristic

Site	Date	n	Mean	U	P
Castle Mall	12th to mid-14thC	13	122.08	276.5	0.96
Dolforwyn Castle	1274–1390	25	123.88	502.5	0.66
Dudley Castle	1262–1321	5	114.00	52.0	0.06
	1321–1397	13	134.46	111.5	0
Launceston Castle	Late 13thC	51	128.41	721.0	0
West Cotton	1100–1250	6	121.83	102.5	0.43
Wigmore Castle	Mid-13th to mid-14thC	43	120.49	-	-

FIGURE 7.59

Mann-Whitney U-tests of chicken tarsometatarsus distal breadth measurements from Phase 5–7 contexts from Wigmore Castle and contemporary medieval sites: Castle Mall (Albarella et al 1997); Dolforwyn Castle (Stephen Rowland pers comm); Dudley Castle (Thomas 2005a); Launceston Castle (Albarella and Davis 1996); West Cotton (Albarella and Davis 1994)

Site	Date	n	Mean	U	P
Camber Castle	1637–18thC	5	150.60	12.0	0.27
Castle Mall	Late 16th–18thC	8	148.25	15.5	0.09
Dudley Castle	1533–1750	12	139.75	36.0	0.37
Launceston Castle	16th century–1650	4	116.50	0	0
Wigmore Castle	16th–17thC	8	135.00	-	-

FIGURE 7.60

Mann-Whitney U-tests of chicken tarsometatarsus distal breadth measurements from Phase 9–10 contexts from Wigmore Castle and contemporary post-medieval sites: Camber Castle (Davis 1987); Castle Mall (Albarella et al 1997); Dudley Castle (Thomas 2005a); Launceston Castle (Albarella and Davis 1996)

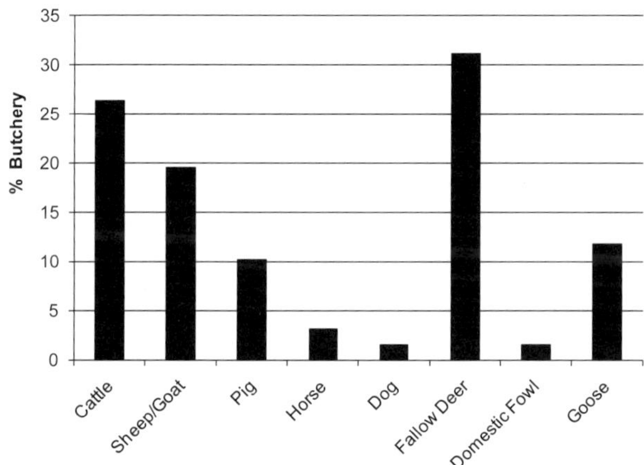

FIGURE 7.61

Proportion of hand-collected, identifiable, post-cranial bones exhibiting butchery marks for the most abundant species

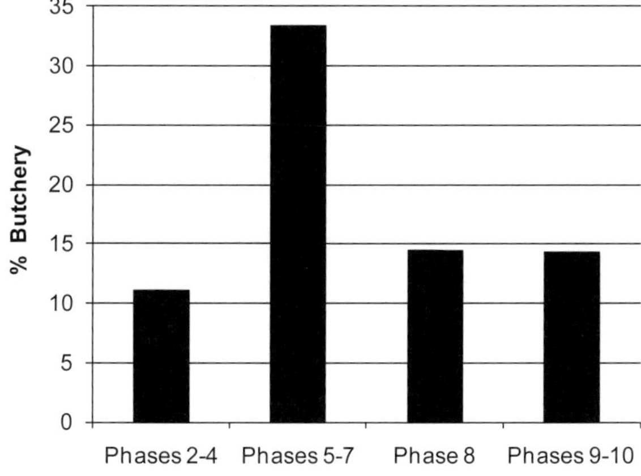

FIGURE 7.62

Proportion of hand-collected, identifiable, cow, sheep/goat and pig post-cranial bones exhibiting butchery marks by phase

of dismemberment and secondary butchery. Only two saw marks were recorded: a fallow deer antler fragment from Phase 11 and a sheep metacarpal from Phase 8.

As Figure 7.61 demonstrates, there is a general correlation between animal size and butchery mark frequency, doubtless a functional reflection of the greater necessity for butchery with larger species. The fact that there is a higher proportion of butchery marks on fallow deer is probably a consequence of the skewed anatomical distribution for this species (Figure 7.36). Only one dog and one horse bone was recorded with butchery marks (chop marks on the proximal radius and mid-shaft of the humerus respectively), suggesting the limited exploitation of their flesh.

Analysis of the proportion of butchery amongst the three major domestic mammals by phase (Figure 7.62) reveals that the greatest frequency occurred in Phases 5–7. This is a consequence of the large numbers of butchered cattle foot bones from the Phase 5 dump: 69/75 metacarpals and 43/48 metatarsals that were chopped through the mid-shaft, while a further eight metapodia had been split longitudinally. This pattern of butchery is most likely a consequence of marrow extraction (Rixson 1989, 52). Cattle metapodials are a good source of marrow and its extraction could reflect the waste of stock, soup or broth preparations. Such food is not necessarily 'high status' and it is possible, therefore, that this deposit indicates the feeding of construction workers during the rebuilding of the castle. However, bone marrow was an important ingredient for some medieval feast dishes. For example, in the late 14th-century *Forme of Curye,* compiled by the master chef to Richard II, there is a recipe for a pastry called 'pety peruaunt' that required extracting beef marrow whole, cutting it raw, and mixing it with ginger, sugar, egg yolk, minced dates and raisins (Hieatt and Butler 1985, 144). As Simon (1952, 457) recounts, bone marrow was 'served to the Lords of the Star Chamber on nearly every "meat day" from 1519'. Major feasts would have doubtless also required stock and soup in abundance. It is possible then that this deposit represents a major food consumption event, one that coincides with the attendance of the Royal Court and the consumption of large numbers of chickens. However, we also have to consider that the marrow was extracted for other purposes. For example, beef marrow could be used to make neatsfoot oil. The putatively 10th-century Welsh Laws of Hywel Dda indicate that hides from the kitchen went to castle officials such as the chief huntsman for dog leashes, the chief groom for halters and the falconer for gloves (Richards 1954, 32–37). Such leather-work would need to be kept supple after use/getting wet in the field, possibly with neatsfoot oil, which is easily absorbed by leather (Louisa Gidney pers comm). Bone marrow could also be used for the manufacture of glue or tallow, for making soap and candles,

FIGURE 7.63

Cattle first phalanx exhibiting a cut mark indicative of skinning

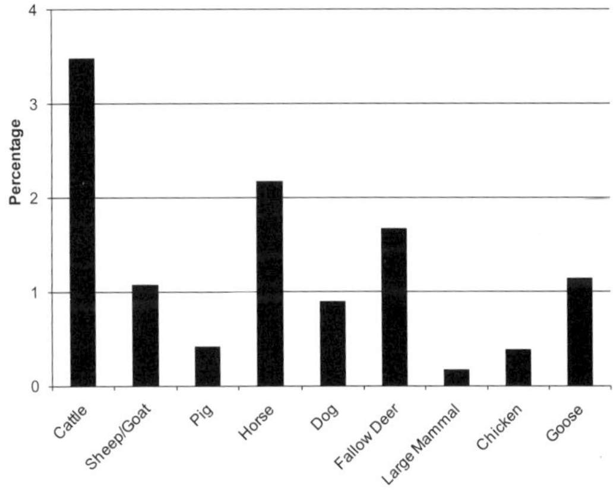

FIGURE 7.64

Relative proportions of all palaeopathological lesions by taxon

Site	Date	Mean PI
Romania		
Draught oxen	Modern	0.32
Young meat bulls	Modern	0.01
Turkey		
Sagalassos	Roman	0.22
Belgium		
Koekelare	Roman	0.19
Liberchies	Roman	0.24
Namur	Roman	0.19
Torgny	Roman	0.28
Britain		
Alchester	Roman	0.06
Colchester	Roman	0.04
Dudley Castle	Medieval	0.17
Wigmore Castle	Medieval	0.04
Wigmore Castle	Medieval (dump removed)	0.05
Wigmore Castle	Post-medieval	0.04

FIGURE 7.65

Comparison of mean Pathological Index values at a range of sites: Romania (Bartosiewicz et al 1997); Turkey (De Cupere et al 2000); Belgium (De Cupere et al 2000); Alchester (Vann 2008b); Colchester (Vann 2008b); Dudley Castle (Thomas 2008)

for example. It is difficult nevertheless to reconcile these latter interpretations with the scale of the deposit, and it is contended that marrow extraction for consumption is the most likely explanation.

The fact that the lowest frequency of butchery occurred in the 12th–13th centuries could be a function of taphonomy; carnivore gnawing was more abundant in this phase (Figure 7.7), which may have hindered the identification of butchery marks.

Aside from the antlers, there was virtually no evidence for craft-working at Wigmore Castle. Four horncores were recovered (two cow, one sheep, one goat), but only the Phase 8 sheep specimen revealed evidence for butchery. A small number of bones also exhibited evidence for hide working, such as a Phase 2 cattle first phalanx presenting horizontal cut marks on the cranial surface of the shaft (Figure 7.63).

Pathology

Evidence for the signs of disease and injury were infrequent amongst the animal bones from Wigmore Castle; only 1.1% of hand-collected and identifiable post-cranial bones were recorded with pathology. Calculation of the prevalence of lesions by species (Figure 7.64) reveals that cattle, horses and fallow deer exhibited the highest frequency. This is probably a consequence of the fact that these animals were slaughtered at an older age and therefore had a greater opportunity to develop (and accumulate) injuries and illnesses that reflected themselves within the skeletal remains; however, as shall be discussed below, it may also reflect the way in which these animals were kept and utilised.

Degenerative joint disease

To investigate whether the cattle at Wigmore were exploited for traction, the presence and severity of lesions in the lower limb were recorded following Bartosiewicz *et al* (1997). For each complete metapodial and phalanx the Pathological Index (PI) value was calculated when all characteristics were present. A PI value of 0 implies no pathological change, while a value of 1 indicates the most extreme form of change. As can be seen from Figure 7.65, which compares the mean PI values for medieval and post-medieval phases at Wigmore Castle with other sites where the method has been implemented, the mean PI is very low. The analysis also reveals no substantive difference between the overall frequency of pathological alteration in medieval and post-medieval phases. However, the mean PI for the Phase 5 cattle dump is noticeably lower (PI=0.020) than the average value for the medieval period.

The broadening of the distal epiphysis of metapodia is also recognised as a potential indicator of traction use (Bartosiewicz *et al* 1997), and can be assessed quantitatively by comparing the difference

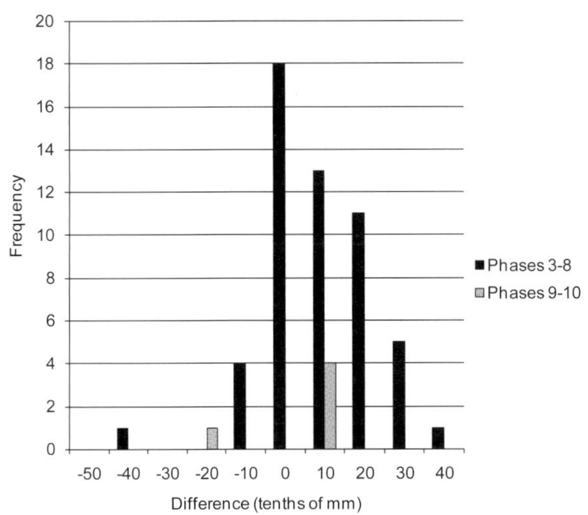

FIGURE 7.66
Frequency of difference between the distal breadth of the medial and lateral condyles of cattle metacarpals

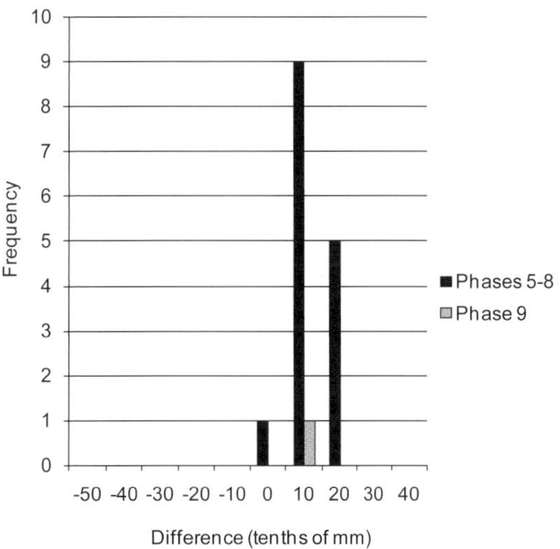

FIGURE 7.67
Frequency of difference between the distal breadth of the medial and lateral condyles of cattle metatarsals

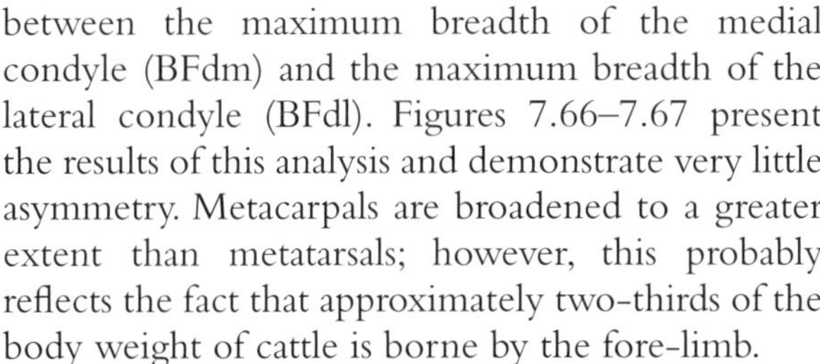
between the maximum breadth of the medial condyle (BFdm) and the maximum breadth of the lateral condyle (BFdl). Figures 7.66–7.67 present the results of this analysis and demonstrate very little asymmetry. Metacarpals are broadened to a greater extent than metatarsals; however, this probably reflects the fact that approximately two-thirds of the body weight of cattle is borne by the fore-limb.

In addition to the systematically recorded pathologies detailed above, two (out of 53) cattle navicular-cuboids (one Phase 5; one Phase 11) exhibited osteophyte formation around the margin of the distal articulation. The later specimen presented a more developed stage of the condition with extensive osteophyte formation and was associated with a rough and eroded distal articular surface, indicative of infective arthritis.

In order to understand the significance of these results, it is necessary to consider the causes of arthritic change in cattle. Pathological conditions such as osteophyte formation and the extension of articular surfaces are adaptive skeletal responses to biomechanical stress; consequently, a range of interdependent factors, both internal (e.g. age, sex and body mass) and external (e.g. the substrate upon which the animal is kept, nutritional health, stalling, traction, harnessing and medical intervention) can affect their formation (Thomas 2008). The low frequency of lower limb pathology at Wigmore Castle can therefore be interpreted in the following, non-mutually exclusive ways:

— the majority of cattle were not exploited for traction,
— the majority of cattle were subject to limited exploitation for traction, which did not put their skeletons under excessive strain,
— the cattle were slaughtered at a relatively early age (following bone fusion) and thus did not attain an age when such lesions become increasingly manifest,
— the cattle were predominantly female,
— the cattle were not very large.

Consideration of the zooarchaeological data above, confirms many of these interpretations: the cattle were slaughtered at a younger age than contemporary elite sites (Figure 7.38); the cattle from the Phase 5 dump were mostly female (Figure 7.47); and the cattle were not especially large by contemporary standards (Figure 7.50). However, the low values would also indicate that ex-traction animals were not frequently supplied to the castle for consumption.

With respect to joint diseases in other species, three Phase 10 horse tarsals (n=17), including the centrale and lateral cuneiform, were ankylosed. The fusion line was visible in some places, but not in others, suggesting that this was a chronic arthritic condition, a fact supported by the smooth appearance of the external bone surface which displayed no evidence of trauma or infection. Spavin is the most likely diagnosis for this lesion, a condition that is more commonly observed in older animals and in horses that are 'ridden hard' (Stashak 2002, 931). A thoracic vertebra from a large mammal (n=32) also exhibited profuse osteophyte formation around the centrum. This bone formation protruded up to 10mm into the intervertebral space, with the nodules extending from the middle and front of the vertebral body. This is most probably osteophytosis, a condition that generally occurs following the degeneration of the intervertebral discs; the bone spurs provide structural support to the destabilised spine.

		Proximal		Distal	
		n	%	n	%
P1	Type 1	0	0	1	1.54
	Type 2	1	1.54	0	0
P2	Type 1	1	1.96	0	0
	Type 2	0	0	1	1.96

FIGURE 7.68

Prevalence of articular lesions on cattle phalanges (lesion types follow Baker and Brothwell 1980)

Articular lesions

Two types of articular lesion that commonly occur on cattle phalanges and metapodials were recorded at Wigmore Castle (Baker and Brothwell 1980, 110–111), Figure 7.68 provides a summary of their frequency. These data are lower than the 3% prevalence noted in modern cattle (Baker and Brothwell 1980, 110) and significantly lower than the 11% and 21% prevalence in medieval and early modern cattle from Dudley Castle (Thomas 2005a, fig 68). These lesions are most likely to be caused during bone development and/or by osteochondrosis (see below); however, it is hoped that the continued publication of prevalence data will shed further light on their aetiology and archaeological significance.

Type 1 lesions were also noted on the proximal surface of a Phase 5 cattle lateral/mid-cuneiform and the proximal lateral facet of a Phase 10 pig radius. These conditions have a prevalence of one out of 53 tarsals and one out of 39 pig radii.

Articular lesions on the proximal end of 31% of cattle metacarpals (n=45) were also noted. Comparable lesions have been identified at Camber Castle, East Sussex (Connell and Davis 1997, 17), Dudley Castle (Thomas 2005a, 38–39), and Lincoln (Dobney *et al* 1996, 38), although the prevalence rate at Dudley Castle was slightly lower. This condition is probably osteochondrosis, caused by 'trauma or biomechanical factors on cartilage that has been weakened by nutritional or hormonal imbalances, vascular disruption, or genetic factors' (Thompson 2007, 136).

Erosive lesions were noted in the centre of the proximal articulation of two fallow deer metatarsals (prevalence=3.8%) and three cattle tarsals (prevalence=7.5%). Evidence for the herniation of the nucleus pulposa was recorded in the caudal articulation of a Phase 9 sheep/goat axis (n=8).

Infection and inflammation

Three examples of periostosis were recorded: a Phase 4 pig fibula (n=2), which exhibited plaques of new bone formation on the medial surface covering an area of around 3.6 x 2.7mm; and two large mammal ribs displaying periostosis on the visceral surface. Periostosis is caused by the reaction and subsequent ossification of the periosteum following inflammation or infection, or the inflammation or infection of adjacent soft tissues. In the case of the ribs, this may be due to one of a variety of pneumonic diseases.

A Phase 6 chicken posterior proximal phalanx exhibited a very swollen shaft that was over 7mm in diameter. There was extensive bone formation mid-shaft, which had a smooth, nodular appearance, but the articular surfaces were unaffected. This is most likely osteomyelitis, an inflammation of the marrow cavity of a bone due to pyogenic (pus-forming) infection. However, there were no cloacae (draining sinuses) to confirm this diagnosis. Similar symptoms were exhibited by a domestic fowl posterior proximal phalanx from a Phase 10 context (n=93). This specimen had nodular new bone formation all over the shaft which protruded up to 2mm from the proximal edge.

Trauma

Evidence for trauma in the faunal assemblage from Wigmore Castle was limited with only a single fractured bone recorded: a Phase 4 goose radius (n=11) that exhibited a healed and remodelled mid-shaft fracture which had left the surface smooth but with a 'lumpy' appearance. Displacement was slight and the limb had remained straight (presumably due to the presence of the ulna which would have acted as a natural splint). Injuries to Roman goose humeri from Bath Lane, Leicester (Baxter 2008), have been associated with male geese fighting with their wings and this might also explain the radius fracture. Fractures of the wing bones may also occur during collisions in flight, either during migration or from flying into trees or other objects (Wood 1941, 68).

A Phase 9 fallow deer metatarsal (n=52) exhibited a raised area on the medial aspect of the inter-metatarsal groove, although taphonomic damage made diagnosis uncertain. Comparable lesions have been found on fallow deer metatarsals from Dudley Castle and are probably traumatic in origin, occurring as a result of an injury below the hock joint causing sub-periosteal bleeding and the development of an ossified haematoma (Thomas 2001, 292).

Developmental anomalies

A five-toed domestic fowl tarsometatarsus (n=324) was recorded from Phase 8 (Figure 7.69). This feature is characteristic of certain breeds of chicken such as the Dorking, Houdans, Silkies, Faverolloes, Sultans and Poland (Bramwell 1975, 18; Brothwell 1993, 34; Sadler 1990, 45). Contemporary examples of five-toed chicken have been recovered from medieval deposits at Baynard's Castle, London (Bramwell 1975), Dudley Castle, West Midlands (Thomas 2005a), and Little Lane, Leicester (Gidney 1993).

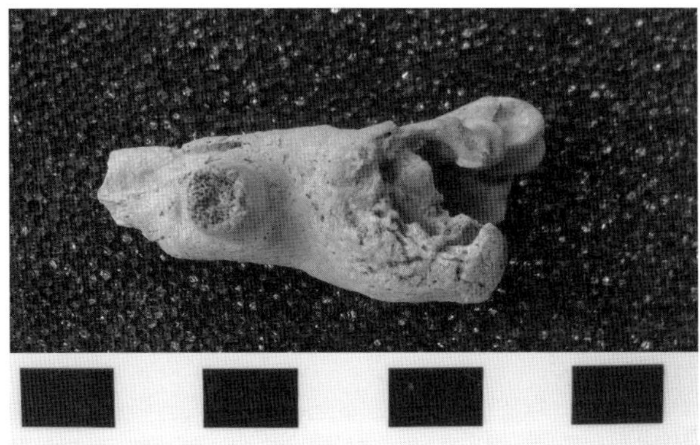

FIGURE 7.69
Male chicken tarsometatarsus displaying 'fifth' toe and profuse new bone formation

It seems unlikely that this breed was introduced because it conferred any particular advantage, since so few specimens have been recorded; however, it may have been bred as a novelty. Like the two specimens with 'fifth toes' from Dudley Castle, the bone from Wigmore Castle exhibited massive proliferation of new bone between the spur and the distal articulation on the posterior aspect of the shaft. The new bone formation was smoother on the outside than on the inside and formed an arc. Brothwell (1993, fig 2) suggests that this condition is an 'age-related new bone formation of unknown aetiology'. However, the emergent evidence suggests that it was a condition that certain breeds may have been susceptible to (see also Sadler 1990, 47).

Four pelves (three cattle, one sheep/goat) exhibited anomalies of the acetabulum. A Phase 10 sheep/goat pelvis (n=21) displayed a facet of the acetabulum on the ilium that was not connected to the rest of acetabulum, leaving a notch in the wall of the joint. This gap was some 8mm wide. The margins of the 'notch' were smooth and rounded and the bone surface looked like normal cortical bone. The three cattle pelves (n=29) displayed similar features, although not always in a precisely identical location; one Phase 11 cattle pelvis displayed the 'notch' on the ischial aspect of the acetabulum. None of the pelves displayed evidence of infection or trauma, suggesting that these anomalies are developmental

Oral pathology

Two examples of oral pathology were found at Wigmore Castle. The first was a Phase 4 dog mandible (n=28), which exhibited a swelling in the molar region; the teeth had been lost post-mortem. This was probably caused by an abscess. Such abscesses can be primary (e.g. caused by trauma) or secondary (e.g. following carious infections of teeth or periodontal disease).

The second example of an oral pathology was a Phase 5 cattle third molar (n=39), the posterior cusp of which was folded back around to run parallel to the central cusp. This may suggest this individual suffered from over-crowding of the teeth within the mandible.

Conclusions

The faunal assemblage from Wigmore Castle exhibits many of the typical characteristics of English castle sites. In terms of species representation there is a greater emphasis on pigs and cattle than on sheep, deer are commonly represented, and there is a diversity of wild birds. The proportion of sheep is noticeably lower than on contemporary castle sites, but this is typical of sites in the region and probably reflects the area's unsuitability for sheep rearing.

Many of the temporal changes that occur at the site are paralleled across English castle sites and reflect wider changes in the environment, consumption habits and agricultural practice, including:

—an increased emphasis on deer and wild birds in the later medieval period connected to changing aristocratic dietary identities,

—a decreased emphasis on pigs and increased emphasis on sheep through the medieval period as woodland declined and the wool and cloth trades expanded,

—increases in the size of domestic livestock from the 14th century, supporting the notion that 'improvements' in medieval agriculture had their origins in the social and economic upheaval following the Black Death,

—an increased reliance on marketed products in the post-medieval period,

—shifting agricultural emphasis between the medieval and post-medieval periods and (for some species) the appearance of earlier maturing forms: sheep slaughtered older as the wool and cloth trade expand; cattle slaughtered younger as they are freed from their roles as traction animals; and chickens slaughtered younger as the emphasis changed from eggs to meat.

Notwithstanding these trends, it is possible to say something about the changing status of the occupants of Wigmore Castle over time. The fact that the highest proportion of deer and wild birds occurs in Phase 1, together with the rare presence of bear, is indicative of high-status living during the early years of the site. The 12th to mid-14th centuries (Phases 2–7) do not share the same high proportions of deer and wild birds, which could reflect the fact that the site was less regularly visited by peripatetic lords or that they were lower ranking. However, comparison of the relative proportion of cattle, sheep and pig indicates that consumption at Wigmore Castle was still typical of medieval castles and distinct from other types of contemporary settlement. The large dumps of cattle and chicken foot bones in Phase 5 and Phase 6 respectively, indicate that large quantities of meat were sometimes consumed in single events, which may have been connected to royal visitations. Despite the description of the derelict state of the castle in the early 15th century, the faunal dataset for Phase 8 indicates continued high-status consumption. This period exhibited the greatest abundance of fish, the highest proportion of wild birds and deer (after Phase 1), the highest proportion of pig after Phases 1 and 2, and the highest proportion of juvenile chickens. High-status dining also continues into the 16th-17th century (Phases 9 and 10). This phase has the third highest relative abundance of pig nationally, the third highest proportion of deer and wild birds (after Phase 1 and Phase 8) and is the period with the second youngest slaughter age for cattle. The fact that Wigmore Castle maintains its elite character in this period probably testifies to the continuation of high-status dining when the castle was managed by the Council of the Marches and kept in repair as a prison.

7.2 FISH BONES

Anthony Gouldwell, Richard Thomas and Stephanie Vann

Wigmore Castle was not sited on a major river although it is not far from the River Teme which runs through Leintwardine and thence through Ludlow; neither is it close to the sea being roughly equidistant from the estuaries of the Severn and the Dee. The castle was doubtless supplied with fish from ponds within the castle estate, although freshwater fish formed only a small component of the fish bone recovered.

The majority of the fish bones were recovered by hand-collection (Figures 7.70–7.74) and, as can be seen from Figure 7.75, a direct relationship exists between recovery method and species presence. Consequently, there will be a bias against some of the smaller species and smaller anatomical elements.

Methods

All fish bone fragments (hand-collected and sampled) deriving from stratigraphically secure deposits were subjected to macroscopic examination. Species identification was achieved using the comparative reference collection of modern specimens at the School of Archaeology and Ancient History, University of Leicester. Fragments of fish bone that could not be attributed to species were attributed to the highest taxonomic level.

The assemblage

In total, 336 fish bone fragments were recovered from Wigmore Castle. Expressed as a percentage of the total number of hand-collected bone fragments recovered from the site, it can be seen that there is very little change in the overall contribution of fish bone to the assemblage over time (Figure 7.76).

	Phase								Total
	2	5	6	7	8	9	10	11	
Thornback ray	-	-	-	-	1	-	-	-	1
Eel	-	-	3	-	-	18	1	0	22
Herring	-	-	-	2	-	26	2	-	30
Salmonid	-	-	-	1	2	1	-	7	11
Roach	-	-	-	1	-	-	-	-	1
Cod	-		2	4	4	4	2	10	26
Cod family (gadid)	1	3	-	1	8	2	1	3	19
Gadiform	-	-	-	-	-	3	-	-	3
Ling	-	-	-	-	2	1	1	-	4
Hake	-	-	-	-	1	-	1	-	2
Plaice/flounder	-	-	-	-	-	1	-	-	1
Unidentified	11	-	4	11	9	34	2	17	88
Total	**12**	**3**	**9**	**20**	**26**	**90**	**10**	**37**	**208**

FIGURE 7.70

Hand-collected fish bone by phase

	Phase			Total
	5	8	11	
Thornback ray	1	-	-	1
Cod	1	-	4	5
Cod family	-	1	4	5
Hake	-	2	0	2
Brown trout	-	1	0	1
Salmonid	-	1	1	2
Unidentified	1	2	5	8
Total	**3**	**7**	**14**	**24**

FIGURE 7.71

Fish bone retrieved from residues (6mm)

	Phase			Total
	2	8	10	
Eel	9	-	1	10
Herring	9	-	-	9
Cod	-	2	-	2
Salmonid	1	-	-	1
Unidentified	1	4	-	5
Total	**20**	**6**	**1**	**27**

FIGURE 7.72

Fish bone retrieved from residues (>4mm)

	Phase			Total
	2	4	6	
Eel	3	-	-	3
Herring	36	5	1	42
Salmonid	5	-	-	5
Unidentified	3	2	-	5
Total	**47**	**7**	**1**	**55**

FIGURE 7.73

Fish bone retrieved from residues (2–4mm)

	Phase			Total
	2	6	9	
Eel	–	1	–	1
Herring	18	1	1	20
Salmonid	1	–	–	1
Total	**19**	**2**	**1**	**22**

FIGURE 7.74

Fish bone retrieved from flots

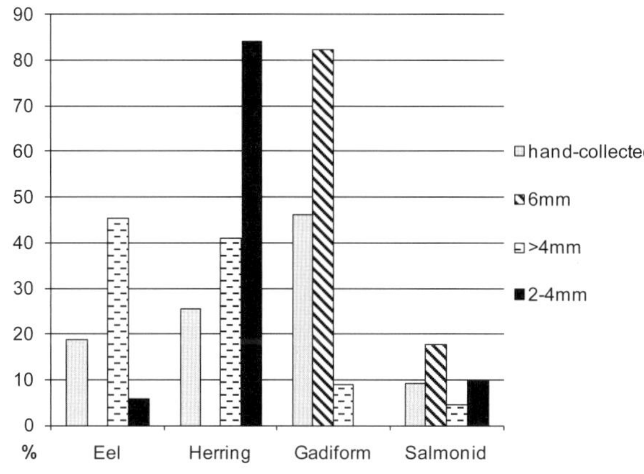

FIGURE 7.75

Relative abundance of key fish taxa by recovery method

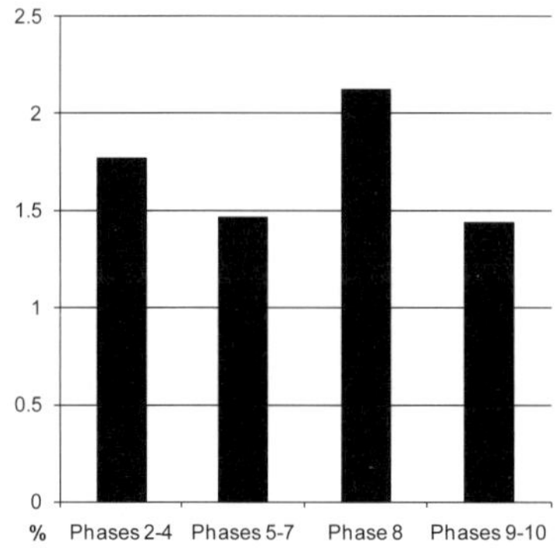

FIGURE 7.76

Percentage of fish bones out of the total number of mammal, bird and fish bone fragments. The dumps of cattle and chicken feet have been excluded

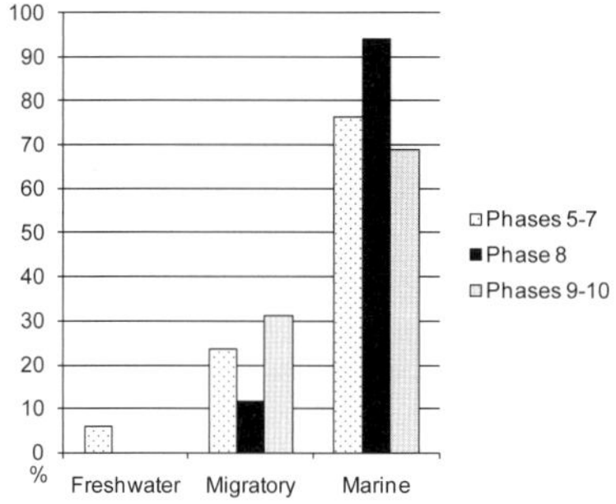

FIGURE 7.77

Relative abundance of freshwater, migratory and marine fish by phase

The highest consumption of fish bone occurs in the mid-14th to 15th century, however, when other indicators suggest high-status consumption.

Virtually the entire fish bone assemblage is composed of migratory and marine species: only one fresh water fish (roach; *Rutilus rutilus*) was recorded. When analysed by phase (Figure 7.77), it can be observed that marine fish dominate all phases with sufficient data, although there is a relatively greater emphasis on migratory species in the post-medieval period. It can also be observed that the greater abundance of fish in the mid-14th to 15th century is composed of marine fish.

Numerically, the most abundant identifiable species was herring (*Clupea harengus*; n=101). This is unsurprising given the fact that this fish was 'the principal staple in Lent' (Hieatt and Butler 1985, 13), and is frequently ranked as the most abundant fish species on sites of medieval and post-medieval date (Serjeantson and Woolgar 2006, tables 8.1–8.5). The herring were almost exclusively represented by vertebrae (the exceptions being a hyomandibular and an anterior maxilla fragment); however, since herring were preserved whole it is not possible to determine whether they were consumed fresh or not (Locker 2007, 317). One abdominal vertebra from a 16th to 17th-century context was laterally compressed, which indicates where it may have been bitten.

The next most numerous identifiable fish was eel (*Anguilla anguilla*; n=36). Although this species is migratory, spending part of its life at sea, it was probably caught in estuaries and rivers (Locker 2007, 316). Eel is regularly recorded as one of the most abundant and frequently present fish species on sites of medieval and post-medieval date (Serjeantson and Woolgar 2006, tables 8.1–8.5; Sykes 2007a, fig 56). Two 16th-century abdominal vertebrae exhibited possible bite marks.

Bones of cod (*Gadus morhua*) and the cod family (Gadidae) were commonly represented and indicate the provision of the site by off-shore fishing. Twelve gadid specimens were qualitatively recorded as large and three were recorded as small. Ling (*Molva molva*) and hake (*Merluccius merluccius*), deep-sea members of the cod family, were also present and may indicate the provisioning of the site from a more distant fishery (Locker 2007, 317). The presence of ling in the mid-14th to 15th century is noteworthy since the first documentary sources for this species appear in the 14th century (Burnley 1992, 438, cited by Sykes 2007a, 58). The supracleithrum of one cod exhibited chop marks suggestive of decapitation; while the remaining cod cleithra were mostly small fragments from around the anterior angle of the bone suggesting a pattern of butchery (for decapitation), especially since these were bones of a substantial size. A ling precaudal vertebra exhibited two cut marks on the ventral aspect of the centrum, which indicates that that the animal was laid on its right side when it was butchered. The fact that the gadids were represented by both cranial and vertebral elements indicates that they were not store fish: as Locker notes, 'head elements … are usually removed during preparation for salting or drying' (2007, 317).

Twenty-one fragments of bones from the salmonid family were recovered, although only one specimen could be more specifically identified: the angular of a trout (*Salmo trutta*). Twelve salmonid specimens were qualitatively recorded as 'small', and may derive from small salmon or trout.

Flatfish was represented by a single specimen: the interhaemal spine of a large plueronectidae, which was within the size range for halibut (*Hippoglossus hippoglossus*). Finally, Thornback ray (*Raja clavata*) — a marine fish that inhabits sedimentary sea floors — was represented by two dermal denticles (bucklers).

7.3 BIRD EGGSHELL

Stephanie Vann

This report presents the results of the detailed analysis of the hand-collected and sieved bird eggshell recovered during the excavation of Wigmore Castle (1996 and 1998). With the exceptions of the recently published assemblage from Causeway Lane, Leicester (Boyer 1999), there have been no other studies of medieval or post-medieval eggshell assemblages from the Midlands. The majority of other studies have instead been conducted on sites located in northern, southern or eastern England (Ayres *et al* 2003; Keepax 1984; Kenward and Hall 1995; Murphy 1985; 1988; 1991; 1992; 2004; Sidell 1997; Sidell and Locker 2000). This site therefore fills an important gap in our knowledge of human-avian interactions, in Herefordshire, central England and nationally.

The main aims of this analysis were to establish the range and abundance of different species of birds as represented by their eggs and to reconstruct the consumption of bird eggs by the occupants of the castle and establish any diachronic variations.

Methodology

All fragments of eggshell (hand-collected and sampled) deriving from spot-dated contexts with no reported residual material, or stratigraphically secure deposits, were subjected to examination under a light microscope (Sidell 1993, 9–10). The colour and texture of the external surface were recorded, although it should be noted that such gross physical characteristics are often affected by taphonomic factors (Sidell 1993, 8–9) and may therefore not always be useful for identification purposes. Shell thickness and number of pores per square millimetre was measured for all but the smallest fragments using an eyepiece graticule at a magnification of x100. These results were used to form the initial groupings of the eggshell. A sub-sample of the assemblage was examined using a scanning electron microscope to test the validity of the initial groupings through analysis of criteria such as the number of mammillae per square millimetre and the characteristics of the internal surface. Species determinations were made through comparison with published data (Boyer 1999; Sidell 1993).

Site	Context	Sample	Phase	Total No.	Colour	Texture	Thickness (microns)	Pores (mm^2)
Wig 96	47	14	9	82	Cream	Smooth	300–400	4
	102	6	6	11	Cream	Smooth	300–500	2
	102		6	79	Cream	Smooth	300–400	4
	220	18	4	1	Cream	Smooth	400	3
	244		4	123	Cream	Smooth	300–400	3
	270	20	3	9	Cream	Smooth	300–400	5
	295	23	2	32	Yellow	Smooth	300–400	2
	305	24	2	50	Cream	Smooth	300–400	2
	338	25	2	63	Yellow	Smooth/uneven	400–700	
	338		2	52	Cream	Smooth	300–400	5
	359	27	2	56	Cream	Smooth	400	
	359	28	2	53	Yellow	Smooth/uneven	300–600	
	390		2	283	Cream	Smooth	300–400	5
Wig 98	518	2110	11	4	Cream	Smooth	300–400	5
	632	2167	8	9	Cream	Smooth	300–400	
	643	2175	10	2	Yellow	Smooth	300	
	647	2204	9	1	Yellow	Smooth	400	
	651	2182	8	1	Cream	Smooth	400	
	656	2186	5	4	Cream	Smooth	300	

FIGURE 7.78
Eggshell from Wigmore Castle

Results

A total of 915 eggshell fragments were analysed from Wigmore Castle (894 fragments from 1996 contexts and 21 fragments from 1998 contexts). Examination under a light microscope showed that there were two broad groups into which the eggshell fitted (Figure 7.78). Most of the shell had a smooth external surface texture and a shell thickness of between 300 and 400 microns. A smaller number of fragments had a more uneven surface texture and a shell thickness of greater than 400 microns. The thinner group falls within the thickness ranges for species such as pheasant (*Phasianus colchicus*), domestic fowl (*Gallus* sp.), duck (*Anas* sp.) and turkey (*Meleagris gallopava*) (Boyer 1999; Sidell 1993). Other species such as herring gull (*Larus argenatus*), razorbill (*Alca torda*) and cormorant (*Phalacrocorax carbo*) also fall within this range, although there was no evidence of these species amongst the bird bones at the site and domestic fowl were predominant (see above).

The thicker group falls within the ranges for species such as domestic goose (*Anser* sp.), guinea fowl (*Numida meleagris*), gannet (*Sula bassana*) and shag (*Phalacrocorax aristotelis*) (Boyer 1999; Sidell 1993). Comparison with the bird bones from the site suggested that goose was the most likely. These thicker fragments were found in only two contexts, both from Wigmore 1996, Phase 2 (Figures 7.79–7.80).

Tentative identifications were confirmed by examination under the scanning electron microscope which showed the sub-sampled specimens to have generally well-defined, regular-shaped mammillae with only moderate fissures (Figures 7.81–7.82). These were particularly comparable to those of domestic fowl (Sidell 1993, 14).

The eggshell from Wigmore 1996 dates from Phases 2-9 (Figure 7.83) with the greatest proportion from the earlier part of that time period (Phase 2). There is no post-medieval material in the 1996 assemblage. In contrast, the eggshell from Wigmore 1998 dates from the Phases 5–11 (Figure 7.84) with the greatest percentage of the assemblage dating to Phase 8. The small size of the 1998 assemblage, however, means some degree of caution is required when interpreting these data.

When the two assemblages are combined (Figure 7.85), it can be seen that over 70% of the eggshell came from Phases 2–4, just over 10% from Phases 5–7 and 9% from Phases 9–10; 1% or less came from each of the other phases.

Discussion

The widespread consumption of domestic fowl and goose began in England during the Roman period and by the medieval period these were being eaten by individuals from all sections of society (Serjeantson 2006, 131). Whilst it cannot be proven that eggshell

Context	Sample	Total no.	Species determination
338	25	63	Goose
338		52	Domestic fowl/duck/pheasant
359	27	56	Domestic fowl/duck/pheasant
359	28	53	Goose
390		283	Domestic fowl/duck/pheasant
295	23	32	Domestic fowl/duck/pheasant
305	24	50	Domestic fowl/duck/pheasant
270	20	9	Domestic fowl/duck/pheasant
220	18	1	Domestic fowl/duck/pheasant
244		123	Domestic fowl/duck/pheasant
102	6	11	Domestic fowl/duck/pheasant
102		79	Domestic fowl/duck/pheasant
47	14	82	Domestic fowl/duck/pheasant
Total		**894**	

FIGURE 7.79
Species determination by context in chronological order, Wigmore 1996

Context	Sample	Total no.	Species determination
656	2186	4	Domestic fowl/duck/pheasant
632	2167	9	Domestic fowl/duck/pheasant
651	2182	1	Domestic fowl/duck/pheasant
647	2204	1	Domestic fowl/duck/pheasant
643	2175	2	Domestic fowl/duck/pheasant
518	2110	4	Domestic fowl/duck/pheasant
Total		**21**	

FIGURE 7.80
Species determination by context in chronological order, Wigmore 1998

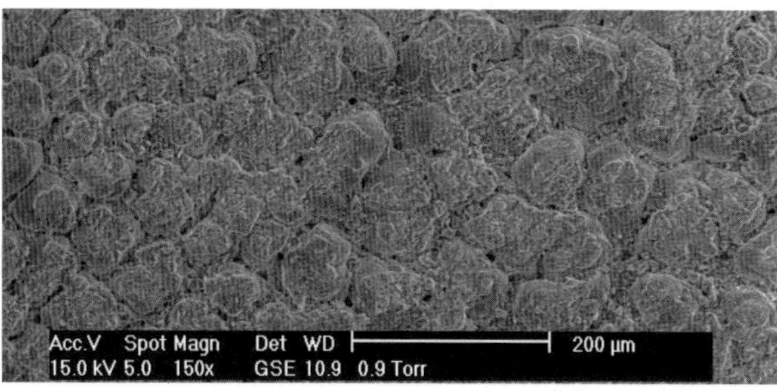

FIGURE 7.81
Archaeological domestic fowl eggshell inner surface showing mammillae (context 244) (150x)

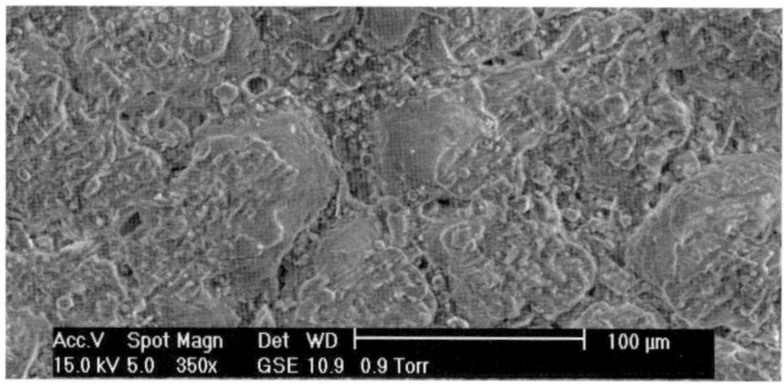

FIGURE 7.82
Archaeological domestic fowl eggshell inner surface showing mammillae (context 244) (350x)

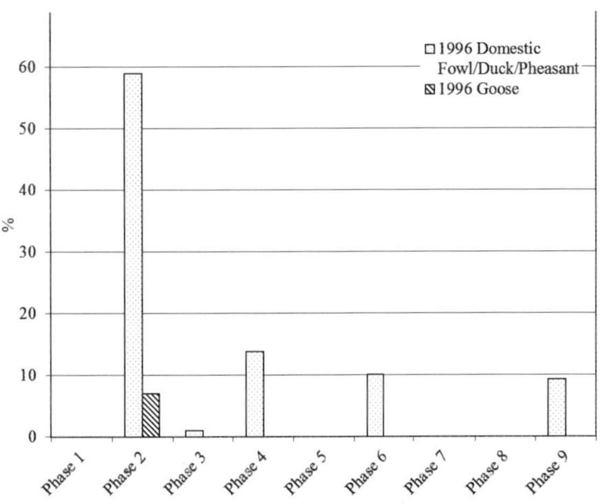

FIGURE 7.83

Relative proportion of eggshell by phase and taxon out of the total egg assemblage from Wigmore 1996

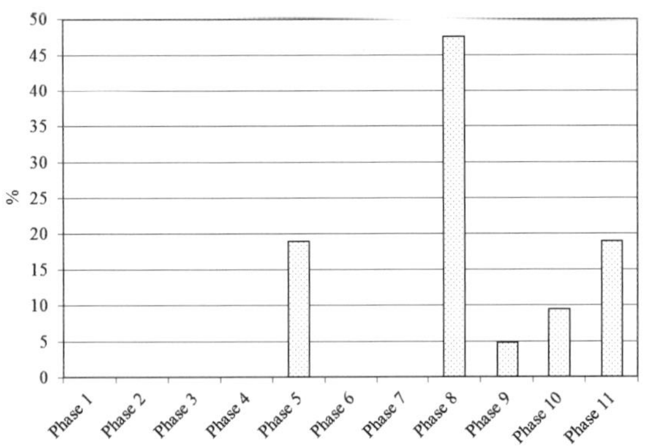

FIGURE 7.84

Relative proportion of domestic fowl/duck/pheasant eggshell by phase out of the total egg assemblage from Wigmore 1998

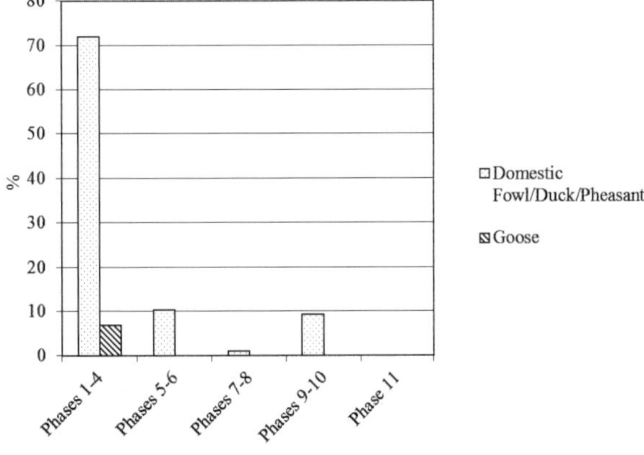

FIGURE 7.85

Relative proportion of eggshell by phase and taxon out of the total egg assemblage from Wigmore 1996 and 1998 combined

from archaeological sites are the remains of eggs that were consumed or that they represent breeding stock, very few avian species were not eaten in medieval England; exceptions being birds of prey and scavengers such as corvids (Serjeantson 2006, 133–134). It seems likely, therefore, that the eggshell found at Wigmore Castle is linked in some form to food supply at the castle. The fact that some of the domestic fowl at Wigmore were in lay is indicated by the presence of medullary bone in four femora found at the site, three dated to Phase 4 and one from Phase 11 (Section 7.1). This, along with the presence of juveniles birds, suggests that there may have been a breeding flock at Wigmore Castle.

The identification of the material from Wigmore Castle as predominantly domestic fowl with some goose is comparable to the assemblage from Causeway Lane in Leicester where the majority of the samples were also identified as domestic fowl, although it was possible that some of the thinner specimens may have been duck or pheasant. Only one goose specimen (dated to the early 12th to mid-13th centuries) was identified in the medieval layers and none was present in the post-medieval layers (Boyer 1999, 332). Similar results were also gained from the analysis of 17th-century eggshell from Tilbury Fort (Sidell and Locker 2000), medieval layers at Eynsham Abbey, Oxfordshire (Ayres *et al* 2003), and Anglo-Scandinavian deposits at Coppergate, York (Kenward and Hall 1995). This indicates the widespread practice of breeding domestic fowl for their meat and eggs during the medieval and post-medieval periods in England.

7.4 THE MARINE MOLLUSCS

Greg Campbell

During the 1996 and 1998 excavations, an assemblage of 1794 marine shells was recovered from 136 deposits. The 1786 shells from the 131 contexts which could be assigned a phase reliably were analysed. A small proportion (173 shells) was recovered by wet-sieving of soil samples, but the great majority were retrieved by hand.

Methods

Whole shells, and quantifiable elements of broken shells (umbones of bivalve shells, and apertures or the bases of apertures of gastropod shells) were extracted from all the material over 4mm available from hand-retrieval and sample wet-sieving. The resulting assemblage was identified to genus (and to species where preservation allowed), by reference to standard works such as Beedham (1972) and Tebble (1966), and to comparative material in the author's own collection. Nomenclature follows Poppe and Goto (1991;1993). English common names are taken from Hayward *et al* (1996). The habitats for these species are taken from these latter references.

The number of shells of each variety recovered in each deposit was counted. Left and right valves of bivalves were not counted separately, but left and right valves were always present in roughly equal numbers for any variety in any deposit.

Types of shells recovered

Oysters were the most common shell, making up nearly four-fifths of the assemblage (Figure 7.86) Oyster preservation was good, with about 20% measurable. About 90% of the hinges were preserved well enough to be identified to species. All of these were of the native, common or flat oyster *Ostrea edulis* L. Native oysters can be common on stable moderately wave-beaten and sheltered low inter-tidal shores and on stable sub-tidal beds to about 50m depth, where they can form extensive beds and reefs when not disrupted by harvesting. Enough deposits produced measureable oysters that a statistical comparison of size and shape between deposits was carried out; the results of that analysis are presented below.

Mussels formed 19% of the sieved assemblage (Figure 7.86). Preservation was good, unusual for this thin fragile shell, and likely caused by hand-retrieval of the largest and most robust shells. The vast majority appeared to be the common mussel *Mytilus edulis* L., with no convincing examples of the warm-water French mussel *Mytilus galloprovincialis* Lamarck. Mussels are common on moderately to strongly wave-beaten inter-tidal shores (where they tend to remain relatively small) and on solid and stable soft sub-tidal beds to 40m depth (where they become relatively large), but can attach to most bare stable surfaces. They often form dense mats which can expand into large beds and reefs when not disrupted by harvesting.

Cockles: some 25 valves were cockles (*Cerastoderma* sp.), usually in deposits containing other shells. Preservation was good, with about half intact. All identifiable valves were of common cockles *Cerastoderma edule* (L.) with no convincing examples of lagoon cockle *C. glaucum* (Poiret). These bivalves live just below the surface of moderately wave-washed or sheltered sandy or muddy beds, from mid-tide to a few metres depth. Population densities are often very high (hundreds per square metre), and harvesting by hand-raking or digging at low tide is simple and productive.

Gastropods: Some 13 shells of common whelk *Buccinum undatum* L. were found, usually from deposits with other shells, more commonly in the later phases. This carnivore-scavenger of muddy sands and stony beds from extreme low tide to 100m is a modern-day delicacy, fished by dredging or potting. Preservation was adequate, so identification was clear. About half were intact, and these were of unusually large size (50–100mm); the fragmentary remains also appeared to be of large whelks.

The only other gastropod was a single flat winkle (*Littorina mariae* Saachi and Rastelli) from Phase 10, deposit 580 CG98 13, along with seven mussels and 15 oysters, from soil sample <2133>. A single mussel and 22 oysters were retrieved by hand from the same deposit. This sea-snail, too small to eat, is plentiful on stable inter-tidal shores covered with seaweed, but can be found occasionally in mussel beds. It is likely that the flat winkle was brought to site accidentally with the mussels.

Phase	**Context**	**Oyster**	**Mussel**	**Cockle**	**Whelk**	**% of total assemblage**
4	2	0.1	-	-	-	0.1
5	5	0.6	-	-	-	0.6
6	4	0.2	-	-	-	0.2
7	1	0.1	-	-	-	0.1
8	21	4.4	6	0.1	0.1	10.5
9	19	5.2	2.3	-	-	7.4
10	45	45.8	7.5	-	0.2	53.5
11	34	21.8	3.6	1.4	0.7	27.5
Total		**78.2**	**19.4**	**1.5**	**1**	

FIGURE 7.86

Percentage of each type of shell by phase

Change over time

Figure 7.86 shows the relative proportion of each type of shell in each phase to the total shell assemblage, in percent. Importation of marine shell to the site began as early as the 13th century (Phase 4), with oysters recovered from deposit 710 CG98 09 and compacted surface 177 CG96 19. Oysters continued to be brought to the site in low numbers during the remainder of the 13th century, and into the early 14th century (Phases 5–7). During the mid-14th to 15th centuries (Phase 8), during and following the reconstruction of the curtain wall, the numbers of shellfish imported increased substantially, and a wider range of shellfish was imported. Mussels became the most common shellfish, and cockles and whelks were definitely consumed for the first time. The quantity fell back during the earlier part of the 16th century (Phase 9), with oysters again the main import.

Over half the assemblage was brought to site during the 16th and early 17th centuries (Phase 10). Most were oysters, with some mussels and rare whelks. Over a quarter of the shells were imported during the 17th century and later (Phase 11) mostly from deposits dating to the era of the English Civil War. Oysters were still the most common, with some mussels; whelks became slightly more common, and cockles were imported again.

The oysters

Those nine contexts in which measurable shells were numerous enough to compare statistically were all from the later part of occupation of the castle. The most common shells in all these shell-rich deposits were oysters. Most of these oyster-rich contexts formed during the time of general decay, localised demolition and gradual abandonment of the castle in the Tudor period, or during or soon after the slighting of the castle defences during the Civil War.

Methods

Dimensions and size

Measurable oyster valves were sorted into left (lower, cupped) valves and right (upper, flat) valves and identified to species. If there were few valves, left and right valves were re-fitted, and the re-fitted shells and the most numerous of the un-paired valves (either left or right) were measured to the nearest 1mm, or to the nearest 0.1mm if less than 10mm. Maximum height (Hmax) (maximum distance from the umbo to the ventral edge) was used to compare sizes between contexts. Frequent damage to the umbones (especially of the right valve) meant that Hmax had to be estimated to ±2mm in approximately 65% of the valves. Distributions of Hmax were expressed as histograms in 5mm intervals and assessed for poly-modality and similarity by eye. Width of the hinge width, Wh (distance across the bourrelets at the hinge's ventral edge) was also recorded. A recent study (Campbell 2010) has shown that dimensions across the plane of commissure are less variable within a given sample of modern native oysters than dimensions of the entire shell, and are consistent between the two valves of the same oyster in spite of these always being different sizes (oysters are therefore said to be 'inequivalve'). The plane of commissure is marked in the left (lower, cupped) valve by a narrow commissural shelf set slightly inernally from the edge, which exactly fits the full size of the right valve (Stenzel 1971, 990 and fig J7, 987). Much of the measurement variability between shells in a sample is due to variation in the size and shape of the hinge and damage to the shell edge, and the plane of commissure does not include the hinge and is seldom damaged. Therefore measurements were taken of closure height, Hc (the distance from the centre of the hinge, across the most distant margin of the adductor scar, to the edge of the plane of commissure) and closure length Lc (the maximum distance across the plane of commissure that is parallel to the hinge axis).

Surface features

Surface features relating to bed conditions (such as traces of encrusting, burrowing or predatory organisms) or to treatment following harvesting (such as opening- or break-marks) were assessed by eye in those deposits rich in shell as either absent, rare, common or severe.

Age and growth rate

To reconstruct the ages of the oysters when harvested, the number of growth-check rings on the surface of each measureable valve was counted. Distributions of age at harvest were expressed as histograms in yearly intervals, and assessed for poly-modality and similarity by eye. To reconstruct shell sizes at previous ages, the height of each growth-check ring in oysters from the selected deposits was measured to the nearest 1mm. Frequent damage to the hinge of right valves (see below) meant that the annual ring heights were estimated to the nearest 2mm in approximately 65% of the valves. Measuring growth-ring heights is an estimate for height at earlier ages, since not all growth-check rings are annual (they can also be caused by disturbance), and not all annual rings are clear (subsequent erosion can remove younger growth rings, and older growth rings in aged shells can be too tightly packed at the shell edge to be discriminated).

Oysters within a deposit were segregated into possible populations according to the number of modes in the fourth annual ring-height distribution. A population was accepted as valid if the possible populations also were responsible for distinguishable height-ranges in the adjacent annual ring-height distributions. For each population, average height at a particular growth ring was calculated, and growth curves (average height at a growth ring, for each ring number) were constructed.

Shape

Oyster shell shape was characterised by calculating a height-length ratio for each population. For oysters, shape can be characterised and compared via ratios of their height to length, with oysters from different habitats having different average ratios (e.g. Kent 1992, 25–27; Winder 1992, 196–197). A recent study (Campbell 2010) showed that measurements of dimensions of the plane of commissure (specified above) are less variable than those of oysters' maximum height and length. Therefore oyster shell shape was reconstructed and compared via closure height-length ratio, cHLR (the ratio of closure height to the closure length, Hc/Lc). The same recent study indicated that the relative hinge size can also vary between habitats. Oyster shape was therefore also characterised by calculating a hinge-length ratio (the ratio of hinge width to closure length, Wh/Lc).

Simple ratios of dimensions are an approximate guide to significant differences in shape. An organism's dimensions tend to change as its size increases, and the relationship between dimensions (the organism's 'allometry') tends to be exponential (Seed 1980, 38–39): $y = m\ x^b$. The ratio of two dimensions can therefore vary depending on the size of the organism: $y/x = m\ x^b/x = m^{(b-1)}$. The ratio of dimensions is independent of size only if the exponent (b) is 1.0 (a condition known as 'isometry'). Since methods for interpreting and comparing straight lines are well-known, allometry is often interpreted using the logarithms of dimensions, because logarithmic transformation converts an exponential relationship to a linear one: $\log(y) = \log(m) + b \log(x)$.

If the relationship between the two variables after log-transformation fits a linear relationship well, the slope of the fitted line is a good estimate for the exponent (*b*), and the intercept is a good estimate of the log-transformed value of the coefficient (*m*).

Statistics and tests

Distributions of dimensions or ratios were plotted as histograms, and assessed as to whether the distribution was likely to be normal (Gaussian). If the distributions were normal, the averages for each context were tested for statistically significant difference (whether the probability of the difference being due to chance alone being less than one in 20, or 5%) by an analysis of variance (anova), along with Levene's test for heteroscedasticity (significantly different distributions around the mean between contexts). If heteroscedasticity was significant, the means were compared using Welch's *F*-test. Significant differences between contexts between pairs of averages were identified using Tukey's Q statistic. Since the number of measured valves were small, and since it was likely that measurements were not normally distributed around their means (an assumption of anova), averages were compared by the non-parametric Kruskal-Wallis test; if a significant difference was likely, these were identified by pair-wise Mann-Whitney U-tests. If a simple ratio of dimensions was found to be significantly different between oysters from different deposits, the allometry was compared via an analysis of co-variance (ancova) test on the $\log_{10}$-transformed dimensions. A straight line was fitted to the $\log_{10}$-transformed dimensions of the oysters in each deposit, using the reduced-major axis method rather than least-squares regression, since there was measurement error in both dimensions. The slope (*b*), intercept (log (*m*)), their standard deviations (s.d.), a measure of goodness of fit to the straight-line approximation (Pearson's 'r'), and the probability (*P*) of isometry (that the slope of the fitted line was exactly 1) were generated as outlined in Hammer and Harper (2006, 56). Statistics were generated and tests performed using the free statistical software package, PAST (version 1.90; Hammer *et al*, 2001).

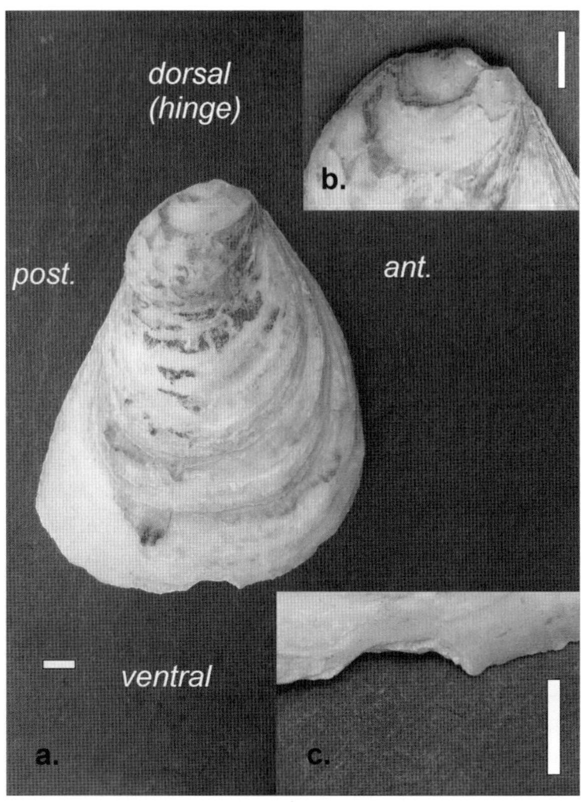

FIGURE 7.87

Oysters from Wigmore Castle: (a) exterior of right (upper) valve from deposit 557, showing shape typical for the site, (b): exterior of umboe, showing damage found in some 60% of the right valves, (c): typical 'old' break to ventral valve edge (scale bars: 5mm)

Results

Surface features

Surface features relating to bed conditions were rare, and very few valves were moderately or densely infested. The burrows of bristle-worms (*Polydora* sp.) were the commonest infestation, but affected only about 5% of the valves. There were rare instances of the complex hollows of *Cliona* (a burrow-etching sponge), oyster spat (very young oysters cemented to larger older shells), small colonies of bryozoans (sea-mats), barnacles and one tube of sand-worm (*Sabellaria* sp.).

No conjoined shells (of similar size cemented together) were observed. Some 40% of the left (lower) valves bore remains or impressions of the surface on which the young oyster had settled, but these were rarely diagnostic of that surface: about 10% showed the curvature typical of settling on mussel shells, with a couple of dozen examples cemented to empty oyster shells, and four shells bore the impression of cockle shells.

About 60% of the right (upper) valves had the umbones broken off, and in many cases the layers had sheared off, so the break extended across the exterior of the valve for some millimetres (Figure 7.87b). Only 10% of left valves had similarly

	Context	25	7	5	566	557	555	538	518	524
maximum	no.	18	15	11	51	43	45	55	37	32
valve	mean	50.4	60.6	53.2	58.3	52.6	51	54.2	54.1	53.9
height	s.d.	10.5	7.5	8.4	9.7	9.6	7.2	9.7	11	13.6
Hmax	min.	36	45	45	24	23	25	23	21	22
(mm)	max.	71	73	73	80	78	69	76	80	83
	mean	4.1	5.5	5.3	4.2	4.6	4.2	4.5	4.5	4.3
Age	min.	2	4	3	2	2	2	1	2	2
(years)	max.	7	7	7	6	8	7	7	8	7

FIGURE 7.88
Contexts with measurable oysters: distribution of maximum size and age

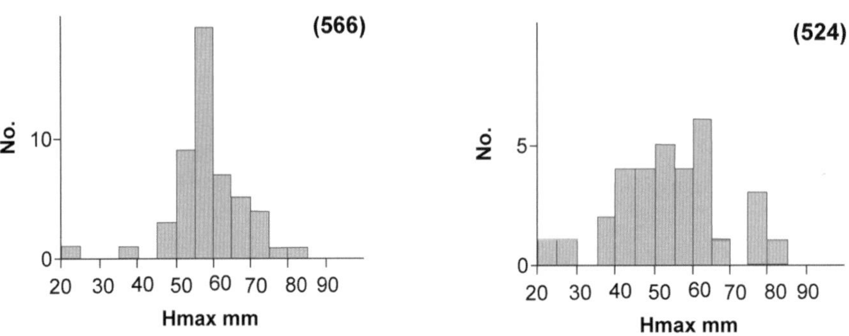

FIGURE 7.89
Oysters: distributions of maximum valve height (Hmax): (566) typical distribution; (524) poly-modal distribution

damaged hinges. Approximately 40% of the right (upper) valves had fresh breaks to the ventral valve edge (the shell margin most distant from the hinge) but a further 30% also had 'old' breaks along this edge, in which the broken surfaces were as encrusted and discoloured as the rest of the shell surface. These 'old' breaks were usually shallow 'U'-shaped notches 2–5mm deep and 4–10mm wide (Figure 7.87c), but about 15% the inset edge of the break was straight and 4–15mm wide.

Size

The mean, standard deviation and range of maximum height (Hmax) and age in each oyster-rich context is presented in Figure 7.88. Figure 7.89 shows a fairly typical distribution of Hmax (566, CG98 04, Phase 10), with a single peak (or mode) between 50 and 60mm, with the number of shells decreasing with increasing size towards a maximum of 80mm. Only 18 of the 307 measureable oysters (5.9%) were above 70mm, the modern legal landing size; and 73 (23.8%) were over 60mm. Figure 7.89 also shows a more unusual distribution (524, CG98 03, Phase 11), with several potential peaks. In all deposits small oysters (less than 37mm) were rare strays, or absent. Statistical tests were therefore performed on oysters over 37mm.

The distributions of Hmax were unlikely to be normal, but were negatively truncated (shells with small values of Hmax expected if the distribution was normal were absent) and positively skewed (there were more large shells, and unusually large shells, than would be expected for a normal distribution). Since the distributions did not appear to be normal (Figure 7.89), and Levene's test showed significant heteroscedasticity ($P = 0.03$), the averages were compared by the Kruskal-Wallis test. This showed that oyster average sizes were different between deposits ($H = 34.91$; H (corrected for ties) = 34.96; $P = 2.8 \times 10^{-5}$). The probabilities that different pairs of deposits could have measurable oysters of the same average size by chance are shown in Figure 7.90. Statistically significant differences are shown in boldface. The shells in Civil War deposit 007, CG96 01, Phase 11, were significantly larger on average than those in the Tudor midden 025, CG96 03, Phase 9 and dump 005, CG96 01, Phase 11. In the dumps (CG98 04) above floor 559, CG98 08, the earliest deposit 566 was significantly larger than 557, 555, and 538; the latter three were not significantly different from each other. The two deposits with the largest averages came from different phases (007 CG96 01, Phase 11 and 566 CG98 04, Phase 10), and were not significantly different. The two fills of 17th-century pit 520, CG98 03, Phase 11, were not significantly different in size.

Valve maximum height (Hmax)

Context	524	518	538	555	557	566	005	007
025	0.32	0.069	0.13	0.66	0.42	**0.0035**	0.657	**0.014**
007	0.0077	**0.043**	**0.016**	**0.00011**	**0.0064**	0.43	**0.017**	
005	0.61	0.10	0.31	1.0	0.70	**0.0051**		
566	0.069	**0.034**	**0.0025**	**6.9×10^{-7}**	0.002			
557	0.66	0.19	0.41	**0.22**				
555	0.17	**0.010**	0.061					
538	0.87	0.39						
518	0.58							

Age at harvest (years)

Context	524	518	538	555	557	566	005	007
025	0.52	0.38	0.22	0.93	0.11	0.59	0.057	**0.0032**
007	**0.012**	**0.010**	**0.0062**	**0.00085**	**0.027**	**0.00058**	0.69	
005	0.11	0.13	0.12	**0.031**	0.26	**0.04**		
566	0.66	0.52	0.27	0.55	0.08			
557	0.37	0.42	0.48	**0.043**				
555	0.50	0.31	0.12					
538	0.68	0.78						
518	0.83							

Closure height-length ratio (cHLR)

Context	524	518	538	555	557	566	005	007
025	**0.0030**	0.56	0.14	0.38	0.92	**0.0002088**	0.14	0.12
007	0.50	0.17	0.40	0.27	0.066	0.22	0.98	
005	0.53	0.26	0.52	0.37	0.11	0.31		
566	0.58	**0.00019**	**0.00088**	**0.00074**	**7.0×10^{-6}**			
557	**0.00069**	0.39	0.065	0.27				
555	**0.0094**	0.69	0.58					
538	**0.025**	0.34						
518	**0.0041**							

Valve height after four years' growth (H4)

Context	524	518	538	555	557	566	005	007
025	0.61	0.15	0.31	0.60	0.94	**0.017**	0.099	0.61
007	0.64	0.77	0.67	0.15	0.13	0.066	**0.013**	
005	**0.013**	**3.7×10^{-4}**	**0.0011**	**0.0046**	**0.01228**	**8.0×10^{-6}**		
566	**0.0026**	**0.041**	**3.7×10^{-4}**	**6.9×10^{-7}**	**7.3×10^{-7}**			
557	0.34	**0.015**	0.088	0.76				
555	0.42	**0.021**	0.19					
538	0.78	0.22						
518	0.24							

FIGURE 7.90

Probability (P) of difference in average occurring by chance (Mann-Whitney U)

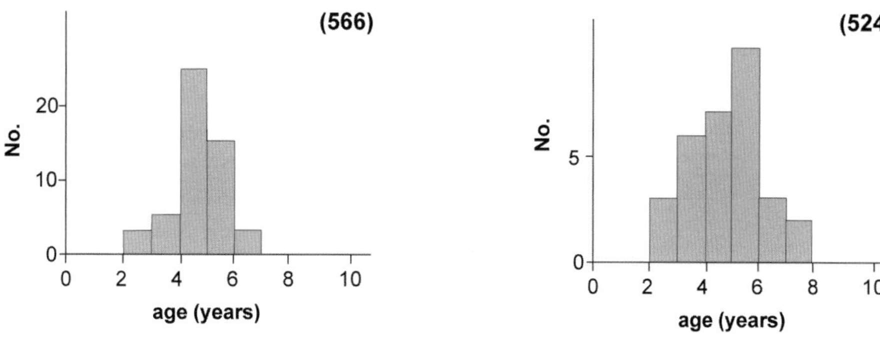

FIGURE 7.91

Oysters distributions of age at harvesting. (566): typical distribution; (524): unusual proportion of 2- to 4-years-old oysters

Context	Hinge-length ratio Wh/Lc	s.d.	cHLR Hc/Lc	s.d.	log (Lc) = log (m) + b log (Hc) slope, b	s.d.	intercept, log(m)	s.d.	P (iso'try)	r
25	0.29	0.05	1.11	0.1	1.23	0.08	-0.43	0.13	0.01	0.96
7	0.26	0.04	1.05	0.13	0.95	0.22	0.07	0.34	0.81	0.59
5	0.28	0.05	1.05	0.11	1.12	0.25	-0.22	0.38	0.64	0.74
566	0.26	0.04	1.01	0.09	1.02	0.07	-0.03	0.11	0.81	0.88
557	0.28	0.04	1.11	0.10	1.04	0.08	-0.11	0.12	0.6	0.88
555	0.26	0.04	1.07	0.11	0.85	0.08	0.23	0.13	0.07	0.78
538	0.27	0.03	1.07	0.09	1.06	0.06	-0.12	0.09	0.33	0.92
518	0.28	0.04	1.09	0.09	1.09	0.06	-0.18	0.10	0.14	0.95
524	0.28	0.05	1.02	0.08	1.10	0.05	-0.17	0.08	0.06	0.97

FIGURE 7.92

Measurable oysters over 37mm: shape and allometry of closure length (Lc) with closure height (Hc)

Age

The mean and range of ages when harvested in each oyster-rich context is presented in Figure 7.88. Figure 7.91 shows a fairly typical age distribution (deposit 566 CG98 04), with most oysters between 4–6 years old, with decreasing numbers with increasing age up to seven or eight years. Figure 7.91 also shows a deposit with an unusually high proportion of 2- to 4-year-old oysters (pit fill 524, CG98 03, Phase 11). In all deposits 1- and 2-year-olds were rare or absent.

The distributions of age were unlikely to be normal, but were negatively truncated (the young shells expected if the distribution was normal were absent) and positively skewed (there were more aged shells, and unusually aged shells, than would be expected for a normal distribution). Since the distributions did not appear to be normal, the non-parametric test was employed. The Kruskal-Wallis test also showed that oyster average age was different between deposits (H=19.68; H (corrected for ties)=21.51; P=0.012). The probabilities that different pairs of deposits could have measurable oysters of the same average size by chance are also shown in Figure 7.90. Statistically significant differences are shown in boldface. The shells in Civil War layer 007 were significantly older on average than any other deposit except the later Civil War layer 005. In the dumps above floor 559, CG98 08, only 557 was significantly older than 555. The two fills of 17th-century pit 520, CG98 03, Phase 11, were not significantly different in age.

Shape

Almost all the oysters were similar in shape regardless of deposit or phase, relatively tall (valve height plainly greater than length), and with a concave curve to the posterior edge. There were no obvious examples of 'round' oysters (with height and length similar), or with convex posterior edges. Approximately one in ten of the smaller shells (Hmax less than 40mm) and one in 20 of the larger shells were very tall with long narrow hinges, resembling the Portuguese oyster *Crassostrea gigas* (Thunberg), but all these also had the weak tooth-ridges and sockets (chomata) diagnostic of *O. edulis* L.

The average hinge-length ratio (Wh/Lc) and its standard deviation is shown for each deposit's oysters in Figure 7.92. There was no significant difference in this ratio between deposits (anova: $F_{[8,298]}$=1.82; P=0.074). Levene's test showed no significant heteroscedasticity (P=0.49). Tukey's test also showed no significant differences between deposits when pairs were compared. The Kruskal-Wallis test also showed no significant differences between deposits (H=14.18; H (corrected for ties)=14.28; P=0.077). Therefore pair-wise Mann-Whitney U-tests were not carried out. The hinge-length ratios for any deposit's measureable oysters was similar to the overall mean of 0.271±0.040, and its range of 0.18–0.40.

The average closure HLR (Hc/Lc) and its standard deviation is also shown for each deposit's oysters over 37mm in Figure 7.92. The distributions of cHLR did not appear to be normal, but were negatively truncated (shells with cHLR less than 0.9 expected if the distribution was normal were rare) and positively skewed (there were more shells with large cHLR, and unusually large cHLR, than would be expected for a normal distribution). The Kruskal-Wallis test showed that oyster shapes were different between deposits (H=36.44; H (corrected for ties)=36.52; $P=1.4 \times 10^{-5}$). The probabilities that different pairs of deposits could have measurable oysters over 37m with the same average cHLR by chance are shown in Figure 7.90. Statistically significant differences are shown in boldface. The shells in Tudor-era deposit 025 and the later Civil War deposits 007 and 005 were not significantly different. The earliest deposit 566, CG98 04 in the Phase 10 dumps above floor 559, CG98 08 was significantly more round than 557, 555, and 538; the latter three were not significantly different from each other. The two deposits with the largest averages (Civil War layer 007 and Tudor layer 566)

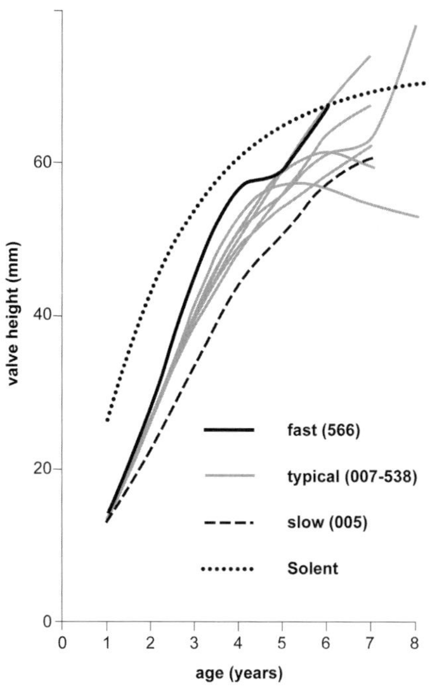

FIGURE 7.93

Oysters' growth curve (max. valve height v. age) of measurable oysters. Light dashed line: slow-growing modern oysters from Solent (after Richardson et al 1993)

did not have significantly different cHLR averages. In the 17th-century pit 520, the oysters in fill 518 were significantly taller on average those in 524.

Length-height allometry

The slopes and intercepts, their standard deviations, the goodness of fit measure ('r') and probability of isometry for each oyster-rich deposit are shown in Figure 7.92. The ancova test comparing the relationships of log_{10}-transformed values of closure length Lc with closure height Hc indicated that the allometry of closure length Lc with closure height Hc was significantly different between deposits (ancova: $F_{[8,282]}=5.05$; $P=7.0 \times 10^{-6}$), and that the slopes were significantly different ($F_{[8,282]}=2.39$; $P=0.016$). The length-height allometry was significantly different from isometry in Tudor deposit 025, with length growing considerably more rapidly than height. The length-height allometry in 17th-century pit fill 524 was the also significantly different from isometry. It was also statistically significantly different from 518, the other fill in the same pit (ancova: $F_{[1,60]}=9.35$; $P=0.0033$), but the slopes were not ($F_{[1,60]}=1.15$; $P=0.28$), implying a significant difference in intercept.

Growth rate

The distribution of maximum valve height at the end of four years' growth (H4) in most deposits had single peaks and a positive skew. The distribution of H4 in deposit 025 had two peaks, suggesting this deposit night have had two populations with different growth rates. However, when the oysters in 025 were separated into two groups based on their relative H4 sizes, these two groups were not significantly different in cHLR, hinge-length ratio, or height-length allometry. Therefore the division into large and small seemed arbitrary, and all the oysters in 025 were treated as a single group. The oysters in some deposits, such as 007 and 566, had similar average sizes but different average ages, which suggested that these were growing at different rates. The Kruskal-Wallis test showed that oyster average size after four years' growth (H4) was different between deposits (H=46.58; H (corrected for ties)=46.67; $P=1.8 \times 10^{-7}$). The probabilities that different pairs of deposits could have oysters of the same average size by chance after four years of growth (H4) are also shown in Figure 7.90. Statistically significant differences are shown in boldface. Deposit 005 oysters were significantly smaller on average at four years old than all other oysters except deposit 007, and deposit 566 was significantly larger on average at four years old than all other deposits. The annual-ring size distributions for each deposit (Figure 7. 93) distinguished three growth rates:

— the fast-growing group of deposit 566, which averaged over 56mm after four years' growth,

— oysters growing at a typical rate for the assemblage, averaging 49-52mm in four years,

— the slow-growing group of deposit 005, which only achieved an average of 44mm maximum height after four years.

The growth curve derived by Richardson *et al* (1993) for relatively slow-growing modern oysters from the Solent is also shown in Figure 7.93; even the fast-growing oysters from Wigmore are quite slow-growing compared to these modern oysters. The growth curve of the oysters in 17th-century deposits 005 and 524 followed the expected form of a gradually flattening curve (like that for the modern Solent oysters), since oysters (like most molluscs) tend to gradually approach a maximum size characteristic of their habitat with increasing age. The growth curve for other deposits did not follow this expected form. Up to an average size of 60mm, the curve followed the expected trend, but once an average size approached 60mm (whatever the growth rate) the curve either underwent a sudden increase to an average over 60mm in subsequent years (implying a growth spurt), or average ages in subsequent years fell to below 60mm (implying oysters began to shrink with age). In those deposits which exhibited the growth spurt, the sudden increase in average size was due to the one or two oysters which had grown beyond 65mm. In those deposits which exhibited a fall in average size in later years, any shells over 65mm in the deposit had achieved this size in the year when the average size had approached 60mm; all older shells were less than 65mm.

Discussion

Surface features

The low infestation meant that little can be said regarding the conditions in which the shells were grown. Some beds were enhanced with cultch (shells deliberately discarded on beds to provide a surface on which young oysters can settle). The low bristle-worm infestation means it was not possible to use their ranges as an indicator of source, a possibility in other assemblages (e.g. Winder 1994). The common loss of the right valve umbo is characteristic of the opening of the oyster by forcing apart the ventral edges of the two valves until the hinge ligament tears. This action crushes together the umbones of the two valves, which tends to snap the weaker umbo (in the right valve). This contrasts with modern practice when preparing oysters 'on the half-shell', in which the partly opened valves are sheared past each other until the hinge ligament breaks due to twisting. The notches along the ventral edge of the right valve would be consistent with the oyster having been opened by the insertion of a fairly long narrow blade between the ventral edges of the valves opposite the hinge. This method of opening is noted in other medieval and later eras in inland towns, such as Oxford (Campbell 2002, 261). This contrasts with usual modern opening practice, in which a short wide blade is inserted between the valves along the posterior edge, behind and below the hinge. Most of the oysters were opened fairly roughly, without concern for their appearance at the table.

Sizes and ages

The sizes and ages of oysters being bought to Wigmore Castle were broadly similar in all the deposits, being typically 50–60mm in size (with an oyster of 70–85mm being large in any group), and between 4–6 years old when harvested (a 7- or 8 year-old being old). One- and two-year-olds and shells less than 36mm were rare or absent. It seems likely that only oysters over three years old and over 36mm were intentionally harvested, with younger smaller oysters accidentally incorporated. The consistent absence of aged oysters from all the deposits would be consistent with the beds having been dredged regularly for some years, and the aged oysters harvested some time previously. While these sizes are quite small by modern standards (the modern legal landing size is typically 70mm), oysters over five years old were still relatively common, so harvesting did not seem unsustainably intensive. Tudor deposit 557 and Civil War deposit 007 contained the largest oysters in the assemblage, with the other deposits of a consistent but smaller size. The Civil War-era deposit 007 oysters were also the oldest on average, similar to those from 566; the other oysters (either Tudor or Civil War-era) were harvested at a somewhat younger age.

Growth rate

The growth rate for all the Wigmore oysters was distinctly slower than slow-growing modern oysters. This might be the by-product of very intense over-exploitation, but it was relatively similar for all the Wigmore oysters, which suggests the slow growth had a common cause for all the oysters, such as a cooler climate. The slowest growth rate was found amongst Civil War oysters (deposit 005) and the fastest (deposit 566) were found in Tudor deposits, but most oysters grew at a similar rate in either phase.

The growth-rate curves were unusual in most deposits, with unexpected departures from a gradually flattening form once an average size neared 60mm. Since oysters cannot shrink with age, in those deposits which exhibited a decrease in average size with age must be due to oysters over 60mm tending to have been selectively removed. Since some younger oysters had achieved a size over 60mm, the chance of an oyster being selected for removal began at about 60mm and increased with increasing size, removing most oysters over 70mm and virtually all those over 80mm. This would be consistent with the oysters being graded for size by hand, possibly using a 'thumb's length' (roughly 2½ inches or 63mm). In those deposits with sudden leaps in average size to well over 60mm, the high averages were due to the one or two oysters over a thumb's length, similar in number to the very small oysters (37mm or smaller) which were probably accidentally included. These larger oysters therefore have been accidentally overlooked in the size grading. It seems probable oysters were being graded by hand for size during these periods, with Wigmore receiving only the lower-grade (smaller) oysters.

Shape

The Wigmore oysters were all relatively tall with concave posterior margins. Oysters of this shape were the common form in some medieval inland towns, such as Oxford (Campbell 2002, 261). Winder (1992, 196–197) found moderately tall oysters more common in off-shore beds, and oysters greater in length than height more common on harbour muds. A recent small study of oyster shape in the modern Solent found that oysters growing off-shore were taller than those growing near the shore and within harbours, but these modern off-shore oysters (with average cHLR values of 0.92–0.93) were not as tall as the Wigmore oysters, with average cHLR values of 1.0–1.12. Modern Solent oysters seem to have proportionally wide hinges when growing off-shore, (Wh/Lc of 0.27–0.29), while oysters from near the shore and in harbours had proportionally small hinges (Wh/Lc of 0.23–0.25) (Campbell 2010). The proportional size of the hinge was similar for all the measurable oyster deposits at Wigmore, around 0.27, which is comparable with modern off-shore Solent oysters. Both the relative hinge size and closure shape of Wigmore oysters suggest they were not gathered from harbours, but from well off-shore.

The oysters in Tudor deposit 025 had a closure length-height allometry significantly different from isometry (Figure 7.92), with length increasing significantly faster than height. In order for the ratio of height to length to still be greater than all the other deposits, this deposit must have been considerably more tall and narrow when young than all other deposits. They may have been more densely packed together in their beds when young than the other deposits. The oysters in 17th-century deposit 524 also had a closure length-height allometry significantly different from isometry, and this allometry was significantly different from those in deposit 518, the other deposit from the same 17th-century pit 520.

In all the other deposits the exponent (*b*) was not significantly different from 1.0 (isometry); in these deposits the cHLR could be used directly to compare shape. The oysters in the Tudor deposit 566 were the most rounded on average (cHLR approximately 1.0, or closure height and length about equal).

Summary

Despite being of similar average age and size, and having similar growth rates, the oysters in the two deposits in 17th-century pit 520 were different shapes, and had achieved those shapes by growing with different allometries. The distributions of ages were also qualitatively different, with 524 having an unusual number of younger oysters. The oysters in the two deposits were therefore from different sources, with similarities in age and size produced by the harvesting and sorting methods. The oysters in deposit 524 were the more rounded, and therefore may have been harvested from nearer in-shore than the other deposits.

There were few contrasts between the Tudor-era and Civil War-era oysters. In both phases length could grow at a greater rate than height (deposits 025, CG96 03, Phase 9 and 524, CG98 03, Phase 11), although most were isometric. Both phases included deposits in which oysters could be relatively rounded in shape (566 and 524), but most were similar in shape, and all were relatively tall, with a shape of oysters from off-shore beds; there may have been some bed management by the addition of cultch, to improve the chances of spat settling on the beds. The Tudor deposits had the both the largest and smallest average oysters, the oldest and youngest average oysters, and the fastest- and slowest-growing oysters; the Civil War-era deposits were similar to the more common Tudor deposits in average size, age, and growth rate. Regular previous dredging for oysters had probably removed the very old oysters from the beds. The minimum sizes being landed, down to about 37mm, were considerably smaller than modern standards, but the wide range of ages showed that harvesting was not leading to over-exploitation. Both phases included deposits with departures from the typical oyster growth pattern that suggest hand-grading for size, with Wigmore receiving the smaller size grade in both phases. The small average sizes compared to modern standards was therefore not simply the result of the generally slower growth rate (possibly due to a cooler climate).

Conclusions

Wigmore lies almost equidistant between the Bristol Channel and the Mersey Estuary, so the importation of marine material, such as shellfish, must have presented a serious logistical challenge. Shellfish have a limited 'shelf-life' and therefore have to be transported at speed, while being kept cool and moist to minimise loss in transit. Shellfish therefore can act as an indicator of the effectiveness of the transport system at a given period. Also, shellfish in the shell constitute a luxury inland, because most of a shellfish is shell and must be discarded. Better sources of protein and animal calories would have been present in locally available animals, or other marine animals with a better proportion of flesh to waste (such as sea fish, or shellfish as preserved flesh). Marine shell therefore constitutes the most plentiful evidence for the changing role of perishable luxury imports in the daily life of Wigmore Castle's past residents, and the changing efficiency of its transportation links to the coast.

The shellfish brought to the castle were all commonly consumed types, familiar in coastal archaeological assemblages of the early medieval and later periods (e.g. Campbell 2009). These shellfish are known on the modern coasts along the Bristol Channel and around the Mersey mouth. There is a modern commercial cockle and mussel fishery in both regions, and British oyster stocks have only recently been decimated by over-exploitation. These shellfish could therefore have been brought to Wigmore from either the Bristol Channel or the coasts of north Wales and north-west England.

Common oysters may survive out of water for some weeks but are unfit to eat after 12 days, even when iced or refrigerated (Aaraas *et al* 2004, 210). Since oysters were being brought to Wigmore from the 13th century (Phase 4), there must have been a desire for luxury foodstuffs at the castle by that time, and the transport of bulky goods from the coast must have then taken about a week. Small numbers of oysters continued to be imported during the 13th and early 14th century (Phases 5–7), so the desire for luxury foodstuffs remained, and the journey to the coast continued to be about a week.

During the mid-14th to 15th centuries (Phase 8) the numbers and range of shellfish brought to the castle increased substantially, with mussels becoming the most common shellfish. Mussels have a shelf-life of about 3–4 days, with 48% mortality after a week at room temperature (Slabyj and Hinkle 1976, 1 and table 2). Bulk transport from as far away as the coasts must have taken much less than a week by this period, and the demand amongst the castle's occupants for fresh shellfish (and potentially their status) must have risen beyond that of the earlier periods. The reduction in the quantity and range of shellfish being brought in during the earlier part of the 16th century (Phase 9) probably shows the castle's importance in the region had diminished.

Shellfish were brought to the castle in their greatest quantities during the 16th to mid-17th centuries (Phases 9–11). Transporting goods across distances as far as the coasts had probably become commonplace. The flat winkle from deposit 580, CG98 13 shows shellfish may have been packed in seaweed for the journey. The range and nature of the shellfish in the two phases was similar. Both phases included oysters with the rounded shape of harbour oysters (566 and 524), but most were the tall shape of off-shore oysters. The variety of shapes, ages, sizes and allometries showed a range of beds were being harvested. The average sizes were small compared to modern standards, but this was not due to over-harvesting (although harvesting was intensive enough to have taken most of the very old oysters). The oysters were probably being hand-graded for size, with the castle receiving the smaller size grade. In both phases damage due to opening was frequent, and the techniques employed were not those that would have produced elegant oysters to impress the diners. During both the Tudor and Stuart-Civil War eras, shellfish had become an everyday food for ordinary folk.

It is not possible at present to compare the pattern of shellfish consumption at Wigmore Castle with other castles in the region in a meaningful way. Traditionally, shellfish are interpreted as a foodstuff rather than a potential luxury import. Their inevitably small contribution to the diet relative to domesticated animals, due to the low meat content of individual shellfish, has led to general under-reporting of shellfish. The only previous report on marine shells from a Welsh Marches castle is a brief note on Dyserth Castle, Clwyd (Jackson 1915). This analysis and that for Dyserth appear to be the only published reports on shellfish for any of the region's castles. There appear to be no published medieval marine shell assemblages from any type of site in Staffordshire, and one or two short reports for each of Herefordshire, Worcestershire and Shropshire. Those for Gloucestershire appear restricted to two or three for Bristol, and those for Cheshire restricted to two or three for Chester. It is hoped that the methods and results presented here will provide some guidance and encouragement for greater use of marine shells to answer questions of archaeological interest in the region.

8

THE PLANT REMAINS

Mariangela Vitolo

8.1 INTRODUCTION

A preliminary assessment of waterlogged plant remains from Wigmore Castle was carried out in 1996 by Lisa Moffett on ten samples. A report and a further assessment on samples from the 1998 excavation never occurred, and the processed and unprocessed samples were first kept at the University of Birmingham/Regional Store and then transferred to Fort Cumberland in 2005. In March 2008 all surviving flots from the 1996 excavations and those from 1998, where the type of sample was given as 'Environmental', were assessed. Eventually those samples that were considered 'moderately rich' to 'fairly abundant' and for which further work was recommended, were analysed in summer/autumn 2009 at Fort Cumberland.

8.2 METHODOLOGY

The samples analysed can be divided into two groups, which have undergone different processing and sorting treatments. The first group included five samples for charred plant remains, the second group three GBA samples, or samples taken for the recovery of waterlogged plant remains and insects. The charred samples were fully floated using a Siraf tank with a 300 micron mesh being used for the flot and a 0.5mm mesh for the heavy residue. The flots were analysed using a binocular dissecting microscope at up to x50 magnification. First of all, the plant remains other than charcoal (including cereal grain and chaff, weed seeds, and some food plants) were sorted from the matrix of charcoal, snail shells and small mammal and fish bones. Then, using English Heritage's modern comparative collection as a reference, they were identified and quantified. For samples <13>, <25> and <28>, all from hearths, an analysis of charcoal was also undertaken.

Of the waterlogged samples, only <26> and <31> had been processed already, whilst sample <38> was processed at Fort Cumberland. Waterlogged samples undergo a different processing method: one litre is bucket-sieved using a simple wash-over technique for the retrieving of plant remains, pouring the wash-over into a 250 micron mesh, and the rest of the sample is processed for insect remains using paraffin. The residue is then sorted and discarded, the wash-over is kept in water and analysed under a binocular dissecting microscope at up to x50 magnification. The plant remains are picked out, identified and quantified, then kept in a 70% alcohol solution and refrigerated. Sample <26> was entirely sorted at Fort Cumberland, whilst of sample <31> the >2 mm fraction had already been sorted, therefore the plant remains recorded for this sample come from the <2 mm fraction.

Nomenclature follows Stace (1997) for plants other than cereals and Zohary and Hopf (2000, tables 3 and 5) for the cereals.

8.3 CHARRED PLANT REMAINS

The charred plant remains species recovered from the flotation samples are shown on Figure 8.1. Sample <13> (137, CG96 15, Phase 6) came from an industrial hearth, associated with lead-working. It produced a fairly small flot, but contained a variety of weed seeds: docks, mallow, sedges, two free-threshing type wheat grains, two rye rachis fragments, and one *Avena* sp. (oat).

Sample <19> (249, CG96 23, Phase 3) despite its large flot size, did not contain many plant remains, other than charcoal. Very few weed seeds, some unidentified grains and 15 *Triticum* sp. were recovered. Mineral concretions and seeds were present in this sample, including one *Myosotis* sp. (forget-me-not), one *Carex* sp. (sedge) and one unidentified seed, plus one *Conium maculatum* (hemlock) and one *Sambucus nigra* (elder) which were definitely not charred and might be either modern or ancient.

Sample <20> (270, pit 271, CG96 24, Phase 3) was small and contained very few indeterminate grains, one wheat, one rye, and a couple of weed seeds: *Atriplex* sp. and *Anthemis cotula* (stinking camomile). This sample also contained a mineral-replaced seed of stinking camomile, an indeterminate seed, and one fly puparium.

Sample <25> (338, CG96 27, Phase 2) was taken from above domestic hearth 351, it was one of the biggest in terms of flot size and it was the richest in cereal grains, although most were not identifiable to genus. It also contained 727 shell fragments of *Corylus avellana* (hazelnut), along with some grasses and very few weed seeds.

Sample <28> (359, CG96 27, Phase 2) from below domestic hearth 351, also produced a fairly

	Sample	**25**	**28**	**20**	**19**	**13**
	Phase	**2**	**2**	**3**	**3**	**6**
	Context Group	**27**	**27**	**24**	**23**	**15**
	Context	**338**	**359**	**270**	**249**	**137**
Taxa	**Common name**					
Ranunculus flammula L.	Lesser spearwort		1			
Corylus avellana L. (shell)	Hazelnut	727	40	1		
Chenopodiaceae/Caryophyllaceae	Goosefoot family/pink family		1		1	
Atriplex sp. L.	Oraches			1		
Agrostemma githago L.	Corncockle		1			
Fallopia convolvulus (L)	Black-bindweed		1			
Polygonum sp.	Knotweed		2			
Persicaria sp.	Knotweeds					1
Rumex sp.	Dock	4	3			3
cf *Rumex* sp.	cf Dock					1
Tilia cordata Mill. C.	Small-leaved lime					1
Malva sp.	Mallow					1
Crategus sp. type	Hawthorn		1			
Crategus/Prunus	Hawthorn/sloe/plum (thorn)		1			
Prunus cerasus type	Sour cherry		1			
Fabaceae indet.	Indeterminate legume	10	65			
Vicia/Lathyrus	Vetch/tare					1
cf *Vicia tetrasperma* (L.) screb.	Smooth tare					1
cf *Cytisus* sp.	Broom		1			
Apiaceae indet.	Carrot family	1			1	
Myosotis sp. L. (m)*	Forget-me-not				1	
Galium sp.	Bedstraw	1	3			
Galium aparine L.	Cleavers	1	1			
Sambucus nigra (L.)	Elder		1			
Anthemis cotula L.	Stinking camomille		2	1	2	
Anthemis cotula L. (m)	Stinking camomille (m)			1		
Lapsana communis L.	Nipplewort		5			
Schoenoplectus lacustris (L.) Palla	Common club-rush		1			
Eleocharis palustris L.	Common spike-rush		1		1	
Cyperaceae indet.	Sedge family				1	16
Carex sp. L.	Sedges					3
Carex sp. L. (m)	Sedge (m)				1	
Cenococcum geophilum	Fungal resting bodies		1	4	3	7
cf *Pteridium* Gled. Ex Scop.	cf Bracken					2
Sprouted Poaceae indet	Sprouted grass indet.	1				
Small Poaceae indet.	Small indeterminate grass		3			
Bromus sp L.	Brome	6				
cf *Lolium* sp.	Cf Rye-grass		2			
Avena sp.	Oat	76	12			4
cf *Avena* sp.	cf Oat	6	25			
Avena (sprouted)	Sprouted oat	2	5			
Large Poaceae indet.	Indet. grass	108	35			
Triticum, free-treshing type (grain)	Free threshing wheat	2	4		1	2
Triticum sp. (grain)	Wheat	3	14	1	15	
cf *Triticum* sp. (grain)	cf Wheat	1	5			2
Secale cereale (rachis)	Rye	9	8	1		2
cf *Secale cereale* (grain)	cf Rye	3	2			
Triticum/Secale sp. (grain)	Wheat/rye	3	2			
Cerealia indet. (grain)	Indeterminate bereal grain		20	7	20	1
	Unidentified seeds		7	1		6
	Unidentified seed (m)			1	1	
	Bark					1
	Pea/bean peduncule					1
	Twig/roots					2
	Herbaceous material					4
	Bud					4
	Abscission scar pad		1			
	Animal dropping		1			
	Burnt bone					1
	Fly puparia (m)			1		

FIGURE 8.1

Charred plant remains: species list (mineralised)*

large flot, although less rich in grains and nutshells. Twenty-two legumes (identified as *Vicia/Lathyrus*) were recovered from this sample, which was also rich in grasses and weed seeds, such as *Galium* sp., *Lapsana communis* (nipplewort), *Anthemis cotula* (stinking camomile), *Ranunculus flammula* (lesser spearwort), *Schoenoplectus lacustris* (common club rush), and indeterminate Cyperaceae. One sour cherry stone was also recovered from this sample.

Samples <13>, <25> and <28> were also analysed for charcoal. Domestic hearths (<25> and <28>) most commonly contained oak and hazelnut, although other species were present in small quantities (Figure 8.2). All the charcoal from sample <13> consisted of oak, some fragments were vitrified or semi-vitrified, possibly because they are derived from lead-working (Figure 8.3).

Discussion of charred plant remains

Samples <25>, <28> and <19> produced the largest flots, although <19> was not very rich in plant remains other than charcoal. The first two samples on the other hand were richer in cereal grains, weed seeds and other plant remains, such as legumes and nutshells.

	Sample	**25**			**28**		
	Context	**338**			**359**		
		>4mm	**>2mm**	**weight in g**	**>4mm**	**>2mm**	**weight in g**
Quercus sp.	Oak	4	9	1.62	11	14	3.49
Quercus sp. semivitifried	Semivitrified oak	0	0	0.00	0	0	0.00
cf *Quercus* sp.	Oak	1	2	0.20		2	0.08
Fagus sp.	Beech	1	2	0.46			
cf *Fagus*	cf Beech		1	0.01			
Corylus sp.	Hazelnut	10	4	1.82	10	3	2.37
Betula sp.	Birch	3		1.02			
Maloideae	Hawthorn, apple, whitbeam etc	2	1	0.49		2	0.14
Ilex sp.	Holly				1		0.06
Acer cf *campestre*	Maple	2	1	0.33	1		0.14
Ligustrum sp.	Privet					1	0.04
Indeterminate		3	4	0.42	1	4	0.68

FIGURE 8.2
Charcoal: samples <25> and <28>

Fraction	Fragment nos	Description	Weight (g)
>4mm	1	Semi-vitried oak	0.61
	2	Oak trunk, not vitrified	0.98
	3	Oak; very minor vitrificaton on one edge	0.32
	4	Oak; some vitrification associated with a knot -structure will be modified in this area anyway	0.46
	5	Fast growing oak, not-vitrified	0.33
	6	Oak twig; not vitrified	0.05
	7	Oak trunk; some vitrification	0.14
	8	Large fragment of oak charcoal, slow growing trunk wood	3.99
	9	Oak trunk; not vitrified	0.64
	10	Oak trunk; slightly vitrified	0.63
	Total		**8.15**
4–2mm	11	cf Oak trunk wood; vitrifed	0.02
	12	Oak; some vitrification	0.01
	13	Oak; vitrified	0.03
	14	Oak; well vitrifed at one edge	0.02
	15	Oak; slightly vitrified	0.04
	16	Oak; deformed and slighlty vitrified	0.01
	17	Oak; slight vitrification at edges	0.01
	18	Oak trunk; well vitrified on one edge	0.03
	19	Oak; well vitirifed/disrupted	0.04
	20	Oak; very slow growing; not vitrified	0.01
	Total		**0.22**

FIGURE 8.3
Charcoal: sample <13>

Sample		**26**	**38**	**31**
Phase		**1**	**1**	**1**
Context Group		**29**	**29**	**29**
Context		**362**	**381**	**376**
Taxa	**Common name**			
Ranunculus acris/bulbosus/repens	Buttercup	16	57	
cf *Ranunculus flammula* L.	Lesser spearwort		3	
Ficus carica L.	Fig		1	
Urtica sp.	Nettle		1	
Urtica dioica L.	Common nettle	4	4	170
Urtica urens L.	Small nettle	2		
Corylus avellana L.	Nutshell	1		
Agrostemma githago L.	Corncockle	36	4	
Cerastium sp.	Mouse-ears		1	
Cerastium fontana/tomentosum L.	Mouse-ear		1	
Lychnis flos-cuculi L.	Ragged robin		2	1
Stellaria graminea L.	Lesser stitchwort		1	
Stellaria media type (L) Vill.	Common chickweed	*		
Chenopodiaceae (embryo)		2		
Aptriplex sp.	Oraches	326	158	
Chenopodium sp.	Goosefoot	178	50	
Atriplex/Chenopodium sp.	Oraches/goosefoot	154	104	
cf *Persicaria lapathifolia* L. Gray	Pale persicaria		1	
Polygonaceae indet.			2	11
Polygonum aviculare agg.	Knotgrass	123	106	24
Polygonum sp.		46		
Rumex sp.	Dock	33	52	34
Rumex acetosella agg.	Sheep's Sorrel	6		
Hypericum perforatum L.	Perforate St John's Wort			1
Viola subg *Melanium*	Violet	8	1	5
Brassicaceae indet.		2		
Small Brassicaceae indet.			1	
Thlaspi arvense L.	Field penny-cress	*		*
Capsella bursa-pastoris L.	Shepherd's-purse			13
Raphanus raphanistrum L.	Wild radish		1	
Anagallis arvensis L.	Scarlet pimpernel			*
cf *Crataegus* sp.	Hawthorns		2	
Crataegus cf *monogyna* Jacq.	Hawthorn	*		
Potentilla sp.	cf Cinquefoil	1	8(1)	1
cf *Potentilla anserina* L.	Silverweed		1	
Prunus spinosa L.	Blackthorn		*	
cf *Rosa* sp.	Rose	*		
Torilis sp.	Hedge-parsleys	2		
Galeopsis tetrahit L.	Hemp-nettles	1		
Rubus sp.	Brambles	10	1	9
Mercurialis perennis L.	Dog's mercury	*		
cf *Linum usitatissimum* L.	Flax		2	
Apiaceae indet.		10		
Aethusa cynapium L.	Fool's parsley		2	
Atropa belladonna L.	Deadly Nightshade			1
Myosotis sp.	Forget-me-not		1	
Prunella vulgaris L.	Selfheal	5	5	
Stachys sp.	Woundworts		2	
Lycopus europaeus L.	Gypsywort		3	
Mentha sp.	Mint		1	
Plantago major L.	Greater Plantain			3
Sambucus nigra L.	Elderberry	1		
Veronica sp.	Speedwell			1
Asteraceae indet.		6		
Achillea millefolium L.	Yarrow			174

FIGURE 8.4A

Waterlogged samples: species list (: mineralised)*

Sample		**26**	**38**	**31**
Phase		**1**	**1**	**1**
Context Group		**29**	**29**	**29**
Context		**362**	**381**	**376**
Taxa	**Common name**			
Anthemis cotula L.	Stinking camomille	104		1
Arctium lappa L.	Greater burdock	*		*
Lapsana communis L.	Nipplewort	26	10	
Sonchus arvensis L.	Corn sow-thistle	1		
Sonchus asper L. (Hill)	Prickly sow-thistle	5		
Sonchus oleraceus/arvensis L.	Sow-Thistles		1	
Tripleurospermum Sch. Bip.	Mayweed	6		1
cf *Carduus* sp.	cf Thistle			1
Carduus sp.	Thistle	2		
Carduus/Cirsium	Thistle			5
Juncus sp.	Rush	3		
Cyperaceae indet.		11	35	
Carex sp.	Sedge	7	264	
Eleocharis palustris L.	Common spike-rush	1	7	1
Isolepsis setacea L.	Bristle club-rush		1	
Small Poaceae indet.		15	7	
Poaceae indet.	Indeterminate grasses			25
Poaceae indet. (charred)	Charred grass	1		
cf *Glyceria* sp.	Sweet-grasses			1
Triticum sp.(chaff)		1		
Cerealia indet (chaff)	Indet cereal chaff	1		
Cerealia indet (bran)	Cereal bran	2		
	Leaf base			1
	Insects	abundant	abundant	abundant
	Worm case	present	present	very present
Cenococcum		present	occasional	fairly abundant
	Mosses	present	present	occasional
	Thorn	1	1	2
	Bark			2
	Indeterminate seeds	30	8	75
	Twigs	2		
	Fish scale	1		
	Bud	24	3	
	Flower base	2		
	Abscission scar pad		1	

FIGURE 8.4B
Waterlogged samples: species list (: mineralised)*

The distortion of most grains, due to the charring conditions, made them unidentifiable, apart from a few grains of *Secale cereale* (rye), *Triticum* sp. (wheat) and *Avena* sp. (oat), of which two were sprouted. Oat seems to be the most abundant grain, although, in the absence of oat chaff, it is not possible to know whether it is a wild or cultivated variety. Many unidentifiable grasses were also recorded in samples <25> and <28>, both from domestic hearths, and, given their size, they might well also be derived from oats.

Barley was totally absent from this assemblage, which is attested at other contemporary sites in the region (Greig, forthcoming). The only chaff recovered consisted of two fragments of rye rachis retrieved from sample <13>, although free-threshing wheat chaff was noted in some of the samples scanned during assessment.

In medieval times it was common to sow mixed crops (maslins) to buffer the risk of crop failure, as they react differently depending on the conditions (Jones and Halstead 1995), but trying to detect a mixed crop presents some problems and it cannot be undertaken on small assemblages like the one from Wigmore. Similarly statistical analysis of the weed seeds that have been used on some prehistoric sites in north-east England (Moffet 2006) cannot be applied here, because the weeds recovered are not necessarily associated with the crops; therefore it is not possible to say whether rye and wheat from Wigmore were grown together, although this is a possibility.

Although some edible plant remains, such as pea/bean, hazelnut and one cherry stone, were recovered, most of the plant remains other than grains consisted of wild grasses and some weed seeds. Many of the seeds recovered generally occur on arable and manured soils, such as corn cockle, black bindweed, nipplewort, cleavers, bedstraw, elder, and some grow in damp places, such as rush seeds, sedges and lesser spearwort. The presence of Cenococcum geophilum (fungi's resting bodies) in all of the samples, except <25>, also suggests arable or disturbed ground (Jensen 1975). The find of a sour cherry stone in sample <28> hints at high status (Dyer 2006). The presence of mineral-replaced seeds and mineral concretions, whose nature is unclear (as in Carruthers 1988), in samples <19> and <20>, from a layer and a pit fill respectively, as opposed to hearths, indicates the presence of faecal matter, either human or animal, in these contexts.

The charred assemblage from Wigmore consisted mainly of hazelnut shells and grasses. Not many weed seeds and very few cereal grains were recovered. The identifiable grains were mostly free-threshing wheat, rye and oats, of which two were sprouted. The only chaff recovered was rye, although a waterlogged wheat chaff fragment was found in one of the GBA samples (< 26 >). One would not expect to find wheat chaff in a medieval context, because of the prevalent use of free-threshing *Triticum*, which does not require exposure to fire during processing.

Most of the seeds recovered consisted of grasses and weed seeds. Apart from the hazelnut shells and the cherry stone, the other plant remains recovered would not be consumed at a table and would be used for cooking or as a fuel. Cherries and nuts may also have been stoned or shelled in the kitchen during preparation of dishes as opposed to placed on the table unprocessed. This suggests the presence of kitchen waste, rather than table waste, possibly coupled with burnt stable waste.

The results from the charcoal analysis show that while both hazel and oak, and small quantities of other woods were used as fuel in the domestic/kitchen fires (<25> and <28>), only oak was used in the hearth associated with lead-working (sample <13>). The presence of only this wood in sample <13> is probably due to its higher calorific value, meaning that it is often used for industrial processes. For domestic hearths high temperature would not be needed, hence the wider mixture of woods used there.

8.4 WATERLOGGED PLANT REMAINS

The three waterlogged samples <26>, <31> and <38> (Figure 8.4) came from a sequence of early deposits associated with the defensive clay bank or rampart of the first timber castle. They were analysed in order to find out what activities were taking place in the vicinity of the site at the time of the construction of the castle and to see if there was a change in the environment throughout the sequence.

Sample <26> (362, CG96 29, Phase 1) came from the the turf line beneath the clay bank; it contained a large number of Chenopodiaceae (identified as *Atriplex* sp. and *Chenopodium* sp.), *Anthemis cotula* (stinking chamomile), *Polygonum aviculare* (knotgrass) and *Persicaria lapathifolia* (pale persicaria). Other seeds occurring in this sample include: *Rumex* sp. (dock), *Rumex acetosella* (sheep's sorrel), *Polygonum* sp., *Aethusa cynapium* (fool's parsley), *Thlaspi arvense* (field penny-cress), *Prunus spinosa* (blackthorn), *Stellaria media* type (common chickweed), *Mercurialis perennis* (dog's mercury), *Arctium lappa* (greater burdock), *Ranunculus* sp. (buttercups), *Tripleurospermum* sp. (mayweed), *Carex* sp. (sedge), *Potentilla* sp.(cinquefoil), *Galeopsis* sp., some indeterminate Apiaceae and indeterminate grasses. Two cereal bran fragments, two cereal chaff fragments (one of wheat) and one charred grass were also recovered, along with sedges and rush seeds.

Sample <38> (381, CG96 29, Phase 1) came from the make up of the bank itself and contained mainly *Polygonum aviculare* (knotgrass), *Carex* sp. (sedges), *Ranunculus acris/repens/bulbosus* (buttercups), *Chenopodium* sp. (goosefoot) and *Atriplex* sp. (oraches) but also some *Urtica* sp. (nettle), *Agrostemma githago* (corncockle), *Lychnis flos cuculi* (ragged robin), *Potentilla* sp. (cinquefoil), *Crategus* sp. (hawthorn), *Prunella vulgaris* (selfheal), *Lycopus europaeus* (gyspywort), *Lapsana communis* (nipplewort), small grasses, *Eleocharis palustris* (spike-rush), and *Myosotis* sp. (forget-me-not). Only evidence of economic plants from this context is one seed of *Ficus carica* (fig).

Sample <31> (376, CG96 29, Phase 1) was taken from the top layer of the sequence; it contained mainly *Urtica dioica* (nettle) and *Achillea millefolium* (yarrow), various Polygonaceae, some *Rubus* sp., 25 indeterminate grasses, and a few identifiable weed seeds, such as *Lychnis flos cuculi* (ragged robin), *Eleocharis palustris* (common spike-rush), *Capsella bursa pastoris* (shepherd's purse), *Atropa belladonna* (deadly nightshade), *Plantago major* (greater plantain) and *Anthemis cotula* (stinking chamomile). These plants were found in the <2mm fraction. In a previous assessment made by Lisa Moffett, a few additional plants were recorded from the >2mm coarse fraction of this sample: *Anagallis arvensis* (scarlet pimpernel), *Rubus* sp., *Thlaspi arvense* (field penny-cress), *Arctium lappa* (greater burdock), *Mercurialis perennis* (dog's mercury), *Ranunculus acris/repens/bulbosus* (buttercups), nutshell fragments and more seeds identifiable to genus but not to species. The seeds were not quantified and are indicated in Figure 8.4 with an asterisk.

Prunella vulgaris is present in samples <26> and <38>, *Tripleurospermum* in <31> and <26>, *Viola* subg. *Melanium, Potentilla* sp., *Rumex* sp., *Polygonum aviculare,* and indeterminate Brassicaceae (small and large) occur in all of them. All of the samples contained insects, earthworm cases, mosses and resting bodies of *Cenococcum geophilum*.

Taxa	Common name	Rumney, 11th to 13thC	Hen Domen, 11th to 13thC	Wiston, 12th to 13thC	Boteler's Castle, 12th to 13thC	Loughor, 12th to 16thC	Wigmore, 13th to 16thC
Avena sp. (grain)	Oat			x(x)	x	x	x(x)
Avena sp. (germinated)	Germinated oat				x		x
Avena sp. (chaff)	Oat chaff			x	x	x(x)	
Avena sp. (awns)	Oat awns			x	x	x	
Avena sativa L. (chaff)	Cultivated oat (chaff)	x		x	x	x	
Avena fatua L.	Wild oat	x		x	x		
Avena strigosa type (pedicels)	Oat pedicels			x			
Triticum sp., free-threshing type (grain)	Free treshing wheat				x		x
Triticum sp., free-threshing type (germinated grain)	Free-theshing germinated wheat				x		
Triticum sp., free-threshing type (rachis)	Free-threshing wheat rachis				*x*		
Triticum sp., cf free-treshing type (rachis)	cf Free-threshing wheat rachis				*x*		
Triticum sp. (grain)	Wheat			x	x		x(x)
Triticum sp. (rachis)	Wheat rachis			x	x		x
Triticum turgidum/durum (rachis)	Bread/pasta wheat				x(x)		
Triticum spelta/aestivum (rachis)	Spelt/bread wheat				x		
Triticum aestivum s.l. (grain)	Bread wheat	x	x	x			
Triticum aestivum s.l.(rachis)	Bread wheat (rachis)			x	x(x)		
Secale cereale L.(grain)	Rye			x(x)	x		x(x)
Secale cereale L. (germinated grain)	Germinated rye				x		
Secale cereale L. (rachis)	Rye rachis			x(x)	x(x)		x
Hordeum vulgare L.	Barley	x	x	x	x		
Hordeum vulgare L. (germinated grain)	Germinated barley				x		
Hordeum vulgare L. (rachis)	Barley rachis			x	x		
Hordeum vulgare (hulled grain)	Hulled barley				x		
Hordeum vulgare (straight grain)	Straight barley			x			
Hordeum vulgare (twisted grain)	Twisted barley			x			

FIGURE 8.5

Cereals: comparison with other castle sites (some spelt was found at Boteler's Castle but in association with Roman pottery, suggesting that it was probably residual)

Discussion of waterlogged plant remains

Most of the plant remains recovered from these samples consisted of weed seeds, whilst cereal remains and other edible plants were limited to two fragments of cereal bran, and two chaff fragments (one identified as *Triticum* sp., wheat) from sample <26>, one seed tentatively identified as flax and one *Ficus carica* (fig) from <38>. The charred grass from<26> is probably residual, given that it is the only carbonised remains in the whole assemblage.

Some plant remains, other than seeds, occur: buds were also fairly frequent, thorns, flower bases, bark, and one abscission scar pad. Resting bodies of Cenococcum geophilum were also present. The state of preservation varied; sample <31> was the one with the worst state, with its 75 *ignota*. Sample <38> had a decent preservation, with only eight seeds that were not identifiable.

The other waterlogged samples from Wigmore were assessed, but they were not very rich and contained the same kind of material discussed above and therefore did not add any further information to the understanding of the environment of the site.

The occurrence of seeds that normally grow on arable land, or occur as crop processing waste, such as corn cockle, stinking camomile, and field penny-cress, shows the presence of arable activity on site. However, as the deposits are the result of human action rather than natural accumulation, the cultivation might have taken place elsewhere. Interestingly, these weed seeds occur only in the bottom and middle layers (samples <26> and <38>), and not in the top one (sample <31>).

Taxa	Common name	Rumney, 11th to 13thC	Hen Domen, 11th to 13thC	Boteler's Castle, 12th to 13thC	Wiston, 12th to 13thC	Loughor, 12th to 16thC	Wigmore, 13th to 16thC
Ficus carica L.	Fig						x
Juglans regia L.	Walnut						x
Corylus avellana L.	Hazelnut		x	x		x	x
Brassica sp.	Cabbage		x			x	
Malus sp.	Apple		x				
Malus sylvestris/domestica	Apple			x			
Prunus cerasus L. type	Sour cherry						x
Prunus spinosa L.	Sloe			x			
Rubus fruticosus L. agg	Bramble		x				
Pisum sativum L.	Pea			x			(x)
Vicia faba L.	Broad bean			x			
cf *Linum usitatissimum* L.	Flax						x
Vitis vinifera L.	Grape	x					
Sambucus nigra L.	Elder	x					x

FIGURE 8.6
Economic plants: comparison with other castle sites

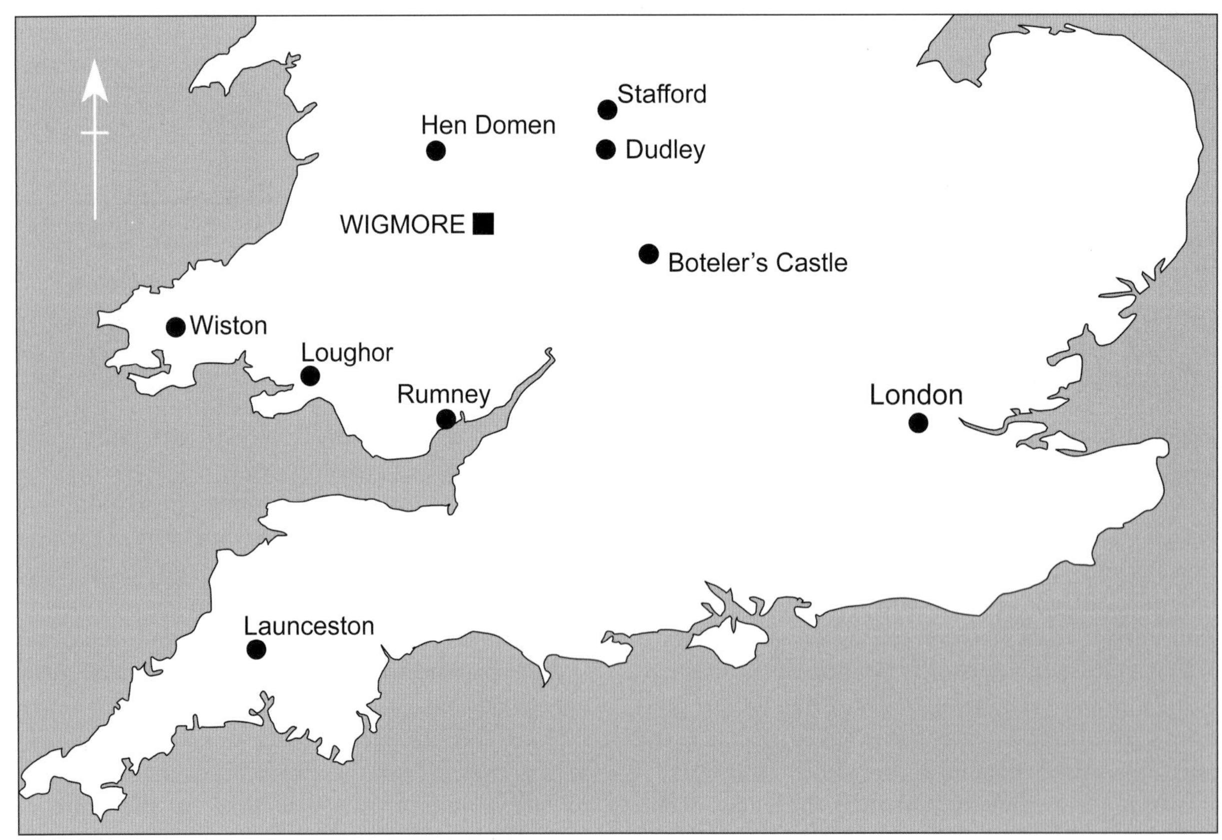

FIGURE 8.7
Map of castle sites mentioned in the text

This might mean that agricultural activity on site tends to cease or lessen in the later stage of site use. This is also shown by the occasional presence of *Cenoccocum geophilum* (resting bodies of fungus) in the top sample and its abundance in the other two. This spore has been proven to be present on arable land (Jensen 1975).

The bottom and middle contexts are also rich in seeds that grow in a damp environment, such as lesser spearwort, forget-me-not, gypsywort, rush seeds and sedges, plus other seeds that are common on pastures, like silverweed, self heal, ragged robin, lesser stitchwort and grasses. These seeds also tend to disappear in the top layer, which contains ruderal seeds, such as nettle, shepherd's purse and yarrow. Plants with an economic nature are also attested: one fig, one flax seed, hazelnut shells and some cereal remains; again they occur in the earliest phases of the sequence.

The evidence gathered from these samples indicates that while layers 362 and 381 were being deposited, the environment was fairly wet, with agricultural land and pasture somewhere in the vicinity, and that by the time layer 376 was being laid down these activities had ceased and there was a predominance of wasteland.

8.5 OVERVIEW

The plant material found at Wigmore is comparable to other roughly contemporary sites in the West Midlands and the Welsh Marches (Figures 8.5–8.7). The exception is the total absence at Wigmore of barley. Barley is attested at other castles, such as Wiston (Caseldine 1997), Hen Domen, (Greig 1982), Loughor (Carruthers 1994) in Wales and Boteler's Castle, Alcester (Moffett 1997), in Warwickshire, whilst barley rachis has been found in assemblages from Boteler's Castle and Wiston. Its absence at Wigmore might reflect a preference given to the cultivation of other cereals, like oats, in the Herefordshire region. *Triticum aestivum* (bread wheat) is attested at Boteler's Castle, Rumney (Williams 1992), Wiston and Hen Domen, but not at Loughor, and is absent at Wigmore as well. Rye is also fairly common, but is absent at Hen Domen, Rumney and Loughor.

Oat is present in all the above mentioned sites, apart from Hen Domen, but only at Wigmore and Boteler's Castle were some of the grains sprouted suggesting that oats may have been malted for brewing. Although in medieval times all large establishments consumed ale in great quantities (Stone 2006), there is not much evidence for brewing at these castles, apart from Boteler's Castle (Moffett 1997) and Wigmore. At Boteler's Castle germinated oat, barley and wheat were found, which hint at their use for making ale, whilst at Wigmore there is only evidence for the use of oats. This is suggested both by the sprouted oats recovered in the samples, the find of a malting quern (see Chapter 5), and the malted oats sold and recorded in the 1322 accounts (Chapter 2).

Some of the plants with an economic nature recovered at Wigmore have been found at other sites, the exceptions being fig, walnut, sour cherry and possibly flax (which are not attested anywhere else), whilst hazelnut is quite common and occurs at all other sites apart from Rumney (Williams 1992) and Wiston (Caseldine 1997). Peas were found at Boteler's Castle and perhaps also Wigmore, although poor preservation precluded definite identification. Broad beans were also found at Boteler's Castle. Seeds of apple (*Malus* sp. and *Malus sylvestris/domestica*) occur at Boteler's Castle (Moffett1997) and Hen Domen (Greig 1982) but are absent from Wigmore.

The presence of fruit suggests the possibility of a garden at Wigmore. In medieval times nearly every household would have had one, and in the case of castles, a garden would have provided supplies for the household and for the market, hence being an important source of income (Dyer 2006).

The lack of work on waterlogged assemblages from other medieval castle sites makes it difficult to compare Wigmore with other castles of the same age. In later times, a wider variety of plants were used, because of the rise in exotic imports. For example, figs and walnuts also occurred in a post-medieval latrine at Dudley Castle in central England (Moffet 1992). More work on medieval assemblages from other high-status sites would surely add to what we already know about diet and nutrition in medieval England.

9

AN OVERVIEW OF THE EXCAVATED EVIDENCE

Stephanie Rátkai

About this noble castle, which involves the great family of Mortimer, Earls of March, a volume might be written. But we must endeavour to compress our materials so as to make them consistent with the nature of our work

Gough (1789 II, 535)

9.1 INTRODUCTION

This chapter draws together some of the information from the specialist reports contained in this volume and from the archive reports commissioned by English Heritage before the final post-excavation project was designed. The actual excavated areas formed only a small percentage of the Inner Bailey of the castle, and the archaeological information from them presents only a small snapshot of the castle's history and development. One of the most interesting datasets, discussed in the first section of this chapter, was provided by the building materials. These can give us not only an idea of how parts of the castle may have looked but also indicate a far more complex sequence of construction and destruction than is evident in the documentary sources and suggest the castle, contrary to expectation, was flourishing in the late medieval period. This information is of particular interest when viewed against the survey of the standing fabric of the castle carried out by Jon Cooke (2008).

The second section of this chapter looks more closely at life in the castle. Again, the picture is necessarily partial, and some information could be broadly described as 'typical of a castle', and yet a study of the minutiae and debris of existence, reveals how the castle may have functioned in its immediate and wider environment. These conclusions are no less relevant, despite being derived from small samples, to the castle as a whole.

There are clearly further lines of research that could be pursued but like Gough (above) we must 'endeavour to compress our materials' and in so doing provide an entrée into the world of Wigmore Castle, not accessible through the documentary record nor through the ruins themselves.

9.2 BUILDING MATERIAL, BUILDINGS AND POSSIBLE BUILDING CAMPAIGNS

The development of the castle presents a complex picture in the two excavated areas which can, to a certain extent, be unravelled by careful consideration of the various building materials recorded, their relative distribution and taphonomy. The 1996 excavations and those within and outside the East Tower present subtly different pictures, even though, necessarily, the data derives from residual finds. The pottery, and to a lesser extent the portable finds, suggests that the demolition material had not been moved great distances and is therefore likely to reflect the buildings which were in the immediate vicinity.

Glazing

Working from the original finds registers prepared by Marches Archaeology and from two lists describing the window glass by context and from Brown's (2008) assessment report, it is apparent that most of the window glass was found in the 1996 excavation (Figure 9.1), a mere 14 pieces coming from the 1998 excavation. The 1996 window glass came, not surprisingly, from the Civil War destruction of the castle and its aftermath (Phases 10 and 11), although Brown (2008) has no record of glass from Phase 11 (at the time of writing she did not have access to all the glass nor the finalised stratigraphic reports). A single undecorated window glass fragment was found in rubble dumps post-dating the Phase 8 Curtain Wall rebuild. There is therefore a marked contrast between the amount of window glass found associated with the earlier building campaign and demolition, and with the Civil War demolition.

Of the 1998 window glass all but one fragment came from Phases 10 and 11, the one remaining fragment coming from Phase 8 (CG98 16). This would indicate a glazed building in the vicinity before the construction of the Tudor plaster floor. Slightly less glass was found within the East Tower but the paucity of glass generally from the 1998 excavations means this is of doubtful significance.

Brown (2008) notes that the glass was in poor condition and very fragmented. Examination by eye and subsequently by X-radiography revealed

Area	Context	Group	Phase	Qty	Area	Context	Group	Phase	Qty
1996	3	1	11	8	1996	28	2	10	1
1996	4	1	11	2	1996	32	2	10	7
1996	5	1	11	29	1996	36	5	9	3
1996	6	1	11	2	1996	47	7	9	1
1996	7	1	11	1	1996	51	6	9	2
1996	9	2	10	1	1996	73	8	8	1
1996	11	2	10	3	1996	u/s			7
1996	15	2	10	6	1998	523	2	11	2
1996	16	2	10	1	1998	518	3	11	4
1996	17	2	10	21	1998	541	4	10	1
1996	18	2	10	10	1998	584	13	10	1
1996	19	2	10	4	1998	580	13	10	1
1996	20	2	10	7	1998	636	16	8	1
1996	21	2	10	31	1998 (E Tower)	556	11	10	1
1996	22	2	10	13	1998 (E Tower)	611	11	10	3
Total window glass recovered from 1996									**162**
Total window glass recovered from 1998									**14**

FIGURE 9.1
Excavated window glass (figures taken from Brown 2008)

that the greater part of the 1996 fragments had borne red-painted decoration and, occasionally, red and black decoration. The decoration was non-figurative and predominantly foliate in character. Brown (2008) considered that the fragments were suggestive of high quality craftsmanship and dated to the 14th century. Three or four decorated sherds were possibly from the previous century.

The difference in the quantity of window glass from the two areas need not be significant. At Portchester Castle (Hampshire) plain and decorated window glass of late 14th century date from the Inner Bailey was dumped with tile and slate in the Outer Bailey as infill for a gully (Kenyon 2005, 171). At Dudley Castle (West Midlands), amidst numerous substantial demolition deposits, only two contained large groups of window glass (Stephen Linnane pers comm). Both deposits were found within the moat at the foot of the motte. Had these particular deposits not been excavated, a very different picture of the castle's appearance would have been surmised. In all likelihood, the windows had been taken to a discrete area where the lead was then removed for recycling and the resultant glass fragments disposed of in a convenient location, like the Portchester example. It is difficult to imagine, given the wealth of other decorative building debris in Wigmore 1998 (see below), that the glazing was not similarly ornate and the example of Dudley Castle provides a reasonable explanation for its absence. One possible significant point is that extensive evidence of lead-working, the melting down of lead scrap, came from the 1996 excavations in Phase 6. Although too early to be directly associated with the window glass from the demolition, it might point to a favoured area for this type of work and might account for the greater quantity of window glass from the 1996 excavations.

Other industrial activity, represented by smithing hearths, was carried out in or adjacent to the area of the 1996 excavations. No such evidence came from the 1998 site.

Wall plaster and mortar

Another class of building material examined during assessment only was the painted wall plaster (Cool 2008). Like the glass, this was very fragmentary and no decorative schemes could be identified. Red paint was the most commonly used but a buff/yellow colour was also found. If some of the painted plaster simply had stone courses outlined in red ('false ashlar'), then this would mirror rather well the actual appearance of the exterior of the red-mortared buildings, which belong to the earlier stone construction phases at the castle.

Decoration appeared to have been applied to a cream ground and there was no evidence of overpainting, indicating that once the painted plaster was in place, it remained so until the demolition of the buildings. Slightly more decorated wall plaster was found in the 1998 excavations which formed a higher proportion of the plaster recovered overall than was the case with the 1996 material. Tentative, prima facie evidence could, therefore, indicate a building with a more complex decorative scheme in the 1998 excavations. False ashlar has been noted at Chepstow (Monmouthshire) and Okehampton (Devon) (Kenyon 2005, 171) and a more complex red-painted geometric design at Hadleigh (Essex). Both Dolforwyn (Powys) and Dryslwyn (Carmarthenshire) castles had buildings decorated with painted wall plaster (Caple 2007, 152). At Dryslwyn, red, blue and yellow colours were used to form non-figurative, patterned designs and there were no examples of false ashlar (Caple 2007, 165). What at first seems like a rather small amount of wall plaster from Wigmore seems less so when compared with a mere 23 fragments recovered from total excavation of the Inner Ward at Dryslwyn. The possibility, therefore, exists that a good number of buildings at Wigmore had decorated wall plaster.

The use of plain whitewashed plaster rendering was attested from Phase 4 and, apart from the Civil War demolition deposits, was most common in Phase 7 (1996), where it must indicate that the building, constructed here after an episode of lead-melting (Phase 6), had a plain lime render, and Phase 8 (1996) the rebuild of the Curtain Wall, which presumably incorporated debris from the Phase 7 building. Limewash was used both on the internal and external walls at Dryslwyn (Caple 2007, 152).

Two types of mortar were identified: the earlier red-coloured, belonging to most of the construction phases of the castle, the later harder and off-white in colour and in use from the 14th century (the Phase 7 building in the 1996 excavations) and in the 15th century (where it is noticeable in the rebuild to the Southern Curtain Wall). The upper sections of the interior of the East Tower are also bonded with this mortar. This was taken by the original excavators as evidence of a rebuild but this is open to question (see Chapter 3).

There is no record of the methodology used in the collection of the mortar samples and most of the mortar from the 1998 excavations has come from the bulk samples, consequently the quantities recorded for 1996 (7072g) and for 1998 (1614g) differ significantly. Secondly, details of the mortar and its colour have not been recorded at any stage in the archive. A detailed survey of the mortar is therefore of little value.

Floor tiles

There were many small fragments of inlaid floor tiles, primarily yellow/white against a brown ground, occasionally with this colour scheme reversed, where the pattern could not be reconstructed. These formed the greater part of the recorded inlaid tiles. Identifiable designs tended towards the heraldic and Vince (2002b) notes the possibility of heraldic inlaid Bredon-type tiles being produced to order for the Mortimer family in the early 14th century. These heraldic tiles are single-tile designs. The probable lion passant design (Figure 6.7, P6) seems to have been inspired by the Wessex School of the 13th to 14th centuries (Eames 1968, plate 6, 2). A repeating four-tile pattern, the only recorded geometric design of this type combining large and small quatrefoils, is illustrated in Figure 6.7, P5. A reconstruction of a pavement tiled in this way is shown in Figure 9.2 (B). The tile pattern is paralleled (see Chapter 6) at abbey sites such as Meaux (East Riding of Yorkshire) and Godstow Abbey (Oxfordshire) (Ganz 1972, plate XVIIA). Inlaid pattern P11 may also be from a four-tile pattern and larger repeating inlaid patterns (possibly 16-tile) are indicated by patterns P4 and P8.

A smaller number of tiles had foliate impressed designs and there was one example of a fourth impressed design (pattern IP4, not illustrated) which may have originally had a central scored cross and rosette design, similar to early 15th century tiles from Basingwerk Abbey (Basingwerk 2003,

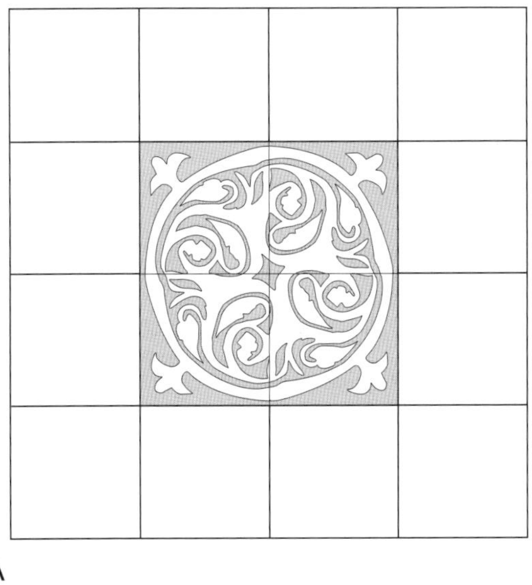

FIGURE 9.2
Suggested reconstruction of floor tile laying patterns

2000.30H/107 and /108) in Flintshire. A complete impressed tile (Figure 6.7, IP1) with a foliate design appears to come from a four-tile design (Figure 9.2, A). A similar impressed pattern was recorded at Stafford Castle (White and Soden 2007, Fig 157, 35) and has parallels elsewhere in Staffordshire and Cheshire.

The floor tile tradition in the West Midlands extends across the Marches into Wales. Tiles found at Dudley Castle and Dudley Priory, for example, occur not only elsewhere in Staffordshire but extend into Wales and are found at sites such as Montgomery Castle (Powys) and Strata Florida (Ceredigion) (see Hodder 1991, 73, fig 27). Given a general regional trend, it is likely that the inlaid tiles date to the 13th to 14th centuries and the impressed tiles to the 15th century.

There can be little doubt that ceramic floor tile was used in a building or buildings on the 1998 site, despite Mills (Chapter 6) conjecture that the material was brought from elsewhere in the castle (Figures 9.3 and 9.4). The single largest group of floor tile came from Phases 10 and 11 demolition and abandonment deposits outside the East Tower. Ceramic floor tile was found in very small amounts in Phase 5 (CG98 21) (including a triangular tile), and Phase 8 (CG98 20) outside the tower, and sporadically in deposits underlying the Phase 9 Tudor mortar floor (CG98 08). Given that these groups seem to have suffered much disturbance, it is possible that these few tile fragments are the remnants of a single early floor, although Mills thinks not (Chapter 6). The tiles appear to have been primarily undecorated and glazed yellow or dark brown. One decorated tile (Figure 6.7, P2) was present from CG98 15, Phase 8. It appears to be a fragment of an heraldic device, probably a lion passant. This design, P2, and the three lions passants design P9a/b seem to be associated with the 1998 excavation, in the area outside the East Tower. Three lions passant gardant were the royal arms, although facing to the left rather than to the right as here. However, we may see here a hint of the Mortimers' belief in their prowess and nobility which underpinned the family motto 'Not we from kings but kings from us'. Although speculative, it is possible that the putative floor was composed of a yellow and dark brown chequerboard interspersed with heraldic tiles.

In contrast to the comparatively large collection of floor tile found outside the East Tower (Figure 9.5), the tower backfill itself produced a somewhat meagre amount, the greater part of which (just over 50% by weight) came from the earliest fill (665). A fragment from two inlaid tiles, one decorated with a *cross bottony* and the other of indeterminate inlaid decoration, were recovered from the context. Later fills contained a complete tile with an impressed design (Figure 6.7, IP1) and a second with an indeterminate impressed design. An inlaid tile with a lion passant (Figure 6.7, P6) was found in a Phase 11 fill of the tower.

In the 1996 excavation considerably less floor tile was recovered than from the 1998 excavations as a whole (Figure 9.6), but more than from the backfill of the East Tower. Just over 65% came from Phases 10 and 11. The earliest fragment was found in Phase 6, associated with lead-melting, and Phase 7 associated with a building. Both fragments were from Bredon-type tiles (Fabric LZ05, Chapter 6): the former an unglazed triangular tile (FT3.2), the latter with a black glaze. A further group of tile was found in rubble post-dating the reconstruction of the Curtain Wall in Phase 8. These consisted principally of fragments from an inlaid heraldic tile showing

CG/Phase	Brick/tile	Brick	Floor tile	Ridge tile	Tile	Total
CG98 05/9	7	-	-	-	-	7
CG98 06/9	-	-	243	-	-	243
CG98 07/9	-	-	191	25	182	398
CG98 08/9	-	-	-	-	70	70
CG98 12/9	-	-	142	73	228	443
CG98 14/9	12	-	5	425	53	495
CG98 15/8	1	-	217	70	25	313
CG98 16/8	-	-	21	2744	4082	6847
CG98 17/8	23	-	-	13	-	36
CG98 20/8	32	-	310	68	587	997
CG98 21/5	98	-	129	28	6	261
CG98 09/4	39	-	-	-	-	39
CG98 23/4	-	293	-	-	-	293
CG98 24/4	39	-	-	-	-	39
CG98 25/4	39	-	-	-	-	39
Total	**290**	**293**	**1258**	**3446**	**5233**	**10520**

FIGURE 9.3
Ceramic building material, by weight, from outside the East Tower, Phases 4–9

CG/Phase	Brick/tile	Brick	Floor tile	Ridge tile	Tile	Total
CG98 01/11	-	-	398	-	-	398
CG98 02/11	116	287	6018	511	314	7246
CG98 03/11	27	196	567	109	3	902
CG98 04/10	-	-	11596	17	167	11780
CG98 13/10	113	-	1684	75	11	1883
Total	**256**	**483**	**20263**	**712**	**495**	**22209**

FIGURE 9.4

Ceramic building material, by weight, from outside the East Tower, Phases 10–11

Context	Brick/tile	Finial	Floor tile	Ridge tile	Tile	Total
665	9	15	1028	344	804	2200
644	4			67	141	212
648	10		21	123	80	234
640			14	246	43	303
630			66	53	113	232
629			187	7		194
622			27	16	46	89
611			25			25
610					63	63
604					75	75
587	4			209	136	349
550			188		125	313
556			376			376
Total	**27**	**15**	**1932**	**1065**	**1626**	**4665**

FIGURE 9.5

Ceramic building material, by weight, from within the East Tower, Phase 10; contexts arranged from earliest to latest. Only four pieces of tile (390g) were recovered from CG10, Phase 11

CG/Phase	B/T	Brick	Floor tile	Ridge Tile	Tile	Total
CG96 01/11	284	479	735	481	373	2352
CG96 02/10	808	1163	2988	702	628	6289
CG96 03/9	143	18	657	669	93	1580
CG96 05/9	20		141	149	46	356
CG96 06/9	47	50	61	28	161	347
CG96 07/9		31	58			89
CG96 08/8			753			753
CG96 09/8					35	35
CG96 10/7			227			227
CG96 11/7	71	117				188
CG96 12/6		78				78
CG96 15/6	52					52
CG96 16/6		111	55			166
CG96 17/5		53				53
CG96 18/4	517	152				669
CG96 19/4		19				19
CG96 20/4	831	77				908
CG96 22/4		108				108
CG96 23/3		66				66
CG96 24/3	314	244				558
CG96 26/2	29	226				255
CG96 27/2	324					324
CG96 29/1	65	338				403
Total	**3505**	**3330**	**5675**	**2029**	**1336**	**15875**

FIGURE 9.6

Ceramic building material, by weight, from the 1996 excavation, Phases 1–10

a cross engrailed (Figure 6.7, P7), unidentifiable fragments from a second inlaid tile both in Bredon-type ware and a black-glazed tile in fabric LZ05.1. The cross engrailed design was only found in the 1996 excavations. Only small amounts of floor tile were found in the Phase 9 context groups. The best group came from CG96 03, primarily a midden-type deposit but which also contained some demolition debris. The gothic cross design, seen on one of the tiles from the East Tower backfill (its only appearance in the 1998 excavations), was represented here.

Although the floor tile recovered from 1996 and 1998 differs markedly in quantity, which could distort any statistical analysis, nevertheless there is evidence that different tiling schemes were used in the two areas. The paucity of floor tile from within the East Tower indicates that it did not originally have a decorated tile floor or floors, or that tiles were removed from the tower when it fell into disrepair and reused. Two designs are only found among the 1996 material: inlaid tiles P7, the cross engrailed, and P11, a probable four tile design (Figure 6.7). Of the remaining inlaid tiles only P5 was found on both sites, with possibly P2 and P6 (single examples queried by Mills, in archive) also present in both. Impressed tiles with dark brown or marbled glazes were mainly a feature of 1998 with only two possible examples coming from Phase 10 in 1996.

If the proposed dating of the tiles is correct then at least two building campaigns are indicated: one using the inlaid tiles and a later programme of works using the impressed tiles. This does not take into account modifications or 'patching up' of buildings, especially in the latter years of the castle. So, for example, even when portions of floor remain *in situ*, as at the Prior's House, Whitefriars, Coventry (Woodfield 2005, 276) the northern section of the decorative scheme has become hopelessly compromised. However, the tiling scheme there of 16-pattern tiles set diagonally within a plain dark green tile background may give some idea of the layout for the multiple-tile patterns found at Wigmore. Likewise at Wigmore Abbey (Breen 2001) part of a tiled floor in the South Chapel of the church was composed of reused tiles Figures 9.7 and 9.8, many with impressed designs. It is of interest that these tiles were set in a chequerboard pattern, that is, the governing scheme was to produce alternate light and dark glazed tiles with no regard to the impressed designs on the tiles. These tiles at Wigmore Abbey also appear to be very similar to the impressed tiles from the castle.

It is unfortunate that so few tile fragments survived, the dimensions of which could be measured. It is possible nevertheless to deduce that the greater part of the tile had measurements of 125/130mm x 125/130mm. The impressed tiles were 130 x 130mm, as was one of the tiles with a 'marbled' glaze. One laying scheme can therefore be suggested for the 1998 material, which comprised the marbled impressed tiles (Mills' patterns IP3 and IP4) and the plain marbled tiles. Tiles with impressed pattern IP1 (Figure 6.7) were glazed dark brown and it is open to question whether both the dark brown and the marbled glazes were used on one pavement, although the obvious propensity for a light and dark laying scheme seen at Wigmore Abbey (above) may support this.

The inlaid tiles were slightly smaller than the impressed tiles and any laying pattern is possible, although the multiple-tile designs may have been set within plain tile surrounds (see above). Only inlaid tile pattern P7 was found on a larger tile of approximately 140 x 140mm. This is the only tile where the heraldic design is set diagonally on the tile. It is also the design which only appears among the 1996 material.

One additional scheme of decoration may be represented by the black-glazed 'mosaic' tile (Chapter 6, Mills' Floor tile 1.1), effectively half the size of a 125 x 125mm tile, and which may have been used as a border and the triangular mosaic tiles (Mills' floor tile FT5.2), whose dimensions are different and incompatible with all the other floor tile. This type of tile was found in 1998 Phase 5 and 1996 Phase 6, throwing up the possibility that some of the earliest floors at the castle were mosaic floors, a conclusion also reached by Mills (Chapter 6).

Stone flagged flooring remained *in situ* in Phase 9 in the 1998 excavations and Shaffrey (Chapter 6) records a possible floor-stone fragment from the 1996 excavations in the same phase. However flagged surfaces were noted much earlier in the Phase 5 Southern Curtain Wall construction trench (see below). Chris Caple (2007) suggests that flagstones were expensive, although hard wearing. At Dryslwyn they are associated with 13th-century occupation of the castle (Caple 2007, 153–155).

Roofing materials

A further component of the buildings was the roofing materials. There seems little doubt that dumps of these bear testament to major episodes of demolition or destruction and in the case of the ceramic component, are unlikely to have been reused, as for example, the floor tiles. Therefore, we can be reasonably sure that a large deposit of roof tile marks an important period of change at the castle.

The single largest group of ceramic roof tile in 1998 comes not from the destruction and demolition of Phases 10 and 11, but from Phase 8 CG98 16 (Figure 9.3). The ceramic roofing material recovered from this group forms some 79% of all the context groups pre-dating the Phase 9 Tudor plaster floor (CG98 08), which effectively sealed the upper deposits outside the East Tower from the lower. There is some ambiguity surrounding the nature of CG98 16 and associated features CG98 15 (a later cut) and CG98 17 (an earlier large pit). Both the original plans and colour slides make it difficult to

FIGURE 9.7
Floor tiles still in situ in the South Chapel area, Wigmore Abbey, looking east (photograph courtesy of Colin Breen, Queen's University, Belfast) (see PLATE *10)*

FIGURE 9.8
Floor tiles still in situ in the South Chapel, Wigmore Abbey, looking south (photograph courtesy of Colin Breen, Queen's University, Belfast) (see PLATE *11)*

distinguish between the three context groups and there is a possibility that all three are essentially one event, such as the digging of a very large pit against the curtain wall.

The pottery from CG98 16 suggested a date in the 15th century (Chapter 4) although a coin from the CG98 15 (SF1996, Chapter 5) predated the early- to mid-15th century. Mould (in archive) notes a runnel of lead with charcoal and mortar present, which she interprets as demolition waste or the result of an accidental fire, and the presence of a moulded stone fragment, a jamb and an ashlar block, a fragment of window glass and floor tile fragments (see above) are consistent with demolition material. A relatively large group of nails was also found. Some of the roof tile fragments are quite large and suggest that the material has not travelled a great distance before being deposited. Likewise cross-joining pottery sherds between this and earlier groups would seem to favour more or less *in situ* deposition of all the finds and demolition material. It would not be unreasonable, then, to suggest that the roof tile recovered might fairly accurately represent how one (albeit quite small) section of the roofline appeared. Mills (in archive) records brown (less commonly green) glazed ridge and crested ridge tile, and mainly unglazed flat tile with two brown-glazed examples and a possible green-glazed tile. The roofline, then, close to the East Tower, may well have consisted of an unglazed tiled roof surmounted by interspaced plain and crested glazed ridge tiles, shading from brown to green, with the first line of tiles below the ridge also being similarly glazed.

One further matter of interest is the relationship between CG98 16 and the lowest fills of the East Tower. In addition to the demolition material found in the the context group, fragments of plate armour were also present, along with horseshoe nails and part of a broken bit. The plate armour may have been disturbed from the earlier context group CG98 20. This group is dated to the 15th century by a Tournai jetton (SF1805, Chapter 5). Disturbance between the groups is certainly witnessed amongst the pottery, which finds sherds from CG98 33, 21, 20 and 17 occurring in CG98 16, but the picture is a little confused and later material could just possibly have intruded into earlier deposits. Rather larger quantities of plate armour were found in the bottom fills of the East Tower, along with ceramic building material which suggest a primary demolition deposit. The ceramic building material is nothing like as abundant as that found in CG98 16 but the basal fill of the tower (665) contains some 47% of all the ceramic building material, a likely indicator of a *bona fide* demolition deposit. The ceramic building material from 665 also contained the single largest group of floor tile, which consisted mainly of plain glazed tiles and two inlaid tiles (one pattern P12). The roof tile from the lowest excavated fill contained green-glazed ridge tile and a brown-glazed crested ridge tile of the same sort found in CG98 16. It is tempting therefore to see a link between the demolition deposit in CG98 16 and the initial decay of the East Tower (see below).

The East Tower backfill also contained yellow-glazed flat and ridge tiles and speckled-glazed flat and ridge tiles. These were a comparatively minor part of the group, with a total of five examples recorded, with two examples from the basal fill. The use of these glaze colours is very uncommon amongst the 1998 material from outside the tower. A speckled-glazed ridge tile and a yellow-glazed ridge tile were found beneath the Phase 9 Tudor floor in CG98 14 and a couple of matching flat roof tiles were found above the Tudor floor in CG98 07. The presence of similar material in CG98 14 and CG98 16 is another link between the East Tower backfill and deposits beneath the Tudor floor. Apart from this, the yellow and speckle glaze tiles would seem to indicate a different and additional roofing colour scheme, to the one suggested above. In aesthetic terms, a green-glazed finial would look well against a yellow/speckled roof.

Once the Tudor floor CG98 08 had been laid, very little ceramic roofing material occurred in disuse groups above it or in the Phase 10 and 11 destruction and abandonment levels (Figures 9.3 and 9.4). Nearly all the ceramic building material consisted of floor tile, which was found primarily in CG98 04.

In the 1996 excavation a very different distribution of roofing material is apparent (Figure 9.6). Roof and ridge tile were only found in any quantity after the Phase 8 rebuild of the Curtain Wall. Several rubble dumps and possible levelling layers were associated with the Curtain Wall, both before and after its construction. It is therefore of some interest that ceramic building materials are so poorly represented. Some of the Phase 9 roof tile may have derived from a 16th-century building campaign, detritus from which ended up in a materially rather mixed dump CG96 03. The 1996 ceramic roofing material is also of interest in that it is the only group where ridge tiles form the greater part of the roofing material. From the limited evidence there is, the roofing scheme in 1996 appears to have been different from 1998. Here, tile glazes were green or speckled, with brown glazes very poorly represented.

In addition to the ceramic roof tile, stone roof tile from a number of local sources was recorded (Chapter 6). A number of complete tiles survived but their dimensions (recorded by Kendrick 2008) show no consistency, ranging from 245mm to 370mm in width, 120mm to 230mm in length, and from 16mm to 29mm in thickness. A substantial tile fragment 370mm x 230mm x 20mm was recorded by Kendrick (2008) in Phase 1 clay dump 393 (Figure 9.9). No explanation can be offered for this. Apart from this, stone roof tile occurred sporadically in the 1996 excavations in Phases 5 to 9, Phase 11 and

Area	Ph	CG	Stone roof	Stone floor	Arch frag	Projectile	Painted stone	Plastered stone	Painted plaster	Pb runnels etc	Vitrified	Hearth bottom
96	1	29	x								x	x
96	3	24			x						x	
96	3	25										
96	4	18	x	?								x
96	4	19									x	x
96	4	20								x		
96	4	22									x	
96	5	17	x	(x)		x				x	x	x
96	6	13								x	x	x
96	6	15								x	x	x
96	6	16	xc									x
96	7	10								x		x
96	7	11	xc			x				x	x	x
96	8	8			x					x		x
96	8	9	x	x	x					x		
96	9	3									x	x
96	9	6	x								x	
96	10	2										x
96	11	1	xc								x	
Outside Tower												
98	4	9	x	x								
98	5	21	x				br					
98	5	33	x									
98	8	15	xc		x					x		
98	8	16	x		x					x		
98	8	20	xc							x		
98	9	12	x									
98	9	14	x	x								
98	9	19	x							x		
98	10	4	xc		x		x	x	x			
98	10	13	xc									
98	11	2	xc		x		br	x		x		
Eastern Tower												
98	10	11	xc		x	br						

FIGURE 9.9

Evidence of construction/destruction: stone building materials, stone projectiles, painted plaster (data from Kendrick 2008; Shaffrey, Chapter 6), lead runnels, vitrified fragments and hearth bottoms (data from Dungworth 2000); br denotes finds only recorded in the Bulk Finds Register (in archive); xc denotes complete example

possibly from Phase 4, although it is possible that all the stone tile from Phase 4 was flooring. Stone roof tile was better represented in the 1998 material, particularly in context groups from outside the East Tower. It occurred first in Phase 4 (CG98 09) in small quantities and then was found in all subsequent periods but particularly in Phases 8 and 10.

The use of ceramic tile and tilestones in the same building complex was noted at Whitefriars, Coventry, by Woodfield (2005), who also noted the difficulty of distinguishing between stone roofing material (in this case Stockingford Shale), tilestone reused as hardcore and Stockingford Shale used as packing and levelling in wall construction. Clearly, the number of perforated fragments at Wigmore testifies to the presence of stone roofing. However, it is noticeable that the majority of the retained stone tile has been perforated. This is particularly clear in the small fragments and may reflect a bias in the collection policy. If so, the overall quantity of tilestone could have been rather greater than now appears. Kendrick suggests that it is 'unlikely that high-status chambers would have been tilestone roofed', although he notes that Stokesay Castle's Great Hall, dated to the 1280s, was roofed with tilestone (Kendrick 2008, 9).

A roof scar on the gatehouse (Cooke 2008) has a shallow pitch indicating a leaded roof and Mould (Chapter 5) notes lead offcuts consistent with sheet lead roofs. However, the very nature of their deposition as scrap for recycling, precludes identifying any area, excepting the gatehouse, where buildings may have been so roofed. Clearly the roofscape at the castle must have been varied. Whether this reflects building status is open to question; availability of roofing materials must play some part. Caple (2007, 155) remarks, however, that Edward I's castles had lead roofs despite the easy availability of slate. At Dolforwyn Castle, roofing appears to have been of lead or of stone tile and no ceramic roofing materials were present (Butler 1997). At Dryslwyn, slate was used from Phase 2a when the castle was still in Welsh hands (Caple 2007, 155) but as at Dolforwyn, ceramic roofing was not used. There was some indication that some of the roofs were leaded, although Caple notes that scrap for recycling could have equally well come from gutters, flashing and down pipes. Wooden shingles were attested at Dryslwyn in the documentary record and split tilestone was used on post-medieval buildings in the Outer Ward. In Phase 11 at Wigmore, squared tilestone is recorded by Shaffrey (Chapter 6) and this may represent roofing material from the 16th century, the time of documented works at the castle.

Brick and architectural stone

In the 1998 excavation only a small quantity of brick fragments was found (11 fragments, 483g), which occurred outside the tower (Figures 9.3–9.5). It is with a certain amount of confidence, therefore, that we can say that there was no brick building in or near the 1998 excavation area. Three brick fragments (225g) came from the construction trench for the East Tower, CG98 23, Phase 4, which is puzzling. However, the industrial use of brick should not be overlooked (see below) and fragments of slag were also found in the construction trench.

Brick fragments (also included in this discussion are the indeterminate brick/tile fragments) were substantially better represented in the 1996 excavations. Unfortunately, this presents some problems. Two fragments found in Phase 1 (one not insubstantial) are clearly difficult to explain. Mortar (see above) was also found in Phase 1. This could be intrusive material but the continuing consistent presence of brick and mortar in subsequent periods before the digging of the Curtain Wall construction trench in Phase 5, throws some doubt on this. Some six hearth bottoms were, however, found in Phase 1 and all but one coming from a grey/brown clay dump (374). This is precisely the context in which the brick was found. There is therefore the very strong possibility that the 'brick' fragments represent part of an iron-working hearth. Fragments of brick from Phase 2 could then quite possibly represent disturbed material from Phase 1 which was redeposited during the construction of the timber building. It is interesting to note that a group of 26 small fragments came from two contexts associated with the Phase 2 hearth. Most of the Phase 3 fragments are from pit 271 and on the face of it seem much more likely to represent detritus from industrial activity rather than evidence for a building of brick. By Phase 4 there is a marked increase in the amount of brick or brick/tile fragments. Some 165 very fragmentary pieces were recorded. The brick fragments were spread across the Phase 4 context groups. Several deposits in this period exhibit signs of burning, including the major burnt horizon CG96 20. Could the brick fragments, therefore, point to an erstwhile oven in the vicinity? At Montgomery Castle (Knight 1991a, 21) hearth and oven tile fragments, some from crude locally produced tiles, were found in the Inner Ward. A group of Herefordshire-type redware tiles was found in a late 13th-century group, also in the Inner Ward. Brick fragments found in Phase 6 are far more likely to be associated with industrial activity (lead-melting) than reflect domestic architecture. In fact, the occurrence of brick or brick/tile fragments before Phase 9 were sparse and must surely indicate industrial activity, ovens, etc rather than represent aspects of domestic architecture. By Phase 9 there is a case to be made for the architectural use of brick; it is found for example in dump CG96 03, which we have seen (above) contained other architectural debris and by Phase 10 there are more substantial fragments of brick recorded. Even so there is not enough to suggest a brick building on the 1996 site, although chimneys and hearths are a possibility.

A small number of architectural fragments (Figure 9.10) was found during excavation and subsequently recorded by David Kendrick (2008). Little can be said about the fragments. Most of the 1998 material, not surprisingly, occurred in demolition and disuse layers of Phases 10 and 11. Three fragments (an ashlar block of the late 11th–early 14th century and an undatable jamb) were found in CG98 16, together with a moulding (undatable) in CG98 15. This is of interest only in that other demolition material was found in these context groups. In the Phase 10 and 11 deposits, fragments from a ridge rib and boss hint at a 'high status, small domestic area, such as a porch, dating from the late 13th century into the 14th century' (Kendrick 2008). There is no reason to assume that these fragments were reused masonry from Wigmore Abbey, a tentative alternative interpretation put forward by Kendrick (2008).

No architectural fragments came from Phases 10 or 11 on the 1996 site. A bead moulding (undatable) and part of a chimney/fireplace (undatable) were found in CG96 09 and CG96 08 respectively. The former context group marks the rebuild of the Curtain Wall in Phase 8 and the latter a build up of rubble against the rebuilt wall. A further, undatable fragment with a curved inner face was found in Phase 3, CG96 24. Kendrick suggests that it may be from a well or possibly part of a fireback, although unsooted. A fireplace back of similar style and dimensions has been found at Kenilworth Castle (Warwickshire) although the date of this feature is

Year	Context	CG	Phase	sf	Type	Description	Date
1996	393	29	1		T19	Tile, no peg hole, 370 x 230 x 20	
1996	270	24	3		T02	Wellstone/fireback not sooted	
1996	196	17	5		T05	Ballista balls	
1996	196	17	5		T05	Ballista balls	
1996	196	17	5		T05	Ballista balls	
1996	147	16	6		T19	Tile, burnt?	
1996	176	16	6		T19	Tile complete 250 x 130 x 16	
1996	88	11	7		T19	Tile complete 325 x 160 x 23	
1996	158	11	7		T19	Tile complete 270 x 175 x 25	
1996	158	11	7		T05	Trebuchet stone	Post 1200
1996	66	8	8	85	T01	Chimney/fireplace	
1996	82	9	8		T20	Stone flag?	
1996	80	9	8	129	T04	Bead moulding	Late 13thC
1996	82	9	8		T03	Curving frag possibly connected to T02	
1998	667	15	8	1875	T17	Moulding	
1998	667	15	8		T19	Tile complete 275 x 150 x 19	
1998	671	16	8	1866	T12	Jamb	
1998	636	16	8	1995	T18	Ashlar	Late 11th–early 14thC
1998	632	20	8		T19	Tile complete? 300 x 120 x 18	
1998	560	12	9		T19	Ttile, reused, 245 x 195 x 16	
1998	638	14	9		T19	Tile	
1998	538	4	10	1564	T08	Rib/vault limewashed	14thC or later
1998	537	4	10	1599	T08		
1998	542	4	10		T19	Tile	
1998	537	4	10	1597	T13	Jamb base	Probably 14thC
1998	538	4	10	7502	T11	Painted stone, resid limewash and scarlet paint	
1998	538	4	10	1563	T10	Painted plaster, purplish red paint	
1998	538	4	10	1570	T09	Boss/vault, reused	Later 13th–early 14thC
1998	604	11	10	1646	T06		
1998	604	11	10	1646	T06	Moulding blind tracery or similar	*c*1250–1325/35
1998	587	11	10		T19	Tile complete 350 x 225 x 20	
1998	556	11	10	1585	T16	Voussoir	*c*1300
1998	556	11	10	1584	T14	Chamfer stop, 13th–early 14thC	13th–early 14thC
1998	563	13	10	1619	T21	Fossil	
1998	519	2	11	1528	T08		
1998	519	2	11	1513	T08		
1998	525	2	11	1587	T08		
1998	517	2	11	1537	T15		13thC
1998	525	2	11	1587	T07	Rib/vault lime-washed, associated with T08 and T09?	13thC, possibly 1290–1300
1998	519	2	11		T19	Tile complete? 360 x 220 x 29	

FIGURE 9.10

Architectural stone (measurements in mm; data from Kendrick 2008)

not given by Kendrick. CG96 24 consisted of three intercutting pits the middle one of which contained the architectural fragment. The pit also contained 244g of brick and 314g of brick/tile (Figure 9.6) which it is suggested may have derived from a hearth or oven (see above) and vitrified building debris indicating demolition or fire debris. The presence of a stone fragment possibly from a fireplace or flue in the same pit is, therefore, of interest and would tend to suggest that it is less likely to be a well stone. Unfortunately it is difficult to date CG96 24 very precisely because there is a strong possibility that the pottery in the pit represents residual material (see Chapter 4).

Although the architectural fragments were somewhat disappointing, there is a glimpse of the possible opulence of Wigmore Castle provided by one fragment with traces of scarlet paint which was found in a demolition deposit CG98 04. Two other painted stone fragments were noted in the bulk finds register from CG98 21, Phase 5 and CG98 02, Phase 11. These are not discussed by Kendrick and it is therefore unclear whether they were incorrectly identified initially or whether they were not seen during the preparation of the archive report. This is unfortunate since painted stonework in Phase 5 would considerably pre-date any embellishments made to the castle by the first Earl of March.

The construction sequence

Taken together, how can the various building materials and other artefact classes inform our understanding of the castle's appearance and development witnessed in the excavated areas? The evidence from 1996 is incontrovertible in establishing that the castle was in existence on its present site in the later 11th century. The ceramics, the fiddlekey horseshoe nail dating to the 10th to 11th centuries and the coin of William II (SF112, even though found residually) all seem convincing and the clay bank and the associated timber, possibly part of a palisade, are also consistent with an early date. However, the Phase 1 clay dumps may not be a single construction event. Three environmental samples were taken from these clay deposits. Two (<26> and <38>) were taken from levels below the putative timber palisade, from material which would have formed the first defensive bank; the third (<31>) came from a layer above the timber post. Vitolo (Chapter 8) observed that the lower samples contained a different suite of plant remains from the upper sample. The lower samples bore the hallmarks of agricultural and pastoral land use whilst the upper she describes as a 'wasteland' (the contents of these samples are discussed more fully below). The upper layers also contain most of the artefactual and ceramic finds (including small fragments of building material), small quantities of mortar and faunal material. Linnane (Chapter 3) suggests that there may be an occupation surface associated with the timber, which by implication suggests a break in the sequence of dumps. He also notes that the marked slope to the south seen in the lower deposits is not apparent in the upper. It is therefore possible that the later clay dumps were infill or levelling material. A possible sequence of events suggests itself, although these are speculative (excavation on the exterior of the Southern Curtain Wall might have elucidated matters). This sequence would begin with the turf line of the virgin site, over which a defensive bank was constructed, surmounted by a timber palisade. This arrangement was modified, presumably in the 12th century, when the bank was partly levelled, and a curtain wall, slightly to the south of the defensive bank could have been constructed. The offset noted by Linnane at the foot of the Southern Curtain Wall may be the vestiges of this original wall. The resultant gap or hollow between the curtain wall and the southern slope of the bank was then infilled with material from inside the Inner Bailey. The presence of (admittedly small amounts of) mortar might favour this interpretation. There is an alternative possibility; that beyond the southern slope of the bank the area was revetted with timber and material dumped to form an extended building platform. At Loughor Castle (Glamorgan), for example, the site (originally a ringwork) was widened in Phase 2 by the addition of layers to form a suitable platform for building (Lewis 1994, 102). Both possibilities would neatly explain the differences in the environmental samples from Wigmore, not least the peak in nettle seeds, a weed associated with human habitation (see below). The six complete smithing hearth bottoms and four fragments of the same, vitrified hearth lining and cinder, found in the upper levels, not only attest to iron smithing within the immediate vicinity but are entirely consistent with an intense period of construction. Further smithing hearth bottoms were found in the Phase 5 construction trench (CG96 17, see below) where they are interpreted as related to the construction (or now possibly reconstruction) of the Southern Curtain Wall, although Dungworth (2000) thought they may have been redeposited from Phase 1.

An earth-fast post timber building CG96 26 and CG96 27 was quickly erected (Phase 2). Only a small area of this building was seen because of the depth of excavation at this point and because of disturbance by later pit-cutting. However, the floor of the building appeared to have been clay. Mortar found in Phase 2 may be evidence that a curtain wall was already standing (see above). The building, if not solely a kitchen (see below), certainly contained one. The evidence for this is varied. Firstly, the largest group of eggshell, including the only incidence of goose egg, and a large group of fishbone were found, mainly associated with the hearth CG96 27 but also with CG96 26. Animal bone, particularly that of domesticated fowl (see below), was also associated with the kitchen. Finds of a possible iron skewer and a copper alloy knife hilt plate are consistent with the preparation or consumption of food (Chapter 5) and the pottery from this period has internal limescale, caused by repeated boiling of water in the vessel (Chapter 4). On the Bayeux Tapestry small birds and other delicacies are shown being cooked on skewers, for example (Figure 9.11). Part of a horseshoe found on hearth 351 is of a type dated to the later 11th and 12th centuries and confirms the early date of the hearth and associated structure. Again, at Loughor Castle (Glamorgan), the earliest identifiable building was a timber kitchen (which was twice destroyed by fire). A slightly later weather-boarded, earth-fast post timber kitchen, remarkably preserved due to water-logging, was excavated at Weoley Castle in the West Midlands (Oswald 1963). Unfortunately, the excavation report contains no information on the faunal remains.

Once the Phase 2 timber building had gone out of use, a series of levelling deposits were laid down in Phase 3 (CG96 25). Much of the material found in the earlier two contexts Groups CG96 25 and 24 (a group of intercutting pits) appeared to have been redeposited from Phase 2. Vitrified building debris was noted in both context groups, which are possible indicators of demolition or fire debris. These groups were sealed by an irregular yellow clay working surface (CG96 23), which was in turn overlain by occupation surfaces. Evidence of faecal matter was found in both CG 23 and 24 (see Vitolo, Chapter 8). Some residual material was also present here, most notably the silver halfpenny

FIGURE 9.11
Detail of the Bayeux Tapestry showing cooking practices

of William II (SF112), which Symons suggests was deposited around 1092–1100/1105. However, this context group marks the first appearance of the locally produced micaceous siltstone-tempered ware (Fabric MS01, see Chapter 4) which was found in the uppermost deposit of CG96 23 and suggests a date in the early 13th century. There was very little animal bone, pottery or other finds from Phase 3. After the removal of the Phase 2 building, therefore, this area appears to have been a vacant lot where domestic debris was periodically dumped.

How much time elapsed between the accumulation of the Phase 3 occupation deposits and the build up of Phase 4 deposits (CG96 22) is difficult to tell. Burnt clay lenses and vitrified building material in CG96 22 attest to clearance of fire or demolition material. Rátkai (Chapter 4) argues for a date in the third quarter of the 13th century for the ceramics from this group. Mould (Chapter 5) believes that the presence of a cuboid horseshoe nail in CG96 22 points to a date towards the end of the 13th century. Horseshoe nails are a better indicator of date and the context group must date, therefore to some time after *c*1270. Mortar in Phase 3 (800g) and Phase 4 (1055g) may be evidence that a stone curtain wall was in existence.

The activity represented by CG96 22 was sealed by a thick layer of charcoal-rich deposits. This clearly represents a major conflagration. The thickness of the burnt layer and the absence of signs of weathering or dissipation of the deposit strongly suggest that it was quickly covered over by the levelling deposits of CG96 19. The probability is that the burning indicates the presence of a building but only a small group of timber nails were found within the burning and there was very little pottery and bone, none of which was burnt. The absence of pottery and bone would seem to indicate that this was not a domestic building. At Loughor Castle, Lewis (1994, 114–115) notes that quantities of domestic and other detritus, found within burnt layers, were unburnt and interprets this as evidence of ransacking. Mould (Chapter 5) notes a trimming of lead sheet and fine-gauge iron wire from within the Wigmore deposit and believes that this may be debris swept up and dumped after the fire. The function of the fine-gauge wire is uncertain. Mould suggests that it may be part of a woman's headdress, which is an attractive theory, but elaborate headdresses appear to be mainly a feature of the 14th and later centuries, although Fairholt (1976, 223–224) gives references to 'horns' and 'bosses' in the literature of the late 13th and early 14th centuries. Whatever the use of the wire, its fine gauge indicates that it would have been time consuming and expensive to produce.

The dumps, occupation surfaces and occasional pit-digging witnessed in CG96 19 and 18, may have occurred in a relatively short space of time. There is clearly much redeposited earlier material. The pottery evidence from CG96 19 indicates a deposition date in the last quarter of the 13th century at the earliest. Amounts of destruction or demolition debris, such as timber nails, vitrified building debris and an iron wall hook, were found in both groups. Animal and fish bone, and eggshell indicate food waste was also present. Most interestingly, smithing hearth bottoms were found in both CG96 18 and 19. The occurrence of smithing hearth bottoms at this and other castle sites seems to be indicative of periods of construction (Kenyon 2005, 164). Although physical remains of new buildings in the 1996 excavations cannot be picked out readily at this time, the hearth bottoms may indicate that a programme of works had already begun at the castle in this general area, in advance of the construction or reconstruction of the Southern Curtain Wall in the following Phase. Any Phase 4 building activity would be roughly contemporary with the construction of the East Tower and associated wall 711 in the 1998 excavations.

The Phase 3 and Phase 4 evidence shows that the Phase 2 timber building had disappeared by the early 13th century at the latest. Evidence for any structures dating to Phase 4 is scant and consists of a 'ditch' (CG96 22) and a possible fence or wattle partition (CG98 21). Stephen Linnane (Chapter 3) notes that the fence/partition was on the same alignment as a Phase 7 wall (CG96 11). This is the only evidence which might indicate that the line of five stake-holes forming the fence/partition might have been more significant than first appears and formed part of a larger structure. The ditch (CG96 22) ran parallel with the Southern Curtain Wall. Unfortunately this was seriously truncated by the Phase 5 construction trench for the Southern Curtain Wall. Linnane (pers comm) feels that although the evidence is equivocal, the surviving sections of the ditch are too insignificant to be the remains of an earlier defensive wall line. From the early 13th century until the late 13th century, various deposits of demolition, domestic and industrial material accumulated, interspersed with pit digging. Small areas of metalling in CG96 19 may indicate attempts to regularise the area.

The advent of Phase 5 marked a major constructional phase at the castle (Figure 9.12). In the 1996 excavation a substantial construction trench (CG96 17) for the Southern Curtain Wall was revealed. The fill sequence was interleaved with red mortar or mortar-like layers, and three stone-slabbed working surfaces, possibly laid to provide a secure footing for scaffolding, and the construction trench appears to have been re-cut at least twice during the construction process. This has been interpreted by Linnane (Chapter 3) as an attempt to 'tidy up' the trench edge as work continued. There is some confusion regarding the east and west section drawings where these cuts are more obvious on the western section, less so on the eastern side, so the interpretation of the cuts is somewhat obscure. However, Cooke (2008), by studying the put-log holes in the extant standing masonry, suggests that the wall construction proceeded in a series of 'lifts', occasioned by the need to allow the mortar to 'go off' before the wall was raised any higher. It is therefore possible that the re-cuts and 'working surfaces' encountered in the construction trench are related to this.

The lower fills of the construction trench were curiously devoid of domestic artefacts, pottery and faunal remains. These do not appear until after the second stone-slabbed working surface (see Figure 9.8). The first finds occurred in the layer immediately below the second working surface and consisted of timber nails and a complete smithing hearth. Dungworth (2000) considered that the hearth may have been redeposited from Phase 1 (see above) but this seems unlikely and it is perhaps best viewed as ancillary to the Southern Curtain Wall construction. Further smithing hearth fragments and timber nails were found in the middle fills along with small amounts of pottery. The later fill containing a smithing hearth fragment was rich in animal bone and also contained structural ironwork, building materials, a knife, an awl and pottery. The layer immediately above this contained three ballista

Construction trench CG96, Period 5	**Finds**
Backfills	Pottery, animal bone*, brick, timber nails
Red-brown gritty layer and rubble layer	None
Backfills	Pottery, animal bone (x1 fragment), vitrified building material
Red gritty layer	None
CUT	
Backfills	Pottery, animal bone, rivet, washer, finial
Red-brown gritty layers, rubble	Pottery, animal bone, brick, ballista balls, shears
Backfill	Pottery, animal bone, fish bone, smithing hearth fragment, building material, structural ironwork, knife, awl
Red gritty layer	None
Backfills	Pottery, animal bone*, fish bone, smithing hearth fragment, timber nails
Stone slabbed working surface	None
Backfill	Complete smithing hearth, timber nails
Red mortar	None
Backfill	None
CUT	
Backfills	One bone fragment
Stone slabbed working surface	None
Backfill	None
Stone slabbed working surface	None
Southern Curtain Wall foundation	None
CUT for the Southern Curtain Wall construction trench	

FIGURE 9.12

Schematic representation of the Phase 5 Curtain Wall construction (denotes a large assemblage)*

balls. Kendrick dates these to after *c*1200, which is too late for the mid-12th-century siege of the castle during the rebellion against Henry II, and possibly too late for William Longchamp's attack on the castle in the early 1190s. They could conceivably be associated with de Montfort's attack on the castle in 1264, which appears from the documentary record may have caused rather more damage to the castle than the previous incursions. Alternatively, rather than 'incoming' missiles, they may have formed part of the castle's stockpile of 'outgoing' munitions. There is, for example, a record of a large amount of war machinery at the castle in the early 14th century (Mortimer 2004, 117) and a possible crannequin of 14th century date (see Mould, Chapter 5) was identified in Phase 8.

Moving to the Phase 4 East Tower and the earlier, Phase 3, associated Curtain Wall, there is only a single 12th-century sherd recorded in the East Tower construction trench (CG98 23). Other finds in the fill consisted of part of a rotary key, a nail shank and iron slag. A further iron artefact may have been from a nailed binding but the possibility exists that this was part of a scale tang knife. If the latter is correct, then the artefact would post-date the mid-14th century. Whatever the interpretation of this artefact and its associated dating, the East Tower construction trench cut deposits containing pottery datable to later than *c*1250. The pottery in these deposits is directly comparable to that recovered from deposits cut by the Southern Curtain Wall construction trench, where the ceramic evidence suggests that the wall is unlikely to have been constructed before *c*1300 (see Chapters 4 and 10). Some corroborative evidence can be found in the fish bone. All three fragments from the Southern Curtain Wall construction trench came from the cod family. Cod does not seem to have become a regular part of the diet (superseding herring, see below) until the later 13th or 14th century. This seems rather late for the first stone defences, particularly as there is some tantalising evidence for Norman stone construction elsewhere on the site (Chapter 2). This directly links Wigmore to Chepstow Castle, like Wigmore, another of William fitz Osbern's castles and notable for its stone hall, part of the original castle construction. It seems likely then that a stone defensive circuit was in existence in the 12th century (see above) but there is no definite archaeological proof for this from either of the two excavated areas at Wigmore. However, we can perhaps see in the offset at the base of the Southern Curtain Wall the possibility of an earlier structure. It is also possible to see in the initial sterile backfill layers of the construction trench a relic of earlier work. These sterile layers (see Figure 9.9) were sealed by a deposit of red mortar which lay immediately below the fill containing the complete smithing hearth. In the 1998 excavations, a 'red gritty layer' was recorded above a layer which apparently predated all construction in the area. These mortar layers may therefore be vestiges of earlier construction work. If so, then the Phase 5 construction trench may represent repairs or modification to the Southern Curtain Wall. We can perhaps see the reason for this in the ballista balls found in one of the later fills, although other interpretations are possible (see above). Although tentative, it is possible that repair to the Southern Curtain Wall was necessary following de Montfort's attack on the castle in 1264. Alternatively, works at the castle may be linked to Roger (V) Mortimer's known presence at Wigmore in 1310, 1314 and 1316. Ian Mortimer (2004, 117–118) notes that in 1322 Roger's finer possessions were at Wigmore Abbey. They may have been moved there earlier for safe-keeping whilst the castle was under reconstruction. However, Caple (2007, 165) notes that at Dryslwyn mortar of identical composition was used for walls and floors and there is a possibility that some of the 'red gritty' and mortary spreads sometimes imperfectly recorded by the excavators were vestiges of floor surfaces.

Once work on the Southern Curtain Wall was completed, a clay surface was laid down. This appears to have been an external surface. Deposits formed over this containing a variety of finds. A rather crude Merels board and stone counter (see Shaffrey, Chapter 5) were found along with other domestic items, a horseshoe and timber nails, animal bone and a small amount of floor tile (its first occurrence on the 1996 site) and a small amount of very fragmentary pottery. The artefactual and pottery evidence suggests that much of the material here was redeposited, rather than being *in situ* occupation deposits.

There then followed an episode of lead-melting. It is clear from the scrap that survives that structural lead was being melted down, including window cames. This indicates glazed windows in the castle before *c*1300. Mould (Chapter 5) feels the lead-melting is indicative of demolition, the resultant lead ingots being taken from the site for sale or reuse elsewhere. However, in the face of the major building programme associated with the Southern Curtain Wall, the lead may have been melted down but then reused elsewhere in the castle. Documentary evidence reveals that Roger (V) Mortimer was granted lead from Hanley Castle by the king in the late 1320s (Chapter 2). The lead-melting at Wigmore may date to this or the previous decade. In *c*1328 Roger was involved in work on Ludlow Castle and possibly also Wigmore. There is therefore the possibility that that the lead from Wigmore was taken to Ludlow in furtherance of the works there. However, Kenyon (2005, 164) notes that building works could result in the setting up of workshops within pre-existing buildings which were subsequently demolished or rebuilt. At Portchester, the Hall was used for lead-melting in the late 14th century, with two hearths set into the floor (Kenyon 2005, 164). A temporary smithy was also constructed in the courtyard. A similar picture is seen at Sandal Castle (Mayes and Butler 1983), where lead- and iron-working hearths were associated with the conversion of the castle from timber to stone.

Vitrified timber associated with the lead-melting hearths was all oak. Vitolo comments (Chapter 8) that oak has a higher calorific value and as such is often favoured for industrial processes. Since lead has a low melting point this would seem to be less germane here and the possibility remains that the oak represents disused structural timbers. This would be consistent with a general period of demolition at the castle. Gill Campbell (pers comm) notes that the vitrified oak bore no sign of insect attack which would be unusual in structural timbers but suggests that the wood used in the hearths as fuel could be offcuts left from the replacement of timbers, that is, the evidence represents construction rather than demolition.

Whilst the lead-melting was underway, further small amounts of domestic rubbish accumulated. Part of a rotary quern (Chapter 5) was found in a pit in CG96 15 and in the same context group CG96 13 a small fragment of possible plate armour was noted. This is the earliest period in which plate armour was found. It is interesting to note that an inventory (de Charlton's Inventory) of Roger (V)'s possessions taken after his arrest in 1322 (Mortimer 2004, 116–117) notes an abundance of plate and other armour at the castle (although a greater quantity of armour, and of better quality, had been temporarily stored at Wigmore Abbey). Very small fragments of pottery were found associated with all the lead-melting hearths, some of which were burnt but other artefacts were few. In the midst of a picture which seems to show a general scatter of redeposited material, one of the more bizarre finds was found. This was a cache of chicken feet (Chapter 7). The feet clearly represent a primary dump of food preparation waste and might be taken to indicate that a kitchen was close by, were it not for the total absence of any other corroborating evidence apart from a butchery knife from occupation layer 168. A single unglazed triangular floor tile from a mosaic floor was found in the same layer 168, together with the butchery knife, a buckle and a key.

In Phase 7, there is, once more, concrete evidence of a building in this area of the castle, the first such evidence since the timber building of Phase 2. It was stone built and faced with white plaster on the interior. The building ran parallel to the Southern Curtain Wall with the main entrance facing the curtain wall. Unfortunately no finds or pottery were recovered from the construction trench of the building. The purpose of the building remains unknown. An irregular mortar surface immediately outside the entrance to the building may have been intended to strengthen the area. If so, this perhaps suggests frequent heavy traffic into the building. From the artefactual and other evidence (below) it is difficult to believe that this was anything but an ancillary building.

The pottery from within the building was little different from that encountered in Phase 6 and again the small sherd size and residual material suggests that this is largely redeposited pottery. This is most apparent in the construction of clay floor 158 which contained the largest pottery group. The floor lay above surface 168 of CG96 16, Phase 6. Definite fragments of plate armour were found in 158, providing another link with the previous period (see above) and possible redeposition. Further finds of an awl, a pierced terminal and part of a trebuchet ball are almost certainly redeposited also. Deposits above 158 may represent occupation. The paucity of animal bone and pottery is consistent with the surfaces having been kept clean whilst the building was in use but the presence of horseshoe nails and ceramic building material may be more consistent with make-up material brought into the building or material disturbed from underlying levels.

The building post-dates the lead-melting of Phase 6. Linnane (Chapter 3) suggests that the building stood for some time. It appears to have had a new clay floor laid over the deposits discussed above. Again very little pottery or bone, and no artefacts were found in layers above the new clay floor. However, two lead-working hearth bottoms were found in the clay floor and fragments in a later clay layer, possibly the final floor surface. Wall plaster above this suggests that the building fell into decay (see below). Were the hearth bottoms redeposited from the Phase 6 lead-melting or do they represent, along with the smithing hearth bottom from a Phase 7 pit (see below), a new bout of building? A lump of lead that had solidified in the bowl of a ladle and been subsequently discarded came from a patch clay 086 close to pit 091(which contained the smithing hearth bottom) and dated to Phase 7. The lead discard seems to indicate that, indeed, there was further lead-working in the vicinity in Phase 7. Although there is no conclusive evidence to show that the Phase 7 building was used for lead-working *in situ*, it may have functioned as something like a workshop, along similar lines to examples given by Kenyon (2005 164).

The Phase 7 rectangular pit CG96 10 (discussed above) which post-dated the lead-working spreads of CG96 13 (Phase 6) contained the fragment of the smithing hearth bottom in its basal fill, evidence of a different metal-working process. Apart from the basal fill, which also contained timber nails and very small amounts of pottery and bone, the remaining fill sequence was devoid of finds. The layer cut by the pit also contained a fragment of a plain, black-glazed floor tile.

No Malvern Chase pottery was found in Phases 6 or 7. It suggests that Phase 7 had come to an end by *c*1350/75 but there is an important caveat. If the pottery is redeposited material then there may be no artefacts which are contemporary with the building. No Malvern Chase ware came from rubble dumps 81 and 82 CG96 09 which sealed the Phase 7 activity. These dumps, the first in a series which continued into Phase 9, are interpreted as a prelude to a rebuild of the Southern Curtain Wall. Some demolition material was found in the dumps and included timber nails, a small amount of ceramic and stone roof tile, pieces of lead sheet (some partially melted), a flagstone and two architectural stone fragments. The first of these was a late 13th-century bead moulding; the second was a curving fragment which Kendrick suggests might be connected with the chimney or wellstone fragment found in Phase 3 (see above). If they are connected, it suggests that material is being churned up and redeposited in quite limited areas. Some of this demolition material must be derived from the Phase 7 building. The moulding is proof that some more elaborate construction work was carried out before Roger (V) Mortimer's tenure of the castle in the early 14th century and is a useful corrective against the assumption that all the major domestic buildings in the Inner Bailey must date from his time.

This rubble was cut by a construction trench for the new curtain wall. The fills were largely devoid of pottery. However, one fill did contain two tiny fragments of Malvern Chase ware (*c*1% by weight of the context group). This context group seems largely analogous to CG98 20 which contained demolition and other debris culminating in the laying of a plaster floor (see below), although this contained slightly more Malvern Chase ware. We can therefore see traces of an 'event', which involved the construction of a new building aligned at right angles to the Curtain Wall by the East Tower, modifications to the tower itself (see below) and the rebuilding of the Southern Curtain Wall. Although it is hazardous to combine both documentary and archaeological evidence, we could perhaps see in the disuse of the Phase 7 building a reflection of the statement of 1425 that 'the castle is derelict and worth nothing' (Chapter 2) and the subsequent works outlined above and below as reflecting 'further repairs to the castle' in 1438–39. Linnane (Chapter 3) is surely correct in viewing further rubble dumps CG96 08 as a general levelling of the area up to the rebuilt Curtain Wall, using demolition and other debris. These dumps contained a much greater amount of Malvern Chase ware (some 66% of the context group by weight), although this is a rather odd spike in an otherwise steadily increasing chronological progression. It seems likely, however, that the levelling took place in the 15th century. Again it is possible that the major demolition horizon CG98 16 (see below) is contemporary with CG96 08. A worked stone from a chimney or fireplace was found in CG96 08 together with a small amount of floor tile. Strangely there was no roof tile in this group and only a very small amount in CG96 09 associated with demolition and the rebuilding of the Curtain Wall. This could suggest that the Phase 7 building was roofed in something other than ceramic tile or, rather less likely, that the tile had been salvaged for reuse elsewhere in the castle.

The Phase 8 Southern Curtain Wall rebuild also contained a niche or alcove set into it. The alcove and the subsequent Phase 9 deposits excavated in the 1996 excavations present somewhat conflicting evidence. The presence of the alcove would logically suggest that this section of the curtain wall was internal to a building but no other evidence exists for such a structure, which presumably would have been of stone. It is possible that the footprint of the building lay outside the area of the excavation trench, in which case it would have run at right angles to the Southern Curtain Wall and have been a fairly substantial structure. The blocking of the niche before the demolition of the castle — the pottery indicates that this was done by *c*1600 — suggests that the building was still standing at this time. The pottery from behind the blocking was quite different from any other group on site. No artefacts were recovered from behind the blocking but a small amount of building debris (window glass, ceramic roof tile, brick and floor tile) were present. However, the date of the pottery does not date the blocking itself but merely gives a *terminus ante quem* for its construction. In fact, the presence of some building debris behind the blocking is symptomatic of a period of dereliction or even demolition which is at odds with an evident repair or modification to the alcove.

It has been suggested by Cooke (2008) that the alcove may have been a fireplace, but there are problems with this interpretation, not least that the base of the alcove does not marry up with any excavated floor surface, yet is insufficiently elevated to have belonged to the first floor of a building. Neither sooting nor burning was noted in the alcove and Linnane (Chapter 3) notes the absence of any dressed stonework. A second proposal by Cooke (2008) that the alcove was a latrine shaft is hard to support on various grounds not least its blocking.

During Phase 9 a series of mainly rubble deposits built up. If the building outlined above existed then these deposits were within the building. Only two contexts were found associated with them which could conceivably have been floor surfaces, 045 CG96 06 and 033 CG96 04. The latter, a plaster surface, could only be dated by reference to the underlying rubble dumps of CG96 07 and 06. There was no coherent structure to these dumps but brown gritty clay surface 045 CG96 06 within the dumps, virtually an interface between the two context groups, on coin and pottery evidence, dated to the later 15th century. The dumps contained an indecipherable amalgam of small amounts of mixed building debris, metalwork, pottery, animal bone (spread unevenly through the various contexts), fish bone, eggshell and marine shell. Mould (in archive) noted some modern disturbance into these deposits and Rátkai (Chapter 4) recorded several pottery cross-joins which linked 045, CG96 06 with CG96 09 and CG96 07 and several cross-joins within each context group, so there is clearly much disturbance. The absence of Cistercian ware in CG96 06 may suggest that it had been deposited before the final two decades of the 15th century. Residual pottery and artefacts were also present. There was no evidence of the dumps having been cut into or reworked, so the obvious conclusion is that they were deposited in fairly short order. However, if CG96 07 and 06 are composed of a series of rapidly disposed dumps, it remains a mystery why in the midst of this someone would wish purposefully to lay surface 045. Neither surface 045 nor the plaster surface, which was only some 3 x 1m, and backed onto the curtain wall, had the appearance of an internal floor surface. There was no evidence that more substantial floor surfaces had been removed, so we are left, effectively, with a building without floors and without any discernible excavated footprint. An increased area of excavation might have been able to answer the conflicting evidence.

The plaster surface appears to have been more or less contemporary with rubbish dump CG96 03, which lay in the central and northern part of the excavation trench. This dump appeared to be a fairly coherent 16th-century group, although there was a small amount of residual material, hardly surprising in view of all the disturbance witnessed in the previous context groups. Food waste (animal bone and marine shell) was well represented and there was a small collection of domestic ironwork including a knife of 15th- or 16th-century date, used for either carving or serving at the table. Yet more building or demolition debris was found in the dump and comprised roof and floor tile, and brick. Vitrified building material was also present and perhaps most surprisingly six complete smithing hearth bottoms, fragments of the same, and iron-smithing slags. This must surely point to Bishop Lee's or Sir Henry Sydney's documented works at the castle.

The presence of CG96 03 within the putative building must indicate, if nothing else, that the building had gone out of use in the 16th century and, as in the 1998 excavations, been seen as a suitable place to dump unwanted detritus. If so, the plaster surface 033 may represent little more than a dump of waste building material.

In essence, Phase 8 saw the reconstruction of the Southern Curtain Wall (with alcove) accompanied by the probable construction of a building running at right angles to it in the 15th century. The building evidently did not last long since by the 16th century it was derelict, possibly by the time of Roland Lee in the 1530s or possibly by the time of Sir Henry Sydney in the 1580s. The food remains perhaps favour the former since he is known to have been resident at Wigmore, and the animal bone, fish and marine shell suggest the diet of a wealthy and influential individual or individuals. By about 1600 decay, dereliction or demolition is witnessed by the deposits trapped between the alcove-blocking and the curtain wall. A turf line 024 CG96 02 formed over CG96 03, further evidence of neglect and decay of the building, after which the whole of the area was sealed by demolition deposits. A similar, but more substantial turf line dating to the 17th century was noted in the 1998 excavations.

Phase 10 demolition deposits, CG96 02, which had built up against the Southern Curtain Wall, sealed all previous activity. As would be expected, these deposits contained a rich array of building material, including the single largest collection of window glass (see above) from the site and the largest group of floor tile from the 1996 excavations. One further complete smithing hearth bottom and associated slags, presumably residual from CG96 03, were recorded. Curiously there is very little ceramic roofing material and it is hard to escape from the conclusion the buildings in this area of the site were roofed with lead. Food waste, domestic artefacts and pottery were found in the demolition. The pottery consisted of mixed 16th- and 17th-century material but only a small amount of the pottery was undeniably Civil War in date. The evidence suggests that the demolition material accumulated rapidly. The disposition of the demolition layers is consistent with the Southern Curtain Wall having been reduced by pick (see Chapter 10). Of interest is an oxshoe found in this group (see Chapter 5). This indicates an animal used for heavy traction and can be seen as evidence for the carting away of building materials for reuse.

Above the Phase 10 demolition was a series of humic layers (Phase 11), which overlay the by now demolished Southern Curtain Wall. However, there is something curious about these layers since they contain large quantities of domestic material (pottery, bone, marine shell, metal artefacts), a forged coin of Charles I and comparatively small amounts of demolition debris, most of this having been deposited in CG96 02, Phase 10. Technically, since these layers overlie the Curtain Wall, they are post-demolition and hence belong to Phase 11, but the abundance of finds suggests that they must represent the final Civil War activity and occupation (albeit short-lived). In addition the sheer quantity of finds, particularly the pottery, which is the largest group from anywhere on site, and the (admittedly small) number of cross-joins between Phases 10 and 11, and within the Phase 11 contexts (although possibly the result of disturbance by tree roots?), is inexplicable if these deposits simply represent build up after the demolition. They must have been deposited by human agency. In contrast, the Phase 11 deposits in the 1998 excavation, contained virtually nothing.

The basal deposits 05 and 07 of Phase 11, effectively an interface between Phases 10 and 11, contained one of the larger groups of marine shell. The shell was curiously uncrushed and was found with large collections of animal bone and the forged coin of Charles I. The deposits overlay 017, Phase 10, which contained clay pipe consistent with a Civil War date (Peacey 2008). Overall, clay pipe was particularly poorly represented, with a single stem that could pre-date the Civil War and only seven stem fragments which by their bore width could date to the time of the Civil War. This food waste, predominantly domesticates such as cattle, sheep and pig, must represent the diet of the final occupants of the castle, possibly even of those who were involved in the slighting or its immediate aftermath.

From Phase 5, in the 1998 excavations, through to the construction of the Tudor plaster floor, 559, in Phase 9, a complex series of deposits and cut features was recorded. The sequence was difficult to understand due in part to the number of cut features, bringing with them the opportunity for intrusion and redeposition of material. From the existing records, plans and photographs it is certainly not clear how many distinct, discrete events are represented or whether these took place in a comparatively short timespan or over centuries. The following discussion is an attempt to find a 'best fit' interpretation of the evidence. The earliest and possibly contemporary context groups were CG98 33 and CG98 21, make-up deposits and a gravel floor surface, 659, respectively. A colour slide of the area and a multi-context plan in archive, reveal the massive extent of pitting and truncation. The detrimental effect of this is demonstrated by a series of cross-joining sherds which run through all the context groups from Phase 5 onwards up to the final make up layers CG98 12 and CG98 14 for the Tudor plaster floor 559, Phase 9. Context groups CG98 33 and CG98 21 are clearly quite separate entities but their integrity has been severely compromised. It is not possible to establish the relationship of the two context groups and it is not clear whether the gravel surface, which abutted the stonework of the East Tower was internal or external, although the occurrence of silty deposits above the gravel surface might suggest an exterior surface was more likely. The greater occurrence of artefacts and pottery in GC98 21 is more consistent with the gravel surface being outside a building than within one also. A mere 11 sherds, a broken horseshoe, a horseshoe nail and two fragments of oyster shell and two of animal bone were all that came from CG98 33. The sherds here also seemed to have been subject to slightly less trample and had an average sherd weight of 11g in contrast to that of CG98 21 at 9g. A variety of debris was also to be found on and above the gravel surface CG98 21. A jeton of Edward II, with a deposition date of the second quarter of the 14th century or even slightly later (SF1762, Chapter 5) came from occupation surface 652. Both 652 and another occupation layer above the gravel floor contained three Malvern Chase ware sherds that post-date the mid-14th century. The ware was not found in CG98 33 but so few sherds came from this context group that its absence may be of no significance. Part of the same bottle (Fabric R10) was found in both context groups. Whether this sherd was intrusive in CG98 33 is difficult to judge. It seems fair to assume that the gravel surface was laid down well before the mid-14th century and by analogy a similar *terminus ante quem* must apply to CG98 33. Perhaps most significantly fragments of window lead (Chapter 5) found in 652 and 646 (the same contexts which produced Malvern Chase ware) provided direct evidence for glazed windows and also a link with the fragment of window glass found in CG98 20, Phase 8 (see above). Further evidence of disturbance was noted by Mould (archive) from the artefactual evidence with pieces of a distinctive, decorative iron binding being found in CG98 21, context 646 and CG98 15, Phase 8.

Context group CG98 33 was cut by pit 675 CG98 17, which was incompletely excavated and was located against the Curtain Wall. There was evidence that the pit had been open for some time before backfilling and the loamy fill may indicate that it was situated outside a building (see Chapter 3). The situation is, however, far from straightforward. There were few artefacts from the fill, which consisted of a broken horseshoe, part of a bone handle and iron nails and little food waste although a small amount of animal bone was present. The pottery indicated links with CG98 21 and the subsequent CG 20. Rátkai (Chapter 4) notes that there was a noticeably early component to the pottery from CG98 33 which was less apparent in CG98 21. Given the very disturbed nature of the deposits — CG98 33 was cut not only by pit 675 but also by a probable post-pit 687 — there is a good chance that it has been contaminated by the introduction of later material such as the Fabric R10 bottle (see above and Chapter 4) and could be a relic of much earlier activity.

The critical factor in characterising the deposits below the Phase 9 plaster floor is the absence or presence of demolition debris. It is absent from CG98 33 apart from a single unworked stone roof tile fragment. Demolition material is absent from CG98 17, the pit-cutting CG98 33. It does, however, contain just under 12% by weight Malvern Chase pottery. This would suggest a date in the final quarter of the 14th century. Small quantities of building debris are present in CG98 21 (see above) and these might conceivably have been intrusive, but it is with the advent of CG98 16, 15 and 20 that the evidence for a major episode of demolition is found, incorporating stone and ceramic roofing material, floor tile, architectural fragments, runnels of lead and part melted lead window fittings, window glass, timber nails (large groups were found in CG98 16 and 20) and mortar. This seems to have culminated in the laying of a plaster floor 631, the last action of CG98 20, in the south of the excavated area. A small cache of floor tiles was found in 632 which immediately underlay the floor. Linnane suggests (Chapter 3) that the floor formed part of a building, running at right angles to the Curtain Wall, and divided by a timber partition.

There were numerous pottery cross-joins across these 'demolition context groups' and it is difficult not to draw the conclusion that they formed in pretty quick succession. The pottery was indicative of a 15th-century date for this activity. Coin evidence is consistent with this and Symons (Chapter 5) suggests a deposition date of 'well into the 15th century' for a heavily clipped and worn half-groat of Edward III, found in CG98 15 (SF1996) and a general 15th-century deposition for the Tournai jeton found in CG98 20 (SF1805). In addition, CG98 16 and 20 mark the first appearance of plate armour fragments in the artefactual record. A small amount of general household detritus and horse furniture was found in these groups, along with more personal items, such as an amber bead. In fact, despite the presence of demolition material in CG98 20 there was also reasonable amounts of food waste. Comparatively little fish bone and marine shell were found in CG98 15 and 16 but CG98 20 produced a good group of fish bone and marine shell representing the consumption of salmon, trout, cod, hake, ray, eel, oysters, mussels and cockles, the greatest concentration of this material being in 632, immediately below the mortar floor. Animal bone, indicative of a high-status diet (see below) was also present and was also reasonably well represented in CG96 16 but slightly less so in CG98 15. It is now difficult to untangle the occupation deposits over the gravel surface (CG98 21) and the make-up layers beneath the plaster floor (CG98 20). Fish and animal bone were found in both. Another denticle from a thornback ray was found in a layer immediately above the gravel surface. These are the only two examples of this fish from the entire site.

The above evidence points to a major episode of demolition and the building of a new structure at right angles to the curtain wall, containing the plaster floor (631) and internal partition, in the 15th century. This building was in turn replaced by another in Phase 9, CG98 08, which backed on to the East Tower and had a plaster floor (559). The absence of occupation deposits above this has led Linnane (Chapter 3) to suggest that the plaster may have been the base for a stone slab floor. The absence of wear or repair to this floor may support this view or suggest that, if unflagged, it quickly fell into disuse. Mortar or plaster floors are not hard-wearing and evidence of patching or repair is to be expected (Caple 2007, 153–155). Such evidence of repair was not seen at Wigmore on any of the plaster surfaces (631 CG98 20, 559 CG98 09 and CG96 033). At Dryslwyn Castle plaster floors were used from the third quarter of the 13th century (Caple 2007, 153–155). At Wigmore there was no evidence to indicate the use of plaster floors before the 15th century.

The lifespan of plaster floor 559 is difficult to judge. As we have seen above, the absence of wear or patching, and the ceramics would seem to suggest a short period of use, assuming that the floor surface was not a bedding for other material. However, the cutting of ten post-holes through the floor, probably for some sort of partition (see Chapter 3), indicates that the building, in which the floor was set, stood for long enough for modifications to be made.

Some building debris was present in CG98 12 and CG98 14, both interpreted as make up for the plaster floor 559, but the range of artefacts found in these groups is very similar to that found in the 'demolition groups' and they have every appearance of having been disturbed and redeposited or at least contain much redeposited material. A penny of Edward I (SF1657) with a deposition date of the first half of the 14th century found in CG98 12 tends to support this interpretation. Indeed, the exact relationship between CG98 14 and the demolition deposits discussed above, has been imperfectly recorded. The unexplained burial of part of an articulated horse skeleton CG98 19, Phase 9, lay beneath CG98 14 but this and the lower section of CG98 14 may have been the uppermost fills of CG98 15.

Food remains were not well represented in CG98 12 and 14. Cistercian ware sherds in the make-up layers indicate that the plaster floor and hence the associated building were constructed after *c*1480. To the north of the plaster floor were the remains of a stone flagged floor. Linnane (Chapter 3), surely correctly, suggests that this was contemporary with the plaster floor and suggests that the flagged floor was intended to take heavier traffic than the plaster floor. The make-up layers below the floor are completely devoid of finds with the exception of 7g of ceramic building material. There is some evidence that there was some attempt to 'patch up' the area whilst the floor was in use (Chapter 3) but the area swiftly fell into disuse and decay (CG98 13, Phase 10). Mortar, rubble, floor tile, window glass, timber nails, stone roof tile, a small amount of ceramic roof furniture and a piece of broken window frame were dumped. A small amount of domestic waste also found its way into the debris, including a spoon bowl of the 16th- or 17th-century, and a large deposit of marine shell (Chapter 7) The adjacent plaster floor was covered with similar deposits, CG98 04, although architectural fragments and painted plaster were also included. This group contained the single largest floor tile deposit from the entire site. Another large group of marine shell was recovered. Ceramic evidence suggests that material had been dumped over the stone-slabbed floor by *c*1550. There was very little pottery from over the plaster floor, however, although it was consistent with a 16th-century deposition date. Rátkai suggests (Chapter 4) that disuse, abandonment and demolition may have followed in quick succession. The marine shell from CG98 13 came from the top of the dumps and presumably represents a by now derelict building being used as a convenient place to dump food debris. The marine shell in CG98 04 is found immediately above the plaster floor but is then interleaved throughout the other demolition deposits. This could conceivably indicate a more gradual accumulation of debris.

Following this initial disuse and decay, a period of neglect followed, allowing a turf line to form over CG98 04. The turf line contained a coin of Henry VIII (SF1803) with a deposition date of *c*1530–50 and a high quality curb bit of 17th-century date (Chapter 5). Other finds suggesting demolition, such as timber nails and lead trimmings, were associated with the turf line. Above the turf line a series of demolition deposits (CG98 02, Phase 11) were found. Before these were deposited, during a period of neglect, the Curtain Wall may have become increasingly unstable and have had to be reinforced with timber props (CG98 03, Phase 11). The pit associated with the timbers' post-holes contained a large deposit of fish bone and marine shell. The remains of two frogs in the fill presumably represent pit-falls rather than a fondness for *cuisses de grenouille*. The presence of frogs may hint at a period of dereliction or abandonment (see Caple 2007, 309) and it is worth noting that amphibian bone was also found in CG98 13, a context group associated with decay or dereliction. A pottery sherd burnt to the point of vitrification, attesting possibly to an episode of intense burning, was found in the fill. A blackware mug sherd gives a *terminus post quem* for the context group of *c*1550, although logically this group should be later, possibly *c*1600, making it roughly contemporary with the blocked alcove backfill in 1996, discussed above.

The demolition deposits (CG98 02) above the turf line contained very little pottery or other artefacts. A solidified runnel of lead and an iron timber nail were found in a deposit with part of a Cistercian ware cup. The demolition deposits mostly contained ceramic building material, particularly floor tile, some stone roof tile and an architectural fragment (a limewashed rib from a vault). The latest pottery from this context group was blackware and Fabric RW12 which, like CG98 03 (above), indicates a *terminus post quem* of *c*1550. There is no pottery which must date to the time of the Civil War, such as the slipwares found in the 1996 excavations. However the 1996 Phase 11 pottery assemblage was much larger than that from 1998 and the slipwares formed only a very small proportion, so statistically the absence of these wares need not be significant. It would certainly seem to be the case that serious and irreversible decay of the castle fabric had already happened by the mid- to late-16th century, despite Roland Lee's efforts in the 1530s (Chapter 2). It is possible that CG98 02 represents the final demolition of the castle by the Harleys at the time of the Civil War but it is certainly not provable and natural decay cannot be ruled out.

The history of the East Tower is rather more complex than at first might appear. Excavation within the tower stopped at a sloping clay deposit, 670, before the bottom of the tower was reached. There was no evidence for the original construction of the tower although it is possible that this was missed during excavation and the clay deposit was part of the original defensive bank. Above this a series of fills (CG98 11) were uncovered. Details of the stratigraphically earlier layers were not recorded in the primary record so it is not clear whether these were also sloping or flattened like the subsequent fills from 630 upwards. The absence of tip lines in the upper fill material, above fill 640, was striking and suggested something other than the random, hasty disposal of debris into the tower.

The initial excavators considered the East Tower infill to be a single action. However, much later in the post-excavation process, a more careful integrated analysis of the stratigraphy, ceramics and artefacts led Linnane (Chapter 3) and Rátkai (Chapter 4) to postulate three episodes of infilling (termed sub-groups a, b and c by Linnane), which may have begun in Phase 8/9, rather than in Phase 10.

Fills sandwiched between 670 and 630 (sub-group a) contained the greater part of the finds. The presence of floor and roof tile (see above) indicated that some demolition material was being used as part of the backfill. Timber nails were also common, particularly the bottom-most excavated fill (665). The most striking aspect of these fills, however, was the presence of several pieces of militaria and horse furniture (Chapter 5). Plate armour fragments found outside the tower in Phase 8 CG98 20 and CG98 16, which were also associated with demolition debris (see above) and were the only other groups to contain plate armour, provide a link with the exterior and interior of the tower. A further link is provided by the pottery. Sherds from the same Malvern Chase ware jar were found in tower fill 629 and CG98 15; sherds from a Fabric MS01 jar (Figure 4.5, 46) were found in fill 630 and CG98 15, CG98 16 and CG98 20; sherds from a Fabric Q40 jug in 665 and CG98 20; sherds from a Q60 jug in 630 and CG98 16 and CG98 17 and sherds from a Fabric Q70 jug were found in tower fill 630 and CG98 17. It seems, therefore, as if demolition and other debris has been removed from the area immediately outside the East Tower and used to backfill and then level the basement of the tower, possibly as an attempt to form a new floor surface within the basement. The pottery from the basal layer 665 appeared to be 15th century in date with very little residual material. The amount of residual material then increased substantially up to the deposition of level surface 630 (Chapter 4). Fill 629 (part of sub-group b) above 630 contained a silver penny (SF1806) with a suggested deposition date in the 1460s, possibly even as late as the 1480s (Chapter 5). However, fill 629 also contained pottery Fabric RW12 which is unlikely to pre-date the 16th century. It would seem, therefore, that the major 15th-century demolition and construction event witnessed outside the tower in Phases 8 and 9 also resulted in works within the East Tower.

Further levelled dumps of material (sub-group b) were deposited above 629 until their increasing depth, ending with deposit 610, would have reduced the basement space between floor and ceiling to an unusable height of some 1.0m. Finds within these deposits were much reduced and some may have been disturbed from the lower levels. Consecutive layers 610, 604 and 587 were particularly unusual in that they only contained Malvern Chase ware (Chapter 4). A dead dog appears to have been dumped above 610 in fill 604 (although a much smaller amount of dog bone was found in fills 622, 629, 630 and 640), which surely suggests that the East Tower was by then semi-derelict. Although ceramic building material was present, there was no floor tile, unlike the earlier fill sequence, where floor tile predominated. Other demolition debris consisted of architectural fragments, stone roof tile, scrap lead and structural ironwork. Fill 587 (sub-group c) was unusual in containing a comparatively large assemblage of animal bone including more dog bone but primarily composed of domestic fowl. This group of deposits seem to date to the 16th century and may link with the decay and demolition witnessed outside the tower in Phase 10, CG98 04 and CG98 13. Linnane (Chapter 3) notes the apparent displacement of hearthstones in 587. The pottery would suggest that this took place in the later 16th century. Deposits above this were virtually devoid of pottery and produced a modern pottery sherd from 509, Phase 11, and sherds from a mottled ware bowl (later 17th to mid-18th century) from 510, Phase 11. Demolition deposits over the passageway leading to the tower contained floor tile, window glass, nails and architectural fragments (a voussoir and a chamfer stop). Significantly there was no animal bone and only a minute scrap (less than 1g) of pottery.

Figure 9.13 attempts to show the archaeological evidence for buildings and possible building campaigns in the two excavated areas by distilling

Area		Date	Evidence
1996	Timber castle	Later 11thC	Clay dumps, timber post
1996	Remodeling of defences, possible stone curtain wall?	12thC	Environmental, smithing hearth bottoms
1996	Timber building	12thC	Post-holes, hearth
1996	Building and early curtain wall?	13thC	Stake holes, 'ditch' and demolition material
1996	Building?	13thC	Burnt horizon (post-1270), suggesting destruction of timber structure
1998	Buildings (hypothetical) agains curtain wall	13thC	Artefactual: floor tile, roof furniture, stone floor tile found residually, window lead and lead runnels, window glass, architectural stone; post-hole? gravel surface (external?)
1998	Construction of Curtain Wall and Eastern Tower	Post-1250	Artefactual
1996	Curtain wall construction	*c*1300	Construction trench, hearth bottoms
1996	Demolition/construction	Early 14thC	Lead-melting hearths
1996	Building	Early 14thC	Structural remains
1996	Curtain wall repair	15thC	Demoliton debris, structural evidence
1996	Building?	15thC	'Alcove' in Curtain Wall
1998	Initial decay/remodelling of Eastern Tower	15thC	Levelling dumps
1998	Demolition	Early to mid-15thC	Building debris
1998	Building at right angle to Curtain Wall	Mid-15thC +	Mortar floor, timber partition
1998	Demolition or ?modification	Late 15thC +	Make up layers containing mainly residual material
1998	Building baking on to Eastern Tower	Post-1480	Plaster floors, post-holes
1996	Building	Late 15thC +	Plaster floor
1996	Demolition/repair	16thC	Dump of demolition debris, complete hearth bottoms
1998	Initial decay/disuse	Mid-16thC	Mortar deposits and rubble dumps
1998	Eastern Tower further decay	16thC	Further levelling
1998	Remedial work?	*c*1600?	Pit and post-holes
1996	Remedial work	*c*1600?	Blocking of 'alcove'
1998	Eastern tower demoliton	17thC	Demolition debris
1996	Final demolition/destruction	1640s	Demolition deposits
1998	Final demolition/destruction	1640s	Demolition deposits

FIGURE 9.13

Suggested castle construction sequence and associated evidence (denotes large assemblage)*

the above information. Clearly, the size of the excavated areas, particularly at their lower levels, provides only the merest snapshot of the castle's history. Nevertheless, a pattern does emerge. There can be no doubt that the first castle stood on the present site and encompassed the lower part of the Inner Bailey. It appears to have had a timber palisade and timber buildings within it. There is no evidence for stone buildings at this early date, although there is the possibility that they once existed on the motte (Chapter 2). Unfortunately, evidence for the transition from timber to stone is very sketchy. The presence of 13th-century masonry and painted window glass, 13th-century demolition debris, smithing hearths and the remains of a major conflagration are all the excavated archaeological evidence we have to go on. Even the date of the first stone curtain wall is problematic, always assuming (although it is highly likely) that the timber defences were remodelled in stone before the 14th century. Some very slight evidence for early stone structures and by inference a stone curtain wall is provided by the wellstone or fireback (see above) found in Phase 3 (early 13th century) and by the presence of mortar from the 12th century onwards.

Analysis of the standing fabric of the castle suggests that the gatehouse dates to the late 12th or early 13th century (Chapter 2; Cooke 2008) and it is suggested that the Curtain Wall adjacent to the East Tower dates to the early 13th century.

The East Tower appears to have been constructed after 1250 and the (?second) Southern Curtain Wall a little later, around 1300. It is tempting to see the impetus to improve the castle defences as the result of de Montfort's attack in 1264 but it is only too easy to hang the narrative thread on documented historical 'facts', without considering that other possibilities exist. It is, for example, in the early 1250s that Montgomery Castle's middle ward timber defences were replaced in stone (the outer defences somewhat later). Emulation of the royal castle at Montgomery may have influenced the Mortimers to upgrade their castle or increasingly hostile relations with the Welsh culminating in Edward I's campaign of 1277 may have made this advisable. This theme is more fully discussed in Chapter 10.

Building work (the construction of the Southern Curtain Wall) was in train at the very end of the 13th century or in the early 14th century. Some of this work must have occurred during the tenure of Roger (V) Mortimer, later the first Earl of March. He was present at the castle in 1310, 1314 and 1316 (Mortimer 2004). However, it is not necessary to see him as the instigator of this episode of construction, which may have been part of a continuing sequence of works. It is worth noting, for example, that extensive rebuilding (including a new keep) at Dudley Castle by the de Somerys was being carried out from *c*1265 to *c*1310, a lengthy period, although exacerbated by periods of insolvency, which were usually remedied by extortion of the local populace. Perhaps these visits by Roger (V) coincided with the final stages of the work at the castle. At any rate it was in a suitable state of repair in 1329 for entertaining royal and aristocratic guests at the Round Table Tournament and for Edward III, after Roger (V)'s death, to stay there in 1332.

With the disgrace and execution of Roger (V) in 1330, the castle may have begun to decline. Maintaining the condition of the castle was probably not helped by forfeiture of Mortimer lands to the Crown and the deaths of several heirs in quick succession. However in 1360 a staff of constables and porters, and perhaps also other officers, is recorded at Wigmore Castle. There is evidence of some building or repair work at the castle in the 14th century, possibly the construction of the Southern Curtain Wall, the Phase 6 lead-melting and the Phase 7 building adjacent to both. There is some evidence that the Phase 7 building fell into neglect which might reflect a general downturn in the castle's fortunes. By 1425 the last Mortimer heir, Edmund, was dead and the Mortimer estates passed to the House of York. The *inquisition post mortem* of Edmund (Chapter 2) contains the familiar phrase from many late medieval documents that the castle was 'worth nothing'. As Thompson (1987, 15) points out, the expression 'worth nothing' has been equated with 'ruinous' by many writers but this is not the case and the phrase means that the castle in question yielded no revenue. This is quite another matter and Thompson (1987, 14–15) lays out how the expenses involved in the upkeep of a castle could effectively nullify the revenues received from its estates. What is surprising at Wigmore is that there seems to have been a flurry of activity in the 15th century, with evidence of demolition and rebuilding on both the 1996 and 1998 sites. Johnson (1991) suggests that in the 1420s to 1450s Richard of York administered the Welsh and Marcher estates from Ludlow. However, the activity at Wigmore might suggest that the castle was 'improved' and the most likely reason for that is the presence, if only periodically, of Richard of York. This is also more fully explored in Chapter 10.

Further work at the castle is evidenced towards the end of the 15th century or at the beginning of the 16th century, too late to be directly associated with the House of York. It is possible that some of this work is attributable to Henry, Duke of Buckingham in 1483, but the works seem to have been fairly extensive and perhaps another candidate should be sought, the most obvious being Henry Tudor, after his accession to the throne.

A further series of works appear to have been carried out in the 16th century, and these seem to be associated with Bishop Roland Lee and possibly Sir Henry Sidney. Remedial works at the end of the century or beginning of the next attest that attempts were made to keep the castle sound but they have the appearance of being somewhat makeshift and may have been too little too late. Viewed dispassionately, it is difficult to believe that, if not totally derelict, the East Tower, the building adjacent to it and the possible building backing on to the Southern Curtain Wall were not in bad repair. Also telling is the formation of turf lines in both the 1996 and 1998 sites before the final phase of demolition.

9.3 THE ARTEFACTUAL, FAUNAL AND ENVIRONMENTAL ASSEMBLAGES: ASPECTS OF LIFE WITHIN THE CASTLE

Diet and environment

The small size of the areas excavated and the concomitant size of the artefactual and other assemblages, precludes a detailed description of life at Wigmore Castle. In many respects the finds from Wigmore are typical of high-status, medieval, fortified sites. Absences of certain artefact classes, such as whetstones and hones, which would be normally expected, may simply reflect the smallness of the artefactual sample and have no greater significance. With this in mind, the following is an attempt to pull together some strands from the various categories of excavated finds, which might throw some light onto Wigmore and to highlight further possible avenues of research.

The faunal remains demonstrate the importance of game in the diet of the castle's inhabitants. Deposits from both the 1996 and 1998 contain the same range of high-status foodstuffs and suggest that the buildings in both areas were themselves high status. The faunal remains stand in direct contrast to the medieval pottery, in particular, which contained little exotica. This aspect of the pottery assemblage is not uncommon and has been noted at other castles in the region (see Chapter 4). A sherd of Ham Green ware, however, indicates contact with Bristol and sherds of French green-glazed ware may have also found their way to the castle from the south-west. This hints at procurement of wine via the south-west ports for use at the castle. It is, however, a slender link.

The consumption of game is rich in meaning and Thomas and Vann (Chapter 7) put much of the art of venery in context. It was the wealthy and aristocratic who owned the forests, parks and warrens from where the game came. It was the aristocrats who had sufficient means to support packs of hunting dogs and horses necessary for the pursuit and capture of certain types of game. Records survive for a hunting party of Roger Mortimer, 4th Earl of March, in the late 14th century. Here, further expenses are indicated by the purchase of green hunting gowns for the aristocratic party, the re-gilding of Roger's hunting knife, further 'furbishments for his belt', a new bow and other archery equipment (Woolgar 1999, 195). Other smaller game was caught using snares, nets and birds of prey. Lead weights found at Dolforwyn Castle (Butler 1990, 94) may have been from birding nets. At Hen Domen, the remains of a goshawk were found in a pit (Browne 2000), representing probably a bird used for hunting; and at Stafford Castle, goshawk remains and those of a golden eagle and buzzard were recorded, the latter two both also possibly used for hunting (Sadler and Jones 2007). Unfortunately, with the exception of the animal bones themselves, only a few remains associated with hunting have been found at Wigmore. Pursuit of larger game is indicated by the remains of possible hunting dogs and a barbed arrowhead, all found quite late in the castle's history. However, turning to de Charlton's inventory of 1322 (see above), small game was evidently acquired using nets and snares (Mortimer 2004, 117). If the proposed building campaigns outlined (see above and Figure 9.12) are correct, then one of the attractions of the castle to Richard, Duke of York, may have been the proximity of good hunting. The remains of game are certainly just as well represented in the 15th century as in earlier centuries, another reason for believing that the castle still had resident aristocrats from time to time.

Thomas and Vann (Chapter 7) note the higher than average occurrence of beef in the diet. This is often the dominant domesticate on castle sites but also seems to be well represented on other sites on the Welsh Marches, such as Cheptow town (Noddle 1991). One of the main reasons for many of the various Welsh incursions into England was cattle raiding. The cultural significance of cattle to the Welsh appears to have been deep and long standing and may have had its roots in the Celtic past. Certainly, cattle and cattle-raiding were celebrated in Ireland, most notably in 'The Cattle Raid of Cooley'. According to Clancy (1999), between 854 and 1603 over 500 cattle raids were recorded in the Annals of the Four Masters. Hagen (1995, 68) notes that a man of rank in Wales by definition owned a cattlefold and in both Wales and Ireland compensation was often determined in terms of numbers of cattle. Hagen (1995, 75), citing Noddle, also draws attention to the fact that even in the Anglo-Saxon period, cattle are a far more important component of the diet in the west and that the relative frequency of cattle appears to be a regional rather than temporal phenomenon. The consumption of cattle at Wigmore may therefore not only reflect a regional bias in animal husbandry nor simply the status of the castle, but also integration into a social and cultural milieu where cattle were especially valued. As we shall see later, there may be other features in the Marcher lordships which reflect 'Welshification', quite apart from the inter-marriage between the Marcher Lords and Welsh aristocracy and royalty.

There are two deposits where cattle bones were particularly well represented. One of these is in the East Tower (along with rabbit bones, domestic fowl and dogs) and the other within the Phase 5 construction trench for the Southern Curtain Wall.

These come from two deposits, 178/179, the final fill of the construction trench, and 203, the layer immediately below that containing the ballista balls (Figure 9.12). A very small amount of deer, sheep, pig, fowl and fish bones were also found here and very small amounts of sheep and dove/pigeon were found in 178/179. Despite the two bone groups being separated by several fills, they both contain a preponderance of cattle foot bones which have been split for marrow extraction. Since there is nothing like this from elsewhere on site, it seems logical to assume that both bone deposits derive from the same source. This would tend to suggest that the final section of the construction trench was filled in short order. Yet if so, why was the backfill sequence cut (interpreted as tidying the trench edge during construction, see above), which would suggest a more drawn out backfill process.

Thomas and Vann (Chapter 7) discuss various uses, other than the purely edible, for bone marrow. Marrow is also mentioned in Anglo-Saxon leechdoms (Hagen 1995, 76), the bones being broken with the back of an axe to aid marrow retrieval. On balance, the conclusion put forward by Thomas and Vann that the bones most likely represent food waste is probably correct. Hagen (1995, 318) notes that at Hamwih (Southampton), the meat probably came into the town on the hoof, but once at the butchers, the flesh was trimmed from the bone and 'the bones chopped to release their fat and marrow before being quickly cast into pits. The bones were probably never cooked'. Although this does not prove that the fat and marrow were for human consumption, it may represent fairly accurately what happened at Wigmore. An extensive purveyance made for Richard II in *c*1387 (Renfrow 1993, II, 335) lists among the comestibles 300 marrowbones, leaving no doubt that they were for human consumption. Other food remains in the Southern Curtain Wall backfills are rare (Figure 9.12), so the cattle bones must be two quite deliberate dumps. The need for quick disposal of the waste may indicate that the two deposits of bones may, therefore, represent two separate lots of food preparation. It is of interest that in the following period a dump of chicken feet was found (see above). This and the cattle bones suggest that somewhere in the vicinity was a building where food was prepared and also probably cooked.

The number, albeit small, of pig and deer bones in deposit 203 seem to be consistent with the marrow being eaten by high-status diners rather than those employed in constructing the Southern Curtain Wall. Modern disgust at offal and marrow has coloured the perception of it as a food source but it is a highly nutritious foodstuff. Thomas and Vann (Chapter 7) note a 16th-century recipe for marrow and many 15th-century recipes are given in Renfrow (1993), where marrow is used in both sweet and savoury pastries and as part of a spiced crust or filling for spit-roasted meats, presumably to help retain the moisture in the meat. At the beginning of the 16th century, the Duke of Buckingham, on entertaining the Burgundian ambassador, purchased 20 calves feet for making jelly. Although the making of calves' foot jelly is unlikely to result in the bone waste seen in Phase 5 at Wigmore, it does again highlight a very different view of what was considered a delicacy in the past.

Evidence of the consumption of fish is found from Phase 1 (a fish scale recovered from sample <26>) through to Phase 11, with a notable group of fish and shellfish remains in CG98 03. The fish bone was not evenly distributed through the periods, the highest incidence being in Phase 2, with comparatively poor representation in Phases 3, 4 and 5, although the distribution of fish bone is probably more indicative of taphonomic factors rather than representing changes in fish consumption. Given the differences in fish bone frequency, one potentially interesting fact emerges: that species representation appears to have a temporal bias. Only one possible member of the cod family (*gadid*) is recorded from Phase 2 and cod does not occur again until Phase 5 (three bones). In 1996, Phase 6, cod and other *gadids* occur with eel and herring but thereafter the latter two species are not encountered again, apart from a single herring vertebra late in Phase 9. On the 1998 site, herring and eel are not represented at all. There is therefore what could be loosely termed a 'cod horizon', which seems to occur towards the end of the 13th century or beginning of the 14th century. A paucity of cod bone was noted at Stafford Castle (Hamilton-Dyer 2007) although the sampling strategy was not perfect and a recovery bias was present. However, work by Rátkai (2007) on the pottery, strongly suggested that the castle was something of a backwater by the mid-13th century and that despite the rebuilding of the keep in the mid-14th century, the inner bailey of the castle (Area B) saw little in the way of occupation thereafter. Thus the majority of the material recovered is likely to pre-date the 14th century. Hagen (1995, 169–171) notes, however, that cod was consumed in the Anglo-Saxon period, although the bias seems to lie to the east of the country or to ports such as Hamwih and Exeter. She (*ibid* 319) also discusses the logistics of moving fresh fish inland before decomposition set in (1995, 319), surely a problem for a remote site like Wigmore, although Woolgar (1999, 118) considers that no part of England was too far from the coast to be supplied with fresh fish. Thomas *et al* (Chapter 7) find no evidence to suggest that the cod was anything other than fresh when brought to the castle, so the increasing frequency of cod and its relatives may have been affected by improvements in communications, although such improvements would have to have been substantial. Even in the later 17th century Daniel Defoe (1927, Appendix to the second volume) commented on the putrid fish brought to Birmingham:

> I might give examples where the herrings, which are not the best fish to keep neither, are, even as it is, carry'd to those towns, and up to Warwick, Birmingham, Tamworth and Stafford, and tho' they frequently stink before they come thither, yet the people are so eager of them, that they buy them, and give dear for them too; whereas were the roads good, they would come in less time...

and it is hard to see travelling conditions being better in the medieval period.

Hammond (1995) only refers to cod in terms of salted and dried cod so perhaps the cranial bones from the cod are misleading. Hammond (1995, 118) does refer to several names for preserved cod 'winterfish, markfish, halfwoxfish, cropling, titling' the exact meaning of which is now lost and perhaps would have included part of the head. On the other hand, remains of a thornback ray found in the 1998 excavation surely indicate that fresh fish reached the castle. The thornback ray is a potentially very large fish (up to 18kg)[1]. Rather surprisingly, according to Hagen (1995, 170) thornback ray is often found on Anglo-Saxon urban sites in Wessex. The thornback ray likes large estuaries, although it can thrive in more than one habitat. Hammond (1995, 118) notes fishtraps in the Severn Estuary that would have caught thornback ray amongst others. As the thornback ray is less common in the waters off the north-west coast of Britain, its presence at Wigmore may indicate that fish (and shellfish) came to the castle primarily from the south-west.

The fish bone assemblage was dominated by marine fish. The only evidence of freshwater fish was represented by bones possibly from *cyprinidae*, that is, members of the carp (*cyprinus carpio*) species group and includes fish such as chub, roach and dace. These are exactly the types of fish which could be kept in fish ponds and such ponds are mentioned in the documentary record (Chapter 2). At Stafford Castle (Hamilton-Dyer 2007) there was definite evidence of freshwater fish in the diet and these were represented by a greater variety of species, such as pike, perch, burbot, tench, roach and chub, again suggesting the availabilty of fishponds to the castle's inhabitants. However, although the sample size at Wigmore is much smaller than that at Stafford, both were dominated by herring and eel.

Marine shellfish, particularly oysters but including mussels, whelks and cockles were recorded at Wigmore (Chapter 7). Oysters and mussels were found infrequently in Phases 4–7 and were totally absent from the first three periods. Mussels were particularly well represented in CG98 20, which dated to the 15th century (see above). The greatest concentration of marine shell was found in Phases 9, 10 and 11 and nine of the larger groups are discussed in detail by Campbell (Chapter 7).

One of the more interesting groups of remains came from the fill of a Phase 11 pit of uncertain purpose, CG98 03, although clearly later used to dispose of food waste. Oysters, mussels, cockles and whelks were found with cod and gadid, and salmonid bone. Given that some of the fish specimens would have been quite large this suggests a reasonable sized congregation of diners. The pit also contained predominantly high-status animal bone (goose, chicken, chicken/guinea fowl/pheasant, snipe, thrush, grey partridge, cattle, pig, sheep, hare and goat) and a small amount of eggshell from domestic fowl. Campbell (Chapter 7) notes that the oysters were roughly opened without care to their appearance at table. This, combined with the smaller size of oyster, he interprets as indicating that the oysters were primarily everyday fare for ordinary people. However this sits oddly with the other undoubtedly high-status food remains with which the oysters were found. It is possible that the oysters were opened roughly because they were destined for cooking, rather than for presenting raw. The pit must date to the 17th century but in many respects, the high-status dining is more consistent with the 16th century. This is one of the few closed groups of material from the site supporting the existence of 17th-century occupation in this area of the castle.

The faunal and environmental remains provide very good evidence of diet in the late 11th and 12th centuries, a period when there is much less documentary evidence (no recipe books, for example) for the foodstuffs consumed in a high-status setting. Judging from the Phase 2 evidence, the diet was both varied and nutritious. Wheat, oats and rye were consumed, with oats being the most dominant and wheat the least. Vitolo (Chapter 8) notes the absence of barley at Wigmore. This finds a parallel at Stafford Castle. At the latter, samples which must be roughly contemporaneous with Wigmore Phase 1 and Phase 2 were processed (Rouffignac 2007). In the former, pea and apple/pear seeds were identified along with faecal matter and canine coprolites. A large pit, which should be roughly contemporary with the Phase 2 hearth and associated deposits at Wigmore, contained many cooking pot fragments, interleaved with tips of ash, presumably representing successive dumps of cooking waste. Here pea (*Pisum sativum*) bean (*Vicia faba*) and hazelnuts (*Corylus avellana*) were found, although it is not entirely clear from the published report whether wheat was also present. The consumption of hazelnuts in particular and legumes is also a feature of the early Wigmore deposits. Hazelnuts could be an important part of the diet, especially in the winter months (Hagen 1995, 53).

Oats were quite widely grown in Anglo-Saxon England (Hagen 1995, 23–24) but were probably used mainly for animal fodder since they are poorly represented on large urban sites and are more frequently encountered on rural or semi-urban sites. However, Gerald of Wales writing in the 12th century, commented that the whole population of

Wales lived almost entirely on oats (Hagen 1995, 23). Oats were also used for brewing and the sprouted oats found in Phase 2 may be a result of this use or could simply indicate spoiled grain which was used for animal fodder. A rather larger deposit of sprouted oats was found in a ditch in the Bull Ring, Birmingham, possibly dating to the late 12th or early 13th centuries (Ciaraldi 2009). Here, both possible interpretations (brewing or fodder) were given, but at Wigmore the malting quern, although found in much later levels, perhaps favours the former, especially as barley is so notably absent from the archaeological record.

If oats favour damp, acid soils, then rye is suited to dry, sandy ones. In the medieval pre-Conquest period it was grown with wheat as maslin but appears not to have been a popular cereal, although, again, the Welsh seem to have grown it frequently as an individual crop (Hagen 1995, 25–26). The occurrence of wheat and rye in Phase 2 samples may then reflect the consumption of maslin. However, Hammond (1995, 2) considers that rye was the main crop grown by peasants for much of the Middle Ages and calls it the 'hardiest grain...[that]... grows in most soils'.

Remains of edible fruits were not common in the Phase 2 deposits at Wigmore. Sour cherry and possibly plum/sloe were found. Of particular interest was the fig seed found in a Phase 1 sample. Although climatic conditions were somewhat warmer in the 12th century and figs could have been grown in this country, it is more likely that the seed represents an imported dried fruit. Figs were a comparatively high-status food, classed as 'spices' and relatively expensive (Hammond 1995, 65). They were often consumed during Lent and on other fast days (Hammond 1995, 74; Woolgar 1999, 130).

Other plants identified in the samples are more difficult to interpret. As with bone marrow, certain plants which are edible and, indeed, were eaten in the past, are now no longer routinely, if ever, consumed. So, for example, orache, *Polygonum*, dock, mallow and hawthorn (berries and young shoots), which are all present in the Phase 2 samples, could have formed part of the diet, especially in the winter months, when they would act as an antiscorbutic. Likewise, buttercup, nettle, goosefoot and sow thistle, among others, all recorded in Phase 1, have a documented history as food sources. It is hard not to see the mint recorded in Phase 1 sample <38> as other than culinary.

Selfheal and woundwort were found in Phase 1 samples <26> and <38> and may represent plants used medicinally, although selfheal has a wide and varied habitat (including modern lawns) and may just represent general vegetation in the area.

Fish was well represented in Phase 2, with herring the most common, followed by eel. A few small salmonids were found and one possible gadid. The roughly contemporary pit 7116 at Stafford Castle (Hamilton-Dyer 2007, 183) contained remains of eel, herring, pike, roach and plaice, showing that even at this early date there was access to marine and freshwater fish on inland sites.

The Phase 2 diet was further enhanced by the consumption of chicken and goose eggs. The presence of these together with fish bones is interesting, since both are fast-day foods. The meat element in Phase 2 is dominated by bird bone, both domestic and wild fowl. Given that the Phase 2 remains are unequivocally food waste it seems reasonable to assume that the thrush or starling was also a food item. The preponderance of bird bone also complements the twisted iron implement, almost certainly correctly identified by Mould as a skewer, since as noted above, skewered birds, possibly spatchcocked, are shown on the Bayeux Tapestry as being cooked in this way (Figure 9.11). A hilt plate from a knife, probably for food preparation, was also found in this period, and a possible bone handle; both reinforce the culinary nature of these deposits. Meat from the hunt was represented by deer and hare. Domesticates such as cattle, sheep/goat and pigs occurred but as a minor element, although clearly providing a greater meat yield than the fowl.

Non-dietary elements in Phase 2 are represented by dog and cat bones. The dog bones are too few in number to draw any firm conclusions but there is a good chance that they are the remains of hunting dogs. They were found in pits within the Phase 2 timber building. Cat bone was slightly better represented. All but one specimen came from a layer below the hearth 351 of CG96 27 and consisted of a group of metatarsals The remaining bone also came from inside the timber building. Hagen (1995) has suggested that cats may have been valued as rodent killers and protectors of grain stores. They are unlikely to have been pets as we use the term today and would have played a role similar to modern farm cats. However, the presence of cat bones beneath a hearth has an almost ritualistic or 'folk magic' aspect to it and a deposition of this sort might repay further study.

Despite the presence of dogs both explicit in the actual remains and implicit in the remains of hunted beasts, and the almost certain presence of rats, the animal bone from Phase 2 showed little sign of gnawing. This suggests that it was not exposed for any length of time after initial discard. Evidence of gnawing was, however, much more common on the animal bone from Phase 1 in material which is likely, by the nature of the deposits, to have been disturbed.

As can be seen from the above, the diet in Phase 2 was wholesome and nutritious. As is often the case, apart from samples taken from cess pits and latrines, vegetable elements of the diet and fruit are not well represented although a possible corrective may be supplied by some of the plant remains such as dock and hawthorn. Food was evidently spit roasted and boiled (Chapter 4) but we should also assume that much larger metal receptacles were used for cooking. Although no archaeological trace of them remains from this early phase, a rim from a copper-alloy cooking vessel and a possible pot suspension hook were found in much later deposits (Chapter 5). The main cereal component of the diet appears to have been oats which may have been served as a porridge but was also probably used for brewing. Wheaten bread may have been eaten but there is an equal chance that maslin bread was eaten. In fact if oat porridge was eaten as a carbohydrate staple, then bread may not have been so regularly consumed. Most of the foodstuffs present in the diet were sourced locally, in other words, the castle was self-sufficient. The exception to this was the herring and possibly the eels.

In Phase 1, Vitolo has convincingly highlighted the differences in the local terrain. Her earliest samples (<26> and <28>) are indicative of a wet environment where there is some pasture and agriculture. The dog's mercury is also suggestive of shady woodland (Rouffignac 2007). Hazelnut, chaff, bran, mint, fig, wild radish (recommended for the warding off of women's chatter!) and flax were recorded and a single fish scale. A very small amount of animal bone (cattle, pig, equid, and cat) was found, all from the initial turf line (bar one bone from 386), but in rather too small a quantity to interpret very securely. These lower levels of Phase 1 must represent the site at the castle's inception. The presence of flax is noteworthy and may suggest some retting nearby. Above these layers were the possible remains of a timber palisade. After this, a further series of layers failed to provide much evidence of foodstuffs although the sudden surge in nettle is probably symptomatic of increasing midden material in the area (Rouffignac 2007). However, there was an increase in the amount of animal bone, showing that dietary components consisted primarily of domesticates (cow, pig, sheep) with wild animals represented by deer and hare. Fowl were conspicuously infrequent and this stands in marked contrast to Phase 2. Perhaps the most astounding find from these deposits was a bear paw. Conventional wisdom is that the bear was extinct in England by this period (Chapter 7). Hagen (1995, 132) notes references to bear flesh in Anglo-Saxon leechdoms but qualifies this by the observation that the leechdoms show Continental influences. Hagen hints that bear may have been consumed occasionally and as a prestige item by the Anglo-Saxons but notes only one occurrence of bear bone on an (unspecified) archaeological site (Hagen 1995, 360, 132). It is still, therefore, unclear as to whether the Wigmore bear paw is tantalising evidence of the continued (rare) existence of bears in post-Roman Britain or an import, and, whether local or Continental, the paw represents food waste or a bearskin.

Military life

At least three attacks on the castle, in 1155, 1191 and 1264, are recorded but the extent of the damage inflicted on the castle fabric is unknown. There is nothing within the stratigraphic record which can be directly and certainly attributed to these events. The castle also seems to have been a strategic base from which campaigns were launched; campaigns against the Welsh in 1192, against Richard Marshall in 1233, against the Welsh again in 1250s, the Siege of Bristol in 1316, rebellion against the Despencers in 1321, the Battle of Shrewsbury 1403 and the Battle of Mortimer's Cross in 1461 to name but a few. In 1483, Henry Duke of Buckingham had authority to place archers and soldiers at Wigmore (and other castles) so a military function was integral to the castle until the end of the Wars of the Roses.

Considering the restricted extent of the excavations, a comparatively large number of horseshoe nails and horseshoes were recovered. The typology of the former begins with the Saxo-Norman fiddle-key type, which is most plentiful on the 1996 site and continues through the earred and cuboid types to post-medieval and modern types (although there are few examples of the latter two). At Wigmore, horse-shoe nails, for which there are few published, quantified comparanda from other castle sites, have proved useful corroborative dating evidence and indicated that the inhabitants of Wigmore were at the forefront of fashion (Chapter 5). Their study serves one other useful function at Wigmore and that is as an indicator of how the castle may have been garrisoned in its early years, before the final subjugation of the Welsh by Edward I. A study by Suppe (1994) of military institutions in the Northern Welsh Marches suggests that the Anglo-Norman Marcher lords were heavily influenced by the Welsh military tactics of fast-moving, lightly armed raiding parties which struck well into English territory and retreated quickly back into Wales with their booty, usually cattle. This influence made itself felt by the formation of small units of lightly armed horsemen, stationed in the Marcher castles. He notes that in the 13th century, 37 tenures in Shropshire were described as owing the service of a 'homo equitans' (Suppe 1994, 75). Such service was owed at Oswestry, Clun, Montgomery and Ludlow, amongst others and also at Wigmore. In the case of Wigmore, documentary references (Cragoe, in archive) to the provision of horsemen do not occur until the 1290s, although there clearly is a differentiation between 'barded', that is, more heavily armed horses, and a more lightly equipped 'horseman' implicit in the entries. Numerous horseshoe nails were recorded at Hen Domen although an exact quantification is not given, but both fiddlekey and earred types are noted (Higham and Barker 2000, 94–95). At Stafford Castle, fiddlekey but not earred types were present. However, only 48 horseshoe nails in total were recovered from the Inner Bailey there, a vastly greater excavated area than at Wigmore. Shoeing nails (and horseshoes) were 'sparse' at Pontefract (Duncan 2002, 268) and the general impression is that castles in less turbulent areas tend to produce much less in the way of horseshoes and horseshoe nails. It could therefore be tentatively suggested that at Wigmore the evidence does point to the use of lightly armed horsemen as part of the garrison in times of need. There is certainly scope for a more detailed study of shoeing nails and horseshoes from a variety of castle sites, to see if Marcher castles during the 12th and 13th centuries are distinguishable by their horse fittings.

Warfare of a later date was represented by fragments of plate armour. The distribution of these fragments and other equipment is of great interest (see below). The earliest possible fragment of plate armour was found in 1996, Phase 6. Also in 1996, plates from a possible gauntlet were found in Phase 7, a hook fastener from armour in Phase 8 and five fragments, one with a hinged hook fastening was found in Phase 9. It is not possible to say whether the armour fragments were residual or not. Ballista and trebuchet balls were found in Phase 5 and Phase 6, a military arrowhead of late 14th century type in Phase 9 and a possible ratchet for a crossbow was found in Phase 8 (but see Chapter 5 for other possible interpretations of this object). River-worn pebbles, not reported on in this volume, may have been manuports and represent incoming or outgoing slingshots.

More numerous fragments of plate armour were recorded in the 1998 excavations. Six fragments were found in the lower fills of the East Tower (see above) together with a mail link, spurs, a horseshoe, horseshoe nails, dating from the Saxo-Norman period to after 1270, four arrowheads, one definitely identified as of military use, a broken knife blade or projectile point and three harness buckles. Similar equipment and militaria were found in layers beneath the Phase 9 plaster floor. Plate armour fragments, a horseshoe, horse-bit, mainly earred horseshoe nails (although one later type was present) occurred in Phase 8. There is some reason to believe (see above) that the Phase 8 deposits are linked to the lower fills of the East Tower. In comparison to the 1996 excavations there is a much greater concentration of militaria and horse equipment in 1998. This could conceivably indicate an armoury in or adjacent to the East Tower. As mentioned above, we know that armour and other paraphernalia associated with warfare and jousting were kept at the castle in the early 14th century. Although many of the 1998 items are not closely datable, the spurs from the lower fills of the East Tower seem to be from the 15th century, with a remote possibility of a 16th-century date. The arrowheads from the tower range in date from the early 13th to the late 14th century, so there certainly has been some mixing of material, although this does not disprove the existence of an armoury.

What exactly does the military and horse equipment represent? Clearly, from the inquisition of 1322 into Roger (V)'s possessions, the Mortimers kept a stock of equipment at the castle, some of which was already quite old at the time of the inquisition. Mould (pers comm) remarked that the excavated armour fragments looked rather battered. There is plenty of evidence in later periods for 'out of date' armour being used by the lower orders in time of war (Robinson 1994, 211). Knight (1993, 114) also reproduces an inventory of 1300, made at Montgomery Castle, which lists various types of militaria, some of which is damaged. A slightly later list remarks 'All manner of armour which should be at the castle ... is defective: 3 hauberks, 4 haubagions, old and perished, 25 chapeaux de fer, perished and of no value, 17 bucklers, 3 lances, all old and perished...' (Knight 1993, 114).

Armour and other accoutrements are also part of the spoils of war. The victory at Mortimer's Cross by the Yorkist forces in 1461 may have resulted in such spoils finding their way to Wigmore. The date of the battle is not inconsistent with the date of the spurs for example. Again at Montgomery Castle, 600 fragments of armour, dating to about 1550 (Robinson 1994) were found in 17th-century destruction debris in the Inner ditch (Knight 1994, 210). Knight (1994, 223–225) believes these were deposited after the Civil War battle of Montgomery and represent not only the spoils of war but demonstrate the use of out of date armour by combatants.

There is no material associated with Civil War warfare. There is, for example, not a single piece of lead shot. A high quality curb bit (Chapter 5) could date to this period or a little earlier. However, the control afforded by the bit would have been mild and as such is unlikely to have been associated with any military activity.

Domestic life

The assemblage of portable finds is of the sort to be expected on a castle site. Although there are some differences in functional composition between the two excavated area (see Figures 5.2 and 5.4), the most notable being the relative frequency of weapons and armour, and horse equipment in the 1998 excavation, there is insufficient evidence to characterise the use to which the buildings in both excavated areas were put. In addition, deposit types of the same period but in different excavated areas are not directly comparable. For example, Phase 5 in the 1996 excavation is the Southern Curtain Wall construction trench and its backfill, whereas in the 1998 excavation, Phase 5 contains occupation deposits. The finds from the two are unlikely to be the same, and in fact, as we have seen (above) the construction trench contained a somewhat anomalous set of fills anyway.

The pottery was of predominantly local manufacture throughout most of the site's history. At the very beginning of the castle, the presence of Worcester-type sandy cooking pot ware (Fabric Q01) suggests that the first castle builders and occupants brought their pottery with them. By the 15th and 16th centuries Malvern Chase ware (Fabric R02) formed an important part of the assemblage but this is part of a general phenomenon in Herefordshire, Worcestershire and Shropshire and attests to the enormous output of the Malvern potters. Continental imported wares were minimal throughout the castle's history and there was nothing which would distinguish the pottery assemblage as having come from a high-status site. Higham (2000, 177) writing about Hen Domen notes 'The high status of Hen Domen is manifest in the faunal remains and metalwork, rather than the ceramics' which could equally well sum up the situation at Wigmore.

Several categories of finds which might be expected on a castle site are absent from the record. There are, for example, no hones or whetstones and no bone or ivory gaming pieces, although a crude Merels board and pebble counters were found (Chapter 5). These are common enough finds on castle sites. A fine gilded chessboard and a gaming board of nutmeg were recorded amongst Roger Mortimer's possessions in the 1322 inventory (Mortimer 2004, 117) and a boxed set of bone chessmen and gaming pieces (partly destroyed by fire) were found at Loughor Castle (Redknap 1994). Indeed, there is a surprisingly low incidence of worked bone objects as a whole from Wigmore. The absence of certain categories of finds almost certainly reflects the small extent of the excavations. The finds assemblage is therefore unrepresentative of what may have been at the castle as a whole, although the assemblage is of interest given the paucity of excavated Marcher castle sites. From the excavated artefacts there is, however, little to indicate the enormous wealth of the Earls of March. Although for the latter we must mainly trust to the documentary record, there are other finds which reveal something about life at the castle which is not apparent in the written record. One small group of finds, the ceramic watering pot (CG98 02 Phase 11; Chapter 4), the iron rake tooth (CG96 08, Phase 9; Chapter 5) and a possible pruning knife (CG96 07, Phase 9; Chapter 5) point to gardens within the castle in the late medieval period. This interpretation is given added weight by Vitolo (Chapter 8) who also suggests the possibility of a garden within the castle, based on the plant remains.

9.4 SUMMARY

The data from the various specialist reports contained in this volume, when viewed together, do throw some interesting light on Wigmore Castle. With the integration of the reports it has been possible to suggest a programme of building works and phases of construction, the most striking of which is the apparent surge of activity in the 15th century. This is a period when Wigmore was thought to be a backwater, eclipsed by Ludlow Castle.

It has been possible to establish that the first fitz Osbern castle stood on the same site as the present castle remains and, at the opposite end of the chronological spectrum, that there appears to have been relatively little happening at the castle in the lead-up to the Civil War. Indeed, if the castle were little used after *c*1600 and probably already partly in a state of decay, it makes the decision of the Harleys to render it untenable even more understandable.

The possible position of an armoury and the provision of a garden in the castle also represent new information. Other elements, such as the use of the castle, probably the gatehouse, as a prison found no corroborative evidence in the archaeological record but the freshwater fish and swan remains find a resonance in the documented fishponds and swans in the moat (Chapter 2). Other documented 'great events' such as the grand tournament based on an Arthurian theme, hosted by Roger, the first Earl of March, have left no material remains within the excavated areas. This demonstrates, if demonstration were needed, as to how wide the gulf can be between the documented history and the archaeological record.

If it has not been possible to provide fresh data on domestic life at the castle, other than to say, it was typical of life at castles elsewhere, the detailed study of the portable finds has revealed some oddities, such as the copper-plated arrowheads. Quita Mould (pers comm) believes that these may be more widespread elsewhere. This demonstrates the importance of close examination and X-radiography of the finds, if the finds record is to be fully understood. Likewise, the fragments of plate armour were only identifiable by X-radiography and it is open to question how many 'iron plates' encountered in many reports, particularly those of an older vintage, could have been more closely identifiable by the use of scientific means. Other categories of finds, such as horseshoe nails, which seem at first sight to be of dubious interest, may hold the key to how a castle was garrisoned and warfare in the Marches. In fact, the small size of the excavations at Wigmore, although disadvantageous to site interpretation in some respects, has, in terms of resources, been advantageous to the close study of most finds categories.

We can see from the finds record that the castle was mostly self-sufficient. Mainstays such as food, ale and pottery were obtained locally but the early introduction of the cuboid horseshoe nails shows that the castle was anything but a backwater in the medieval period.

Notes

[1] www.worldseafishing.com, www.fishing.co.uk

10

WIGMORE CASTLE IN CONTEXT

Stephanie Rátkai

> ...chief stronghold of the mighty Mortimer family but now it stands strangely forlorn, covered in undergrowth and populated only by sheep
>
> Kightly (1979, 95).

10.1 WIGMORE CASTLE IN CONTEXT

A close study of the castle fabric at Wigmore does not form part of this volume. This research, as previously stated, has been undertaken by Jon Cooke (2008) on behalf of English Heritage. Aspects of the standing fabric and of the history of Wigmore Castle have been summarised by Cragoe in Chapter 2, drawing both on her own research and that of Jon Cooke. This chapter, therefore, does not encroach on either but seeks to set only the excavation results from Wigmore, and the interpretation thereof, in a broader setting.

There is, of course, no shortage of castles in the Marches, although few in the Central March have undergone detailed survey, much less extensive excavation. Figure 10.4 tabulates castles primarily in the Central March, details from which have been used in this discussion. The data sources are given in Figure 10.5 to save repeated referencing within the text. Castles in the Marches and beyond, such as Hen Domen, Montgomery, Dolforwyn, Dryslwyn and Loughor, which have been more fully excavated are referenced within the text. Figure 10.1 shows the location of all these sites. These comparanda form the basis for this chapter. It should be noted that the information available for many of these sites varies enormously. As an aid to the following discussion, the lords of Wigmore are listed in Figure 10.2 following the accepted lineage. New data, received after the final draft of this publication is summarised in Figure 10.3. Figure 10.5 summarises the sources for the data used in Figure 10.4[1].

The Welsh Marches are thickly clustered with the remains of motte and bailey castles (see Renn 1973). Wigmore, however is not a true motte and bailey and is described by Renn (1973) as a ringwork. The position of the castle, occupying a rising spur of land with steep drops along most of its length, is one which was utilised elsewhere by the founder of the castle, William fitz Osbern. This can be seen most famously, for example, at Chepstow, but also at lesser known sites such as Clifford Castle (a natural knoll lying adjacent to a steep drop to the River Wye) and Kington Castle (a crag above the Back Brook), both in Herefordshire. Cragoe (Chapter 2) notes the very deep drop at the north of Wigmore as it plunges down into the, now largely obscured, defensive ditch. It is unclear how much of the northern eminence of the Wigmore site was artificially heightened and indeed it may never have been so. For example, at Cymaron Castle (Radnorshire), built by Ralph (Ranulph) Mortimer in *c*1093, the 'motte' is in fact a natural rocky eminence that has been scarped. Caple (2007, 349) notes that Welsh castles are sited on small hills or on the edge of scarps so that they are very visible from the valley floor. Wigmore is not really sited in quite so commanding a position and the best vantage point of the castle would probably have been had from travelling south along the Roman road, a little to the north of Wigmore.

The lower part of the Inner Bailey at Wigmore was originally defended by a clay bank, only the outer slope of which was uncovered during excavation, so its original dimensions are unknown. As noted previously, the area open to excavation for the first castle was very small, so any conclusions are necessarily tentative. There is some evidence nevertheless for a timber palisade associated with the bank. The highly defensible nature of the site would have made a timber palisade more than adequate and the impetus to replace timber with stone defences not necessarily as great as elsewhere. In the previous chapter we have seen that the evidence for the construction date of the first stone defences is anything but clear. It has been suggested that this may have occurred in the 12th century but several considerations need to be factored in. Early stone defences occur at Ludlow in Shropshire (11th century), and at Chepstow (Monmouthshire), the stone hall-keep (11th century) is as much a defensive structure as a symbol of prestige; Knight (1991b, 4) also seems to indicate that the hall-keep was contemporary with a stone-walled bailey. Builth Wells (Breconshire) and Elmley (Worcestershire) had timber defences replaced with stone in the 12th century. Castles such as Hen Domen (Montgomeryshire) and Kington (Herefordshire)

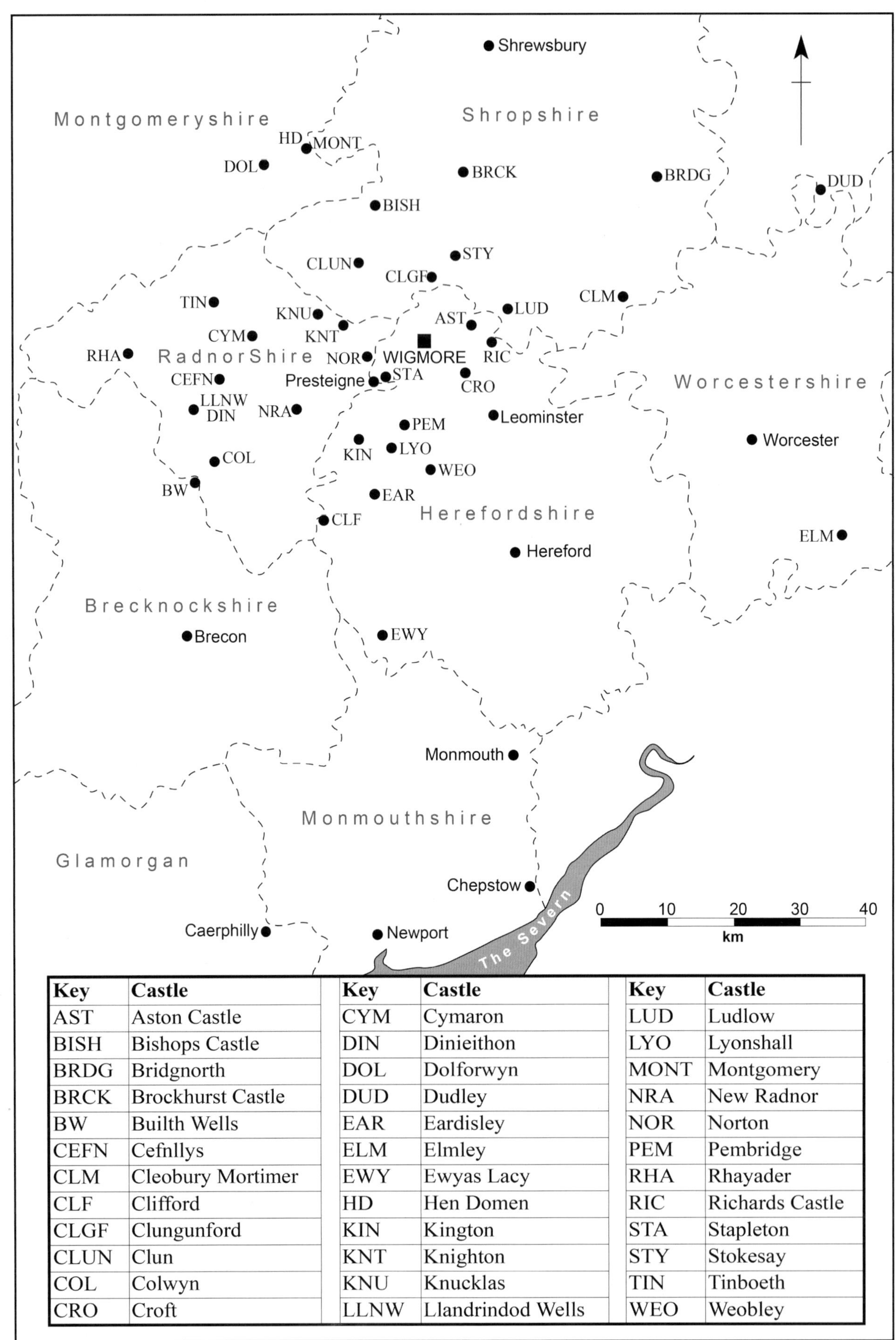

Key	Castle	Key	Castle	Key	Castle
AST	Aston Castle	CYM	Cymaron	LUD	Ludlow
BISH	Bishops Castle	DIN	Dinieithon	LYO	Lyonshall
BRDG	Bridgnorth	DOL	Dolforwyn	MONT	Montgomery
BRCK	Brockhurst Castle	DUD	Dudley	NRA	New Radnor
BW	Builth Wells	EAR	Eardisley	NOR	Norton
CEFN	Cefnllys	ELM	Elmley	PEM	Pembridge
CLM	Cleobury Mortimer	EWY	Ewyas Lacy	RHA	Rhayader
CLF	Clifford	HD	Hen Domen	RIC	Richards Castle
CLGF	Clungunford	KIN	Kington	STA	Stapleton
CLUN	Clun	KNT	Knighton	STY	Stokesay
COL	Colwyn	KNU	Knucklas	TIN	Tinboeth
CRO	Croft	LLNW	Llandrindod Wells	WEO	Weobley

FIGURE 10.1
Location map of the castles mentioned in the text

Name	Title	Lordship	Born	Died	Buried	Spouse
William fitz Osbern		to 1071	?			
Roger de Breteuil	Earl of Hereford	1071–?1075	?	1075?		
Ralph Mortimer		?1075–?1104	?	?1104	Normandy?	(1) Millicent (2) Mabel
Hugh I Mortimer		?1104–1148/50	?	1148–1150	?	Maud le Meschine
Roger I Mortimer		1148/50–?1153	before 1117	? 1153	?	?
Hugh II Mortimer		?1153–1180/81	?	1181x85	Wigmore Abbey	?
Roger II Mortimer		1180/81–?1214	before 1153	by 1214	Wigmore Abbey	Isabel Ferrers
Hugh III Mortimer		1214–1227	?1183		Wigmore Abbey	Eleanor Braose
Ralph II Mortimer		1227–1247	before 1198		Wigmore Abbey	Gwladus Ddu
Roger III Mortimer		1247–1282			Wigmore Abbey	Maud Braose
Edmund I Mortimer		1282–1304			Wigmore Abbey	Margaret Fiennes
Roger V Mortimer	1st Earl of March	?1305–1330			Greyfriars, Coventry	Joan de Geneville
Edmund II Mortimer		1330–1331	1302–1303?		Wigmore Abbey?	Elizabeth Badlesmere
Roger VI Mortimer	2nd Earl of March	1331–1360			Wigmore Abbey	Philippa Montacute
Edmund III Mortimer	3rd Earl of March Earl of Ulster	1360–1381			Wigmore Abbey	Philippa Plantagenet
Roger VII Mortimer	4th Earl of March Earl of Ulster	1381–1398			Wigmore Abbey	Alianore Holland
Edmund IV Mortimer	5th Earl of March Earl of Ulster	1413–1425			Clare Priory, Suffolk	Anne Stafford
Richard Plantagenet	Duke of York	1432–1460			Fotheringhay	Cecily Neville

FIGURE 10.2
The lords of Wigmore from the Conquest to 1460

Name	Title	Lordship	Born	Died	Buried	Spouse
William fitz Osbern		to 1071	?			
Roger de Breteuil	Earl of Hereford	1071–?1075	?	1075?		
Ralph Mortimer		?1075–post 1115?	*c*1050?	post 1115	Normandy?	(1) Millicent (2) Mabel
Hugh I Mortimer		post 1120–1180/81	*c*1100?	1181x1185	Wigmore Abbey	Maud le Meschine
Roger I Mortimer		1180/81–1214	*c*1150?		Wigmore Abbey	(2) Isabel Ferrers
Hugh II Mortimer		1214–1227	?1183		Wigmore Abbey	Eleanor Braose
Ralph II Mortimer		1227–1246	before 1198		Wigmore Abbey	Gwladus Ddu
Roger II Mortimer		1246–1282			Wigmore Abbey	Maud Braose
Edmund I Mortimer		1282–1304			Wigmore Abbey	Margaret Fiennes
Roger III Mortimer	1st Earl of March	?1305–1330			Greyfriars, Coventry	Joan de Geneville
Edmund II Mortimer		1330–1331	1302–3?		Wigmore Abbey?	Elizabeth Badlesmere
Roger IV Mortimer	2nd Earl of March	1331–1360			Wigmore Abbey	Philippa Montacute
Edmund III Mortimer	3rd Earl of March Earl of Ulster	1360–1381			Wigmore Abbey	Philippa Plantagenet
Roger V Mortimer	4th Earl of March Earl of Ulster	1381–1398			Wigmore Abbey	Alianore Holland
Edmund IV Mortimer	5th Earl of March Earl of Ulster	1413–1425			Clare Priory Suffolk	Anne Stafford
Richard Plantagenet	Duke of York	1432–1460			Fotheringhay	Cecily Neville

FIGURE 10.3
The lords of Wigmore: revised lineage (after Ian Mortimer)

never had anything other than timber defences. At other sites the replacement of timber with stone occurred at different points: Clun in Shropshire (late 12th to early 13th century), Croft (*c*1400), Lyonshall (13th century) and Weobley (12th and 13th centuries) in Herefordshire. At the royal castle of Montgomery, the Middle Bailey had stone defences built in 1251–53 (Knight 1993, 112) but the Outer Bailey was still defended by a timber palisade. It is clear from this brief survey that the transition from timber to stone in the Marches was piecemeal and occurred over at least two centuries.

At Loughor Castle, Glamorgan (Lewis 1994), constructed *c*1106, a levelling of the ringwork, extending the area within the castle and forming a platform for building, seems to be the closest parallel for what may have happened at Wigmore. This remodelling of the castle also marked the construction of the first stone curtain wall. Lewis (1994, 120–121) suggests that this may have taken

Castle	Location	History
Aston Castles	Herefordshire	Disuse *c*1155?
Bishops Castle	Shropshire	Leland 'well maintained'
Bridgnorth	Shropshire	1102 surendered to Henty I
		1155 surrendered to Henry II
		1166–74 repairs
		1211–12 barbican and turning bridge constructed
		15th century completely neglected
		Leland 'totally ruined'
		1647 slighted
Brockhurst Castle	Shropshire	1194–95 repairs
		1255 disuse
Builth Wells I & II	Breconshire	1168 castle (BW I) destroyed by Welsh
		Re-founded (BWII) in early 13th century
		1219 re-fortified
		1223 besieged
		1229 besieged and destroyed by Llywelyn
		1240 rebuilt
		1256 attacked by Welsh
		1260 demolished
		1277 rebuilt
		1294 besieged
		16th century Leland 'a fair castle of kings'
		1550+ demolished after fire
Caerphilly	S Wales	1270 attacked by Llywelyn
		1296–1316 minor Welsh attacks
		16th century Leland 'ruinous'
Cefnllys	Radnorshire	1262 taken by Welsh, Leland 'now down'
		1294 taken by Welsh
		1403 garrisoned and armed
		1425 'worth nothing'
		1430s repaired
		Leland 'now down'
		1588 ruined
Cleobury Mortimer	Shropshire	Destroyed 1155, Leland 'there was a castle'
Clifford	Herefordshire	1311+ left to decay
		1426 worth nothing
Clun	Shropshire	1196 burnt by Welsh
		1402? attacked by Glyn Dŵr
		16th century Leland 'somewhat ruinous'
Colwyn I & II	Radnorshire	1135 captured by Welsh
		1144 rebuilt by Hugh Mortimer
		1148+ in Welsh hands
		1195 rebuilt by William de Braose
		by 1397 abandoned
		16th century Leland 'ruins'
Croft	Herefordshire	1647 slighted
Cymaron	Radnorshire	1134 destroyed by Welsh
		1144 repaired
		1154 in Welsh hands
		1179 Cadwallon ap Madog, Lord of Cymaron, murdered by Roger Mortimer
		1179 in Crown hands
		1182 in Welsh hands
		1195 re-fortified
		1215 destroyed by Llywelyn
		Pre-1297 courthouse built
Dinieithon	Radnorshire	Sister castle to Cymaron, did not outlast 12th century
Elmley	Worcestershire	Leland 'there standeth but one tower and that partly broken'
Ewyas Lacy	Herefordshire	16th century Leland 'It hath been a notable thing'

FIGURE 10.4A

Marcher and Welsh castle history comparanda

Castle	Location	History
Kington	Herefordshire	1172 forfeited to crown 1180s wooden palisade repaired 1195 used as base for attacks against the Welsh 1216 destroyed by King John
Knighton	Radnorshire	1262 surrendered to the Welsh and destroyed
Knucklas	Radnorshire	1262 surrendered to the Welsh 1282 garrisoned by Edmund Mortimer ruined by the time of Glyn Dŵr's campaigns 1425 said to be derelict
Lyonshall	Herefordshire	13th-century timber motte and bailey replaced in stone
New Radnor	Radnorshire	1196, 1216, 1231, 1262 destroyed by the Welsh 1282 garrisoned against the Welsh 1402 captured by Glyn Dŵr and left to decay 1425 worth nothing 16th century Leland 'in ruin' but a 'piece of the gate was late amended'
Norton	Radnorshire	1262 surrendered to the Welsh
Rhayader	Radnorshire	1194 rebuilt 1194–1202 changed hands between English (Mortimers) and Welsh 1202 regained by Prince Rhys 1231 burnt by the Welsh 1425 (derelict) 'scitus castri veteris'
Richards Castle	Herefordshire	16th century Leland ' the keep, the walls and towers of it yet stand but going to ruin'
Stapleton	Herefordshire	1403 prepared against attack by Glyn Dŵr 1500s upgraded to a fortified manor house 1640s slighted
Tinboeth	Radnorshire	14th century decay 16th century Leland 'great ruins'
Weobley	Herefordshire	1138 captured by King Stephen, Leland 'somewhat ruinous'

FIGURE 10.4B
Marcher and Welsh castle history comparanda

place after 1151, when Loughor was burnt and captured by the Welsh, and before 1215, when the castle was once more captured by the Welsh. He suggests that the curtain wall construction could have been the work of Henry II in the period 1184–89, or of William de Braose (a powerful Marcher lord and rival in the Central March of Roger (II) Mortimer) in 1203–8.

At Wigmore, the extent of the Inner Bailey was seriously constrained by its geography and the levelling of the defensive bank and placement of the stone defensive circuit outside the defensive bank would have considerably increased the space within the lower section of the Inner Bailey for building. The very great depth of deposits uncovered in the Inner Bailey, some 8.50m, a prodigious amount seemingly unparalleled elsewhere, is in part explained by the bank and its levelling, which amounted to some 2.5m of deposits.

It is also germane to consider what might prompt the replacement of timber with stone. Although it has become fashionable to view castles less as strongholds of a mainly military and strategic purpose and more as symbols in the landscape, it is an inescapable fact that the Welsh Marches were an unruly, strife-torn area at least until the final decade of the 13th century. Even then Glyn Dŵr's revolt in the early 15th century, rekindled hostilities and the history of the area is also marked by petty feuding between the Marcher lords and the Welsh, and between the Marcher lords themselves — particularly acrimonious relations developed between Hugh (II) Mortimer and Joce de Dinan of Ludlow at the time of the Anarchy. As Suppe notes (1994, 52): 'Baronial castles and their guard schemes became anachronistic and militarily useless by the 13th century except in the Marches'. Clun Castle, for example, was stormed by the Welsh in 1195 and this may have provided the impetus for the construction of stone defences there. Wigmore was besieged, but not taken, by Henry II in 1155, although Mortimer castles at Cleobury and Bridgnorth (Shropshire) were. Hugh (II) Mortimer fortified Bridgnorth before the siege and may already have strengthened Wigmore's defences in stone. Wigmore, held by Roger (II) Mortimer in alliance with the Welsh, was again attacked in 1191, by William Longchamp, although by 1194 Roger received 10 marks from the king to fight against the Welsh. A further grant of 20 marks was made to Hugh (III) de Mortimer in 1223 from the Crown for the castle at Wigmore, which may well have been to improve its defences. It is certainly a period when the Welsh were on the offensive under Llywelyn and besieged New

Radnor castle in 1216, Builth Wells castle in 1223 and were again to invest New Radnor in 1231. Even before the Welsh incursions of the 1190s, Colwyn Castle (Radnorshire) had been captured twice by the Welsh, in 1135 (at the time the castle was a Mortimer possession) and 1148. Cymaron Castle, another Mortimer possession, fell to the Welsh in 1134 and was repaired by Hugh (II) Mortimer in 1144, before falling to the Welsh again in 1154. Hugh also rebuilt Colwyn in 1144. Added to this, disturbances during the Anarchy and its aftermath, and rebellion against Henry II in the middle of the century would add to the feeling that at Wigmore, defences of stone, for the Inner Bailey at least, might not be such a bad idea.

A general overview of the castles in the region indicates that there was a constant ebb and flow in castle fortunes against which probable building programmes and life at Wigmore can be viewed. A number of castles fell to the Welsh in the 12th century and their life ended then; castles such as the first ones at Builth Wells and Colwyn, and Dinieithon Castle (Radnorshire), which seems not to have outlasted the 12th century. The latter two both had Mortimer connections. In the castles surveyed only Aston Castle (Herefordshire) seem to have been demolished by Henry II *c*1155. A few castles fell to the Welsh in the early 13th century but most rose again, although Cymaron (another Mortimer castle) did not. The Welsh campaigns of the second half of the 13th century damaged several castles, such as Knighton, Cefnllys, Knucklas and New Radnor, (Knighton never recovered) and were responsible for the construction of Dolforwyn by the Welsh, although this was destroyed in 1277 by Roger (III) Mortimer. The latter then became a Mortimer possession, was rebuilt but by 1392 was described as 'worth nothing' and 'ruinous' in 1398 (Butler 1990, 82). After the final defeat of Llywelyn by Edward I, despite sporadic outbreaks of Welsh insurgency into the early years of the 14th century, the removal of the Welsh 'menace' led to a decline in many of the Marches' castles, proof, if proof were needed, of the important strategic role they had played. Caerphilly (Glamorgan) fell into decline after *c*1327 and was derelict by the 16th century. Clun seems to have been largely neglected by the fitz Alans after the 1270s, Colwyn was abandonned by 1397, Dolforwyn was ruinous by 1398, Knucklas, ruined before *c*1400 and Tinboeth, an isolated castle of little but strategic value, was in decline in the 14th century, the final mention of it being in 1322, before Leland's observation in the 16th century that it was ruinous. The castles at Clun and New Radnor received a body blow from Glyn Dŵr's rebellion at the beginning of the 15th century from which they never fully recovered. Montgomery Castle also appears to have been in decline in the 14th century (Knight 1993, 114). The Great Tower, the chief tower and the chapel were said to be 'defective' in 1310. This is particularly remarkable, as, by then, the castle was less than 100 years old. From 1359 to 1425 the castle was in Mortimer stewardship and like several castle listed below, was garrisoned during Glyn Dŵr's revolt. In 1381, Sir John de Ludlow obtained the right to live in the bailey with his wife, two esquires, a chamberwoman and a laundress (Knight 1993, 115), which gives some idea of how few people may actually have been living in the castles at this period. By 1402, at a time of war, the numbers had been increased by 60 men-at-arms and 124 archers.

A fascinating insight into cycles of dereliction and upkeep of a castle can be gained from records relating to Dryslwyn Castle (Caple 2007, 41–46). From 1287, when the castle fell into English hands, until at least the mid-14th century, the necessity for constant vigilance and repairs seems unending. The first stage of repairs, beginning after the siege of 1287 was complete in 1290. Ten years later money was spent re-roofing buildings damaged in a gale. A major period of neglect occurred under the ownership by the Despencers. Despite refurbishment in 1312, repairs were necessary again in 1329. Some ten years later the castle had undergone about 20 years of neglect, which led to extensive remedial works. The curtain wall was rebuilt in 1342 under the auspices of the Black Prince. Further repairs were necessary in the 1350s and the castle continued to be maintained as a defensive strong point until after Glyn Dŵr's revolt. By 1455 it was no longer a defensible site. Caple's exposition demonstrates admirably the amount of work and expense required to keep a fully functioning castle on the go and, just as importantly, how quickly the rot could set in. Both these aspects are particularly relevant to any discussion of the fortunes of Wigmore Castle.

Another important aspect of the history of Wigmore Castle, is the somewhat analogous position occupied by the Mortimers themselves. Of all the great borderland magnates, the Mortimer family was the only one whose power and focus lay predominantly in the Marches (Davies 2000, 313). As such, their *honorial caput*, would probably have received far more attention and for a longer period than many of the castles of the Central March.

Those castles that survived the 14th century were mostly ruinous by the 16th. New Radnor was the subject of Roland Lee's attentions in the 16th century (along with Wigmore and Montgomery). At New Radnor, Bishop Lee advised that the gatehouse be repaired and used as a prison, seemingly one of his preferred options, and we find a similar reference to the use of Wigmore as a gaol in 1537, perhaps using the gatehouse also. Similarly, Lee used stone from Chirbury Priory for repairs to Montgomery and from Wigmore Abbey at Wigmore.

By the time of the Civil War, only a few castles were tenable such as Montgomery, Ludlow, Croft Castle and Stapleton Castle, the latter being slighted by the owners to prevent it falling into the hands

Castle	Sources
Aston Castle I	Remfry 1994–2007, http://www.castles99.ukprint.com/Essays/aston.html
Bishops Castle	Renn 1973, Thompson 1987
Bridgnorth	Renn 1973, Thompson 1987
Brockhurst Castle	Renn 1973, Remfry 1994–2007, http://www.castlewales.com/brockhst.html
Builth Wells I & II	Renn 1973, Thompson 1987, Remfry1994-2007, http://www.castles99.ukprint.com/Essays/builth.html
Caerphilly	Thompson 1987, Renn 1989
Cefnllys	Thompson 1987, Remfry 1994–2007, http://www.castles99.ukprint.com/Essays/cefnllys.html
Cleobury Mortimer	Thompson 1987
Clifford	Renn 1973, Remfry 1994–2007, http://www.castles99.ukprint.com/Essays/clifford.html, Thompson 1987
Clun	Renn 1973, Thompson 1987, Renfry 1994-2007 http://www.castles99.ukprint.com/Essays/clun.html
Colwyn I & II	Renn 1973, Thompson 1987, Remfry 1994-2007 http://www.castles99.ukprint.com/Essays/colwyn.html
Croft	Northall 2009 http://www.castlewales.com/croft.html
Cymaron	Renn 1973, Remfry 1994–2007, http://www.castles99.ukprint.com/Essays/cymaron.html
Dinieithon	Renn 1973
Elmley	Renn 1973, Thompson 1987
Ewyas Lacy	Renn 1973, http://www.castles99.ukprint.com/Essays/longtown.html, Thompson 1987
Kington	Renn 1973, Remfry 1994–2007, http://www.castles99.ukprint.com/Essays/kington.html
Knighton	Renn 1973, Northall 2009, http://www.castlewales.com/knighton.html
Knucklas	Thompson 1987, Remfry 1994–2007, http://www.castles99.ukprint.com/Essays/knucklas.html
Lyonshall	Fry 1996, Renn 1973
New Radnor	Renn 1973, Remfry 1994–2007, http://www.castles99.ukprint.com/Essays/radnor.html, Thompson 1987
Norton	Renn 1973
Rhayader	Renn 1973, Thompson 1987, Gatehouse 2012, http://www.gatehouse-gazetteer.info/Welshsites/904.html http://www.rhayader.co.uk/index.php/rhayader/aboutdetail/more_about_rhayader/
Richards Castle	Renn 1973, Remfry 1994–2007, http://www.castles99.ukprint.com/Essays/richards.html, Thompson 1987
Stapleton	Renn 1973, Thompson 1987
Tinboeth	Thompson 1987, Remfry 1994–2007, http://www.castles99.ukprint.com/Essays/tinboeth.html
Weobley	Fry 1996, Renn 1973, Thompson 1987

FIGURE 10.5
Sources for Figure 10.4

of the enemy (in this case, the Parliamentarians), exactly the same as at Wigmore Castle, although in the latter case to prevent it from falling into Royalist hands.

As can be seen from the above, circumstances in the Marches were entirely conducive to active building programmes at Wigmore throughout the 12th and 13th centuries and the establishment of a 12th-century stone curtain, updated and enhanced towards the end of the 13th or beginning of the 14th century seems entirely plausible. Although after the de Montfort rebellion there were no further attacks against Wigmore, the Marches were sufficiently volatile to have made the upkeep of the castle defences a primary consideration. The Mortimers were certainly active militarily and besieged the short-lived Welsh castle of Dolforwyn in 1277, garrisoned New Radnor and Knucklas against the Welsh in 1282 and briefly lost possession of Cefnllys to the Welsh in 1294.

In addition, the loss of Mortimer lands in Normandy in 1205 may have focussed the family's attention on their *honorial caput* in England. We could perhaps see the laying of the mosaic tile pavements as an attempt to turn the castle from a functional fortress into a habitation with a greater degree of adornment. The visit of Henry III to Wigmore in 1233 may add some weight to this. From the time of Roger (V) Mortimer, the castle clearly was a well furnished place, although not necessarily more so than other flourishing castles of the period. Evidence of the range of goods and furnishings are provided by the inventories of 1322 and 1330 but there is also some corroborative evidence from the excavations, such as the drape rings, the possible headdress wire, the inlaid shears, book clasp and the amber beads. A reference to the Duke of Kent and his retinue being granted free access to Wigmore during Roger (V) Mortimer's exile in the early 1320s (Cragoe, in archive), also suggests that Wigmore must have been well-appointed at this time. In the light of the decline of many of the castles in the Marches during the 14th century, including those held by the Mortimers, and, excluding the revolt against the Despensers in 1321 and against Edward II in 1326, in the outbreak of peace which came to the Marches following Edward's subjugation of the Welsh, there was ample opportunity for Mortimer attentions to be turned to Wigmore. The staging of the Arthurian Tournament there in 1329 reveals not only the personal pride of Roger (V) but also the pride in his castle. The Arthurian legends were, of course popular *leit motifs* running through aristocratic culture of the Middle Ages, but the Mortimers may have held a special affection for them, perhaps through their Welsh inheritance from the time of Gwladus Ddu, wife of Ralph (II) Mortimer. Caple (2007, 350) remarks that 'Wales in the 12th and 13th centuries was a land of legends, lineage and prophecy'. It may be apposite that Meyrick (1836a, 27) remarks, in reference to the alliance between Glyn Dŵr, Percy and Mortimer, that 'We may be amused at the superstition of the age, that these great personages conceived themselves to be the parties prophesied, by Merlin, as those among whom the kingdom was to be divided'.

Roger (V) appears to have been involved in building works in 1328, adding a chantry to Leintwardine church, extending Wigmore church and building a chantry and improving the lodgings at Ludlow. However, from the excavated remains there is no very clear indication of major building work at Wigmore apart from the Phase 6 lead-melting hearths at this time and the subsequent construction of a seemingly modest new building in Phase 7. It is by no means certain that the lead was destined for reuse at Wigmore and could just as easily have been transferred to Ludlow Castle for works there. However, a few of the fragments of architectural stone (Kendrick 2008) are consistent with works carried out in the late 13th and early 14th centuries. Decorated window glass found in the final demolition rubble was also dated to the 14th century, with only three pieces of possibly earlier date. We should, therefore, be open to the possibility that the reconstruction of the Southern Curtain Wall is unconnected with Roger (V). Elsewhere, a Court House was built at the Mortimer castle of Cymaron in 1297 and works may have been carried out at another Mortimer castle at Cefnllys by Maud Mortimer (Roger (V)'s grandmother) in 1303. Both events pre-date Roger's assumption of the title. Caple (2007, 351) notes that in the Southern March from the 1290s the powerful Marcher families of Valence, de Clare and Bigod were competing in architectural display and it is possible that renewed building at Wigmore may have been part of this 'spirit of the age', rather than the expression of an individual such as Roger (V) Mortimer.

After Roger's execution in 1330, the fate of the castle is uncertain. There appears to be a period of disuse in Phase 7 as the building found in the 1996 excavations apparently decayed to the extent that plaster had fallen from the walls to the ground and there is no very clear evidence of prolonged occupation detected in the 1998 excavations. It should also be borne in mind that by the early 14th century Ludlow Castle had passed into Mortimer control through the marriage of Joan de Geneville to Roger (V) Mortimer. Accounts suggest that not only did Roger build at Ludlow but that he also held court there in some opulence (see Mortimer 2004, 207–209) and it has always been assumed that with the acquisition of Ludlow Castle, the fate of Wigmore was sealed. Certainly, in 1333, there is a somewhat mysterious inquiry into damage and repairs necessitated at Wigmore Castle, although in contrast, the previous year Edward III was at Wigmore Castle, which not only suggests that the castle was in good order but is also interesting for the fact that Wigmore was chosen rather than Ludlow Castle. Knight (1993, 111) pertinently notes that 'acts of God' can be equally responsible for decay to the castle fabric and 'damage and repairs' may not, therefore, be the harbingers of disuse and terminal dereliction. Emery (2000, 597–598) is of the opinion that building at Wigmore was instigated by Roger (V) and by his grandson Roger, the 2nd Earl of March, but that well before the end of the 14th century the Mortimers were no longer patrons of building works. In the case of Roger (V), Emery (2000, 597–598) believes that building at Wigmore was primarily driven by the desire to embellish the ancient *honorial caput*. This is eminently believable but there is a caveat in that Roger would have needed to have undertaken a substantial amount of building work (see above) in a short period of about three years.

Decline at Wigmore after the death of Roger (V) would match the pattern of 14th-century decline seen at other castles, and, in the case of Wigmore this may have been exacerbated by the death of Roger's heir Edmund in 1331 and the lengthy minority of his heir, Roger (VI), who regained the title of 2nd Earl of March only in 1354. Wigmore Castle had been in the custody of William de Bohun, Roger (VI)'s stepfather, and was not returned to Edmund until 1343. However, it was not until 1356, at the death of his grandmother, Joan de Geneville, that he gained possession of Ludlow Castle. Roger's heir Edmund, 3rd Earl of March, was born in 1354 at Llyswen, Breconshire, (not Wigmore nor Ludlow) and the assumption therefore that any decline at Wigmore before *c*1360 was linked to the pre-eminence of Ludlow, seems unfounded. In 1359, Montgomery Castle was granted to Roger (VI) and subsequently passed to the House of York (see below). The period of 14th-century ownership by the Mortimers saw a programme of building at Montgomery with a kitchen and brewhouse being constructed in the Inner Ward and 'manorial-type' buildings in the Middle Ward (Knight 1993, 102). The construction of a kitchen and brewhouse suggests that works at Montgomery were not merely cosmetic and that they were associated with intended occupation of the castle. It is therefore not inconceivable that some work could also have been carried out at Wigmore. Whatever the truth of the matter, attention was not solely focussed on Ludlow Castle at a time when it is generally seen to have been of paramount importance to the Mortimer family.

A further intimation of the hand of Roger (VI) Mortimer in building works is afforded by the now lost stained glass from Wigmore Church (see Chapter 2) which depicted the arms of Bohun, Montacute,

Mortimer and Badlesmere and which must have been commissioned by him. It seems unlikely that under the circumstances no work at all was carried out at the castle. The point raised by Cooke (2008) that the consistency of the architectural detailing indicates a single building campaign under Roger (V) Mortimer need not be true. It is unfortunate that no mason's marks survive which could corroborate the single build theory. At Weoley Castle, for example, a large number of such marks survived which seemed to link a specific phase of building with a particular family of masons (Kirsty Nichol pers comm).

Like the 3rd Earl, the 4th and 5th Earls of March, inherited in their minority, but in adulthood became important players on the stage of English and Irish politics. It is unlikely that their attention was directed to Wigmore to any great extent (but see above), although the Earls of March continued to be buried at Wigmore (see Figures 10.2 and 10.3 , as they had been from at least the time of Hugh de Mortimer (died *c*1181), the exception being the 5th earl, who was buried in Suffolk in Clare Priory, which he had founded. Woolgar (1999, 160) notes that the choice of burial place emphasised the connections of the deceased and, as such, continued interment at Wigmore Abbey suggests that Wigmore still occupied an important place in the hearts and minds of the Mortimers at least until the 15th century. It is also worth noting that by the end of the 14th century the Mortimers obtained two-thirds of their income from their Marcher and Welsh estates (Davies 2000, 395) which might have occasioned more than a passing interest in Wigmore, and in 1393 Roger, the 4th Earl of March, had a 40 day progress through his Welsh lands. Such visits were not necessarily welcome and Davies terms them 'grand and profiteering' progresses. In the course of the 14th century the number of great Marcher families was seriously reduced (Davies 200, 395) so, despite the series of Mortimer minorities mentioned above, the lords of Wigmore flourished and indeed profited by the diminishing pool of rival Marcher estate holders. As both Caple (2007, 140–146) and Thompson (1987, 14–16) amply demonstrate, significant resources were required to keep a castle in reasonable repair; the addition of new buildings or rebuilding of existing buildings must have required considerably greater resources and the Mortimers were in the happy position of being extremely wealthy.

Probably in 1401–2, Wigmore Castle is recorded as being garrisoned (Cragoe, Chapter 2) presumably in response to Glyn Dŵr's revolt. In 1402, Sir Hugh Burnell was appointed keeper of the castles of Cefnllys, Dolforwyn and Montgomery (Knight 1993, 116), all of which were Mortimer castles, although the future 5th Earl of March was still in his minority. Knight (1993, 116) records that Burnell's keepership of the castles contained a clause concerning the maintenance of the buildings. It is therefore possible that some degree of maintenance was also carried out at Wigmore. In 1425 Richard Plantagenet (the 3rd Duke of York) inherited the Mortimer estates, although he too was in his minority. The *inquisition post mortem* for Edmund, 5th Earl of March, declared Radnor, Knucklas, Cefnllys, Clifford and Wigmore castles to be 'worth nothing'. Wigmore, Cefnllys and Radnor were all apparently garrisoned in 1402–3. Knucklas, the only castle described as 'completely derelict' in 1425, was not garrisoned, which seems to imply that Wigmore, Cefnllys and Radnor were in a reasonable state of repair at the beginning of the 15th century. As we have seen in Chapter 9, the term 'worth nothing' is not synonymous with derelict or decayed, which the preceding tends to confirm.

The excavation results, however, reveal something quite remarkable at Wigmore and that is a major episode of demolition and construction in the 15th century. It seems unlikely that these can have occurred before 1425, although a building campaign before this date might have sufficiently stretched resources to make the castle 'worth nothing'. An interesting parallel is seen at Cefnllys Castle, a Mortimer castle from the outset. Repairs were undertaken here in the 1430s. This would coincide with Richard, Duke of York, attaining his majority and it would seem quite plausible that the rebuilding and repair to the Southern Curtain Wall at Wigmore, which consists of a particularly well-ordered stretch of masonry, which could not be considered a botched repair or stop-gap, belong to this period also. If so, this throws a new light on how Richard administered his Welsh and Marcher estates. It has always been assumed that this had been done from Ludlow but the building works at Wigmore are found in conjunction with the type of animal bone assemblage which can only be associated with aristocratic occupancy. Why then would the fortunes of Wigmore (and Cefnllys) have been revived? At this stage, the military importance of the castle was redundant in the Marches but several other possibilities present themselves. Perhaps the most compelling of these is both psychological and symbolic. Wigmore had, since time immemorial, been the principal seat of the Mortimer family. From the time of Roger (III) in the mid-13th century, the family had been closely associated with the Crown. Roger, 4th Earl of March, was named heir presumptive to the English throne in 1385 and on his death in 1398, his son Edmund 5th Earl of March, was similarly named. The usurpation of the Crown by Henry IV, effectively removed the Earl of March's claim but on the death of Henry V he became a member of the Council of Regency during the minority of Henry VI. Richard of York would also have seen the benefit of emphasising his Mortimer connections — he also styled himself Earl of March — and what better way to do this than to restore the *honorial caput* of the Mortimers? Similar symbolic acts can be seen in the construction of a new stone keep at Stafford Castle in the mid-14th century (Soden 2007, 219–220), the construction of the Sharrington Range at Dudley Castle in the 1530s by John Dudley (Stephen Linnane pers comm) and, to return to Stafford, the reconstruction of Ralph's stone keep in the early 19th century by the Jerningham family (Soden 2007, 225), in order to boost their claim to the title. In all three cases, however, subsequent occupation of the newly refurbished castles seems to have been short lived or sporadic. At Wigmore, it would appear that the 15th-century rebuilding and modifications were not purely symbolic but were also accompanied by some occupation. This is unlikely to have been continuous and the high quantity of game consumed in the 15th century may reflect that the castle was a good base from which to go hunting. Nevertheless, the presence of 15th-century Tournai tokens is indicative of an exchequer and hence some administrative functions. Emery (2000, 598) makes the salient point that the Marcher, Welsh and Irish estates were the financial and military mainstay of the House of York's power which it used to pursue its national ambitions.

As for Cefnllys, it stood in the ancient Welsh *cantref* of Maelienydd, which the Mortimers had long campaigned for, and provides a direct link back through Gwladus Ddu (Gladys the Dark), wife of Ralph Mortimer, to Llywelyn the Great, Prince of Wales. Thus Wigmore and Cefnllys together neatly link Richard of York to both English and Welsh royalty.

Meyrick (1836b, 246) notes that Richard Plantagenet, Duke of York, was at Wigmore in 1461; here he received a letter from his sons Edward and Edmund, who were at Ludlow. A further tangential link to the House of York's involvement in Wigmore can be found in a grant of 1462 to the king's (Edward IV) servant for services to the king and his father (Richard of York) at Northampton, Wakefield and Wigmore (Cragoe, Chapter 2). Last but not least, in a grant of lands to Edward IV's first born son (the future Edward V), the list is headed by the castle, lordship and honour of Wigmore and again in 1493, this time relating to the then Prince of Wales, Arthur. If Wigmore did hold a symbolic status then Henry Tudor was also keen to keep the symbolism alive.

Curiously, Thomas Wright, an early 19th-century antiquarian, appears to have been far less dismissive of the later role of Wigmore Castle. In his *History and antiquities of Ludlow* he remarks 'Edward [later Edward IV] ...spent all the leisure time he could spare in the castles of Ludlow and Wigmore' and 'Lady Anne Neville...kept her court at Wigmore Castle' (Wright 1826, 60). The sources for these statements are, of course, not given. However much veracity we attach to these observations, it is demonstrable that in the popular imagination of the time, Wigmore was given an importance which is completely at odds with interpretations in more modern writings.

A further episode of building or refurbishment occurred at Wigmore probably towards the end of the 15th century, but thereafter the site is marked by the steady accumulation of dumps and rubble, most of which are difficult to place in any context. Larger areas of excavation might have made these sequences clearer. It is impossible within the constraints of the areas excavated to be certain how much of the rubble represents natural collapse and how much was placed by human agency. The apparently somewhat sudden decay and dereliction would seem to bear out observations about the ruinous state of Wigmore in 1528 and later by Bishop Lee in 1534.

Wigmore Castle passed from the female descendants of Edward IV on the death of Anne of York, wife of the 3rd Duke of Norfolk in 1511 and the widowhood of Catherine of York, Countess of Devon, in the same year (Cragoe, in archive). Any link between the House of York and their Mortimer antecedents, and Wigmore had been completely severed. This could have rendered the castle totally redundant, although Henry VIII retained the castle (see Chapter 2) and it was held by Princess Mary (later Mary I). The documentary evidence could be read to suggest that the princess was at times resident at Wigmore.

Of the other Mortimer castles in the Marches, Cefnllys, which was repaired in the 1430s, was ruinous by 1588, Stapleton was turned into a fortified manor house in the 1500s and by the 1540s Richards Castle was standing but ruinous. Builth Wells, a royal castle, built by Edward I in the 1270s, was demolished after a fire in the second half of the 16th century. The castles at Ludlow and Montgomery were still functional in the 16th century, particularly Ludlow, which was the seat of the Council of the Marches.

Bishop Roland Lee, a ruthless careerist who became Lord President of the Council of the Marches and something of Henry VIII's 'enforcer' in the West, surveyed many of the Marcher castles. As we have seen, he instigated works in the 1530s to both Radnor Castle and Wigmore, providing them with a gaol, and to Montgomery Castle. Lee seems to have been particularly antipathetic to the Welsh, as his enthusiasm for prisons suggests. Fines levied by the Council of the Marches were the chief means by which royal castles were repaired and Ludlow seems to have been the main beneficiary of this system (Williams 1989, 4). However, Lee spent at least two years engaged in works at Wigmore but hard and fast evidence for these works is not very apparent from the excavations. A possible plaster surface in the 1996 excavation may belong to this period and it is just possible that the patching of the stone-slabbed floor, and the mortar and rubble dumps above it, in the 1998 excavations, are associated with Lee's work. Strangely, during the 16th century, the faunal remains and marine shell suggest a continuing high-status diet. Some of this could be associated with Bishop Lee's presence but surely not all of it. With the death of Lee in 1543, documentary evidence concerning the castle is in short supply. Under the Lord Presidency of Sir Henry Sidney (1560–86), further buildings were erected at Ludlow but as Cragoe points out (Chapter 2), Sidney carried out further repairs to Wigmore in the 1580s, though by this time it appears to have fallen into further decay. Who then was resident at Wigmore? The evidence of the type of diet enjoyed at Wigmore does not accord with that of prisoners in the gaol. A constable and porter are mentioned in connection with Wigmore and Radnor Castles in 1589 which not only provides possible candidates for occupancy but also suggests that neither castle was in particularly bad shape. Evidence for a seemingly luxurious lifestyle for the Constable at Dudley Castle, was provided by both faunal (Thomas 2005a) and artefactual remains (personal inspection by the author), in roughly the same period. This may also have been the case at Wigmore. In addition, Cragoe notes gentry occupation in the early 1530s and 1590s (Chapter 2). And yet, the archaeological evidence is strongly indicative of decay and dereliction in both excavated areas in the 16th century (see Chapter 9).

A useful summary of the state of Welsh castles in the later 16th and 17th centuries is provided by Williams (1989, 4–5). He quotes from George Owen's *The dialogue of the government of Wales* published in 1594, where the latter trenchantly observes that the castles had hitherto been the bane of people's lives but that all now stand 'in ruyn and decaye'. It is at this time that it is noted that Montgomery Castle is out of repair and that there was 'noe householde stuff in the castle' (Knight 1993, 118). In the period 1618–24, further surveys into the condition of royal castles in Wales continue to present a picture of decay and ruination, with the fabric of the castles being continually pilfered for lead, timber, iron and stone (Williams 1989, 5).

By the early 17th century the evidence for the state of repair and the degree of occupation at Wigmore is contradictory. The East Tower and the adjacent excavated area were probably ruinous but this is, after all, but a small area of the castle. Artefacts and pottery relating to this period are very poorly represented in this area. In the case of the 1996 excavations, the evidence is less clear cut and there is without doubt some pottery which must date to the Civil War and a high quality curb bit is consistent with some high-status occupation in the first half of the 17th century. In addition, there was at least one repair to the castle fabric (the blocking of the 'alcove' in the Southern Curtain Wall) and the possible propping of the Curtain Wall by the Eastern Tower. Unfortunately the alcove, its function and, more pertinently, the date and reason for its construction and blocking is largely inexplicable.

A reference exists (Hinds 1909, 597–608) to the office of a 'castellan of the castle' at £15 4s 2d in the period 1617–19. By this date, the castle appears to have been in the private ownership of Robert Harley, inherited from his father, who had been steward of the castle in the late 16th century and who had subsequently purchased the castle in 1601, after its forfeiture by Gelly Merick to the Crown (see Chapter 2). The office of Wigmore castellan in the second decade of the 17th century is of interest in that it suggests that not long after its purchase the castle was not the primary residence of the Harleys.

For matters of comparison, at Radnor the same office of castellan is recorded at £10 and is the same for Cardigan. Most of the castles listed have the office of steward, castellan or keeper at between about £6 and £10, so the office at Wigmore was somewhat better remunerated and hence may indicate a rather better preserved castle. The castellan of Windsor was paid at £20 (but several other officers there make a much higher annual expenditure), the keeper at Bristol £28, but it is the North Welsh castles that command the most with Conway at £50 and Caernarvon at £60. The document seems to suggest that Wigmore was 'holding its own' against some of the other royal castles and it is difficult to reconcile this with continued reports of the ruinous state of the castle in the 16th century.

Thompson (1987) points out that by the time of the Civil War, the existence of a sound defensive curtain wall is sufficient to allow a castle to be garrisoned regardless of the condition of the internal buildings. In the early years of the Civil War, the Royalists believed that they could hold an uninterrupted line of castles and garrisons from Chester to Bristol (Williams 1989, 2) and it is against this that we must view the perceived strategic importance of Wigmore. Any attempt to hold such a fortified place was usually accompanied by the construction of earthen outworks, as was the case at Montgomery (Williams 1989, 13). We cannot know for certain the state of the curtain walls at Wigmore but the castle site is not an obviously advantageous one for mid-17th century warfare. None of the correspondence between Robert and Brilliana Harley mentions any work at the castle and the absence of the large quantities of artefactual and other debris of the type which is found on other sites used during the Civil War, even allowing for the fact that only small areas at Wigmore were excavated, suggests that the castle cannot have been garrisoned in any effective way during the unrest. The letter from Brilliana to Robert Harley quoted by Cragoe (Chapter 2) is somewhat opaque in its meaning. Readings of this letter mark yet another divergence in interpretation, and as with the 16th century, it becomes increasingly difficult to reconcile the documentary and archaeological record.

Pre-emptive slighting is certainly known at other sites (see Thompson 1987) and there is a logical rationale for this course of action. The text of the letter seems to suggest, however, keeping the castle, with what appears to be an inadequate force of eight men (with a promise of more to follow, although we do not know if this was honoured). Their *materiel* — a single barrel of gunpowder and a small quantity of match — also seems scarcely adequate for either a garrison or for a wrecking party. The single barrel of gunpowder may reflect the general paucity of powder and artillery in the early years of the war noted by Williams (1989, 16). In the excavated areas of the castle there is no evidence that the walls or buildings were brought down by gunpowder, which surely would have blown the masonry out ie the resultant cascade of stone would have been displaced beyond the confines of the Inner Bailey.

The usual method of slighting appears from the records, to have been by either undermining and/or dismantling. This was usually a long, drawn out and expensive affair. Owen (quoted in Williams 1989, 11) opined 'yt ys more easie to digg stones out of the mayne rock, than to pull down an old wall'. The records from Montgomery Castle show (Thompson 1987, Appendix 4) that the demolition there was in part achieved by undermining the fabric. However time consuming, dismantling by mining or picking did allow the cost of the slighting to be defrayed against the profit from the resale of building stone, lead and other salvaged materials. On the other hand, Montgomery was slighted after the Civil War not during the conflict, as at Wigmore, where time and resources were at a premium. Bridgnorth Castle was blown up during the Civil War, so the use of gunpowder is not unknown but a single barrel of gunpowder at Wigmore hardly seems sufficient to slight the castle to any appreciable extent and the letter should be treated with a certain amount of circumspection. If, however, the castle was very ruinous indeed by the 1640s, then a small party may have been able to inflict further, more effective damage to the castle fabric. It is noticeable that the maximum area of damage to the Inner Bailey is to the north of the Eastern Tower (1998 excavations) which is evident from present-day conditions and the Buck engraving of 1733. If this was a result of slighting it is paradoxically the one excavated area that had no finds demonstrably datable to the Civil War. The area where this material is found (1996 excavations) is the area that seems to have survived relatively well. If, however, we assume that the eastern side of the Inner Bailey was at best partly derelict in the 16th century this may have been the area to which the slighting was directed, nature having progressed the state of disrepair.

If material of Civil War date is in short supply at Wigmore Castle, then material of the second half of the 17th century and later is even rarer and there is nothing to suggest occupation on the site. The removal of stone from the castle in 1647 which Cragoe notes (Chapter 2) indicates not only the ruinous state of the castle but also the absence of interest on the part of Robert Harley in the castle in general and in restoration in particular. The find of an oxshoe in the 1996 demolition deposits suggests that material was salvaged and carted away. In the light of all the evidence, undated documents relating to the 'repayre of the old house in the castle and the old gate for a house of correction' (Chapter 2) cannot relate to works after the end of the Civil War. The reference is in itself an oddity, since the amount of money stipulated for the repairs is only 2s 2d. Referring to the accounts for the slighting of Montgomery Castle (Thompson 1987, 186–193), this would pay for roughly a day and a half's labour for a mason, roughly a day's labour for a carpenter or two days for an unskilled labourer, excluding material costs. Again two different interpretations are possible. Cragoe (Chapter 2) sees the small expenditure as evidence that the buildings were in good repair and hence needed little doing to them to make them good. An alternative view is that this sounds less like a repair and more of a rough and ready stabilisation of unsound structures. When viewed alongside the archaeological evidence, it appears insufficient evidence on which to predicate the continued existence of a functioning prison at the castle in the 17th century, especially since the penal role of several castles appears to have been primarily associated with Roland Lee's 16th-century reign of terror, under the aegis of the Council of the Marches.

By the time of Buck's engraving of 1733 the castle was already very ruinous (see Figure 2.2). It appears to have been bypassed by those in search of the 'picturesque', and the rugged, overgrown, steep contours of the Inner Bailey and the isolation of the site, were clearly ill-suited to casual picnickers. Sherds from a teapot and a minimum of three drinks bottles (Cool 2008) bear evidence that by the 20th century some intrepid visitors made their way to the site but, in general, modern material was seldom encountered during the excavations.

10.2 CONCLUSION

In many ways, Wigmore Castle still remains something of an enigma. The bold step, taken by English Heritage of returning the castle to its 'wild' state has much to recommend it, and the site now facing the visitor retains much of its grandeur and romance, lost at other more traditionally well-tended sites. And yet, the scope of the excavations was really too narrow, before the site was made safe and returned to Nature's care, to reveal a fully coherent picture of life at the castle. Much of the detail from the faunal and artefactual assemblages conforms to a pattern seen not just at Marcher castles but of castles generally. The one difference is that Marcher castles retained their military function long after those in less marginal areas had ceased to do so. All is totally in keeping with the quotidian life of the aristocracy and their households. Lacunae in the finds record can assume no significance given the small sample size provided by the restricted excavation. Nevertheless new information has come to light. There can be no doubt that the castle stands on the original site chosen by fitz Osbern nor can there be any doubt that the castle was flourishing in the 15th century. Both of these conclusions could only have been reached as a result of archaeological intervention. The extent of the decay in the 16th century, which is far from clear in the documentary record, is more concretely manifest in the excavated deposits in and around the East Tower. The fulsome and excellent range of documentary evidence collated by Dr Cragoe provides an interesting counterpoint to that recovered from excavation. Without allowing the documentary sources to bind the excavation results into too prescriptive a scheme, it is, nevertheless, possible to hazard an opinion linking the two sets of data in many cases. As Kenyon (2005, 180) remarks 'What is important is that the two sources, archaeological and historical, should be used in conjunction'. Of course, loose ends remain and contradictions between the strands of information are observable. It would be strange if it were otherwise.

As with so much archaeology, there are still many avenues of research to be pursued. Large-scale excavations of medieval sites of any sort, much less castles, are woefully under-represented in North Herefordshire and South Shropshire. The pottery report in this volume is therefore invaluable for publishing a distinct regional tradition not reported on elsewhere. In terms of the artefactual assemblages there are very few closely comparable excavated castle sites in the Marches. A further complication arises because of the differences in the way artefacts have been summarised for publication in the past, making it difficult to establish a clear quantification of the object types recovered on occasion (Quita Mould pers comm). Nevertheless, there is nothing which marks out the finds assemblage as substantially different from other castles whether in England, the Marches or Wales, nor anything which would hint at the enormous wealth of the Earls of March. When, for example, Roger Mortimer, 4th Earl of March, assumed his title, there were 40,000 marks in his treasury (Gough 1789) and the extensive lands acquired in Wales by Roger Mortimer, the 1st Earl of March (see Davies 2000), during the brief period he was virtual ruler of England, remained in the family, despite Roger's subsequent fall from grace and execution. With the acquisition of the Mortimer inheritance, the Duke of York became the wealthiest magnate in the kingdom, second only to the king.

Comparisons with 'wholly Welsh' castles are also difficult to come by. Caple (2007, 352) notes the 'dearth of archaeological evidence' for 11th- and 12th-century castles in Wales. At Dolforwyn (Butler 1990, 95), built in the second half of the 13th century, the Welsh phase of the castle, which at most lasted 12 years (see Butler 1997, 199, regarding discussion of the castle's construction date), was notably aceramic and without metal finds. It then came into the possession of the Mortimers for most of its remaining history. Dryslwyn Castle built in the early to mid-13th century was rebuilt in the later 13th century by Rhys ap Maredudd. This was a substantial structure comparable to Wigmore and Pembroke castles (Caple 2007, 350) but its 'Welsh phase' ended when it was besieged and taken into Crown ownership in 1287. As we have seen (above and Chapter 9), the castle differed very little, in terms of artefactual and faunal remains, from Wigmore. Life then at Dryslwyn, when the castle was the residence of a Welsh prince was typical of that enjoyed by aristocratic Marcher and English neighbours. There is some evidence from the ceramics (Webster 2007) that standards dropped when the castle fell into the hands of the English and the castle became part of a complex state supply system (Caple 2007, 351) with a gradually diminishing garrison. Any differences at any phase in the castle's history when compared to Wigmore can be primarily ascribed to geographic factors. Thus, for example, the greater quantity of shellfish consumed at early periods in Dryslwyn's history are more likely to have arisen because of the comparative proximity to the coast rather than reflect an ethno-cultural diversity.

In spite of the small scale of the excavations at Wigmore Castle, it is hoped that this volume goes some little way to expunge Kightly's (1979) perception of Wigmore as 'strangely forlorn, covered with undergrowth and populated only by sheep' and replaces it instead with a view of its former glory — an important fortress and the home of one of the most influential families in English, Welsh and Irish history.

10.3 POSTSCRIPT

The early history of the Mortimer family is particularly tangled. The over-abundance of Ralphs, Rogers and Hughs in the documentary record has led to numerous discrepancies in the literature. A complete revision of the accepted chronology of the early Mortimers has been written by Ian Mortimer in *The early history of the Mortimer family of Wigmore: a reappraisal*. The arguments presented are convincing but unfortunately a copy of the draft article only became available after the final edit of this volume was completed. It was therefore too late to incorporate Dr Mortimer's reassessment. As a result, both Dr Cragoe and I have used the 'official' lineage as a framework for our discussions.

The revision of the lineage has much to recommend it. In essence it removes a Roger and a Hugh from the lordship (Roger (I) and Hugh (II) in Figure 10.2), who seem to be unsupported constructs necessitated by the refusal to accept the longevity of Ralph, the first Lord of Wigmore and his son Hugh, and misreadings of certain key documents, thus 'The Complete Peerage genealogy is a theory that is doubly if not trebly contradicted by contemporary evidence — by the Norman charters as well as the Wigmore chronicles, as well as the lack of references to a Roger [the putative Roger (I) in Figure 10.2] as head of the family'. Figure 10.3 shows the revised lineage proposed by Dr Mortimer.

If Dr Mortimer is correct then the sudden activity of Hugh in the Welsh Wars of the 1140s, after a youth passed in Normandy — and a consequent weakening of Mortimer control of the family's Marcher estates — becomes more understandable and may, in fact, provide a framework in which to set the remodelling of the defensive rampart in Phase 1 at Wigmore and the construction of the Phase 2 timber building. In addition, the revised lineage makes Hugh's dismissal of Henry II as 'a mere boy' (see Cragoe, Chapter 2) more comprehensible if at the time Hugh was a man in his 50s, who was a seasoned campaigner against the Welsh.

The problem of the Mortimer lineage has also been addressed by Paul Remfry (2009) resulting in a similar conclusion to that reached by Ian Mortimer.

Notes

1 Figure 10.5 tabulates the references for castles in Figure 10.4 and mentioned in the text. Although an unorthodox approach, it was felt that removing the majority of the references from Chapter 10 would make a more easily readable text. Most of these data are drawn from the work of Renn (1973) and Thompson (1987). In addition, a substantial amount of information was taken from the work of Paul Remfry, the author of several books and pamphlets about Marcher castles and the Mortimer family (Remfry 1995; 2008). Synopses of the histories of various castles have been made available on-line by Remfry (1994–2007) on the website Anglo-Norman Castles http://www.castles99.ukprint.com/index.html. It is this site that was accessed in 2012 by the author for the data for Figure 10.4. Some of the data had previously been available on www.castleswales.com, copyright J L Thomas (2009) and was accessed by the author in 2010.

BIBLIOGRAPHY

ABBREVIATIONS FOR PRIMARY SOURCES

BL: British Library
CCR: *Calendar of Close Rolls*
CFR: *Calendar of Fine Rolls*
CLP: *Calendar of Letters and Papers Henry VIII*
CIPM: *Calendar of Inquisitions Post Mortem*
CPR: *Calendar of Patent Rolls*
DB: Domesday Book
DNB: Oxford Dictionary of National Biography, revised on-line edition
EH: English Heritage
HCL: Hereford City Library
HRO: Herefordshire Record Office
LPR: *Letters and Papers, Foreign and Domestic, of the Reign of Henry VIII*
LPL: Lambeth Palace Library
NA: Nottinghamshire Archives
NMP: National Mapping Programme, English Heritage
NMR: National Monuments Record, English Heritage
NRO: Nottinghamshire Record Office
SMR: Herefordshire Sites and Monuments Record
TNA: The National Archives (formerly the Public Record Office)

OTHER ABBREVIATIONS

BAR: British Archaeological Reports (British Series unless otherwise noted)
CUP: Cambridge University Press
HBMC: Historic Buildings and Monuments Commission for England
HMSO: His Majesty's Stationary Office
OUP: Oxford University Press
RCHM: Royal Commission for Historic Monuments (England)

REFERENCES

Aaraas, R, Hernar, I J, Vorre, A, Bergslien, H, Lunestad, B T, Skeie, S, Slinde, E and Mortensen, S, 2004 'Sensory, histological and bacteriological changes in flat oysters, *Ostrea edulis* L., during different storage conditions', *Journal of Food Science* 69, 205–210

Albarella, U, 1997 'Size, power and veal: zooarchaeological evidence for late medieval innovations', in G de Boe and F Verhaeghe (eds), *Environment and subsistence in Medieval Europe, 'Medieval Europe Brugge 1997' conference volume 9*, Zellik, I A P Rapporten 19–30

Albarella, U, 2006 'Pig husbandry and pork consumption in medieval England', in C Woolgar, D Serjeantson and T Waldron (eds), *Food in medieval England: diet and nutrition*, OUP, Oxford, 72–87

Albarella, U, Beech, M and Mulville, J, 1997 *The Saxon, medieval and post-medieval mammal and bird bones excavated 1989–1991 from Castle Mall, Norwich, Norfolk*, English Heritage Ancient Monuments Laboratory Report 72/97, London

Albarella, U and Davis, S, 1994 *The Saxon and medieval animal bones excavated 1985–1989 from West Cotton, Northamptonshire*, English Heritage Ancient Monuments Laboratory Report 17/94, London

Albarella, U and Davis, S, 1996 'Mammals and birds from Launceston Castle, Cornwall: decline in status and the rise of agriculture', *Circaea* 12, 1–156

Albarella, U and Pirnie, T, 2008 'A review of animal bone evidence from Central England', http://ads.ahds.ac.uk/catalogue/archive/animalbone_eh_2007

Albarella, U and Thomas, R, 2002 'They dined on crane: bird consumption, wild fowling and status in medieval England', *Acta Zoologica Cracoviensa* 45, 23–38

Allen, M, 2005 'The interpretation of single-finds of English coins, 1279–1544', *British Numismatic Journal* 75, 50–62

Almond, R, 2003 *Medieval hunting*, Sutton, Stroud

Anon, 1911 'Notes of the fourth field meeting, August 28th, 1906: Wigmore and neighbourhood', *Transactions of the Woolhope Naturalists' Field Club for 1905–7*, 300–306

Appleby, J T, 1963 *The chronicle of Richard of Devises of the time of King Richard the First*, Tomas Nelson & Son, London

Appleton-Fox, N, 1998 *Wigmore Castle, Wigmore, Herefordshire. Interim archive report on the excavation of Area B*, Marches Archaeology unpublished report 036, July 1998

Archibald, M M, 1970 'Wyre Piddle (Worcs) 1967 hoard of fifteenth century silver coins', *Numismatic Chronicle* series 7 volume 10, 133–162

Archibald, M M, 1988 'English medieval coins as dating evidence', in J Casey and R Reece (eds), *Coins and the archaeologist*, Seaby, London, 264–301 (2nd edition)

Armitage, E, 1904 'Early Norman castles of England: part II', *English Historical Review* 19, 417–455

Armitage, P, 1977 *The mammalian remains from the Tudor site of Baynard's Castle London. A biometrical and historical analysis*, Unpublished PhD thesis, Royal Holloway College/British Museum of Natural History, London

Auden, T, 1909 'Wigmore castle', *Transactions of the Shropshire Archaeological and Natural History Society* 39, xviii, 367–372

Ayres, K, Locker, A and Serjeantson, D, 2003 'Phases 2f–4a, the medieval abbey: food consumption and production', in A Hardy, A Dodd and G D Keevil, *Aelfric's Abbey: excavations at Eynsham Abbey, Oxfordshire 1989–1992*, Thames Valley Landscapes 16, Oxford, 360–406

Bailey, M, 1988 'The rabbit and the medieval East Anglian economy', *Agricultural History Review* 36, 1–20

Barker, D and Crompton, S, 2007 *Slipware in the collection of the Potteries Museum and Art Gallery*, A & C Black, London

Baker, J and Brothwell, D, 1980 *Animal diseases in Archaeology*, Academic Press, London

Barker, P A, 1970 *The medieval pottery of Shropshire from the Conquest to 1400* Shropshire Archaeological Society Monograph Series 1, Salop

Barker, P and Higham, R, 1982 *Hen Domen, Montgomery. A timber castle on the English-Welsh border, volume 1*, The Royal Archaeological Institute, London

Barratt, G, 1998 'Wigmore Castle Topo Enhancement Survey Shell Keep and Inner ward Interiors', in J Cooke, *Wigmore Castle, Herefordshire*, unpublished draft English Heritage Research Report

Barton, K J, 1963 'Some evidence for two types of pottery manufactured in Bristol in the early 18th century', *Transactions of the Bristol and Gloucester Archaeological Society* 82, 160–168

Bartosiewicz, L, van Neer, W and Lentacker, A, 1997 *Draught cattle: their osteological identification and history*, Annales Sciences Zoologiques 281, Tervuren

Basingwerk 2003 *Gathering the jewels 2003*, National Museum and Galleries of Wales, http://education.gtj.org.uk/search/simpleSearch.php?lang=en&srch=floor%20tiles&pg=3, accessed April 2013

Baxter, I L, 2008 'Injuries to Roman goose humeri resulting in bone necrosis: the result of fighting amongst males?', http://www.alexandriaarchive.org/icaz/icazForum/viewtopic.php?t=1067

Bayliss, D G, 1958–60, 'The lordship of Wigmore in the fourteenth century', *Transactions of the Woolhope Naturalists' Field Club* 36, 42–48 and 137–39

Beedham, G E, 1972 *Identification of the British Mollusca*, Hulton, Amersham

Beresford, M, 1967 *New towns of the Middle Ages*, Lutterworth Press, London

Berry, G, 1974 *Medieval English jetons*, Spink and Son, London

Biddle, M, 1990 *Object and economy in medieval Winchester*, Winchester Studies 7.ii, Clarendon Press, Oxford

Blount, T, 1675 *History of Herefordshire*, unpublished manuscript, HRO CF50/248, formerly HCL FLC 942.44

Boessneck, J, 1969 'Osteological differences between sheep (*Ovis Aries* Linne) and goat (*Carpra hircus* Linne)', in D Brothwell and E Higgs (eds), *Science in Archaeology*, Thames and Hudson, London, 331–358 (2nd edition)

Booth, P, 2000 *Oxford Archaeology Roman pottery recording system: an introduction*, Oxford Archaeology, unpublished report

Bosworth, J and Toller, T N, 1898 An Anglo-Saxon dictionary, Clarendon Press, Oxford (updated online edition at http://lexicon.ff.cuni.cz/texts/oe_bosworthtoller_about.html)

Bosworth, J and Toller, T N, 1921 (supplement), *An Anglo-Saxon Dictionary, Clarendon Press, Oxford* (updated online edition at http://lexicon.ff.cuni.cz/texts/oe_bosworthtoller_about.html

Botzum, R and Reeves, N C (eds), 1997 *The 1675 Thomas Blount Manuscript History of Herefordshire*, Hereford

Bound, T M, 1876 *The history of Wigmore and the adjacent neighbourhood*, Orphan's Printing Press, Leominster

Boyer, P, 1999 'The eggshell', in A Connor and R Buckley, *Roman and medieval occupation in Causeway Lane, Leicester: excavations 1980 and 1991*, Leicester Archaeology Monographs 5, Leicester, 329–333

Brayley, E W and Britton, J, 1805 *The beauties of England and Wales, or delineations topographical, historical and descriptive volume VI*, Thomas Maiden, London

Brakspear, H, 1933 'Wigmore Abbey', *Archaeological Journal* 90, 26–51

Bramwell, D, 1975 'Birds remains from medieval London', *The London Naturalist* 54, 15–20

Brears, P C D, 1983 'The post-medieval pottery', in P Mayes and L A S Butler, *Sandal Castle excavations 1964–1973*, Wakefield Historical Publications, Wakefield, 215–224

Breen, C, 2001 *Wigmore Abbey: interim excavation report*, University of Ulster archive report for Specialist Arts Section, BBC, London

Brewer, E, 1992 *Sir Gawain and the Green Knight: sources and analogues*, Boydell & Brewer Ltd, Woodbridge

Brie, E A (ed), 1908, *The Brut or the chronicles of England 2*, Early English Text Society 136, Oxford

Brothwell, D, 1993 'Avian osteopathology and its evaluation', *Archaeofauna* 2, 33–43

Brown, D L, 1996 'The Roman small town of Leintwardine: excavations and other fieldwork 1971–1989', *Transactions of the Woolhope Naturalists' Field Club* 48, 510–572

Brown, G, 2002 *An earthwork survey and investigation of Wigmore castle, Herefordshire*, English Heritage Archaeological Investigation Report Series A1/14/2002, Swindon

Brown, S, 2008 'The window glass', in H E Cool and S Rátkai, *Wigmore Castle: an assessment and Project Design*, Barbican Research Associates, September 2008

Browne, S, 2000 'Animal bones', in R Higham and P Barker, *Hen Domen, Montgomery: a timber castle on the English-Welsh border. A final report*, Exeter University Press, 126–134

Brydges, E, 1789 *The topographer: containing a variety of original articles, illustrative of the local history and antiquities of England, Volume 1*, printed for Robson & Clarke, London

Buchanan-Brown, J, 1999 'The natural history of Herefordshire: John Aubrey's projected tract', *Transactions of the Woolhope Naturalists' Field Club* 49, 379–403

Bull, G and Payne, S, 1988 'Components of variation in measurements of pig bones and teeth, and the use of measurements to distinguish wild from domestic pig remains', *Archaeozoologia* 2, 27–65

Burnley, D, 1992 'Lexics and semantics', in N Blake (ed), *The Cambridge History of the English Language II, 1066–1476*, CUP, Cambridge, 409–499

Butler, L, 1990 'Dolforwyn Castle, Montgomery, Powys. First Report: the excavations 1981–86', *Archaeologia Cambrensis* CXXXVIII, 78–98

Butler, L, 1997 'Dolforwyn Castle, Powys, second report', *Archaeolgia Cambrensis* CXLIV, 133–203

Camden, W, 1637 *Britain, or a Chorographicall Description of the Most Flourishing Kingdomes, England, Scotland and Ireland*, (P Holland trans), London

Campbell, B M S, 1991 'Land, labour, livestock, and productivity trends in English seignorial agriculture 1208–1450', in B M S Campbell and M Overton (eds), *Land, labour and livestock: historical studies in European agricultural productivity*, Manchester University Press, Manchester, 144–182

Campbell, B M S and Overton, M, 1993 'A new perspective on medieval and early modern agriculture: six centuries of Norfolk farming *c*1250–*c*1850', *Past and Present* 141, 38–105

Campbell, G E, 2002 'The marine shell', in Z Kamash, D R P Wilkinson, B M Ford and J Hiller, 'Late Saxon and medieval occupation: evidence from excavations at Lincoln College, Oxford 1997–2000', *Oxoniensia* 67, 260–261 (199–286)

Campbell, G E, 2009 'Southampton French Quarter 1382 specialist report Download E3: marine shell', in R Brown (ed), *Southampton French Quarter 1382 specialist report downloads*, Oxford Archaeology OA Library EPrints, Oxford (http://library.thehumanjourney.net/42/1/SOU_1382_Specialist_report_download_E3.pdf)

Campbell, G, 2010 'Oysters ancient and modern: potential shape variation with habitat in flat oysters (*Ostrea edulis* L.), and its possible use in archaeology' in E Álvarez-Fernández and D Carvajal Contreras (eds), *Not only food: Proceedings of the 2nd ICAZ Archaeomalacology Working Group Meeting, Santander, 2008*, Munibe 31, 176–187

Cantor, L M, 1965 'The medieval parks of South Staffordshire', *Transactions and Proceedings of the Birmingham Archaeological Society* 80, 1–9

Caple, C, 1991 'The detection and definition of an industry: the English medieval and post-medieval pin industry', *Archaeological Journal* 148, 241–255

Caple, C, 2007 *Excavations at Dryslwyn Castle 1980–95*, The Society for Medieval Archaeology Monograph 26, Leeds

Carpenter, D A, 2000 'A noble in politics: Roger Mortimer in the period of baronial reform and rebellion, 1258–1265', in A J Duggan (ed), *Nobles and nobility in medieval Europe*, The Boydell Press, Woodbridge, 182–203

Carruthers, W, 1988 'Mystery object number 2: animal, mineral or vegetable?', *Circaea* 6.1, 20

Carruthers, W, 1994 'Charred plant remains', in J M Lewis, 'Excavations at Loughor Castle, West Glamorgan 1969–73', *Archaeologia Cambrensis* CXLII, 173–177 (99–181)

Caseldine, A E, 1997 'The charred plant remains from layer 63, pit 49', in K Murphy, 'The castle and borough of Wiston, Pembrokeshire', *Archaeologia Cambrensis* CXLIV, 86–88

Channer, J, 2001 'Wigmore Castle', *Society for the Protection of Ancient Buildings Newsletter* 22, 21–25

Chaplin, R E and White, R W G, 1969 'The use of tooth eruption and wear, body weight and antler characteristics in the age estimation of male wild and park fallow deer (*Dama dama*)', *Journal of Zoology* 157, 125–132

Chapman, D and Chapman, N, 1975 *Fallow deer: their history, distribution and biology*, Terence Dalton Ltd, Lavenham

Ciaraldi, M, 2009 'Plant macroremains', in C Patrick and S Rátkai, *The Bull Ring uncovered: excavations at Edgbaston Street, Moor Street, Park Street and The Row, Birmingham City Centre 1997–2001*, Oxbow, Oxford, 239–258

Clanchy, M, 1993 *From memory to written record, England 1066–1307*, Blackwell, Oxford (2nd edition)

Clancy, S, 1999 Cattle in early Ireland, *Celtic Well e-journal* www.applewarrior.com/celticwell/ejournal

Clark, G T, 1874 'Wigmore', *Archaeologia Cambrensis* 4th series 18, 97–109

Clark, G T, 1884 *Mediaeval military architecture in England*, 2 vols, Wyman & Sons, London

Clark, J (ed), 1995 *The medieval horse and its equipment c1150–c1450*, Medieval finds from excavations in London 5, HMSO, London

Clarke, P V, 1982 'The pottery: a preliminary report', in P Barker and R Higham, *Hen Domen, Montgomery. A timber castle on the English-Welsh border, volume 1*, The Royal Archaeological Institute, London, 73–86

Clarke, S, Jackson, R, Jackson, P, Jemmett, D and Jemmett, J, 1985 'Post-medieval potteries in North Gwent', *Medieval and Later Pottery in Wales* 8, 49–63

Clay, P and Salisbury, C R, 1990 'A Norman mill dam and other sites at Hemington Fields, Castle Donington, Leicestershire', *Archaeological Journal* 147, 276–308

Coad, J C and Streeten, A D F, 1982 'Excavations at Castle Acre Castle, Norfolk, 1972–77', *Archaeological Journal* 139, 138–301

Colvin, H M, 1968 'Castles and government on Tudor England', *English Historical Review* 83, 225–234

Connell, B and Davis, S J M, 1997 *Animal bones from Camber Castle, East Sussex, 1963–1983 excavations*, English Heritage Ancient Monuments Laboratory Report 107/97, London

Cooke, J, 2008 *Wigmore Castle, Herefordshire*, unpublished draft English Heritage Research Report

Cooke, J, forthcoming *Wigmore Castle, Herefordshire: Fabric Survey*, English Heritage Research Report 13/2012

Cool, H E M, 2008 'Painted plaster and mortar', in H E M Cool and S Rátkai, *Wigmore Castle: an assessment and Project Design*, Barbican Research Associates, September 2008

Cool, H E M and Rátkai, S, 2008 *Wigmore Castle: an assessment and Project Design*, Barbican Research Associates, Sept 2008

Coplestone-Crow, B, 1989 *Herefordshire place-names*, BAR 214, Oxford

Coppack, G, 2002 'Conserved in the gentle hands of nature', *Context (Journal of the Institute of Historic Building Conservation)* March 73, http://ihbc.org.uk/context_archive/73/nature_dir/nature_s.htm

Coppack, G, 2005 'Wigmore Castle: new approaches to conservation', *English Heritage Conservation Bulletin* 49, 29–30 (http://www.english-heritage.org.uk/publications/conservation-bulletin-49/)

Coppack, G, nd *Wigmore castle: historical and archaeological information*, unpublished notes in EH Registry file MP/0017/02/01

Cowgill, J, de Neergaard, M and Griffiths, N, 1987 *Knives and scabbards,* Medieval finds from excavations in London 1, HMSO, London

Croft, R A, 1987 *Graffiti gaming boards*, Finds Research Group AD700–1700, Datasheet 6, Oxford

Crump, J J, 1997 'The Mortimer family and the making of the March', *Thirteenth Century England* 6, 117–126

Cumberpatch, C, 2002 'The pottery', in I Roberts, *Pontefract Castle excavations 1982–86*, West Yorkshire Archaeology Service, Exeter, 169–226

Cummins, J, 1988 *The hound and the hawk: the art of medieval hunting*, Weidenfeld and Nicholson, London

Curtler, W H R, 1908 'Agriculture', in W Page (ed), *The Victoria History of the Counties of England. A History of the County of Hereford 1*, Constable, London, 407–428

Dalwood, H, 2005 'Archaeological assessment of Wigmore, Hereford and Worcester', in H Dalwood and V Bryant, *Extensive Urban Survey: The Central Marches Historic Towns Survey 1992–1996* (archaeologydataservices.ac.uk/archive/viewmarches_eus_2005/downloads)

Davies, R R, 2000 *The Age of Conquest: Wales 1063–1415*, OUP, Oxford

Davis, H W C, 1924 *Medieval England: a new edition of Barnard's Companion to English History*, Clarendon Press, Oxford

Davis, S J M, 1987 *Prudhoe Castle: a report on the animal remains*, English Heritage Ancient Monuments Laboratory Report 162/87

Davis, S J M, 1992 *A rapid method for recording information about mammal bones from archaeological sites*, English Heritage Ancient Monuments Laboratory Report 19/92, London

Davis, S J M, 1996 'Measurements of a group of adult female Shetland sheep skeletons from a single flock: a baseline for zooarchaeologists', *Journal of Archaeological Science* 23, 593–612

De Cupere, B, Lentacker, A, van Neer, W, Waelkens, M and Verslype, L, 2000 'Osteological evidence for the draught exploitation of cattle: first applications of a new methodology', *International Journal of Osteoarchaeology* 10, 254–267

Defoe, D, 1927 *A tour thro' the whole island of Great Britain, divided into circuits or journies*, Dent, London

Dickinson, J C and Ricketts, P T, 1969 'The Anglo-Norman chronicle of Wigmore Abbey', *Transactions of the Woolhope Naturalists' Field Club* 39, 413–446

Dobney, K, Jaques, S D and Irving, B G, 1996 *Of butchers and breeds: report on vertebrate remains from various sites in the City of Lincoln*, Lincoln Archaeological Studies 5, Nottingham

Dobney, K and Reilly, K, 1988 'A method for recording archaeological animal bones: the use of diagnostic zones', *Circaea* 5(2), 79–96

Doonan, R C P, 1999 *Evidence for lead working from Wigmore Castle*, Ancient Monuments Laboratory Report Series 66/1999

Driesch, A von den, 1976 *A guide to the measurement of animal bones from archaeological sites*, Peabody Museum Bulletin 1, Cambridge, Massachusetts

Dryburgh, P R, 2002 *The career of Roger Mortimer, first earl of March (c1287–1330)*, unpublished PhD thesis, University of Bristol

Dugdale, W, 1830 *Monasticon Anglicanum: a history of the abbies and other monasteries, hospitals, frieries and cathedral and collegiate churches*, 6 vols, J Caley, H Ellis and B Bandinel (eds), Longman, Hurst, Rees, Orme & Brown, London

Duncan, H B, 2002 'Domestic metalwork', in I Roberts, *Pontefract Castle: archaeological excavations 1982–86*, West Yorkshire Archaeology 8, Wakefield

Dungworth, D, 2000 *Assessment of metal working debris from Wigmore Castle Hereford and Worcester*, Ancient Monuments Laboratory Report Series 38/2000

Dyer, C C, 1988 'Change in diet in the Late Middle Ages: the case of harvest workers', *Agricultural History Review* 36, 21–38

Dyer, C C, 2006 'Gardens and farden produce in the Later Middle Ages', in C M Woolgar, D Serjeantson and T Waldron (eds), *Food in medieval England*, OUP, Oxford, 27–40

Eales, J, 1990 *Puritans and roundheads: the Harleys of Brampton Bryan and the outbreak of the English Civil War*, CUP, Cambridge

Eames, E S, 1968 *Medieval tiles: a handbook*, British Museum, London

Eames, E, 1980 *Catalogue of medieval lead-glazed earthenware tiles in the department of Medieval and Later Antiquities*, British Museum, London

Egan, G, 1995 'Buckles, hasps and strap hooks', in J Clark (ed), *The medieval horse and its equipment c1150–c1450*, Medieval finds from excavations in London 5, HMSO, London, 55–61

Egan, G and Pritchard, F, 1991 *Dress accessories c1150–c1450*, Medieval finds from excavations in London 3, HMSO, London

Ekwall, E, 1990 *The concise Oxford dictionary of English place-names*, 4th edition, Oxford

Ellis, B, 1995 'Spurs and spur fittings', in J Clark (ed), *The medieval horse and its equipment c1150–c1450*, Medieval finds from excavations in London 5, HMSO, London 124–150

Emery, A, 2000 *Greater medieval houses of England and Wales II: East Anglia, Central England and Wales*, CUP, Cambridge

English Nature, 1997 *Clun and north-west Herefordshire hills*, unpublished report

Fairbrother, M, 2000 'Objects of iron', in C J Young, *Excavations at Carisbrooke Castle, Isle of Wight, 1921–1996*, Wessex Archaeology Report 18, Trust for Wessex Archaeology Ltd, Salisbury, 140–155

Fairholt, F W, 1976 *A glossary of costume in England*, EP Publishing, Wakefield (reprinted from volume II of F W Fairholt, 1885 *Costume in England*)

Felter, M and Bartindale, S, 2009 *Wigmore Castle Report on the investigative conservation of metal small finds*, York Archaeological Trust Conservation Laboratories report 2009/55

Fry, P Somerset, 1996 *Castles of Britain and Ireland*, Abbeville Press, New York

Gaimster, D, 1997 *German stoneware 1200–1900*, British Museum, London

Galbraith, V H and Tait, J, 1950 *Herefordshire Domesday c1160–1170*, printed for the Pipe Roll Society by J W Ruddock, London

Ganz, B, 1972 'The buildings of Godstow Nunnery', *Oxoniensia* XXXVII, 150–157

Gelling, M, 1984 *Place-names in the landscape*, Dent, London

Gidney, L J, 1991a *Leicester, the Shires 1988 excavations: the animal bones from the medieval deposits at St Peter's Lane*, English Heritage Ancient Monuments Laboratory Report 116/91, London

Gidney, L J, 1991b *Leicester, the Shires, 1988 excavations: the animal bones from the medieval deposits at Little Lane*, English Heritage Ancient Monuments Laboratory Report 57/91, London

Gidney, L J, 1991c *Leicester, the Shires 1988 excavations: the animal bones from the post-medieval deposits at St Peter's Lane*, English Heritage Ancient Monuments Laboratory Report 131/91, London

Gidney, L J, 1992 *Leicester, the Shires 1988 excavations: the animal bones from the post-medieval deposits at Little Lane*, English Heritage Ancient Monuments Laboratory Report 24/92, London

Gidney, L J, 1993 *Leicester, the Shires 1988 excavations: further identifications of small mammal and bird bones*, English Heritage Ancient Monuments Laboratory Report 92/93, London

Giffin, M E, 1941 'Cadwalader, Arthur, and Brutus in the Wigmore manuscript', *Speculum* 16, 109–120

Given-Wilson, C (ed and trans), 1997 *The chronicle of Adam Usk 1377–1421*, Clarendon Press, Oxford

Goodall, A, 2007 'Copper alloy and lead artefacts', in C Caple, *Excavations at Dryslwyn Castle 1980–95*, The Society for Medieval Archaeology Monograph 26, Leeds, 257–263

Goodall, I H, 1983 'Iron objects', in P Mayes and L Butler, *Sandal Castle Excavations*, Wakefield Historical Publications, Wakefield, 240–253

Goodall, I H, 1990 'Locks and keys', in M Biddle, *Object and economy in medieval Winchester*, Winchester Studies 7.ii, Clarendon Press, Oxford, 1001–1036

Gough, R, 1789 *Britannia: or a Chorographical Description of the Flourishing Kingdoms of England, Scotland and Ireland by William Camden, Translated and Enlarged*, 3 vols, London

Grant, A, 1982 'The use of tooth wear as a guide to the age of domestic ungulates', in B Wilson, C Grigson and S Payne (eds), *Ageing and sexing animal bones from archaeological sites*, BAR 102, Oxford, 91–108

Grant, A, 1985 'The large mammals', in B Cunliffe and J Munby (eds), *Excavations at Portchester Castle IV. Medieval, the Inner Bailey*, Reports of the Research Committee, Society of Antiquaries of London 34, London, 244–256

Grant, A, 1988 'Animal resources', in G Astill and A Grant (eds), *The countryside of medieval England*, Basil Blackwell, Oxford, 149–187

Greig, J, 1982 'The plant and insect remains', in P Barker and R Higham, *Hen Domen, Montgomery. A timber castle on the English-Welsh border, volume 1*, The Royal Archaeological Institute, London, 60–62

Greig, J, forthcoming 'Research issues in the medieval period within the West Midlands' environment', in J Hunt (ed), *The Archaeology of the West Midlands: The West Midlands Regional Research Framework for Archaeology*

Hagen, A, 1995 *Anglo-Saxon food and drink*, Anglo-Saxon Books, Hockwold cum Wilton

Haines, R M, 1978 *The church and politics in fourteenth-century England: the career of Adam of Orleton, c1275–1345*, CUP, Cambridge

Halstead, P, 1985 'A study of mandibular teeth from Romano-British contexts at Maxey', in F Pryor, F French and C French (eds), *Archaeology and environment in the Lower Welland Valley 1. Cambridge*, East Anglian Archaeology Report 27, 219–224

Hamilton-Dyer, S, 2007 'The fish bone', in I Soden (ed), *Stafford Castle. Survey, excavation and research 1978–98, volume II: the excavations*, Stafford Borough Council, Stafford, 179–184

Hamilton, J and Thomas, R, 2012 'Pannage, pulses and pigs: isotopic and zooarchaeological evidence for changing pig management practices in 14th-century England', *Medieval Archaeology* 56, 234–259

Hammer, Ø and Harper, D A T, 2006 *Paleontological data analysis*, Blackwell, Oxford

Hammer, Ø, Harper, D A T and Ryan, P D, 2001 'PAST: Paleontological Statistics Software Package for Education and Data Analysis', *Palaeontologia Electronica* 4(1), http://palaeo-electronica.org/2001_1/past/issue1_01.htm

Hammon, A, 2010 'The brown bear', in T O'Connor and N Sykes (eds), *Extinctions and invasions: a social history of British fauna*, Windgather Press, Oxford, 95–103

Hammond, P W, 1995 *Food and feast in medieval England*, Alan Sutton Publishing Ltd, Bridgend

Hands, R (ed), 1975 *English hawking and hunting in the Boke of St Albans*, OUP, Oxford

Harcourt, R A, 1974 'The dog in prehistoric and early historic Britain', *Journal of Archaeological Science* 1, 151–175

Harding, D A, 1985 *The regime of Isabella and Mortimer, 1326–1330*, unpublished MA thesis, Durham University

Hare, J N, 1985 *Battle Abbey: the eastern range and the excavations of 1978–80*, HBMC, London

Harland, J F, Barrett, J H, Carrott, J, Dobney, K and Jaques, D, 2003 'The York System: an integrated zooarchaeological database for research and teaching', *Internet Archaeology* 13 (http://intarch.ac.uk/journal/issue13/harland_index.html)

Haslam, J, 1988 'The Anglo-Saxon burh at *Winingamere*', *Landscape History* 10, 25–36

Hayward, P, Nelson-Smith, T and Shields, C, 1996 *Sea shore of Britain and Europe*, HarperCollins, London

Hibbert, C, 1988 *The English: a social history 1066–1945*, Paladin Grafton Books, London

Hieatt, C B and Butler, S, 1985 *Curye on Inglysch: English culinary manuscripts of the fourteenth century (including the Forme of Curye)*, OUP, Oxford

Higham, C, 1969 'The metrical attributes of two samples of bovine limb bones', *Journal of Zoology, London* 157, 63–74

Higham, R, 2000 'Introduction to the pottery report', in R Higham and P Barker, *Hen Domen, Montgomery: a timber castle on the English-Welsh border. A final report*, Exeter University Press, Exeter, 82–83

Higham, R and Barker, P, 2000 *Hen Domen, Montgomery: a timber castle on the English-Welsh border. A final report*, Exeter University Press, Exeter

Higham, R and Barker, P, 2004 *Timber castles*, Exeter University Press, Exeter

Hill, P, 1997 *Whithorn and St Ninian: the excavation of a monastic town, 1984–91*, The Whithorn Trust, Sutton Publishing, Stroud

Hinds, A B, 1909 *Calendar of State Papers and manuscripts relating to English affairs in the archive collection of Venice and in other libraries of northern Italy*, vol 15, Longmans, London

Hislop, M, Kincey, M and Williams, G, 2011 *Tutbury: a castle firmly built*, Birmingham Archaeology Monograph Series 11, BAR 546, Oxford

Hodder, M, 1991 *Excavations at Sandwell Priory and Hall 1982–88*, South Staffordshire Archaeological and Historical Society Transactions 31

Hopkinson, C, 1989 'The Mortimers of Wigmore 1086–1214', *Transactions of the Woolhope Naturalists' Field Club* 46, 177–193

Hopkinson, C, 1991 'The Mortimers of Wigmore 1214–1282', *Transactions of the Woolhope Naturalists' Field Club* 47, 28–46

Hopkinson, C, 1995 'The Mortimers of Wigmore 1282–1330', *Transactions of the Woolhope Naturalists' Field Club* 48, 303–334

Houston, M G, 1965 *Medieval costume in England and France*, A and C Black, London

Howlett, R (ed), 1884–89 *Chronicles of the reigns of Stephen, Henry II, and Richard I, IV: the chronicle of Robert of Torigni, Abbot of the Monastery of St Michael-in-Peril-of-the-Sea*, Rolls Series 84, London

Howse, W H, 1950 'A short account of Wigmore castle', *Transactions of the Radnorshire Society* 20, 19–20

Hughes, T G, 2003 *A tour of the stone slate regions, Silurian*, accessed March 2009 from http://www.stoneroof.org.uk

Hunt, J (ed), forthcoming *The archaeology of the West Midlands: The West Midlands Regional Research Framework for Archaeology*

Hurst, D, 1992 'Pottery', in S Woodiwiss (ed), *Iron Age and Roman salt production and the medieval town of Droitwich*, CBA Research Report 81, 132–157

Hurst, D, 2005 *Sheep in the Cotswolds: the medieval wool trade*, Tempus, Stroud

Hurst, J D and Rees, H, 1992 'Pottery fabrics: a multi-period series for the County of Hereford and Worcester', in S Woodiwiss (ed), *Iron Age and Roman salt production and the medieval town of Droitwich*, CBA Research Report 81, 200–209

Hurst, J D, Pearson, E A and Rátkai, S 2001 'Excavation at the Buttercross, Leominster, Herefordshire', *Transactions of the Woolhope Naturalists' Field Club* XLIX Part II, 215–261

Hurst, J G, Neal, D S and Van Beuningen, H J E, 1986 *Pottery produced and traded in north-west Europe 1350–1650*, Rotterdam Papers VI 1986, Rotterdam

Insley, C, 2008 'Kings, lords, charters, and the political culture of twelfth-century Wales', *Anglo-Norman Studies* 30, 133–153

Jackson, J W, 1915 'Appendix A. Notes on the vertebrate and molluscan remains from Dyserth Castle', in T A Glenn, 'Prehistoric and historic remains at Dyserth Castle', *Archaeologia Cambrensis* 15, 77–82 (47–86)

Jensen, H A, 1975 'Cenococcum Geophilum fr. in arable soil in Denmark', *Saertryk af Friesia* X, 4–5, 300–314

Jessop, O, 1996 'A new typology for the study of medieval arrowheads', *Medieval Archaeology* 40, 192–205

Jessop, O, 2007 'Weapons', in C Caple, *Excavations at Dryslwyn Castle 1980–95*, The Society for Medieval Archaeology Monograph 26, Leeds, 197–208

Johnson, P A, 1991 *Duke Richard of York, 1411–1460*, Clarendon Press, Oxford

Jones, C, Eyre-Morgan G, Palmer S and Palmer, N, 1997 'Excavations in the outer enclosure of Boteler's Castle, Oversley, Alcester, 1992–93', *Transactions of the Birmingham and Warwickshire Archaeological Society* 101, 1–98

Jones, G and Halstead, P, 1995 'Maslins, mixtures and monocrops: on the interpretation of archaeobotanical crop samples of heterogeneous composition', *Journal of Arcaheological Science* 22, 103–114

Jones, R, Sly, J, Simpson, D, Rackham, J and Locker, A, 1985 *The terrestrial vertebrate remains from the Castle, Barnard Castle*, English Heritage Ancient Monuments Laboratory Report 7/85, London

Jones, T (ed and trans), 1973 *Brut y Tywysogyon or The chronicle of the princes, Red Book of Hergest Version*, Cardiff (2nd edition)

Keepax, C, 1984 'The avian egg-shells', in B Philp, *Excavations in the Darent Valley, Kent: the excavation of the south-east area of the Archbishops of Canterbury's medieval manor-house and Tudor palace at Otford*, Kent Monograph Series Research Report 4, Dover Castle, Fiche M16

Kendrick, D J, 2008 *The worked stone and tilestones*, archive and assessment report prepared for English Heritage, February 2008

Kent, B, 1992 *Making dead oysters talk: techniques for analyzing oysters from archaeological sites*, Maryland Historical and Cultural Publications, Crownsville, Maryland

Kenward, H K and Hall, A R, 1995 *Biological evidence from the Anglo-Scandinavian deposits at 16–22 Coppergate*, The Archaeology of York 14: The Past Environment of York, Fascicle 7, York Archaeological Trust and the Council for British Archaeology, York

Kenyon, J R, 2005 *Medieval fortifications*, Continuum Studies in Medieval History, Continuum, London

Kiesewalter, L, 1888 *Skelettmessungen am Pferde als Beitrag zur theoretischen Grundlage der Beurteilungslehre des Pferdes*, PhD dissertation, Leipzig University

Kightly, C and Cheze-Brown, P, 1979 *Strongholds of the Realm*, Thames and Hudson, London

Knight, J K, 1991a 'The pottery from Montgomery Castle', *Medieval and Later Pottery in Wales* 12, 1–100

Knight, J K, 1991b *Chepstow Castle*, Cadw, Cardiff

Knight, J K, 1993 'Excavations at Montgomery Castle, Part I' *Archaeologia Cambrensis* CXLI, 97–180

Knight, J K, 1994 'Excavations at Montgomery Castle, Part II: the finds (metalwork)', *Archaeologia Cambrensis* CXLII, 182–242

Knight, J K, 1996 'Excavations at Montgomery Castle, Part III: the finds: other than metalwork', *Archaeologia Cambrensis* CXLIII, 139–203

Kratochvil, Z, 1969 'Species criteria on the distal section of the tibia in *Ovis ammon* F. *aries* L. and *Capra aegagrus* F. *hircus* L.', *Acta Veterinaria (Brno)* 38, 483–490

Laborderie, O de, Maddicott, J R and Carpenter, D A, 2000 'The last hours of Simon de Montfort: a new account', *English Historical Review* 115, 378–412

Langdon, J, 1986 *Horses, oxen and technological innovation: the use of draught animals in English farming from 1066 to 1500*, CUP, Cambridge

Langdon, J, 2004 *Mills in the medieval economy: England 1300–1540*, OUP, Oxford

Larking, L B, 1858 'Inventory of the effects of Roger Mortimer at Wigmore Castle and abbey, Herefordshire', *Archaeological Journal* 15, 354–362

Lauwerier, R C G M, 1988 *Animals in Roman times in the Dutch Eastern River area*, Nederlandse Oudheden 12, Amersfoort

Lentacker, A and van Neer, W, 1996 'Bird remains from two sites on the Red Sea coast and some observations on medullary bone', *International Journal of Osteoarchaeology* 6, 48–49

Lewis, J M, 1994 'Excavations at Loughor Castle, West Glamorgan 1969–73', *Archaeologia Cambrensis* CXLII, 99–181

Liddiard, R, 2005 *Castles in context: power, symbolism and landscape, 1066 to 1500*, Windgather Press, Macclesfield

Lightfoot, K W B, 1992 'Rumney Castle, a ringwork and manorial centre in South Glamorgan', *Medieval Archaeology* 36, 96–163

Locker, A, 2007 'Fish bones', in C Caple, *Excavations at Dryslwyn Castle 1980–95*, The Society for Medieval Archaeology Monograph 26, Leeds, 314–318

LPR: *Letters and Papers, Foreign and Domestic, of the Reign of Henry VIII*, ed J S Brewer, J Gairdner and R H Brodie, 22 volumes (London, 1862–1932)

Luff, R, 1993 *Animal bones from excavations in Colchester, 1971–85*, Colchester Archaeological Report 12, Colchester

Lyman, R L, 1994 *Vertebrate taphonomy*, CUP, Cambridge

MacDonald, K, 1992 'The domestic chicken (*Gallus gallus*) in sub-Saharan Africa: a background to its introduction and its osteological differentiation from indigenous fowls (*Numidinae* and *Francolinus* sp)', *Journal of Archaeological Science* 19, 303–318

Maltby, M, 1979 *The animal bones from Exeter 1971–1975*, Exeter Archaeological Reports 2, Sheffield

Maltby, M, 1982 'Animal and bird bones', in R A Higham, J P Allan and S Blaylock (eds), 'Excavations at Okehampton Castle, Devon', *Devon Archaeological Society* 40, 114–135 (19–152)

Mandl, F, 1999 *Depictions of nine men's morris on rock in the northern part of the Kalkalpen*, TRACCE Online Rock Art Bulletin

Mayes, P and Butler, L A S, 1983 *Sandal Castle excavations*, Wakefield Historical Publications, Wakefield

Meyrick, S R, 1836a 'Historical memoranda of Wigmore Castle Herefordshire', *The Analyst: a Quarterly Journal of Science, Literature, Natural History and the Fine Arts* IV, 3–28

Meyrick, S R, 1836b 'Historical memoranda of Wigmore Castle Herefordshire', *The Analyst: a Quarterly Journal of Science, Literature, Natural History and the Fine Arts* VI, 243–266

Miller, E, 1965 'The fortunes of the English textile industry during the thirteenth century', *The Economic History Review* 18, 64–82

Mills, A D, 2003 *A dictionary of British place-names*, OUP, Oxford

Mills, P, 2000 *The CBM from Newark Castle Gardens*, unpublished archive report for Archaeological Project Services

Mills, P J E, 2006 *The role of brick and tile in the ancient Mediterranean city economy: a case study in Carthage and Beirut*, Unpublished PhD Thesis, University of Leicester

Mitchiner, M, 1988 *Jetons, medalets and tokens. The medieval period and Nuremberg. Volume 1*, Seaby, London

Moffett, L, 1992 'Fruits, vegetables, herbs and other plants from the latrine at Dudley Castle in central England, used by the Royalist garrison during the Civil War', *Review of Palaeobotany and Palynology* 73, 271–286

Moffett, L, 1997 'Plant remains', in C Jones, G Eyre-Morgan, S Palmer and N Palmer, 'Excavations in the outer enclosure of Boteler's Castle, Oversley, Alcester, 1992–93', *Transactions of the Birmingham and Warwickshire Archaeological Society* 101, 111–126

Moffett, L, 2006 'The archaeology of medieval plant foods', in C M Woolgar, D Serjeantson and T Waldron (eds), *Food in medieval England*, OUP, Oxford, 41–55

Moore, S, 1999 *Cutlery for the table. A history of British table and pocket cutlery*, The Hallamshire Press Ltd, Sheffield

Mortimer, I, 2003 *The greatest traitor: the life of Sir Roger Mortimer, 1st Earl of March, ruler of England, 1327–1330*, Jonathan Cape, London

Mortimer, I, 2004 *The greatest traitor*, Pimlico, London

Mould, Q, 1979 'The iron nails', in G H Smith, 'The excavation of the hospital of St Mary of Ospringe, commonly called Maison Dieu', *Archaeologia Cantiana* 95, 148–152 (81–184)

Mould, Q, 2006 'The metal finds', in A Saunders, *Excavations at Launceston Castle, Cornwall*, The Society for Medieval Archaeology Monograph 24, Leeds, 301–339

Mould, Q, 2011 'An appraisal of the portable finds', in S Rátkai, S J Linnane and Q Mould with Richard Morris, *An archaeological overview of Weoley Castle, Birmingham*, archive report for Birmingham Museum and Art Gallery (http://archaeologydataservice.ac.uk/archives/view/weoleycastle_eh_2011/downloads.cfm)

Murphy, K, 1997 'The castle and borough of Wiston, Pembrokeshire', *Archaeologia Cambrensis* CXLIV, 71–102

Murphy, P, 1985 'Avian eggshell', in M Atkin, A Carter and D H Evans, *Excavations in Norwich 1971–78, Part II*, East Anglian Archaeology Report 26, 68 and Fiche Tables 28–29

Murphy, P, 1988 'Avian eggshell', in B Ayers, *Excavations at St Martin-at-Palace Plain, Norwich, 1981*, East Anglian Archaeology Report 37, 113–114 and Fiche Table 16

Murphy, P, 1991 *Hertford Castle: molluscs and other macrofossils*, AML Report New Series 58/91

Murphy, P, 1992 'Avian eggshell', in P Crummy, *Excavations at Culver Street, the Gilberd School, and other sites in Colchester 1971–85*, Colchester Archaeology Report 6, 280

Murphy, P, 2004 'Avian eggshell', in R Havis and H Brooks, *Excavations at Stansted Airport, 1986–9*, East Anglian Archaeology Report 107, volume II, 459–460

Noddle, B, 1991 'The animal bones', in R Shoesmith, *Excavations at Chepstow 1973–74*, Cambrian Archaeological Monographs 4, The Cambrian Archaeological Association, 150–155

North, J J, 1991 *English hammered coinage. Volume 2: Edward I to Charles II, 1272–1662*, Spink and Son, London (3rd edition)

North, J J, 1994 *English hammered coinage. Volume 1: early Anglo-Saxon to Henry III, c600–1272*, Spink and Son, London (3rd edition)

Nowakowski, J A and Thomas, C, 1992 *Grave news from Tintagel: an account of a second season of archaeological excavations at Tintagel Churchyard, Cornwall, 1991*, Cornwall Archaeological Unit, Cornwall County Council Institute of Cornish Studies, University of Exeter, Truro

O'Donnell, J, 1970 'Market centres in Herefordshire 1200–1400', *Transactions of the Woolhope Naturalists' Field Club* 40, 186–194

Oswald, A, 1963 'Excavation of a thirteenth-century wooden building at Weoley Castle, Birmingham 1960–61', *Medieval Archaeology* 6, 109–134

Ottaway, P, 1992 *Anglo-Scandinavian ironwork from 16–22 Coppergate*, The Archaeology of York: the small finds 17/6, CBA, London

Owen, G, 1594 *The dialogue of the government of Wales* (published 2010, Cardiff, University of Wales Press)

Owen, H D, 1991 'Wales and the Marches', in E Miller (ed), *The Agrarian History of England and Wales Volume III (1348–1500)*, CUP, Cambridge, 238–253

Patrick, C and Rátkai, S, 2009 *The Bull Ring uncovered: Excavations at Edgbaston Street, Moor Street, Park Street and The Row, Birmingham City Centre 1997–2001*, Oxbow, Oxford

Payne, A, 2007 *Wigmore castle, Herefordshire: report on geophysical surveys, August 1998*, English Heritage Research Department Report series 42/2007, Swindon

Payne, S, 1972 'Partial recovery and a sample bias: the results of some sieving experiments', in E S Higgs (ed), *Papers in Economic Prehistory*, CUP, Cambridge, 49–64

Payne, S, 1973 'Kill-off patterns in sheep and goats: the mandibles from Aşvan Kale', *Anatolian Studies* 23, 281–303

Payne, S, 1975 'Partial recovery and sample bias', in A T Clason (ed), *Archaeozoological Studies*, North Holland Publishing Company, Amsterdam, 7–17

Payne, S, 1985 'Morphological distinctions between the mandibular teeth of young sheep, *Ovis*, and goats, *Capra*', *Journal of Archaeological Science* 12, 139–147

Payne, S, 1987 'Reference codes for wear states in the mandibular cheek teeth of sheep and goats', *Journal of Archaeological Science* 14, 609–614

Peacey, A, 2008 'The clay pipes: Appendix 9', in H E M Cool and S Rátkai, *Wigmore Castle: an assessment and Project Design*, Barbican Research Associates, September 2008

Peacock, D P S (ed), 1977 *Pottery and early commerce: characterisation and trade in Roman and later ceramics*, London, Academic Press

Pearce, J and Vince, A, 1988 *Surrey whitewares*, London and Middlesex Archaeological Society Special Paper 10, London

Peck, C W, 1970 *English copper, tin and bronze coins in the British Museum 1558–1958*, Trustees of the British Museum, London (2nd edition)

Pickering, D, 1762 *The statutes at large from the fifteenth year of King Edward III to the thirteenth year of King Henry IV, vol 2*, Joseph Bentham, Cambridge

Poppe, G T and Goto, Y, 1991 *European seashells I (Polyplacophora, Caudofoveata, Solenogastra, Gastropoda)*, Verlag Christa Hemmen, Hackenheim

Poppe, G T and Goto, Y, 1993 *European seashells II (Scaphopoda, Bivalvia, Cephalopoda)*, Verlag Christa Hemmen, Hackenheim

Pounds, N J G, 1990 *The medieval castle in England and Wales: a social and political history*, CUP, Cambridge

Rackham, O, 1986 *The history of the countryside: the classic history of Britain's landscape, flora and fauna*, J M Dent, London

Rátkai S, 1987 'The post-medieval coarsewares from the motte and keep of Dudley Castle', *Staffordshire Archaeological Studies, Museum Archaeological Society Report*, New Series 4, 1–11

Rátkai, S, 2001 'The pottery', in J D Hurst, E A Pearson and S Rátkai, 'Excavation at the Buttercross, Leominster, Herefordshire', *Transactions of the Woolhope Naturalists' Field Club* XLIX 1998, Part II, 229–244 (215–261)

Rátkai, S, 2003 'The pottery', in J Wainwright, *Palmers Hall, Ludlow College, Ludlow, Shropshire: a report on an evaluation*, Marches Archaeology Internal Report 311, November 2003

Rátkai, S, 2004 'The pottery', in J Kenney, *Land to the rear of 9–10 King Street, Ludlow, Shropshire: a report on an archaeological evaluation*, Marches Archaeology Internal Report 321, February 2004

Rátkai, S, 2005 'The pottery', in H Sherlock, *Excavations at Mill Street, Leominster*, Archenfield Archaeology Internal Report AA03/35

Rátkai, S, 2006a 'The pottery', in J Wainwright, *Palmers Hall, Ludlow College, Ludlow, Shropshire. A report on a programme of archaeological works*, Marches Archaeology Internal Report 411, February 2006

Rátkai, S, 2006b 'The pottery', in J Wainwright, *Concord College, Acton Burnell, Shropshire. A report on a programme of archaeological works*, Marches Archaeology Internal Report 418, May 2006

Rátkai, S, 2007 'The medieval and early post-medieval pottery', in I Soden (ed), *Stafford Castle. Survey, excavation and research 1978–98, volume II: the excavations*, Stafford Borough Council, Stafford, 59–62

Rátkai, S, 2009 'The pottery', in C Patrick and S Rátkai, *The Bull Ring uncovered: excavations at Edgbaston Street, Moor Street, Park Street and The Row, Birmingham City Centre 1997–2001*, Oxbow, Oxford, 55–102

Rátkai, S, 2011a 'Appendix 5: sandy and sandy micaceous wares', archive report for Birmingham Museum and Art Gallery, in S Rátkai, S J Linnane and Q Mould with Richard Morris, *An Archaeological Overview of Weoley Castle, Birmingham* (http://archaeologydataservice.ac.uk/archives/view/weoleycastle_eh_2011/downloads.cfm)

Rátkai, S, 2011b 'The medieval pottery', in M Hislop, M Kincey and G Williams, *Tutbury: a castle firmly built*, Birmingham Archaeology Monograph Series 11, BAR 546, Oxford, 200–210

Rátkai, S, forthcoming a, 'Appendix 2: the pottery, in K Crooks, *The former Leominster Poultry Packers site: archaeological evaluation*, Archaeological Investigations Report HAS329

Rátkai, S, forthcoming b, 'The pottery', in J West and N Palmer, *Haughmond Abbey, Shropshire*

RCHM, 1932 Unpublished notes and drawings in NMR, filed under Wigmore Castle

RCHM, 1934 *An inventory of historical monuments in Herefordshire 3*, HMSO, London

Redhead, N, 1990a 'Wigmore castle: a resistivity survey of the outer bailey', *Transactions of the Woolhope Naturalists' Field Club* 46, 423–431

Redhead, N, 1990b 'Wigmore castle: geophysical prospecting in the Welsh marches', *The Manchester Archaeological Bulletin* 5, 71–80

Redknap, M, 1994 'The bone gaming pieces', in J M Lewis, 'Excavations at Loughor Castle, West Glamorgan 1969–73', *Archaeologia Cambrensis* CXLII, 150–156 (99–181)

Reeves, A C, 1983, *The Marcher Lords*, Christopher Davies, Llandybïe

Reitz, E J and Wing, E S, 1999 *Zooarchaeology*, CUP, Cambridge

Remfry, P M, 1995 *The Mortimers of Wigmore 1066–1181*, SCS Publishing, Worcester

Remfry, P M, 2000 *Wigmore Castle Tourist Guide*, SCS Publishing, Worcester

Remfry, P M, 2008 *The castles and history of Radnorshire*, SCS Publishing, Worcester (2nd edition)

Remfry, P M, 2009 'The early Mortimers of Wigmore, 1066–1181', http://www.castles99.ukprint.com/Essays/earlymort.html

Renfrow, C, 1993 *Take a thousand eggs or more: a collection of 15th century recipes*, 2 vols, published by author, USA

Renn, D, 1968 *Norman castles in Britain*, John Baker, London

Renn, D, 1973 *Norman castles in Britain*, John Baker, London (2nd edition)

Renn, D, F, 1989 *Caerphilly Castle*, Cadw, Cardiff

Richards, M, 1954 *The Laws of Hywel Dda*, Liverpool University Press, Liverpool

Richardson, C A, Collis, S A, Ekaratne, K, Dare, P and Key, D, 1993 'The age determination and growth rate of the European flat oyster, *Ostrea edulis*, in British waters determined from acetate peels of umbo growth lines,' *ICES Journal of Marine Science* 50, 493–500

Ritchie, A, 2008 'Gaming boards', in C Lowe, *Inchmarnock: an early historic island monastery and its archaeological landscape*, Society of Antiquaries Scotland, Edinburgh, 116–127

Rixson, D, 1989 'Butchery evidence on animal bones', *Circaea* 6(1), 49–62

Rixson, D, 2000 *The history of meat trading*, Nottingham University Press, Nottingham

Roberts, I, 2002 *Pontefract Castle: Archaeological Excavations 1982–86*, West Yorkshire Archaeology 8, West Yorkshire Archaeology Service, Wakefield

Robinson, H R, 1994 'The armour: introduction', in J K Knight, 'Excavations at Montgomery Castle, Part II: the finds (metalwork)', *Archaeologia Cambrensis* CXLII, 210–211 (182–242)

Rooney, A (ed), 1987 *The Tretyse of Hunting*, Medieval and Renaissance Texts and Studies 19, Brussels

Rosenbaum, M, 2007 'The building stones of Ludlow: a walk through the town', *Proceedings of the Shropshire Geological Society* 12, 5–38

Rothwell, H (ed), 1975 *English historical documents: 1189–1327*, Routledge, London

Rouffignac, C de, 2007 'The plant remains', in I Soden (ed), *Stafford Castle. Survey, excavation and research 1978–98, volume II: the excavations*, Stafford Borough Council, Stafford, 184–188

Ryder, M L, 1983 *Sheep and man*, Duckworth, London

Sadler, P, 1990 'The use of tarsometatarsi in sexing and ageing domestic fowl (*Gallus gallus* L.), and recognising five toed breeds in archaeological material', *Circaea* 8, 41–48

Sadler, P, 2007 'The bird bone', in I Soden (ed), *Stafford Castle. Survey, excavation and research 1978–98, volume II: the excavations*, Stafford Borough Council, Stafford, 172–179

Sadler, P and Jones, G, 2007 'The mammal bone', in I Soden (ed), *Stafford Castle. Survey, excavation and research 1978–98, volume II: the excavations*, Stafford Borough Council, Stafford, 161–172

Salisbury, J E, 1994 *The beast within: animals in the Middle Ages*, Routledge, London

Salzman, L F, 1952 *Buildings in England down to 1540. A documentary history*, Clarendon Press, Oxford

Saunders, A, 2006 *Excavations at Launceston Castle, Cornwall*, The Society for Medieval Archaeology Monograph 24, Leeds

Scard, M A, 1990 *The building stones of Shropshire*, Swan Hill Press, Shrewsbury

Schmid, E, 1972 *Atlas of animal bones for Prehistorians, Archaeologists and Quarternary Geologists*, Elsevier Publishing Company, New York

Searle, E (ed), 1980 *The chronicle of Battle Abbey*, OUP, Oxford

Seed, R, 1980 'Shell growth and form in the bivalvia', in D C Rhoads and R A Lutz (eds), *Skeletal growth of aquatic organisms: biological records of environmental change*, Plenum, New York, 23–67

Serjeantson, D, 2006 'Birds: food and a mark of status', in C M Woolgar, D Serjeantson and T Waldron (eds), *Food in medieval England*, OUP, Oxford, 131–147

Serjeantson, D and Woolgar, C, 2006 'Fish consumption in medieval England', in C M Woolgar, D Serjeantson and T Waldron (eds), *Food in medieval England*, OUP, Oxford, 102–130

Shipman, P, Foster, G and Schoeninger, M, 1984 'Burnt bones and teeth: an experimental study of colour, morphology, crystal structure and shrinkage', *Journal of Archaeological Science* 11, 307–325

Shirreff, A G, 1953 'The Sparsholt nine men's morris', *Berkshire Archaeological Journal* 53, 110–115

Shoesmith, R, 1985 *Hereford City Excavations, volume 3: the finds*, CBA Research Report 56

Shoesmith, R, 1991 *Excavations at Chepstow 1973–74*, Cambrian Archaeological Monographs 4, The Cambrian Archaeological Association

Shoesmith, R, 1998 *Wigmore castle, Herefordshire: notes for the visit of the Cocked Hat Club, Friday 18th September, 1998*, unpublished typescript

Sidell, E J, 1993 *A methodology for the identification of archaeological eggshell*, MASCA, The University Museum of Archaeology and Anthropology, University of Pennsylvania Papers 10 Supplement, Pennsylvania

Sidell, J, 1997 'The eggshell', in C Thomas, B Sloane and C Philpotts, *Excavations at the Priory and Hospital of St Mary Spital, London*, MOLAS Monograph 1, 248

Sidell, J and Locker, A, 2000 'The animal bones and eggshell', in P Moore, 'Tilbury Fort: a post-medieval fort and its inhabitants', *Post-Medieval Archaeology* 34, 72–77 (3–104)

Simon, A L, 1952 *A concise encyclopaedia of gastronomy*, Collins, London

Simpson, G G, Roe, A and Lewontin, RC, 1960 *Quantitative Zoology*, Harcourt Brace, New York

Skeel, C A J, 1904 *The Council in the Marches of Wales*, Hugh Rees, London

Slabyj, B M and Hinkle, C, 1976 'Handling and storage of blue mussels in shell', *Research in the Life Sciences*, University of Maine, Orono 23(4), 1–13

Smith, B S, 2002 'Wigmore fairs', *Transactions of the Woolhope Naturalists' Field Club* 50, 356–385

Smith, G H, 1979 'The excavation of the hospital of St Mary of Ospringe, commonly called Maison Dieu', *Archaeologia Cantiana* 95, 81–184

Soden, I (ed), 2007 *Stafford Castle. Survey, excavation and research 1978–98, volume II: the excavations*, Stafford Borough Council, Stafford

Spavold, J and Brown, S, 2005 *Ticknall pots and potters*, Landmark, Ashbourne

Stace, C, 1997 *Flora of the British Isles*, CUP, Cambridge (2nd edition)

Stamper, P, 1988 'Woods and parks', in G Astill and A Grant (eds), *The countryside of medieval England*, Basil Blackwell, Oxford, 128–148

Stashak, T S, 2002 *Adams' lameness in horses*, Lippincott, Williams and Wilkins, Philadelphia

Stenzel, H B, 1971 'Oysters', in R C Moore (ed), *Treatise on invertebrate palaeontology Part N(3): Mollusca 6 (Bivalvia)*, Geological Society of America, Lawrence, Kansas, 953–1218

Stirling-Brown, R, 1988 'Wigmore castle', *Herefordshire Archaeological News* 48, 30–33

Stone, D J, 2006 'The consumption of field crops in Late Medieval England', in C M Woolgar, D Serjeantson and T Waldron (eds), *Food in medieval England*, OUP, Oxford, 41–55

Stone, R and Appleton-Fox, N, 1998 *Wigmore Castle, Wigmore, Herefordshire: Archive report on the excavation of Area A*, Marches Archaeology Report 009A, January 1998

Stubbs, W (ed), 1870–80 *The historical works of Gervase of Canterbury*, Rolls Series 73, London

Suppe, F C, 1994 *Military institutions on the Welsh Marches: Shropshire 1066–1300*, Studies in Celtic History Series XIV, Boydell Press, Woodbridge

Swynnerton, C, 1914 'Certain chattels of Roger Mortimer of Wigmore', *Notes and Queries*, 11th series 10, 126–127

Sykes, N J, 2001 *The Norman Conquest: a zooarchaeological perspective*, unpublished PhD thesis, Southampton University

Sykes, N J, 2004a, 'The dynamics of status symbols: wildfowl exploitation in England AD 410–1550', *Archaeological Journal* 161, 82–105

Sykes, N J, 2004b 'The introduction of fallow deer to Britain: a zooarchaeological perspective', *Environmental Archaeology* 9(1), 75–83

Sykes, N J, 2006 'From *Cu* and *Sceap* to *Beffe* and *Motton*', in C M Woolgar, D Serjeantson and T Waldron (eds), *Food in medieval England*, OUP, Oxford, 56–71

Sykes, N J, 2007a *The Norman Conquest: a zooarchaeological perspective*, BAR International Series 1656, Oxford

Sykes, N, 2007b 'Taking sides: the social side of venison', in A Pluskowski (ed), *Breaking and shaping beastly bodies: animals as material culture in the Middle Ages*, Oxbow, Oxford, 148–160

Symonds, R, 1859 *Diary of the Marches of the Royal Army during the Great Civil War, kept by Richard Symonds*, printed for the Camden Society, London

Tebble, N, 1966 *British bivalve seashells: a handbook for identification*, Natural History Museum, London

Thomas, A and Boucher, A (eds), 2002 *Hereford City Excavations. Volume 4: 1976–1990*, Hereford City and County Archaeological Trust Ltd, Logaston Press, Logaston

Thomas, R, 2001 'The medieval management of fallow deer: a pathological line of enquiry', in M La Verghetta and L Capasso (eds), *Proceedings of the 13th meeting of the European Palaeopathology Association, Chieti, Italy: 18th–23rd September 2000*, Edigrafital SpA, Teramo, 287–293

Thomas, R, 2005a *Animals, economy and status: the integration of zooarchaeological and historical evidence in the study of Dudley Castle, West Midlands (c1100–1750)*, BAR 392, Oxford

Thomas, R, 2005b 'Zooarchaeology, improvement and the British Agricultural Revolution', *International Journal of Historical Archaeology* 9(2), 71–88

Thomas, R, 2005c 'Perceptions versus reality: changing attitudes towards pets in medieval and post-medieval England', in A Pluskowski (ed), *Just skin and bones? New perspectives on human-animal relations in the historical past*, BAR International Series 1410, Oxford, 95–104

Thomas, R, 2006 'Of books and bones: the integration of historical and zooarchaeological evidence in the study of medieval animal husbandry', in M Maltby (ed), *Integrating Zooarchaeology*, Oxbow, Oxford, 17–26

Thomas, R, 2007a 'Maintaining social boundaries through the consumption of food in medieval England', in K C Twiss (ed), *The Archaeology of Food and Identity*, Center for Archaeological Investigations Southern Illinois University Carbondale Occasional Paper 34, Carbondale, 130–151

Thomas, R, 2007b 'Chasing the ideal? Ritualism, pragmatism and the later medieval hunt', in A Pluskowski (ed), *Breaking and shaping beastly bodies: animals as material culture in the Middle Ages*, Oxbow, Oxford, 125–148

Thomas, R, 2008 'Diachronic trends in lower limb pathologies in later medieval and post-medieval cattle from Britain', in G Grupe, G McGlynn and J Peters (eds), *Limping together through the ages: joint afflictions and bone infections*, Documenta Archaeobiologiae 6, Rahden/Westf, 187–201

Thomas, R N W, 1988 'A statistical evaluation of criteria used in sexing cattle metapodials', *Archaeozoologia* 2, 83–92

Thompson, E M (ed), 1889 *Adae Murimuth Continuatio Chronicarum Robertus de Avesbury de Gestis Mirabilibus Regis Edwardi Tertii*, Rolls Series 93, London

Thompson, K, 2007 'Bones and joints', in M G Maxie (ed), *Kennedy, and Palmer's pathology of domestic animals*, Saunders Elsevier, Philadelphia, 1–184

Thompson, M W, 1987 *The decline of the castle*, CUP, Cambridge

Toghill, P, 1990 *Geology in Shropshire*, Swan Hill Press, Shrewsbury

Tolley, R, with Channer, J, Coppack, G, Thompson, J and Weston, K, 2000 'Wigmore castle, Herefordshire, the repair of a major monument: an alternative approach', *Association for Studies in Conservation of Historic Buildings Transactions* 25, 21–49

Tonkin, J W, 2002 *Church of St James, Wigmore*, privately printed

Tonkin, M, 1975 'Wigmore Enclosure Act and Award 1772–1774', *Transactions of the Woolhope Naturalists' Field Club* 42, 282–296

Tonkin, M, 1984 'The Wigmore Enclosure Act and Award 1810–28', *Transactions of the Woolhope Naturalists' Field Club* 43, 283–300

Trow-Smith, R, 1957 *A history of British livestock husbandry to 1700*, Routledge and Kegan Paul, London

Vann, S, 2008a *Recording the facts: a generic recording system for animal palaeopathology*, unpublished PhD thesis, Leicester University

Vann, S, 2008b 'Animal palaeopathology at two Roman sites in central Britain', in Z Miklíková and R Thomas (eds), *Current Research in Animal Palaeopathology: Proceedings of the Second Animal Palaeopathology Working Group Conference*, BAR International Series S1844, Oxford, 27–39

Vann, S and Thomas, R, 2006 'Humans, other animals and disease: a comparative approach towards the development of a standardised recording protocol for animal palaeopathology', *Internet Archaeology* 20 (http://intarch.ac.uk/journal/issue20/vannthomas_index.html)

VCH, 1908 *Victoria County History of Herefordshire 1*, Constable, London

Veale, E M, 1957 'The rabbit in England', *Agricultural History Review* 5(1), 85–90

Vince, A, 1977 'The medieval and post-medieval ceramic industry of the Malvern Region: the study of a ware and its distribution', in D P S Peacock (ed), *Pottery and early commerce: characterisation and trade in Roman and later ceramics*, Academic Press, London, 257–305

Vince, A, 1982 'A comparison of medieval pottery from Hen Domen and Montgomery Castle', in P Barker and R Higham, *Hen Domen, Montgomery. A Timber castle on the English-Welsh border, volume 1*, The Royal Archaeological Institute, London, 81–82

Vince, A, 1985a 'The pottery', in R Shoesmith, *Hereford City Excavations, volume 3: the finds*, CBA Research Report 56, 35–65

Vince, A, 1985b 'Roof furniture and building materials', in R Shoesmith, *Hereford City Excavations, volume 3: the finds*, CBA Research Report 56, 65–69

Vince, A, 1985c 'Floor tiles', in R Shoesmith, *Hereford City Excavations, volume 3: the finds*, CBA Research Report 56, 70

Vince, A, 1997 'The floor tiles', in R Shoesmith and R Richardson, *A definitive history of Dore Abbey Hereford*, Logaston Press, Logaston, 77–84

Vince, A, 2002a 'Ceramic building materials and roof furniture' in A Thomas and A Boucher, *Hereford City Excavations, volume 4: 1976–1990*, Logaston Press, Logaston, 93–94

Vince, A, 2002b 'The floor tiles', in A Thomas and A Boucher, *Hereford City Excavations, volume 4: 1976–1990*, Logaston Press, Logaston, 97–98

Vince, A and Wilmott, T, 1991 'A lost tile pavement at Tewkesbury abbey and an early fourteenth-century tile factory', *Antiquaries Journal* 71, 138–173

Ward Perkins, J B, 1940 *London Museum medieval catalogue*, HMSO, London

Watts, S, 2006 *Rotary querns c700–1700*, The Finds Research Group AD700–1700, Datasheet 38, Oxford

Webster, P, 2007 'Pottery', in C Caple, *Excavations at Dryslwyn Castle 1980–95*, The Society for Medieval Archaeology Monograph 26, Leeds, 236–245

White, H and Soden, I, 2007 'Medieval floor tiles', in I Soden (ed), *Stafford Castle. Survey, excavation and research 1978–98, volume II: the excavations*, Stafford Borough Council, Stafford, 152–158

Whitehead, R, 1996 *Buckles 1250–1800*, Greenlight Publishing, Chelmsford

Williams, D, 1992 'Plant macrofossil remains', in K W B Lightfoot, 'Rumney Castle, a ringwork and manorial centre in South Glamorgan' *Medieval Archaeology* 36, 155–156 (96–154)

Williams, J G, 1989 'The castles of Wales during the Civil War, 1642–47', *Archaeologia Cambrensis* CXXXVII, 1–26

Wilson, C A, 1973 *Food and drink in Britain from the Stone Age to recent times*, Constable and Company Ltd, London

Winder, J M, 1992 'The oysters', in I P Horsey, *Excavations in Poole 1973–1983*, Dorset Natural History and Archaeological Society Monograph 10, Dorchester, 194–200

Winder, J M, 1994 'Oyster and other shells', in J W Hawkes and P F Fasham (eds), *Excavations on the Reading Waterfront Sites 1986–87*, Wessex Archaeological Reports 5, Wessex Archaeological Trust, Salisbury, 90–92

Wiseman, J, 2000 *The pig: a British history*, Duckworth, London

Wood, H B, 1941 'Fractures among birds', *Bird-Banding* 12(2), 68–72

Woodfield, C, 1981 'Finds from the Free Grammar School at the Whitefriars, Coventry *c*1545–*c*1557/58', *Post-Medieval Archaeoogy* 15, 81–159

Woodfield, C, 2005 *The Church of Our Lady of Mount Carmel and some conventual buildings at the Whitefriars, Coventry*, BAR 389, Oxford

Woodfield, P and Woodfield, C, 2005 'Slate', in C Woodfield, *The Church of Our Lady of Mount Carmel and some conventual buildings at the Whitefriars, Coventry*, BAR 389, Oxford

Woodiwiss, S (ed), 1992 *Iron Age and Roman salt production and the medieval town of Droitwich*, CBA Research Report 81

Woolgar, C M, 1999 *The great household in late medieval England*, Yale University Press, New Haven and London

Woolgar, C M, Sejeantson, D and Waldon, T (eds), 2006 *Food in medieval England*, OUP, Oxford

Wright, B, 1998 *The execution and burial of Roger Mortimer, First Earl of March (1287–1330)*, privately printed

Wright, T, 1826 *History and antiquities of Ludlow*, J Morton, Manchester

Yalden, D, 1999 *The history of British mammals*, T & A D Poyser Ltd, London

Yalden, D W and Albarella, U, 2009 *The history of British birds*, OUP, Oxford

Young, C J, 2000 *Excavations at Carisbrooke Castle, Isle of Wight, 1921–1996*, Wessex Archaeology Report 18, Trust for Wessex Archaeology Ltd, Salisbury

Zalkin, V I, 1960 'Metapodial variation and its significance for the study of ancient cattle', *Bulletin Moskovskoe Obsčhestvo Ispytatelei Otdel Denii Biologischeskei* 65, 109–126

Zohary, D and Hopf, M, 2000 *Domestication of plants in the Old World*, OUP, Oxford (3rd edition)

INDEX

Peter Brown